READINGS IN THE PSYCHOLOGY

OF CHILDHOOD AND ADOLESCENCE

A BLAISDELL BOOK IN PSYCHOLOGY

CONSULTING EDITOR • *Raymond G. Kuhlen, Syracuse University*

Readings in the Psychology of Childhood and Adolescence

Edited by

William J. Meyer

Syracuse University

BLAISDELL PUBLISHING COMPANY

A Division of Ginn and Company

WALTHAM, MASSACHUSETTS · TORONTO · LONDON

Preface

A BOOK OF readings, such as this one, really serves two not unrelated purposes: (1) It provides large numbers of students with ready access to the original sources of research, and (2) It saves costly wear and tear on library facilities. The more skeptical student may wonder, however, why he is required to read original sources regardless of whether they appear in an anthology or not. There are of course certain obvious values in reading original source reports. For example, an examination of original sources provides an opportunity to assess the methods and procedures used by an investigator which will familiarize students with this important aspect of child psychology. An awareness of the methods used permits an assessment of the adequacy of an investigator's procedures and, perhaps of greater interest, provides a means of determining why the investigator selected the particular method. A second value of reading original studies is the opportunity of assessing whether the author's conclusions are consistent with, or warranted by, the empirical results of his study. Investigators are often guilty of over generalizing their results and of making inferences that are several steps removed from the data. It is also possible that a specific investigator overlooked an especially pertinent inference inherent to his data which the student can only become aware of by careful reading of the original paper. There is still a third value in reading original sources. Typically, an anthology is used in conjunction with a general textbook in which the author summarizes the results of numerous research studies in a particular area and where the author cites studies to support a favored hypothesis. Even the best-intentioned and thorough author will tend to include only those aspects of a study of particular relevance to the point he is developing, with the consequence that other aspects of the study may be overlooked. It is also possible that a textbook author will use the results of a study in a way that is incompatible with the results of the study.

The papers included in this book of readings have been carefully selected. Although an effort was made to sample studies employing various methods and strategies, there is a somewhat greater number of experimental than correlational or descriptive studies. Where important theoretical differences exist in the field, stress was placed on those studies empirically dealing with the issues. Finally, some attention was given to the interest value of the studies by selecting some papers related to the social issues of the day.

There are a greater number of studies using younger children as opposed to adolescents, especially in those chapters dealing with cognitive-perceptual development. This is the case because these behaviors become stabilized prior to the adolescent years. The chapters dealing with social-emotional development include more studies of adolescents because of the presumed influence of pubescence on social-emotional aspects of behavior.

It is recognized that the papers included in the book are not of uniform quality. In large measure this discrepancy occurs because a specific area is especially difficult to study, therefore requiring crude and imprecise procedures. Each of the papers in this book was edited or abridged to some degree. In most cases redundant material was deleted, as well as lengthy reviews of the literature. Key references, cited in each of the studies, were maintained, and a complete listing of them can be found in the bibliography at the end of the book. In no instance does the editing or abridging change or modify the substance or intent of any paper.

The major credit for a book of readings must go to the authors and publishers who consented to have their material reproduced and who agreed to the editing and abridging of their work. My grateful acknowledgment is extended to each of them. More detailed acknowledgment will be found as footnotes to the individual selections. I also wish to acknowledge the diligent and time-consuming editorial work of my assistants, Dale Goldhaber and Barbara Swanson, in assembling this book, and of the people who typed all of the manuscript, Julie Bright, Anne Rock, and Nan Renner.

W. J. M.

Contents

CHAPTER 1

Issues in Child Development and

Behavior Research

CHILDREN's development and behavior is of considerable interest to philosophers, scientists, child-care workers, educators, and parents. Each views the child with a different set of interests and theoretical conceptualizations. Certainly the current concern in the United States for helping culturally deprived children and the emphasis given to improving education for all children underscores the important status of children. In view of this intense concern for children, it is imperative that our present theories, methods, and research strategies be systematically examined. The objective of such a sysematic examination is not merely to uncover weaknesses but also to identify those aspects of the scientific endeavor that show promise. The ensuing discussion may help the reader to identify the strengths and weaknesses of the papers included in this book.

Theories of Developmental Psychology

It is generally acknowledged by scholars concerned with human development that the sophistication and imagination shown in developing research methods far exceeds that shown in developing theories. Those developmental theories which deal with broad aspects of behavior typically involve basic concepts which are loosely defined and difficult to examine at an empirical level. The theoretical relationships among the concepts are generally unspecified. Typically this type of developmental theory places great reliance on elapsed-time as an explanatory concept on the untenable assumption that *time per se* influences behavior or causes behavioral change. Logically, time cannot cause anything. Rather, it is the events that occur during a time interval that are more salient; it is these events that are not specified. Reliance on elapsed time is, nevertheless, consistent with the predominantly biological and organismic nature of these theories as exemplified in the work of Freud, Gesell, Werner, and Piaget. Despite their weaknesses, the biologically oriented theories serve as powerful reminders that students of child development and behavior are concerned with a biological entity which influences all aspects of development and behavior.

The second general theoretical approach provides greater precision of conceptual formulations, but at the cost of a considerable narrowness of focus. These

1

theories are typically referred to as behavior or stimulus-response theories and include the work of Hull, Spence, Guthrie, Mowerer, Estes, and Skinner. These theories focus mainly on the variables influencing learning, especially among laboratory animals. Although recent efforts to broaden the scope of these theories has blunted the criticism of narrowness, the criticism remains valid especially when considered in relation to the study of child development. Whereas the organismic theories tend to rely almost exclusively on biological predeterminism, behavior theories mostly ignore the biological foundation of behavior (see the paper by Hirsch in Chapter 3 for a detailed discussion of this issue). Thus, it is assumed that specific environmental manipulations will uniformly influence behavior within a species. When, as is typically the case, specific manipulations lead to variations in performance, the observed variation is interpreted as the result of errors of measurement.

The stimulus-response orientation has contributed to developmental theory by emphasizing the importance of rigorously defining terms and specifying the interrelationships among terms. Finally, stimulus-response theories are cast in terms that are more testable and more amenable to experimental manipulation than is true of organismic theories.

There exists, obviously, a distinct difference in the basic theoretical views concerning children's behavior and development. This state of affairs often disturbs students because it suggests that no one really *knows* very much about child development and behavior. Actually, it is almost a certainty that no one theory is either completely accurate or inaccurate; but each theoretical position, and the empirical relationships it helps generate, contributes to knowledge. As new knowledge accumulates, some theories diminish in importance because they are unable to incorporate the new data, while other theories are forced to modify previously assumed concepts. The more carefully constructed theories survive the data for longer periods of time regardless of whether they are organismic or stimulus-response theories. Ultimately, empirical relationships more clearly define the behaviors subsumed by diverse theoretical concepts. A frequent outcome of behavior analysis of concepts is the realization that seemingly diverse labels and concepts actually refer to the same variables and the same behavioral outcomes. It should be clear from this discussion that advances in theory rely on the systematic accumulation of data where the antecedent variables and behavioral outcomes are carefully described. Some of the issues involved in accumulating data are examined in the next section.

Methods of Studying Child Development and Behavior

No matter what specific technique or experimental procedure an investigator determines is most appropriate for his research, he must offer evidence of its *reliability* and of its *validity*. Reliability refers to the degree of consistency with which an aspect of behavior is measured on at least two different occasions. The reliability of most psychological tests is usually estimated by one of the split-half methods (the correlation of scores on odd vs. even items, or the correlation of scores on the first half vs. the second half of the items); the test-retest method, where the scores on two administrations of the same test to the same subjects on two different occasions are correlated; and the parallel forms method, where two comparable (same means and standard deviations) forms of the same test are given to the same subjects and the scores correlated. The use of comparable forms provides the most accurate estimate, and the split-half methods the least accurate estimate, of reliability.

Reliability is also important in laboratory studies involving the experimental manipulation of independent variables and the measurement of the manipulation effects on one or more dependent variables. Since the outcome of the manipulations changes the child's behavior, the methods of estimating test reliability cannot be used. Actually, reliability must be inferred from the outcome of the experiment; that is, if the difference on the dependent variable is statistically significant, it can be reasonably assumed that the dependent variable measure and the manipulation of the independent variable are reliable. If the differences are not statistically significant, then the measures and manipulations may or may not be unreliable and/or the independent variable did or did not influence the specific dependent variable. Negative results have meaning when the experimental techniques are highly precise.

The concept of reliability is also used in observational studies of children. Some investigators estimate the stability of observed behavior, a legitimate and important concern; but more often investigators determine observer reliability, that is, observer agreement. Estimation of observer reliability usually involves at least two persons recording observations independently on the same group at the same time and is typically reported in terms of per cent agreement. The degree of observer agreement varies in terms of the complexity of the behavior being observed and the amount of training given the observers.

Since reliability refers to the consistency of behavior and is also an estimate of the error involved in measurement, it follows that reliability is crucial for valid measurements. Simply stated, validity refers to the degree to which a test, methodological procedure, or set of observations measure the intended behavioral attribute. Thus it is possible to have reliable measures that lack validity, a problem which is especially difficult to unravel in the case of experimental methods. Before exploring the complex issues involved in the validation of experimental research, the discussion will intially focus on the three types of validity usually associated with test construction: *content validity, predictive validity,* and *construct validity.*

In developing a series of test items for an arithmetic achievement test, the most logical procedure is to first determine the skills or behaviors that the children are to learn. The items are then constructed in accordance with the required skills. Thus the content of the test provides evidence for validity which is called content validity. Of course, the items could be ambiguously stated (this would reduce reliability), or the range of behaviors measured could be either overly narrow or overly inclusive. Content validity is also involved when making direct observations of behavior. A category of behavior such as aggression, should be defined, including an enumeration of specific behaviors. Each specific behavior comprises the content of the category and constitutes content validity. Finally, most experimental studies rely heavily on content validity in terms of the manipulations of both the independent and the dependent variables. In a study of the effectiveness of reward and punishment on discrimination learning, the reward operation (giving the subject a rewarding stimulus or withdrawing an aversive stimulus) and the punishment operation (giving the subject an aversive stimulus or withdrawing a positive stimulus) are the basis for content validity. Counting the number of correct responses, errors, or response latencies are possible outcome measures having content validity.

Predictive validity refers to the ability of one measurement to account for performance on a second subsequent measure. The predictive validity of the Stanford-Binet Intelligence Scale, for example, is estimated by correlating scores with performance on an achievement test. It should be noted that, unlike content validity, it is not necessary that the items on the predictive instrument have any obvious relationship to the criterion task. A frequent problem in establishing predictive validity is the difficulty of defining a criterion task, especially when the relevant theoretical conceptualizations are vaguely defined. Researchers rely, to a considerable extent, on the outcomes of predictive validity studies when matching subjects on the same attribute or when they are interested in identifying subjects with particular attributes.

Construct validity, a more complex type of validity, is of considerable importance in child development and behavior research. Essentially, construct validity involves the derivation of a set of test items or experimental operations from properties of theoretical concepts. These test items or operations then operationally define the theoretical concept. The theoretical concept also provides a basis for predicting behavioral outcomes from which dependent variable measures can be derived. If the test or operations successfully predict behavior, then confidence in the theoretical formulation is increased. If the predicted behavioral outcomes are not substantiated, then it cannot be determined whether the failure is attributable to poor theory or to inadequate operational definitions of the theoretical construct. Several excellent examples of studies involving construct validity are concentrated in Chapter 7 of this book, which deals with motivation. Motivation is a central concept in theories of learning, but a motivational state is not directly measurable and must be inferred from behavior. In the studies by Davitz and by Walters and Ray, motivation is influenced by manipulation of the experimental situation. Palermo *et al* determine motivational state by using the Children's Manifest Anxiety Scale. In all instances the predicted differences in behavior are supported, thus lending support to the various theoretical formulations associated with the concept of motivation.

There is one issue concerning the validity of experimental studies that until recently has been largely ignored. Most experimental studies include an adult experimenter who is responsible for setting into operation the independent variable and for recording observations. Thus the experimenter becomes a variable in the experiment, including his biases and predefined expectancies about the outcome. These biases do, in fact, influence experimental outcomes, as well as do such other experimenter characteristics as sex. As long as only one experimenter is used, it is impossible to statistically demonstrate an experimenter effect. The solution is to use at least two experimenters with different characteristics and whose knowledge of the anticipated outcomes is negligible. A second alternative is the wider use of replication in psychological research.

The specific issues involved in selecting research methods with children are thoroughly reviewed in Mussen (1960), a volume which should be consulted. There is, however, one methodological issue of relevance to all the studies in this book, and that concerns sampling. Ideally, of course, every study should involve randomly selected children where randomization is based on an entire population. This approach is obviously not feasible; the fact is that subjects for most research are secured from cooperating school districts and from university nursery schools. Both sources of subjects introduce bias into the research outcome, especially children from university nursery schools. The argument that a biased sample does not influence the general form of a law of development or the variables influencing behavior, except to shift the distribution in one or another direction, is probably untrue. As we gain new knowledge about children's cognitive behavior, for example, it becomes increasingly clear that patterns of development and the variables influencing that development are highly individualistic. We suspect that the behavioral predispositions of "culturally disadvantaged" children are sufficiently different from the middle-class norm that the variables which influence one group in a particular way may have very different effects on the other. The importance of sampling effects are shown rather clearly in the paper by Moss and Kagan (Chapter 15), who conclude that the stability of achievement-oriented behavior, as observed in their study, may be unique to the upper-middle-class culture from which their subjects were selected. These comments are intended as a caution not to overgeneralize research findings unless it is known that the variables interact with subject characteristics in a uniform way.

Issues Related to Research Strategies

The approach used by an investigator in studying a general problem area is called a research strategy. Terrell and Harris, for example, propose opposing strategies for studying children which should be carefully read (Chapter 2). Terrell believes that research should be conducted in highly controlled laboratory settings involving relatively simple behaviors; that is, behaviors such as discrimination learning involving geometric figures. Certainly a discrimination learning task is not simple in terms of the psychological processes involved, but the psychological processes are probably less complex than those involved in learning arithmetic. Terrell also argues for the laboratory setting, as opposed to the classroom, because of the large numbers of variables known to operate in the classroom. Not the least of these variables is the teacher, who undoubtedly influences the outcome, in unknown ways, of any research done in the classroom setting. As noted earlier in this chapter, the experimenter also influences the outcome of laboratory experiments; but it is much easier to use several experimenters than it is to use several teachers. Finally, Terrell contends that our knowledge of behavior is so limited that broad-scale studies in naturalistic settings are likely to yield inaccurate findings.

Harris' position is that a great deal of important knowledge can be gained from studying children in naturalistic settings where the dependent variable involves "real-life" behaviors. A basic contention is that knowledge gained in artificial laboratory settings may not apply when other influences are permitted to operate. When learning arithmetic, for example, the child's emotional responses to the material may significantly modify the implications derived from laboratory studies. If behavior is to be completely understood, the total configuration of variables must be included in our research. None may be artificially removed. The strategy is one of observing behavior and teasing out the variables in the current situation, as well as the relevant historical variables, influencing current behavior. Eventually it should be possible to demonstrate how the multitude of interacting variables leads to individual patterns of behaviors.

Another important strategy issue involves the difference between accumulating descriptive data as opposed to manipulating independent variables and testing for effects on dependent variables. Studies of child development rely heavily on the first strategy and include the development of age norms, correlational studies, and studies where subjects are selected on the basis of scores on a test. This strategy is sometimes labeled "response-response" (R-R) because it involves the relationship among two sets of responses or, in the case of normative data, two variables. Thus in developing age norms, the investigator examines behavioral change in terms of age change, often without regard for the variables correlated with age change. A clearer example of the response-response strategy is the study involving the correlation between two test scores or two observations of behavior. Correlational studies are descriptive because they show what classes of behavior tend to cluster; that is, correlational analysis describes the similarities among behavioral attributes. Factor analysis, which relies on the intercorrelations of many variables, is a highly sophisticated technique for describing the similarities among diverse measures of behavior. Finally, studies which categorize subjects on a variable, such as anxiety, and then test for differences in behavior among the categories are also response-response in approach.

The response-response strategy has made important contributions to knowledge about children and is widely used. Correlational studies, in showing relationships among behaviors, have generated many hypotheses about the causes underlying the behaviors. Knowledge about the components of intellectual ability have been derived from correlational analysis which has led to innovations in intelligence testing. Despite the many contributions, the strategy has certain limitations: (1) cause-effect interpretations cannot be ascribed to R-R relationships, and therefore little knowledge is gained about significant antecedents influencing the behavor; (2) there is a high risk that other variables mediate the R-R relationship so that a relationship is more apparent than real. The problem is especially difficult in the case of research where subjects are categorized and the extremes of the distribution are used in the experiment. Using extreme groups enhances the probability that the subjects possess unique attributes, correlated with the categorized variable, which are crucial in determining a behavioral outcome. Unfortunately these unspecified variables are subsumed under the general categorical rubric (anxiety, cognitive style, etc.) giving the appearance of a direct cause-and-effect relationship.

The stimulus-response (S-R) and/or experimental strategy involves the direct manipulation of independent variables. Although most S-R studies with children are conducted in laboratory settings, the strategy is by no means restricted to that setting. S-R studies permit the direct assessment of antecedent conditions on behavior, providing evidence about the generality of specific environmental manipulations. The logic underlying this statement is that among *randomly selected* children, the effect of an environmental manipulation may modify behavior in some systematic way that, because of sample randomization, is relatively independent of other variables. Thus, anxiety may be manipulated by varying shock strength and the effects on behavior assessed.

The S-R strategy is receiving considerable attention among investigators because of the importance of more directly assessing the impact of stimulus variables on behavior. Critics of the strategy have focused primarily on the lack of sample randomization, arguing that antecedent manipulations may very well interact with variables unique to particular samples. This criticism has received empirical support; lower-class children, for example, frequently respond to experimental conditions differently from middle-class children. Secondly, S-R studies frequently deal with "trivial" problems because of the restrictions placed on investigators in manipulating antecedent variables. (Intensity of shock cannot be used as an antecedent condition because of possible adverse effects on a child.) Finally, critics contend, with some justification, that antecedent manipulations are often perceived differently by the investigator and by the children, leading to erroneous conclusions.

Each of the issues described in this chapter provides a basis for evaluating the research procedures and theoretical positions reflected in the papers included in this book. The objective of this evaluative activity should not be the outright acceptance or rejection of the research findings but rather an assessment of the findings in terms of their contribution to understanding the variables influencing behavior. It is just possible that the suggested approach to evaluation may generate many interesting, and testable, hypotheses.

CHAPTER II

Concepts and Methods
in Child Development

THE STUDIES included in this book represent a broad range of research strategies and methodologies. A research strategy relates to the general design employed by an investigator and is largely determined by the investigator's conceptual biases. There is an additional consideration, not unrelated to conceptual orientation, which involves the nature and scope of the questions asked by the investigator. It is possible, for example, to study children's concept learning in a naturalistic setting, such as the classroom, on the assumption that this behavior is influenced by a variety of stimuli. The specific concept examined is typically relevant to academic achievement (quantity concepts, for example) because these behaviors have important practical significance. It is also possible, however, to study concept behaviors in the laboratory. This strategy is based on the assumption that concept behavior is sufficiently complex without the addition of "naturalistic" variables whose effects are unknown. Studies of this kind are likely to use nonacademic behaviors (learning a size concept using geometric forms, for example) and include the manipulation of specific independent variables. A rationale for the former view is described in Professor Harris' paper, while the latter view is presented by Dr. Terrell. Both papers are included in this chapter.

There are two general methods employed in developmental studies which derive from a basic concept of human development. Briefly, this concept views development as continuous over time, resulting from the interaction of heredity and environment. Behavioral change is tied closely to changes in chronological age, which fact suggests that research will be concerned with a description of age differences. A strategy consistent with this predeterministic concept involves studying children of different chronological ages with respect to one or more behavioral attributes. One method consistent with this strategy is called "cross-sectional," meaning that children are randomly selected from each of several age levels. The average performance of each age group is compared and inferences about systematic age changes are made. This procedure permits the investigator to obtain the data necessary to test his hypothesis in a very short period of time. One disadvantage of this technique is the difficulty of obtaining comparable samples at each of the successive age groups, especially during the latter part of the teens (less intelligent children leave school). A similar, but more subtle, disadvantage is the fact that no two age groups are ever exposed to exactly the same environmental variables. This difficulty is perhaps less serious when two contiguous age groups are compared; but when the age range spans more than four or five years, comparability of experiences is very difficult to obtain.

A second approach, consistent with a concept of age-related changes in behavior, is called the "longitudinal method" and involves repeated observations on the same individuals. This method provides comparability of sample (typically there is some attrition due to death, distinterest, or inaccessibility) because the same children are used at each age level. The effect of cultural variation is not resolved in this method because specific events can modify behaviors at a particular age point, producing age-related behavior which might appear to be the result of normal development. In the paper by Professors Kodlin and Thompson in this chapter, several extremely important methodological considerations and problems associated with the longitudinal method are examined.

The development of psychological theories pertinent to age changes in behavior has not occurred as rapidly as has the accumulation of empirical data. Psychoanalytic theory and Piaget's model of cognitive development represent the major integrated theories with respect to human development. Central to both theories is the concept of "stages" which, in general, refers to specific, more or less nonoverlapping, levels of behavioral patterns. This view has not gained wide acceptance among American students of human development, who prefer the hypothesis that development is continuous. William Kessen describes the various meanings of the "stage" concept, showing some of its fundamental weaknesses as well as its merits. He is especially concerned about the failure of "stage" theorists to specify the rules of transition from stage to stage — a failure which he believes must be overcome before the concept can be integrated into modern behavior theory.

The final paper in this chapter, by Yvonne Brackbill, is an excellent description of the concepts and methods used by child psychologists in the Soviet Union. Briefly, the foundation of Soviet psychology is based on the philosophy of dialectical materialism as developed by Marx and Engels. This view rejects the mind-body dualism, accepting instead "the view that mental phenomena are inseparably connected with the functioning of the brain and that they can be investigated by the same objective methods as are other phenomena of nature" (Simon 1957, p. 2). Concepts such as the unconscious, spontaneous drives and impulses, or any other formulation outside the material realm are rejected on the grounds that they are nonobjective (nonmaterial) and therefore not in the realm of science. Consciousness, that is, an awareness of objective stimulation, derives from an external material world that is independent of the perceiver.

Indeed, perception reflects a unique organization of matter, in this case matter being the brain. Cortical matter is organized and changed by external conditions in the material life of the society and is developed in practical activity. The implications of this doctrine for research and educational practices are described in Professor Brackbill's paper.

The Developmental Viewpoint

Dale B. Harris

Children are an extremely important resource to any nation and consequently are assigned a position of special status in most societies. A consequence of this position for the scientist is to determine whether more is gained from using children as subjects to test specific hypotheses or whether children should be studied for their own sake. In his Presidential Address to the members of the Division on Developmental Psychology of the American Psychological Association, Professor Dale B. Harris takes the position that a great deal more of importance can be learned about children when they are the main purpose of the research than when a specific theoretical issue is of greater salience. He also raises many important and thoughtful questions about the adequacy of modern learning theory as a means of accounting for the complexity of human behavior. The developmental viewpoint, which has not yet generated a well-defined theoretical model, serves to remind investigators that human development is a complex interaction of biological and environmental variables.

The behavior theorist working in child psychology affirms the value of unitary concepts, the prime importance of theory, and the power of the hypothetico-deductive method in child psychology. He sees the behavior of all living things as subject to one set of laws; one set of general behavior principles suffices for rats and men. Children become convenient, not necessarily essential, subjects for the study of behavior. Within this framework of thinking, child psychology truly is anomalous, and it is difficult to discern any definitive meaning for the term "development." This viewpoint often accuses many child psychologists of being too much concerned with application, too little with conceptual formulation and experimentation, for the health of their science.

Child vs. Developmental Psychology

There are others who hold that the developmental point of view in psychology contributes something unique which general behavior theory as presently con-

SOURCE: Adapted and abridged from Dale B. Harris, "Child Psychology and the Concept of Development." Presidential address read before the Division on Developmental Psychology of the American Psychological Association, September 3, 1956. (With permission of the author and publisher.)

ceived does not supply. Not only may it be necessary to phrase somewhat
different principles for the explanation of behavior when we move from rats to
men; it may also be necessary to redefine the principles according to which
behavior becomes organized as we move from lesser to greater maturity of
subjects. Thus, children become essential subjects for the understanding of
human behavior. The study of animal behavior, on a comparative basis, is also
essential in a truly developmental psychology, but cannot substitute for the study
of children, of adults, and of older people. The child psychologist with a developmental point of view has a somewhat different approach in theory, method, and
application than the child psychologist who is more strictly oriented in behavior
or learning theory. Furthermore, he affirms that a developmental interpretation
of behavior will contribute effectively to psychology by conceptualizing certain
problems and phenomena which the behavior theorist tends to overlook or to
by-pass.

At the present time, a developmental conceptualization of behavior differs
somewhat from behavior or learning theory with respect to the use of components of formal theory, though ultimately both the behavior or learning
theorist and the developmental theorist would hope to phrase their formulations
in terms of basic axioms. The behavior theorist presently goes beyond the developmentalist in his use of analytical terms; in so doing he achieves the appearance
of a more elegant and formal structure, but whether he actually has attained
greater flexibility in manipulating formal concepts is perhaps debatable.

In this contrast of viewpoints there is also implied a distinction which has
troubled life sciences for many years. It was rife in the mechanistic-vitalistic
arguments of the last century. The implication that this difference is real and
significant is found again in many contemporary discussions, though it takes a
different form from the earlier controversy. The behavior theorist primarily seeks
to discuss phenomena in terms of cause. He hopes ultimately to derive the
behavior phenomena commonly subsumed by "purpose" from a set of constructs
not themselves purposive. But at the present he concentrates on the experimental
manipulation of antecedents. The developmentalist more frankly thinks in terms
of "ends" or "purposes," albeit uneasily, because of his intellectual traditions
which rule out teleology. The developmentalist, like the biologist, cannot escape
the fact that predictable end states results from origins in which these states,
though not discernible, are somewhat implicit; that function is circumscribed by
structure, yet serves to maintain that structure. It should be clear that the
modern biologist in speaking of "purpose" invokes nothing outside the material
universe. Rather, his "purpose" is in the configurations themselves. It is seen in
the intrinsic forces which operate to give characteristic form and function to the
growing organism.

For the behavior theorist, useful constructs are inferred states or processes
such as perception or motivation. The constructs offered by the developmentalist
cut across such processes, taking the form of motor behavior, social development,

and intellectual growth — classes of behavior described phenomenally, and more readily susceptible to the language of the "purpose" or functions ultimately served.

The methodology of the behavior theorist is one of theoretical formulation, the conceptual isolation of variables, and the crucial experiment; the developmentalist leans much more heavily upon directed observation and upon the use of the experiment empirically to define and isolate variables as well as to test the significant relationship of variables. The ideal of behavior theory is systematic design and the laboratory experiment; the developmental viewpoint perhaps comes closer to Egon Brunswik's concept of the representative design and insists that in many instances we may be forced to rely upon experiments of nature. When phenomena have remote historical antecedents, as those revealed in the psychotherapeutic session for example, it may not be possible fully to replicate them, or to formulate suitable principles to understand them in the phenomena available in the laboratory surrogate for the life history. Behavior theory focuses its attention relatively more on the specific stimulus conditions which elicit behavior and on the effect of variability in the stimulus condition on a given behavior response. The developmental viewpoint, while recognizing the importance of the environment and paying considerable attention to variability in stimulus conditions, studies both constancy and variability in responses of the organism in relation to the complexity of the environing situation, especially as complexity alters over time.

Because the developmentalist is interested in global phenomena and tends to use a phenomenistic terminology, he inevitably becomes more concerned with practical applications than does the behavior theorist, who usually wishes to avoid them. In the field of child psychology this problem is especially acute. Children are socially significant, and the developmentalist tends to take his cues from the attention given the problems of growth and adjustment which practical workers from many professions continually face. These problems, they insist, have their most definite meaning in the context of the child's experience; and, at any rate for the developmental psychologist who works with human behavior, the problems must be phrased in a language which treats of the phenomenon of "purpose" or "goal-seeking." Hence, these problems are scientifically meritorious as they occur. The behavior theorist wishes to restate the problems in conceptual terms which are not themselves intrinsically purposive. The developmentalist has no fundamental quarrel with this position except that he believes that at the present state of knowledge, it is not possible to work at such a reduced level of analysis and still deal with certain pressing scientific issues.

In drawing these opposing positions, we are, of course, not affirming an all-or-none position. We see each of these distinctions as a matter of relative emphasis. Perhaps this relative emphasis bespeaks differences in habits of thinking in two groups. Lest it seem that this statement merely charges off to "personality differences" some rather vague distinctions which one cannot otherwise assign, it may be well to recognize that a similar division in viewpoint appears in the biological literature. Perhaps we are saying the difference is due merely to differences in the sets of constructs which the proponents have been trained to use. However, this may be, in biology as in most science, there is no disposition at the moment to put all eggs into one theoretical basket, although this is what some behavior theorists apparently wish to do.

Theory in Contemporary Child Psychology

Of today's child psychologists who are most concerned with theory, Sears and his colleagues come closer than most to bridging the gap between a formal behavior theory and the phenomena of development and change in child behavior. By giving descriptive terms quite carefully delimited definition, Sears (1957) constructs a systematic theory of behavioral or action change which goes far to account for molar phenomena. His recent contributions are taking form as a carefully wrought scientific contribution to developmental theory. His identification of the dimension of action permits study of the person-as-a-whole, one primary omission of most behavior theories, and his accounting for both dependency and aggression in terms of learning theory goes a long way toward handling two particularly complex phenomena.

Baldwin's (1955) recent contribution to developmental theory is frankly based on intuitive or common sense understanding of child behavior. Theory grows out of such understanding by the scientist concerning himself with observable phenomena and by developing ever broader principles which will embrace more phenomena. Baldwin's approach thus attempts to take account of the phenomena of behavior as it occurs; he tries to translate the child in his phenomenal world into general and abstract principles; he does not develop a system of theorems which are then tested by crucial experiments. Baldwin, then, stays closer to the developmental tradition.

Werner's (1948) idea of differentiation from primitive wholistic or global responses into more specific responses calls attention to the progressive emergency of more complex forms from simpler antecedents. Piaget's work, calling attention to the significance of early sensory experience in the infant's exploratory contacts with his world, shows how these more complex forms may be shaped by the circumstances under which the simpler antecedents have occurred.

John E. Anderson's (1957) description of principles of a developmental theory go far toward stating the problems of child behavior study in terms of biological principles and models. Of particular value is his treatment of development as process, involving the environing conditions. In this, he comes close to the concept advanced by the ecologist which embraces the totality of living and non-living things in the natural world in one vast, complexly interwoven web of relationships. Barker and Wright have made good use of ecological principles in their program of research on child behavior.

The Concept of Development in Psychology

With these general precautions let us take a closer look at concepts of development as applied to the study of human behavior. Several of these concepts have their origin in biological science.

Modern biology tends to be organismic — that is, it regards the living capable of maintaining its existence as a unitary system and of reproducing itself. Likewise, the developmental concept in psychology deals with the human individual as a living system and within an environing system. Although the developmentalist in psychology pays attention to the complexly patterned character of the stimulus situation, his primary emphasis is on the tendency of the organism to organize its responses in a self-maintaining fashion over major divisions of the life span. He is concerned with continuities in behavior as well as variability among responses. In the case of the human being, he is particularly interested that the individual develops a highly complex symbolic representation of its self.

Development and the Open System

In studying the living system, the developmentalist regards it as "open." Physical or "closed" systems tend toward an equilibrium which is attained from reversible reactions, usually chemical in nature. Living systems, on the contrary, are said to be never truly in equilibrium, but rather in a steady state attained by irreversible reactions. By importing complex organic molecules, using their energy and turning back simpler end products to the environment, the living system builds irreversible changes into itself. It is this feature which possibly makes the mechanical model unsuitable for the living organism and accounts for the complexity which so impresses the developmentalist. Once changes are built into the organism, they modify permanently the relationship of the organism to the environment, changing the probabilities that other sorts of changes will or will not occur. Over time, these changes become cumulative and modify the character of the organism's behavior. But this modification occurs slowly; the very complexity of the system gives it behavioral durability without complete rigidity.

Thus, the organism itself becomes a factor in its own development. To say that the organism acts in part as an agent in shaping its developmental course may merely group a number of antecedents and relegate them to the background, unanalyzed. Yet the concept of organism, which by the character of its organization up to a given point of the developmental process serves as an agent to shape the further course of that process, can be an important corrective for the notion that behavior is simply reactive, and situationally determined, the produce of forces acting at the moment. The developmentalist tends to see determinism as much more complex. Furthermore, with his emphasis on history, the developmentalist sees deterministic sequences reaching far back in time. To enable himself to move forward in this thinking, the developmentalist, it must be admitted, sometimes invokes concepts which have been called "mentalistic." Biologists and philosophers of science also struggle with such concepts as "determinism" and "purpose." Some such term as "purpose" is difficult to avoid in discussing motivated human behavior.

Organization in the System

The concept of organization is the second major contribution of the developmental point of view in psychology. Behavior is seen as having a complex, diversified structure made up of many parts; that is, any one behavior response is made up of many part movements woven together in complex fashion. Behavior development consists in the modification, the elaboration of this structure. It is not merely additive. The fundamental question is, how do these units combine and change their combination over time? Can this best be described by such terms as differentiation or integration, or both? For the developmental view stresses the fact that over long reaches of time the simple paradigms of learning theory seem not to describe adequately the patterned responses which increase in complexity, yet show greater specificity of parts, as an infant and youthful organism matures. This is not the occasion to rehearse the familiar difficulties with the concepts of differentiation and integration. Here the developmentalist's use of figurative language and analogy undoubtedly have created part of the trouble. And although we use these expressions less often now than formerly, the phenomena they were coined to express still perplex us.

The possibility that complexity itself may become a limited factor in further differentiation and organization must be recognized. John E. Anderson (1957) has pointed out that through learning the organism becomes progressively less multi-potential, more efficient, but also more rigid. The child who spends his hours after school playing baseball rather than practicing music is not likely to gain skill with an instrument in adult life. Whether or not the baseball skill becomes "significant," in Anderson's sense, depends on still other events which have their own probabilistic character. The changing probabilities occasioned by these irreversible sequences in development thus exercise a cumulative, constraining character on development. No current learning theory adequately considers these "built in" limitations on behavior organization which the developmentalist recognizes.

Another important limitation on development is found in the competition among growth processes within the individual. We see this illustrated functionally in the arrest sometimes occurring in language development at the onset of rapid motor development. Still another limitation on development is found in the demands made on the individual by his social context. Here the formulations of sex and class role have a particularly meaningful connotation. Such concepts represent a different order of phenomena than those which relate only to the limits imposed on the subject by a piece of candy, the discrimination box, and the exhortation of the experimenter.

The Importance of Symbolic Processes in Development

Finally, the developmentalist calls particular attention to the symbolic processes of which the human organism alone is capable. While the symbolic function of signs as a language of expression or of command is found in lower animals, the reference of symbols to content or things is found only in man. This symbolic function is essentially the function of "mind," with which the psychologist has traditionally been concerned. Even when we consider such "mental" activities only as a form of behavior, we must admit that symbolizing behavior constitutes a great share of human behavior.

The developmentalist emphasizes for general psychology the fact that the aspects of the internal environment which we call psychological, to distinguish them conveniently from the physiological or biochemical, owe much of their constancy to this symbolizing process. This symbolizing capacity of man enables him to develop a concept of himself and to elaborate this self-concept as he grows more complex over time. Child development has always stressed the significance of language in conceptual processes and in the development of the self-image. The psychoanalytically inclined student of the self-image emphasizes the nonverbal aspects of the body image, such as organic sensations, id drives, and the like. While recognizing the importance of these, the developmental psychologist stresses the significance of the so-called higher mental processes which are implemented and carried forward by this symbolic function. The clinician notes that conflicts between biologic drives and emotionalized social controls lead to adjustment difficulties, and the developmentalist points out that social controls are mediated by symbol systems, that conflicts between symbol systems can themselves cause trouble and that various performance skills acquired and evaluated within the framework of a complex symbolic system, have distinct adjustive functions.

The capacity to represent experience by symbols and to deal with it apart from its context permits man to some extent to manipulate the future through goal-setting activities. Thus symbols become controlling devices and, in man, are clearly the basis of "purpose" or of the end-serving activities which are so important to social psychologists, clinical psychologists, and educational psychologists. The developmentalist thus inevitably becomes concerned with the "phenomenal world." The biological capacity of the organism to resist damage and to heal itself from environmental insults appears to have its psychological counterpart. The symbol system, being the basis of the self-image, permits man a good deal of psychological maintenance and self-repair. The developmentalist, along with the phenomenologist, remarks on the capacity of the personality to perceive experience in such a way as to support its organization or integration. Modifications are resisted, particularly if those modifications threaten the unitary character of the personality or its capacity to maintain its integrity over time. We see this behavioral characteristic vividly in young children, denoting it as resistance or negativism when it comes athwart our purpose. It is this concept of behavioral durability which the developmentalist recommends to the clinical worker, or to anyone prone to analyze behavior in terms of a simple situational determinism.

We have noted how the organism's history becomes an important determiner of its future development. In man, the symbolic capacity gives his personal history a particular significance. To experimental psychology's concern with present states and functions the developmental viewpoint adds a concern with process, how the organism came to its present state. The developmentalist has a point to make to the educator, the clinician, the social worker when he discusses behavior change or therapy as fundamentally a process of reorganization brought about either by change of external forces or by change of the internal organization, or by both.

Increasingly we are coming to see that the scientist cannot pursue the truth with indifference to its application. Children matter very much to a vast multitude of parents, teachers, and others. What the parent or teacher believes about the contribution by the child himself to his learnings as compared with the contribution by the stimulus situations matters very much to what the adult does with the child and eventually to what the child requires.

The Behavior-Theorist Viewpoint

Glenn Terrell

A fundamental question that involves almost all scientists is whether the problems of society are best solved by direct attack with immediate application or by the systematic investigation of the variables related to the problem. The history of psychology reveals too many instances where the former approach generated practices that were subsequently shown to be inadequate or, at best, appropriate to only a limited group who happened to incorporate certain antecedent traits. Dr. Terrell carefully argues that knowledge, which can be appropriately applied, results from the painstaking accumulation of empirical relationships. From the behavior-theorist's viewpoint, studies of broad complex problems are premature because the basic relevant variables are as yet not well understood. Dr. Terrell reflects this attitude in his call for simple measures of behavior.

Perhaps the best way to begin this paper is to explain what the writer means by simple research in child psychology. A few examples should suffice: (a) the effects of interference on crank-turning behavior; (b) an experiment involving the learning of concepts of size; (c) an investigation of reinforcement variables

SOURCE: Adapted and abridged from Glenn Terrell, "The Need for Simplicity in Research in Child Psychology." *Child Development,* 1958, 29, 303–310. (With permission of the author and the Society for Research in Child Development.)

affecting the resistance to extinction of a simple response of placing a ball in a hole. In each of these problems the behavior studied is relatively simple, particularly in relation to far more complex responses involved in studies of social development, or in investigations of the effects of child-rearing methods on personality growth. It is felt that the best way to begin the argument for the current need for simple research in child psychology is to make an analysis of a characteristic area of research involving exceedingly complex variables. For this purpose, the writer has selected the general area involving the effects of child-rearing variables on personality development. Out of this analysis and subsequent argument should come the impression that the writer's main reason for favoring "basic" research is a methodological one. Following this discussion, the writer will present some of the important uses of the study of simple processes in child psychology, and will follow this with a treatment of the advantages that such a research orientation has.

To illustrate what the writer considers the prematurity of research at a complex level in child psychology, perhaps the analysis of a hypothetical example will prove helpful. Let us suppose that an investigator wishes to study, among other things, the relationship between the duration of breast feeding in infancy and the frequency of dependency behavior of elementary school children. Measures of duration of breast feeding are obtained by the interview, while measures of dependency are taken in a standardized projective doll-play situation. For the sake of the argument, let us assume that the investigation is conducted with the greatest possible care. Much preparation has gone into the interview and the doll play procedures in order that the research reduce to a minimum the invalidities and unreliabilities of the study due to these factors. Further, let it be assumed that the investigator finds a significant inverse correlation between duration of breast feeding and the frequency of dependency behavior.

To what extent is he justified in claiming the discovery of a relationship between these variables? Obviously the experimenter is not manipulating the independent variable. Though a relevant variable can be isolated and studied without the experimenter's manipulating it, the difficulty with this procedure, as McCandless and Spiker (1956) recently pointed out in an appeal for more experimental research in child psychology, is greatly increased as the number of relevant variables affecting the dependent system is increased. And as McCandless and Spiker in the same paper further pointed out, "That a very large number of variables affects the behavior of the living organism is a fact that has long been recognized" (p. 76). Here is the crux of the difficulty: the number of relevant variables affecting the dependent system in complex research, as in the hypothetical example, is undoubtedly far greater than those affecting relatively simple responses. Furthermore, they are infinitely more difficult to isolate and control. In fact, the control of variables associated with the study of the effects of child-rearing techniques on adjustment is in most cases impossible at the present stage. Indeed, it is highly probable that the great majority of these variables are as yet unidentified. Some of the possible variables more obviously relevant to dependency, other than the duration of breast feeding, are the character structure of the parents, friendship patterns, socioeconomic class, genetic and constitutional factors, and the nature of sibling relationships. Variables such as these are more often than not unconsidered in studies at this level, and even if efforts to study them were made, the outlook would indeed be bleak, since it would be difficult if not impossible to say which has affected the dependent variable, and to what degree. The end result of this state of affairs is, of course, that the experimenter thinks he has discovered a relationship in child-rearing variables, when in reality there is a good chance that one or more of the unconsidered variables mentioned above has brought about the change in the dependent variables. Any well-trained scientist must admit that because of the above reasoning, there is, at the very best, only a slight, highly equivocal suggestion in the results of the above described hypothetical study that there is a meaningful relationship between the variables studied, certainly not enough to warrant the confident statements about child-rearing problems one frequently sees emanating from such research. It is not at all unlikely that many child psychologists have been misled into conducting further research along these lines, to say nothing of the possibly more serious consequences of parents being misled by reports of these studies.

It is unmistakably clear that one of the newer trends in developmental psychology is a preoccupation with basic research problems that relate to some of the significant problems in general psychology, particularly within a stimulus-response framework. Two of these problems will be described briefly, along with some of the research that has been performed with children bearing on these issues.

First, there is the principle of stimulus generalization, which has been used in general behavior theory to explain, among others, such phenomena as the occurrence of sudden or insightful solutions of problems and the persistence of behavior that is not rewarded, or is even punished. One of the important variables assumed to affect the generalization of a response is the number of reinforcements given on the training stimulus. The evidence from classical conditioning with infrahuman and adult human subjects demonstrates fairly conclusively that an increase in the number of reinforcements on the training (conditioned) stimulus results in an increased amount of generalization to the test stimuli. Spiker (1956) has developed a simple technique to extend these findings to the young child. The Ss, preschoolers, were trained to pull a lever repeatedly to a stimulus of a given hue in order to receive marbles. They were then tested on stimuli of different hues to determine the number of responses that would be made to the test stimuli without received reinforcement. A group given 24 reinforcements to the conditioned stimulus prior to the generalization test averaged nearly twice as many responses to the test stimuli as did a group given only 12 preliminary reinforcements. Thus, the same relationship found to exist at the infrahuman and human adult levels was found to apply to the preschool child. In a later experiment it was found that the steepness of the generalization gradient was also a positive function of the number of reinforced training trials as well as the intensity of the stimuli used in the training. These results are in agreement with experiments at the infrahuman level, and with the prediction made by Hull (1952) on the basis of the principle of stimulus dynamism.

The second principle from general psychology which has received recent attention in child psychology is the principle of secondary or mediated generalization, sometimes referred to as acquired equivalence of cues. In brief, this principle states that if S has been trained to make the same response to two or more dissimilar stimuli, there will be an increased tendency to generalize to the other stimulus other responses subsequently learned to one of the stimuli. In other words, if S is taught to make response 1 to stimuli 1 and 2, then taught to make response 2 to stimulus 1, he will make response 2 to stimulus 2. Jeffrey (1953) has demonstrated the role of mediating responses in generalization. He trained his Ss to move a lever, again a simple dependent variable, in one direction to a white stimulus, and in the opposite direction to a black stimulus. He then taught some Ss to call a gray stimulus "white" and others to call it "black," and next retrained the Ss on the lever-moving task to the white and black stimuli. Following this, he presented the gray stimulus interspersed with black and white stimuli to determine how the Ss would respond to the gray stimulus. He found that if the Ss had been taught to call the gray stimulus "white," they reponded to it as they did to the white stimulus; if they had been taught to call the gray stimulus "black," they responded to it as they did to the black stimulus. He found a similar tendency for another group of Ss who instead of using the names "black" and "white" had been taught to turn the handle to the right or the left for the white, black, and gray stimuli. Thus, Jeffrey demonstrates that either verbal or motor responses may serve as mediating responses.

The study of simple responses like the ones described in the experiments above may be made in more applied, pragmatic research with children. For example, in the important area of incentives in children's learning, the writer and Kennedy (1957) have shown that a candy reward results in quicker learning and more consistent transfer of a "larger-than" concept than either praise, reproof, a light flash, or a delayed reward. The only exception to this latter statement was the nonsignificant difference that existed in the consistency of transfer between the candy reward group and the group that was given a delayed reward. In this experiment the behavior studied was a simple button-pushing response to the larger of two three-dimensional geometric objects. The nonsignificant difference in the candy (immediate) and delayed reward group of the aforementioned study led to an experiment comparing two types of delayed rewards with each other and with an immediate reward in the learning and transferring of a "larger-than" discrimination (Terrell 1958). It was hypothesized that Ss assigned to a delayed reward condition which permitted them to observe progress toward the to-be-received reward would learn more quickly and transfer more consistently than would Ss assigned to a delayed reward condition that did not allow them to observe their progress in the learning situation. This hypothesis was convincingly supported by the results of the experiment.

Now what advantages do the studies of simple behaviors in the experiments cited above have, other than their contributions to general psychology? As was stated previously, they are mainly methodological. First of all, when we study basic responses, the variables, both independent and dependent, are easier to manipulate. Compare, for example, the difficulties associated with isolating, controlling, and measuring complex child-rearing and adjustment variables with the relative ease and rigor of control in (a) Jeffrey's study of the effects of simple verbal instructions, "say white" or "say black," on crank-turning responses, or (b) Spiker's experiment with the generalization of lever-pulling responses to lights of varying hues, intensities, and frequencies. Because of the more rigorous control exercised in the latter experiments, the experimenter minimizes the danger of masking the basic processes. That we can be less equivocal about interpreting the results of these experiments is obvious.

In most experiments the researcher has a choice in the matter of selecting responses to be studied. For example, Spiker may well have studied the principle of stimulus generalization within a more complex, clinical framework, by obtaining measures of generalization of responses of children from maladjusted teachers to peers or love interests, instead of studying the generalization of lever-pulling responses to lights of differing intensities and hues. Or again, the writer may have studied the effects of various incentives on the solution of higher mathematics problems, or on some of the more intricate aspects of social development in childhood. That we are all interested in the latter problems is a foregone conclusion. In fact, the critics of the writer's position will ask the question, "Of what practical value is it to investigate these simple, trivial behaviors? What we need to know, indeed what society is demanding of us now, is the solution of important practical problems in developmental psychology, such as the complex factors involved in learning and personality development." The writer's answer to this argument is that he believes that ultimately we will be able to supply answers to the complex, immediately relevant social problems associated with child psychology more quickly if we first systematize our knowledge of relationships existing at an elementary behavior level. By doing this we do not get ahead of our limited methodological resources, which has always been one of the greatest tendencies of researchers in child psychology. And what is even more important, we do not run the serious risk of misleading society.

The Concepts of "Stage" and "Structure"

William Kessen

It is not unusual for a child to be described as being in a particular "stage" of development. Describing children in terms of "stages" conveys more than a convenient categorization of behaviors. For example, in the personality theory of Freud or the theory of cognitive development of Piaget, the concept of "stages" is used to indicate a more or less unique set of structures or processes which are discontinuous with either previous or subsequent stages. Dr. Kessen analyzes the meaning and usefulness of "stage" theories for developmental psychology. His recommendations for how current "stage" theories should be modified will serve as an important guideline for serious students of developmental theory.

Men seem always to have felt a need to impose segmentation on the complicated course of human development. Although it has usually been argued that development is "continuous" and without discrete shifts, more often than not the arguer has early called on the notion of "stage" or "level" to help him understand the speed and fluidity of change in children.

Two theories of human development demand and receive wide attention — the speculations of Piaget and of Freud — and both make use of the "stage" construct in ways that are certainly nontrivial and that may be crucial. It is not necessary to stipulate the usefulness or adequacy of these formulations; their very visibility requires that we attend to their devices of segmentation.

The pages to follow present in some detail a critical examination of the "stage" construct, not chiefly from a historical or a textual-analytic basis, but rather in exploration of the theoretical range of the notion. What burden of theory is carried by statements about stages? Are there variations in use of the terms which stand in need of separation? What formulations are available as alternatives to segmentation by stages? Discussion of these and related questions will uncover many traditional puzzles in the study of development; in fact, the ubiquity of the segmentation issue is well demonstrated by the variety of problems with which it is linked. One in particular — the theoretical status of statements about mental structure — is particularly relevant to the work of Jean Piaget and will be examined later in this paper.

The Several Uses of "Stage"

Literary-Evocative

Unhappily, one common use of "stage" carries no more weight than a meta-

---

SOURCE: Adapted and abridged from William Kessen, " 'Stage' and 'Structure' in the Study of Children." *Monographs of the Society for Research in Child Development*, 1962, 27, No. 83, 65–82. (With permission of the author and the Society for Research in Child Development.)

phor. To speak of children as being in the chimpanzee stage is to achieve a joke at best; there are no known and expressable relations between phylogenesis and the behavior of children that advance our understanding. It would doubtless be much too hard-nosed to demand the excision of literary-evocative descriptions of children, but it is worth our while to recognize that the game is limited in its usefulness. Nor is the metaphorical classification of children's behavior restricted to zoological comparisons; one may reasonably ask for any scheme of developmental segmentation whether it depends for its convincingness more on poetical suggestion than on accurate and useful description.

"Stage" as a Paraphrase for Age and as a Paraphrase for Observation

Can we substitute for an expression "The child is in stage x" the alternative expression "The child is y years old"? To the degree that such a substitution is appropriate, the forms are redundant and the "stage" usage unnecessary. By and large, it has been the view of the child psychologists who use the constructions of learning theory that the notion of stage can be dispensed with on exactly these grounds of redundancy with age. The argument typically goes: Age, as a major factor in learning, may have to enter as a parameter to many of our fundamental equations, but this does not justify the invocation of a superfluous and probably empty theoretical term. We must return to this argument later, but there should be noted in it one of the truisms of behavior study, a platitude we forget. Segmentational terms, whether on the model of "response" or on the model of "stage," are not observation words like "black" and "blue," or even easily determined variables like age; they are theoretical terms and, like other theoretical terms, do not name things or events but take their meaning from the context of theory in which they appear. Briefly then, when the language of stages is used merely as a paraphrase for age variation, it is not useful — particularly if such a substitution affords either the psychologist or his audience no more than the satisfaction of apparent new knowledge.

A closely related paraphrastic device, which occurs frequently in parental or natural child psychology and altogether too commonly among professionals as well, consists in using the language of stages to describe observations. The sequence:

Q: Why did Johnny say "no" to me?

A: Because he's in the negativistic stage.

is formally parallel with the well-rubbed example of the child who fights because of his pugnacity instinct. It should be added, however, that explanations of this order are not necessarily, or even usually, vacuous and meaningless; they fulfill an important function that some writers on method have missed. When we say that a child said "No" because he is in the negativistic stage, we are saying something about what explanations will not work (e.g., it is not the case that he said "No" because his Uncle John gives him a dollar for each negation), usually suggesting that our knowledge of the antecedent events that could explain the behavior is incomplete. We also express the fact that there were times in Johnny's life when he did not say "No" so frequently; that is, his no-saying is not universally the case. But it is easy to transmute this device into a mere professional spasm when "He's at the teething age" can be translated as "He's teething," or when "Children at age x enter a tool-using stage" can be translated as "Children at age x begin to use tools."

An exception to the foregoing argument, and one not without interest, can be seen in the use of the "stage" construct to represent *sequence*. The knowledge, for instance, that the stage of tertiary circular reactions (Piaget) occurs after the stage of secondary circular reactions helps us to think coherently about the course of development and, of vastly more consequence, it suggests to us the descriptive or theoretical basis on which the behavior is seen as segmented and developing. For example, Piaget's treatment of changes in the response of the young child to inanimate objects presents a description of sequence which suggests the operation of organizing — i.e., theoretical — principles. Take another example. A statement about "the stages of locomotor development" is, first of all, an abstracted and highly compressed *description* of a limited aspect of infantile behavior, but it also expresses the proposition that there is some nontrivial reason — some theoretical justification — for collecting these segments together in a chronological line. In the best case for sequential statement, there may be underlying regularities (e.g., cephalocaudal progression) which are demonstrated or suggested by the expression of sequence.

Reference to locomotor development leads to another use of the "stage" notion which, though it expresses sequence, aims at being more than a paraphrase for age or observation — the developmental norm or ideal. When it is said that a child is at such-and-such a stage on a normative basis — whether in a relatively primitive way such as "He's a typical 3-year-old" or in the highly sophisticated fashion of intelligence-test mental age scores — more is meant than the statement of succession of behaviors. The scope of the discourse is about differences among children of the same chronological placement (e.g., the typical 3-year-old) and not about inevitable and synchronous succession in all children. This is not an appropriate place to open a discussion of the meaning of the intelligence test norms, but it is appropriate to emphasize that the normative use of "stage" is different from the use of the stage construct in a general developmental theory. Only when we have discussed "stage" as a theoretical construct can we return to a treatment of its proper relevance to the determination of individual differences.

Description of the Environment

The typical occurrence of "stage" has dealt with some unfolding of behavior in the child more or less without reference to his surroundings, but there are relatively frequent occasions in which the notion has to do with the environment as much as with the child. Thus, when Erikson speaks of "crises in development," his emphasis is often on what is happening *to* the child as much as on what is happening *in* the child — witness the case of "trust vs. mistrust" and its relation to the mother's giving and withholding. Similarly, when there is mention of the "school-age child," we normally mean not merely an elliptical specification of age, but the presence of a typical environment — i.e., school — in which the child behaves. The list of examples can be extended almost indefinitely; what bears noting is that the characterization of stage is rarely, if ever, free of the environment in which the child acts, though there may be no explicit treatment of the dimensions of significant variation in behavior ascribable to environmental variations. Perhaps under lead of the ethologists, there is abroad in child psychology a renewed emphasis on the stimulus; that is, on the specification of environmental events antecedent to behavior which shows "maturational" change.

Specification of the Parameters of Variation

In the dissection of the construct "stage," a dramatic shift in generality and scope is seen when stages are taken as parametric variations of a fundamental set of theoretical statements. Before examining this species of stage in psychological usage, let us distort theoretical mechanics to provide a clear, even if absurd, analogous example. An object propelled upward within the earth's atmosphere will, at the top of its trajectory, begin to fall. Now, it would be possible to speak of its "upward-moving stage" and its "downward-moving stage," but this formulation would be favored by relatively few physicists, largely because the formulas for computing position and velocity are the same whether the object is going up or down. Once we know its initial velocity and direction, we can solve the problem. It is toward this use of the construct "stage" that general theorists of development tend to develop general and inclusive formulas about changes in behavior which are operative across the entire course of human development and, further, to reduce the notion of "stage" to parametric variation in these formulas.

There seems little doubt that much of Freud's developmental theory can be put in this form of general formulations combined with parametric variation. The pleasure principle is invariably relevant to behavior; there is a general pattern of reaction to danger, the occurrence of anxiety, and the elaboration of defenses; there are "standard" regularities in gratification and in object relations; all of these are conceptually independent of the specific stage of psychosexual development. The statement, then, that a child is in the oral or the phallic stage is a theoretical instruction to change the parameters of the fundamental equations in a specified way. Noteworthy too is the great economy of this use of the "stage" idea; there is no question that when we say that a child is in the oral stage we mean more than "He is *x* years old," or "He sucks." Translated in the fashion proposed here, the specification of stage makes a statement based on a theory about the child's behavior in diverse settings, relating the special and particular facts about orality to the general theoretical formulations applicable to any phase of development. Psychoanalysis is liable to the charge of imprecision and irregularity in the "fundamental equations" of its descriptive schemes, and this looseness seriously prejudices the usefulness of the theory. But in idealized form, at any rate, psychoanalysis presents "stages" as relatively complicated sets of theoretical statements.

A second example of this more fruitful way of conceiving developmental phasing has been mentioned earlier. Although largely programmatic in its applications to child psychology, the approach of the learning theorists has been of this order. In brief, there are postulated a set of general principles which apply to all ages of man (and, incidentally, of all other mammalian species as well); yet there are clear differences in behavior that can be related to age; therefore, if a theorist aims at a fully generalizable theory of behavior, it will be necessary to make changes in the generalized constants of the fundamental equations in order to predict variation with age. At the empirical level, a good deal of work has been done on age-related variations in behavior having to do with amount, delay, and schedule of reinforcement, generalization and discrimination, responses to changes in drive, and so on; but there remains an obvious gap in the pattern — there is no clear sign of a theory of developmental change derived from the associationistic or more narrowly stimulus-response schools.

General parametric formulations play an important part in Piaget's developmental theories. More specifically than either psychoanalysis or learning theory, Piaget states that there are ubiquitous processes — the functional invariants — which exert their effect throughout the course of development. The stages of Piaget's formulation are explicitly said to vary with variation in mental structure, and it is on mental structures that these unyielding and unvarying processes work. In his work with Inhelder on the growth of logical thinking, Piaget asserts again that the child's striking and often saltatory increases in skill at problem solving, particularly problem solving of a kind that involves the application of physical principles, can be organized around the development of an understanding of logical operations. The stages of the child's mental development, then, are determined by the elegance and advance of his comprehension of negation, reciprocity, and so on. The similarity to the Freudian schema is clear: To say that a child is in a preoperational stage is to say much more than that he is such and such an age or that he can solve such and such a problem. There is included in the statement, based on theory, that his approach to, and competence with, all problems demanding abstract operations will be of a particular and specific kind.

The Operation of Different Rule-Systems

Suppose that one is studying some aspect of behavior in which there is good control over the input of stimulation and with which a fairly simple index or measure of responding is used — the case of probability learning or, more generally, of concept formation may serve as examples. Under some circumstances, it is possible to express the observations in a highly condensed and regular set of rules; that is, a group of equations that contain terms dealing with variation in stimulus input and which lead to prediction of certain response outcomes. Suppose further that this set of equations or operations is so precise that we can write a computer program containing them and that, by acute selection of steps, we can simulate with fair accuracy the performance of human subjects. Take the suppositional game one step further, and the relevance to development will become manifest. If, as a function of age or of correlated change in the development of the child, different programs must be written for the simulation of his behavior, then the notion of "stage" can be given very exact definition. A "stage," under this dispensation, would be a simulation program different from the one which was adequate for the younger child. It may be a matter of some murkiness to decide how much of a change in the program will be called a change in "stage," and it may very well be that this approach to the problem of cognitive development will obliterate the theoretical need for the construct.

Stages, States, and Transitions

With some of the theoretical uses of "stage" outlined, and with the purely literary or paraphrastic uses put to one side, it is possible to make a generalized statement of the problem of stages. From this base, we can move to a discussion of problems and policies in the segmentation of development.

Understanding the problem of segmentation entails remembering some primitive facts about the history of psychology, facts that would have only esoteric and antiquarian interest were it not true that these primitive facts demark continuing rifts among psychologists. Put in briefest compass, and largely to jog memories of old arguments, the divisive dimensions of child psychology (and perhaps of the field at large) can be stated in the following ways.

The psychologist may study *states* of the organism, in a sense catching the bird at the moment in flight and saying, "At this moment, the organism has such and such characteristics." In the language of contemporary psychology, the psychologist of states would, for example, speak of "anxiety state," "defensive structure," or "MMPI profile"; much closer to an interest in children's thinking, he would speak of "mental structure," "levels of cognitive development," and so on.

A colleague of the state-psychologist, and very often a colleague sharing the same skin, is concerned with stable *differences among people* in state-characteristics. This is the traditional view of the clinical psychologist and the psychologist of personality; his central task is in making meaningful segregations of people in terms of state-characteristics. This permits him, at least in program, to make predictions about the behavior of this or that particular person.

Still a third member of our little academic faculty is often out of agreement with his fellows about strategy. He sees the basic psychological problem to be the formulation of general rules for *transition* from one stage or state to another, and his concentration on understanding how the organism gets from one condition to another often makes him less than sympathetic with the psychologist of stage and the psychologist of individual differences.

Piaget, and to some degree Freud, have tried to deal with the disjunction in attack presented by the psychologists of state on one side and the researchers of transition on the other. Piaget has specified, at least for the very young child, certain functional generalizations which govern the transition from one stage to another. These are apparently held to be invariant across development and have differential effect at different points in the development of the child only because they operate on a different initial point. For this reason, it is critical to Piaget's model that an accurate description of stages be possible; assimilation and accommodation lead to widely separated ends if they begin at different stages. Perhaps it is for this reason that Piaget is sometimes seen as using the traditional techniques of merely listing the behavior of the child as it changes with age; paradoxically, the "stage" notion is *formally* relatively unimportant for Piaget. In this regard, it should be noted that Piaget has little interest in individual variation among children in the rate at which they achieve a stage or in their overall capacity during it; he is a student of the development of thinking more than he is a student of children.

In brief, the problems of the child psychologist in his search for segmentational systems can be seen from three points of view — the description of states or stages, the specification of stable individual variation, and the formulation of rules for transition from one state to another. Even though these ways of approaching the problem are apparently interrelated, and very closely so, theorists of child behavior have only occasionally made it their business to include all three in their purview. One of Piaget's important incidental achievements has been to demonstrate the necessary interrelation of stage and transition in the investigation of children's thought.

The Longitudinal Method

Dankward Kodlin and Donovan J. Thompson

The longitudinal method of studying developmental problems typically represents a long-term commitment on the part of the investigators. Such a commitment of time and money requires that the research design and methodology be planned with extreme care. Perhaps more so than in any other research method, the longitudinal method demands careful selection of subjects, detailed specification of independent and dependent variables, the development of sensitive and appropriate measuring

SOURCE: Adapted and abridged from Dankward Kodlin and Donovan J. Thompson, "An Appraisal of the Longitudinal Approach to Studies in Growth and Development." *Monographs of the Society for Research in Child Development*, 1958, 23, No. 67, 47 pp. (With permission of the authors and the Society for Research in Child Development.)

instruments, and careful planning of data processing. Drs. Kodlin and Thompson, who are public health research workers, provide in this paper a concise and detailed analysis of the longitudinal method. Despite the large number of problems typically involved in this method, it is their considered opinion that the returns in the form of very meaningful data justify the means.

It is an accepted tenet in public health field investigations that the longitudinal approach, i.e., repeated observations on the same individual over a period of time, is one of the most valuable approaches for the investigation of factors which influence growth and development. This opinion stems from the realization that conditions which affect physical, emotional, and intellectual maturation or the occurrence of disease may antecede by a long interval of time the overt manifestation of these phenomena. Consequently, the identification of these conditions and the measurement of their influence on the phenomena under study require repeated and long-term observations.

While there is little disagreement in principle regarding the value of this approach, actually there is considerable reluctance to undertake longitudinal studies or to finance them adequately. Experience has shown that to obtain and evaluate observations made over a long period of time on the same group of subjects presents many practical and theoretical problems, as will be pointed out later. Because of this, the attempt is made to substitute for longitudinal studies those based essentially on the cross-sectional approach, i.e., either (a) observations made at one particular point in time on individuals who have different time-exposure characteristics, or (b) repeated observations at various points in time on different groups of individuals. In some respects this approach reduces the difficulties of obtaining the observations.

The possibility of an alternative to the longitudinal approach immediately raises the question: When are the longitudinal and the cross-sectional approaches interchangeable, if at all? The study reported here was aimed at answering this question. We have focused attention on investigations relating to child growth in this country because it is in this field that most of the experience in longitudinal studies has accumulated. However, basically the answers to the question posed should have general application whenever one seeks to examine changes in relation to the passage of time or the long-term influence of specified factors.

The results of the study have led us to frame a series of questions aimed at judging how well a study satisfies basic criteria of field research. We hope that these questions will serve as a useful guide to those who plan to undertake longitudinal studies. Finally, we hope that the findings and discussions of this study will stimulate further research in the statistical aspects of long-term study.

An Appraisal of Methodology of Longitudinal Studies: Summary Considerations

The term *longitudinal studies* is used here to designate those studies in which repeated observations over a period of time are made on the same individuals.

We exclude from this term those studies in which repeated observations over a period of time are made on groups or samples of individuals without concern as to the inclusion of the same individuals in each series of observations.

Longitudinal studies may involve the examination of data already collected (retrospective longitudinal studies) or of data to be collected (prospective longitudinal studies).

Review of the major longitudinal growth studies in this country reveals that increasing attention is being given to improving the methodology of these studies. Experience has shown that:

1. the accumulation of data without frequent analysis precludes the opportunity for reevaluation of objectives and techniques;

2. when subjects and observations are chosen primarily on the basis of expediency, severe limitations are imposed on the value of the study;

3. inadequate analytical techniques have at times prevented the full exploitation of the unique features of longitudinal data;

4. a sharp distinction must be made between study objectives which require the longitudinal approach and those which can be achieved by the cross-sectional approach.

Because of the importance of the last point we have examined the logical aspects of the two approaches and from this examination the following statements can be made:

1. The longitudinal approach is the *only* approach which gives a complete description of the growth phenomenon.

2. The cross-sectional approach never can satisfy the objective of a study which requires the measurement of the change in a trait through time on a given individual. This means that when the objective of the growth study is to arrive at predictions of individual growth, generally, or, to establish the correlation between measurements obtained at successive ages, it is necessary to employ the longitudinal approach.

3. A cross-sectional approach may provide data for a retrospective longitudinal study when the variables are of a nature that can be recalled.

4. It should be obvious that generalizations from a longitudinal study of a single cohort to other comparably defined cohorts cannot be made unless one assumes a stable universe.

5. If the assumption of a stable universe holds, then the cross-sectional approach can be used in place of the longitudinal approach except for the type of measurements listed under (2).

6. In both longitudinal and cross-sectional studies generalizations from samples to cohorts or parts thereof require that the samples be randomly selected or be considered such.

7. If the assumption of a stable universe holds and random samples of the cohorts are studied, considerations of relative precision (in a statistical sense) and relative economy may be used to arrive at an optimal sampling scheme,

which may be either longitudinal or cross-sectional depending on the particular estimate desired.

From these considerations, we are led to conclude that far more emphasis should be placed on the methodology of longitudinal studies than has generally been the case. The effectiveness of longitudinal studies will be increased when it is accepted that they should satisfy the criteria that are basic for the conduct of all field studies.

How well these criteria will be met by a longitudinal study may be judged by considering the following questions:

1. Does the stated objective of the study demand measurement of the relationship (a) between successive observations, as, for example, a measurement of correlation between stature at successive ages; or (b) between "early" events and the variable trait under study at a subsequent point of time, as, for example, a measurement of correlation between early illness history and performance on mental or physical tests at maturity?

If the answer is "Yes," it means that only a longitudinal approach can achieve the objective stated. If the answer is "No," that is, if it it desired only to obtain the average stature of children at specific ages, or the average increments in growth at successive ages, then the longitudinal approach may be unnecessary. An unequivocal answer to this question requires a precise and detailed statement of the objectives of the study.

2. What evidence is there to suggest the hypothesis of some relationship between an "early" event and changes in the traits under study? For example, what facts or theories are there to indicate some correlation between illness history and subsequent performance?

The answer to this question, we feel, provides a basis for anticipating the potential contribution of this project. If it reveals that the existing evidence to support the hypothesis of a relationship is meager, it leads to the following question:

Can repeated observations on samples of individuals, but not necessarily the same persons, or a one-time cross-sectional study give evidence to support the hypothesis? The purpose of this question is to elicit information as to whether or not further preliminary studies should be made before undertaking an operation which will last several years and may turn out to be unproductive. In experimental laboratory work it is a well-established principle to undertake long-term experimentation only after short-term experiments have indicated specific points to test.

3. Are the traits under study irreversible or at least easily recalled?

The relationship of such permanent traits (ossification, dentition, signs of sexual maturity) to other variables could under certain circumstances be investigated cross-sectionally. If stored information (i.e., age at menarche) is utilized, cross-sectional inquiries attain the character of retrospective longitudinal studies. Inaccuracies in recollection may well limit the utility of such information.

Thus, the answer to this question allows us to judge the extent to which we can consider some substitution for the prospective longitudinal approach.

4. Are the measurements of the traits under study meaningful and of proven validity?

This is a most important question and refers to both the traits such as stature or intelligence that we observe repeatedly, and the "early" events or factors that we wish to relate to them. If the measurement of a trait, let us say, a serological test, has no clear-cut physiologic meaning or has not been "standardized," i.e., will show significant variation in time even when applied to the same constant material, there is considerable risk that at the end of a study the observer will not be able to analyze the observations. This has been the case particularly in studies dealing with behavior or traits for which measurements were not objective or were later found to have little meaning. If there is doubt on these points, a subsidiary question may be raised: Can the validation of the test be carried out through preliminary explorations using the cross-sectional approach?

5. What generalizations can be made from the findings on the subjects observed?

Two aspects of this question deserve emphasis.

First, what are the characteristics of the population from which the subjects are selected and how are they selected?

An answer to this aspect of the question reveals the limitations to which generalization of the findings is subject. When children are selected at random from the population of a community, it would seem safe to generalize the findings to all the children of that community. On the other hand, when children are selected simply on the basis of their presence in a certain school and their willingness to cooperate, difficulties may well arise in trying to characterize the universe to which the findings may be generalized.

Secondly, how many subjects have been or will be lost during the project and what effect will this loss have on the findings of this study?

It is not only the amount of loss that is preoccupying but primarily the bias that may be introduced by the peculiar traits of either the subjects who remain or those that leave the study. This question will elicit information regarding plans that have been made about the minimum number of subjects required by the study, follow-up of the subjects, and examination of the differences between those that remain and those who leave. If the answer reveals that the loss, actual or anticipated, is large and that it is or will be difficult to assess the significance of the losses relative to the objective of the study, it is doubtful that the longitudinal approach is appropriate for the study.

6. What analytic techniques will be employed?

The unique contribution which the longitudinal approach can make is in measuring the relationship between successive changes in the traits studied or between some "early event" and changes in these traits. To obtain these measurements requires, in many instances, elaborations of statistical analytic techniques beyond current usage or actually the development of new techniques. If these tools are not available, preferably in the designing stage of the study, investigators are likely to be swamped by a large body of data of which only limited amounts of information, and with considerable delay in time, are going to be extracted.

7. To what extent can the objectives of the study be satisfied by a series of "short-term" longitudinal studies?

This question serves further to clarify the degree to which the objectives have been precisely and correctly indicated. If these objectives can be segregated into several, each of which can be studied in sequence, then a series of short-term longitudinal studies, one after the other and each on a new sample, is likely to have greater assurance of achieving adequate results than a single study extending over a long-time period and performed on a single sample. With a series of short-term studies we would anticipate greater retention of interest on the part of the investigator, smaller rates of loss of subjects, an accumulation of data more easily handled, more frequent formulation of specific hypotheses based on the findings of the preceding surveys or of the surveys or experiments currently carried out by others, and greater opportunity to improve on study design and analysis in line with progress in statistical methods.

Methods in the Soviet Union

Yvonne Brackbill

The earlier papers in this chapter pointed to a rather sharp difference of opinion among American child psychologists as to the merit of experimental research with children. According to the observations of Dr. Brackbill during her visit to the Soviet Union, this difference of opinion does not exist; Soviet child psychologists are committed to the experimental method. It is also noteworthy that the more promising laboratory findings are rather quickly translated into educational programs which are then systematically tested in the classroom. This procedure, it would appear, substantially reduces the lag between laboratory discovery, program implementation, and the establishment of a thoroughly tested curriculum in the school system. In the United States the lag between these phases of research and development often is as great as ten years.

I recently visited several centers of psychological research in Moscow and Leningrad. I went to the Soviet Union not as an official visitor, but through the usual Intourist channels. My trip was neither financed by any organization nor

SOURCE: Adapted and abridged from Yvonne Brackbill, "Experimental Research with Children in the Soviet Union." *American Psychologist*, 1960, 15, 226–233. (With permission of the author and the American Psychological Association.)

was I under any obligation to report my observations. Indeed, I had no intention of writing an article about them. However, once there, I was sufficiently impressed by what I observed and, more important, found my observations so much at variance with what I had expected to observe after reading the literature currently available in English that I felt constrained to pass along some of my information in the interests of both American and Soviet psychologists.

Visits to these institutions made up my agenda: In Moscow, the Institute of Defectology, Institute of Psychology, Institute of Pediatrics, and Department of Psychology, University of Moscow; in Leningrad, the Institute of Physiology and the Institute of Evolutionary Physiology. (Please note that since my visits were limited to these institutions, the use of such general terms as "Soviet" and "USSR" in this article puts a greater stress on brevity than accuracy.) All of these centers, with the exception of the Department of Psychology, are devoted exclusively to research. Similarly, most of the 25 scientists with whom I spoke at length were engaged in full-time research. Our conversations were most frequently concerned with procedural details and results of recently completed investigations; they less frequently dealt with ongoing or contemplated projects, and still less frequently with topics other than research.

Use of S-R Rather than R-R Design

Soviet research with children typically employs an experimental or S-R design, and at least one of the variables under investigation is more apt to be drawn from and the results are more apt to contribute to the field of experimental psychology than is the case for child research in this country.

For discussion purposes, let me define as the limiting case of an S-R design, a study in which there is at least one independently or experimentally manipulated variable with at least two values or levels. "Experimentally manipulated" is not meant to include variables based on subject characteristics that existed prior to the experiment, e.g., intelligence level. Using this criterion, I categorized by type of design 24 Soviet studies on which I have notes extensive enough to permit this. (Replications were excluded from the tally). All designs were of the S-R type. For comparison, I scanned the last two issues I had received of five American journals, using the same criterion to classify by design all research articles by using children as Ss (arbitrarily, twelfth graders or younger). The 10 issues yielded a total of 42 studies using children; of these, 17 were classifiable as S-R designs and 25 as R-R designs.

Does the absence of R-R designs mean that at least Soviet psychologists have taken Spence and Bergmann seriously? Or does it represent a sampling artifact for which I am to blame? A sampling artifact is certainly possible, but the arguments favoring representativeness do seem to outnumber those against it. For example, more than once I was told in essence: For many problems, a clinical or observational method is, of course, a necessary preliminary step. But one must never stop here; the problem must then be brought to the laboratory and formulated in experimental terms. And indeed, I listened to several research accounts that illustrate this nicely: e.g., experimental studies concerned with problems of personality development or with pathological conditions — research areas that in this country typically bear a heavy annual crop of R-R designs.

As one example, L. I. Bozhovich told me of work in progress in her laboratory, Institute of Psychology, concerned with the cumulative effect of *negative verbal reinforcement*[1] on the child's personality development. The impetus for this work came from observations of cases of "defense" against or failure to internalize adult requirements. To use her example: a child offers to help with the dishes, he breaks one, his mother scolds or criticizes him without thanking or praising him for having volunteered in the first place. This event appears to have two effects: first, the future probability of the child's offering help is reduced; and, second, the affectional bond between child and parent is loosened. Bozhovich is now studying this problem within the laboratory (in the face of acknowledged difficulties arising from the lack of previously established close contact between E and S). As the nucleus of the experimental situation, she will use adult criticism of the child's play products. The main variable under investigation will concern types of verbal contingencies that, when added to adult criticism, cancel out deleterious effects on personality development. In addition, she will study personality differences leading to differential reactions to negative reinforcement.

Again, in Luria's laboratory, Institute of Defectology, a considerable amount of work within the experimental paradigm has been and is being done on mental retardation. O. S. Vinogradova related her work on semantic generalization along the dimensions of rhyme, synonymity, and word relatedness, using type of context as an independent variable and bulb pressing, GSR, and EEG as dependent measures. V. I. Lubovsky has also used retarded children in an extensive investigation of acquisition, extinction, and reversal learning of both simple *operants* (bulb pressing) and complex discriminations as a function of increasing complexity of response and *discriminative stimuli* — all under verbal reinforcement conditions.

Associated with the differential propensity for using S-R vs. R-R designs are certain other methodological points that distinguish Soviet from American work. One such concerns the number of variables that either type of design can comfortably accommodate in a single study. In this country, it is not uncommon to find projects in which variables outnumber subjects; while in the Soviet centers I visited, there was no mention of studies of comparable complexity. Apparently, if a problem or area is to be investigated extensively, the tendency has been up to now to stick to the S-R design and to try for a series of small, interlocking studies.

Likewise absent from Soviet research are retrospective studies and studies using parents — either as Ss or as founts of child-rearing data. (There is no *logical* reason why parents could not be used as Ss in experimental studies, but in practice it rarely happens.)

Hypothesis Testing

Although there is a growing interest among some Soviet psychologists in the use of inferential statistics, they are not yet commonly employed. Certainly, in none of the research reports I heard were inferential statistics included. My questions about analysis of results were answered either in terms of simple descriptive statistics (frequently percentages, sometimes means) or in terms of frequencies. In the reprints and books given to me, the typical form for presentation of results is a frequency distribution of raw data — in a table of either grouped or ungrouped data, or as histograms or bar diagrams.

The absence of statistical evaluation has already been commented on by American reviewers of Soviet psychological literature. But what has not received equal publicity is the widespread emphasis in Soviet research on experimental replication as a means of assessing reliability of results.

Further, when results are to be put to practical use, replication of laboratory-obtained results in extra-laboratory situations is definitely the paradigm. N. A. Menchinskaya, Deputy Director, Institute of Psychology, was quite explicit about the ideal methodological sequence for research at the institute: first, observation; then experimentation outside of the laboratory under natural conditions, whenever possible. Also, I was given to understand by other psychologists as well that the Institute of Pedagogy, for example, could not be expected to accept the results of a single, laboratory experiment.

Use of Infants and Younger Children in Experimental Research

By way of introduction, it might first be noted that in the United States the most striking age gap in experimental research with children is the period from infancy to early childhood. Undoubtedly a major reason for this is that from the time neonates are discharged from the hospital to the time their mothers enroll them in preschool or kindergarten, their availability as *groups of normal* Ss is practically nil. The choice comes down to the single, normal, home infant vs. the increasingly rare institutional group of highly selected infants. Using Ss from either population poses its own peculiar set of difficulties that I will not detail here. Suffice it to add that, no matter what the source of young subjects, getting permission to use mechanical equipment on them is typically as difficult as catching marlin with a drop line: a Skinner crib apparently looks like an iron maiden to infant caretakers, and the mere mention of electrodes is generally enough to terminate any further negotiations. It is for this reason too, no doubt, that experimental work with young children has been curtailed in this country.

If such obstacles exist in the Soviet Union, they are not apparent. In the matter of subject availability, for example, both the Moscow and Leningrad Institutes of Pediatrics maintain infant residence centers in connection with their research laboratories. For example, N. M. Schelovanov's laboratory, Institute of Pediatrics, Moscow, is devoted to research on the ontogeny of higher nervous activity; and within the laboratory there is a residential center accommodating 25 children, aged birth to three years. Such an arrangement has helped to make it possible for Schelovanov to secure a vast amount of longitudinal, experimental data on sensory development and on the development of both innate and conditioned responses. (He is particularly interested in "defense" responses, i.e., escape, avoidance.)

As for the brass instruments issue, Schelovanov's four experimental rooms contain more remarkable child research equipment than it has so far been my privilege to see. Each room contains a special crib and accompanying mechanical equipment. Although the four rooms have certain features in common, each differs from the others to the extent of its intended special function. One of the experimental cribs includes apertures in its housing, which can be used for taking motion pictures, fixing apparatus for stimulus presentation, etc. The crib rests on a round, revolvable platform. Strips of linen can be passed through the two slots in the crib sides to secure older, restless infants. (Loose swaddling without attachment to crib sides is also effectively used.) At one end of the crib is a head rest; underneath the head rest pad is a stabilometer, leads from which connect with a kymograph outside the housing. (Head turning is frequently used as a conditioned response.)

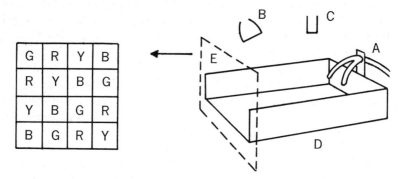

Figure 2.1 Second type of experimental crib, Institute of Pediatrics, Moscow. A. Two-pronged rubber tubing for delivery of air puffs; a universal joint clamp secures this to the headboard and also allows for easy height adjustment. B. Lamp (bright white light) for avoidance conditioning. C. Small, low-intensity red light lamp—as in first described apparatus. D. Equipment for auditory stimulation—as in first described apparatus. E. Panel, for presentation of primary colors, by means of low intensity lights; sections may be activated singly, in any combination, or in any desired sequence.

Figure 2.1 contains a sketch of another experimental crib, minus housing. The use of this crib was demonstrated by a veteran S of seven months, who obliged with such a repertoire of differential responding as would make the average American rat fear for its job.

Work of a similar nature has been done by the late Bronstein and by N. I.

Kasatkin, of the Institute of Evolutionary Physiology, Leningrad. For a conditioning measure, Kasatkin has made extensive use of the anticipatory sucking response, recording sucking movements by means of a Marey capsule and kymograph. Fifteen to 20 grams of milk are used per reinforcement during conditioning. This is administered through a nipple that remains in S's mouth throughout the session. The average number of trials per session is 10. The average number of reinforced trials needed for stable responding is about 200–250 at age 1 month, and about 10 at age 3 months.

M. M. Kolzova,[2] at the Institute of Physiology, Leningrad, has been using slightly older Ss for her work. As an interesting contrast to American studies on the effect of verbal mediation in the acquisition of motor responses in 4- to 5-year-olds is Kolzova's study on what might be called the effect of motor mediation in the acquisition of verbal responses in 1- to 2-year-olds. For example, in one of her experiments two groups of 10 Ss each were run individually. The task for both groups required S to respond to E's instruction: "Show me the book." The groups differed in terms of the variety of movements available to them in responding (also in terms of amount of effort?) during training periods of equal length. Only two alternative responses were allowed Ss of Group I throughout training: turning the head to look at the book or holding the book when it was handed to S by E. Twenty responses were used during training for Group II: holding the book, picking it up, carrying it, etc. In a test for generalization, S was placed before a selection of books (including the training book) as well as objects other than books; E repeated the instruction, "Give me the book," following each choice. Generalization from training to test books occurred in 0% of the Ss in Group I, and in 80–90% of the Ss in Group II. (The experiment was replicated, using another word.)

Interdisciplinary Cooperation

In the United States, "interdisciplinary cooperation" is generally used to refer to a working situation in which people from several different professional fields work together on the same research project. The disciplinary crossovers that I observed in Soviet psychological research were of two kinds — both different from the American conception:

1. Psychological research is often done by people other than psychologists and in institutions other than those whose titles would indicate a close affiliation with psychology. Thus one can find research on learning and conditioning in children being done by physiologists, physicians, biologists, etc., and in institutes of physiology, pediatrics, gynecology and obstetrics, and evolutionary physiology.

2. More important than the matter of names and titles is the fact that in the Soviet Union much psychological research is so formulated (either in terms of problem or operations or both) as to be clearly applicable to the concerns of other disciplines; and concomitantly, other disciplines actually do use the results. A most striking illustration of this is the interchange between Soviet educators

in the Institute of Pedagogy and learning psychologists in the Institute of Psychology, Moscow. The Institute of Psychology often functions in a consultant or cooperative role, as in the following ways: (a) Educators may and do solicit research help with learning-teaching problems, e.g., most effective methods of programing textbook material, special methods of programing course material to maximize efficiency of acquisition in slow learners. (b) If the initial research idea comes from the learning psychologist and if the project is thought to bear on educational problems, the psychologist may consult with the educator during the design stage. (c) If the psychologist has already run the study and feels the results show implications for education, he may then point these out to the educator. A demonstration of applicability and replicability are the educator's requisites in accepting the results for use.

Stress on Practical Applications

No doubt a contributing factor in the large amount of interdisciplinary give and take is the importance placed by Soviet psychologists on implementing research problems in such a way as to maximize applicability of results to practical problems: e.g., Prokina's study on methods of training children to be on time, Institute of Psychology. But the emphasis on application also extends to laboratory research on more "basic" problems, where it appears as an affinity for using those methods or operations that most closely approximate natural conditions, i.e., will allow maximum confidence in generalizing to real life situations. For example, in a learning experiment, foreign language words are more apt to be used than nonsense syllables. Menchinskaya feels that the ideal research design is one that both tests a theoretical proposition and, through a judicious choice of experimental material and operations, contributes to the solution of some practical problem. Some of the research projects done within the Institute of Psychology provide pertinent illustrations of the general attempt to hybridize applied and basic research.

One such concerned the effects of training sequence and type of task on initial learning and transfer in problem solving. Using physical problems — such as determining the weight of a car on the pavement — the investigator, Kalmikova, asked if there were any difference in efficiency of solution attributable to the sequence in which two training conditions were presented. The two training conditions were (a) verbal attempts at solution and (b) "perceptual-motor practice," i.e., allowing S to manipulate a concrete model or object representing the task, e.g., a toy car. (Beyond the fact that physical problems were used as tasks, note that the experimental variable itself is a direct reflection of an age-old educational argument about the relative values of "verbal" vs. "manual" learning.)[3]

The results, by the way, proved to be a joint function of training sequence and type of task, for both initial acquisition and transfer. When the most important features of solution were salient in the visual representation of the problem, the sequence, manipulation-verbalization, was more effective. The opposite sequence proved superior when the visual representation emphasized details irrelevant to solution.

In another proposed project, the entire staff of D. B. Elkonin's laboratory will take full charge of a first-year elementary-school class (7-year-olds) in an experimental teaching project, tentatively scheduled to continue for four years. The project will be concerned with both the use and teaching of learning principles. Specifically, one of its aims is to field test learning principles applicable to curriculum organization and presentation (active participation, spaced practice, etc.). The second aim is to incorporate the same principles into the curriculum — in other words, the first-grade Ss will start learning *how* to learn.

As I began to see the quantity and quality of Soviet research, I kept asking myself during interviews with the Soviet scientists: "What's wrong with Soviet-American communication that I had to come all the way to Moscow to find out that Soviet experimental child research is both competently done and of considerable interest to me?"

Probably the most likely reasons concern the paucity of translated material coupled with a predominant use of the summary form in its presentation. To explain this point: Summaries of one type or another are currently the chief source of information on Soviet psychological research. They appear in the form of reviews written by American psychologists, e.g., the *Annual Review of Psychology;* surveys written by Soviet psychologists, e.g., a book edited by Simon (1957): abstracts, e.g., *Psychological Abstracts;* or sometimes as translated summaries appearing at the end of full-length, Russian-language articles, e.g., the book edited by Luria. In any form, their use creates at least two problems for the English-speaking reader. First, the material in them may be quite understandable, but too brief for use by itself. If the summaries referred to English-language publications, they could be used as summaries should be used: i.e., as leads or screening devices for original articles. But the language barrier and low ceilings on translation funds generally prove effective obstacles here.

The second problem is that the contents of the summary may not be quite understandable — even misleading, in this particular sense: If a summary is to be brief, it must necessarily depend on abstract terms to convey maximum information in minimum space. But the abstractions (terms, concepts, constructs) that Soviet psychologists use tend to be somewhat unfamiliar or different from those used by American psychologists. Therefore, the net impression from a translated summary is apt to be that the research project is unrelated to either the problems or methods currently in vogue in this country — that it looks uninteresting.

These comments are meant to point out an intercultural problem in semantics that deserves consideration in the interests of better communication and hence better appreciation of Soviet contributions to the literature in experimental and child psychology.

NOTES

[1] Terms appearing in italics are my own.

[2] In a personal communication, Kolzova indicates that she would like to add and to emphasize a general point of major importance: "We regard the physiology of higher nervous activity (and psychology also) as an auxiliary science for pedagogy." Kolzova cites as examples her own experiments, which are conceived and designed with the goal in mind of gaining new knowledge in the search for means of ". . . directing the development of the integrative function of the cortex." She goes on to say: "We can develop more specific forms of integration in the child by means of using stimuli of different functional meaning. And we can make this integration wider, i.e., generalized, involving a great number of conditioned connections."

[3] I was told when visiting the National Foundation for Educational Research, London, that an educational problem of major importance in England today is the inability of present teaching-learning methods to foster creativity in mathematics and that the most tenable hypothesis in trying to account for this failure was the practice, in the early elementary grades, of teaching arithmetic exclusively by "verbal" means: e.g., visual presentation of the arabic numerals $2 + 2$ without concomitant or prior opportunity to manipulate objects in terms of their number, e.g., 2 oranges $+$ 2 oranges.

CHAPTER III

Biological Correlates of Behavior

MANY DEVELOPMENTAL psychologists assume, at least implicitly, that children are born with essentially the same potential to profit from environmental stimulation. Investigators of personality development, for example, typically ascribe observed variability in personality patterns to variations in child-rearing practices. There can be little doubt that some part of observed personality variation is attributable to different child-rearing practices; but surely part of the variability is attributable to biological variations in behavioral predispositions. There are other developmental psychologists, of course, who believe that environmental influences play little or no role in the course of human development. These psychologists subscribe to the notion that behavioral change is genetically programed and relatively impervious to modification. This view overlooks such known facts as the effects of nutrition on physical stature or medical advances on longevity.

During the 1930's, a considerable amount of attention was directed toward determining the relative contribution of environment, as opposed to heredity, on behavior. Many of these studies, because of poor research designs, generated equivocal results. But fundamentally, as Anastasi so clearly shows in her article, the question of relative contribution could not really be answered. Those favoring genetics failed to recognize that the impact of environment can be observed as early as intrauterine life with effects that can be of long-term duration. The environmentalists failed to recognize that the effectiveness of environmental manipulations depended upon specific hereditary characteristics; that is, environmental manipulations have never been equally effective for all children, nor were they equally successful in modifying different behaviors within the same child. The failure of this research question to generate any substantive knowledge, and the fact that recent research has shown that environment can modify behavior potential, have led to the generally accepted view that heredity and environment interact to produce a unique set of behavioral capabilities.

The interaction view, then, poses different sets of questions, as indicated in the papers by Anastasi and Hirsch. The study by Jones and Bailey shows the importance of patterns of physical growth and development on general psychological

adjustment. Assuming these patterns of physical growth are genetically determined, this study shows that late-maturing, as opposed to early-maturing, boys
have quite different experiences with their peers and with adults, which influences
their adjustment during the teen and young adulthood years.

The extremely interesting paper by Professor Tanner describes some of the
physiological processes occurring within human beings. Principally, this study
demonstrates the importance of built-in biological mechanisms that regulate the
development of the human organism. Although this study demonstrates the
importance of biological systems, it in no way permits the interpretation that
environmental variables are unimportant.

The papers included in this chapter represent examples of how the interaction
viewpoint is being translated into research procedures. It should be recognized,
however, that extremely important breakthroughs are occurring in the physiology
of memory, genetic structure, and in brain functioning. These breakthroughs
are sufficiently new that their implications for the science of human behavior are
just now beginning to be explored. There is little doubt that they will have
broad implications for students of developmental psychology.

Heredity, Environment, and the Question "How?"

Anne Anastasi

In the middle 1930's a great deal of time and effort was spent in determining in what
proportion heredity and environment contributed to the variability of human behavior.
This question generated little in the way of a definitive answer for reasons carefully
detailed in this important paper. Professor Anne Anastasi, well known for her work
in the psychology of individual differences, argues for the view that heredity and
environment interact in a way that makes the old questions unanswerable. She describes the kinds of research that are consistent with an interaction view and explains
why these problems will further our understanding of individual differences.

Two or three decades ago, the so-called heredity-environmental question was
the center of lively controversy. Today [1958], on the other hand, many psychologists look upon it as a dead issue. It is now generally conceded that both
hereditary and environmental factors enter into all behavior. The reacting
organism is a product of its genes and its past environment, while present environment provides the immediate stimulus for current behavior. To be sure, it can be
argued that, although a given trait may result from the combined influence of
hereditary and environmental factors, a specific difference in this trait between

SOURCE: Adapted and abridged from Anne Anastasi, "Heredity, Environment and the Question 'How?'" *Psychological Review*, 1958, 65, 197–208. (With permission of the author and
the American Psychological Association.)

individuals or between groups may be traceable to either hereditary or environmental factors alone. The design of most traditional investigations undertaken to identify such factors, however, has been such as to yield inconclusive answers. The same set of data has frequently led to opposite conclusions in the hands of psychologists with different orientations.

Nor have efforts to determine the proportional contribution of hereditary and environmental factors to observed individual differences in given traits met with any greater success. Apart from difficulties in controlling conditions, such investigations have usually been based upon the implicit assumption that hereditary and environmental factors combine in an additive fashion. Both geneticists and psychologists have repeatedly demonstrated, however, that a more tenable hypothesis is that of interaction. In other words the nature and extent of the influence of each type of factor depend upon the contribution of the other. Thus the proportional contribution of heredity to the variance of a given trait, rather than being a constant, will vary under different environmental conditions. Similarly, under different hereditary conditions, the relative contribution of environment will differ. Studies designed to estimate the proportional contribution of heredity and environment, however, have rarely included measures of such interaction. The only possible conclusion from such research would thus seem to be that both heredity and environment contribute to all behavior traits and that the extent of their respective contributions cannot be specified for any trait. Small wonder that some psychologists regard the heredity-environment question as unworthy of further consideration!

But is this really all we can find out about the operation of heredity and environment in the etiology of behavior? Perhaps we have simply been asking the wrong questions. The traditional questions about heredity and environment may be intrinsically unanswerable. Psychologists began by asking *which* type of factor, hereditary or environmental, is responsible for individual differences in a given trait. Later, they tried to discover *how much* of the variance was attributable to heredity and how much to environment. It is the primary contention of this paper that a more fruitful approach is to be found in the question "How?" There is still much to be learned about the specific *modus operandi* of hereditary and environmental factors in the development of behavioral differences. And there are several current lines of research which offer promising techniques for answering the question "how"?

Variety of Interaction Mechanisms

Hereditary Factors

If we examine some of the specific ways in which hereditary factors may influence behavior, we cannot fail but be impressed by their wide diversity. At one extreme, we find such conditions as phenylpyruvic amentia and amaurotic idiocy. In these cases, certain essential physical prerequisites for normal intellectual development are lacking as a result of hereditary metabolic disorders. [Since the original publication of this paper an effective treatment procedure for phenylpyruvic amentia has been discovered. It is thus no longer true that children with this deficiency will be mentally retarded.]

A somewhat different situation is illustrated by hereditary deafness, which may lead to intellectual retardation through interference with normal social inter-action, language development, and schooling. In such a case, however, the hereditary handicap can be offset by appropriate adaptations of training procedures. It has been said, in fact, that the degree of intellectual backwardness of the deaf is an index of the state of development of special instructional facilities. As the latter improve, the intellectual retardation associated with deafness is correspond-ingly reduced.

A third example is provided by inherited susceptibility to certain physical diseases, with consequent protracted ill health. If environmental conditions are such that illness does in fact develop, a number of different behavioral effects may follow. Intellectually, the individual may be handicapped by his inability to attend school regularly. On the other hand, depending upon age of onset, home conditions, parental status, and similar factors, poor health may have the effect of concentrating the individual's energies upon intellectual pursuits. The curtailment of participation in athletics and social functions may serve to strengthen interest in reading and other sedentary activities. Concomitant circumstances would also determine the influence of such illness upon personality development. And it is well known that the latter effects could run the gamut from a deepening of human sympathy to psychiatric breakdown.

Finally, heredity may influence behavior through the mechanism of social stereotypes. A wide variety of inherited physical characteristics have served as the visible cues for identifying such stereotypes. These cues thus lead to behavioral restrictions or opportunities and — at a more subtle level — to social attitudes and expectancies. The individual's own self-concept tends gradually to reflect such expectancies. All of these influences eventually leave their mark upon his abilities and inabilities, his emotional reactions, goals, ambitions, and outlook on life.

The geneticist Dobzhansky illustrates this type of mechanism by means of a dramatic hypothetical situation. He points out that if there were a culture in which the carriers of blood group AB were considered aristocrats and those of blood group O laborers, then the blood-group genes would become important hereditary determiners of behavior (1950, p. 147). Obviously the association between blood group and behavior would be specific to that culture. But such specificity is an essential property of the causal mechanism under consideration.

More realistic examples are not hard to find. The most familiar instances occur in connection with constitutional types, sex, and race. Sex and skin pigmentation obviously depend upon heredity. General body build is strongly influenced by hereditary components, although also susceptible to environmental modification. That all these physical characteristics may exert a pronounced effect upon behavior within a given culture is well known. It is equally apparent, of course, that in different cultures the behavioral correlates of such hereditary physical traits may be quite unlike. A specific physical cue may be completely unrelated to individual differences in psychological traits in one culture, while closely correlated with them in another. Or it may be associated with totally dissimilar behavior characteristics in two different cultures.

It might be objected that some of the illustrations which have been cited do not properly exemplify the operation of hereditary mechanisms in behavior development, since hereditary factors enter only indirectly into the behavior in question. Closer examination, however, shows this distinction to be untenable. First it may be noted that the influence of heredity upon behavior is always indirect. No psychological trait is ever inherited as such. All we can ever say directly from behavioral observations is that a given trait shows evidence of being influenced by certain "inheritable unknowns." This merely defines a problem for genetic research; it does not provide a causal explanation. Unlike the blood groups, which are close to the level of primary gene products, psychological traits are related to genes by highly indirect and devious routes. Even the mental deficiency associated with phenylketonuria is several steps removed from the chemically defective genes that represent its hereditary basis. Moreover, hereditary influences cannot be dichotomized into the more direct and the less direct. Rather do they represent a whole "continuum of indirectness," along which are found all degrees of remoteness of causal links. The examples already cited illustrate a few of the points on this continuum.

It should be noted that as we proceed along the continuum of indirectness, the range of variation of possible outcomes of hereditary factors expands rapidly. At each step in the causal chain, there is fresh opportunity for interaction with other hereditary factors as well as with environmental factors. And since each interaction in turn determines the direction of subsequent interactions, there is an ever widening network of possible outcomes. If we visualize a simple sequential grid with only two alternatives at each point, it is obvious that there are two possible outcomes in the one-stage situation, four outcomes at the second stage, eight at the third, and so on in geometric progression. The actual situation is undoubtedly much more complex, since there will usually be more than two alternatives at any one point.

In the case of the blood groups, the relation to specific genes is so close that no other concomitant hereditary or environmental conditions can alter the outcome. If the organism survives at all, it will have the blood group determined by its genes. Among psychological traits, on the other hand, some variation in outcome is always possible as a result of concurrent circumstances. Even in cases of phenylketonuria, intellectual development will exhibit some relationship with the type of care and training available to the individual. That behavioral outcomes show progressive diversification as we proceed along the continuum of indirectness is brought out by the other examples which were cited. Chronic illness *can* lead to scholarly renown or to intellectual immaturity; a mesomorphic physique *can* be a contributing factor in juvenile delinquency or in the attainment of a college presidency! Published data on Sheldon somatotypes provide some support for both of the latter outcomes.

Parenthetically, it may be noted that geneticists have sometimes used the term "norm of reaction" to designate the range of variation of possible outcomes of gene properties. Thus heredity sets the "norm" or limits within which environmental differences determine the eventual outcome. In the case of some traits, such as blood groups or eye color, this norm is much narrower than in the case of the other traits. Owing to the rather different psychological connotations of both the words "norm" and "reaction," however, it seems less confusing to speak of the "range of variation" in this context.

A large portion of the continuum of hereditary influences which we have described coincides with the domain of somatopsychological relations, as defined by Barker, Wright, Myerson, and Gonick (1953). Under this heading, these authors include "variations in physique that affect the psychological situation of a person by influencing the effectiveness of his body as a tool for actions or by serving as a stimulus to himself or others" (Barker *et al.*, 1953, p. 1). Relatively direct neurological influences on behavior, which have been the traditional concern of physiological psychology, are excluded from this definition, Barker being primarily concerned with what he calls the "social psychology of physique." Of the examples cited in the present paper, deafness, severe illness, and stereotypes would meet the specifications of somatopsychological factors.

The somatic factors to which Barker refers, however, are not limited to those of hereditary origin. Bodily conditions attributable to environmental causes operate in the same sorts of somatopsychological relations as those traceable to heredity. In fact, heredity-environmental distinctions play a minor part in Barker's approach.

Environmental Factors: Organic

Turning now to an analysis of the role of environmental factors in behavior, we find the same etiological mechanisms which were observed in the case of hereditary factors. First, however, we must differentiate between two classes of environmental influences: (a) those producing organic effects which may in turn influence behavior and (b) those serving as direct stimuli for psychological reactions. The former may be illustrated by food intake or by exposure to bacterial infection; the latter, by tribal initiation ceremonies or by a course in algebra. There are no completely satisfactory names by which to designate these two classes of influences. In an earlier paper by Anastasi and Foley (1948), the terms "structural" and "functional" were employed. However, "organic" and "behavioral" have the advantage of greater familiarity in this context and may be less open to misinterpretation. Accordingly, these terms will be used in the present paper.

Like hereditary factors, environmental influences of an organic nature can also be ordered along a continuum of indirectness with regard to their relation to behavior. This continuum closely parallels that of hereditary factors. One end is typified by such conditions as mental definciency resulting from cerebral brain injury or from prenatal nutritional inadequacies. A more indirect etiological mechanism is illustrated by severe motor disorder — as in certain cases of cerebral palsy — *without* accompanying injury to higher neurological centers. In such instances, intellectual retardation may occur as an indirect result of the motor handicap, through the curtailment of educational and social activities. Obviously this causal mechanism corresponds closely to that of hereditary deafness cited earlier in the paper.

Finally, we may consider an environmental parallel to the previously discussed social stereotypes which were mediated by hereditary physical cues. Let us suppose that a young woman with mousy brown hair becomes transformed into a dazzling golden blonde through environmental techniques currently available in our culture. It is highly probably that this metamorphosis will alter, not only the reactions of her associates toward her, but also her own self-concept and subsequent behavior. The effects could range from a rise in social poise to a drop in clerical accuracy!

Among the examples of environmentally determined organic influences which have been described, all but the first two fit Barker's definition of somatopsychological factors. With the exception of birth injuries and nutritional deficiencies, all fall within the social psychology of physique. Nevertheless, the individual factors exhibit wide diversity in their specific *modus operandi* — a diversity which has important practical as well as theoretical implications.

Environmental Factors: Behavioral

The second major class of environmental factors — the behavioral as contrasted to the organic — are by definition direct influences. The immediate effect of such environmental factors is always a behavioral change. To be sure, some of the initial behavioral effects may themselves indirectly affect the individual's later behavior. But this relationship can perhaps be best conceptualized in terms of breadth and permanence of effects. Thus it could be said that we are now dealing, not with a continuum of indirectness, as in the case of hereditary and organic-environmental factors, but rather with a continuum of breadth.

Social class membership may serve as an illustration of a relatively broad, pervasive, and enduring environmental factor. Its influence upon behavior development may operate through many channels. Thus social level may determine the range and nature of intellectual stimulation provided by home and community through books, music, art, play activities, and the like. Even more far reaching may be the effects upon interests and motivation, as illustrated by the desire to perform abstract intellectual tasks, to surpass others in competitive situations, to succeed in school, or to gain social approval. Emotional and social traits may likewise be influenced by the nature of interpersonal relations characterizing homes at different socioeconomic levels. Somewhat more restricted in scope than social class, although still exerting a relatively broad influence, is amount of formal schooling which the individual is able to obtain.

A factor which may be wide or narrow in its effects, depending upon concomitant circumstances, is language handicap. Thus the bilingualism of an adult who moves to a foreign country with inadequate mastery of the new language represents a relatively limited handicap which can be readily overcome in most cases. At most, the difficulty is one of communication. On the other hand, some kinds of bilingualism in childhood may exert a retarding influence upon intellectual development and may under certain conditions affect personality development adversely. A common pattern in the homes of immigrants is that the child speaks one language at home and another in school, so that his knowledge of each language is limited to certain types of situations. Inadequate facility with the language of the school interferes with the acquisition of basic concepts, intellectual skills, and information. The frustration engendered by scholastic difficulties may in turn lead to discouragement and general dislike of school. Such reactions can be found, for example, among a number of Puerto Rican children in New York City schools. In the case of certain groups, moreover, the child's foreign language background may be perceived by himself and his associates as a symbol of minority group status and may thereby augment any emotional maladjustment arising from such status.

A highly restricted environmental influence is to be found in the opportunity to acquire specific items of information occuring in a particular intelligence test. The fact that such opportunities may vary with culture, social class, or individual experiential background is at the basis of the test user's concern with the problem of coaching and with "culture-free" or "culture-fair" tests. If the advantage or disadvantage which such experiential differences confer upon certain individuals is strictly confined to performance on the given test, it will obviously reduce the validity of the test and should be eliminated.

In this connection, however, it is essential to know the breadth of the environmental influence in question. A fallacy inherent in many attempts to develop culture-fair tests is that the breadth of cultural differentials is not taken into account. Failure to consider breadth of effect likewise characterizes certain discussions of coaching. If, in coaching a student for a college admission test, we can improve his knowledge of verbal concepts and his reading comprehension, he will be better equipped to succeed in college courses. His performance level will thus be raised, not only on the test, but also on the criterion which the test is intended to predict. To try to devise a test which is not susceptible to such coaching would merely reduce the effectiveness of the test. Similarly, efforts to rule out cultural differentials from test items so as to make them equally "fair" to subjects in different social classes or in different cultures may merely limit the usefulness of the test, since the same cultural differentials may operate within the broader area of behavior which the test is designed to sample.

Methodological Approaches

The examples considered so far should suffice to highlight the wide variety of ways in which hereditary and environmental factors may interact in the course of behavior development. There is clearly a need for identifying explicitly the etiological mechanism whereby any given hereditary or environmental condition ultimately leads to a behavioral characteristic — in other words, the "how" of heredity and environment. Accordingly, we may now take a quick look at some promising methodological approaches to the question "how."

Within the past decade, an increasing number of studies have been designed to trace the connection between specific factors in the hereditary backgrounds or in the reactional biographies of individuals and their observed behavioral characteristics. There has been a definite shift away from the predominantly descriptive and correlation approach of the earlier decades toward more deliberate attempts to verify explanatory hypotheses. Similarly, the cataloguing of group differences in psychological traits has been giving way gradually to research on *changes* in group characteristics following altered conditions.

Among recent methodological developments, we have chosen seven as being particularly relevant to the analysis of etiological mechanisms. The first represents an extension of selective breeding investigations to permit the identification of specific hereditary conditions underlying the observed behavioral differences. When early selective breeding investigations such as those of Tryon (1940) on rats indicated that "maze learning ability" was inherited, we were still a long way from knowing what was actually being transmitted by the genes. It was obviously not "maze learning ability" as such. Twenty — or even ten — years ago, some psychologists would have suggested that it was probably general intelligence. And a few might even have drawn a parallel with the inheritance of human intelligence.

But today investigators have been asking: Just what makes one group of rats learn mazes more quickly than the other? Is it differences in motivation, emotionality, speed of running, general activity level? If so, are these behavioral characteristics in turn dependent upon group differences in glandular development, body weight, brain size, biochemical factors, or some other organic conditions? A number of recent and ongoing investigations indicate that attempts are being made to trace, at least part of the way, the steps whereby certain chemical properties of the genes may ultimately lead to specified behavior characteristics.

An example of such a study is provided by Searle's (1949) follow-up of Tryon's research. Working with the strains of maze-bright and maze-dull rats developed by Tryon, Searle demonstrated that the two strains differed in a number of emotional and motivational factors, rather than in ability. Thus the strain differences were traced one step further, although many links still remain to be found between maze learning and genes. A promising methodological development within the same general area is to be found in the recent research of Hirsch and Tryon (1956). Utilizing a specially devised technique for measuring individual differences in behavior among lower organisms, these investigators launched a series of studies on selective breeding for behavioral characteristics in the fruit fly, *Drosophila*. Such research can capitalize on the mass of available genetic knowledge regarding the morphology of *Drosophila*, as well as on other advantages of using such an organism in genetic studies.

Further evidence of current interest in the specific hereditary factors which influence behavior is to be found in an extensive research program in progress at the Jackson Memorial Laboratory, under the direction of Scott and Fuller (1951). In general, the project is concerned with the behavioral characteristics of various breeds and crossbreeds of dogs. Analyses of some of the data gathered to date again suggest that "differences in performance are produced by differences in emotional, motivational, and peripheral processes, and that genetically caused differences in central processes may be either slight or non-existent" (Scott and Charles 1953, p. 225). In other parts of the same project, breed differences in physiological characteristics, which may in turn be related to behavioral differences, have been established.

A second line of attack is the exploration of possible relationships between behavioral characteristics and physiological variables which may in turn be traceable to hereditary factors. Research on EEG, autonomic balance, metabolic processes, and biochemical factors illustrates this approach. A lucid demonstration of the process of tracing a psychological condition to genetic factors is provided by the identification and subsequent investigation of phenylpyruvic amentia. In this case, the causal chain from defective gene, through metabolic disorder and consequent cerebral malfunctioning, to feeble-mindedness and other overt symptoms can be described step by step. Also relevant are the recent researches on neurological and biochemical correlates of schizophrenia. Owing to inadequate methodological controls, however, most of the findings of the latter studies must be regarded as tentative (Horwitt 1956).

Prenatal environmental factors provide a third avenue of fruitful investigation. Especially noteworthy is the recent work of Pasamanick and his associates (Pasamanick, Knobloch, and Lilienfeld 1956), which demonstrated a tie-up between socioeconomic level, complications of pregnancy and parturition, and psychological disorders of the offspring. In a series of studies on large samples of whites and Negroes in Baltimore, these investigators showed that various prenatal and paranatal disorders are significantly related to the occurrence of mental defect and psychiatric disorders in the child. An important source of such irregularities in the process of childbearing and birth is to be found in deficiencies of maternal diet and in other conditions associated with low socioeconomic status.

An analysis of the data did in fact reveal a much higher frequency of all such medical complications in lower than in higher socioeconomic levels, and a higher frequency among Negroes than among whites.

Direct evidence of the influence of prenatal nutritional factors upon subsequent intellectual development is to be found in a recent, well-controlled experiment by Harrell, Woodyard, and Gates (1955). The subjects were pregnant women in low-income groups, whose normal diets were generally quite deficient. A dietary supplement was administered to some of these women during pregnancy and lactation, while an equated control group received placebos. When tested at the ages of 3 and 4 years, the offspring of the experimental group obtained a significantly higher mean IQ than did the offspring of the controls.

Mention should also be made of animal experiments on the effects of such factors as prenatal radiation and neonatal asphyxia upon cerebral anomalies as well as upon subsequent behavior development. These experimental studies merge imperceptibly into the fourth approach to be considered, namely, the investigation of the influence of early experience upon the eventual behavioral characteristics of animals. Research in this area has been accumulating at a rapid rate. In 1954, Beach and Jaynes surveyed this literature for the *Psychological Bulletin,* listing over 130 references. Several new studies have appeared since that date. The variety of factors covered ranges from the type and quantity of available food to the extent of contact with human culture. A large number of experiments have been concerned with various forms of sensory deprivation and with diminished opportunities for motor exercise. Effects have been observed in many kinds of animals and in almost all aspects of behavior, including perceptual responses, motor activity, learning, emotionality, and social reactions.

In their review, Beach and Jaynes pointed out that research in this area has been stimulated by at least four distinct theoretical interests. Some studies were motivated by the traditional concern with the relative contribution of maturation and learning to behavior development. Others were designed in an effort to test certain psychoanalytic theories regarding infantile experiences, as illustrated by studies which limited the feeding responses of young animals. A third relevant influence is to be found in the work of the European biologist Lorenz on early social stimulation of birds, and in particular on the special type of learning for which the term "imprinting" has been coined. A relatively large number of recent studies have centered around Hebb's (1949) theory regarding the importance of early perceptual experiences upon subsequent performance in learning situations. All this research represents a rapidly growing and promising attack on the *modus operandi* of specific environmental factors.

The human counterpart of these animal studies may be found in the comparative investigation of child-rearing practices in different cultures and subcultures. This represents the fifth approach in our list. An outstanding example of such a study is that by Whiting and Child, published in 1953. Utilizing data on 75 primitive societies from the Cross-Cultural Files of the Yale Institute of Human

Relations, these investigators set out to test a number of hypotheses regarding the relationships between child-rearing practices and personality development. This analysis was followed up by field observations in five cultures, the results of which have not yet been reported.

Within our own culture, similar surveys have been concerned with the diverse psychological environments provided by different social classes (Davis and Havighurst, 1946). Of particular interest are the study by Williams and Scott (1953) on the association between socioeconomic level, permissiveness, and motor development among Negro children, and the exploratory research by Milner (1951) on the relationship between reading readiness in first-grade children and patterns of parent-child interaction. Milner found that upon school entrance the lower-class child seems to lack chiefly two advantages enjoyed by the middle-class child. The first is described as "a warm positive family atmosphere or adult-relationship pattern which is more and more being recognized as a motivational prerequisite of any kind of adult-controlled learning." The lower-class children in Milner's study perceived adults as predominantly hostile. The second advantage is an extensive opportunity to interact verbally with adults in the family. The latter point is illustrated by parental attitudes toward mealtime conversation, lower-class parents tending to inhibit and discourage such conversation, while middle-class parents enourage it.

Most traditional studies on child-rearing practices have been designed in terms of a psychoanalytic orientation. There is need for more data pertaining to other types of hypotheses. Findings such as those of Milner on opportunities for verbalization and the resulting effects upon reading readiness represent a step in this direction. Another possible source of future data is the application of the intensive observational techniques of psychological ecology developed by Barker and Wright (1955) to widely diverse socioeconomic groups.

A sixth major approach involves research on the previously cited somatopsychological relationships (Barker, Wright, Myerson and Gonick, 1953). To date little direct information is available on the precise operation of this class of factor in psychological development. The multiplicity of ways in which physical traits — whether hereditary or environmental in origin — may influence behavior thus offers a relatively unexplored field for future study.

The seventh and final approach to be considered represents an adaptation of traditional twin studies. From the standpoint of the question "How?" there is need for closer coordination between the usual data on twin resemblance and observations of the family interactions of twins. Available data already suggest, for example, that closeness of contact and extent of environmental similarity are greater in the case of monozygotic than in the case of dizygotic twins. Information on the social reactions of twins toward each other and the specialization of roles is likewise of interest. Especially useful would be longitudinal studies of twins, beginning in early infancy and following the subjects through school age. The operation of differential environmental pressures, the development of specialized roles, and other environmental influences could thus be more clearly identified and correlated with intellectual and personality changes in the growing twins.

Parenthetically, I should like to add a remark about the traditional applications of the twin method, in which persons in different degrees of hereditary and environmental relationships to each other are simply compared for behavioral similarity. In these studies, attention has been focused principally upon the amount of resemblance of monozygotic as contrasted to dizygotic twins. Yet such a comparison is particularly difficult to interpret because of the many subtle differences in the environmental situations of the two types of twins. A more fruitful comparison would seem to be that between dizygotic twins and siblings, for whom the hereditary similarity is known to be the same. In Kallmann's monumental research on psychiatric disorders among twins (1953), for example, one of the most convincing bits of evidence for the operation of hereditary factors in schizophrenia is the fact that the degrees of concordance for dizygotic twins and for siblings were practically identical. In contrast, it will be recalled that in intelligence test scores dizygotic twins resemble each other much more closely than do siblings — a finding which reveals the influence of environmental factors in intellectual development.

Behavior Genetics

Jerry Hirsch

An implicit, if not explicit, assumption often made in studies of child development is that variations in environmental variables account for variations in observed behaviors. In the experimental situation, within-group variation is typically treated as error variance; that is, lack of precise measurement. Such assumptions as these are examined critically by Professor Hirsch, a psychologist interested in the correlates of genetic behavioral variation. He convincingly argues that behavior theorists must change their assumptions and methods in dealing with biological organisms. His position that heredity and environment interact to produce unique phenotypes has important implications for basic psychological theory, educational practice, and social action.

Individual differences are no accident. They are generated by properties of organisms as fundamental to behavioral science and biology as thermodynamic properties are to physical science. Much research, however, fails to take them into account. The behavioral sciences have attempted to erect a superstructure without

SOURCE: Adapted and abridged from Jerry Hirsch, "Behavior Genetics and Individuality Understood." *Science,* 1963, 142, 1436–1442. (With permission of the author and the American Association for Advancement of Science.) Copyright 1963 by the American Association for the Advancement of Science.

paying sufficient attention to its foundation. A uniformity of expression over individuals, and even across species, has too often been assumed for behaviors under study. . . . . . . In this article I consider some effects that such assumptions about heredity, individuality, and behavior have had on the behavioral sciences.

Three Approaches to Behavior

In the study of behavior, three points of view can be distinguished. (i) Only common properties of behavior are studied among individuals and species. (ii) Only common properties of behavior are studied among individuals, while both similarities and characteristic differences are studied among species. (iii) Similarities and differences are studied among individuals, populations, and species.

The first view prevails when an organism is used as a tool for studying behavioral correlates of stimulus conditions, reinforcement schedules, deprivation regimens, pharmacological agents, or physiological mechanisms. It is hopefully assumed that the form of any relation observed — for example, that between stimulus and response — will have universal generality. The organism's role is essentially that of an analyzer, like the role of the Geissler tube in physics. In their illuminating discussion "The misbehavior of organisms," the Brelands (1961), drawing on over 14 years of faithful application of the methods and assumptions of behaviorism, show that behaviorism also assumes "that the animal comes to the laboratory as a virtual *tabula rosa,* that species differences are insignificant, and that all responses are about equally conditionable to all stimuli." They relate a history of "egregious failures" which they feel "represent a clear and utter failure of conditioning theory."

From the second viewpoint the behavior of animals is as characteristic of their species as is their form. This view prevails in ethologically oriented studies — for example, studies of such instincts as reproductive, parental, or territorial behavior. All members of a species are assumed to manifest a given behavior pattern, in some typical way. In Mayr's cogent analysis (1963) this represents typological thinking whose replacement "by population thinking is perhaps the greatest conceptual revolution . . . in biology."

The third approach characterizes behavior genetics: the study of the relations between the genetic architecture of a taxon and the distributions of its behavioral phenotypes. It employs the methods of both the behavioral sciences and genetics. The growth of this field can be attributed to protest against the counterfactual uniformity postulate, combined with the realization that we can now have a description and analysis of behavior based on a deeper understanding of the materials on which the behavioral sciences make their observations.

The key to our present understanding of the structure of life came during the first half of this century, from investigations of transmission cytogenetics and population cytogenetics. Through study of cell division and reproduction (mitosis, meiosis, and fertilization), together with statistical analysis of variations in the expression of traits among offspring of specified matings, transmission cytogenetics gave us our first picture of the fundamental units of life (genes and chromosomes) and of the variation-generating probability mechanism (meiosis) by which lawfully combined random samples of these units are passed on from parents to offspring. Through study of (i) the distributions of genes in populations, (ii) the mechanisms responsible for both stability and change in gene frequencies, and (iii) the role of such mechanisms in evolution, population cytogenetics has given us some understanding of ensembles of these units that comprise the gene pools of populations and species — the taxa that are natural units of evolution.

Understanding Individuality

The phenotype (appearance, structure, physiology, and behavior) of any organism is determined by the interaction of environment with its genotype (the complete genetic endowment). Each genotype is the end product of many mechanisms which promote genotypic diversity in populations.

Ordinarily members of a cross-fertilizing, sexually reproducing species possess a diploid, or paired, set of chromosomes. Most species whose behavior we study are sexually dimorphic. The genetic basis of this dimorphism resides in the distribution of the heterosomes, a homologous pair of sex chromosomes (XX) being present in the mammalian female and an unequal pair (XY), in the mammalian male. Sexual dimorphism guarantees that any population will be variable to the extent of at least two classes. Whether sex-chromosome or other genotypic differences are involved in any particular behavior remains an empirical question to be investigated separately for every population. It can no longer be settled by dogmatic attitudes and assumptions about uniformity.

Chromosomes other than sex chromosomes are called autosomes. Every autosome is normally represented by a homologous pair whose members have identical genetic loci. Alternative forms of a gene any of which may occupy a given locus are termed alleles. If an individual receives identical alleles from both parents at homologous loci, he is said to be homozygous for that gene. If he receives two alleles that differ, however, he is said to be heterozygous for that gene. The process by which a gene changes from one allelic form to another is called mutation.

When a gene is represented in the population gene pool by two allelic forms, the population will be genotypically polymorphic to the extent of at least three classes. That is, individuals may be homozygous for either of two alleles or heterozygous for their combination.

Study of populations has revealed that often extensive series of alleles exist for a locus. Well-known examples are the three (actually more) alleles at the ABO-blood locus in man and a dozen or more alleles at the white-eye locus in *Drosophila*. Benzer (1961), in his study of the internal genetic architecture of *one* "gene" with a corresponding physical structure of probably less than 2000 nucleotide pairs, the *r*II region of the T4 bacteriophage, found 339 distinguishable mutational sites, and he expects to eventually find some 428. There is no reason to believe that we shall find less complexity in cellular organisms as further refinement increases the resolving power of our techniques for analyzing them. In general, for each locus having n alleles in the gene pool, a population will contain $n(n + 1)/2$ genotypic classes. Mutation insures variety in the gene itself.

Sexual reproduction involves meiosis — a complex cellular process resulting in a meristic division of the nucleus and formation of gametes (reproductive cells) having single genomes (a haploid chromosome set). One homolog in every chromosome pair in our diploid complement is a paternal origin and the other is of maternal origin. In meiosis, the homologs of a pair segregate and a gamete receives one from each pair. The assortment to gametes of the segregating homologs occurs independently for each pair. This process insures diversity because it maximizes the likelihood that gametes will receive unique genomes. For example, gametogenesis in *Drosophila willistroni* produces eight alternative gametic genomes, which, if we represent the three chromosome pairs of this species by Aa, Bb, and Cc, we designate ABC, ABc, AbC, aBC, Abc, aBc, abC, abc. In general, n pairs of chromosomes produce 2^n genomes (if we ignore the recombination of gene linkages that actually occurs in crossover exchanges between chromosomes). Man, with 23 chromosome pairs, produces gametes with any of 2^{23} alternative genomes. This makes vanishingly small the chances that even siblings (other than monozygotes) will be genetically identical. Since the gamete contributed by *each* parent is chosen from 2^{23} alternatives, the probability that the second offspring born to parents will have exactly the same genotype as their firstborn is $(1/2^{23})^2$, or less than 1 chance in over 70 trillion! The probability that two unrelated individuals will have the same genotype, then, is effectively zero (Hirsch 1962).

The argument for genotypic uniqueness of members of populations is even more compelling, since other conditions also contribute to diversity. So, it is clear, the organisms which the behavioral sciences study are intrinsically variable before they undergo differentiating experiences. The mechanisms responsible for this variety are mutation, recombination, and meiosis. Add to these individual experience, and it becomes evident why individuals differ in behavior. In fact, the more reliable our methods of observation become, the more evident will this variety be.

The Abnormality of the Normal

. . . Physiological systems are variable, not uniform. Williams (1956) amply documents this and points out that implicit in our use of "normal" is reference to some region of a distribution arbitrarily designated as not extreme — for example, the median 50 per cent, 95 per cent, or 99 per cent. We choose such a region for every trait. Among n mathematically independent traits — for example, traits dependent on n different chromosomes — the probability that a randomly selected individual will be normal for all n traits is the value for the size of that region raised to the nth power. Where "normal" is the median 50 per cent and

$n = 10$, on the average only 1 individual out of 1024 will be normal (for ten traits). When we consider at one time the distributions throughout a population of large numbers of physiological systems, we should expect negative deviates from some distributions to combine with positive deviates from others, both kinds of extreme deviates to combine with centrally located ones, and deviates of similar algebraic sign and magnitude to combine. Each individual's particular balance of physiological endowments will be the developmental result of the genotype he draws in the lotteries of meiosis and the mating ritual. Because of crossing over, most genes assort independently. Hence, we cannot expect high correlations among the systems they generate.

If, underlying every behavior, there were only a single such system — for example, if the male "sexual drive" were mainly dependent on the seminal vesicles or if escape behavior were mainly dependent on the adrenals — then the same kind of distribution might be expected for both the behavior and the underlying system. Whatever uniformity might exist at one level would be reflected at the other. The last few decades of research on the biological correlates of behavior have made it increasingly clear that behavior is the integration of most of these systems rather than the expression of any one of them. Therefore, there is little reason to expect that the many possible combinations and integrations of those systems that go to make up the members of a population will yield a homogeneously normal distribution of responses for many behavioral measures. An organism richly endowed with the components of one subset of systems and poorly endowed with those of another is not to be expected to behave in the same manner as an organism with an entirely different balance of endowments. The obviousness of this fact is well illustrated by the differences in behavior among the various breeds of dogs and horses.

. . .

Behavior Genetics

There now exists a substantial and rapidly growing literature on the behavior genetics of many organisms, from *Drosophila* to man what Tryon (1963) calls "the basic science of individual differences." It comes from research far less hampered by unsound premises. In Fuller and Thompson's useful summary (1960) we can see "its documentation of the fact that two individuals of superficially similar phenotype may be quite different genotypically and respond in completely different fashion when treated alike." This field, like others, is passing through stages. The goal of the early work was a genetics *of* behavior. It took a while to learn that heritability is a property of populations and never of behaviors: the relation between behavioral variation and relevant genetic variation is never constant. It must be measured in specific populations under specific conditions, because it varies with both.

. . .

Many strains of small mammals (mice, hamsters, rats, guinea pigs, and rabbits) are maintained under varying inbreeding regimens for purposes of medical and other research. When different strains within a species are compared, it actually becomes a challenge *not* to find differences in one or more behaviors. When strain comparisons are followed by appropriate genetic crosses, genetic correlates of behavioral differences are demonstrated. Such experiments have been performed for a large variety of behaviors: alcohol preference, hoarding, mating competition, susceptibility to audiogenic seizure, exploratory tendency, and various learning measures.

Paralleling the animal research are studies of human pedigrees, studies of family resemblances, twin comparisons, population surveys, and studies of race differences. Again, heritabilities have been demonstrated for many behaviors; for example, nature-nurture ratios were computed for intelligence test and personality test performance. Kallmann (1962) and his associates have pioneered, and others have joined, in collecting an impressive body of evidence on genetic factors in schizophrenia and other psychopathologies.

In 1963, with the wisdom of hindsight, we can ask why so many demonstrations were necessary. Should it not have been common knowledge that within each population the variation pattern for most traits will be conditioned by the nature of the gene pool, and that this will differ among populations? The answer lies in one phrase: the heredity-environment controversy.

The "opinion leaders" of two generations literally excommunicated heredity from the behavioral sciences. Understandably, they objected to amateurish labeling of behaviors as instincts without proper experimental analyses. Also, they were repelled by the pseudogenetics of Hitler and other purveyors of race prejudice. On the other hand, impressed with the power of conditioning *procedures,* they proclaimed their faith in analysis of experience as the starting point for behavioral science — as though experience, like the Cheshire Cat's grin, could exist without the organism. "Our conclusion . . . is that we have no real evidence for the inheritance of traits," said Watson (1959). While acknowledging that there are heritable differences in form and structure, he claimed there is no evidence that those differences are related to function, because "hereditary structure lies ready to be shaped in a thousand different ways." Behaviorism still makes the gratuitous uniformity assumption that all genetic combinations are equally plastic and respond in like fashion to environmental influences.

We are now in a more fruitful period. Experimental analysis is yielding information about genes and chromosomes and how they act. The way is open to understanding molecular — ultimately submolecular — mechanisms and to following metabolic pathways between genes and phenotypes. . . .

Our laboratory has made the most detailed analysis, to date, of relations between the genome and a behavioral phenotype in studies of geotaxis (gravity-oriented locomotion) in *Drosophila*. Selective breeding from a geotactically and genetically heterogeneous foundation population has produced the two strains shown in Figure 3.1, which have diametrically opposite response tendencies.

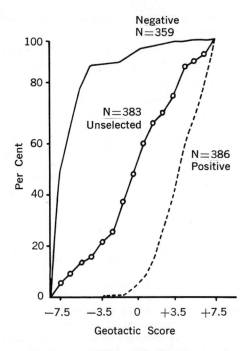

Figure 3.1 Cumulated percentages of animals (males and females) that received geotactic scores in a 15-unit maze. From an unselected foundation population (middle curve) and from the two selected strains (outer curves.) (Hirsh and Erlenmeyer-Kimling 1961.)

Other methods produced three populations differing with respect to both degree and kind of similarity in chromosome constitution among their members. Two parameters of their behavioral distributions were thus controlled. The least dispersion occurred in the population in which all members carried two of the three large chromosomes in identical form. The other two populations, differing from each other with respect to the single chromosome distributed in identical form to all their members, differed in central tendency but not in dispersion, which was twice that of the first population. Figure 3.2 shows, for this model situation, the kind of prediction and control that an understanding of population structure and its genetic basis may yield. . . .

The study of man is also moving beyond the stage of wondering whether we can find a heritability for this or that behavior. Phenylpyruvic oligophrenia, a form of mental deficiency accompanied by a high concentration of phenylpyruvic acid in the urine, had early been traced to a gene-controlled enzymatic deficiency in phenylalanine metabolism. Now, Down's syndrome (mongolism) has been associated with the presence of extrachromosomal material.

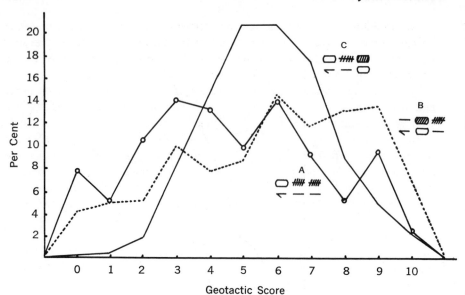

Figure 3.2 Distributions of geotactic scores in a 10-unit maze for males of three populations (described in text). Rectangles: chromosomes carried in identical form by all members of a population; dashes: chromosomes varying at random; hatching: heterozygosity; half-arrowhead: the Y chromosome of males. (The abscissa scale was reversed and the zero point was shifted to the center of the distribution.) (Hirsch 1959.)

Race Differences

A problem of continuing social importance, for an understanding of which most behavioral scientists have lacked a proper conceptual basis, is the question of race differences. To the liberals this question has been a continuing source of embarrassment. They have made little progress in answering it since the signing of our Constitution and Bill of Rights, when it was *asserted* that all men are created equal. To the prejudiced the question has presented no difficulties, because they *know* other races are inferior to their own; this seems as obvious to them as the flatness of the earth did to our ancestors.

This question appears in another perspective when it is examined in the light of current knowledge of population structure. Dobzhansky (1962) has clearly called attention to the difference between equality and identity. Genotypic uniqueness creates biochemical individuality. Without enforcing conformity — irrespective of heredity, training, or ability — a democratic ethicosocial system offers to all equality of opportunity and equal treatment before the law. Genetics explains both individual and population uniqueness. Even though reproductively isolated populations belong to the same species and have the same genes, the relative frequencies of different alleles of genes in their gene pools are almost certain to differ. Mutations and recombinations will occur at different places, at different times, and with differing frequencies. Furthermore, selection pressures will also vary. In analyzing data from such populations we have learned to ask, not whether they are different, but, rather, in what ways they differ.

Races are populations that differ in gene frequencies. Observations on populations are summarized in distributions, so often assumed to be normal. When we add the assumption of common variance, or make transformations to obtain it, the data fit into the ever popular analysis-of-variance models. *The* difference between two populations must then be a difference between means, because the assumptions of normality and homogeneity of variance for the model leave no other property with respect to which the distributions can differ. The final step in this fantastic chain of reasoning has recently been taken in *Science* by Garrett (1962). He ignores individual differences and claims that wherever two populations differ on some scale of measurement, no matter how vague, any individual from the population with *the* higher mean is better than any individual in the other population, and that intermarriage will "be not only dysgenic but socially disastrous"!

Distributions have other properties, such as dispersion, skewness, and kurtosis (peakedness), and no single one is exclusively important. Where these other properties have been examined, the inadequacy of a preoccupation with the central tendency and a hasty assumption of normality has been easy to document. There is no reason to expect two populations with different heredities and different environments to have precisely the same distribution for any trait. We can expect to find varying combinations of similarities and differences in the several properties of distributions when we compare different populations for a given trait, or any set of populations for different traits. Furthermore, the number of traits for which we could make comparisons is effectively unlimited, and many of the traits will be uncorrelated. Again, a lack of intrinsic correlation would come as no surprise to a behavioral science that understands its materials, because traits are the developmental results of thousands of genes, most of which, because of crossing over, sooner or later undergo independent assortment.

For ease of exposition, I have not considered environment in discussing race. Certainly, it is no less important than genetic endowment. The ontogeny of a responsible and effective citizen requires prolonged socialization, highly dependent upon the socializing agency. A genotype must have an environment in which to develop a phenotype. But the same genotype can produce quite different phenotypes, depending on the environments in which it may develop. Furthermore, a given environment can nurture quite different phenotypes, depending on the genotypes which may develop there. This fact is attested daily by parents and teachers who find that a method of tuition admirably successful with one child may be worthless with another, who nevertheless can learn by a different method. So while environment makes an undeniably important contribution to the particular values obtained in phenotypic measurements, consideration of particular environments should not change our general picture of population structure. Without an appreciation of the genotypic structure of populations, the behavioral sciences have no basis for distinguishing individual differences that are attributable to differences in previous history from those that are not; and no basis for understanding any differences whatsoever where there is a common history.

Physical Maturing among Boys as Related to Behavior

Mary Cover Jones and Nancy Bayley

The importance of physical growth on how one is perceived by peers and adults is clearly demonstrated in this classic study by Professors Jones and Bayley. This report derives from a significant longitudinal study at the Institute of Child Development, University of California at Berkeley. Early-maturing and late-maturing boys are compared on several aspects of social behavior with the general conclusion that early-maturing boys display more mature patterns of behavior and superior levels of adjustment. One might argue that these findings reflect an overall psychological superiority inherent to the early-maturing boys. It is also possible that because of their advanced physical status, cultural expectations demand more mature social behaviors. When the late-maturing boys catch up, the same social demands would generate mature behavior. This latter interpretation is consistent with the finding that by the age of 21 to 25, the observed differences between the two groups are minimal.

The problems of adjustment which are usually attributed to the adolescent period center around the youth's need to develop heterosexual interests, to select a vocation, and in general to acquire the status of adulthood in the eyes of his peers and of his elders. The impetus for the attainment of independent and mature status is undoubtedly related to the adolescent's physical changes, but the process of growing up is so complex and so interwoven with cultural factors that we have not yet been able to demonstrate more than a rather general relationship between physical and psychological phases of development.

It is well known that children mature at different rates, and reach the period of pubescence at different chronological ages. Although the psychological accompaniments of these differences in maturing can be examined in terms of mass statistics, this approach to the problem is often disappointing because of its tendency to obscure the intricacies of the growth pattern and the dynamics involved in the process of integration. Case reports of individual children have

SOURCE: Adapted and abridged from Mary Cover Jones and Nancy Bayley, "Physical Maturing among Boys as Related to Behavior." *Journal of Educational Psychology,* 1950, 41, 129–148. (With permission of the authors and Abrahams Magazine Service, Inc.)

been somewhat more successful in their attempts to disclose the processes involved in the attainment of maturity, but the accumulation of individual life histories is a slow way in which to arrive at useful generalities.

The present report deals with two groups of boys who fall at opposite ends of a normal sample distributed on the basis of one developmental characteristic (skeletal age). In an attempt to find differentiating behavior characteristics, statistical comparisons of the two groups have been made and illustrative case material has been assembled for individuals falling at each extreme. The method, while providing no touchstone, does enable us to consider group differences without losing sight of the individual behavior patterns of members of the group.

There are several ways in which children's physical maturity status may be expressed. One of the most commonly used for girls is the age of menarche. As a possibly comparable measure for boys, some investigators have used the age of appearance of pubic or of axillary hair. Shuttleworth classified children in the Harvard Growth Study according to age at maximum growth in height. Height and weight have also been used as an index of physical maturity, although maturity differences may be obscured by genetic differences in measurements of gross body dimensions. This difficulty is avoided by the use of skeletal age norms, from x-rays of the long bones of the hand and knee. Skeletal age has the advantage of being a stable and reliably assessed indicator of physical maturity, closely related to other aspects of physical maturing, and applicable at all ages from birth to young adulthood.

Physical Characteristics of the Early- and Late-Maturing Groups

The selection of contrasting extreme groups for the present study was on the basis of physical maturity assessments by the Todd standards for hand and knee. The groups included 16 boys who were most consistently accelerated and 16 who were most consistently retarded during the four and a half years for which we had cumulative skeletal x-rays, beginning at an average age of 14 years. The total distribution from which these extremes were truncated consisted of 90 cases, a normal classroom sample of boys in an urban public-school system.

On the average, the physically accelerated and the physically retarded boys are seen to be of the same age, but are separated by about two years in skeletal age (the criterion variable). Although some overlapping was noted in the height of individual children at each age, the means of the groups are widely different. Even as early as 11 years all of the late-maturing are shorter than the mean for the early-maturing. At the mean age of 14 years the distributions show an extreme separation; in the later years of adolescence the differences tend to decrease, and the predicted mature heights of the early- and late-maturing are very similar.

There is also an obvious divergence (with no overlap) when the two groups are compared in terms of physical maturity ratings. This is seen when Greulich's five-point standards of maturity[1] are applied to photographs taken at 14 years of age. The characteristic rating at this age is 3. The mean of 16 early-maturing boys was 4.5 (close to the maximum), with no rating below 4. The mean of the 16 late-maturers was 2.0, with only two ratings of 3.

The boys who matured late were relatively very small from 13 to 15 years. In agreement with Bayley's study of body build in relation to skeletal maturing, they were characteristically slender built and long legged at all ages. Furthermore, their strength tests show them to have been relatively weak at the ages when they were lagging in size, and their scores in the Espenschade tests of athletic ability were in most instances below average. The early-maturing boys, on the other hand, were usually large, broad-built, and strong, and tended to show good athletic skill throughout the period of our records. Their superiority in strength and physical skills was greatest at ages 13 to 15, when their early growth spurt accentuated their differences in size as compared with the slower-growing average and late-maturing boys. This is in agreement with a report by H. E. Jones, who presents a variety of data for groups of boys in the Adolescent Growth Study, considered in relation to static dynamometric strength. Strong boys were found to be relatively mature in skeletal age, weak boys were immature.

Social Behavior in Boys' Groups

The psychological records examined in connection with the present study include both observational measures and reputation scores. We shall present first the ratings made independently by three staff members when the boys were in small groups (usually 6) in a same-sex "free play" situation. These will be referred to as ICW (Institute of Child Welfare) ratings. The observations and ratings were concerned, in general, with social behavior and personal attributes which are important in social relationships.

The ratings have been converted into standard scores in which 50 represents the mean of the total group, with an SD of 10 points. The direction and the degree of a child's deviation from the mean of his group are thus expressed in such a way that comparisons can readily be made between accelerated and retarded subgroups.

Figures 3.3 and 3.4 present cumulative standard score curves, from ages 12 to 17, for four traits involving personal appearance, and attention-seeking behavior. (A summary of all the traits studied is presented in Table 3.3.) As shown in Figure 3.3, the early-maturing are consistently rated as superior in physical attractiveness, with average scores which reach their highest value at age 15. In general, the group is about one SD above the mean total sample of boys. The late-maturing fall somewhat below the group mean, increasingly so from age 12 to age 15 or 16. These differences in attractiveness of physique are complexly influenced by factors of size and of body build. Early maturing is not only associated with a more rapid growth in height, but also with mesomorphy. The boys in this group tend to be "well built," muscular, and athletic. By contrast, the more slender, poorly muscled build of the late-maturers was rated as relatively "unattractive" by the adult observers.

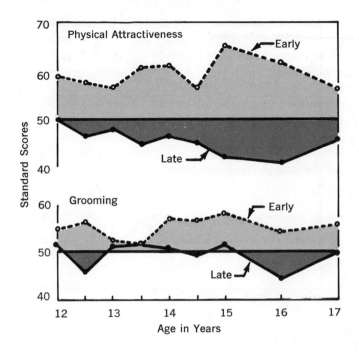

Figure 3.3 Mean standard scores for early- and late-maturing groups in physical appearance.

When a comparison is made of the androgynic qualities of the builds of these two groups, the early-maturers are found to be on the average more "masculine," the late-maturers more "childish" in their build. As shown in the lower half of Figure 3.9.1, early maturing, as might be expected, is also associated with a somewhat greater attention to the amenities of personal grooming. This is expressed in cleanliness, attention to hair and nails, and neatness of clothing.

When the distributions at age 16 for a composite based on physique, grooming, and attractiveness of facial appearance are compared, the separation of the early- and late-maturing is so marked that all but one of the former fall above the average of the latter. Only two cases among the late-maturing are rated above the central tendency of our total group of boys.

Another group of traits which may have developmental significance are those related to expressiveness. In these characteristics the early-maturing are close to the group average, but the late-maturing are consistently above the average. Similar differences were found for other traits involving expressiveness; comparisons were made for behavior defined, at contrasting extremes, as talkative-silent; active-stationary; busy-idle; peppy-indifferent; and laughing-sober. In each of these the early-maturing boys were distributed similarly to the total sample of boys, the late-maturing were consistently on the "expressive" side of the scale.

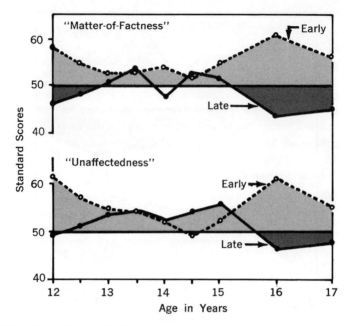

Figure 3.4   Mean standard scores of early- and late-maturing groups in attention-seeking behavior.

At least two factors are probably involved in determining this deviate position of the late-maturing. The first is a persistence of a childish activity pattern. A busy scurrying about and noisy interchange of shouts and comments is more characteristic of preadolescence than of later years; the adolescent often looks down upon such behavior as undignified, and adopts instead the role of a lounger, observing with tolerant superiority the childish antics of those younger than himself. A second factor is a reaction formation to inferiority. The "active small boy" may be expressing through his activity not merely a survival of an immature culture pattern. He may also use this as the only technique he knows to hold the attention of others and to compensate for a physically less favored status.

In this connection, it is instructive to consider the evidence concerning attention-seeking behavior, as presented in Figure 3.4. In the upper half of this figure, the late-maturing boys tend to vary around the average in the trait "matter-of-factness." Their lowest score is at age 16, when they fall on the "show-off" side of the scale. In the lower half of the figure, their scores also vary around the average on the trait "unaffectedness." Again, they attain a low score at age 16; their expressiveness is judged to have a more affected quality at ages 16 and 17 than in the years immediately preceding. Although the differences are small, this would be consistent with an interpretation emphasizing a "natural" or "childish" expressiveness in the earlier years of adolescence, and a more compensatory attention-seeking expressiveness in the later years. In contrast, the early-maturing are at these ages judged to be relatively non-attention-seeking: unaffected and matter-of-fact.

Also pertinent are the ratings for inhibition and relaxation in social situations. The late-maturing are relatively uninhibited, but they are also judged to be relatively tense. At age 16, the early-maturing are on the average approximately one SD above the group mean, in the direction of "relaxation," and the late-maturing are a similar distance below the mean, in the direction of "tenseness." The early-maturing are consistently well adjusted in this trait, while the late-maturing are in most semesters on the less well-adjusted side of the scale.

Table 3.1 presents the significance of the differences between the early- and

TABLE 3.1. *Mean Standard Scores for Early- and Late-Maturing Boys*

TRAIT	EARLY	LATE	SIGNIFICANCE OF DIFFERENCE
Attractiveness of Physique	60.6	45 0	.01
Grooming	54.6	49.8	.05
Animation	49.6	61.2	
Eagerness	47.9	59.3	.05
Uninhibitedness	52.5	60.2	
Matter-of-factness	60.5	43.6	.02
Unaffectedness	60.7	46.2	.05
Relaxation	61.1	40.6	.01

late-maturing at age 16, based on t ratios. For all but two traits on this list, differences are significant at the 5 per cent level or better. In these two traits (animation and "uninhibitedness") significant differences are obtained when results are considered for all nine semesters in which ratings have been recorded, from age 12 to 17, and analyzed in terms of the binomial test for consistency. In attractiveness of physique, grooming, and relaxation (higher for the late-maturing) differences are in the same direction in each of nine semesters, with a significance level of .002. Differences of the same consistency were obtained for a number of other traits; these results show that the late-maturing are significantly more busy, more active, more peppy, and more talkative. Differences at the 2% level (in the same direction for eight of the nine semesters) were found for eagerness, social initiative, and sociability, in favor of the late-maturing. Differences at the 7% level (in the same direction for seven of the nine semesters) occurred in several additional traits, indicating a possibly greater tendency for the early-maturing to be good-natured, and for the late-maturing to be attention-seeking and to enjoy games.

It may be noted that the two maturational groups show similar rather than different records in a number of traits of social importance. Thus, they present no marked or consistent differences in observed popularity, leadership, prestige, poise, assurance, cheerfulness, or social effect on the group.

In view of the relation of maturing to physical abilities, and of high valuation placed upon athletic performance in the adolescent culture, it is perhaps surprising that differences in maturing are not reflected in such traits as popularity, leadership, or prestige. Case reports have made it clear that late maturing is sometimes a primary source of social and personal maladjustment. On the average, however, the late-maturing boy succeeds in maintaining a fairly adequate status among his age-mates; very likely he is helped in this by his activity and other compensations, and it is also probable that some of the early-maturing are handicapped at times by the fact that they have outgrown their age group.

Reputation with Classmates

Another source of evidence concerning adolescent behavior and status is from the Reputation Test. For the same age range previously presented, data are available from a series of tests in which classmates were asked to write down the name of anyone in the class conforming to certain descriptions. For example, "Here is someone who finds it hard to sit still in class," or at the other extreme, "Here is someone who can work quietly without moving around in his seat." Scores were obtained by determining the percentage of times a person was mentioned on a given trait description, and these measures were then transformed into standard scores in which 50 represented the "indifference point" (indicating no mentions at either extreme of the trait). Reputation scores are less differentiating than ratings; they tend to identify outstanding individuals, but may fail to distribute the middle range of cases who receive few or no mentions from their classmates. As a result differences between early- and late-maturing in average reputation scores are less marked than in average ratings by adults. However, a number of traits show differences which occur in the same direction on six testings, and are significant by the binomial test.

The late-maturing are consistently more "attention-getting," more "restless," more "assured in class," more "talkative," less "grown-up," and less likely to have older friends. On five out of six tests they are more "bossy," and less "good-looking."

Less consistency is found for traits which have been established as especially important for adolescent prestige. On judgments of "popular," "reader," "friendly," "daring," "active in games," and "humor about self," the late-maturing stand relatively well until the middle period of junior high school, and then tend to drop to lower status.

Table 3.2 presents a comparison of average standard scores for the two groups in the E 10 and L 11 grades. The differences are not statistically significant but they present a picture which is in general similar to that already found in the observations by adults: the late-maturing appears as assertive (in a small-boy extroverted way) but at this age are somewhat lower in prestige traits.

At the earlier ages the more active and energetic of those in the late-maturing

TABLE 3.2. *Mean Standard Scores for Reputation Traits*

TRAIT	EARLY-MATURING	LATE-MATURING
Attention-getting	48.1	52.2
Restlessness	45.3	52.9
Talkativeness	47.9	53.0
Bossiness	47.1	52.6
Assurance in class	45.6	50.0
Popularity	54.0	50.7
Leadership	51.3	47.5
Humor (about self)	53.5	48.7
Having older friends	56.2	42.3
Good appearance	54.4	49.3

group were not unsuccessful in winning social recognition. But the early-maturing were much more likely to get and maintain the kind of prestige accorded to athletes and officeholders. Two of the 16 early-maturing boys became student body presidents, one was president of the boys' club (a position next in importance to that of student body president), several were elected to committee chairmanships, and four attained outstanding reputations as athletes. The 16 late-maturing boys produced only one somewhat "important" officeholder (a class vice-president), and one athlete.

NOTE

[1] Based on ratings of pubic hair and external genitals.

The Regulation of Human Growth

James M. Tanner

Recent advances in the understanding of the biological processes of human behavior have generated many interesting, and in some respects speculative, hypotheses. In general, these various theories postulate a central preplanned or coded mechanism which, upon appropriate stimulation, triggers various processes. Appropriate stimulation, it should be understood, is not simply the result of heredity but relies upon a sufficiently nutrient environment. This paper by Professor Tanner, which was originally given as a speech, presents data showing the presence of built-in mechanisms with respect to patterns of physical growth and development. A theory is also presented which attempts to explain the fascinating phenomena of physical growth patterns reported. This study contributes to our knowledge of the biological coding systems that apparently influence many aspects of human behavior.

SOURCE: Adapted and abridged from J. M. Tanner, "The Regulation of Human Growth." *Child Development*, 1963, 34, 817–847. (With permission of the author and the Society for Research in Child Development.)

The most striking and perhaps most fundamental characteristic of the growth of an animal is that it is self-stabilizing, or, to take another analogy, "target-seeking." Children, no less than rockets, have their trajectories, governed by the control systems of their genetical constitutions and powered by energy absorbed from the natural environment. Deflect the child from its natural growth trajectory by acute malnutrition or a sudden lack of a hormone, and a restoring force develops so that as soon as the missing food or hormone is supplied again the child catches up toward its orginal curve. When it gets there, it slows down to adjust its path onto the old trajectory once more.

There was a time when self-correcting and goal-seeking capacity was thought to be a very special property of living things, but now that we understand more about the dynamics of complex systems consisting of many interacting substances we realize that it is not, after all, such an exceptional phenomenon. Many complex systems, even of quite simple lifeless substances, show such internal regulation simply as a property consequent on their organization. Indeed the activity of the rocketeers has made us all too dismally familiar with the general notions of cybernetics and equifinality. Animal geneticists and auxologists have in the last decade introduced this approach into their ways of thinking, and among developmental psychologists Piaget at least has endeavored to do the same. But though new models and a new mathematical symbolism are powerful aids to thought, they do not of themselves tell us anything about the mechanisms of regulation that are at work. We know very little as yet about how these intricate growth patterns are organized.

Let me begin by illustrating how regular is the growth of a healthy well-nourished child. The upper section of Figure 3.5 shows the measurements of height of a boy in the Harpenden Growth Study taken every 6 months from ages 4 to 10 by a single observer, Mr. R. H. Whitehouse. The circles represent the measurements, and the solid line is a simple mathematical curve of the form $h = a + bt + c \log t$ (where h is height and t age) fitted to them. None of the measurements deviates more than 4 mm from this line, although the experimental error of measuring height may be 3 mm even in experienced hands. The lower section of Figure 3.5 shows the same data plotted as 6-monthly velocities; the continuous curve is the first derivative of the fitted curve in the upper section. This child shows a slightly better fit than average, but it is by no means exceptional; the curves of many others in the Harpenden Growth Study are very similar. A curve of this form fits height data very well from about 6 months to around 10 years. If there were any periods of acceleration common to most children during this time, then they would be shown by the deviations of velocity from the fitted curves being mostly positive at that age and negative before and after. When we average the deviations for 19 boys and 13 girls each fitted from 4½ years to 9 years, we find no age at which these averages depart significantly from zero. In other words we can find no satisfactory evidence of a midgrowth or juvenile spurt in height occuring at 6 or 7 to 8. At adolescence a different curve

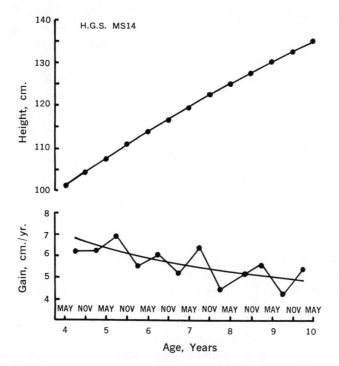

Figure 3.5 Growth of a boy in the Harpenden Growth Study measured every 6 months by R. H. Whitehouse. Above, "distance" plot of height achieved at each age; below, velocity plot of average velocities each 6 months. Solid lines: above, curve of form height = $a + bt + c \log t$ ($t =$ age) fitted to individual's height-achieved points; below, the derivative of the fitted curve.

is needed, but we have confirmed that the Gompertz function, which is a sigmoid curve with four parameters, fits just as well at that time as the simple curve does earlier.

Seasonal Effect

A number of children show greater deviations from the fitted curve than does the child in Figure 3.5, but when they are investigated most of the deviations turn out to be regular. The fluctuations of velocity from 6½ onward represent the effect that season of the year has on growth in height of many, but not all children. (Small and irregular 6-monthly fluctuations could be caused by measuring error, a low value on one occasion causing a low velocity followed by a compensatory high one.) In the case of one boy, deviations from the distance curve amounted to 5 mm above and below it, and the velocity of April to October growth averaged no less than 1.6 cm/year more than growth from October to

April. But this seasonal rhythm is only superimposed on the basic regularity. In fact a small seasonal effect can be seen in Figure 3.5, where the average May to November growth rate is .2 cm/year more than the rate from November to May.

The cause of the seasonal effect is not known. Presumably the endocrine system is affected by light or temperature or some other climatic or just possibly some nutritional factor. The most likely endocrine mediators are probably the thyroid and the adrenal cortex, thyroxine possibly accelerating growth and increased cortisol secretion possibly decelerating. We have no sure evidence, however, that a seasonal change in rate of secretion of either of these hormones takes place in man. Growth hormone could be another possibility and perhaps insulin a fourth. All we can say for certain is that there are marked individual differences in this response to seasonal change.

Illness

This is a simple example of the regulation of growth. Similar individual differences in the ability to regulate seem to occur in response to illness. We have fitted curves to 6-monthly height measurements of children who have suffered relatively minor illness, but omitting the first measurement following the illness. We then tested whether the post-illness measurement was significantly below the fitted nonillness curve. In the great majority of cases it was not; either the illness had had no effect or the catch-up had been complete within a few months. But in a few children the postillness point was depressed and these children were not apparently any sicker than the others, nor apparently eating less or behaving in any obviously different way in the uniform environment of the children's home where all were resident. Apparently some children are less well regulated than others.

Figure 3.6 shows the effect on growth of a young child of two periods in which food intake was much reduced for psychological reasons. Above is the curve of body length at successive ages ("distance" curve) and below, the average rates of growth at successive periods plotted against the 50th percentile lines for length growth velocity (for details, see Prader, Tanner, and von Harnack, 1963). The velocity during each period of catch-up reached more than twice the average velocity for the chronological age; it was nearly twice average for the skeletal age, which was retarded in parallel with the retardation in length and caught up as the length caught up. The catch-up is apparently complete in that the child is quite normal in both length and velocity of length growth by age 5.

Birth Catch-Up

This capacity to catch up in growth seems to be used normally around the time of birth in man. There is evidence that the growth rate of the fetus at least in weight slows down during the last four weeks of pregnancy. The prenatal values are calculated from data on birth weights of live children born after a shorter

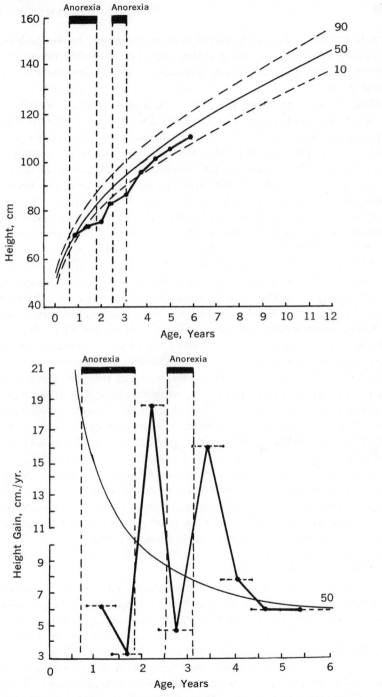

Figure 3.6 Two periods of catch-up growth following episodes of Anorexia Nervosa in a young child.

gestation than average. In using them we are assuming that these early-delivered children's weights are the same as the weights of fetuses of the same age as yet still in the uterus; in other words that among healthy singletons the early-born are not especially big or small children for their gestational age. Such an assumption may be challenged. But there is good evidence also of a catch-up occurring after birth, particularly in small babies. This is shown in a partially longitudinal survey of some 17 thousand babies in which babies below average in birth weight gained more than the others, thus reducing the range of weight in the whole group. The catch-up finishes by about 5 months in these data and is distinctly more marked in boys than in girls. Thus there is a negative correlation between birth weight and weight gain from birth to 3 months or from birth to 6 months of the order of about .15. The negative correlation is still present, though lower, by the time 1 year is reached. The catch-up occurs also in length, indeed probably to a greater extent than in weight.

The catch-up mechanism at birth is of much genetical importance. It seems to be the chief means by which variability in adult size is maintained in the population. Most of the adult size variability is established by 2 years after birth, since by then the individual's adult size is to a large extent fixed (presuming adequate environmental conditions). The correlation coefficients between length of child at 2 years and length of the same child when adult is nearly .8; it approaches .7 even at age 1. (Genetical differences in the time and intensity of the adolescent spurt account for the remainder of the adult variability.) Thus there would be many genetically large children developing in the uteri of small mothers and constituting a problem at the time of birth, unless selection for assortative mating were very strong, a solution which would produce other genetically undesirable effects. The problem is solved by birth size being controlled almost entirely by uterine factors, the correlation of birth length and adult length being only about .2. The catch-up after birth does the rest. Note that this is a true regulatory problem because only some of the small babies catch up. A proportion of them need little or no catch-up to reach and continue on their natural growth curves, since they are genetically small; it is those aimed, so to speak, at largeness who catch up on their proper track.

Control of Catch-Up

We do not know what the catch-up stimulus is but the characteristics of catch-up require, it seems to me, that this signal represents the degree of mismatch between the actual size (or for the sake of clarity actual height) of the organism and the size (or height) required at that age by the hypothetical built-in or "target" growth curve. Lack of growth of a limb, as in poliomyelitis, or hypertrophy of a limb, as in arteriovenous aneurysm, does not cause any catch-up or slow-down of the body as a whole. (Though in certain organs such as the liver and kidney local factors are additionally operative, causing hypertrophy of the corresponding organ alone following removal or disease of part of it.) As the target curve is approached, so the mismatch diminishes and the catch-up slows down. For the mismatch to be read, both actual size and target size must somehow be represented in the organism. At present we do now know how either representation is made. It is possible that the mismatch is a peripheral phenomenon, and occurs in all cells in all tissues, the cells themselves each carrying the code for their own maturity. The catch-up in treated hypothyroidism might indeed be explicable on this basis. But it seems an unlikely hypothesis for explaining most catch-ups, and for explaining the normal control of growth in size, which is our ultimate objective. I should like to suggest a possible and I believe more plausible hypothesis for investigation.

Consider "target" size. Suppose that somewhere in the brain a tally is kept of the time passed since conception, or rather since the age, perhaps about 3 months after conception, when the mechanism of the tally begins to function. This tally can represent the target curve, for both are fundamentally series of signals made against a continuing time base. Suppose, purely for simplicity's sake, that the tally consists of a steady increase in the amount of a substance in certain nerve cells, then the form of the growth curve may be represented at any time by (some function of) the concentration of this substance.

Now as to actual size: it is scarcely conceivable that the body can represent its actual extension in space. Suppose instead that the organism measures its actual height or size by the concentration of some form of circulating substance produced by cells as an inevitable accompaniment to the process of growth or protein synthesis. In this supposition I follow the most provocative and stimulating ideas of Paul Weiss (Weiss and Kavanau, 1957) except that he envisages these substances — which he calls anti-templates — as numerous and tissue-specific and acting directly on peripheral cells, whereas I prefer to think primarily of a single substance acting at the brain level. In the simplest model then, the concentration of this substance (which we will call "inhibitor") would be proportional to the size of the organism. Its actual concentration can be measured against the concentration expected on the basis of the time tally and the discrepancy used as the mismatch signal for release of growth-stimulating factor. If, for simplicity's sake, we suppose that the time tally consists of a steady increase in the number of receptive sites for growth-inhibitor substance, then the mismatch signal would consist of the number of unoccupied sites.

The tally need not, of course, represent clock time; on the contrary it will represent the maturation rate for each individual organism. The rate of tally, and rate of change of that rate, will be an individual, presumably inherited characteristic.

The growth inhibitors are purely hypothetical substances. Neither their origin nor their site of action is known. Weiss supposes that each type of tissue produces inhibitors as it grows, and these diffuse out into the blood and inhibit the growth of the same tissue elsewhere in the body by local action at the cellular level. This is doubtless a valid model for lower animals. It may also be valid for certain aspects of shape in mammals. One might even suppose, at least a priori, that the general correspondence of development throughout the whole body of a given individual of a tissue such as muscle or bone might be brought about in this way. But in the control of mammalian growth, certainly in size and probably even in bone and muscle, it seems more likely that the inhibitors act centrally. Furthermore it seems unlikely that many tissues produce tissue-specific inhibitors (though kidney and liver may). Clearly the limbs contribute nothing important, for children with poliomyelitis, or even entirely missing limbs, grow perfectly normally in the rest of their bodies: they do not hypertrophy due to lack of inhibitors. Thus bone muscle and fat seem not to be the source of inhibitor production. The liver is the obvious choice; but it is very difficult to provide evidence for this, since damage to the liver diminishes the ability to metabolize substances essential for growth and hence may result in a slowing down of growth even if inhibitor production is also diminished.

We may reasonably think that the same mechanism underlies the form of the normal velocity curve of growth, wherein a baby grows faster than a 9-year-old. Suppose, again for simplicity, that the tally accumulates at a constantly decreasing rate. Suppose also that the inhibitors develop in proportion to the sites of synthesis used up in the cells as they pack in more protein, each turn of the RNA wheel, as it were, throwing off a molecule of inhibitor. Then the inhibitor concentration would rise in an exponential fashion, fast at first and slowly later. The mismatch (M) between these two concentrations would be large at first and decrease after the manner of the growth velocity curve. In this simple model the concentration of growth-stimulating factor is directly proportional to the mismatch and the velocity of catch-up is supposed to be directly proportional to the concentration of growth-stimulating factor. (Really one or other of these relationships might well be logarithmic.)

The model represents the chief feature of catch-up correctly. The catch-up velocity seems usually to be not only greater than the velocity expected at the age of catch-up, but also greater than the velocity expected at the age at which growth stopped. The model predicts that the mismatch and hence the catch-up velocity will be the velocity appropriate to a younger age than this, how much younger depending on the relative curvatures of the time tally and inhibitor lines. The model also predicts that catch-up growth, following a given time of growth arrest, will be more intense at young ages than at older ones. This is generally thought to be the case, although our own data give no direct evidence for it.

We have so far ignored the existence of the adolescent spurt and dealt with growth as though it gradually ceased at the end of its exponential preadolescent curve, as it does in fishes and reptiles. In primates particularly there is a secondary growth system superimposed on this basic one, causing a new increase of growth rate to occur just when the impetus of the basic system is nearing its end. There is no reason to suppose that the adolescent growth cycle is organized in a different manner from the basic cycle, but it uses different substances. Its time tally and

its inhibitors must be distinct from those of the basic cycle, just as its growth-stimulating factor is also distinct. But it is linked to the basic cycle in that its beginning occurs when the basic cycle has reached a certain point in its evolution.

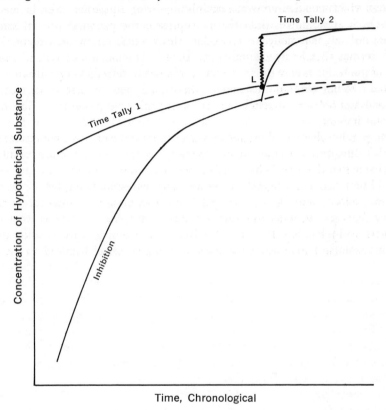

Figure 3.7 Hypothetical linkage of two systems. The switch to the new system occurs at L, a point supposed governed by the velocity of the integral of the time tally.

Linkages such as these occur between many systems during growth, and we must try to form some idea of how they may work. The simplest way in which the linkage could occur is illustrated in Figure 3.7. Here it is supposed that when the threshold point L on the time tally is reached a new tally is activated and the switch made. L might be specified either by the velocity or the integral (or accumulated amount) of the time tally. We could explain early and late maturing by variation in the place of L on the curve. We could account also for the fact that early maturers have a great adolescent spurt velocity than late maturers; since when L is placed nearer the origin of the curve the total mismatch will be greater than when it is placed far from the origin.

Of course, this model may be quite wrong, and, if not quite wrong, is certainly much oversimplified. The true situation is without doubt more complex. For example we have assumed that the tally continues unaltered even under circumstances which stop the rest of the organism growing altogether. This is somewhat unrealistic. Catch-up is probably incomplete if the period of growth arrest by starvation, say, is prolonged. To explain this we may assume that the time tally is somewhat affected by the starvation, though to a much lesser extent than the rest of the body. It may fail to resume its old rate at refeeding, or it may return to its old rate but without a catch-up. Alternatively we can assume that catch-up depends not only on mismatch but also on the time tally's velocity (or its integral or total amount).

On purely cybernetical grounds we may expect at least two complications. To combat sluggishness in the response to the mismatch (under normal conditions), it is likely that the rate of change of the mismatch rather than its absolute amount would be taken as the signal for release of growth-stimulating factor. Secondly we may expect multiple feedback pathways from tissues to center rather than a single feedback, in order to ensure stability of the system. This is what cyberneticists call reliability through redundancy, and we may expect it to complicate our physiological analysis here as elsewhere in analyses of feedback in the body.

CHAPTER IV

Prenatal and Neonatal Behavior

A CURSORY examination of the research literature related to prenatal and neonatal behavior indicates a greater accumulation of knowledge about motor behaviors as contrasted with sensory behaviors. The reason for this difference is that motor capabilities can be directly observed whereas knowledge about sensory capabilities relies more on inference. It is not possible, for example, to ask an infant which of two light sources is brighter. Thus, traditional psychophysical experiments have not been done with infants because these experiments often require complex motor manipulations and/or verbal report. Until recently, most of the conceptualizations about the infant's sensory world would have been based primarily on speculation rather than empirical fact.

The studies included in this chapter demonstrate the capabilities of prenatal and neonatal organisms, and they also demonstrate the ingenuity of scientists in developing techniques and methods for studying difficult and complex problems. Spelt developed a technique by which it was possible to classically condition fetuses in utero. Olfactory discrimination was found by Engen, Lipsitt, and Kaye by recording changes in the infants' activity level, and respiratory and cardiac reactions to the stimuli.

The experiment by Fantz is of particular interest because of the provocative nature of the findings (newborn infants preferred looking at human faces to other stimulus patterns) and because of the importance of the findings to certain theoretical issues. Fantz's conclusions about the infants' preference for the human face should be read carefully because, as he argues rather clearly, this is not evidence for an instinctive preference for human faces; other complex patterns of stimuli may have been more effective than the human faces. The results can be interpreted, however, as consistent with the theoretical view that many perceptual processes are present and operative in newborn infants without benefit of prior experience or external stimulation.

The final study in this chapter, by Melzack and Thompson, demonstrates the potential importance of early experience on subsequent social development. These and other related experiments indicate that among animals the effects of early experiences can define the course of subsequent development and have long-lasting effects on behavior. This experiment is related to the concepts of "imprinting" and "critical periods," both of which have been extensively studied. The term "imprinting" refers to the establishment of certain behaviors, early in the organism's life, which are maintained for substantial periods of time. Imprinted behaviors are apparently learned, but the learning process is different from other learning situations such as instrumental conditioning. Massed practice, for example, generates stronger "imprinting," but spaced practice is usually more effective in instrumental learning. "Critical periods" refers to the observation that "imprinting" occurs with greater strength during specific age periods of the organism's early history. Thus, too early or too late an imprinting experience reduces the effectiveness of the experience. The Melzack and Thompson experiment, as well as the work on imprinting and critical periods, may provide a basis for explaining seemingly "instinctive" behavior.

Finally, the various experiments in this chapter attest to the broad range of capabilities of infants and they further lend support to the notion that infancy is at least as an important period as any other in the life span.

The Conditioning of the Human Fetus in Utero

David K. Spelt

A generally held view of the human fetus and neonate is that they are incapable of acquiring even the simplest kind of conditioned response. Research using neonates (the neonatal period extends from birth to the end of the first two weeks of life) indicates, in fact, that they are capable of acquiring a classically conditioned response. The data do not permit the conclusion, however, that any neonatal behavior pattern results from conditioning as opposed to biological predispositions. It can be concluded that at least some simple conditioned response (learning) is possible during the latter stages of prenatal existence. This experiment is especially interesting because of the imaginative techniques and procedures that were developed to measure the conditioned response, and because of the careful use of control groups.

It is commonly recognized that environmental factors influence the organism from the moment of fertilization, but experimental studies of their effects on the behavior of mammalian fetuses have usually disturbed the fetal environment severely. The possibility that conditioned response techniques provide a method which would eliminate resort to surgery has long been seen. Ray (1932) made the first attempt, using the previously reported fetal response to loud sound which he sought to condition to a vibrotactile stimulation applied to the maternal

SOURCE: Adapted and abridged from D. K. Spelt, "The Conditioning of the Human Fetus in Utero." *Journal of Experimental Psychology*, 1948, 38, 338–346. (With permission of the author and the American Psychological Association.)

abdomen. Although results on his single case were inconclusive, his use of individual receiving tambours, taped to the maternal abdomen over the fetus, eliminated much distortion of records by maternal breathing. This study was suggested by Ray's work and resembles it in general procedure.

Apparatus

The source of noise (US) was a box 29¾ inches square, 10⅝ inches deep, made of ½ inch pine stock. It stood on one side, surmounted by a metal framework which carried an oak clapper 5 inches wide, 22½ inches long, and 1 inch thick. Pivoted 1 inch from the top, the clapper had a narrow steel handle 9 inches long. A steel spring ran from each edge of this handle to the supporting framework, so that a pull of some 8 pounds was necessary to raise the clapper, through an arc of 85 degrees, to the stop which limited its excursion. When released the clapper struck the face of the box sharply, closing a circuit through a dry cell and signal marker. On top of the box were mounted all the controls for E's use.

Vibrotactile stimulation (CS) was provided by an ordinary doorbell, with the gong removed, the striker bent outward at an angle of 90 degrees to its original position, and the interrupter soldered shut. The striker vibrated strongly but almost silently in response to four volts of 60-cycle A.C. This stimulator, fastened to a block of wood, was held in an adjustable metal clamp at the end of a movable support affixed to the side of the bed in which the Ss lay. Thus, the striker could be made to vibrate perpendicularly to the surface of any part of the abdomen. A dual key controlled the transformer-stimulator circuit and a dry cell-signal marker circuit.

Fetal movements were recorded by means of three pairs of 50-mm receiving tambours taped to the maternal abdomen, each pair connected to a one-inch recording tambour. The method of placing the tambours is described below. S operated a signal marker whenever she felt fetal movement by pressing a push button which she held in her hand. A Manning pneumograph connected to a 1-inch recording tambour supplied records of maternal breathing. An electric clock and signal marker provided a time line marked in intervals of five seconds.

All recording devices were vertically moving ink-writers which bore upon an electrically driven long-paper kymograph. The kymograph, apparatus controls, and E were screened from S's view when she lay in bed, as indicated in Figure 4.1.

Subjects and Procedure

Except for three nonpregnant control Ss and one of the pregnant Ss, all 16 Ss were selected from patients attending the obstetrical clinic of an urban hospital. All but two were past the seventh calendar month of gestation. Only patients whose histories were free from evidence of pathology during pregnancy were considered, and only those willing to participate actually served as Ss. Not that Ss

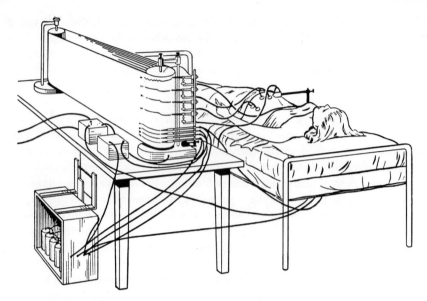

Figure 4.1 A sketch of apparatus arrangement for fetal conditioning study.

knew they were taking part in an experiment, for the word was scrupulously avoided by everyone who dealt with them. Ss were told that since confinement was approaching and since their progress thus far had been excellent, the staff wanted some special information to be obtained from X-ray pictures and from records of fetal movements to be made twice daily for 10 days or two weeks. They were told that no cost was involved, and that they would be guaranteed free care in the hospital's obstetrical ward when they came to term. Since the hospital was sufficiently crowded to admit only a fraction of the group attending the clinic, certainty of admission was an important reward. It was made quite clear, however, that they were free to decline without jeopardizing the normal chance of admission, for no record was made of their decision on the clinic card. A few of those interviewed did so decline.

Procedure during the first experimental periods varied slightly for different Ss. Most Ss had two sessions daily, lasting from 30 to 75 minutes each, depending largely on S's comfort. Three Ss in the experimental group (Group 1, Nos. 10, 12, 15) received 8–16 successive US, followed by 3–10 successive unreinforced CS (five seconds each) as a control for the possibility of pseudoconditioning. The other Ss in Group 1 (Nos. 16, 17) received 5–15 successive unreinforced CS without prior US. Actually, only three CS were needed to demonstrate the indifference of the vibrotactile stimulus, since it never elicited a response, without reinforcement, after three successive failures. Ss were warned about the noise on the first trial or two, but very few were startled, even on the first day.

Conditioning procedure involved presentation of CS for five seconds, terminated by the loud noise (US). Since Ray had shown that successful stimulation of the fetus induces a "refractory period" lasting some four minutes, the principle of separating successive stimulations by intervals of somewhat greater length was followed, except on one or two occasions when the validity of the principle was checked.

Special control groups were treated somewhat differently. Thus, Group II consisted of six Ss (Nos. 1, 3, 4, 8, 9, 14) with whom the CS alone was tested for indifference during the last two months of pregnancy. Group III included three nonpregnant Ss (Nos. 19, 20, 21), each of whom served for two "conditioning" periods. In Group IV were two Ss (Nos. 5, 18) with whom the effect of fetal age on the response to sound (US) alone was investigated by beginning presentation in the seventh month of gestation.

Results

Group I. Two Ss in this group had displayed indications that the conditioning procedure had been effective, when the experiment was interrupted by labor. S-10 during the first four sessions received 16 successive US followed by 10 successive CS. Although the fetus responded regularly to the noise, the vibrotactile stimulus was ineffective. By the eighth session three successive responses to CS alone appeared, but labor began the following day. Similarly, with S-17 three successive responses to CS alone appeared by the eighth session, but the onset of labor precluded further experimenting.

Results with the other three Ss in Group I will be presented in greater detail. Records of S-16 showed the first fetal response to CS alone after 21 paired stimulations, and others appeared at intervals until in the sixth session, after 59 reinforced presentations, a series of seven successive CR occurred. At the beginning of the seventh session the next morning, and with no reinforcement, four more CR were elicited, followed by irregularly spaced responses as experimental extinction developed. There was no indication of recovery of the response the following day, although US was still effective.

S-15 received 10 successive US followed by three successive CS during the first two sessions. As before, the noise was effective, the vibrotactile stimulus ineffective. The first response to CS alone occurred in the sixth session after 16 paired stimulations. Others occurred irregularly, but since this S was still in the eighth month of gestation, she was allowed to leave the hospital at her own request after the eleventh session. She returned two weeks later and the experiment was resumed. The CS alone was ineffective, but after 31 reinforcements six successive CR appeared, followed by experimental extinction. With 12 more reinforcements the CR was reinstated at the end of the session.

S-12 was perhaps the most interesting of the group, because of the extensive study of the CR which was possible. During her first two sessions, eight successive US were followed by four successive CS, which were ineffective. The earliest response to CS alone came in the seventh session after 21 paired stimulations, when on two successive trials CR occurred. Three more CR were obtained at the beginning of the ninth (Nos. 40–44). When four successive CS produced no direct record of fetal response (Nos. 55–58), S was permitted a 24-hour rest period to see whether spontaneous recovery would develop. That such recovery occurred is evident. Eleven successive CS alone produced six clear reactions in the fetal records and on two other trials the maternal signal was pressed. The response was then extinguished again, although the fetus still responded to the noise. S was then discharged, but returned to the hospital 18 days later as a result of false labor. Hence it was possible to resume experimental work exactly three weeks after the last previous session. In the next two periods, CS was presented alone 12 times in succession; seven of the first nine stimuli were effective, showing retention of the response over this interval, while the last three were ineffective. On the next day only two CR were elicited in eight trials, and S was again discharged. She returned 13 days later, when X-rays showed that the fetus was probably past term, but it was possible to run one more experimental session before labor was medically induced. There was no response to CS alone although the two stimuli together were effective.

Group II. This group included six Ss, all in the late eighth or the ninth month of pregnancy, with whom the CS alone was tested to discover whether it became effective simply as a result of advancing fetal maturity. Although each S received 4–7 unreinforced vibrotactile stimuli, none of the 32 trials elicited a response.

Group III. In this group were three nonpregnant Ss, members of the hospital's staff, each of whom served for standard experimental periods. Presentation of the two stimuli in varying combinations, for 16–23 trials per S during the two sessions, yielded no records remotely resembling those obtained with pregnant Ss.

Group IV. This group consisted of two Ss whose records indicated that the US used (noise) was ineffective before the eighth calendar month of gestation. S-5, in whom gestation had progressed to the latter part of the seventh month, was exposed to 39 successive US. On only one occasion did the records show what might have been a fetal response. On eight other trials the maternal signal appeared without evidence of movement in the fetal records.

S-18 was tested at intervals from the middle of the seventh month to the middle of the eighth. During the seventh month 60 US yielded no indication of movement, either in the fetal or the maternal records. During the eighth month the US was presented four times during the first week, with the maternal signal indicating fetal movement unsupported by the direct records. In the third week, seven stimuli produced three definite fetal reactions and one indicated by the maternal signal only.

Olfaction in the Human Neonate

Trygg Engen, Lewis P. Lipsitt, and Herbert Kaye

The systematic study of infant sensory processes such as olfaction has been impeded by numerous technical difficulties. In working with adult subjects it is a simple matter of asking them to verbalize their reactions to odors. Quite obviously, this procedure is not possible with infants and therefore other response indicators must be used. Professors Engen, Lipsitt, and Kaye, at Brown University, have developed measures that have proven to be both reliable and sensitive to differences in stimuli input. They were also careful to use stimuli which would not be painful to the infants, thus confounding the results. One of the more interesting findings in this report is the evidence for the emergence of adaptive responses (learning) to the more physically irritating stimuli employed. The experiment also clearly demonstrates that human infants are capable of olfactory discriminations.

This paper reports the results of research in olfaction related to a general study program of sensory and learning processes of infants currently carried out at Brown University in cooperation with the Providence Lying-In Hospital. The purpose of this study was to observe human neonates' responses to olfactory stimulation during the first few days of life and the change in such responses with repeated stimulation.

There is a lack of data concerning the newborn's capacity to smell, for virtually no research on this topic has been done in the past three decades. Until about 30 years ago, there had been a few such studies, but with ambiguous findings. Definite responses were obtained only to such stimuli as acetic acid and ammonia, but it was believed these responses were largely the result of pain or irritation (i.e., through stimulation of the trigeminal nerve) rather than smell. Some investigators believed they observed responses to so-called pure odor stimuli, e.g., valerian, mint, and essence of lavender, but others could not verify the observation. Some suggested that newborn infants are able to discriminate between pleasant and unpleasant odors, but others held that olfactory sensitivity is not present or is poorly developed at birth.

Perhaps the chief reason for the lack of clear-cut conclusions is that many of these studies relied on E's rapid judgment rather than on automatically recorded responses which could be viewed repeatedly; and most failed to establish inter-observer reliability of the observations made. Recent developments in apparatus make possible a study of this sensory process under more objective experimental

SOURCE: ˙ Adapted and abridged from Trygg Engen, Lewis P. Lipsitt, and Herbert Kaye, "Olfactory Responses and Adaptation in the Human Neonate." *Journal of Comparative and Physiological Psychology*, 1963, 56, 73–77. (With permission of the authors and the American Psychological Association.)

conditions, especially with respect to measures of the infant's responses (Lipsitt and DeLucia 1960).

The present paper reports the results of two related experiments, the first designed to compare the responses made to acetic acid and phenylethyl alcohol, and the second to compare responses made to anise oil and asafoetida. On the basis of adults' reports, acetic acid would be classified as irritating or painful, but phenylethyl alcohol would probably be described as a pure odor. Anise oil is typically called a "pleasant" and asafoetida an "unpleasant" odor. However, few describe asafoetida as "irritating" or "annoying," as in the case of acetic acid. Moreover, one investigator obtained conditioned responses in the dog for asafoetida and anise only through the olfactory nerve and not through the trigeminal nerve. On the other hand, recent dual-channel electrophysiological recordings from animal preparations have indicated that a so-called odor stimulus (e.g., phenylethyl alcohol) in relatively high concentration might elicit a response in *both* the trigeminal and olfactory nerves, while a lower concentration of the same stimulus might produce a response in only the olfactory nerve. There is reason, therefore, to question the present classification of chemical agents into irritants vs. olfactory stimuli, for the neural mechanisms mediating the response are not yet clearly understood. The present concern is to determine (a) to what extent the neonate responds to these stimuli and (b) how the response changes with repetitive stimulation.

Method

Subjects

Twenty apparently normal infants, 10 for each experiment, were Ss. There were 4 boys and 6 girls in each experiment. The average age of the infants was 50 hours with a range from 32 to 68 hours.

Response Measures

Portions of the apparatus used to measure the infant's responses have been described earlier (Lipsitt and DeLucia 1960), and only the essential details will be discussed here. The major device sensitively measures leg-withdrawal and general bodily activity. Respiration was recorded by attaching a Phipps and Bird infant pneumograph around the abdomen. Heart rate was measured in the second experiment in connection with the possibility of differential activity resulting from anise oil and asafoetida, and was recorded from the wrists with EEG electrodes prepared with Bentonite paste. All recordings were made on a four-channel Grass polygraph, Model 5.

Stimuli

The experiments employed full-strength acetic acid, phenylethyl alcohol, anise oil (Anethol, U.S.P.), and tincture asafoetida. One cubic centimeter of each odorant was kept in a 10 × 75 mm Pyrex test tube stopped with a cork wrapped in aluminum foil. The stimulus was presented to S on a commercial Q-Tip, one end of which was attached to the cork, the other end containing cotton saturated with and positioned just above the liquid odor.

Procedure

The experiments were performed in a ventilated laboratory with the temperature at about 80 degrees F. The Ss were tested individually between 10 and 11 A.M., 15 to 90 minutes after feeding. Noise and illumination were kept at a minimum. After S had been placed in the apparatus, Es waited until S appeared to be asleep (i.e., eyes were closed), respiration was steady and regular, and activity was at a minimum. This state was required before the presentation of all stimulus and control trials.

Each S was presented two odors, either acetic acid and phenylethyl alcohol (first experiment), or anise oil and asafoetida (second experiment). Half of the Ss received, for example, 10 trials with acetic acid first and then 10 trials with phenylethyl alcohol, while for the other half this order was reversed. A stimulus presentation consisted of E removing the cork with the attached Q-Tip and placing it between and about 5 mm away from the S's nostrils. The control trial involved the presentation of a clean (dry) Q-Tip in exactly the same manner. Presentation of stimulus and control trials was alternated. The duration of trials was recorded on the polygraph and was, with one exception, 10 seconds. Responses to acetic acid were of such amplitude that the Q-Tip was maintained in the prescribed position for no more than 2.5 seconds. The time between trials was approximately 1 minute; a longer period was required occasionally before S's behavior returned to pretrial standards.

With one minor exception, the procedure was the same in both experiments. In the second experiment, 4 posttest trials were added to obtain further data on order effects in the presentation of different odors. Two trials of the odor presented first in the session were reintroduced and again alternated with two control trials at the end of the session. There were thus a total of 40 trials per S in the first and 44 in the second experiment.

Results

The raw data consist of simultaneous tracings of leg-withdrawal, general activity, respiration, and heart rate on the polygraph with paper speed at 5 mm per second. For each odor two methods were used to evaluate individual records. Both methods yielded essentially the same results, and in both cases the frequency of response was evaluated with the Wilcoxon matched-pairs signed-ranks tests. All p values reported are two-tailed. The three judges evaluating the records independently agreed on 86% of the total number of individual trials. Whether a response was ultimately judged to have occurred or not depended on the majority rule, i.e., the judgment of the two agreeing judges was taken as correct in the 14% of the trials where unanimity did not prevail.

The *Es* first judged whether or not any or all of the polygraph tracings during stimulus and control trials were larger than those observed for the 10-second interval immediately preceding the trial. The response measures tend to be correlated, although respiration appeared to be most sensitive with this particular stimulus material. The first analysis revealed a significantly higher frequency of differences for stimulus trials than for control trials ($p < .01$). However, the information of basic interest from this analysis was that about 15% of the controls gave a larger response than that obtained during the 10-second period immediately preceding it. This difference is not significant, nor are the differences among the control trials for the four odors. The responses observed on control trials appear to reflect the infants' "baseline activity"; the fact that they sometimes do occur emphasizes the necessity for including such control trials in any study of olfactory responses in infants.

The control trial was used as baseline and a response on a stimulus trial was judged positive only when it was *greater* than that observed on the accompanying control trial. The average results of this analysis are presented below. Figure 4.2 presents the results obtained with the 10 Ss in the first experiment with acetic acid and phenylethyl alcohol. The points plotted indicate the percentage of Ss giving a larger response on a stimulus trial than on the control trial. Averages of two successive trials produce a smoothed but undistorted picture of the trend of individual trials. It is evident that responses were obtained to both stimuli, but significantly more to acetic acid than to phenylethyl alcohol ($p < .001$). In the case of neither stimulus was there a reliable diminution of response from early to later trials, as determined by a *t* test for related proportions. Nor was there a reliable effect of presentation order of the two odors. In the second experiment heart rate was recorded along with leg-withdrawal, stabilimeter activity, and respiration, but the former measure seemed to show no differential effects of anise oil and asafoetida, nor did it prove feasible to count accurately changes in heart rate resulting from the olfactory stimuli. (This difficulty was probably due to the relatively slow speed at which the polygraph had to be run to record the other three measures accurately. The heart rate record was often buffered by movement artifacts.)

Figure 4.3 presents the percentage of responses as a function of trials for anise oil and asafoetida when each of them is presented first and second in the session to subgroups of five Ss. A greater percentage of responses was obtained with asafoetida than anise oil ($p < .001$), and for both there is a decrement in response from the first to the last block of trials ($p < .001$ for asafoetida, and $p < .02$ for anise oil, all 10 Ss combined). The effect of order of presentation (i.e., first or second) on the frequency of response can also be observed. There is evidence of an interaction effect, for the order of presentation seems to affect response to anise oil significantly, ($p < .001$) but not to asafoetida ($p > .05$). Finally, it can be seen in Figure 4.3 that in the posttest trials, the percentage of responses returns to nearly the level observed for the first several trials with

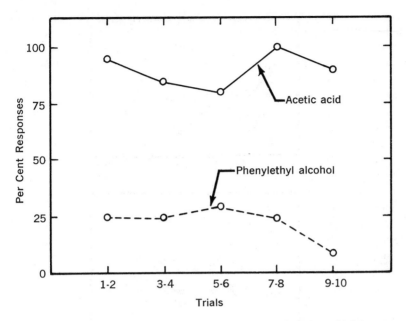

Figure 4.2 Percentage of responses as a function of trials.

each odor ($p < .08$ for anise, and $p < .05$ for asafoetida, based on five Ss, two-tailed t test for proportions between last block of trials and posttest trials). There occurred, then, both a decrement in response as a function of repeated stimulus presentations and recovery following stimulation with another odor.

Discussion

The present experiments yielded clear-cut evidence that the neonate responds to olfactory stimulation. As might be expected on the basis of past findings, the largest number of responses was elicited by acetic acid, with asafoetida next and followed by phenylethyl alcohol and anise oil. The reason for this rank order is not clear. It could reflect differences in intensity of the odors, for intensity was not controlled in the present experiments. Another possibility is that magnitude of response is inversely related to pleasantness of the stimuli. However, an attempt to judge the obtained records as well as the behavior of the infant, e.g., facial expression and posture, provided no support for such speculation. In brief, infants can smell soon after birth, but the quantitative and reinforcing properties of various chemical agents are problems for future research.

The observed decrement in response as a function of trials presents an interesting problem of interpretation, because it is difficult to distinguish operationally between *sensory* adaptation (i.e., changes in receptor organs produced by repeated stimulation) and *response* habituation or adaptation (i.e., extinction of

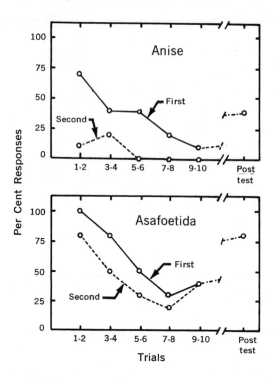

Figure 4.3   Percentage of responses as a function of trials.

a response to an originally novel or effective stimulus) in the present experiment. The recovery from the adaptation observed in the posttrials and the cross adaptation indicated by the effect of order of presentation of the stimuli seem consistent with a phenomenon of sensory adaptation, as does the relative absence of adaptation to a noxious stimulus, acetic acid. Only further study can illuminate the distinction between these two types of adaptation phenomena, and determine which of the two is occurring here.

One final observation may be made concerning qualitative aspects of the infants' responses to the odor stimuli. It was often observed that with successive presentations of some stimuli, mostly acetic acid, but often asafoetida, S's response changed progressively from a diffuse, seemingly disorganized response (similar to a mild startle) to a smooth, efficient response in escaping the odor stimulus. In early trials the baby's entire body seemed to respond, while in later trials, a simple retraction or turn of the head from the locus of the odorant was executed. It is quite likely that this *response differentiation*, similar to that obtained by others in older infants, is a rudimentary form of learning resulting from differential reinforcement of different response components. Further studies should attempt to document either photographically or mechanically these changing characteristics of the infants' head-movement responses.

Pattern Vision in Newborn Infants

Robert L. Fantz

William James once remarked that the visual world of the newborn infant is probably characterized by an undifferentiated mass of confusion. In all probability he meant by this comment that the infant is unable to translate visual input into anything meaningful. If his intent, however, was that the infant is incapable of differentiating stimuli visually in his environment, then this experiment by Robert L. Fantz casts doubt upon his speculations. Dr. Fantz demonstrates through the use of a specially developed "looking chamber" that newborn infants display differential preferences for patterns of stimuli. Of interest is the finding that the infants spent more time looking at a human than at a competing stimulus pattern. However, as Fantz indicates, this should not be considered as evidence for an instinctive recognition of a face.

It is usually stated or implied that the infant has little or no pattern vision during the early weeks or even months, because of the need for visual learning or because of the immature state of the eye and brain, or for both reasons. This viewpoint has been challenged by the direct evidence of differential attention given to visual stimuli varying in form or pattern. This evidence has shown that during the early months of life, infants (i) have fairly acute pattern vision (resolving $\frac{1}{8}$-inch stripes at a 10-inch distance); (ii) show greater visual interest in patterns than in plain colors; (iii) differentiate among patterns of similar complexity; and (iv) show visual interest in a pattern similar to that of a human face.

The purpose of the present study was to determine whether it was possible to obtain similar data on newborn infants and thus further exclude visual learning or postnatal maturation as requirements for pattern vision. It is a repetition of a study of older infants which compared the visual responsiveness to patterned and to plain colored surfaces. The results of the earlier study were essentially duplicated, giving further support for the above conclusions.

The subjects were 18 infants ranging from 10 hours to 5 days old. They were selected from a much larger number on the basis of their eyes remaining open long enough to be exposed to a series of six targets at least twice. The length of gaze at each target was observed through a tiny hole in the ceiling of the chamber (Figure 4.4) and recorded on a timer. The fixation time started as soon as one or both eyes of the infant were directed toward the target, using as criterion the superposition over the pupil of a tiny corneal reflection of the target; it ended when the eyes turned away or closed. The six targets were pre-

SOURCE: Adapted and abridged from Robert L. Fantz, "Pattern Vision in Newborn Infants." *Science*, 1963, 140, 296–297. (With permission of the author and the American Association for the Advancement of Science.) Copyright 1963 by the American Association for the Advancement of Science.

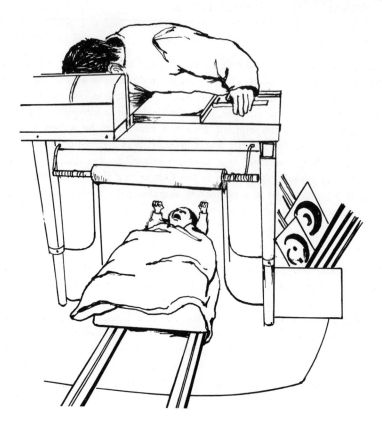

Figure 4.4 Infant "Looking Chamber" for testing visual responsiveness to targets exposed under controlled-stimulus conditions. The patterned objects are visible in a box on the table, each with a handle for sliding it in the chamber. Observer is looking on one side of the target through the peephole, which is hidden by the timer.

sented in random order for each infant, with the sequence repeated up to eight times when possible. Only completed sequences were included in calculating the percentage of total fixation time for each target.

The targets were circular, 6 inches in diameter, and had nonglossy surfaces. Three contained black-and-white patterns — a schematic face, concentric circles, and a section of newspaper containing print $\frac{1}{16}$ to $\frac{1}{4}$ inch high. The other three were unpatterned — white, fluorescent yellow, and dark red. The relative luminous reflectance was, in decreasing order: yellow, white, newsprint, face and circles, red. Squares containing the patterns or colors were placed in a flat holder which slid horizontally into a slightly recessed portion of the chamber ceiling to expose the pattern or color to the infant through a circular hole in the holder. The chamber and underside of the holder were lined with blue felt to provide a contrasting background for the stimuli, and to diffuse the illumination (between 10 and 15 feet-candle) from lights on either side of the infant's head. The subject was in a small hammock crib with head facing up directly under the targets, one foot away.

The results in Table 4.1 show about twice as much visual attention to patterns as to plain colored surfaces. Differences in response to the six stimulus objects are significant for the infants both under and over 2 days of age; results from these groups do not differ reliably from each other, and are similar to earlier results from much older infants. The selectivity of the visual responses is brought out still more strikingly by tabulating the longest-fixated target for each newborn infant: 11 for face, 5 for concentric circles, 2 for newsprint, and 0 for white, yellow, and red. For comparison, the first choices of infants 2 to 6 months were distributed as follows: 16, 4, 5, 0, 0, 0.

TABLE 4.1. *Relative Duration of Initial Gaze of Infants at Six Stimulus Objects in Successive and Repeated Presentations*

		Mean Percentage of Fixation Time						
AGE GROUP	N	FACE	CIRCLES	NEWS	WHITE	YELLOW	RED	P*
Under 48 hours	8	29.5	23.5	13.1	12.3	11.5	10.1	.005
2 to 5 days	10	29.5	24.3	17.5	9.9	12.1	6.7	.001
2 to 6 months	25	34.3	18.4	19.9	8.9	8.2	10.1	.001

* Significance level based on Friedman analysis of variance by ranks.

Three infants under 24 hours could be tested sufficiently to indicate the individual consistency of response. Two of these showed a significant (p .005 and p .05) difference among the targets in successive sets of exposures, one looking longest at the face pattern in 7 or 8 exposures, the other looking longest at the "bulls's-eye" in 3 of 6 exposures. The third infant 10 hours after birth looked longest at the face in 3 of 8 exposures.

It is clear that the selective visual responses were related to pattern rather than hue or reflectance, although the latter two variables are often thought to be primary visual stimuli. Specification of the prepotent configurational variables is unwarranted at this time. The results do not imply "instinctive recognition" of a face or other unique significance of this pattern; it is likely there are other patterns which would elicit equal or greater attention. Longer fixation of the face suggests only that a pattern with certain similarities to social objects also has stimulus characteristics with considerable intrinsic interest or stimulating value; whatever the mechanism underlying this interest, it should facilitate the development of social responsiveness, since what is responded to must first be attended to.

Substantiation for the visual selection of patterned over unpatterned objects is given in an independent study of newborn infants in which more visual attention was given to a colored card with a simple figure, when held close to the infant, than to a plain card of either color.

The results of Table 4.1 demonstrate that pattern vision can be tested in newborn infants by recording differential visual attention; these and other results call for a revision of traditional views that the visual world of the infant is initially formless or chaotic and that we must learn to see configurations.

Early Experience and Social Behavior

Ronald Melzack and William R. Thompson

The effects of early experiences on subsequent development have always played an important role in theoretical formulations; especially that of Sigmund Freud. It is unfortunate that a concept of such central importance is not amenable to direct experimental analysis at the human level. It would not be possible, for ethical reasons, to perform on people the kinds of treatments used by Drs. Melzack and Thompson with animals. Experiments, such as the one reported in this paper, are being conducted in various centers around the country and have contributed to a greater understanding of the impact of early social experience on subsequent social behavior. It is especially noteworthy that the effects of these early social experiences tend to vary somewhat among species, suggesting that environmental events necessary for optimal social development may vary, depending upon behavioral predispositions.

Perceptual experience acquired early in life has been shown in many recent studies to have a profound influence on the intellectual, perceptual, and emotional behaviour of the mature organism. There is one area of mammalian behavior, however, which is relatively unexplored: social behaviour. Reviews of animal studies point out the paucity of evidence on the effects of early perceptual and social experience on adult social behaviour.

There is experimental evidence that mice raised with experience in competitive social situations show more aggressive behaviour at maturity than litter-mates raised without such experience. Similarly, it has been shown that dogs deprived of normal social and perceptual experience during development are later consistently submissive to their normally reared litter-mates. Part of the present study, then, is an attempt to investigate more systematically the effects of early experience on dominance behaviour in the dog.

SOURCE: Adapted and abridged from R. Melzack and W. R. Thompson, "Effects of Early Experience on Social Behavior." *Canadian Journal of Psychology*, 1956, 10, 82–91. (With permission of the authors and the Canadian Psychological Association.)

Method

Subjects

Nine litters of purebred Scottish terriers, all descendants of one litter of Bar Harbor strain, were used. Each litter was randomly divided into two groups. One group, containing a total of 21 dogs (14 males and 7 females), was placed in restriction cages. The 16 dogs (8 males and 8 females) which comprised the "free environment" or control group were raised normally as pets in private homes and in the laboratory.

Rearing

Three different methods of restriction were used during this study. (a) Four dogs were reared separately in ordinary metal dog cages, and were able to look out at the other kennel cages and dogs. But, apart from a monthly 15-minute grooming period, they were never removed from their cages. (b) Seven dogs were reared in cages which were covered with heavy cardboard. The only part of the laboratory room that these dogs could see was the ceiling directly above an air- and light-vent at the top of each cage. Two or three dogs were kept in a single cage; but the only contacts they had with human beings until maturity occurred briefly during the daily feeding and cleaning period. (c) Ten dogs were reared in complete social isolation in cages like those used in (b). Only one dog was kept in a cage, and contact with human beings was eliminated. Each cage contained two compartments, and when the sliding partition between them was opened once a day, the dog was allowed to enter a freshly-cleaned compartment containing a pan of food. By means of these three methods, then, 21 dogs were deprived of a normal social and sensory experience from the time when weaning was completed at the age of four weeks until they were removed from their cages at from seven to ten months of age.

After the restricted dogs were released from their cages, they received the same opportunities for social and sensory stimulation as their normally reared litter-mates. They had long walks and play periods outdoors and in the laboratory, and had frequent contacts with other dogs and with human beings. Testing began about three weeks after the restricted dogs were released and was completed within six months. Since the litters used in this study were born at different times over a five-year period, it was not possible to use each litter for all of the tests.

Experiment I: Social Relations with Dogs (Dominance)

Subjects

Twenty-one restricted and 15 free-environment dogs were used.

Procedure

To test for dominance behaviour, a restricted and a normally reared dog, both food-deprived for 24 hours, were held at two opposite corners of the testing room by two experimenters. Either a large bone or a dish of food was located at the centre of the floor. Both dogs were brought up to the food and allowed to smell it. They were then returned to their corners and released at the same time.

The results for each contest, which lasted for five minutes, were classified as a *win* for one of the dogs, or a *tie*. A dog scored a *win* when he drove the second dog away from the food by growling or barking, and remained in control of the food for all or most of the time. A *tie* was recorded when the contest did not yield manifest dominance on the part of either dog.

In order to test only dogs of like ages, dominance contests were held within each of four groups of restricted and free-environment dogs. There were approximately the same number of males and females among the restricted and free-environment dogs of each group.

The normally reared dogs made 57 "wins," as against 7 made by the restricted dogs. It is interesting to note that the highest number of wins made by restricted dogs occurred in Group 1, in which two or three dogs were reared in a single restriction cage. The 5 wins made by these dogs were all scored against the same female control dog. However, no consistent sex differences could be discerned in the results. The difference in number of wins between restricted and control dogs for the four groups is significant at the .001 level.

The behaviour of the restricted dogs was such that the results cannot be attributed to their submissiveness alone; the dogs seemed also to be highly confused by the situation. Growling or snapping by the normally reared dogs, whose responses always seemed oriented toward the food and the competing dog, rarely elicited any comparable, organized, competitive behaviour in the restricted dogs. Indeed, most of them appeared unaware that there was any "contest." They tended to sit and watch the other dog eat, or move off and explore the room. At times they went to the food when the dominant dog was present, but most often they were easily pushed out of the way. Only occasionally did they compete by actually fighting.

Supplementary Observations

The observations of sharing among restricted dogs were confirmed in the present study. A number of contests were held between pairs of restricted dogs and between pairs of normally reared dogs. It was observed that when two restricted dogs were pitted against each other, they frequently shared the bone or food dish. Such sharing of food was only rarely observed among the normally reared dogs. Further evidence of the ineptitude of the restricted dogs in competitive situations was observed when they were tested against normally reared dogs which were six months younger. The restricted dogs consistently lost the bone or food to the younger control animals.

Experiment II: Relations Among Dogs (Social Curiosity)

Subjects

Sixteen restricted and 11 normally reared dogs were used.

Procedure

Each dog was led into a testing room containing two dogs which were kept separately behind two wire-mesh barriers. Chalk lines were drawn 1½ feet in front of each barrier, and the amount of time during a 10-minute period which each dog spent across the chalk lines near the two other dogs was recorded. This test was repeated next day with the same dogs behind the barriers.

Results

On the first testing day, the normally reared dogs ran almost immediately to the dogs in the room. They sniffed and looked at them, sometimes growled and barked, and usually followed them closely on the other side of the barrier. They spent a mean of 97.7 seconds in such social investigation. During the remaining time they tended to explore the room or sit at a distance from the other dogs. On the second day, 9 of the 11 normally reared dogs spent less time near the two dogs than they did on the first (mean: 64.6 seconds): this suggests a diminution in "social curiosity."

The restricted dogs, in comparison, showed a high degree of excitement in the presence of the dogs behind the barriers, but rarely followed them closely, or showed behaviour which seemed oriented with respect to these dogs. Indeed, a restricted dog would often wander close to one of the pens and urinate on it without taking any notice of the dog inside. At times the restricted dogs explored quietly around the room, then suddenly dashed toward one of the dogs in the barriers and spent considerable time running around in circles and moving rapidly back and forth, with gross, excited body movements, suggesting a diffuse emotional excitement. They spent a mean of 64.5 seconds across the chalk lines close to the two dogs. This type of behaviour increased on the second day without the emergence of more sustained, socially-organized curiosity behaviour. Eleven of the 16 restricted dogs spent more time across the line than they did on the previous day, giving a mean of 72.9 seconds. The difference in shift of means (Day 1 to Day 2) between the restricted and the normally reared dogs is significant at the .01 level of confidence ($x^2 = 6.68$).

Experiment III: Social Relations with Man

Subjects

Fourteen restricted and 14 free environment dogs were used.

Procedure

Three social roles, representing "typical" human behaviour toward animals, were played by an experimenter in the presence of each dog. (1) *Friendly man:* E tried to pat the dog and gently stroke his head and back. (2) *Timid man:* E retreated and tended to "cringe" after every approach that the dog made toward him. (3) *Bold man:* E moved directly and continually toward the dog with short, rapid stamping steps. Each role was played for a period of two minutes, with about a five-minute interval between roles for recording the dog's behaviour.

Every attempt was made to present identical testing conditions to all dogs of both groups. E first walked slowly around the room for two minutes to make sure that no dog avoided him in advance of testing. The same E subsequently played all three roles, in the above sequence, to both the restricted and the normally reared dogs of any given litter. He was not told, prior to testing, whether a dog had been reared normally or in restriction, although this could sometimes be inferred from its behaviour.

The recorded observations of each dog's behaviour toward the "friendly man" and the "timid man" were tabulated under one of four categories of socio-emotional response: *friendly behaviour, avoidance, diffuse emotional excitement,* and *aggressive stalking*. The responses made to the "bold man" were classified as *avoidance* or *escape*.

Results

(1) Behaviour to the "Friendly Man"

Thirteen of the 14 normally reared dogs showed *friendly behaviour* to the "friendly man."

They permitted E to pat them and play with them throughout the period; they approached at E's call, and remained at his side, frequently turning onto their sides or backs while E stroked them. None of the restricted dogs showed this type of behaviour.

Ten of the 14 restricted dogs made responses which were classified as *diffuse emotional excitement*. They moved excitedly and rapidly near and around E, with short, jerky, to-and-fro movements. Whenever they tried to lick or "nuzzle" any part of E's body, however, they assumed a characteristic bodily posture: the front part of the dog's body lay close to the floor, with the neck, head and forelegs stretched far forward; the hind-quarters were walking height, with the hind legs pushed back slightly, so that the dogs always appeared to be in a "springing" or "stalking" position. Rudimentary forms of friendly behaviour, avoidance, and aggressive stalking could sometimes be discerned in their profoundly excited behaviour, but its most striking feature was that no consistent, organized, adient social responses to the "friendly man" ever emerged from it. Any attempt by E to pat or touch the dogs produced only jerky withdrawal movements with a marked concomitant increase in excitement. This tended to be followed by rapid, circular, prancing motions, until they resumed their excited licking behaviour, usually in the characteristic "stalking" stance.

One normally reared and four restricted dogs showed *avoidance* of the "friendly man"; they continually withdrew from E and always maintained a distance of at least two feet between E and themselves. These differences in behaviour between the restricted and the free-environment dogs are significant at the .001 level.

(2) Behaviour to the "Timid Man"

Of the 14 dogs in each group, 8 restricted and 9 normally reared dogs displayed a type of behaviour which appears closely related to diffuse emotional excitement, but is much better described as *aggressive stalking*. These dogs moved excitedly and rapidly to and from in the characteristic "stalking" position, making short, jerky jumps, and constantly facing E. As the "timid man" retreated, however, this behaviour became a progressive, excited, forward approach, often with vigorous stamping movements of the forelegs in fitful starts and stops. And, as they moved nearer to E, they began to bark, growl, and snap their jaws with increasing frequency. However, the dogs rarely came within two feet of E.

This *aggressive stalking* gave the impression that the dogs were trying to "tease" a response out of E. They maintained the "stalking" posture almost continually in the presence of the "timid man," executing forward and backward movements with equal facility. Although they tended to spring forward toward E, they were also poised to spring backwards, and any sudden movement by E, even though in retreat, often elicited a sudden, short jump backwards by the dog. For the combined groups, the probability of such a high proportion of aggressive stalking occurring by chance in response to the "timid man" is .001 ($x^2 = 31.28$).

(3) Behaviour to the "Bold Man"

The responses of the dogs to the "bold man" were classified as *avoidance* or *escape*. Of the 14 dogs in each group, 8 normally reared and 2 restricted dogs showed *avoidance*: they would usually stand quietly as the "bold man" approached, and then suddenly dash out of his way, never getting caught in a corner or against the wall. The remaining dogs (12 restricted, 6 free-environment) showed *escape behaviour*: they ran out of the way of the "bold man" only after they were nudged or pushed by his foot during his aggressive approach. Many of them got caught in corners or against the wall; others simply did not move and would have been stepped on by E had he not stopped. These differences between the two groups are significant at the .05 level of confidence.

(4) Supplementary Observations

Seven restricted dogs, which had been reared two or three in a cage, were tested a year after their release along with four of their normally reared littermates. The restricted dogs still showed more diffuse emotional excitement to the "friendly man," and more escape behaviour to the "bold man," than did the free-environment dogs. But four restricted dogs showed friendly approach to the "friendly man," and two of them showed avoidance behaviour to the "bold man." Thus there were no longer any statistical differences between the two groups in their behaviour toward these two roles.

Discussion

The outstanding feature of the behaviour of the restricted dogs in these tests was their obvious ineptitude in coping with the social situations presented to them. The dominance tests showed clearly that they were incapable of responding adequately in a competitive social situation with other dogs. Indeed, most of the restricted dogs appeared not even to know how to *try* to be dominant, thus putting themselves at the very bottom of the dominance hierarchy in their canine society. They also differed markedly from the control animals in their capacity to perform responses which would be instrumental in satisfying such a basic need as curiosity toward other dogs. They showed a general excitement in the presence of other dogs, but did not exhibit sustained, well-oriented curiosity toward them.

A similar lack of adequate social behaviour was observed in the responses of the restricted dogs to the three roles portrayed by the experimenter. They did not know how to accept and reciprocate the friendly approaches of the "friendly man." Nor were they able, in the threatening social situation presented by the "bold man," to avoid physical contact in the unexcited, organized manner typical of the normally reared dogs. After a year of living in a normal environment, however, there was a decrease in the high level of emotional excitement which characterized their earlier responses, and several of them exhibited friendly behaviour to the "friendly man" and avoidance of the "bold man."

It may be concluded, then, that restriction of early social and perceptual experience has a definite retarding effect on the emergence of normal, adult social behaviour in dogs, whether toward members of their own or other species. With opportunities to gain such experience, however, dogs reared in moderate isolation, at least, can overcome to a significant degree the adverse effects of restriction on their social responses to man.

CHAPTER V

Perceptual Development

Perception is an extremely complex psychological process involving more than mere sensory acuity. Psychologically, perception involves a significant component of cognitive capabilities; that is, stimulus input, be it visual, auditory, tactual, or kinesthetic, has meaning because of previously acquired conceptualizations about the environment. There is considerable disagreement about the degree to which the cognitive component modifies or influences stimulus input. The controversy, drawn along lines already discussed in previous chapters of this book, is essentially concerned with the degree to which perceptual capabilities develop independently of environmental experience. Dr. Eleanor Gibson and her associates at Cornell University take the view that perceptual processes are relatively uninfluenced by previous experience or learning. The experiment by Rosenblum and Cross with infant monkeys supports this view.

Professor Hebb, of McGill University, takes the experiential view in this controversy, contending that what is perceived by the various sensory systems depends upon previous experience with the stimuli. Nissen and his associates provide support for the Hebb view as does the study by Zeigler and Leibowitz. In this experiment the effects of sensory deprivation are quite evident, indicating that such sensory experiences are essential during the early part of life if perceptual processes are to develop normally.

In addition to experiments concerned with the variables underlying perceptual processes, developmental psychologists have also studied the relationship between perceptual processes and the important behavior of reading. Early research produced a series of norms for behavioral capabilities assumed to be related to the reading process. In one such study, for example, it was concluded that the average child could not discriminate between *b* and *d* until the age of 7½ years. This finding was generally interpreted as meaning that no matter what environmental circumstances existed, developmental processes prohibited the discrimination. Professors Hendrickson and Muehl, after careful analysis of what behavioral capabilities were necessary for discriminating *b* from *d*, developed a training

103

situation by which children younger than 7½ years were able to successfully discriminate *b* from *d*. These results suggest that careful manipulation of the environment can augment the perceptual capabilities of children.

The Development of Size Constancy

H. Philip Zeigler and Herschel W. Leibowitz

Most adults, having some notion of the distance of an object from them, make reasonably accurate estimates of the actual size of the object. There is a question as to whether this ability develops over time as a function of experience and cognitive growth, or whether the ability is essentially present from birth. Professors Zeigler and Leibowitz compared the size constancy behavior of a group of boys, ranging in age from 7 to 9 years, with a group of men ranging from 18 to 24 years. Comparisons of both groups with a hypothetical curve derived from the law of size constancy indicates that the children, but not the adults, diverged significantly from the hypothetical curve. The results are interpreted as supporting the view that size constancy increases with age, but the results do not indicate why this improvement occurs.

There is some question in the literature as to whether size constancy varies with age. Data are, however, lacking from an investigation of size constancy for which a wide range of distances is available and for which a functional relationship can be plotted. The present study was designed to obtain such results.

Procedure

A series of standard stimulus-objects, made from 1-inch diameter wooden dowels, were prepared such that at the distances used in the study, the objects subtended a visual angle of 0.96 degrees at S's eye. The comparison object, also a 1-inch diameter dowel, was so arranged that the visible portion of its length could be continuously varied by moving it up or down through a hole cut in the center of a board. The remainder of the comparison object was hidden from S by a suitably placed curtain. S was seated at a distance of 5 feet from the comparison object, which was approximately at eye level. The standard objects were fitted into small black wooden blocks and mounted on a black metal stand 3 feet from the floor in front of and slightly to one side of the comparison object.

The experiment was conducted in a room 108 × 22 feet. From S's position three windows were visible on one side of the room and one at the extreme

SOURCE: Adapted and abridged from H. Philip Zeigler and Herschel W. Leibowitz, "Apparent Visual Size as a Function of Distance for Children and Adults." *American Journal of Psychology*, 1957, 70, 106–107. (With permission of the authors and the *American Journal of Psychology*.)

end. There were several pieces of furniture visible along the walls. Illumination was provided by six 100-watt bulbs in addition to the windows, and the experiments were conducted in the early afternoon and only on sunny days.

Five distances were used: 10, 30, 60, 80, and 100 feet. For each distance S made four judgments, two ascending and two descending. (The actual manipulation of the comparison stimulus was done by E at S's direction.) The distances were presented in a random order and, between successive trials with new distances, S was so blindfolded that he could not see E setting up the standard objects.

The instructions for both children and adults were as follows.

> I am going to move this stick (pointing to the comparison object) up and down. I want you to tell me when it looks as high as the one out there (pointing to the standard object).

S was told to disregard the stand or the wooden block and to base his judgments on the height of the standards. E avoided giving any information as to whether the standards were of the same or different sizes. S was also instructed to make all judgments with binocluar regard and to wear glasses if needed.

The Ss were 13 in number (8 boys, ranging from 7 to 9 years of age, and 5 men, from 18 to 24 years of age) all resident at a summer camp. The men were told they were to serve as controls for the experiment with the children. For the boys, the experiment was part of a "scouting" game which included outdoor as well as indoor estimates of the sizes of various objects.

Results

The results for the children and for the adults are plotted in Figure 5.1. On this plot a horizontal line represents the law of the visual angle; a theoretical condition in which perceived size can be predicted on the basis of geometrical optics. The law of size constancy is represented by a line of slope 0.017 (tan 0.96°). If perceived size were independent of distance, i.e. perfect size constancy, the data would fall along this theoretical function.

It can be seen from Figure 5.1 that the data for the adults fall very close to the prediction in terms of size constancy as previously reported by Holway and Boring. The data for the children, however, fall at positions on the matched-size axis closer to the line representing the law of the visual angle. Differences between the means of matched sizes for adults and children were calculated for all distances above 10 feet. A Mann-Whitney nonparametric u-test indicates that these differences are significant ($u < 0.01$ for 30, 80, 100 ft.; $u < 0.05$ for 60 ft.)

Discussion

The present experiment indicates that the differences between children and adults increases with the distance of the test object. This can be clearly seen from the shape of the curve in Figure 5.1. The function for the adults is

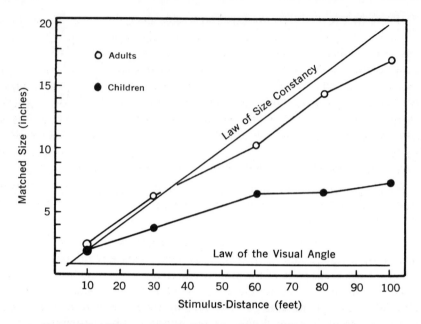

Figure 5.1　Mean matched size as a function of stimulus-distance for a group of adults and of children. The size of the test-object was adjusted so as always to subtend a constant visual angle.

nearly linear, and lies close to the line representing the law of size constancy. The curve for the children rises less rapidly with distance and approaches a limiting value at about 60 feet. The differences between the mean are significant for the adults ($p < 0.01$).

With respect to inter-S variability, the present results are consistent with those of previous investigators. As has been pointed out by Smith, studies of size constancy typically demonstrate an increase in variability with distance. This also holds true for the present investigation.

The present results, obtained over a range of 90 feet, demonstrate that the functional relationship between matched size and distance is different for adults and children. Such results are interpreted as supporting the view that size constancy increases with age.

The Visual Cliff Situation

Leonard A. Rosenblum and Henry A. Cross

An important question in the study of perceptual development is whether depth perception occurs without extensive experience. Since this problem must be examined with very young nonverbal children, it is important that the test situation provide behavioral evidence that clearly differentiates between the presence or absence of depth perception. The visual cliff situation, developed by Professor Eleanor Gibson, provides an interesting and valid method for studying depth perception with young children. The authors of this study use the visual cliff with neonatal monkeys and find that the animals are capable of depth discrimination during the first 20 days of life. Apparently the visual mechanisms necessary for depth perception are operative early in life; a generalization which includes both animals and man.

Presented with the opportunity of stepping onto a transparent surface over a shallow area as opposed to one which is suspended a considerable distance off the floor, young animals of a variety of species choose the shallow side (Gibson and Walk 1960). Their work on this problem has led them to the conclusion that the survival of a species requires the development of depth discrimination by the time independent locomotion appears. In the rhesus monkey, the early presence of rudimentary locomotor ability and a partially arboreal habitat suggest that high survival value would attach to the early appearance of visual depth discrimination. The present study was designed to measure the appearance of differential reaction to depth in the neonatal rhesus monkey during the first 20 days of life.

Subjects

The Ss were 11 infant rhesus monkeys born at the Wisconsin Regional Primate Research Center. Each S was separated from its mother during the first two days post-partum and housed individually in a wire-mesh cage whose dimensions were 24 × 19 × 15 inches. A heating pad was placed on the floor of each cage during the first 15 days of the experiment.

Apparatus

The test-situation was a wooden chamber, 53 inches high, 46 inches wide, and 10 inches deep. The chamber was divided vertically into halves by an opaque partition extending from the floor to within 9 inches of the top, and at this height the entire apparatus was covered by a clear Plexiglas shelf. Two identical Masonite panels, 23 inches long and 10 inches wide, were painted with a

SOURCE: From Leonard A. Rosenblum and Henry A. Cross, "Performance of Neonatal Monkeys in the Visual Cliff Situation." *American Journal of Psychology,* 1963, 76, 318–320. (With permission of the authors and the *American Journal of Psychology.*)

checkerboard of green and white squares, each 1 inch on a side. One panel was placed flush on the underside of the Plexiglas shelf and the other placed on the floor of the apparatus, 44 inches beneath the Plexiglas surface. The entire apparatus was illuminated by a twin 36-inch fluorescent reflector fixed 15 inches above the center of the Plexiglas; thus, during testing there was a single Plexiglas surface which presented a floor directly beneath its surface for half its extent and an apparent drop on the other half, the so-called "visual cliff" side. During the choice trials, a 10-inch square plywood panel covered with black, coarse sand-paper was centered on the Plexiglas surface. Latencies on choice trials defined as the time elapsed from the placement of S on the sandpaper until a choice was made, were obtained by means of a Standard Electric timer, operated by a hand-switch held by E. A synchronous-motor timing device connected to a small bulb unseen by S indicated 15-second intervals to E.

Procedure

Every S was tested daily throughout Days 3–20 of life. Each day's testing consisted of two direct-placement trials separated by two choice trials, with the order of the trials alternated from day to day for each S. A direct-placement trial consisted of the following: S was placed directly onto either the visual cliff or the shallow side of the apparatus, its head facing the opposite side, and allowed to remain for 90 seconds. The right-left position of the shallow side and visual cliff side was alternated daily. Each trial was divided into six 15-second periods, and E recorded on a check-sheet the appearance or nonappearance of a series of behaviors previously shown to be indicative of emotional disturbance in infant rhesus monkeys. The four behaviors recorded in the context were crouching, vocalization, self-clasping, and rocking (rhythmic, stereotyped movements of the body or its parts). Three disturbance levels were recorded; a zero level, a low level, and a high level, characterized by no disturbance, a single disturbance, and two or more disturbances, respectively. These levels were given numerical values of 0, 1, and 2. A second kind of measure recorded during each 15-second period was "freezing," defined as a failure to locomote or to change position.

The procedure for the choice trials was as follows: The sandpaper covered panel was positioned; S was placed on it, with its head parallel to two sides, and then allowed 200 seconds to make a choice, each choice being defined as the movement of any three limbs off the sandpaper. When a choice was made, the trial was terminated. Intertrial intervals were approximately 2 minutes.

The significance of differences for all tests was measured by analysis of variance. Since the data did not meet all the assumptions underlying the F-test, a confidence-level of 0.01 was set.

Results

Table 5.1 shows the mean disturbance scores for the two direct-placement trials. The analysis of variance indicated a significantly higher frequency of disturbance on the visual cliff than on the shallow side. The failure of the inter-action to reach significance showed that there was no significant change in this differentiation during the 18 days of testing. Similar results were obtained for freezing (Table 5.1), the difference again significant and the interaction not.

TABLE 5.1. *Mean Response in the Visual-Cliff Situation as a Function of Age*

RESPONSE	3–5	6–8	9–11	12–14	15–17	18–20
Disturbance						
cliff	1.40	1.50	1.55	1.42	1.41	1.37
shallow	1.16	1.16	1.20	1.26	1.09	1.13
Freezing						
cliff	2.83	3.04	3.22	3.11	2.85	3.15
shallow	2.32	1.61	1.96	2.00	2.04	1.71
% Choice						
cliff	11.3	3.3	9.3	9.0	3.6	0.0
shallow	62.0	65.0	55.6	59.3	59.3	57.3
no response	26.7	31.7	35.1	31.7	37.1	42.7

For the choice trials, the percentage of responses made to each side, and the percentage of trials on which there was failure of choice, are shown in Table 5.1. The difference between visual cliff and the shallow side was significant while the interaction was not. (A number of accidental and presumably spurious responses were made on the choice trials. These occurred as a result of the Ss bolting off the sandpaper without looking, or backing off the sandpaper onto the visual cliff.) One further indication of a clearcut preference for the shallow side is the fact that of the 11 animals tested, 9 made fewer than three choices of the visual cliff during the 18 days of testing.

Discussion

Locomotion, climbing, and even jumping appear early in the behavioral reper-toire of rhesus monkeys. Since, in the feral state, part of this behavior must occur in trees some distance from the ground, the importance of the ability to discriminate depth for the survival of the young rhesus is obvious. Despite the fact that the first days of life of the infant are spent in comparative safety at the mother's breast, the neonate seems capable of discriminating and reacting to visual depth. Further work is required to analyze the cues on which the dis-crimination revealed in the present study is based.

The Effects of Sensory Deprivation

Henry W. Nissen, Kao Liang Chow, and Josephine Semmes

Studies of sensory deprivation involve the restriction of stimulation into one or another sensory system. For ethical reasons, an investigator would not wish to apply such procedures to a human being because of the possible serious consequences to his subsequent development. It is possible, however, to employ such techniques with infrahuman organisms and have the resulting effects suggest the consequences to human beings. This is the strategy employed with one chimpanzee in this study by Nissen and his colleagues at the Yerkes Laboratories of Primate Biology. In general terms, it can be concluded that the sensory-deprivation procedures employed had deleterious effects on the subsequent perceptual capabilities of the chimpanzee. The results also lend support to the theoretical position that normal sensory development requires external stimulation and does not rely entirely on genetic predeterminants.

The problem of how experience contributes to the development of behavior may be approached from either of two opposite directions: opportunities for experience, training, or practice may be either restricted or enriched, the resulting behaviors then being compared with the performances of normal controls. Restriction of experience is usually accomplished (a) by sensory deprivation — temporary (by environmental control or drugs) or permanent (by surgical interference with sense organs or afferent pathways), or (b) by surgical, chemical, or mechanical interventions in the normal activity of effectors. Either (a) or (b), or both, may be effected by central nervous system extirpations. In the case of the distance receptors, it is relatively easy to eliminate sensory inlets without directly interfering with motor functions; in the case of tactual stimuli and especially kinesthesis, the alteration of either sensory or motor function alone, without affecting the other, is usually impossible.

The present study represents a first approximation toward analysis of the role of experience in the development of tactual-kinesthetic-visual perceptions and of motor coordinations in a young primate. Beginning soon after birth, and continuing for a period of 30 months, use of the hands and feet in climbing, grasping, and other manipulative behavior was made physically impossible and the sensory stimulation from these parts was radically reduced.

Subject

The S of this study was a male chimpanzee, Rob. He was born March 19, 1948, after an estimated gestational period of 212 days, about 2 weeks shorter

SOURCE: Adapted and abridged from Henry W. Nissen, Kao Liang Chow, and Josephine Semmes, "Effects of Restricted Opportunity for Tactual, Kinesthetic, and Manipulative Experience on the Behavior of a Chimpanzee." *American Journal of Psychology*, 1951, 64, 485–207. (With permission of the authors and the *American Journal of Psychology*.)

than average. His birth weight was 1.13 kg, as compared to an average of 1.79 kg. By the age of 6 months Rob's weight was about 80% of the average, and at 30 months was almost 90% of the average weight of nursery-raised chimpanzees. Roentgenograms, made at 6-month intervals, show that in respect to onset of ossification in the epiphyses and short bones he was somewhat retarded. Eruption of the deciduous teeth occurred within the normal age-range.

Rob was separated from his mother 36 hours after birth and was reared in the nursery under routine conditions of diet and care. In general, his health has been better than average, and he has had no serious illnesses. A mild inguinal hernia (not uncommon among nursery-reared male infants) had disappeared without treatment by the age of 6 months. His food-intake had usually been somewhat less than average; from age 15 to 21 months he was given supplementary B-complex vitamins, and this seemed to increase his appetite slightly.

Methods of Restriction

Starting at the age of 4 weeks, Rob's opportunities for tactual and manipulative experiences were artificially restricted. At first this was done by use of a sort of straightjacket which held his arms folded across his chest. This method proved to be impracticable. From age 5 to 14 weeks Rob's hands and feet were encased in cloth bandages held in place by adhesive tape. This procedure also was unsatisfactory: it prevented almost all movement of the digits, and the exclusion of air (by the adhesive tape) resulted in peeling of the skin of the volar surfaces of hands and feet.

Beginning July 1 (at age of 15 weeks), cardboard cylinders (mailing tubes) were placed over all four extremities. The first tubes used had an inside diameter of 2 inches; tubes of 2¾ and finally 3⅛-inch diameter were employed as Rob increased in size. The length of the cylinders was so adjusted that when the fingers or toes were fully extended they did not quite reach the distal end of the tube. Until February, 1949 (age 11 months), the proximal end of the tubes extended to an inch or so above the knee and elbow joints. At that time the edge of the tube on his left leg produced a deep gash in the thigh. For two weeks, while this was healing, no tube was used on that extremity, but a cloth bandage was kept over his left foot. Thereafter, and until they were finally removed (October 24, 1950, age 31 months) the lengths of the tubes were so adjusted that the proximal ends came just below the knee and elbow joints. The tubes were kept in place by four strips of adhesive tape running the length of the tube and then fastened to a ring of tape wound around the middle of the upper arms and thighs. Figure 5.2 shows Rob with the tubes in place. By cutting or loosening the four longitudinal strips of tape, the tube could be removed easily for periods of testing. Until December, 1948 (age 9 months), the distal ends of the tubes were open; by that time Rob's fingers were long enough so that when fully extended they reached to the edges of the cylinders. The ends of the four tubes were therefore closed by taping a circular piece of thin sheet-metal over the ends. Since the proximal ends of the tubes were open, there was still sufficient circulation of air to prevent damage to the skin of hands and feet.

Results

Various testing and training procedures were employed during and after the 31-month period of restriction. Other nursery infants, reared under normal routine conditions, were available for comparison. The effects of the restriction were assessed by (1) observations of general behavior exhibited during the 30 months that the cylinders were in place; (2) training in visual discrimination of size, form, and depth; (3) training in a tactual discrimination; (4) series of tactual-motor tests (with cylinders removed) at ages 14 and 31 months; and (5) observations of behavioral changes during the 4 months following permanent removal of the cylinders.

Figure 5.2   Rob's sitting posture, cylinders in place.

(1) Except for activities made impossible by the tubes, the development of general behavior during the first 31 months of life was fairly normal. Pronograde and orthograde standing and walking occurred about as usual in nursery reared infants. In sitting, however, S adopted a highly atypical posture (see Figure 5.2).

(2) Rapid learning of the visual discrimination habits indicate that lack of

opportunity for manipulation and for association of visual with tactual-kinesthetic sensations from the hands (and feet) did not noticeably handicap S in developing perceptions of size, form, and depth.

(3) S had great difficulty in learning a problem which required the discrimination of two widely separated loci (i.e. the two hands) of tactual-pressure stimulation. A younger control animal reached a much higher level of performance in one-tenth as many trials.

(4) The tests of tactual-motor coordinations indicated a number of deficiencies by comparison with the normal. S did not even attempt to bring his fingers to a stimulated region on the dorsal trunk or head. Approximation of the fingers to a locus of stimulation on the ventral trunk or limbs was slow, halting, and inaccurate; apparently vision was a distinct aid in this performance. He did not grasp or cling to the attendant who carried him. He did not groom; the lip movements and sounds which are part of this presumably instinctive pattern were completely absent, and his rough-and-ready poking with a finger showed none of the precision and perseverance which is typical of the behavior. There was some behavior suggestive of forced grasping. When the tubes were removed at age 31 months, it was found that instead of using the usual plantigrade position of the feet, he stood (and walked) on the dorsal surfaces of the middle joints of his toes — a posture well adapted to the limitations imposed by the cylinders.

(5) During the four months following permanent removal of the tubes, S's ability to bring his fingers to a given place improved in speed and accuracy. He did not bring his hand to the back of his trunk, however, and rarely to his head. A tendency to cling to the attendant developed, but very slowly. Grooming behavior did not appear. Plantigrade position of one or both feet occurred with increasing frequency. Climbing, which the tubes had made impossible, appeared, but the amount of locomotion in the vertical plane remained far below average. Use of the hands, first in scooping or shovel-like movements, and then for grasping objects, occurred quite soon after removal of the restriction. The atypical sitting posture persisted.

The results of the study demonstrate that the general approach used is a feasible and promising one for the study of perceptual development and of the genesis of sensory-sensory and sensory-motor coordinations. Within the limits of a less-than-perfect technique of restriction, and the use of only one S, the data indicate the areas in which experience is important for achieving integration.

The Discrimination of *b* and *d* in Kindergarten Children

Lois N. Hendrickson and Siegmar Muehl

Research indicates that the discrimination between *b* and *p*, or *q* and *d*, is present in children before the discrimination of *b* and *d*. The former discrimination requires an up-down orientation whereas the latter requires a left-right orientation. Professors Hendrickson and Muehl of the State University of Iowa offer the hypothesis that young children develop an up-down orientation prior to the left-right orientation and therefore make the *b-p* discrimination earlier. They suggest that if children's attention was drawn to the left-right discrimination they would readily learn to discriminate *b* and *d*. Procedures were developed in their experiment which varied the degree of attention to the left-right discrimination, resulting in a greater degree of *b-d* discrimination as a function of the degree to which the left-right orientation was stressed.

Davidson (1935) reported that up-down inversions illustrated by "q" and "d" were discriminated by more than 50% of the kindergarten-aged children. At the same age, left-right inversions, illustrated by "b" and "d," were discriminated by less than 10%. It was not until 7½ years that 50% of the children identified left-right inversions correctly.

Developmental norms of this type require careful interpretation, particularly if they are to be used as the basis for making statements about children's "readiness" to learn certain tasks. Do the norms reported on the left-right inversion mean that preschool and early school-aged children: (a) literally cannot "see" the difference between two figures so inverted, or (b) lack the instructional set to realize that this kind of difference is important? Since research has shown that the same age children do discriminate, and therefore see, an up-down inversion, it is likely they could also see a left-right inversion, providing they have a set to attend and differential responses to associate with this difference. Although children of this age do not usually have left and right as meaningful directional labels in their vocabulary (which is the case with up and down), they may well have other distinctive verbal or nonverbal responses they could learn to associate with this directional difference.

An experimental study reported by Jeffrey (1958) offers support for this assumption. Jeffrey's subjects learned names for two stick figures differing only in the direction an arm pointed — left or right. The results showed that the subjects given motor-response pretraining in pushing a button (one of two) that was on the side to which the stick figure pointed performed better on the naming task than a control group lacking the motor pretraining.

SOURCE: Adapted and abridged from L. N. Hendrickson and S. Muehl, "The Effects of Attention and Motor Response Pretraining on Learning to Discriminate *b* and *d* in Kindergarten Children." *Journal of Educational Psychology*, 1962, 53, 236–241. (With permission of the authors and the American Psychological Association.)

Jeffrey's results suggest two types of responses, and response-produced cues, that the children may have learned to associate with the directional difference of the arms in the motor-response pretraining: "attention" cues produced by an instructional set to observe the directional element of the arm, a necessary condition for making the correct button response; or kinesthetic cues produced by reaching left and right for the buttons. In either case the assumption would be that these distinctive response-produced cues, separately or in combination, became an implicit part of the response pattern to each of the stick figures; that this acquired distinctiveness transferred to the naming task, facilitating learning.

The purpose of the current study was to investigate further the relative effectiveness in kindergarten-aged children of attention- and motor response-produced cues on learning to associate verbal labels with the letter inversion "*b*" and "*d*."

Method

Pretraining

The basic piece of equipment was a Hunter Cardmaster. The Cardmaster is designed to present 3½ × 6¼ inch plastic cards in a viewing aperture. By means of a separate timer unit, two metal shutters can be used to cover or expose the viewing aperture to secure the following exposure intervals: an anticipation interval, with one shutter open to expose half of the card; a joint presentation interval, with both shutters open to expose the entire card; and a between-cards interval, with both shutters closed during which time a new card is automatically positioned behind the viewing aperture.

For the pretraining task, an additional response unit was placed in front of the Cardmaster; an opening in this unit allowed the subject to view the Cardmaster aperture. The frame of this response unit was 20 inches wide, 18 inches high, and 12 inches deep. A low, slanted platform extending below the Cardmaster window was cut with two parallel slots, 3½ inches apart, to allow the traverse of the two handles. The handles were covered by rubber tricycle handle-grips. Microswitches at the ends of the slots were connected with a doorbell chime, controlled via a remote switch by the experimenter. This chime indicated and rewarded correct responses in pretraining. The sides and top of this apparatus were designed to minimize the possible effects of cues in the experimental room.

For pretraining, three different sets of Cardmaster cards were used, one for each of three pretraining groups. On each card were three stimuli of the same relative size and in the same relative positions. Each set contained a series of eight cards. These three sets are shown in Table 5.2.

The stimuli for two of the sets of cards were the lower-case, sans-serif letters *b* and *d*. The letters were ¾ inch high and were centered on the cards. One-eighth inch below and ⅜ inch to either side of the letters were two arrows, ¾ inch long. The letters and arrows were printed on the cards in black ink.

For the group designated the Attention-Consistent Motor Response (A-CM)

TABLE 5.2. *Order of Stimulus Presentation for Three Groups in Pretraining*

TRIALS	ATTENTION-CONSISTENT MOTOR (A-CM)	ATTENTION-INCONSISTENT MOTOR (A-IM)	IRRELEVANT-CONTROL (Ir-C)*
1	d	b	r
	← →	← →	r–o
2	b	d	o
	← →	← →	r–o
3	b	d	l
	← →	→ ←	p–l
4	d	b	p
	← →	→ ←	p–l
5	b	d	r
	← →	→ ←	o–r
6	d	b	l
	← →	→ ←	l–p
7	d	b	o
	← →	← →	o–r
8	b	d	p
	← →	← →	l–p

* Letters here indicate color of patches; no letters actually appeared on these cards
r = red; o = orange; p = pink; l = lavender).

group the arrows below the stimulus letters always pointed outward. For the
Attention-Inconsistent Motor Response (A-IM) group, half the arrows below the
letters pointed inward and half pointed outward.

On the third set of cards were three patches of color. Paired colors cut from
construction paper were used: pink (p) paired with lavender (l), and red (r)
with orange (o). On each card, one of the smaller patches was the same color
as the larger center patch. These cards were used with the Irrelevant-Control
(Ir-C) group.

At the beginning of pretraining each subject was seated in front of the apparatus so that either handle could be reached readily. The subjects were instructed
to watch the window. The two groups receiving letter stimuli were instructed
as follows:

See this letter. This part of the letter (the experimenter traced the round part
of the letter) points this way (the experimenter pointing). Now see these two
arrows. They point in different directions. Show me which way this arrow
points. And this one. That is right. One of the arrows points the same way
that the letter does. Can you find it? Now each time I show you a card, I will
want you to find the arrow that points the same way as the letter. But you will
not need to point to the arrow each time. Instead you can push the handle that
goes to the arrow (the subject was guided to place left hand on left handle;
right hand on right handle). Since this is the arrow that goes the same way as
the letter, you would push this handle. Try it. Hear the bell? The bell rings to
tell you that you are right. Here is another letter. Find the arrow that goes the
same way as the letter, and push the handle towards the arrow.

The pretraining stimuli for the A-CM groups (see Table 5.2) were designed to elicit attention responses to the directional difference between the letters, and to elicit a consistent left-arm motor response to letter *d* and a consistent right-arm motor response to letter *b*. The stimuli for the A-IM group were designed also to elicit attention responses to the directional differences in the letters; however, the motor responses to the letters were inconsistent; e.g., the left arm response was required on half the presentations of *d*; the right arm response on the other half.

Instructions for the Ir-C group were similar in form to the above and adapted to the task of matching the color stimuli.

Relevant parts of the instructions were repeated throughout the training whenever the subject made an incorrect response. The subject was also told to use only his right hand to push the right-hand handle, and his left hand to push the left-hand handle. This instruction was conveyed without the use of the words left and right.

Both shutters on the Cardmaster opened simultaneously on each trial, exposing the entire card. Each card was presented (via remote control operated by the experimenter) only after the subject had completed his response to the previous card. Thus, there was no fixed time during which the subject was required to respond.

The subjects were given 30 trials following the 2 instructional trials. A trial consisted of a single stimulus presentation.

Transfer Task

The pretraining apparatus was removed, and the Cardmaster placed directly before the subject. The transfer task consisted of the paired-associate presentation of the letters *b* and *d* paired with pictures of a snowman and a pumpkin, respectively. The actual letter names were not used due to the possible difficulty in discriminating the subject's responses. Eight cards with the letter-picture pairs were arranged in the following order: *b, d, d, b, d, b, b, d*. The pairs were presented with a 3-second anticipation interval (only the letter exposed), a 3-second joint-presentation interval (letter and picture exposed), and a 2-second between-trial interval. The first two trials were instructional. The subject was shown the first two pairings and told that the letter *b* went with the snowman, the letter *d* with the pumpkin. The subject was then instructed to look at the letter each time and try to guess the picture that went with it before he saw the picture.

The subjects were given a maximum of 30 trials following the 2 instructional trials. A trial consisted of the presentation of a letter-picture pair. The transfer task was terminated if the subject reached a criterion of 8 consecutive correct responses; at this point he was credited with correct responses for the remaining trials. Verbal encouragement by the experimenter constituted the reward for correct responses. In addition to correct responses, the subjects were scored for errors and omissions.

Subjects

The subjects were 52 kindergarten children, drawn from a public school in Iowa City. The age range was 5–4 to 6–11 years, with a mean age of 5–11. The subjects were taken from the classroom in alphabetical order and assigned in rotation to one of three groups. Children judged by the teacher to be mentally retarded or who were expected to repeat kindergarten were not used. Two subjects were dropped due to failure to follow instructions in the transfer task, and one was dropped due to apparatus failure. Thus, 49 subjects were retained; 2 groups contained 16 subjects, and the third group, 17 subjects. Testing was done in the spring.

Results

Pretraining

The means in percentage of correct responses and standard deviations for the three groups are shown in Table 5.3.

TABLE 5.3. *Pretraining Results Based on Percentage of Correct Responses in 30 Trials*

GROUPS	M	SD
Attention-Consistent Motor	98.35	4.94
Attention-Inconsistent Motor	86.52	10.22
Irrelevant-Control	98.57	3.94

Harley's Test for homogeneity of variance among the groups was significant ($p < .01$), leading to the rejection of the null hypothesis. To offset the effect of heterogeneity of variance, the significance level on subsequent statistical tests was set at .025.

A Type I analysis of variance for correct responses over trials showed a significant groups effect ($p < .001$). The trials and interaction effects were not significant. The t test scores between the groups showed the percentage of correct responses for the A-IM group to be significantly less when compared to both the A-CM and Ir-C groups ($p < .001$). The latter groups did not differ significantly.

Transfer Task

Table 5.4 will show the means in percentage of correct responses and standard deviations for the three groups. The learning curves over trials are shown in Figure 5.3. A Type I analysis of variance of these data indicated a significant groups ($p < .025$) and trials ($p < .001$) effect. The interaction was not significant. The t test scores between the groups showed that when Group A-CM was compared with Group A-IM, the mean difference was not significant. Comparing Group A-CM with Group Ir-C, the difference was significant ($p < .01$). The subjects reaching a criterion of 8 consecutive correct responses

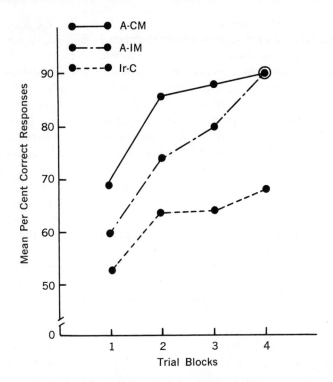

Figure 5.3   Percentage of correct responses in the transfer task. All trial blocks, except the first, contain 8 trials. The first trial block contains 6.

in the groups were compared. There were 12 each of the 2 attention groups; 4 in the Ir-C group. This distribution yielded a significant chi square ($p < .02$) when each of the attention groups was compared with the control.

Table 5.4 shows the means in percentage of errors and standard deviations for the three groups. A Type I analysis of variance for errors over trials showed

TABLE 5.4. *Transfer Task Results Based on Percentage of Correct Responses and Errors in 30 Trials*

GROUP	Response Measure			
	CORRECT RESPONSE		ERROR	
	M	SD	M	SD
Attention-Consistent Motor	82.96	18.66	11.34	15.01
Attention-Inconsistent Motor	76.23	18.56	15.37	14.89
Irrelevant Control	62.30	20.68	27.99	17.66

a significant groups effect ($p < .025$). The trials and interactions effects were not significant. The *t* test scores between the groups showed that Group Ir-C made a significantly greater percentage of errors when compared to Group A-CM ($p < .01$) and Group A-IM ($p < .05$). The latter groups did not differ significantly.

There were no reliable differences among the groups on the omissions measure.

Discussion

The findings of the present study showed, first, that pretraining in attending to the directional differences between the letters b and d facilitated learning names for these same letters in a paired-associate transfer task. This result agrees with Jeffrey's (1958) study with children approximately 1½ years younger, and provides additional evidence that a left-right inversion can be identified considerably before Davidson's (1935) normative age of 7½. Second, the findings showed that pretraining in making a consistent motor response to the directional differences between the letters b and d did not add significantly to the transfer task performance. Although there was an apparent difference early in learning on the correct response measure favoring the A-CM group compared to the A-IM group (see Figure 5.3), it is not clear whether this effect was due to A-CM group facilitation or A-IM group interference resulting from the more difficult pretraining task for this group (see Table 5.3).

Some evidence for the modality of the so-called attention cues was provided by questioning the children, after the transfer task, as to how they knew that a particular letter went with a particular picture. All but two children who reached criterion, irrespective of groups, indicated they used the direction of the letters to tell them apart. Most of these children used gestures to indicate this directional difference. By contrast, two-thirds of those who did not reach criterion gave answers indicating they did not recognize the difference between the letters. None of the children used the letter names or the words left or right in describing the difference. These verbal reports suggest that the attention cues were, at least in part, implicit verbal responses which served to identify each letter by its directional component.

In conclusion, the results of the present study, in conjunction with Jeffrey's (1958) findings, suggest caution in the application of the concept of readiness when this concept is used to prescribe appropriate age levels at which children can optimally learn a particular task. Age norms derived from tests built to assess a given skill level provide no certain evidence as to what age the skill might first be taught and learned provided that the learning conditions were effectively arranged.

CHAPTER VI

Learning Variables: Reinforcement

MOST LEARNING theorists in the United States treat reinforcement as a crucial element in the learning process. Some of these theorists assume that a stimulus can be reinforcing only if it reduces a drive, while others contend that if a stimulus strengthens a response it is an effective reinforcer. The latter position is less concerned with the specific drive state of the organism than the former. Despite these differences in opinion, there can be little doubt that reinforcement does indeed influence and modify children's behavior.

The experiment by Brackbill and Jack demonstrates the importance of individualizing reinforcer stimuli. These investigators show that stimuli, traditionally viewed within a culture as highly reinforcing, may be variably effective among a random selection of children. Indeed, there is evidence from other sources (for example, see the paper by Terrell, Durkin, and Wiesley in Chapter 7 of this book) that reinforcer effectiveness varies in accordance with social class level and chronological age.

The experiment by Offenbach and Meyer suggests that there may be many stimuli about which adults have little or no awareness, that serve as both positive and negative reinforcers. Thus, these investigators show that when a child receives positive reinforcement following some of his behaviors and a neutral stimulus (a buzzer in this case) for other behaviors, the initially neutral stimulus acquires negative reinforcement value. Conversely, when a child receives negative reinforcement for some behaviors and a neutral stimulus for other behaviors, the initially neutral stimulus acquires positive reinforcement value. One might argue that adults who take a predominantly negative approach with children may actually be providing the children with positive reinforcement when they remain silent on any particular occasion.

The experiments by Stevenson and his colleagues and by Gilmore and Zigler are derived from a drive-reduction approach to reinforcement. Essentially these investigators contend that children experience different patterns of reinforcements from their environments. Some children are accustomed to receiving many reinforcements while others customarily receive few if any. Children in the

121

former category, it is reasoned, become satiated on the reinforcers; therefore they are at least less motivated to perform in anticipation of receiving reinforcement. Stevenson, Keen, and Knights assumed that strangers would be more effective reinforcing agents than parents because children satiate on parental reinforcement. Gilmore and Zigler assumed that first-born children receive more reinforcements than later-born children and are therefore more satiated for reinforcers. As one might expect, however, first-born children are apparently more susceptible to adverse criticism from adults. All the assumptions were supported by the experiments.

Reinforcement and Discrimination Learning

Yvonne Brackbill and Donald Jack

Theoretically, all stimuli are potential positive reinforcers, even those that we traditionally think of as aversive. Although there may be universal reinforcers, as some theorists have suggested, the majority of stimuli acquire their reinforcing value by means of learning. In this experiment, the investigators permitted one group of children to select the stimulus they would like to earn, but a second group (the control group) was not given a choice. Although the differences in average performance were small, the experimental group displayed less variability. This finding suggests that parents and teachers should attempt to individualize their use of reinforcing stimuli rather than rely on the assumed reinforcement value of a stimulus.

The present study is concerned with the influence of reinforcement value on learning. Reinforcement value is defined as the individual S's relative preference for various types of reinforcers, when amount of reinforcement and probability of occurrence of reinforcement are held constant.[1]

The results of several studies show that, on the average, different types of reinforcers are differentially effective for learning. For example, Terrell and Kennedy (1957) found that children learn faster when rewarded with candy rather than with praise. However, despite the fact that children as a *group* learn more effectively on candy reinforcement, it is hardly conceivable that any one type and amount of reinforcement has an exactly equal reinforcing effect for all Ss of any such group. Given one group of Ss and one type of reinforcement, there must still be some intragroup variability in effectiveness of that reinforcement as a function of variability in value of the reinforcer for the Ss. In other words, for different people, the same objective or external reinforcer may have

SOURCE: Adapted and abridged from Yvonne Brackbill and Donald Jack, "Discrimination Learning in Children as a Function of Reinforcement Value." *Child Development*, 1958, 29, 185–190. (With permission of the authors and the Society for Research in Child Development.)

different reinforcement values, and if so, the within-group variability in reinforcement value should be reflected statistically as a large standard deviation in number of trials to learning criterion.

The present experiment used a discrimination learning situation to compare the relative effects of two experimental treatments: identity of reinforcement *value* vs. identity of external reinforcing object. Ss run under the first condition (Group RV) were allowed to choose the most preferred one of three reinforcers: M & M candies, varicolored marbles, or varicolored plastic trinkets. Ss of the second experimental group (Group R) were reinforced with candies. It was predicted that although there would be no significant mean difference between the two treatment groups in trials to criterion, Group RV would show greater within-group homogeneity than Group R, i.e., there would be a significantly smaller standard deviation for Group RV.

Candy was used as the standard reinforcer for Group R in order to make the experimental comparison a conservative one. The reasoning behind this was as follows: First, from a logical consideration, it would seem that if sigma were to vary in size at all with differences in *average* reinforcement value, it should be smallest for that reinforcer having the highest average value (and hence, the greatest facilitating effect on learning). Second, from a statistical consideration, if means and standard deviations are positively correlated in size, that treatment producing lowest mean number of trials to criterion should also show the smallest standard deviation.

Method

Subjects

The Ss were 60 male children. They were obtained from the eight kindergarten classes of two elementary schools within a single school district. Mean age of Ss was 63.6 months, SD, 3.4. The sample was relatively homogeneous in terms of race (white) and socioeconomic status (middle class). Mean California Mental Maturity Scale IQs for second graders at each school was 106. Goodenough Draw-A-Man tests were available for all kindergartners, and were used in the selection process to eliminate potential Ss of subnormal intelligence, as follows: The school psychologist submitted a list of names of children with extremely low scores on the Goodenough test. A short-form WISC was then administered to these 17 children. Using a cutting score of 70 IQ, eight of the 17 were eliminated from the total pool from which Ss were drawn.

Selection of Ss and placement into one of the two experimental groups was in alphabetical order. In order to have the total RV group composed of equal numbers of Ss preferring each of the three reinforcers, a quota was established of 10 Ss per type of reinforcer. This quota imposed no practical difficulties, since, on the average, the three reinforcers were approximately equal in attractiveness. Only two potential Ss were discarded because they chose a reinforcer (trinkets) for which the quota had already been reached.

Experimental Procedure

S was seated opposite *E*, at a small table on which were three boxes, the discriminative stimuli. The boxes were of different colors (dark red, light red, and red-orange). Two boxes, No. 1 and No. 2, were the same size but different in size from the third box. Color and size, however, were irrelevant cues, as was also the presence of box No. 3, since the correct response was a simple position alternation sequence of the reinforcement between boxes No. 1 and No. 2. For presentation, the boxes lay open side down on a large piece of brown felt approximately four inches distant from each other; the end boxes, No. 1 and No. 3, were equidistant from *S*. Position of the boxes was constant for all trials.

On a second table, to *S*'s right, lay a small pillow on which *S* rested his head between trials. This served two purposes: (a) it eliminated the necessity of placing a screen in front of *S* while *E* reloaded the boxes, and (b) it reduced sound localization in the event of any auditory cues during reloading.

As soon as *S* entered the experimental room, *E* gave the following instructions:

(*Group R*) Do you know what these are? (*E* paused and indicated an open box of M & M candies.) They're candy; they're chocolate. I have something very special for you to do, and if you can do it you can have some of the candy.

(*Group RV*) Here are some marbles; here are some charms; here are some candies. (*E* paused and indicated the appropriate boxes; placement and naming order were rotated by Ss.) Now I have something very special for you to do, and if you can do it you can have some of the charms *or* some of the candies *or* some of the marbles. You can't have some of all of them, just some of one kind. *Now think hard*: if you could have *just one kind*, which kind would you rather have — would you rather have some candies *or* would you rather have some charms *or* would you rather have some marbles?

(*Both groups*) I'm going to put one ___ at a time under one of these boxes. And every time you pick up the box that has the ___ under it, you can keep the ___. Understand? Now! *There is a way to find the right box every single time. See if you can find the way.*

Put your head down on that pillow and wait until I say "ready.". . . Ready. Pick up the box that you think has the ___ under it. . . . Now every time you get a ___, pick it up and put it in this envelope, and all the ___ that you put in there will be for you to keep . . . Head down . . . Ready.

(After the last trial, the following statement was repeated until *S* indicated agreement. The purpose of the statement was to "jam" inter-*S* communication.)

Well, you found the way, didn't you? You found out that the candy was always under the *red* box. (*E* indicated simultaneously all boxes.) Yes, the candy was always under the *red* box.

Two learning criteria were used: (a) number of trials taken before *S* no longer chose the irrelevant or never-reinforced box No. 3; and (b) the number of trials taken to a run of 10 consecutive correct choices. An experimental session ended either when *S* reached the second criterion or after the 150th trial. In the latter case, the score assignment was 150. Session length ranged from 10 to 25 minutes per S, depending upon time taken to reach the second criterion.

Results

Table 6.1 shows the means and standard deviations for both groups on both learning criteria. As predicted, there were negligible differences between means

TABLE 6.1. *Means and Variance Estimates for Discrimination-Learning Criteria*

VARIABLES	FIRST CRITERION: NUMBER OF TRIALS TO ELIMINATE IRRELEVANT BOX			SECOND CRITERION: NUMBER OF TRIALS TO AND INCLUDING 10 CONSECUTIVE CORRECT RESPONSES		
	Group			*Group*		
	R		RV	R		RV
N	30		30	30		30
M	58.30		43.57	72.47		60.97
σ_{D_M}		11.15			10.55	
t		1.32			1.09	
p		.19			.27	
σ^2	2503.96		1351.25	2283.13		1167.34
F		1.85			1.96	
p		.05*			.05*	

* One-tailed test.

and relatively large differences between standard deviations. That is, on both measures, the RV group showed significantly less variability than did the R group. Although the evidence is by no means overwhelming in support of the hypothesis, it ought to be pointed out that the experimental comparison was a conservative one in two ways. The first — the use of a high average value reinforcer for Group R — was mentioned above. Second, the true variability was underestimated by assigning to nonlearners the limiting score of 150. This restriction worked against the hypothesis since there was a disproportionately larger number of nonlearners in Group R than in Group RV (six as compared to one).

The correlation between CA and number of trials to the second criterion was —.12. The insignificant size of this correlation is no doubt attributable to restriction of age range in the sample. Last, there was no significant difference in mean performance between the 10 candy reinforced Ss of Group RV and the 30 candy reinforced Ss of Group R.

Discussion

The results of the present study are relevant to some common methodological problems. First, an experimenter who employs a simple analysis of variance design, using children as Ss, frequently finds that between-group differences are large, but that the size of the within-group variability is even more impressive.

The present findings suggest that the use of individually determined reinforcers will reduce such error variance.

Second, experimenters working with young children often report some difficulty in maintaining sufficient motivation to ensure Ss' cooperation, or even to keep them in the experimental room. The method of allowing S to choose that reinforcer he would most like to work for, probably maximizes motivation as a function of high incentive value.

A third methodological problem concerns the fact that the effectiveness of any given type of reinforcer varies with age. For example, trinkets are not effective reinforcers at age 2½, but are effective at age 4. What is needed, then, is a "methodological cookbook" of normative data, listing relative effectiveness of all possible reinforcers by successive age levels. But this information is not available, except for the limited data provided by Terrell and Kennedy. At present, selection of the most effective reinforcer for a given problem and age group depends on a good guess or a pilot study. The present results suggest that it would be less hazardous and/or time-consuming to hold reinforcement value constant for any experimental group rather than reinforcement type, i.e., to offer Ss a selection of reinforcers.

The above data may also lend themselves to practical application. For example, in the classroom situation, teachers depend principally on one type of reinforcement — the grade. However, grades are not equal in reinforcement value for all students. In view of this, teachers might obtain better academic results from their poorer students by offering other, individually determined incentives. As an incidental note, one of the authors has tried informal remedial training with a few children deficient in either arithmetic or reading. In all cases, the underachievement appeared to be a function of insufficient motivation, not of inability. Rapid improvement was noted when the procedure involved (a) reinforcement with individually determined reinforcers, and (b) a combined reward-punishment technique.

NOTE

[1] From a conceptual point of view, *reinforcement value* might be considered as roughly analogous to *incentive motivation* (K), insofar as the latter intervening variable is used to account for performance differential as a function of differences in quality of reinforcement. There are operational differences, however, since the present procedure does not involve a consummatory response, the classical conditioning of which is assumed to be the basic mechanism underlying incentive motivation.

Parents and Strangers as Reinforcing Agents

Harold Stevenson, Rachel Keen, and Robert M. Knights

Assuming that the supportive behaviors of parents toward their preschool youngsters generate satiation effects, the authors hypothesized that parents are less effective reinforcing agents than strangers. A second hypothesis was that females, either the child's mother or a stranger, are more effective reinforcing agents than males. The task involved placing marbles in a hole, and the measure of the dependent variable was rate. In general, the results supported the hypothesis. The evidence also showed that girls were more influenced by reinforcers from females, both their mothers and female strangers, than boys were influenced by males. As the authors suggest, this may be because girls identify more with their mothers than boys identify with their fathers.

The results of a study (Stevenson 1961) indicate that sex of the experimenter is a significant variable in determining the rate of response of preschool children in a simple motor task. Larger increments in response were obtained for both boys and girls when supportive statements concerning the children's performance were delivered by female experimenters than when they were delivered by male experimenters. These results were interpreted as supporting the assumption that the reinforcing effectiveness of the mother, derived from her role in satisfying the child's basic needs, generalizes to other women, thereby increasing their effectiveness as reinforcing agents. The father, on the other hand, plays a less significant role in the early caretaking of children, and it was assumed that fathers — and in turn other men — acquire less capacity for reinforcing behaviors not associated with primary drives. The question remains whether similar results would be found if the parents themselves were to serve as experimenters. The purpose of this study is to determine the effects of social reinforcement on the performance of preschool children when the agents of social reinforcement are the children's parents, and to compare these effects with those obtained in the study employing strangers as experimenters.

There is reason to believe that in this type of task parents would be less effective as reinforcing agents than strangers. Several recent studies have indicated that familiarity with a supportive adult established during a pretraining period reduces the effectiveness of the adult as a social reinforcer of performance on subsequent tasks. Because of the continuing supportive role played by most parents of preschool children, the children may be partially satiated for parental support and consequently show smaller increments in response with parents

SOURCE: Adapted and abridged from Harold Stevenson, Rachel Keen, and Robert M. Knights, "Parents and Strangers as Reinforcing Agents for Children's Performance." *Journal of Abnormal and Social Psychology*, 1963, 67, 183–186. (With permission of the authors and the American Psychological Association.)

than with strangers as reinforcing agents. Strangers may, therefore, acquire their reinforcing effectiveness because of generalization from parents, but may be more effective social reinforcers because of the children's partial satiation from parental support.

Method

Subjects

The subjects were 116 boys and 116 girls within the CA range from 3–0 to 5–0 years, attending nursery schools in Minneapolis and St. Paul. All of the children of the appropriate CAs in each group visited were used as subjects. The schools enrolled children of above average socioeconomic and intellectual level, and they were selected on the basis of availability rather than any other criteria.

Experimenters

The experimenters were either parents of the children or adults whom the children had not met prior to the experimental session. Sixteen boys were tested by their mothers and 16 by their fathers; 16 girls were tested by their mothers and 16 by their fathers. The remaining subjects were tested by one of six men or six women who served as experimenters and who were involved in some phase of the Institute of Child Development program. Forty-two of these boys were tested by a male experimenter, 42 by a female experimenter; 42 of the girls were tested by a male experimenter, 42 by a female experimenter. The data for subjects not tested by their parents have been utilized in a prior study (Stevenson 1961).

Apparatus

The apparatus consisted essentially of a table of adjustable height with two bins, 8 × 10 inches, and a short transverse upright panel to shield the experimenter's record from the subject. The left bin contained approximately 1600 orange, blue, and green marbles. The right bin was covered by a plate with six ⅝-inch holes placed randomly about the surface. Below the right bin was a mechanism which counted each marble as it fell to the bottom of the bin.

Procedure

The procedure has been described in detail (Stevenson 1961). The experimenter seated the subject at the table and instructed the subject that the marbles were to be placed in the holes one at a time, that any marble could be put in any hole, and that the experimenter would tell the subject when to stop.

The first minute of the game was used to establish a baseline rate of response for each subject. During this minute the experimenter was instructed to play the role of an attentive but nonreinforcing observer of the subject's performance. After the first minute the experimenter delivered supportive statements about the subject's performance twice a minute for the next 5 minutes of the game. The statements were made after approximately 15 seconds and 45 seconds within each minute, and five statements were used: "You're doing very well," "That's very good," "You know how to play this game very well," "That's fine," "You're really good at this game." The statements were arranged according to a series of predetermined random orders. The experimenters were instructed not to respond to the subject's overtures for interaction, but to repeat relevant parts of the instructions or to tell the subject that the matter could be discussed later.

A letter and a telephone call were used to recruit parents for the study. Excellent cooperation was obtained; the only parents unable to serve as experimenters were those who had no free time during the nursery school hours. The parents were not previously informed of the nature of the study and were not told that it would involve participation with their children. The parent was met by a research assistant and taken to the experimental room. The procedure was explained in detail and the parent practiced the task with the assistant as a subject. The parent was told that the purpose of the study would be explained in a follow-up letter. The assistant then went with the parent to the nursery school room. The session was observed through a oneway mirror. The remaining experimenters were given the same instructions prior to testing subjects and practiced the procedure with an experienced experimenter as the subject.

Response Measures

The number of marbles inserted during each minute of the experimental session was recorded. The number inserted during the first minute when the experimenter made no supportive comments provided a base rate of response. For each subject the base rate was subtracted from the number of marbles inserted during each subsequent minute, and the mean of the sum of these difference scores was used as the index of the effectiveness of the social reinforcement.

Results

Base Rate

An analysis of variance of the mean base rate for each subgroup indicates that the average number of responses made during the first minute of the task was significantly higher when the subjects were tested by a male experimenter than by a female experimenter ($F = 5.24, df = \frac{1}{2}24, p < .05$). None of the other main effects or interactions was statistically significant.

Difference Scores

The mean difference scores summed across the 5 minutes are presented in Figure 6.1 according to sex of experimenter, sex of subject, and type of experimenter. The prediction that fathers would produce lower increment scores (or, as it resulted, higher decrement scores) than mothers was supported by the results of a one-tailed t test ($t = 1.88, df = 62, p < .05$). An analysis of variance of these data indicates the difference between male and female experimenters is statistically significant ($F = 8.98, df = \frac{1}{2}24, p < .01$). Performance also dif-

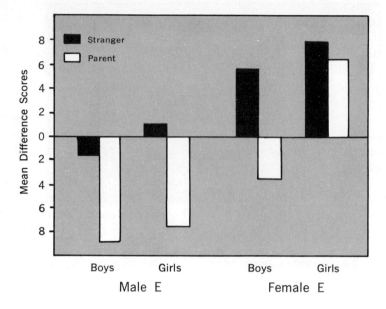

Figure 6.1   The mean difference score for each of the subgroups.

fered significantly, depending upon whether the subject was tested by a stranger or by a parent ($F = 4.99, df = \frac{1}{2}24, p < .05$). There was no significant difference associated with sex of subjects, and none of the interaction terms was significant.

Raw Scores

A third measure of performance is the number of responses made during the 6 minutes of the game. The mean number of responses made each minute by each subgroup is presented in Figure 6.2. An analysis of variance of these data indicates that boys made significantly fewer responses during the game than girls ($F = 6.39, df = \frac{1}{2}24, p < .05$). The subjects tested by strangers made a greater number of responses than did subjects tested by their parents ($F = 4.40, df = \frac{1}{2}24, p < .05$). The main effect associated with sex of experimenter and the interaction terms were not significant.

To determine whether performance changed significantly across trials the data were separated according to type of experimenter. Lindquist (1953) Type III analyses of variance indicated a significant difference across trials for subjects tested by their parents ($F = 2.27, df = \frac{5}{3}00, p < .05$), and for subjects tested by strangers ($F = 2.26, df = \frac{5}{8}20, p < .05$). In the former case performance decreased across trials, while in the latter it increased. In the first analysis there was a significant difference according to sex of subjects ($F = 3.88, df = \frac{1}{6}0, p < .05$). None of the other main effects or interactions in the two analyses was significant.

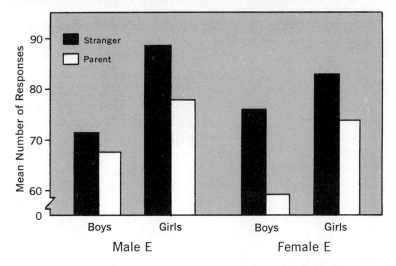

Figure **6.2** The mean number of responses made by each subgroup.

Discussion

The results indicate that supportive statements have a reinforcing effect in increasing rate of response in this task only for certain adult-child combinations. Fathers, and male experimenters in general, were less effective as reinforcing agents than were mothers or other females. Of the children tested by their parents, only girls tested by their mothers showed an increase in rate of response after the introduction of the supportive comments. This is in contrast to the results for children tested by strangers, where the only group showing a decrease in rate of response was boys tested by male experimenters. It is of interest that the rank orders of the various adult-child combinations were identical when the parents and strangers served as experimenters; the least effective combination in both cases was a male adult with a boy, and the most effective combination was a female adult with a girl (Figure 6.1). The greater effectiveness of female experimenters and of strangers compared to parents is in line with the assumptions made prior to the study.

It is difficult to interpret some of the other findings. The first question is why the initial rate of response was higher for children tested by male experimenters than for children tested by female experimenters. The uncommonness of fathers and other males visiting nursery schools and the lower incidence of interaction in game situations with adult males may have led to the children's being more excited at the prospects of playing a game with male experimenters than with female experimenters. It might be assumed that children were made more anxious by their fathers (and by men in general) and that the higher motivation derived from the anxiety was evidenced in a higher initial rate of response. In turn, the consequence of the males' initiating supportive statements may be to reduce the children's anxiety, with a resultant decrease in their rate of response. Supportive comments thus may function to reduce anxiety in a tense situation or to reinforce performance where there is less evidence of tension. The function of the statements appears, therefore, to depend upon the type of initial motivation induced by the experimenter.

Another question is why girls tested by strange female adults or by their mothers showed the greatest increments in response. Preschool girls are assumed to be more highly identified with their mothers than boys with either their mothers or fathers. As a consequence of this, the supportive comments delivered by females in the present study may have had an enhanced effect on girls' performance, for here the girls receive not only the supportive comment made by the mother but also their own self-approval derived from their identification with a supportive figure.

Adult Silence as a Reinforcer

Stuart I. Offenbach and William J. Meyer

Discrimination-learning studies typically involve the presentation of a positive reinforcer for correct responses and silence for incorrect responses. It is also possible to punish incorrect responses and remain silent for correct responses. Professors Offenbach and Meyer demonstrate that adult nonreaction rather quickly acquires reinforcement value. Children exposed to rewards interpret silence as punishment, while children exposed to punishment interpret silence as reward. The evidence does not indicate whether adult silence following punishment is as effective a positive reinforcer as the use of a tangible reinforcing stimulus.

Studies using the reinforcement combinations "Right"-(Nothing) (RN) and (Nothing)-"Wrong" (NW) suggest that children learn to differentially interpret E's failure to respond according to whether E previously dispensed reward or punishment. Thus in the combination RN, E's failure to respond (or the occurrence of any initially neutral stimulus combined with "Right") is interpreted as punishment whereas (Nothing) or any initially neutral stimulus, in the combination NW is interpreted as reward. These studies, however, do not provide evidence that (Nothing) is an effective reinforcer in a new learning situation.

In an effort to demonstrate the effectiveness of reinforcers acquired in the manner described, two experiments are reported in which a pretraining task is given to the experimental groups. This task, presented for 10 trials, utilized a randomized noncontingent reinforcement procedure permitting all Ss to receive

SOURCE: Adapted and abridged from Stuart I. Offenbach and William J. Meyer, "A Neglected Source of Reinforcement in Discrimination Learning." *Journal of Experimental Child Psychology*, 1964, 1, 294–300. (With permission of the authors and the Academic Press.)

identical reinforcement patterns. Five of these trials were followed by a buzzer, assumed to be a neutral "reinforcer"-stimulus, while the five remaining trials were followed by a verbal statement. The verbal statement for the BNE groups (Buzzer-Nothing-Experimental) was "Wrong" and the verbal statement for the NBE groups (Nothing-Buzzer-Experimental) was "Right." Immediately following the 10 pretraining trials, a discrimination learning task was presented in which the buzzer, now combined with (Nothing), was the reinforcing stimulus. The BNE groups heard the buzzer for correct responses and NBE groups for incorrect responses. In each experiment, Buzzer Control groups (BNC: Buzzer-Nothing-Control) and (NBC: Nothing-Buzzer-Control) were given the acquisition task without the pretraining experience. The BNC groups heard the buzzer for correct choices and NBC groups for incorrect choices. In Experiment I, additional controls consisted of "Right"-(Nothing) and (Nothing)-"Wrong" groups who were given only the acquisition task.

Experiment I

This experiment was designed to answer three questions: (1) does an initially neutral stimulus (a buzzer) acquire reinforcing value in a direction opposite to the verbal statement with which it is combined; (2) are there age differences in the effectiveness of the reinforcers; and (3) is the effectiveness of the acquired reinforcers similar to the effectiveness of the verbal reinforcers "Right" and "Wrong"?

Meyer and Offenbach (1962) have shown that the NW combination is superior to the RN combination only when the discrimination learning task involves multiple irrelevant dimensions. In order to demonstrate that the buzzer acquires reinforcement value in the predicted direction and that punished groups will learn faster than rewarded groups, it is necessary to provide a learning task with multiple irrelevant dimensions.

Method

Subjects

A total of 120 children, 60 kindergarteners and 60 fourth graders, served as Ss in this experiment. Approximately as many boys as girls were included at each age level. The Ss were all from the same suburban school district.

Procedure

Ten children were randomly assigned to each of the 12 groups in this experiment. The children were seen individually in a schoolroom which was relatively free from distractions. The Ss in the BNE and NBE groups received the following instructions for pretraining: "We are going to play a game with these flashlights. Each time that I say 'ready,' you turn on one of the lights. The way that you turn them on is by pressing one of these red buttons on the top. Remember, one of the lights is the right one to turn on and one is the wrong one to turn on.

Any questions? OK, now we will begin to play the game." The experimental groups received 10 pretraining trials with the flashlights. The same sequence of verbal and buzz-type reinforcement was used for each S.

The acquisition task consisted of 15 pairs of blocks with three irrelevant dimensions (height, color, and shape) and one relevant dimension (position). A constant value of each irrelevant dimension appeared in each pair of blocks. The side (left or right) reinforced was determined randomly for each child. The instructions for the acquisition task were: "(Now) We are going to play a game with some blocks. I am going to show you two blocks at a time and I want you to choose, by pointing your finger, which block is the correct one. The block may be correct because of its color, red or blue; its shape, triangle or rectangle; its position, left or right; or because of its height, taller or shorter. Remember, one of the blocks is the right one to choose and one is the wrong block to choose. Any questions? OK, now we will begin to play the game." All questions were answered by repeating the relevant part of the instructions. Additional apparatus consisted of a buzzer (Speed-X, Model 450) and a large box containing the pairs of stimuli. Ss were tested until they reached a criterion of 10 out of 10 correct responses or until 75 trials elapsed.

Design

There are 6 treatment groups at each age level: buzzer experimental groups BNE and NBE, buzzer control groups BNC and NBC, and the verbal control groups RN and NW. The groups were used in different combinations according to the purpose of the analysis. There are two major analyses: (1) a $2 \times 2 \times 2$ factorial analysis involving pretraining vs. no pretraining (BNE + NBE vs. BNC + NBC); reward vs. punishment (BNE + BNC vs. NBE + NBC); and kindergarten vs. fourth grade; and (2) a 4×2 factorial analysis involving 4 reinforcement treatments, RN, NW, BNE, and NBE; and kindergarten vs. fourth grade.

Results

A $2 \times 2 \times 2$ analysis of variance was performed on the data. Effects attributable to pretraining were statistically significant ($F = 9.56; df = 1, 63; p < 0.01$) indicating that the experimental groups (BNE and NBE) learned faster than did the control groups (BNC and NBC).[1] All age and interaction effects were nonsignificant. The prediction that the NBE group would learn in fewer trials than the BNE group was supported by a one-tailed t-test ($t = 1.80; df = 38; p < 0.05$).

The analysis of the experimental groups and the verbal control groups is summarized in Table 6.2. The nonsignificant Fs for the RN vs. BNE and the NW vs. NBE comparisons indicate that the acquired reinforcers do not differ in effectiveness from the verbal reinforcers. The significant T_3 comparison indicates that the punished groups learned significantly faster than did the rewarded

TABLE 6.2. *Analysis of Variance for Experiment I — Experimental (Pretraining) Groups and Verbal Reinforcement Groups*

SOURCE	df	ms	F
RN vs. NW vs. BNE vs. NBE	3	2067.0	3.45*
(T₁) RN vs. BNE	1	3.6	
(T₂) NW vs. NBE	1	211.6	
(T₃) RN + BNE vs. NW + NBE	1	5985.8	9.99**
Kndg. vs. 4th grade	1	3511	5.86*
Age × Treatments	3	84.9	
Within Groups (Error term)	72	598.975	

* $p < 0.05$.   ** $p < 0.01$.

groups. Age differences were also significant, indicating that the task was more difficult for the kindergarten children.

The results of the first analysis support the original hypothesis that a neutral stimulus acquires reinforcing value in a direction opposite to the verbal statement with which it is combined. Inspection of Table 6.2 indicates that little, if any, learning took place in the BNC and NBC groups. Secondly, the acquired reinforcers were as effective as the verbal statements "Right" and "Wrong." The anticipated difference between positive and negative reinforcement occurred (the groups with negative reinforcement learned in fewer trials).[2]

Experiment II

This experiment was designed to test, using acquired reinforcers, the information interpretation of the effectiveness of verbal reinforcement combinations suggested by Meyer and Offenbach (1962). Briefly, this interpretation assumes

> that each S approaches the task with a certain response set. Acquisition for the punishment group occurs as incorrect response tendencies are eliminated. The effect of punishment is to make it very clear to the Ss that a particular mode of responding is incorrect or inadequate. Acquisition for the reward-alone group occurs when a particular response set is confirmed. However, it must be remembered that all dimensions, relevant and irrelevant, are present in one of each pair of stimuli presented the Ss. When an RN S makes a rewardable response in this situation, it is highly probable that an incorrect response set will be confirmed and thus strengthened. Eventually learning occurs as the Ss, in an effort to maximize reward, respond to a different dimension. For the situation, then, where the task involves at least two irrelevant dimensions, the elimination of incorrect sets, as provided by punishment, is superior to the confirmation of sets, provided by reward. When the number of alternative response tendencies is limited (to two dimensions), the rewarded group can only choose between two dimensions. Under this condition confirmation can and apparently does occur rapidly. Even so, learning still should be somewhat more rapid for the punishment group . . . because of the presence of the one irrelevant dimension" (Meyer and Offenbach, 1962, pp. 533–534).

Experiment II employed a simple acquisition task (one relevant and one irrelevant dimension) to determine if the differences between reward and punishment can also be eliminated with acquired reinforcers.

Subjects

The Ss for this experiment were 80 children, 40 kindergarteners and 40 fourth graders, from the same suburban school district as the children in the first experiment.

Procedure

A $2 \times 2 \times 2$ factorial design two age levels, two reinforcement conditions (buzzer-positive and buzzer-negative), and two pretraining levels (0 and 10 trials) permitted random placement of 10 Ss in each group. The pretraining task and instructions were identical to those used in Experiment I. The acquisition task consisted of 15 pairs of blocks with one irrelevant dimension, height. Again, a position response, randomly determined for each S, was reinforced. The reduction in the number of irrelevant dimensions necessitated the following change in the acquisition task instructions: ". . . The block may be the correct one to choose because of its position, left or right, or because it is taller or shorter than the other. . . ."

Results

The only significant effect in the analysis of variance was that attributable to pretraining ($F = 14.72; df = 1, 63; p < 0.01$) and indicates that learning was significantly faster for the experimental groups. The differences between BNE and NBE were nonsignificant ($t = .34; df = 38; p > .05$). Age differences were not significant ($F = 2.14; df = 1, 63; p > .05$) (Note 1). These results also support the conclusion that an initially neutral stimulus acquires reinforcing value in a direction opposite to the verbal reinforcer with which it is combined. As in Experiment I, little learning took place in the BNC and NBC control groups. The absence of differences between the reward and punishment experimental groups is consistent with the information interpretation of Meyer and Offenbach (1962).

Discussion

The results of both experiments support the hypothesis that stimuli which are purposely or otherwise combined with a rewarding stimulus or a punishing stimulus acquire effective reinforcer value in an opposite direction. These results support the interpretation that the failure to observe extinction in (Nothing)-"Wrong" reinforcement groups is attributable to (Nothing) being interpreted as reward. It is also possible that the extinction observed where positive reinforcement alone was used in acquisition may have been the result of acquired punishment. One can speculate that this acquisition occurs by means of a "mediational system" activated by the instructions. For example, Ss in the NBE group were informed in the instructions that each of their responses would be either right or wrong — but, and this is crucial, during pretraining they were only told "Right." Thus not being told "Right" appears to lead to the implicit response that the choice is wrong, and this implicit response is then associated with the "buzzer." This analysis is similar to the secondary reinforcement paradigm except that the S's implicit response (Wrong) replaces the overt occurrence of the "primary" reinforcer (Wrong) by E.

Although the design of the present experiments does not permit direct inferences about the effectiveness of E's failure to respond (Nothing), it is plausible to assume that (Nothing) acquires reinforcement value. Thus as (Nothing) in the combination "Right"-(Nothing) acquires punishing value, performance should improve and the differences between RN and NW groups should diminish. Examination of the acquisition curves reported by Meyer and Seidman (1960) support this expectation. They found that the difference between the "Right"-(Nothing) and (Nothing)-"Wrong" groups was substantial after 20 acquisition trials but that this difference diminished rapidly during the next ten trials, so that differences between the groups vanished. No effect attributable to acquired reward, in the combination (Nothing)-"Wrong," is anticipated since, when this acquisition occurs, the correct response has already been learned. E's failure to respond then serves only to maintain the correct response.

NOTES

[1] In Experiments I and II none of the 10 Ss within one of the subgroups reached 10 out of 10 correct responses before the 75th trial. Consequently, the trials-to-criterion scores of these subgroups had a zero variance and could not contribute to the within subgroups error sum of squares in the analyses of variance. This was corrected by subtracting from the error degrees of freedom the 9 df associated with the group with zero variance, i.e., dividing the error sum of squares by 63 df rather than 72 df in computing the error mean square.

[2] In both Experiments I and II, analyses of variance of the number of errors yielded results identical with the analyses of the number of trials to criterion.

Birth Order and Reinforcer Effectiveness

J. B. Gilmore and Edward Zigler

First-born children, as opposed to their siblings, typically receive more attention and/or general social reinforcement, especially during the time they have status as the only child. Gilmore and Zigler hypothesize that the behavior of first-born children is less influenced by generalized social reinforcement than is that of later-born children, and that first-borns are more reactive to the withdrawal of social reinforcement than later-borns. This hypothesis, derived from a homeostatic deprivation-

SOURCE: Adapted and abridged from J. B. Gilmore and Edward Zigler, "Birth Order and Social Reinforcer Effectiveness in Children." *Child Development*, 1964, 35, 193–200. (With permission of the authors and the Society for Research in Child Development.)

satiation theory of motivation, is supported by the outcome of this experiment. Apparently one consequence of being a first-born is a greater degree of dependency behavior.

Several investigators have recently turned their attention to the relation between birth order and such variables as the need for affiliation, efficacy of social reinforcement, and susceptibility to social influence. When discovered, birth order effects were attributed to differential dependency training during childhood, with the first-borns being viewed as more dependent than later-borns, and thus having a greater need for social contact and social reinforcers, and being more susceptible to social influence.

The specific aspects of the parent-child interaction that give rise to birth order effects are far from clear. One possible explanation of the birth order findings is that first-borns are more likely than later-borns to have been continually satiated on social reinforcers early in their lives. Such continuous satiation would then be viewed as interfering with the child's independence training. That is, if the support, warmth, and approval of social agents are continually available, there is little need for the child to develop mechanisms other than dependent ones in dealing with environmental stresses.

The results of several studies may be employed to derive specific predictions from this view that first-borns receive more reinforcers and are therefore relatively more satiated on them than are later-borns. These studies, employing a simple deprivation-satiation paradigm, have found that children who are satiated on social reinforcers have less motivation to secure such reinforcers, or be influenced by them, than do children who have been deprived of such reinforcers. Thus, the view of first- and later-borns advanced above, in conjunction with the Brown and Farber (1951) formulation concerning the motivating effects of frustration, generate the following specific predictions:

1. On a simple satiation-type game, first-borns will play for a shorter period of time than later-borns when the game is played under a support condition.

2. The absence of social reinforcers will be more frustrating to children who are more accustomed to receiving them than to children who are not. In a non-support condition, first-borns should respond to this situation by playing the game longer than first-borns playing in the support condition, in the hope that such play will eventually lead to the usually administered social reinforcers. However, for the later-born child this should not be a particularly frustrating condition, and he should view it as a relatively typical situation in which no social reinforcers are available. The later-borns should therefore respond to this situation by playing the game for a shorter period of time than did later-borns under a support condition. What is being predicted here is an interaction effect between birth order and the reinforcement condition under which the game is played.

These predictions were tested in the present study by having groups of first-

and later-born children play a simple game under either support or nonsupport conditions.

Method

Subjects

The subjects consisted of a group of 20 first-born children and a group of 20 later-born children matched on CA. The mean CA for each group was 6.9 years, with each group having a range of 5.5 to 8.5 years. All subjects came from the kindergarten, first, and second grades of the Columbus School in New Haven, and the subjects' parents' occupations indicated that both groups were homogeneous and comparable in respect to socioeconomic class. Subject availability made it impossible to equate the groups on sex. The first-born and later-born groups contained 6 boys and 14 girls and 13 boys and 7 girls, respectively. Each of the two groups was divided into subgroups of 10 subjects each, with the four groups being equated on age. Within each group the two subgroups were equated as closely as possible on sexual composition.

Apparatus

Each subject played three pre-experimental games: the Card game, the Nursery School game, and the Nail Board game. The Card game consisted of turning over cards whose faces were either red or black. The Nursery School game involved mounting pictures of children on two wooden boards. The Nail Board game involved the child's rolling a marble down an inclined plane covered with nails.

The experimental task was the Marble-in-the-Hole game. It is a repetitive and monotonous game and was constructed to reduce relatively quickly the subject's desire merely to "play the game," thus allowing the motivation to obtain social reinforcers to become the dominant variable in determining how long the child would continue to play. The game was constructed so that there was no defined goal toward which the child could work; rather the game was open-ended, and the subject could reasonably terminate it whenever he wished. The game consisted of a green box, 9 by 8 by 7 inches, with two small holes 2 inches apart in the lid and an open green box containing 300 marbles, half red and half yellow.

Procedure

Each subject was tested individually. The experimenter met the subjects in their respective classrooms and took each child upstairs to a familiar classroom that was used as the experimental room. Once in the test room the experimenter said: "We are going to play some games today. These are all fun games, and I think you will like them." The subject then played the three pre-experimental games. The instructions for each of these games were as follows:

> The first game we are going to play is called the Card game. We will use these cards. (Holds up whole deck so S can see a few of the faces.) Some of

these cards are red and some of them are black. You point to a red one. (*S* points.) Now point to a black one. (*S* points.) There. Now I am going to put some of these cards face down like this. (Spreads half of deck out in front of *S*.) Then I'm going to pick one like this. (Picks out card and turns it over. The card picked by *E* is always red). There, I got a red one. Now you pick one and see if you can get a red one. (*S* then picks five cards during this game.)

. . . The next game that we are going to play is called the School game. (Brings over Nursery School game.) These are two school houses and these are pictures of eight children that go to these school houses. (Points.) Some of these children go to the school house with the red roof. (Points to red roof.) And some of these children go to the school with the yellow roof. (Points to yellow roof.) You take each picture and if you think it goes to the school with the red roof then you put it like this (demonstrates); if you think it goes to the school with the yellow roof then you put it like this (demonstrates). Now you do it for each picture.

. . . Now let's play the Nail Board game. This is the Nail Board game. Here's the marble for the Nail Board game. You put it here and see if you can make it come down here (points) and end up in this box, the red/white one. (Points.)

For half the subjects in each subgroup, every response made on the pre-experimental games was called "correct," while none of the responses of the remaining subjects was so rewarded. This manipulation was introduced in the hope that it might accentuate the effects of the support and nonsupport conditions administered during the experimental task proper. However, preliminary analysis revealed that the effect of this manipulation, and all interaction effects involving it, were insignificant (all Fs less than 1.00).

Upon completing the pre-experimental games, the subject was immediately introduced to the experimental task with the following instructions:

The next game is called Marble-in-the-Hole. That is this game, here. I'll tell you how to play it. See, some of these marbles are red and some of them are yellow. The red ones go in this hole, here. (Points.) The yellow ones go in this hole, here. (Points.) Now show me a red marble and show me what hole it goes in. (*S* does so.) Good. Now show me a yellow marble and show me what hole *it* goes in. (*S* does so.) Good. Now in this game you can put as many marbles in the holes as you want to. *You tell me when you want to stop.*

The subject was allowed to play the game until he stated that he wished to stop or until he had played continuously for 10 minutes. Half of the first-borns and half of the later-borns played the experimental game under a nonsupport condition, with the remaining subjects playing under a support condition. In the nonsupport condition the instructions were given, and the experimenter watched the subject but did not interact further with him during the game. No verbal support was given to the subject, and care was taken to avoid nodding, smiling, or giving other types of nonverbal support. In the support condition the following statements were used: "You really know how to play this game." "Fine." "Good." "You really know how to play Marble-in-the-Hole, don't you?" One of these statements was made after every tenth marble was inserted, beginning with the fifth marble. (Upon completion of the experiment all subjects who played the pre-experimental games under the success condition and/or the experimental game under the nonsupport condition played the pre-experimental games again. This time they were verbally rewarded for their responses and were told they had done very well on all the games.)

The experimenter was a male, advanced psychology graduate student with experience in testing children in experimental problems. Prior to undertaking the study, the experimenter tested a number of children in order to establish thorough familiarity with the experimental procedures.

Results

Analysis of Predictions

The mean times spent on the experimental task by each group in the two reinforcement conditions are presented in Figure 6.3. In order to test the first prediction, the performance of the first-borns (mean = 160 seconds) and the later-borns (mean = 411 seconds) in the support condition was compared. This difference of 251 seconds was found to be a significant one ($t = 294; p < .005$). To test the second prediction, a 2×2 analysis of variance (birth order $\times$ reinforcement condition) was run. While the effects associated with birth order ($F = 2.26$) and reinforcement condition ($F < 1.00$) were not significant, the interaction effect was significant ($F = 3.86; p < .05$, one-tailed test). As can be seen in Figure 6.3, this interaction is congruent with the prediction derived from the position advanced that first-borns are more satiated on social reinforcers than are later-borns.

Other Findings

The data were analyzed for sex effects, since the two groups were not equated on sex and since recent studies have indicated a sex of experimenter by sex of subject interaction effect in the effectiveness of social reinforcement. Again employing the length of time spent on the game as a dependent variable, a median test was run comparing the performance of boys and girls. The resulting x^2 (< 1.00) was not significant. Ignoring birth order, a further inspection was made of the possible effects of sex, support condition, and their interaction on the length of time played. This analysis revealed no significant relationships (all $Fs < 1.00$).

Product-moment correlations were run between CA and time played for first-borns ($r = -.11$) and later-borns ($r = -.07$). These correlations do not differ significantly from zero nor from each other, and it may be inferred that differences in CA among the subjects had no systematic effect on length of time spent on the game.

Since the findings supported the view that first-borns can be appropriately viewed as children who have been satiated on social reinforcers, further analyses were conducted in the hope of clarifying the nature of this satiation. Two possi-

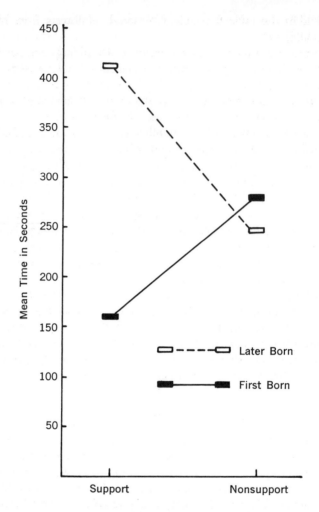

Figure 6.3   Mean times spent on the experimental task by each group under conditions of support and nonsupport.

bilities present themselves. It is possible that first-borns have fewer siblings than later-borns and as a consequence receive more social reinforcement from their parents than do later-borns, who must share the supply of social reinforcers with more siblings. Thus, the relative satiation on social reinforcers demonstrated by first-borns would be viewed as the product of family size rather than birth order. The second view is that, independent of number of siblings, the first-born will manifest the satiation phenomenon. Here the view would be that the first-born receives a great deal of caretaking early in his life and this influences his behaviors for social reinforcers later in life; or that, regardless of the number of siblings, the first-born child is the favored recipient of social reinforcers from his parents throughout childhood.

An initial analysis revealed that the mean of 4.3 siblings possessed by later-born subjects was significantly more than the mean of 1.3 siblings for the first-born subjects ($t = 6.30; p < .001$). This finding lends credence to the view that it is family size rather than birth order that produced the effects found in this study. However, further analysis revealed that such was not the case.

In order to assess the relative efficacy of birth order and number of siblings, an r_{pb} (point bi-serial correlation) was run between birth order and the length of time played by the subjects in the support condition ($r_{pb} = .57; p < .01$), and an r was run between the number of siblings and the length of time played in this condition ($r = .23; p > .20$). Again employing the subjects in the support condition, an r_{pb} of .63 ($p < .01$) was found between birth order and number of siblings. Employing these correlations, partial correlations were run between birth order and time played, partialing out the effect of number of siblings ($r12.3 = .56; p < .01$), and between number of siblings and time played, partialing out the effect of birth order ($r1.32 = -.20; p > .20$). These correlations indicate that first-borns play the game under the support condition less long than later-borns, independent of the number of siblings. The relation between number of siblings and time played, independent of the birth order effects, was not a significant one. Although not significant, the direction of this relation is contrary to the number-of-siblings position advanced above, i.e., the greater number of siblings, the less time spent on the game.

Discussion

The most striking finding of the present study was that first-borns evidenced less need for social reinforcers than did later-borns when such reinforcers were readily available. A second finding of consequence was an interaction effect between birth order and reinforcement condition, indicating a reversal in the two groups' need for social reinforcers when such reinforcers should be forthcoming but are not. These results support the hypothesis that the first-born child is more satiated on social reinforcers than is the later-born child.

The social reinforcement satiation view of first-borns appears capable of explaining the heightened dependency of such individuals upon the contact and opinions of others when placed in stressful situations. As noted earlier, the caretaking experiences of the child continuously satiated on social reinforcers are such that the learning of more mature mechanisms for handling stress is hindered.

The intriguing problem remains as to the particular sequential aspects of the caretaking of first-borns that produce the reported findings. The present study indicates that it is birth order, rather than a correlate such as number of siblings, which produces the effects. The question of whether the first-born child receives social satiation early in his childhood only, or is the recipient of social satiation as a preferred child throughout childhood, is an open one. The fact that birth order effects are found in adults long after such subjects have been regularly satiated on early dependency needs suggests that the dynamics of birth order are established in a relatively early period in life. Such a view is not only in keeping with that advanced by several personality theorists, but is also consistent with recent findings that both the effectiveness of social reinforcers later in life and differences in the enhanced effectiveness of social reinforcers with a constant length of institutionalization were related to the caretaking experienced during the first few years of life.

CHAPTER VII

Learning Variables: Motivation

MOTIVATION has proven to be one of the more difficult concepts to define in psychology. Human motives were once ascribed to biological instincts; more or less each category of human behavior, such as aggression or love, had its corresponding instinctive basis. Conceptualizing human motives in terms of instincts failed to explain the diversity of human behavior except in a highly circular fashion; that is, the difference between a youngster displaying aggression and another youngster not displaying aggression was explained in terms of differences in the strengths of the instinct to aggression. How these children happened to have different instinctive strengths could not, obviously be answered in terms of the general theoretical model. Psychology rejected the instinct model and turned to the concept of drives derived from the concept of homeostasis. Initially, these drives included hunger, thirst, and sex. It was now possible to define motivation in terms of deprivation; the greater the deprivation, the more intense the drive state. This model provided a means of experimentally manipulating the strength of a drive and, in general, led to empirical verification of the hypothesis that the greater the drive — up to a certain point — the greater the learning behavior of the animal.

It soon became obvious, however, that primary drives could not explain the enormous complexity of human behavior, especially in a society where behavior is not obviously directed by strivings for primary drive satisfaction. The concept of acquired or secondary drives was introduced within the general homeostatic model which led to the derivation of such acquired drives as achievement, aggression, and dependency. Indeed, there are some theoretical models that postulate as many acquired drives as there are overt behaviors. Such models share certain problems of circularity with the instinct model.

More recently, there has been an attempt to reduce the number of postulated human motives by introducing the concept of a generalized drive state, which for many theorists means anxiety. According to this view, behaviors postulated as acquired drives (aggression, dependency, etc.) are viewed as instrumental responses; that is, the person is aggressive because in the past that response has been reinforcing. The papers by Davitz and by Palermo, Castaneda, and

McCandless, and by Walters and Ray derived from the concept of a generalized drive state. Davitz's study shows that postfrustration responses are modifiable — a finding which should be of considerable interest to parents and teachers. Palermo et al. show the deleterious effects of intense anxiety on complex learning, indicating that overly strong motivation is not always good. Walters and Ray examine an important methodological issue that raises some question about the manipulation of secondary drives.

Another aspect of motivation theory is considered by Professor Harlow and his associates. In this study, evidence for the presence of a built in manipulation drive that has some similarity to the concept of a curiosity drive is shown. The position taken in this paper with respect to a homeostatic view of motivation is in contrast with the study by Terrell et al., which is derived from a homeostatic model.

The Effects of Previous Training on Postfrustration Behavior

Joel R. Davitz

A variety of theoretical formulations postulate that frustration has negative influence on behavior. Two of the better-known theories perceive frustration as the antecedent to aggression or as an antecedent to regressive behaviors. The view presented by Dr. Davitz is that frustration is a generalized instigator or motivator of behavior to which a variety of responses can be attached. From this viewpoint it is possible that adaptive and positive behaviors can follow frustration, provided that such responses were originally associated with the stimuli surrounding frustration. Dr. Davitz describes an experiment in this paper which supports his theoretical contentions and which casts serious doubt on the hypothesis that frustration effects only specific behaviors.

In recent years the concept of frustration has been central in both mental hygiene and social psychology. Psychologists and other social scientists have shown their interest in frustration and its effects by developing several theories, by performing a number of experiments, and by using the concept of frustration to account for the deviant behavior of persons and of social groups. In spite of this extensive interest, many issues relating to the effects of frustration remain unresolved, and the current theories remain incompletely tested.

The research reported here deals with the influence of one variable upon reactions to frustration. The principal hypothesis is that a person's response to frustration will be affected by his previous experience in situations similar to that in which frustration is encountered. Specifically, the experiment studies the

SOURCE: Adapted and abridged from Joel A. Davitz, "The Effects of Previous Training on Post-Frustration Behavior." *Journal of Abnormal and Social Psychology*, 1952, 47, 309–315. (With permission of the author and the American Psychological Association.)

differential effects of *aggressive training* and of *constructive training* on the responses to frustration made by children 7 to 9 years of age.

In order to develop the theoretical rationale for the present study, three major theories of frustration presented in the recent literature will be critically reviewed. The frustration-aggression hypothesis, which assumes a high degree of correlation between frustration and an "instigation to aggression," interprets postfrustration behavior in terms of direct aggression, displaced aggression, or substitute activity (Dollard, Doob, Miller, Mowrer, and Sears 1939, 1941). That direct or indirect aggression is not a universal response to frustration has been wide discussed in the literature of frustration-aggression criticism. Thus, the category of "substitute activity" necessarily covers an extremely wide range of behavior. The interpretation of this wide range of nonaggressive behavior as substitute activity — "substitute" only from the perspective of a theoretician anticipating aggression — requires the manipulation of unverified inferred variables, and does not provide an adequate general theoretical framework within which to analyze, predict, and understand this behavior.

The frustration-regression theory suggests that the change of behavior which occurs after frustration is predominantly in the direction of regression. While there is little question that regression may occur as a result of frustration, a change of behavior in this direction is certainly not the only possible change in direction. There are instances in the classroom every day in which the change of behavior after frustration is in the direction of growth rather than regression. There would seem to be no general factor in frustration *per se* which determines the direction of behavioral change, and the a priori assumption that the change is always in one direction is not consistent with everyday observations. Therefore, because it predicts a change of behavior after frustration in only one direction, *viz.* regression, the frustration-regression theory does not provide a general theory of frustration.

Maier (1949) has suggested that postfrustration behavior is nonmotivated behavior without a goal. This challenge of the postulate that all behavior is motivated rests on Maier's experiments with animals forced to respond in insolvable problem situations. Maier observed that these animals developed consistent patterns of behavior, yet there was no apparent goal; and he concludes that postfrustration behavior is qualitatively different from motivated behavior because it is behavior without a goal. Maier's theoretical position restricts the definition of motivation to goal-seeking, neglecting the widely recognized definition of motivation in terms of antecedent conditions. The chief criticism of Maier's position is that his basic experimental data, upon which he bases his fundamental postulate of motivated and nonmotivated behavior, can be adequately interpreted and predicted in terms of avoidance behavior, utilizing the concepts of learning theory and without invoking a new theoretical sphere of nonmotivated behavior.

Having briefly examined these theories of frustration, it is suggested that a general theory of frustration cannot be restricted to the prediction of a particular mode of response or to a particular directional change of behavior after frustration. This critical examination also suggests that frustration theory may be most fruitfully treated in terms of a more general theory of adjustment, rather than in terms specific to frustration alone.

It is suggested that postfrustration behavior tends toward adjustment, and that the process of adjustment may be analyzed in terms of learning theory. For purposes of this study, frustration is defined as the blocking of drive-evoked behavior. When this behavior is blocked and the drive continues, the cumulative intensification of the drive evokes an emotional response. The particular pattern of behavior evidenced by the organism is a function of the organism's hierarchy of responses related to the emotional stimulation and the particular situation in which frustration is encountered. While it is suggested that this hierarchy of responses is a significant determinant of the organism's postfrustration behavior, it is recognized that this is not the only determining factor. The intensity of the original frustrated drive and the resultant emotional response, the degree to which the original drive-evoking situation continues to impinge upon the organism, and the degree of active punishment involved in the frustrating circumstances may be several other factors involved in this complex process.

Frustration theory is treated as merely one case of a general adjustment theory employing the concepts of learning theory. No specific behavioral responses are predicted as general results of frustration, nor is the direction of behavioral change, either in terms of regression or growth, suggested as a general rule. As in all cases of behavior, the analysis of postfrustration behavior involves the interaction of a particular organism and a particular situation, and the theoretical framework suggests general relationships among the various factors involved in this interaction.

The principal focus of the present research was the development of differential response tendencies, prior to subjecting the subjects (Ss) to frustration. One group of Ss was trained aggressively before frustration, and another group was trained to act constructively. All Ss were trained in the same physical setting as that in which the effects of the frustration were observed. It was assumed that the training received would develop in the individuals of each group a specific behavioral tendency related to that physical situation, and it was hypothesized that their learned behavioral tendencies would differentially affect the behavior of each of the groups following frustration.

The two major hypotheses of the study were:

1. Subjects trained aggressively will behave more aggressively after frustration than will subjects trained constructively.

2. Subjects trained constructively will behave more constructively after frustration than will subjects trained aggressively.

Procedure

The experimental procedure may be divided into four major sections: (a) free play; (b) training; (c) frustration; and (d) free play. In the first experimental session each of the ten groups was allowed free play with any of the materials in the experimental playroom. This was followed by a series of training sessions in which five groups were trained aggressively and five groups were trained constructively. The final sequence of the experiment consisted of a frustrating situation followed by a second period of free play.

The experimental population consisted of 40 subjects, 24 girls and 16 boys between the ages of 7 and 9, selected from a group of children in residence at a summer camp. The mean age of the subjects was 100 months and the standard deviation of age was 9 months. The total population was divided into five pairs of experimental groups (10 groups), each pair matched on the basis of age and sex. There were four Ss in each group, and the particular type of training, aggressive or constructive, assigned to each group was determined in a random manner.

The playroom was twelve feet long and nine feet wide, and it was bounded on one end by a black wire screen which permitted cameras, placed at a small opening in a wall fourteen feet from the screen, to record the behavior during the pre- and postfrustration play sessions. The play materials, which were arranged in an identical fashion before each free play session, consisted of clay, three dolls, building logs, dump truck, large plastic punching doll, hammer, saw, nails, and wood. Each group received seven thirty-minute training sessions.

Aggressive training is defined as that which encourages and rewards behavior the goal of which is injury to some object or person. The aggressive training was a series of games designated as: Cover the Spot, Scalp, and Break the Ball. These games are briefly outlined below.

Cover the Spot. At the center of a mat placed on the floor was a small *x* marked in black chalk. Each S was instructed to cover the spot with some part of his body, and that person covering the spot at the end of the game was the winner. Only one person could cover the spot at one time, and it was emphasized to the Ss that there were no rules limiting their aggressive behavior during the game.

Scalp. A piece of cloth was tied around the arm of each subject and he was informed that his was his scalp. The object of the game was to tear the scalps from the other S's arm while protecting one's own scalp.

Break the Ball. Each S was provided with a ping pong ball which was placed on the floor and could not be touched by hand. The object of the game was to break everyone else's ping pong ball while protecting one's own ball.

The several games described above were played for a period of ten minutes and repeated during the seven training sessions. During these training sessions a chart for each group was kept on the wall, and the winner of each game was awarded a star on this chart. Throughout these sessions aggressive behavior was praised and encouraged by the experimenter (E), and, in general, there was a high degree of aggressive behavior evidenced.

Constructive training is defined as that which encourages and rewards behavior involving the use of materials for the construction of designated objects. The constructive training consisted of drawing murals and completing jigsaw puzzles. During four sessions a long sheet of paper was placed on the wall and a box of crayons was placed on the floor. Instructions were given to draw a single picture on the entire sheet of paper, and E emphasized the constructiveness of each S as well as the cooperation of the group. During the remaining sessions, each group was presented with a jigsaw puzzle containing thirty pieces. The Ss were told that if the pieces were put together correctly, they would form a picture of American Indians or a familiar fictional character. When the group completed the first puzzle, a second puzzle was provided, and this was continued until the end of each training period. Throughout the training periods all aggressive behavior was discouraged by E, while constructiveness, on the other hand, was praised and encouraged.

The final phase of the experiment consisted of the frustration and a second free play session. The Ss were seated on the floor next to a projector outside of the playroom and told that they were to see movies. Five reels of film, arranged next to the projector, were contained in boxes which displayed the titles of the film and a picture of the leading character. The first reel was shown completely. At the start of the second reel, each S was given a bar of candy, and at the climactic point of the film, E stepped in front of the seated Ss, removed the candy from their hands, and ushered them into the playroom. As E locked the screen door of the playroom, he made the following statement: "You cannot have any more candy or see any more films, but you can play with anything in the room." Although the Ss could see the projector, which continued to run, through the screen door, and movie screen was not visible. E did not answer any questions and made no comment on behavior. In no case was there any contact between groups during the final phase of the experiment.

The behavior evidenced in the pre- and postfrustration free play sessions was recorded on moving picture film for a period of eighteen minutes, starting in each case with the moment the Ss entered the playroom. Two 8-mm cameras with automatic self-winding devices and wide angle lenses were used for this purpose. In order to analyze the data, the pre- and postfrustration behavior recorded on film was observed and written protocols of the behavior of each S were made. Pre- and postfrustration periods were not identified, and the observations were made independently by two observers. During each viewing of the film the observers made a continuous record of a single S. These protocols were compared, differences between observers noted, and the procedure was repeated until agreement between observers was reached concerning the behavior of each S.

Results

The data were analyzed in terms of the two major hypotheses, and the statistical analysis pertaining to each hypothesis will be presented separately.

Aggressiveness

It is hypothesized that Ss trained aggressively will evidence more aggressive behavior after frustration than will Ss trained constructively. The 80 protocols of behavior, including the records of pre- and postfrustration behavior of all 40 Ss, were presented to four judges, who were asked to rank the protocols in order of aggressiveness. The playroom and materials were described to the judges; however, the pre- and postfrustration sessions and the individual Ss were not identified. The 80 protocols were presented in random order, and the protocols were ranked independently by each judge. The judges were doctoral students in psychology who had previous experience in ranking procedures.

The agreement among judges was determined by the coefficient of concordance. All four judges agreed that 20 protocols evidenced no aggression and could not be ranked along the aggression continuum. Including these protocols in the evaluation of agreement among judges would result in a spuriously high coefficient of concordance, since the concordance of judges on protocols not on the continuum is $+1$. Therefore, in computing the coefficient of concordance these protocols were omitted. The value of the coefficient of concordance, corrected for ties, for the four rankings of 60 protocols was found to be .903, indicating an extremely high degree of agreement among judges.

In the following analysis of the data, the pre- and postfrustration ranks of each S were determined by summing the ranks assigned to each protocol by the four judges and arranging these summed ranks in order from the lowest to the highest sum. It should be noted that the form of the population of ranks cannot be specified; therefore, the analysis of the data is in terms of nonparametric inference.

In order to test the major hypothesis concerning aggressiveness, the pre- and postfrustration ranks of each S were compared, and a gain of rank was indicated by a $+$; a loss in rank, by a $-$. The null hypothesis which was tested may be stated as follows: The probability of gains after frustration of the aggressively trained group is less than, or equal to, the probability of gains of the constructively trained group. The null hypothesis would be rejected for a high number of gains in the aggressive group.

Only pairs of ranks (the pre- and postfrustration ranks of each individual) were considered. Therefore, these observations may be treated as independent, and the significance of the difference of gains and losses between the two groups may be tested by the ordinary method of chi-square. In computing chi-square, the ties for each group were split, half added to the number of gains and half to the number of losses in each group. This procedure increased the numerator of chi-square, thus providing the most conservative estimate of probability. The obtained chi-square corrected for continuity is 3.63. However, the hypothesis under consideration is a one-sided hypothesis, and the chi-square value is in terms of a two-sided hypothesis. For moderate samples, if chi-square has one degree of freedom, the square root of chi-square has a distribution which is the right hand half of a normal distribution. Therefore, in order to test the present one-sided hypothesis, the chi-square value must be converted into the equivalent value in terms of a unit normal deviate. This value is 1.90; therefore, the null hypothesis is rejected at the .05 level of significance. It is concluded that aggressively trained Ss behaved more aggressively after frustration than constructively trained Ss.

The equivalence of the location of prefrustration ranks of the two groups is evaluated by the *median test*. The hypothesis that the two population medians are equal is tested. The resulting value of chi-square is 1.6, and the hypothesis cannot be rejected even at the .10 level of significance. Therefore we may conclude that in terms of the location in the rank order of aggressiveness before frustration, the aggressive and constructive groups were equivalent.

Constructiveness

It is hypothesized that the constructively trained Ss will behave more constructively after frustration than the aggressively trained subjects. The analysis of the data in terms of this hypothesis is essentially the same as the procedure discussed above in terms of aggressiveness. The 80 protocols were ranked from most to least constructive by five judges, and the agreement among judges was determined by the coefficient of concordance. The value of the coefficient of concordance was found to be .904, indicating an extremely high degree of agreement among judges.

The pre- and postfrustration protocols were arranged in rank order of constructiveness by taking the sum of ranks assigned to each protocol by the five judges. Correcting for continuity, the resulting value of chi-square was 5.10. This value was converted to the corresponding value in terms of a unit normal deviate and the value 2.25 was obtained. Therefore the null hypothesis, that the probability of gains of the constructively trained group is less than, or equal to, the probability of gains of the aggressively trained group, was rejected at the .02 level of significance. It may be concluded that the constructively trained Ss behaved more constructively after frustration than the aggressively trained Ss.

The equivalence of the location of prefrustration ranks of the two groups is evaluated by the *median test*. The hypothesis that the population medians are equal is tested. The resulting value of chi-square is 0.4, and the hypothesis cannot be rejected even at the .10 level of significance. Therefore, it may be concluded that in terms of location in the rank order of constructiveness before frustration, the constructive and aggressive groups were equivalent.

Conclusions

Both hypotheses were supported by the experimental results. Therefore it may be concluded that under the conditions specified in the present experiment previous training in situations similar to that in which frustration is encountered is a significant determinant of the organism's postfrustration behavior. These results are in contrast with past studies of frustration which have interpreted postfrustration behavior primarily in terms of the frustrating situation itself.

The experimental results do not seem to be consistent with the frustration-aggression hypothesis as a general theory of frustration. While 14 of the Ss of the aggressively trained group behaved more aggressively after frustration, the post-frustration behavior of 5 subjects was ranked as less aggressive than their pre-frustration behavior. The evidence countering the frustration-aggression hypothesis is even more striking when the constructively trained group is considered; 11 of the 20 Ss in this group behaved less aggressively after frustration, while only 6 behaved more aggressively. Furthermore, it does not seem reasonable to interpret the general decrease of aggressiveness evidenced by the constructive group and the increase of constructiveness evidenced by 12 members of this group as "substitute activity." It would seem to be more consistent with objective psychological theory to interpret these results in terms of a general theory of adjustment rather than in terms of a specific mode of response such as aggression.

The frustration-regression theory and Maier's interpretation of postfrustration behavior as behavior without a goal are not supported by the data. While growth and constructiveness as defined in this study are not synonymous, there is a close relationship between these two concepts. Therefore, to interpret the increase of constructiveness as evidenced by 16 of the 40 subjects in this experiment in terms of regression or behavior without a goal does not seem to be a valid theoretical procedure. While 22 Ss did evidence less constructiveness after frustration, it is obvious that the change of behavior is not necessarily in the direction of regression. Previous training is at least one factor which determines this change of direction.

It should be noted that in the experiment presented here the two major hypotheses are interdependent. The data used for testing the two hypotheses were obtained from the same population and the behavior of each S was treated in terms of aggressiveness and constructiveness. All other things being equal, a high degree of constructiveness was associated with a low degree of aggressiveness, and vice versa, as indicated by a rank order correlation of $-.83$ between aggressive and constructive ranks of the 40 subjects.

The effects of prefrustration training in this experiment were not invariant. Six individuals within the constructively trained group behaved more aggressively after frustration, and four Ss in the aggressively trained group behaved more constructively after frustration. This indicates that while the experimental training was a significant factor in terms of the behavior of the group, the total past history of the individual must be considered in predicting and understanding his behavior after frustration.

It has been demonstrated that postfrustration behavior cannot be treated only in terms of the stimulus conditions associated with the frustration. The external stimulus conditions of the frustrating situation were identical for the aggressive and constructive groups, while the previous training of the groups differed.

Therefore, in this case the previous training was the significant factor which determined the differences of the change of behavior in the two groups after frustration. It is suggested that previous experience in situations similar to that in which frustration occurs is one factor which must be considered in the understanding of postfrustration behavior.

The results of this single experiment are presented neither as conclusive evidence of the inadequacy of present frustration theories nor as final evidence of the effects of previous experience on postfrustration behavior. For the writer, the most significant result is a realization of the need for further experimental study in this area.

Anxiety and Complex Learning

David S. Palermo, Alfred Castaneda, and Boyd R. McCandless

Although motivation is one of the more important variables in the learning process, it is at the same time one which is not particularly well understood. Systematic investigation involving the manipulation of the strength of motivation through the use of shock or anxiety-producing instructions has produced much useful data. Procedures such as shock, however, are not employed, for ethical reasons, with children. Professors Palermo, Castaneda, and McCandless circumvent this problem by administering a paper-and-pencil inventory, the Children's Manifest Anxiety Scale (CMAS), and select children at the extremes of the distribution and determine their rates of learning on a complex task. Their assumption is that children scoring high on the CMAS are more highly motivated than low-scoring children. Their theoretical formulations are supported empirically.

The Taylor scale of manifest anxiety, a measure of motivation, has been used to relate the effects of different motivational levels to the performance of adult Ss in a variety of learning situations. The results of these experiments suggest that the performance of high anxious Ss, when compared with low anxious Ss, is superior in simple learning situations such as classical conditioning but inferior in more complex tasks such as trial-and-error learning.

In an attempt to broaden the use of the Taylor scale, Castaneda, McCandless, and Palermo (1956) have recently revised the scale so that it is applicable to children in the fourth, fifth, and sixth grades. It was felt that problems similar in nature to those investigated with adults might be studied with children if such a scale were available.

SOURCE: Adapted and abridged from D. Palermo, A. Castaneda, and B. McCandless, "The Relationship of Anxiety in Children to Performance in a Complex Learning Task." *Child Development,* 1956, 27, 333–337. (With permission of the authors and the Society for Research in Child Development.)

According to the theory based on Hull (1943) and extended by Spence (1953), the effects of increases in motivational level on performance depend upon the relative strength of the correct and incorrect or competing responses. If the correct response is dominant (strongest) over those incorrect responses competing with it, or if it is the only response aroused in the situation, then an increase in motivation should facilitate performance. Thus, in the case of eyelid conditioning, if it is assumed that the correct response is dominant and there are few competing responses, it would be expected that an increase in motivation would lead to superior performance.

However, in more complex learning situations where one or more competing incorrect responses are dominant, the theory would predict an impairment in performance as a result of an increase in motivation. The present investigation is concerned with attempting to determine the relationship of anxiety or motivation in children to performance in such a situation. Ss were required to learn to turn off different colored lights by the buttons which were connected to them. In this situation, if the correct response is not dominant, it would be expected that an increase in motivation should lead to poorer performance.

Method

Subjects

A total of 36 Ss from the standardization population of the children's form of the Taylor scale were used as Ss. These Ss were selected from four fourth grade classes in three Iowa City public schools on the basis of extreme scores on the scale. The anxious group consisted of 9 girls and 9 boys drawn at random from those Ss who participated in this study and whose scores fell approximately in the upper 20 per cent of the total standardization group, while the nonanxious group was composed of 9 girls and 9 boys drawn at random from those Ss who participated in this study and falling approximately in the lower 20 per cent. Anxiety scores ranged from 3 to 11 for the nonanxious group, and from 23 to 33 for the anxious Ss.

Apparatus and Procedure

The apparatus consisted of a box 13 by 12½ inches painted flat black. Projecting from its base was a sloping response panel approximately 7½ by 9½ by 13 inches. Two push buttons were arranged on this panel on a horizontal plane spaced 6 inches apart and 2 inches from S's edge of the panel and toward its center. On the panel between, but 2½ inches above, the two push buttons was a green jeweled reflector illuminated by a 6.3 volt pilot lamp. Centered 4 inches above the panel was a 1-inch diameter aperture of flashed opal glass. Housed behind the aperture were four colored lights: red, blue, amber, and white. The construction of the apparatus was such that by means of a rotary selector switch any single light could be activated, and by means of a toggle switch either one of the two buttons could be set to turn it off. If the correct button was selected, the light went off and the green light on the response panel was activated. Incorrect responses affected neither the stimulus light nor the green light on the response panel.

All Ss were given 20 trials. All of the lights did not appear with equal frequency, but the order was random except that no single light appeared twice in succession. Each light remained on until the correct response was made. Two of the lights were turned out by one button, and two were turned out by the other button.

The instructions were designed to indicate to S that he was to learn which button turned off each light, and that if an error was made, correction would be allowed.

Results and Discussion

Figure 7.1 presents the learning curves of the anxious and the nonanxious Ss in terms of errors in four blocks of five trials. It will be observed that with respect to each block of trials the nonanxious Ss were superior to the anxious Ss.

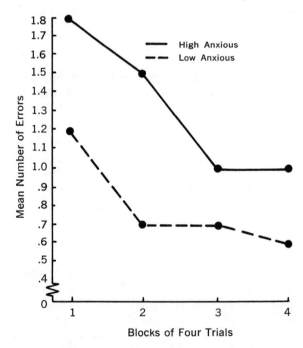

Figure 7.1 Error curves for the anxious and nonanxious Ss plotted in blocks of 5 trials.

An analysis of variance based upon these data indicate there is a significant decrease in errors over blocks of trials ($F = 5.49$; $df = 3$ and 102; $p < .005$). More important, however, is the fact that the over-all differences between the errors made by the anxious and nonanxious groups is significant $(F = 4.71; df = 1$ and $34; p < .05)$.

Previous experiments using the adult form of the Taylor scale have indicated that in complex learning situations where the dominant response is not correct, the anxious (high motivation) Ss show inferior performance to that of the non-anxious (low motivation) Ss. The present results are in line with previous work, suggesting that the theory applied to adult Ss is applicable in the present study with children and that the children's anxiety scale is a useful measure of motivational level.

As was stated previously, according to the theory the effects of increases in motivation on performance depend upon the relative strength of the correct and incorrect responses aroused by the experimental situation. The results of the present study and those of previous studies suggest that specific attention should be given to the performance of anxious and nonanxious Ss in situations where the strength of the correct and incorrect responses may be determined. For example, with problems such as the present one, it might be expected that the differences between the anxious and nonanxious Ss would increase with increases in the number of light-button combinations, since there would be a greater probability that more strong competing responses would be aroused. In discrimination-learning problems it would be expected that difficult discriminations would be easier for the nonanxious than for the anxious. In the area of verbal learning it might be expected that a list of words of high association value and low intralist similarity would be easier for anxious Ss than for nonanxious Ss.

Anxiety, Isolation, and Reinforcer Effectiveness

Richard Walters and Edward Ray

The concept of secondary—or acquired—drives plays a crucial role in many theories of child behavior. Since acquired drives are given the same theoretical properties as primary drives, it is necessary to conduct experiments to determine if this assumption is valid. Professor Walters and his colleagues report an experiment in which the strength of a dependency need or motive was manipulated under two conditions. According to the theory, the two conditions should not have influenced the strength of the dependency drive. The results failed to support this expectation, prompting the investigators to hypothesize a more generalized drive theory in which anxiety plays a crucial role.

SOURCE: Adapted and abridged from Richard Walters and Edward Ray, "Anxiety, Isolation, and Susceptibility to Social Influence." *Journal of Personality*, 1960, 28, 358–367. (With permission of the senior author and Duke University Press.)

During the past two decades there have been numerous reports of the effects of maternal deprivation on the social development of children. The majority of studies are either psychoanalytically oriented or employ neo-Hullian concepts involving the assumption of an acquired dependency drive. The evidence for the latter position consists only of the occurrence of dependency behavior that does not appear to reduce a biological drive.

More recently, Gewirtz (1956, 1957) has employed Skinner's (1953) concepts in a learning-theory analysis of the effects of maternal deprivation on dependency behavior. This analysis involves a definition of drive in terms of experimental operations that affect the relative efficacy of reinforcers. Unfortunately, it also involves the questionable assumption that social deprivation operates analogously to food deprivation and arouses a social drive that is, in turn, analogous to primary appetitive drives, e.g., hunger and thirst.

Gewirtz' analysis has been tested in two experiments. In the first of their reports the authors demonstrated that children who had experienced a brief period of social isolation conditioned more readily in a simple discrimination-learning situation than did children who had not been isolated. In their second experiment they found that children who had experienced a brief period of social interaction with an adult conditioned more slowly than either isolated or non-isolated subjects. Gewirtz and Baer interpret these results as showing that brief social isolation arouses a social drive and that this drive is reduced through social satiation.

These studies can be criticized on the grounds that the isolation procedure aroused anxiety and that the findings attributed to the arousal of a social drive could, in fact, have been due to the arousal of anxiety. This position is consistent with Brown's (1953) formulation that the important motivating component of many so-called acquired drives is, in fact, anxiety.

There is evidence that first-born Ss appear to be more anxious about social isolation than are later-born Ss, a finding which was interpreted as the result of differential dependency training. In light of this finding, some control of birth order appeared desirable in an experiment designed to investigate the effects of social isolation and anxiety on reinforcer effectiveness.

The present study may be regarded, in some respects, as a replication of the Gewirtz and Baer experiments. Two groups of socially isolated Ss, one anxious and one nonanxious, were compared with two equivalent socially satiated groups; equal numbers of first-born and later-born Ss were assigned to each group. It was predicted that anxiety, rather than social isolation, would prove to be the major determinant of the effectiveness of social reinforcers.

Method

Subjects

Ss were 20 first-born and 20 later-born Grade I and Grade II boys. Their ages ranged from 6 years, 1 month, to 8 years, 8 months, with a mean age of 7 years,

2 months. Five first-born Ss and five later-born Ss were assigned randomly to each of the four experimental conditions.

Procedure

Isolation with anxiety. A male graduate student in his middle twenties served as E's assistant. He was a complete stranger to the children and appeared at the school only when his services were required in the experiment. The assistant knocked on the classroom door and, unless the teacher herself answered, asked for the teacher by name. By prior arrangement the teacher called S to the door and said, "I want you to go with this man." The assistant then said to S: "Come with me into the next building." He did not introduce himself or explain why S was being taken out of the class. He initiated no conversation, answered S's questions in a brief, aloof manner, and deliberately avoided giving any information about the nature of the experiment. He conducted S through the primary school, across the school yard, and into the basement of an adjacent junior high school building where the conditioning procedures were carried out. S was brought to the outer of two adjoining rooms and told:

"We have something for you to do, but we are not ready yet. You wait in this room until we fix the machine. You sit here (indicating an adult-size chair), and I shall be back for you in a little while when the machine is ready. Do not touch anything in the room and do not leave the room until I come for you."

The assistant then joined E in the inner room, from which observation of S was possible. At the end of a 20-minute isolation period, the assistant came out of the inner room, brought S into the experimental room, and, without any other introduction to E, said: "I want you to stay with this man. He will show you what to do."

Isolation without anxiety. The school secretary, who was well known to all the children, went to the classroom and asked S if he would like to come to the next building to play a game. During the walk to the junior high school, she offered to hold S's hand and did everything possible to make him feel at ease. She conducted S to the exeperimental room and introduced E by saying:

"This is a friend of mine, Mr. Ray. I want you to play a game with him, but I'm afraid the game is broken right now. I do not want you to miss your turn, so why don't you wait in this room (indicating the adjoining room) while we fix it. It won't take long. You can sit here (indicating a child-size chair), and Mr. Ray will call you as soon as the game is ready. Be a good boy and don't come out until you are called."

The secretary then returned to her office. After 20 minutes had elapsed, E brought S into the experimental room, introduced himself once more, and proceeded with the "game."

Satiation with anxiety. Gewirtz and Baer used interaction with an adult E as a satiation condition. In their experiment, E conversed with S in a friendly manner, offered cutting and drawing materials, and extended praise and approval whenever it could be given appropriately. This procedure was not used in the present experiment on the grounds that it might have reduced the extent to which the presence of a strange adult would serve to arouse anxiety. Instead, it was decided to allow S to be satiated by his playmates on the playground or in the classroom.

The assistant fetched S immediately after a midmorning or noonhour break, during which period, subsequent questioning revealed, all Ss had been interacting with their friends for a minimum of 20 minutes. Activities consisted of playing hockey or tag, sliding on the ice, or playing indoor games in the classroom. Ss in this group were treated in exactly the same manner as Ss in the isolated-anxious group except that, immediately on arrival at the experimental room, E's assistant presented S to E, saying: "You stay with this man. He will show you what to do."

Satiation without anxiety. The secretary called for S immediately after the midmorning or the noonhour break. She treated him in the same manner as she treated isolated nonanxious Ss. Upon entering the experimental room she introduced S to E by saying: "This is a friend of mine, Mr. Ray. He wants to play a game with you. He will show you how it works. You stay here and play, and I shall see you later."

Conditioning Procedure

Following the experimental treatments, S was conditioned by a procedure that has been described in detail by Gerwitz and Baer. S's task was to drop a marble into one of two holes at the forward top of a box, from which S picked it up and again dropped it into one of the holes. To prevent the possible operation of clicks as secondary reinforcers, the box and tray were lined with felt; otherwise, the apparatus was essentially the same as that used by Gewirtz and Baer. Only one marble was used, in contrast to the six differently colored marbles used in the Gewirtz and Baer experiment; during the pretesting period it was found that, if more than one marble was available, S sometimes tried to pick up two at once and, as a result, would drop one marble on the floor. The use of a single marble thus safeguarded against unnecessary interruptions of the conditioning procedure.

The conditioning procedure was the same as that used by Gewirtz and Baer. E told S to keep dropping the marble into one of the holes. During the first four minutes (the baseline period) E gave no reinforcement. Beginning with the fifth minute, E proceeded to dispense reinforcers according to a predetermined schedule whenever S dropped the marble into the hole preferred *least* during the last minute of the baseline period (the correct response).

Using verbal approval ("Hm-hmm!" "Good!" "A good one!" or "Fine!") as a reinforcer, E reinforced each correct response until S had made 10 consecutive correct responses. He then reinforced every other correct response until five additional correct responses had been made. After this, E gave five more reinforcements, one for each third correct response. Finally, E reinforced only every fifth correct response, the latter schedule being continued until 10 minutes of reinforced play had been completed. The above procedure was qualified by three conventions, again in accordance with the procedure of Gewirtz and Baer: (a)

Every correct response that immediately followed an incorrect response was reinforced. (b) If S made five consecutive incorrect responses, E began the schedule again, halving the number of reinforcers called for at each ratio level until the reinforcement ratio last employed was again in effect. (c) If S made 20 successive incorrect responses, E said, "You can put the marbles in either hole."

Reinforcer-Effectiveness Score

The numbers of marbles dropped in the correct and incorrect holes during each minute of play were recorded. The relative frequency of a correct response was calculated for each minute by dividing the number of correct responses by the corresponding total number of responses. The relative frequency of the correct response of the fourth (last unreinforced) minute of play was then subtracted from the median relative frequency of the correct response during the ten 1-minute reinforcement periods. This manner of assessing reinforcer effectiveness is the same as that used by Gewirtz and Baer.

Results

Table 7.1 presents the mean reinforcement-effectiveness scores for the experimental groups. It is quite evident that reinforcement was most effective for those Ss for whom isolation had been associated with anxiety.

TABLE 7.1. *Mean Reinforcer-Effectiveness Score*
(N = 5 in Each Group)

GROUP	CATEGORY	ANXIOUS	NONANXIOUS
Isolated	First-born	0.337	0.081
	Later-born	0.345	0.159
Nonisolated	First-born	0.247	0.120
	Later-born	0.100	0.087

Bartlett's test showed that slight heterogeneity of variance was present $(x^2 = 10.255; p < .05 < .01)$. In view of the Norton study, cited by Lindquist (1953), analysis of variance was nevertheless carried out. This analysis yielded a highly significant difference between anxious and nonanxious Ss $(p < .005)$ and a smaller difference between isolated and nonisolated Ss $(p < .05)$. No difference was found between first-born and later-born Ss.

Figure 7.2 indicates the relative effectiveness of the conditioning procedure for Ss under each of the four experimental conditions. Both anxiety groups show evidence of acquisition; by contrast, the two nonanxiety groups show little change in performance.

Discussion

The results of this study give strong support to the hypothesis that anxiety, not isolation by itself, is the major factor affecting rate of conditioning. The relatively small difference between isolated and nonisolated Ss has to be interpreted with

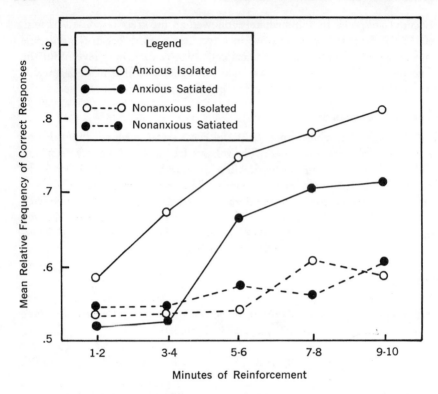

Figure 7.2 Mean relative frequency of correct responses on each of 5 pairs of trials for each of the 4 experimental groups.

caution. With heterogeneity of variance present, a difference significant only at the .05 level may not justify rejection of the null hypothesis. Moreover, any difference that exists may represent a secondary effect of anxiety. Some anxiety was perhaps aroused in the supposedly nonanxious isolated Ss as a result of their being left alone in a strange setting for 20 minutes. In addition, the anxiety aroused in anxious isolated Ss may have been increased both by their being left alone and by the statement that the "machine was being fixed."

In recent years psychologists have tended to postulate more and more acquired drives — dependency, aggression, curiosity, affiliation, dissonance. The major difficulty with these constructs is that there are no discriminable antecedent conditions which would allow them to be defined without reference to the behavior they are called upon to explain. The process by which fears are acquired is, on the other hand, relatively well understood. It seems reasonable to believe that during the history of the individual certain types of response are differentially reinforced as a result of anxiety reduction. Among these responses are undoubtedly those that are usually classed as dependent or affiliative. As these responses become more and more prepotent in the individual's repertory, they probably receive reinforcement even in situations in which anxiety reduction does not take place. In this way, strong habitual patterns of response are built up, e.g., patterns of behaving dependently or aggressively. There is no reason to suppose, however, that in this process "habits have become drives."[1]

Gewirtz (1957) has carefully analyzed the possible effects of schedules of reinforcement on the dependency behavior of socially deprived — i.e., institutionalized — children. To assume, however, that isolation (and, by implication, separation or maternal deprivation) activates a social drive in no way advances his analysis. In contrast, the concept of anxiety (in the sense of an emotional response to stimuli that have been associated with discomfort and pain) may help to explain differences among children in their initial responses to separation. If experiences of isolation (e.g., as a technique of punishment) or separation have been previously accompanied by pain, the child's emotional response should be relatively strong. The behavior initially elicited will presumably depend on the child's past history in terms of positive and negative reinforcements. His subsequent behavior during the separation period, as Gewirtz has pointed out, will depend on the manner in which reinforcers are dispensed by his substitute caretakers.

NOTE

[1] The senior author has, in previous publications (e.g., Bandura and Walters 1959), employed concepts such as dependency drive, aggressive drive, and drive to identify. It now appears to him, however, that the phenomena that such "drives" are called upon to explain can be equally well, and more parsimoniously, explained by reference to the concept of anxiety and to the effects of a variable interval reinforcement schedule during which reinforcements are dispensed only when the individual is responding at a high rate or with very great intensity.

Social Class and Incentive Effectiveness

Glenn Terrell, K. Durkin, and M. Wiesley

The basic hypothesis tested in this study is that socioeconomic level is related to motivation. More specifically, the authors hypothesize that middle-class children are motivated by a broad variety of material and nonmaterial incentives, while lower-class children are more motivated by material incentives. The results of the experiment support the hypothesis. One might speculate that middle-class parents emphasize achievement values for their own sake, or it is possible that the middle-class children, having had considerable prior experience with the material incentives, are not usually motivated by them. The outcome of the experiment is also consistent

SOURCE: Adapted and abridged from Glenn Terrell, K. Durkin, and M. Wiesley, "Social Class and the Nature of the Incentive in Discrimination Learning." *Journal of Abnormal and Social Psychology*, 1959, 59, 270–272. (With permission of the authors and the American Psychological Association.)

with a homeostatic theory of drive and drive reduction. Finally, the study has implications for dealing with culturally deprived children in the schools.

Previous research has suggested interesting differences in the relative effectiveness of material and nonmaterial incentives for children of different social-class backgrounds. In an experiment involving the solution of a series of tasks, it was found that middle-class subjects (Ss) maintained approximately the same level of achievement motivation when told they had reached a norm as when they were promised a sum of money. The motivation of lower-class Ss, on the other hand, dropped significantly when the material reward was absent. Terrell and Kennedy (1957) found that children, a preponderance of whom were from a rural background, require significantly more trials to learn a "larger-than" response when given only a light flash as an indication of a correct response than when given a series of material incentives, including candy, praise, token, and reproof. In a similar experiment performed with middle-class children, Terrell (1958) found that children assigned to the light flash condition learned somewhat faster than those who received candy.

From the foregoing, it would be predicted that an interaction exists between social class and the nature of the incentive. Specifically, it was believed that a nonmaterial incentive is as effective as a material incentive for middle-class Ss, whereas for lower-class Ss a material incentive is more effective than a nonmaterial one. The present experiment was designed to test this belief. It is important to note that while Douvan studied the relationship between these variables, using a measure of motivation as a criterion variable, this paper is a report of a discrimination learning experiment, involving an acquisition measure as a dependent variable.

Method

Subjects

There were 12 Ss in each of the following age categories: 5-, 6-, 10-, and 11-year-olds, with an equal number of boys and girls in each age group. The school from which Ss for this experiment were drawn very appropriately contains children from a wide variety of social-class backgrounds. Warner's Index of Status Characteristics (Warner, Meeker, and Eels 1949) was the measure used to define class position. In the present study, all Ss designated as middle class fell into either the upper-middle or the lower-middle classes of Warner's schema, while Ss with scores placing them in Warner's upper-lower and lower-lower classes constituted the lower class.

Materials

There were three pairs of three-dimensional geometric figures in the shape of cubes, cones, and cylinders. The small member of each stimulus set had a basal area of 4 square inches, while the large member had a basal area of 8 square inches. These stimuli are hereafter referred to as the training stimulus sets. A third cube with a basal area of 16 square inches was used in a transposition test, along with the 8-square-inch cube. These stimuli are hereafter referred to as the test stimuli. The order of presenting the stimuli and the position of the positive, large-size, stimulus were randomized alike for each S.

Additional apparatus consisted of a 16 × 24 × 4 inch box which contained the batteries and circuits necessary to operate a signal light. Two jacks and two push-button mounts were on top of the box. The stimuli were placed into the jacks on each trial. Locked onto the rear edge of the box was a 10 × 16 × ¼ inch panel board which contained the signal light. The circuits were arranged so that a correct response, pushing the button at the base of the large stimulus, caused the light to go on.

Design

There were two experimental groups. Following each correct response, one group of Ss received a nonmaterial reward, a light flash, while the Ss of the other group received a material reward, a small piece of candy, in addition to the light flash. Within each of the two levels of social class, Ss were randomly assigned to the two incentive conditions, making a total of 12 Ss in each treatment-level combination.

Procedure

The Ss were tested individually. Each S received the following instructions: "This is a game where I want you to try to choose one of these (E points to the training stimulus sets), and push the button in front of the one you choose. If you are right, this little light will go on. If you are wrong, the light will not go on. Now remember, the game is to see how quickly you can learn to choose the one that makes the light go on."

The last sentence was repeated after every tenth trial. Immediately after reaching a criterion of 9 of 10 correct responses, each S was given a four-trial transposition test on the test stimuli. The same differential incentive conditions employed during the acquisition trials were continued during the test trials.

Results and Discussion

The original design called for an analysis of variance of the mean number of trials to the criterion and mean number of transposition responses. All Ss except one transposed on every trial, making an analysis of transposition data useless. In the case of the number of trials to the criterion, the homogeneity and normality assumptions were far from met. Also, the criterial means and variances were correlated. For these reasons, it seemed advisable to subject these data to a nonparametric test. Wilson's chi-square technique makes possible the test of hypotheses concerning main and interaction effects ordinarily tested by a two-way analysis of variance.

Table 7.2 contains the training means and SDs. As can be seen from this table, a striking interaction exists between social class and the type of incentive. Middle-class children learn more quickly when given a nonmaterial incentive than when given a material incentive, while the reverse is true of lower-class children. The overall means for social class are identical, while the difference between over-all incentive means is negligible.

TABLE 7.2. *Means and SDs of Trials to Criterion in Training*
(Each treatment group $N = 20$)

	Material Incentive					
	PRESENT		ABSENT		TOTAL	
	Mean	SD	Mean	SD	Mean	SD
Middle	7.91	8.33	3.50	2.58	5.70	6.72
Lower	3.41	3.02	8.00	5.15	5.70	4.80
Total	5.66	6.66	5.75	4.65		

Table 7.3 contains frequencies above and below the median for each of the incentive-class combinations in number of trials to the criterion. All analyses

TABLE 7.3. *Frequencies Above and Below the Median in Number of Trials to Criterion for Each Incentive-Class Combination*

FREQUENCY	INCENTIVE			
	Middle Class		Lower Class	
	Material	Nonmaterial	Material	Nonmaterial
Above Median	6	7	5	12
Below Median	6	5	7	0

and subsequent discussion are based on the data of Table 7.3. The predicted interaction is apparent in this table, and to a significant degree. The chi-square value for the interaction is 5.17, which with one degree of freedom reaches significance at about the .03 significance level. The direction of the interaction is the same for ages 5 and 6 as well as for ages 10 and 11. No analyses of interaction effects were made for these ages independently, since the frequencies were very small. The chi-square test for main effects of class was nonsignificant, while the test of main effects of incentive was significant at the .05 level. There was a significant tendency for Ss assigned to the material incentive condition to learn more quickly than those Ss assigned to the nonmaterial incentive treatment. This finding is rendered rather meaningless in view of the significant interaction present in this experiment.

Several interesting implications arise from this experiment. There is evidence to indicate that parents of middle-class children place a greater emphasis on learning for learning's sake than do parents of lower-class children. Additional evidence in support of this hypothesis was found in the aforementioned experiment by Terrell (1958), in which middle-class Ss indicated in a questionnaire given to them following the experiment that they would rather "do something for the fun of it" than to be "promised or given something for doing it." It would appear that the most important feature in the learning of middle-class Ss is merely some indication that they are progressing. It is strikingly apparent in Table 7.3, however, that the presence of a material incentive is very important to lower-class Ss. It is possible that the lower-class child is too preoccupied with obtaining the material, day-to-day necessities of life to have the opportunity to learn the value of less material, symbolic incentives. Davis (1941, 1943) suggests such a possibility. Additionally, since it is likely that the lower-class child generally is more deprived of the specific material incentive, candy, used in the present study, this deprivation may result in an intensification of his desire for candy. It would be interesting to know whether or not the same results would be obtained in experiments employing other material incentives such as toys, clothing, movie tickets, and the like.

Finally, there is a possibility that the middle-class child is more adept than the lower-class child at engaging in effective imaginative activity during learning.[1] If this be the case, it would seem that the middle-class child would learn more effectively under a symbolic, nonmaterial type incentive than lower-class children.

NOTE

[1] The writers are indebted to Howard E. Gruber for this interesting suggestion.

Manipulation Drive

Harry Harlow, Margaret K. Harlow, and D. R. Meyer

Most theories of learning, that include reinforcement as a basic condition, usually accept a homeostatic position. According to this position an organism is motivated by a state of physiological or psychological imbalance and is reinforced by a stimulus that produces homeostasis. Professor Harlow and his associates provide evidence for the existence of an externally elicited drive, manipulation, which is not channeled by an external reinforcer. This evidence is consistent with those theories of child behavior postulating an intrinsic curiosity motive. Many child development experts are concerned that the curiosity drive of young children is systematically repressed. Professor Harlow shows that such repression may also inhibit the occurrence of important learning experiences.

source: Adapted and abridged from Harry Harlow, Margaret K. Harlow, and D. R. Meyer, "Learning Motivated by a Manipulation Drive." *Journal of Experimental Psychology*, 1950, 40, 228–234. (With permission of the authors and the American Psychological Association.)

A preliminary study of puzzle solution in four rhesus monkeys suggested that a manipulation drive might operate in these animals, and with sufficient strength to provide adequate motivation for learning. Psychologists have traditionally utilized the homeostatic drives in learning studies with subhuman animals, and have neglected, if not actually been blind to, the importance of externally elicited drives in learning.

The primary purpose of this study is to investigate the performance of monkeys on mechanical puzzles whose manipulation is accompanied by no extrinsic reward. A secondary purpose is to investigate the effect of the subsequent introduction of a food reward.

The study is comparable to the Blodgett (1929) and the Tolman and Honzik (1930) latent learning experiments, and the repetition of the Blodgett experiment by Reynolds (1945), in that the initial training was conducted without special incentives, and later on training food incentives were introduced. The study differs from the earlier studies, however, in that the design of the present investigation places emphasis on the performance during the nonreward periods, whereas the design of the other investigations places emphasis on the performance after the introduction of reward.

Method

Subjects

Subjects in this investigation were eight rhesus monkeys with previous laboratory experience confined to discrimination, delayed reaction, and multiple discrimination reversal learning problems. The animals were matched in pairs and assigned to two groups on the basis of emotionality as judged by one person familiar with all the subjects under both living cage and experimental conditions. Group A, the experimental animals, contained Monkeys 138, 143, 150, and 151. Group B, the matched control subjects, included Monkeys 140, 146, 142, and 147.

Apparatus

The essential experimental apparatus, illustrated in Figure 7.3, consisted of a metal-edged unpainted wooden base to which was attached, flush, a hasp restrained by a hook which was, in turn, restrained by a pin. The pin and hook are referred to as Restraining Devices 1 and 2, respectively, and had to be opened in serial order before the hasp, referred to as Device 3, could be raised. The apparatus was screwed to a wooden perch 24 inches long and 6 inches wide fastened to one side of an inside living cage 6 feet long, 2½ feet wide, and 6 feet high. The animals at all times had access, through a runway, to an outside living cage 4 by 2½ by 6 feet.

For tests conducted in the experimental room a puzzle identical with the one described except for a food-well one inch in diameter cut in the board and covered by the hasp, was screwed onto a 24 by 10 inch test tray placed on the floor of a

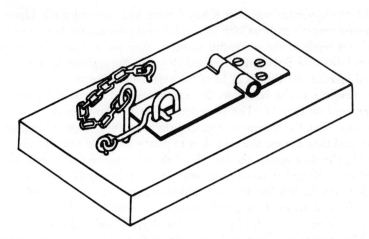

Figure 7.3 Mechanical puzzle apparatus. See text for a description of apparatus used for tests conducted in the experimental room.

24 by 24 by 24 inch cage. A restraining cage 27 by 26 by 16½ inches adjoined the test cage.

Procedure

Throughout the experiment each subject was housed in individual quarters consisting of an inside and outside cage, and fed daily, as is the customary procedure for the colony, between 5:30 and 6:00 P.M.

Tests without food reward. During the first 10 days of the investigation, Group A subjects had the assembled puzzle attached to their perches, and Group B subjects had the puzzle attached with the restraining devices unassembled and the hasp raised. At convenient times, an experimenter checked the puzzles in all the cages and recorded any successful manipulations that had occurred. Approximately 50 checks were made on each animal in the 10-day period. Any devices released by Group A subjects were reset at the time of the check. It was planned to unfasten any devices found assembled at the checking time for Group B subjects, but no instance of assembling behavior occurred. On both the 11th and the 12th days, 10 checks were made on each subject at hourly intervals.

On both Days 13 and 14 five 5-minute observations one hour apart were made on each subject. For the observation, the experimenter assembled the puzzle, left the cage, started the stopwatch, and observed from outside the cage without staring directly at the animal. A record was made in seconds of the time the subject initially touched the puzzle, released the restraining devices, and lifted the hasp. The order in which the parts were touched or manipulated was also recorded. At the conclusion of each of the observations except the last one on

Day 14, the apparatus was reset if any devices had been released. Upon the experimenter's return an hour later or the following day for the next observation, a record was made of the successful manipulations accomplished in the interval.

Tests With and Subsequent to Food Reward. Approximately one hour before the daily feeding on Days 4 to 13 of the experiment, the animals in both groups were brought into the laboratory for adaptation to a special test situation to be administered on Day 14. The procedure on each adaptation day was to release the animal from the transport cage into the restraining cage, giving him a few raisins, and then to raise the cage door to permit entrance into the adjoining test cage. On the floor against the far side of the test cage rested a standard test tray 24 inches by 10 inches, containing two 1-inch food-wells 12 inches apart, center to center. On the first five days, the subject obtained raisins from both food-wells, took additional raisins introduced through the cage bars, then returned to the restraining cage. On each of the next five days, 20 delayed reaction trials were run. The monkey was kept in the restraining cage until the experimenter baited one food-well and covered both wells with identical objects. The restraining cage door was then opened and the monkey allowed to displace the object and take the raisin. He then returned to the restraining cage and awaited the next trial. These tests were run merely to accustom the Group A animals to obtaining hidden raisins in the experimental cage situation. Group B animals were given identical training so that general adaptation would be constant for both groups.

The special puzzle test with food reward was conducted on Day 14 approximately two hours after the last living cage observation. Each Group A monkey was released into the restraining cage as on previous days. The tray in the test cage, however, now had the puzzle apparatus attached to it. While the animal watched, the food-well was baited with a raisin, the hasp lowered, and the restraining devices set. The restraining cage door was opened and the animal allowed to enter the test cage. A record was made of behavior for a period using the procedure described for Days 13 and 14 on the nonreward tests. The monkey was then returned to the living cage and immediately given a trial on his own puzzle apparatus, which was baited in his presense with a raisin crushed beneath the hasp. A five-minute observation was made from outside the cage. The apparatus was reassembled immediately (this time without food) while the animal watched, and behavior was once more observed for five minutes.

Results

Tests Without Food Reward

The data of Table 7.4 present for each subject the total number of Day 13 and 14 solutions in 10 tests. A solution is defined as release of both restraining devices. The table also shows the number of solutions accomplished within 60 seconds of initial contact with the apparatus.

The Group A monkeys made a total of 31 solutions and the Group B monkeys

TABLE 7.4. *Puzzle Solutions on Days 13 and 14*

Total Solutions

Group A			Group B
SUBJECT	SOLUTIONS	SOLUTIONS	SUBJECT
138	8	1	140
143	6	1	146
150	9	2	142
151	8	0	147
Total	31	4	

Solutions Attained Within 60 Seconds

Group A			Group B
SUBJECT	SOLUTIONS	SOLUTIONS	SUBJECT
138	5	0	140
143	3	0	146
150	7	0	142
151	7	0	147
Total	22	0	

a total of 4 solutions in 40 trials. The difference is significant at the 1 per cent confidence level as determined by a *t*-test for related measures. There was no overlapping in the scores made by the individual animals of the two groups. None of the Group B monkeys ever solved the problem within 60 seconds of initial contact, whereas all the Group A monkeys solved the problem three or more times within this time limit. Over 50 per cent of all solutions by the Group A monkeys were made in 20 seconds or less, and over 35 per cent were made in 10 seconds or less. Monkey 151 twice failed to touch the puzzle in the five-minute test period but solved the problem without error in less than five seconds when the experimenter passed to the next cage.

The number of errors made before initial solution on Days 13 and/or 14 were examined. An error is defined as contact with or manipulation of any device out of sequence, or any incorrect manipulation of the restraining devices. Three of the four Group A animals made the initial solution in the first observation period and without error. All Group B monkeys made errors before the initial solution, and one monkey failed to solve the problem during the 10 five-minute tests. The difference between the two groups as determined by a *t*-test of related measures, is significant at the 1 per cent confidence level.

A comparison of the total number of correct and erroneous responses of the Group A and Group B monkeys indicates that all Group A monkeys made more than twice as many correct as incorrect responses, whereas all Group B monkeys made more than twice as many incorrect as correct responses. The differences are again significant at the 1 per cent confidence level as measured by a x^2 test of independence.

A further indication of the difference in proficiency of the two groups lies in the finding that the Group A monkeys made *no errors* in 21 of the 38 times that puzzle manipulations were observed, while the Group B monkeys always made errors in the 25 times that puzzle manipulations were observed.

TABLE 7.5. *Total Correct and Incorrect Responses on Days 13 and 14*

			CORRECT R
SUBJECT	CORRECT RESPONSES	ERROR RESPONSES	INCORRECT R
140	7	16	0.4
146	4	24	0.2
142	7	19	0.4
147	2	15	0.1

(Group B)

Solution of the problem, it will be recalled, was defined in terms of releasing both Restraining Devices 1 and 2. Responses to Device 3 in the five-minute observation periods were available (a finding confirmed in subsequent study), even though all Group A monkeys invariably displaced the hasp in the one-hour period between observations. Subject 138 ignored the hasp in 1 of 8 solutions, Monkey 143 in 2 of 6 solutions, Monkey 150 in 8 of 9 solutions, and Monkey 151 in none of 8 solutions.

Tests With and Subsequent to Food Reward

The data show that in three of the four Group A subjects, the introduction of food rewards seriously disrupted the efficient puzzle solution which they had repeatedly demonstrated previously. In the experimental room test with food reward, Monkey 143 touched the apparatus and then retreated and refused to work, while Monkeys 138 and 150 worked on the problem, but failed after making 5 and 9 errors, respectively. On the food trial in the home cage, Subject 138 failed again, and the other three subjects made errors before their successful manipulations. It is to be noted that Monkey 143 performed very poorly in the subsequent home cage test without food.

The degree of disruption of the acquired puzzle responses in the case of Monkeys 138, 143, and 150 during and following the introduction of food is indicated by their total of 39 errors in these three five-minute tests, although they had made a total of only 17 errors in the previous 10 five-minute tests. The differences in the *kind of errors* is also very striking. In the initial 10 tests without food reward, the monkeys *never* approached the problem by touching the hasp first; in the subsequent tests, all three monkeys *always* erred by attacking (literally) the hasp first. In the initial 10 tests without food reward the three monkeys had made a total of 2, 2, and 0 hasp errors, respectively in contrast to the 8, 8, and 7 hasp errors made by the same monkeys subsequently.

Discussion

The behavior obtained in this investigation poses some interesting questions for motivation theory, since significant learning was attained and efficient performance maintained without resort to special or extrinsic incentives. It is obvious, of course, that a number of physiological drives might have operated to activate the animals. Hunger must certainly have been present, since 14 to 22 hours had elapsed between the last feeding and the puzzle performances. Thirst may have been present, at least part of the time, for water bottles occasionally run dry during the day. Data obtained in a subsequent study suggest that temperature drive played a role. Sex drive might also have operated. Granted that these physiological drives were present, the problem remains of explaining how such drives could operate to direct behavior on the puzzle problem. Solution did not lead to food, water, or sex gratification. The precise serial manipulations or locomotor behavior.

Whether one assumes a reinforcement or nonreinforcement theory of learning, the behavior of the monkeys is not explained by attributing their performance directly to the homeostatic drives. The reinforcement theorist is left to account for the drive or drives reduced by performance. The nonreinforcement theorist is faced with the problem of explaining the channeling of behavior.

The authors propose that an externally elicited drive operated to channel behavior on the mechanical puzzle, and that the performance of the task provided intrinsic reward. The idea of an externally stimulated drive eliciting intrinsically motivating behavior is not, of course, a new one. The exploratory-investigatory drive proposed by previous workers would fit in this category. The curiosity motive frequently attributed to human infants and children can also be characterized in this way. Tolman (1941) has proposed play and aesthetic drives in apes and, presumably, human beings as primary drive conditions which might be externally elicited.

In spite of previous suggestions of such drives, little experimental work has been conducted relating to them, and the work that has been done appears to be limited to the exploratory drive. Nissen (1930) obtained data on the behavior of rats in crossing a charged grid to a Dashiell checkerboard maze, and attributed the behavior to an exploratory drive. This same drive has been proposed by some to explain latent learning in the studies of Blodgett (1929), Haney (1931), Buxton (1940), and others. In several of these experiments control over the possible escape incentive was obtained by housing the animals in the maze during the "latent" learning response of naive rats after an initial trial without food reward on the Graham and Gagne elevated runway. Because of lack of food reinforcement, however, the investigators did not interpret this improvement as a learning phenomenon.

An exploratory drive might have operated, in the present experiment, to initiate behavior toward the puzzle, but some motivation in addition to the exploratory drive must be adduced to account for the persistence of the puzzle solving behavior through the course of the experiment without suggestion of extinction.

A secondary reinforcement explanation seems inadequate for a number of reasons. The only extrinsic incentive previously provided these subjects was food, and so presumably any secondary reinforcement would be derived from hunger reduction. Introduction of food in the present experiment served to disrupt performance, a phenomenon not reported in the literature on secondary reinforcement. Furthermore, the animals' history raises serious doubts about a secondary reinforcement interpretation. The previous experimental experience of the animals includes no problems of manipulation beyond pushing an object on a tray, and no problems of any kind presented in the living quarters. Some monkeys have been noted to reach through their living cages and manipulate the latches on the doors, but such responses have never led to solution and escape, and would thus provide no opportunity in the present experiment for secondary reinforcement of manipulatory responses based on escape. Additional evidence against a secondary reinforcement interpretation lies in the relative indifference during the observation tests of three of the four monkeys to the hasp, the only device that in any way resembled discrimination or delayed reaction to objects. Finally, no evidence of extinction appeared after numerous trials without food or other extrinsic incentives. It seems far fetched to propose that secondary reinforcement derived from hunger reduction in discrimination learning and delayed reaction problems conducted in the test rooms generalized to the puzzle problem presented in the living quarters, and once generalized, was maintained for 80 trials without any primary reinforcement.

Persons unfamiliar with monkeys might suspect social reinforcement of the responses, and theoretically it is possible that the experimenter might serve as a secondary reinforcing agent to provide reinforcement for a derived or secondary motive. The animals' history provides opportunities for such motivation, for taming procedures utilize food, and the human being is also associated with the daily feeding and watering. During the previous experimental work, however, interaction between S and E was minimized through the use of screens in all but one group of delayed reaction problems. General observation of the Ss has not suggested an affectional attachment to the Es which might have motivated performance. In the puzzle study, the E was not present during the trials on the first 12 days, and during the observations on Days 13 and 14, the presence of the E produced negative rather than positive effects. Certainly for Animals 146 and 151, the departure of the E was a stronger stimulus than his presence to puzzle attack and solution. Social motivation is a possible explanation, but it appears to be an unlikely one.

It is the opinion of the Es that a manipulation drive can best account for the behavior obtained in this investigation. The stimuli to the drive are external and, in conjunction with the animals' capacities, set the pattern of behavior. The manipulation is conceived of as having reinforcing properties that account for the precision and speed the subjects acquire in carrying out the solution, and the persistence they show in repeated performances. Observations of subhuman animals and human beings provide abundant illustrations of directed manipulatory behavior unassociated with homeostatic drive reduction or social approval, but to the authors' knowledge no previous investigations have utilized this drive experimentally.

In conclusion we would like to emphasize the strength and the persistence of the manipulatory drive as described in this paper. It would appear that that drive, and probably a broad category of drives to which manipulation belongs, may be as basic and as strong as the homeostatic drives. Furthermore, there is some reason to believe that these drives can be as efficient in facilitating learning as the homeostatic drives.

The homeostatic drives have been such convenient drives for the comparative-theoretical psychologist that the potentialities of other drives have been ignored and their role in behavior has been neglected or belittled. The unsatisfactory nature of modern drive theory may stem in large part from the biases of Es who have tended to cast all studies in a limited common mold.

CHAPTER VIII

Complex Learning

ALTHOUGH it can be succcessfully argued that a classically conditioned response is an instance of complex learning, the term "complex learning" is usually used in reference to the acquisition of behaviors requiring abstract conceptualizations. There is not yet any one theory of sufficient breadth and depth to account for the apparent diversity of variables influencing complex learning processes. One might broadly classify available theories into two categories: (1) theories that emphasize hypothetical structures presumably located in the cortex and derived from a combination of experiences and biological growth; and (2) stimulus-response theories which frequently use the concept of "generalization" to explain complex behavior, as shown in White's paper, and which have been recently expanded to include processes that mediate between presentation of a specific stimulus and the emergence of a particular response. These mediational processes include verbal symbols to which specific categories of responses have been attached through a process of conditioning.

Each of these broad categories of models have strengths and weaknesses. Structure models, as best exemplified by the work of Jean Piaget, provide a basis for understanding developmental changes in conceptual behaviors. One kind of conceptual behavior, mainly conservation, is systematically examined in the paper by Elkind, whose methods are directly derived from Piaget's theory. It should be noted that even though this study supports Piaget's conceptualizations, there are other studies which fail to do so. As a consequence, the status of this theory in the United States is somewhat equivocal. In describing children's conservation behaviors, great reliance is given to stage differences. It is precisely in this area, however, that the theory is in need of expansion. Piaget hypothesizes that children move from stage to stage, each higher stage being dependent upon but autonomous from the previous stage. Piaget does not, however, specify under what conditions this transition occurs. (See the paper by Kessen in Chapter 2 for an analysis of this problem.) It would not be helpful, incidentally, to explain transitions in terms of chronological age since time *per se* is not a meaningful variable unless the specific events occurring during the time period are specified.

That there are developmental changes in the complex learning processes of human beings is amply demonstrated in the studies by Sigel and by Crandall and his associates. Each of these studies demonstrates not only an age difference in overt behavior, but also that the underlying cognitive processes are different. In many respects this inference is entirely consistent with Piaget's thinking and consistent with the educational practice of presenting young children with concrete examples of concepts rather than relying on verbal abstract concepts.

The paper by Lee, Kagan, and Rabson demonstrates the importance of one variable, cognitive style, upon concept acquisition. This study, in conjunction with other similar kinds of research, indicates that children are highly variable in their approaches to solving problems. Some children are typically impulsive and respond before they have considered all of the alternatives available. Other children may be described as more reflective and taking the time to consider alternatives before responding. There is evidence to suggest that middle-class parents reinforce the latter approach, whereas lower-class parents tend to reinforce the former type of behavior. The potential importance of cognitive styles for child-rearing practices and educational practices seem, at this time, enormous.

Generalization of an Instrumental Response with Variation in Two Attributes of the CS

Sheldon H. White

Stimulus generalization is the degree to which a response made to one stimulus is also made to other stimuli on the same dimension. The slope or steepness of the generalization gradient is influenced by such variables as motivation (the greater the motivation the flatter the gradient), strength of original learning (the greater the original training the steeper the gradient), and chronological age (older children evidence steeper gradients than younger children). In this experiment Dr. White demonstrates that when the generalization stimuli differ from the training stimuli on more than one dimension, the gradient of generalization is steeper.

The stimuli involved in a discrimination usually differ on one physical dimension but have common values on others. If the difference between the distinguishing components of the stimuli is made larger, the discrimination is learned more easily. This can be explained by the principle of stimulus generalization, as used in discrimination learning theory (Spence, 1937).

To date, studies of generalization have always involved the gradual alteration

SOURCE: Adapted and abridged from Sheldon H. White, "Generalization of an Instrumental Response with Variation in Two Attributes of the CS." *Journal of Experimental Psychology,* 1958, 56, 339–343. (With permission of the author and the American Psychological Association.)

of one component of a CS while holding the others constant. Theory, however, has recognized the possibility that more than one component may be so varied and, by postulating summative rules for generalized reaction tendencies, can predict that discrimination learning will be superior with multiple, as opposed to single, dimensions of variation between discriminanda. This has been confirmed in several studies.

This experiment was an attempt to demonstrate that novel stimuli differing from a training stimulus along two physical dimensions will elicit fewer generalized responses than will novel stimuli which differ only on one of those dimensions.

Method

Apparatus

The apparatus was a modification of one developed by Spiker (1956) to study generalization with children. It allows S to respond by repeated pulls of a handle during trial.

The stimuli were presented by an experimental model of the Hunter Cardmaster, a device for the timed presentation of cards. This is a gray metal box, 14 × 14 × 14 inches, with a stimulus aperture 6 inches wide and 3 inches high. Within, a conveyor system slides a 6¼ × 3½ inch card from the bottom of a stack and presses it against the aperture. Black cloth curtains part to either side to reveal the card to S. When the curtains close, the card is returned to the top of the stack and a new one brought up. Each stimulus exposure lasted 3.8 seconds, an interval which preliminary testing indicated would allow a sufficiently high rate of response for gradations in generalization to manifest themselves. Each intertrial interval lasted 3.5 seconds.

The opening of the curtains closed a switch in the circuits of an impulse counter and a marble delivery device; these circuits were then completed when S pulled the response handle ¾ inch towards himself. (A 3-pound pull would close the microswitch.) Thus, when the curtains were open, each pull would register an impulse counter and cause a marble to be delivered. When they closed, the counting and marble delivery stopped. A hidden button enabled E to lock out marble delivery during any given trial.

The handle protruded from the lower right-hand corner of a black wooden box on which the cardmaster rested, and varied from waist to chest height for different Ss. Tubing, housed in a black box to the left, held a reserve of about 300 marbles. These were delivered into a plastic pail at S's left.

Stimuli

The stimuli were 3 × 5 inch sheets of Munsell colored paper, covered with library tape and mounted on white plastic cards. In Table 8.1, the colors were schematized in the Munsell notation, which is of the form: Hue Value/ Chroma. The colors were illuminated by a 100-watt bulb about 2 inches above, shielded to prevent glare. The blinds of the various schoolrooms used were drawn, to make this the principal source of illumination of the stimuli.

Procedure and Ss

The children were told they were to play a game, and that the way to win it was to fill a pail with marbles. The E pulled the handle to two exposures of the training stimulus, and S was encouraged while pulling to six more exposures. Occasionally, when S had not given three or more responses on each of the consecutive trials, he was given up to four more. Marbles were delivered on all pretraining trials.

All Ss were then given 6 reinforced trials with the training stimulus and, without pause, a sequence of 8 nonreinforced test trials distributed among 12 reinforced presentations of the training stimulus. Either 1, 2, or 3 reinforcements separated one test trial from the next.

TABLE 8.1. *Munsell Values of Colors Used as Stimuli Value (Lightness)*

HUE	8/	7/	6/	5/
10GY	10GY 8/6	10GY 7/6	10GY 6/6	10GY 5/6
5GY	5GY 8/6	5GY 7/6		
10Y	10Y 8/6		10Y 6/6	
5Y	5Y 8/6			5Y 5/6

NOTE: Group L's test stimuli along row. HL's along diagonal, H's in column. The training stimulus was 10GY 8/6.

The transition to testing produced a change in incidental stimulation. The color used in training, being always the same, was presented by opening and closing the curtains on one card. During the last training trial, E closed a switch causing the Cardmaster thereafter to change cards at the end of each trial. Card changing produced a sound noticeable to S. The first trial of the testing sequence was, therefore, a reinforced presentation of the training stimulus, in an attempt to counteract any change in behavior which might be produced by the new sound.

There were three testing groups. Group H had four test stimuli: the training color and three others differing in hue, but of the same lightness. Group L had test stimuli varying in lightness, but of the same hue. The novel stimuli for Group HL differed from the training color in both hue and lightness. Each HL color contained a Group H hue and a Group L lightness (Table 8.1).

The Ss were kindergarten children in the Cedar Rapids public schools who met a criterion of not more than one error on Plates I-VI of the ISCC Pseudoiso-chromatic Colorblindness Test, administered before an experimental session. The data for 24 children were not used. Fourteen Ss — 4 from H, 4 from L, and 6 from HL — were interrupted by mechanical failure of the apparatus. Three HL Ss were dropped because of procedural errors, and 3 other HL Ss because an extremely rapid rate of response overfilled their marble container. One S from H, and another from L, were eliminated because of distractions within the school. Two children failed to meet the color-blindness criterion. There remained a total of 72 Ss, 24 in each group.

Results

During training Group H, L, and HL averaged, respectively, 6.4, 6.5, and 6.6 pulls per trial. Analysis of variance did not reveal a significant difference between the groups.

TABLE 8.2. *Analyses of Variance Comparing Groups H vs. HL, and L vs. HL, on Number of Responses to Their Four Test Stimuli*

		H vs. HL		L vs. HL	
SOURCE	df	MS	F	MS	F
Between Ss	47				
Groups (G)	1	9.69	1	150.00	9.12**
Error (b)	46	11.04		16.44	
Within Ss	336				
Stimuli (S)	3	64.34	30.21***	47.04	23.76***
Cycles (C)	1	83.44	71.93***	45.37	18.52***
GxS	3	2.40	1.13	3.81	1.92
GxC	1	1.63	1.41	1.26	1
SxC	3	3.11	2.80*	2.57	2.40
GxSxC	3	0.03	1	0.64	1
Error (w)	322				
Error (w)	138	2.13		1.98	
Error (w)	46	1.16		2.45	
Error (w)	138	1.11		1.07	
Total	383				

* P .05.   ** P .01.   *** P .001.

The left half of Figure 8.1 shows the mean number of pulls per test stimulus, cycles given separately, for Groups H and HL. There is little difference between them on their two test values, but Group H gives more responses than Group HL on the two further points. For both groups, responses to the 10GY (training) value in test trials were markedly greater than to the three novel test stimuli, which did not differ greatly in numbers of responses elicited. There is a decrease in response rate from the first to the second cycle of test trials. These effects, except for the difference between groups, were found to be significant in an analysis of variance (Table 8.2).

An analysis of variance with the factors shown in Table 8.2, but using only the data of the three novel test stimuli, was performed. In this analysis, only the cycles effect was significant, at the .001 level.

From the right half of Figure 8.1, it is seen that (a) Group L gave more generalized responses to all four of its test stimuli than did Group HL to its corresponding stimuli; (b) a gradient of generalized responses sloping away from

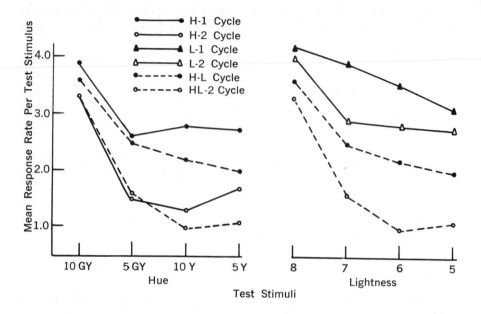

Figure 8.1   Mean response rates per test stimulus in Groups H, L, and HL as a function of variation in hue and brightness.

the training value is indicated; (c) there is a decrease in responses from the first to the second cycle. Analysis of variance indicated these effects to be significant (Table 8.2).

A repetition of this analysis using only the data of the three novel test stimuli of each group again showed these three effects, and no others, to be significant.

Discussion

The fact that more Ss were eliminated from Group HL than from the H and L groups together raises the possibility that some sampling bias was inadvertently introduced. The most serious contamination would be in the selection of slower responders into Group HL, since evidence of this and other studies tends to show low positive correlations between rates of response during acquisition and test trials. However, the acquisition data shows that all three groups gave about the same rate of response during training, and suggests that the group differences in generalization were probably not produced by selection of Ss.

The hypothesis of the present study can be predicted by considering each attribute of the training stimulus to be a separably conditionable component, with its habit strength summating with that of other attributes to produce the habit strength for the compound CS. Hull's laws of primary stimulus generalization and habit summation would then predict that: (a) the three groups should respond identically on test trials to the training color; (b) the HL generalization gradient should be below those of the other two groups; and (c) the HL gradient should be steepest.

For Prediction a, we may note that the H, L, and HL groups averaged, respectively, 3.6, 4.1, and 3.5 responses over their two test trials to the training color, with nonsignificant differences. For Prediction b, we note that Group L was significantly above, and Group H tended to be above, Group HL in numbers of responses on their generalization test trials. With regard to Prediction c, it is evident in Figure 8.1 that the differences between Groups H or L and HL are greater at the furthest test point than at the training point, as would be expected. However, the Groups X Stimuli effect fails to approach significance in either analysis of Table 8.2.

The above discussion of theory and test has disregarded the extinction effects which resulted from a counterbalanced testing procedure, and which affect the generalization curves. The comparison of test stimuli with Ss was based, as it usually is, upon a consideration of the great economy of Ss which the method provided. In terms of theory, at least, the predicted effects should usually manifest themselves despite distortions produced by this method. The prediction which is most vulnerable to distorting effects of extinction is c. that of differing slope for the HL, as compared to the H or L gradients.

Developmental Trends in the Abstraction Ability of Children

Irving E. Sigel

Abstract behavior is an attribute that requires many years before attaining maturity, and one which passes through several levels. Very young children's abstraction behavior is generally stimulus bound and frequently is referred to as perceptual. More mature abstract behavior is shown in the quality of stimulus organization where categorization is not bound by stimulus similarity. Dr. Sigel of the Merrill-Palmer Institute empirically describes the developmental changes that occur in the abstraction behavior of elementary-school-age children. His data provide a basis for developing methods of teaching concepts at different age levels.

Abstraction is "a mental process in which some attribute or characteristic is observed independently of other characteristics of an experience as a whole." Werner (1948) emphasizes that the ability to abstract does not appear suddenly in the course of the individual's development; rather it is present from the very beginnings of life but changes qualitatively with progress in maturation.

SOURCE: Adapted and abridged from Irving E. Sigel, "Developmental Trends in the Abstraction Ability of Children." *Child Development*, 1953, 24, 131–144. (With permission of the author and the Society for Research in Child Development.)

Different organizational patterns of response to environmental stimuli are observed in children of varying age levels. The abstraction behavior of very young children seems to be primarily on a sensori-motor level and can be designated as *perceptual*. In such a response the individual yields to demands of the situation, and the organization of the material is determined by the nature of the stimuli as well as by the limited maturity of the subject. A more mature individual would be expected to consciously impose organization on the material and classify the material into deliberately conceived categories. This is the *conceptual* level of abstraction.

The hypothesis that the younger the child, the more perceptual are his organizations has been stated, but a search for specific details of the development encounters a paucity of data. The present study was undertaken to obtain information regarding changes in abstraction ability during the elementary school period.

Method

Procedure

Candidates for study were boys of lower-middle-class background who were in the correct grades for their ages and whose percentile ranks on the Raven Test of Progressive Matrices were between 25 and 75. From candidates 7, 9, and 11 years old, 20 were chosen at random to represent each age group.

Toy objects were selected as the basic item for the grouping tests, and pilot exploration resulted in assembly of 24 items which were familiar to all of the children. Except for the snake, which was about 12 inches long, the maximum dimension of any object was 5 inches. The following objects were used: Blue and red plastic lounge chair, red plastic office chair, brown and white plastic arm chair, red plastic stool, white plastic dining table, red plastic end table, plastic man in black suit and white shirt, plastic woman in blue dress, flesh-pink rubber baby doll, flesh-pink celluloid child doll, brown metal soldier, metal boy in blue suit, green plastic truck, blue plastic baby carriage, purple plastic airplane, red and yellow plastic tractor, blue metal train engine, red and blue plastic boat, brown metal chicken, red celluloid fish, pink celluloid duck, red plastic horse, green wood snake, black and white plastic dog.

Five variants of the test situation were used:

Form I — Tactual-motor. The subject was permitted to handle the objects while making his groupings.

Form II — Visual-nonmotor. The subject was not allowed to touch the objects but was asked to point to or name the objects and instruct the tester on grouping.

Form III — Pictures. Black and white photographs mounted on cards approximately 3.5 × 4.5 inches were substituted for the objects, and the subject was allowed to group the cards manually.

Form IV — Names. The name of each object was printed in large, black block letters on a card approximately 3 inches square, and the subject was asked to group the cards.

Form V — Names listed. The names of all objects were typewritten on the upper one-half of a sheet 11 × 13 inches, and the subject was asked to write the names in groups on the lower one-half of the sheet.

Within each age group the order in which the five forms were given was rotated so that four subjects of the twenty did Form I first, four did Form II first, etc. In the presentation of each form the materials were arranged in a circle on a table so that two objects obviously of the same class were not adjacent. The same arrangement of materials was employed with all subjects.

Before testing, each child was asked to identify the objects as they were placed on the table or to read the names on cards as listed. Before each test a subject was told to "put those things together in a pile (or list) that belong together or go together or are alike in any way, and those other things that go together or belong together or are alike in another way in another pile (or list). You may have as many or as few piles as you wish. Do you understand?" Some 7-year-olds found the concept of "belongingness" or "likeness" difficult to grasp. Examples were not given because they might set a pattern and deter spontaneous grouping. When a child seemed not to understand or asked whether there was a right way to group, the directions were repeated. Judged by the performances of the children, the task was comprehended.

Minimum control was exerted by the experimenter in the first test situation, the child being left to determine what made things similar or belong together. Trials were completed in not more than ten minutes. After completion of the first trial, a subject was asked to explain the reason for each group. The names of objects in each classification and the reasons for groups were recorded verbatim. To determine the upper limits of grouping and the effects of pressure, additional trials were used.[1] Each child was instructed to "group the things that are alike or belong together into fewer groupings than you made the first time," until the children could not reduce the number of groupings. After the objects were grouped, the reasons for grouping again were recorded verbatim. The identical procedure was followed with each of the five test forms. Each child was given one test daily for five consecutive days to reduce fatigue and perseveration.

Upon completion of the five test forms, each subject was given a class recognition test to determine his ability to recognize bases of groupings possibly more inclusive than any he had devised. Successively, a child was introduced to the groups of objects which could be classified as animal, human, vehicle, and furniture and was asked, "Do these things go together or belong together or are they alike in any way?" If these were identified, the experimenter presented to the child the 24 objects in two groups, those "living" and "nonliving," and asked the same question. If these were identified, the 24 objects were placed in a single group, and the child asked the basis of it. Finally, the subject was exposed to the classifications "red" (office chair, stool, horse, fish, end table) and "metal" (train engine, soldier, boy, chicken).

For scoring on the basis of the number of objects placed in each category, designations of groupings were classified as perceptual, conceptual, and miscellaneous; subcategories were required for the first and last of the three classifications.

A. *Perceptual*

1. Affective — grouping based on feeling.

2. Identity — grouping based on identity of structure or function.

3. Partial identity — grouping based on identity of certain aspects of structure or function.

4. Centroid — grouping based on belongingness in a geographical area.

5. Functional — grouping based on use.

B. *Conceptual*

Grouping in which the objects were treated as members of a class even though gross structural differences were apparent. Designation by a class name was required for a grouping to be scored conceptual.

C. *Miscellaneous*

1. Mixed-1 — grouping in which conceptual and perceptual classifications are combined and treated as perceptual.

2. Mixed-2 — grouping in which two or more perceptual groupings are combined into a third perceptual category.

3. Thematic — grouping based on a story.

4. Pseudogrouping which appeared incorrect in interpretation and information of reality.

5. Nongroupings — objects which were not found to belong to any grouping and which were isolated intentionally.

The miscellaneous categories were derived from a pilot study and are recognized as a heterogeneous combination of subcategories necessary to demonstrate adaptations in sorting behavior when "pure" conceptual or "pure" perceptual organization was not exhibited.

Results

The frequency with which the children of three age groups made use of the perceptual and conceptual classifications in Trials 1 and 2 is shown in Figure 8.2. By an analysis of variance technique the age differences indicated in the chart for conceptual classifications in Trial 1 were significant at the .01 level of confidence. Differences in the use of conceptual categories also were significant for every age comparison in Trial 2. The age differences in perceptual classification in Trial 1 were significant between the group of children 7 years old and both of the older groups but were not significant between groups 9 and 11 years old. In no instance were dependable differences found between tests.

Comparisons between Trials 1 and 2 for groups of children 7, 9, and 11 years old did not show significant changes in the use of perceptual type classifications, although the direction of change was toward an increased use in Trial 2 by the 9-year-olds and decreased use by the other two groups. With respect to conceptual classifications all groups showed changes significant between the two trials

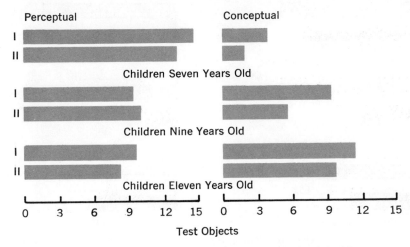

Figure 8.2 Comparisons of mean numbers of objects placed in perceptual and conceptual categories by children of three age groups.

at least at the .05 level of confidence. However, in both trials the trends with increasing age were similar downward for use of the perceptual categories and upward for the conceptual classifications.

The percentages of objects grouped according to the subcategories of the perceptual and miscellaneous classifications are shown in Figure 8.3. The children never used the "affective category," and the "identity" category was omitted because with the test objects employed, identity might have been a conceptual approach in some instances and a perceptual approach in others.[2]

In both trials the children 7 and 11 years old employed the partial identity category as a basis of grouping significantly more than did the 9-year-old children. Similarity is apparent between the results for 7- and 11-year-old groups, yet one would expect to find differences, since maturity is a factor in differentiating the types of classificatory approaches used. If the reasons offered for the groupings are considered, the 7-year-olds classified significantly more frequently on the basis of partial identity of action than did the 9- and 11-year-olds. The two older groups tended to use partial identity of structure, although the differences between the 9- and 11-year-olds is not significant. Partial identity of structure was used significantly more by the 11-year-olds than by the 7-year-olds.

The centroid grouping was employed by the youngest children more significantly, and use of that category was less for each older age group. Typical reasons given for the groupings were: "all belong in air," and "all belong in the house." Objects were organized in ways familiar to the child from his own experience or from stories and explanations. The trend described occurred in Trial 2 also, although the 9-year-old children increased their use of this type of classification.

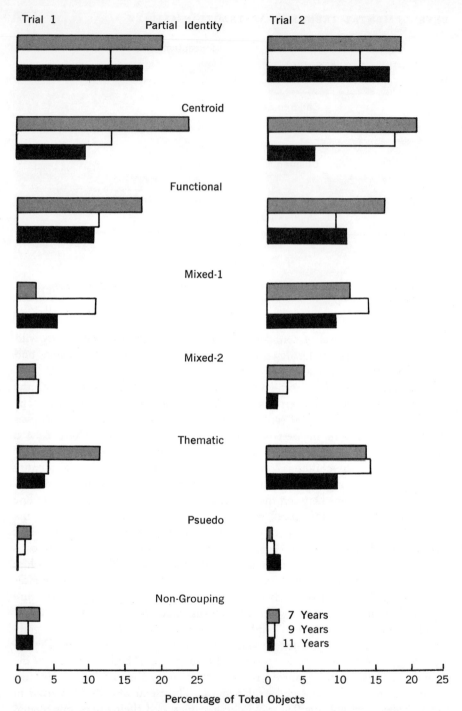

Figure 8.3 Comparisons of percentages of total number of objects placed in perceptual and miscellaneous categories in trials 1 and 2 by children of three age groups.

The 7-year-old children also employed functional grouping significantly more than did the older children. Nine- and 11-year-old children used the category almost equally. Under pressure to reduce the groupings, the 11-year-olds increased the frequency of their use of this classification, but the other two groups did not.

Examination of the uses of the miscellaneous groupings shows that in the first trial the combining of the perceptual and conceptual approaches (mixed-1) occurred most frequently among 9-year-old children. The combination of two or more perceptual categories (mixed-2) was used almost equally by the 7- and 9-year-olds, but rarely by the older children. In Trial 2, however, all groups increased their use of the mixed categories, the greatest increase being for the oldest children.

Use of the thematic category decreased with age, the 7-year-old group using it most frequently. In Trial 2, however, the 9-year-old children increased their use of this approach to an extent that results for the 7- and 9-year-old groups do not differ significantly. The 11-year-old children also increased their use of thematic groupings in Trial 2.

Subsumed under the category "pseudo" are the groupings meaningless to us. This and "nongrouping" appeared rarely and most frequently in the 7-year-old group. The children had the most difficulty with the category "vehicle," which some did not use at all. More frequently, the failure involved only the baby buggy. Even 11-year-old children often did not think of this classification. The difficulty may have stemmed from the fact that baby buggies have no motors, as do the other vehicles represented. Another possibility is that the children may have considered it part of the family's furniture. The boat, the snake, and the fish also presented difficulties and frequently were left ungrouped, especially by the 7-year-old children.

The question arises, can the child who does not in spontaneous groupings

TABLE 8.3. *Percentages of Groups of Children Who Identified Groupings in Recognition Test*

GROUPINGS	AGE GROUPS (YEARS)		
	7	9	11
Animal	50	75	90
Human	60	85	95
Vehicle	0	40	50
Furniture	40	90	90
Living	0	40	35
Nonliving	0	15	15
Single Group	0	0	25
Red	5	20	10
Metal	0	0	10

use such categories as animal, vehicle, furniture, human, redness, and metal, identify such classifications when the groupings are made by the experimenter?

The results of the recognition test are summarized in Table 8.3 and demonstrate that the ability to identify groupings increases with age. The similarity between scores of the 9- and 11-year-old children is greater than between those of either group and the 7-year-old children. Only the 9- and 11-year-old youngsters were able to identify the category "living things," and only 11-year-old children were able to give some adequate reason for grouping all the objects into one category. More of the 9-year-old group were able to identify the "red" category than either of the other two age groups. Only two 11-year-old subjects were able to identify "metal" as a basis of classification, perhaps because the metal objects were painted. All children gave some basis for their designations of the groupings, but their reasons were not always correct in terms of conceptual response. Usually, the explanations were not different from those offered for their own classifications.

Discussion

The classificatory behavior represented in the first trial indicates the child's ability in a situation which is minimally structured. The children were free to use the approaches they "felt most comfortable" with in determining similarity or belongingness. The trends are clear that regardless of the nature of the material, perceptual classifications declined and conceptual ones increased with age. This finding substantiates the hypothesis that with increases in age significant changes in classificatory behavior occur. The specific determinants effecting this change are difficult to isolate. Although the group trends reported are clear, individual variations within the groups in the use of "more mature" classificatory approaches were found. Some 7-year-olds were able to utilize conceptual as well as perceptual approaches. What accounts for the individual variations becomes a highly relevant and pertinent question. Since chronological age and social class are controlled, and since the mental ability range within the groups did not include extremes, the questions point to areas of experiential, personality, and organic forces as possible determinants of the difference. Factors such as quality of experience with similar problems, early learnings of concepts, reality "boundness," and rate of constitutional maturation offer themselves as possible determinants of the variations observed. Further experimentation with variables such as these is necessary.

NOTES

[1] The first and second trials were used only for analysis since too few children in the sample were able to reduce the groupings in Trial 3.

[2] Nevertheless, the use of what might be considered "identity" was rare. This might have been a function of the materials, since no two objects were identical.

Patterned and Nonpatterned Probability Learning

Vaughn J. Crandall, Dan Solomon, and Richard Kellaway

The concept of probability is sufficiently complex that perhaps only a relatively few individuals understand it fully. Nevertheless, daily living requires constant assessment of the probabilities of events. One can observe probability-like behavior even among young children even though the processes involved may be distinctly different from those involved with adults. The late Dr. Vaughn Crandall and his associates at the Fels Research Institute examined age differences in probability learning under conditions of patterned and nonpatterned event sequences. Their results indicate that all the children, in this case 15-, 16-, and 17-year-olds as opposed to 6-, 7-, and 8-year-old children, developed expectations that were consistent with reality whereas the younger children did not. The performance of the older group can be characterized as evidencing higher mental processes whereas the younger children tended to be bound to the immediate stimulus situation.

Brunswik (1943) has argued convincingly that research on human learning should be as representative of everyday life as possible. He has pointed out that classical learning studies employing 100 per cent reward or 100 per cent punishment of responses do not represent natural learning situations, where partial reinforcement is the rule, not the exception, and where most events occur with some probability of less than one. In recent years, following Brunswik's suggestion, a growing body of research on probability learning and decision-making has eventuated. With a few exceptions studies of children's probability learning and decision-making have yet to be conducted. Research of this nature is necessary for several reasons. First, research with children will provide information for comparative psychology by ascertaining similarities and differences between the probability-learning capacities and processes of children and those of adults, on the one hand, and between those of children and subhuman organisms, on the other. Second, research in this area should contribute to genetic psychology by determining changes with age in children's probability learning processes and abilities. Third, research regarding children's probability learning may ultimately provide valuable information regarding basic learning mechanisms underlying children's early social learning and personality development; that is, the social learning of children characteristically takes place in a probabilistic environment.

The present study was primarily concerned with one parameter of children's probability learning — age differences. Secondarily, it explored possible differences in children's abilities to learn in patterned and nonpatterned probability situations.

SOURCE: Adapted and abridged from Vaughn J. Crandall, Dan Solomon, and Richard Kellaway, "A Comparison of the Patterned and Nonpatterned Probability Learning of Adolescents and Early Grade School-Age Children." *Journal of Genetic Psychology*, 1961, 99, 29–39. (With permission of the authors and the Journal Press.)

Method

Forty children participated in the experiments. One group was comprised of 20 15-, 16-, and 17-year-old adolescents; a second group contained 20 6-, 7-, and 8-year-old children. All of the children came from middle-class socioeconomic backgrounds and were above national averages in intellectual ability. The mean Stanford-Binet IQ of the older children was 124.8; that of the younger group, 118.6. The difference between the IQ's of the two groups of children was tested with Wilcoxon's test of unpaired replicates and was not statistically significant.

Experiment I

This experiment was conducted in individual sessions. Each child was seated at a table facing an upright board on which were mounted two half-inch jewel lights, one red and one green. At right angles to this board and attached to it was a second board. A metal chute extended diagonally downward from this second board to a metal container in front of the child. The lights and the container were shown to the child and he was given the following instructions:

> On the board in front of you are two lights, a red light and a green light. Today we want to see how well you can guess which one of the lights will flash when we ask you to guess. Each time before one of the lights goes on, I will say, "guess." Say "red" if you think the red light will flash, say "green" if you think it will be the green one. After you guess, one of the lights will flash. If your guess is right, a poker chip will slide down the chute into the container in front of you. If your guess is wrong, you won't win a chip. When we are all done, we'll count all the chips you have won and give you one cent for every four chips. Since you will have a large number of chances to guess, you can win as much as seventy-five cents depending on how well you guess. Remember, each time you win a chip if your guess is right, but you won't win one if your guess is wrong.

The program of guessing trials was prearranged and the same for all children. Each child was presented an 80–20 probability learning situation for 80 trials in which, during each block of 10 trials, one light flashed on eight trials and the other light flashed on two trials. As a control for possible position and color preferences, the red (and left) light was employed as the more frequently occurring stimulus for half of the younger and half of the older children, while the green (and right) light was the more frequent stimulus for the remaining children. The 80–20 probability learning situation was immediately followed by an 80-trial 50–50 probability condition. During this latter learning situation, each of the two lights flashed five times in each 10-trial block. Throughout the total series of learning trials, the temporal order of occurrence of the lights was non-patterned.

Results

Each child's statements regarding which light he expected to flash on each trial were recorded. Expectations for the more frequently occurring light were designated *Ep,* and constitute the basic data of the experiment. The mean of the *Ep*s was tabulated for each block of 10 trials for both the 80–20 and 50–50 learning situations. Wilcoxon's nonparametric tests were applied to these data; the unpaired replicates test was used for between-group comparisons and the paired replicates test for within-group tests.

The learning curves of the two groups of children are presented in Figure 8.4. The probability learning of the older children appears superior during

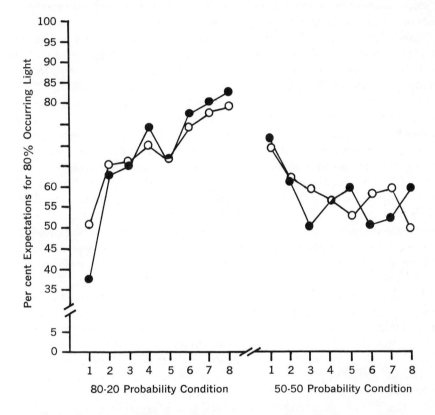

Figure 8.4 Percentage of expectations for the 80% occurring light during 80–20 and 50–50 nonpatterned probability learning plotted in 10-trial blocks. The open circles represent the learning curves of the younger children; the closed circles, those of the older children.

the 80–20 learning situation. This is evidenced in two ways. First, the older children's expectations for the more frequent stimulus developed more rapidly during latter blocks of learning trials than those of the younger children. Second, like adult Ss in previous two-event probability learning experiments, the mean expectation of these older children ultimately approximated the objective frequency of occurrence of the two stimuli while the mean expectation of the younger group of children did not. During the subsequent 50–50 probability learning period, the learning curves of the two groups of children were essentially the same. Statistical tests of the data produced the following results. (a) In previous two-event probability research, expectations for the two stimuli at the beginning of learning have been found to approximate 50–50. In the present experiment, however, during the first block of trials of the 80–20 probability condition, while the mean Ep of the younger children did approximate 50–50, that of the adolescent children did not. Their mean Ep was less than .40, and significantly less than that of the younger children ($p < .01$). The writers have no ready explanation for this phenomenon. (b) The Ep of both groups of children increased rapidly during subsequent trials; significant increases occurred for both groups between the first and second block of 80–20 learning trials ($p < .01$). (c) While the initial rate of Ep development was similar for both groups, i.e., no statistically significant differences for the first six blocks of trials, the final Ep strength of the older children was greater than that of the younger children. The older children expected the more frequent stimulus to occur more often during the seventh and eighth blocks of trial than did the younger children ($p < .05$). (d) Finally, during the subsequent 50–50 probability learning situation no statistically significant differences were found between the expectations of the two groups of children. It should be noted that there was no significant difference in spite of the fact that the older group of children had previously developed stronger expectations for the occurrence of the more frequent stimulus during the 80–20 conditions and thus had a greater shift to make in their expectations.

Immediately following the experiment, each child was interviewed regarding his guessing behavior during the experiment. One interesting point arose from these interviews: while the stimuli in the experiment were actually presented in a nonpatterned sequence, a number of children reported that they expected, looked for, and (sometimes) thought they found the stimuli occurring in some consistent temporal pattern. These "higher-order" pattern expectations were reported by the adolescent children more frequently than by the younger children; 18 of the 20 adolescents said they had held pattern expectations while only 6 of the 20 younger children did so. It is, of course, possible that still others of the younger children may have employed such pattern expectations but did not, or could not, verbalize them. However, the interviews did suggest the possibility that the *process* of the children's probability learning, as well as the effectiveness of their learning, may have differed with age. A second experiment, employing patterned probabilities, was designed to provide information regarding this question.

Experiment II

The same children participated in the second experiment as in the original one, with an interval of approximately one year transpiring between the two experiments. The procedures of the two experiments were the same with one exception. In Experiment I the stimuli were presented in a nonpatterned sequence; in the second experiment, consistent temporal patterns were employed. In the second experiment, during the 80–20 probability learning situation, the more frequent light flashed on four successive trials followed by a single occurrence of the other light on the fifth trial. This 4–1, 4–1 pattern was maintained throughout the 80 trials of this condition. During the subsequent 50–50 probability condition, the more frequently occurring stimulus of the preceding 80–20 learning condition was presented five successive times and was followed by five successive presentations of the other light. This 5–5 pattern continued for the duration of the experiment.

The learning curves of the two groups of children during the 80–20 condition indicates that the adolescent children's Ep developed much more rapidly than those of the younger children. However, in contrast to Experiment I, the younger children continued to increase their Ep throughout the 80–20 condition. Again, as in Experiment I, the learning curves of the two groups were essentially the same during the subsequent 50–50 condition. Statistical tests found: (a) The older children's initial rate of Ep acquisition was superior in the patterned 80–20 probability situation (Block 2, $p < .01$; Block 3, $r < .01$; Block 4, $r < .01$; Block

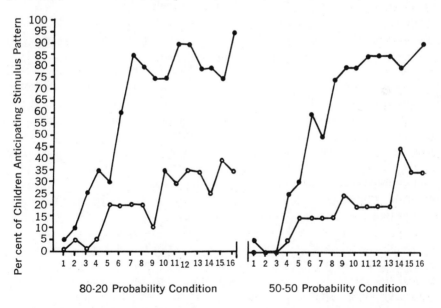

Figure 8.5 Percentage of children correctly anticipating stimulus patterns during 80–20 and 50–50 patterned probability learning plotted in 5-trial blocks. The open circles represent the anticipations of the younger children; the closed circles, those of the older children.

5, $p < .02$; Block 6, $p < .01$). (b) By the end of the 80–20 condition, however, Ep of the two groups of children were similar; no significant differences were found in the seventh and eighth blocks of trials. (c) No significant differences occurred between the Ep of the two groups during the 50–50 patterned probability learning situation.

While the above analyses pertain to the children's probability learning in respect to their Ep, a product-measure of their probability learning, they provide no information regarding the children's ability to correctly anticipate the *stimulus patterns* presented to them. Figure 8.5, divided into five-block learning trials corresponding to the unit of the patterns presented, summarizes data regarding this question. Figure 8.5 indicates that during both the 80–20 and the 50–50 learning conditions the older children's performances were markedly superior. For example, in no block of trials in either learning condition did as many as half of the younger children correctly anticipate a pattern. In contrast, in all of the last 10 blocks of 80–20 probability learning trials and in all of the last nine blocks of 50–50 probability trials, three-fourths or more of the adolescents correctly anticipated the patterns presented. The median number of correctly anticipated patterns during the 80–20 probability condition was 10.38 for the older children as compared with 1.50 for the younger group. During the subsequent 50–50 condition, the median number of correctly anticipated patterns by the two groups of children was 9.00 and 1.50 respectively.

The total number of correctly anticipated patterns was tabulated for each child for each of the two learning situations. Unpaired replicates tests were run on these data. The older children significantly identified more patterns in both probability learning conditions ($r < .01$). These results, when combined with the results of the previous Ep analyses of the children's patterned probability learning, suggest the following conclusions: (a) The superior rate of Ep development of the adolescents in the 80–20 probability learning situation can be attributed, to a large degree, to the fact that they expected and correctly anticipated patterned probabilities while most of the younger children did not. The younger children more often employed molecular, trial-by-trial expectations; the older children were more likely to bring "higher-order" pattern expectations to the learning situation, and to employ them effectively. (b) In the subsequent 50–50 probability situation, while the mean Ep of the two groups of children were essentially the same, the *process* of their learning was dissimilar. More of the younger children characteristically responded to the 50–50 presentation of the two stimuli as though these were chance occurrences, i.e., these children ignored the possibility of temporal patterning and reacted with more or less random guessing. Most of the adolescents, on the other hand, anticipated and correctly identified the temporal regularity of the stimulus condition before the end of the learning period. The responses of these older children clearly reflected the use of "higher-learning" expectations to a greater degree than did those of the younger children.

Discussion

The study found children's probability learning capacities to be a function of age in several ways. (a) In the nonpatterned two-event probability learning experiment, the mean expectation of the adolescent children during the 80–20 probability learning situation ultimately approximated the objective occurrence of the two stimuli (as has been previously found with groups of adult Ss). The Ep of the early grade-school-age children did not; these younger children anticipated the more frequently occurring stimulus less often than did the adolescents, and anticipated it less frequently than the stimulus actually occurred. (b) During the subsequent 50–50 nonpatterned probability condition, in spite of the fact that the older children had previously developed stronger expectations for the more frequent stimulus, they were able to shift these expectations rapidly enough so that they did not differ significantly from those of the younger children, who had less of a shift to make. (c) In the second experiment, when temporal patterning of the stimuli was introduced to investigate age differences in the use of pattern expectations, significant differences were also found. When temporal patterning was introduced during the 80–20 probability learning situation, the younger children's Ep developed more slowly than those of the adolescents and were less often based on pattern expectations. (d) In addition, during the subsequent 50–50 patterned probability learning condition, while the Ep of the two groups of children were essentially the same, the *process* of their probability learning, as in the previous 80–20 learning situation, was not. During the 50–50 patterned probability condition, the younger children frequently responded as though the probable occurrences of the two stimuli were random; the adolescent children, on the other hand, more frequently held expectations of possible pattern relationships and, as a result, more often correctly anticipated the actual temporal patterning of the stimuli.

Analytic Categorization and Concept Acquisition

Lee C. Lee, Jerome Kagan, and Alice Rabson

Knowledge and conceptualizations of the environment initially derive from the processing of stimuli. It follows that what conceptualizations develop are related to the stimulus components selected by the child for processing. The authors of this paper, using children from the Fels Research Center, investigated the approaches to processing stimuli among a group of third-grade boys. Some of the boys processed the stimuli by searching for areas of similarity requiring careful attention to specific

SOURCE: Adapted and abridged from Lee C. Lee, Jerome Kagan, and Alice Rabson, "Influence of a Preference for Analytic Categorization upon Concept Acquisition." *Child Development*, 1963, 34, 433–442. (With permission of the authors and the Society for Research in Child Development.)

properties of the stimuli. This process is labeled "analytic." Other boys responded in terms of the total stimulus, especially their functional characteristics. Educational practices may need modification in terms of fitting methods to the cognitive styles of individual children.

Cognitive activity involves at least three different processes that generally occur in the following sequence: the initial categorization of external information, the storage of encoded information, and the imposing of transformation upon the encoded data. The specific categorizations and transformations are governed, of course, by the nature of the problem. Students of cognitive development have often assumed that the striking differences between the cognitive products of children of different ages (or among children of the same age) were attributable to differences in the availability of the rules of reasoning and mediational diversity. Thus, the superior performances of older, in contrast to younger, children on problem tasks is assumed to reflect the generally greater knowledge repertoire of the older children. This supposition is both reasonable and empirically verified. It is not surprising, therefore, that psychologists have not entertained seriously the possibility that other factors may contribute to age and individual differences in cognitive products. Specifically, there has been a tendency to neglect the relevance of interindividual differences in the processing of information — differences in the kinds of stimuli that are initially selected for labeling. For it appears that children and adults do have a preference hierarchy with respect to the stimulus characteristics they will initially attend to in situations where the individual has several degrees of freedom.

One relevant variable that describes a mode of information processing involves the classical dimension of analytic versus nonanalytic (i.e., nondifferentiated or global) categorizations.

One of the central problems in working with this dimension is that markedly different sets of measurement operations have been labeled as indexes of analytic tendencies. Since these different test procedures are probably not assessing identical constructs, it is necessary to refine this phenomenon into its simpler processes and to restrict one's statements about analytic tendencies to the operations that are used in any particular study.

In a series of investigations with school age children, it was found that some children showed a consistent tendency to analyze visually presented stimuli and to group familiar objects together *on the basis of objective elements of similarity that were parts of the total stimulus*. The measure of this preference for analytic conceptualizations is a set of 30 stimuli, each with three black-white line drawings of familiar objects (hereafter called the Conceptual Style Test). Figure 8.6 illustrates some of the stimuli from this instrument.

In this test, the child is asked to "pick out two pictures that are alike or go together in some way." These stimuli have been constructed to elicit two major

Figure 8.6 Illustrations of 16 stimuli from the Conceptual Style Test.

classes of responses — analytic and relational concepts — and, to a lesser degree, inferential-categorical concepts. The analytic concept involves pairings based on similarity in an objective attribute that is a differentiated part of the total stimulus. Examples of this category are "Animals with their tongues out," "Objects with a leg missing," or "Animals with one ear flopped down." Notice that in each of these examples the basis of similarity involves a part of the total stimulus (e.g., the tongue, the missing leg, the ear).

The relational category involves pairings based on a functional relationship between the stimuli. For these particular pictures, a functional relationship is an obvious aspect of the total stimulus. The two stimulus members in a relational concept are not independent conceptually; rather, each derives its meaning from the relationship between them. Examples of relational concepts are "The dog goes in the doghouse," "The man wears the watch," "The man and the woman are married," "The boy wears the glasses."

The inferential-categorical class includes conceptual pairings that are based, not on similarity of differential parts, but on some inferred quality or language convention. In addition, each stimulus in the pair is an independent instance of the conceptual label. Examples of inferential concepts are "Furniture," "Animals," "Clothes," "Men."

Analysis of the responses to this test by children in Grades 1 through 5 has revealed that, with age, analytic responses increase while relational responses decrease. Moreover, analytic and relational responses are always inversely correlated with each other and independent of inferential-categorical concepts. However, the test was designed specifically to suppress inferential-categorical responses, and it may be misleading to dwell on the data for this category. Thus, analytic and relational responses behave as if they were on opposite ends of a continuum. The reliability of an analytic tendency over a 12-month period (Grades 3 to 4) was .70 ($p < .001$) for 24 girls and .43 ($p < .05$) for 22 boys. Relational responses showed parallel stability coefficients ($r = .64$, $p < .001$; $r = .40$, $p < .06$ for girls and boys, respectively). The intratest (split-half) reliability of analytic and relational responses for samples of children in Grades 1 through 5 were in the low nineties.

The present study attempted to assess whether the preference for analytic groupings would be associated with different rates of learning different concepts (analytic, relational, or inferential) in a standard concept formation task.

Method

Subjects

A total of 30 third grade boys was selected from a group of 39 who had been administered the Conceptual Style Test by a female examiner. The group of 30 was composed of the 15 boys who had the largest number of analytic responses (7 to 18) and the 15 with the lowest number of analytic responses (0 to 2). All Ss had intelligence test scores between 105 and 134. Several weeks after the administration of the Conceptual Style Test, each S was administered a concept acquisition task by a different female examiner.

Apparatus

A set of 54 3½ by 5 inch white poster cards were used to present the stimuli (S-R cards). A picture (chromatic and achromatic pictures were used) was pasted on the stimulus half of each card, and a nonsense syllable was printed in black on the response half of the card. The response half of the card was covered by a second card (2½ by 3½ inches) which was attached to the S-R card by means of a cellophane hinge. The cover card was easily lifted, exposing the nonsense syllable. All stimuli were cutouts from magazines and were chosen to represent one of six conceptual classes. There were two analytic, two relational, and two inferential concepts. Each concept category contained nine different stimulus members, making a total of 54 stimuli. Each of the six concepts was paired with a three-letter nonsense syllable selected from the Glaze list of nonsense syllables with 47 per cent association value. The six concepts, three exam-

TABLE 8.4. *The Six Concepts and Their Paired Nonsense Syllables*

CONCEPTUAL CLASS	STIMULUS CONCEPTS	EXAMPLES OF STIMULI	NONSENSE SYLLABLE
Analytic	Objects with a missing leg	Table Boy Bird	CES
	Objects with a black band	Dog Barrel Bowl	ZIM
Inferential-Categorical	Three of a kind	Pears Bottles Mail boxes	PEQ
	Wearing apparel	Dress Hat Trousers	KIX
Relational	Objects with which a baby interacts	Baby Bottle Crib	NEF
	Objects related to school	Teacher Crayons Globe	HIB

ples of the stimulus members in each concept, and the six nonsense syllables appear in Table 8.4.

Procedure

Each S was seated across a table from E, who read the following instructions:

This is a learning game. I'm going to show you a series of cards one at a time. There is a picture on one half of each card and a word on the other half. These are words that don't make any sense, such as B-E-P (spelled), "BEP." There will be different pictures that have the same word; this is because the pictures belong together in some way. Now, you are to learn which word goes with which picture; that is, why these different pictures have the same word. The first time through, look at the picture and word carefully and then read the word out loud. After the first time, you'll see only the picture and you are to try and call out the word that goes with the picture. After you've answered, I'll show you the word that goes with that kind of picture. Do you have any questions? Now, before we start, here is a list of the silly words we will be using. Will you read them aloud so that I will know for sure that you can read these silly words.

A list of nine nonsense syllables was then presented to each S, the six used in the learning task plus three additional syllables.[1] This list was randomized in 10 different sequences. Each S was asked to read each syllable aloud. Two practice trials on three practice S-R pairs followed. The stimuli in these S-R pairs were colored forms unrelated to the stimuli in the learning task to follow. If Ss had difficulty understanding the procedure during these trials, the instructions were reread.

The learning task followed immediately. The Ss were presented the S-R cards one at a time manually. The anticipation method was used in presenting the S-R pairs with picture stimulus and response word each exposed for 5 seconds. All stimuli were randomized with the restriction that one instance of each of the six concepts be presented in one series, and this series was defined as one trial. There was a brief pause at the end of each set of nine trials (the complete presentation of the 54 S-R cards), and then the 54 S-R cards were presented again in the same order. This procedure continued until S learned the task to a criterion of *three errorless trials*. At the end of the learning period, Ss were asked to verbalize the concepts appropriate to each nonsense syllable. Each S was required to learn the task within 40 trials or his data were discarded. The data for two Ss were discarded for failure to meet this criterion, and two additional Ss were run to bring the total sample size to 30 again. A response was correct when an S gave the correct syllable within the 5-second stimulus presentation interval.

Results

The number of trials to criterion was determined for each S on each of the six concepts. In order to determine if the two concepts within the same class (i.e., analytic, relational, inferential) were being learned at similar rates, correlations were computed (for high and low analytic Ss separately) between the trial of attainment for each of the two members of the three conceptual classes.

The correlations suggest that analytic boys learned the analytic concepts at similar rates ($r = .72$) and the relational concepts at moderately similar rates ($r = .59$). The nonanalytic Ss showed the reverse pattern. They learned the relational concepts at highly similar rates ($r = .75$) and the analytic concepts at moderately similar rates ($r = .47$). Neither the analytic nor the nonanalytic boys learned the two inferential concepts with similar ease. Since the hypotheses of this study pertained specifically to the differential learning of analytic concepts, the significant relation between the acquisition of the *black band* and *missing leg* concepts justified a pooling of the learning data for the three pairs.[2] The learning scores for each pair of concepts (i.e., analytic, relational, inferential) were combined for each S and all statistics were computed on the basis of these combined scores.

The mean trials to criterion and the respective standard deviations for the two groups over the combined analytic, inferential, and relational concept classes appear in Table 8.5. A test for heterogeneity of variance among the values did not yield a significant ratio. An analysis of variance of these data show that the main effects for analytic preference (i.e., high or low analytic) and for acquisition of the three concept classes were not significant. ($F = .11$; $df = 1$ and 28; $p < .05$; $F = .56$; $df = 2$ and 56; $p < .05$). However, the interaction between a preference for analytic categorizations and concept acquisition was highly significant ($F = 19.1$; $df = 2$ and 56; $p < .005$), indicating that the differential ease of attainment of the three concepts was intimately related to the tendency to be analytic in grouping the stimuli on the Conceptual Style Test. Analytic boys attained the analytic concepts *earlier* than other two concept classes; whereas the reverse held true for the nonanalytic boys. Although the interaction between the preferred style of the subject and concept attainment was highly significant, separate computations of the three possible t tests between the two groups yielded only one significant ratio ($t = 3.83$, 28 df,

TABLE 8.5. *Mean Trials to Criterion*

| | Concept Classes | | | | | |
| | ANALYTIC | | INFERENTIAL-CATEGORICAL | | RELATIONAL | |
GROUPS	Mean	SD	Mean	SD	Mean	SD
Analytic	20.3	11.3	33.7	12.6	35.4	12.3
Nonanalytic	38.7	19.2	28.7	9.8	27.9	13.4

$p. < .01$). The analytic boys learned the analytic concepts significantly earlier than the nonanalytic boys.

Discussion

These data indicate that some boys are predisposed to search for elements of similarity between objects that are embedded in larger stimulus contexts. These boys tend to ignore initially those properties of objects that involve the entire stimulus. The functional characteristics of babies and teachers or the fact that a "dress" belongs to the general class "wearing apparel" is not regarded initially as the most profitable way to classify diverse objects. Rather, the analytic child's strategy of choice is to fractionate the total stimulus and search for subelements that have a common characteristic. The nonanalytic boy, on the other hand, attends initially to those attributes that involve the total stimulus, especially the functional characteristics of objects (i.e., how each object might relate, as a whole, to another object). The search for elements of similarity within the whole is a much weaker conceptual habit for these boys. The analytic and nonanalytic boys were both bright (IQ scores between 105 and 134), and it is not suggested that one strategy is better than another. However, these are different ways of categorizing experience.

These results suggest that the final outcome of a conceptualization task is not merely a function of the ability to form associations between stimuli and responses or the availability of mediational labels that are relevant to the content of the class being formed. Conceptual products are also influenced by the individual's preferred focus of attention during the initial stages of learning. Children with equivalent ability and mediational structures might arrive at *different end states* in a problem situation because of differences in the initial processing of stimuli. It is certainly possible that the stages of cognitive organization described by Piaget and Inhelder reflect not only differences in the acquisition of complex rules (conservation, serial ordering operations), but also important individual differences in the ways that the problem relevant stimuli are categorized.

NOTES

[1] It became evident during pilot work that during early learning trials the Ss were learning the nonsense syllables rather than the S-R associations. It was decided therefore to familiarize each S with the syllables prior to the learning task.

[2] The correlation between rate of acquisition of the analytic concepts and either the inferential or relational concepts was considerably lower than the correlation of .72 found for the two analytic concepts for analytic Ss. For example, the correlation between trial of attainment for the *black band* and *school concepts* was only .35.

The Conservation of Mass, Weight, and Volume

David Elkind

The principle of conservation refers to an understanding of the fact that changing the shape or form of an object without adding or subtracting from it does not change its mass, weight, or volume. According to Piaget, the noted Swiss psychologist, an understanding of the principle of conservation develops in stages over a period of time. Piaget's microgenetic methodology provides substantial support for his theoretical formulations, but this approach has been criticized by American psychologists because of its reliance on a comparatively few number of children. In this experiment by Professor Elkind, the Piaget techniques are replicated using larger numbers of children. The outcome of the experiment lends support to Piaget's formulation, suggesting that his concepts have broad application.

SOURCE: Adapted and abridged from David Elkind, "Children's Discovery of the Conservation of Mass, Weight, and Volume: Piaget Replication Study II." *Journal of Genetic Psychology,* 1961, 98, 219–227. (With permission of the author and the Journal Press.)

This study is the second in a series devoted to the systematic replication of experiments originally performed by the Swiss psychologist, Jean Piaget. For its starting point the present study takes one of Piaget's investigations (Piaget and Inhelder, 1940) dealing with the ages at which children discover the conservation of mass, weight, and volume. Piaget assumes that concepts develop and that the discovery of conservation earmarks the final stage of their development. By studying children's responses to demonstrations of the conservation of mass, weight, and volume Piaget sought to uncover the genetic stages in the formation of these concepts. The present study differs from Piaget's investigation in its standardization of his procedures and in its use of statistical design.

In his investigation Piaget tested for the conservation of mass, weight, and volume by means of the "sausage" experiment. The purpose of this experiment was to determine whether the child could tell that a quantity remained the same (was conserved) after it was changed in appearance. For example, in testing for the conservation of mass Piaget showed the child two clay balls identical in size, shape, and weight. After the child agreed that both balls had equal clay, Piaget made one of the balls into a sausage. Then he asked the child to judge whether the ball and the sausage contained the same amount of clay. Piaget also asked the child to predict — while both pieces of clay were shaped as balls — if they would be the same were one made into a sausage and to explain his judgments and predictions.

Using the sausage experiment to test 5- to 12-year-old children, Piaget found that the discoveries of conservation followed a regular order that was related to age. The conservation of mass was discovered at ages 7 and 8; the conservation of weight was discovered at ages 9 and 10; and the conservation of volume was discovered at ages 11 and 12. These findings, together with his theoretical interpretations, Piaget reported with the aid of a great many illustrative examples but without statistics.

Starting from Piaget's procedures and results the present study was designed to test the hypotheses that, other things being equal, (a) the number of conservation responses does not vary significantly with the type of response (prediction, judgment, and explanation) required; (b) the number of conservation responses varies significantly with the type of quantity (mass, weight, and volume); (c) the number of conservation responses varies significantly with age level; (d) the number of conservation responses varies significantly with the joint effect of type of quantity and age level (the statistical test of Piaget's age-order of discovery finding). In addition children's explanations were categorized for comparison with the explanations given by Piaget's Ss.

Method

Subjects

One hundred and seventy-five children attending the Claflin School in Newton, Massachusetts, were tested. Twenty-five children were randomly selected from each of the grades from kindergarten to sixth. The mean age and standard deviation for each grade were: Kindergarten, M = 5:8, SD = 3.0; Grade 1, M = 6:8, SD = 3.9; Grade 2, M = 7:7, SD = 3.6; Grade 3, M = 8:6, SD = 3.8; Grade 4, M = 9:7, SD = 3.0; Grade 5, M = 10:7, SD = 2.5; Grade 6, M = 11:9, SD = 4.46 months. Hereafter the grades will be referred to by their age level.

For 125 children at the five oldest age levels, Kuhlmann-Anderson Intelligence Test scores were available. The mean IQ for this group was 109 and the SD was 11.0 points. Most of the children came from middle-class to upper-middle-class homes.

Procedure

Each S was seen individually and questioned three times on each type of quantity. For each quantity S was asked first to predict, next judge, and then explain his conservation or nonconservation responses. The order of the questions and the order of presenting the quantities — mass, weight, volume — was the same for all Ss. A fixed order of presentation was used to provide a more rigorous test of Piaget's findings. Any practice effects resulting from the fixed order should have worked against the differences Piaget found. On the other hand if differences were developmentally determined, as Piaget assumes, then the minimal practice effect over a brief time span should have had little effect.

Tests

In the test for the conservation of mass, two clay balls identical in size, shape, and weight were on the table. E: "Do both balls have the same amount of clay, is there as much clay in this ball as in this one?" S was encouraged to "make them the same," if he doubted the equality of the balls. When S agreed that the two balls were equal E asked, "Suppose I roll one of the balls out into a hot dog, will there be as much clay in the hot dog as in the ball, will they both have the same amount of clay?" (Prediction question.)

After S's prediction E actually made one of the balls into a hot dog while S looked on. E: "Is there as much clay in the ball as in the hot dog, do they both have the same amount of clay?" (Judgment question.) Then E asked "Why is that?" to S's response. (Explanation question.)

Exactly the same procedure was used to test for the conservation of weight and volume. To test for the conservation of weight E asked, "Do they both weigh the same, do they both have the same amount of weight?" etc. And to test for the conservation of volume E asked, "Do they both take up the same amount of space, do they both take up as much room?" etc. On each test the child was initially given the opportunity to handle the balls and to add or subtract clay as he liked, to "make them the same."

Scoring

Each conservation response was scored one, and all nonconservation responses were scored zero. For each S there was a total possible conservation score of nine, and for each type of quantity and type of response there was a total possible score of three.

Statistical Analyses

To test for the effects of type of response an analysis of variance design was used. In this design chance differences between Ss were controlled by testing all Ss on all types of response.

To test for the separate and combined effects of age level and type of quantity a different analysis of variance design was used. In this design chance differences between Ss were controlled, for the type of quantity variable only, by testing all Ss on all types of quantity.

Results

Type of Response

In his investigations Piaget used children's predictions, judgments, and explanations interchangeably as signs of conservation or nonconservation. In the present study the statistical test (F) for type of response did not approach significance. This finding agreed with Piaget's use of these three types of response as equivalent signs of conservation.

Type of Quantity

Piaget found that, other things being equal, the conservation of mass was easiest to discover; the conservation of weight was of intermediate difficulty; and the conservation of volume was the most difficult discovery of all. The F for type of quantity obtained in the present study was 255.55 and was significant beyond the .01 level. Individual t tests between the type of quantity means revealed that the mean for each type of quantity was significantly different than every other. For all Ss the average number of conservation responses given for mass was 2.08, the average number given for weight was 1.75, and the average number of conservation responses given for volume was 0.25. The order of difficulty obtained in the present study was the same as the order that Piaget observed.

Age Level

The Swiss children tested by Piaget showed that, other things being equal, their conservation responses increased with age. For the children in the present study the same held true. The F for age level was 14.38 and was significant beyond the .01 level. Individual t tests of age level means showed that the magnitude of the age level means increased significantly with age in agreement with Piaget's finding.

Type of Quantity-Age Level Interaction

Piaget's illustrative examples indicated that age group differences varied with the type of quantity in question. For mass there was a marked difference between the 5- and 6- and the 7- and 12-year-old groups; for weight there was a marked difference between the 5- and 8- and the 9- and 12-year-old groups; and for volume there was a marked difference between the 5- and 10- and 11- and 12-year-old groups in their number of conservation responses.

In the present study the variations in the differences between age groups for each type of quantity appeared as the interaction effect of type of quantity and age level. This interaction F was 6.93 and was significant beyond the .01 level. Individual t tests for age group differences showed that: (a) for mass the 5-to-6- and the 7-to-11-year-old groups differed significantly; (b) for weight the 5-to-8- and 9-to-11-year-old groups differed significantly; and (c) for volume the 5-to-10- and the 11-year-old groups differed significantly from each other in number of conservation responses given. These findings agreed with expectations based on Piaget's results.

In Piaget's earlier studies (1951a) he assigned different tests to the age level at which the per cent passing was 75. Although he gave no percentages for the conservation experiments, one can assume that he used the same criterion for assigning the conservation of mass to ages 7–8; the conservation of weight to ages 9–10; and the conservation of volume to ages 11–12. The results of the present study were converted into percentages for comparison with Piaget's criterion, and these are presented in Table 8.6.

TABLE 8.6. *Per Cent* of Conservation Responses for Mass, Weight, and Volume at Successive Age Levels*

($N = 25$ at Each Age Level)

TYPE OF QUANTITY	AGE LEVEL						
	5	6	7	8	9	10	11
Mass	19	51	70	72	86	94	92
Weight	21	52	51	44	73	89	78
Volume	0	4	0	4	4	19	25

* Of 75 possible responses.

Table 8.6 shows that the 70 per cent point for mass was reached at the 7-year level but that the 75 per cent point was not reached until age 9. For weight the 73 per cent point was reached at age 9 and the 75 per cent point by age 10. In this study the 75 per cent point for volume was not reached at the 11-year level.

The slight discrepancies between Piaget's results and those in Table 8.6 for weight and mass could easily be due to the small size of the samples used in the present study. The relatively low number of conservation responses at the 11-year level may be due to the fact that Piaget used a somewhat different procedure in his test for the conservation of volume. Piaget had his Ss say whether the ball and the sausage would displace the same amount of water. As a check the same procedure was used with some of the subjects of the present study (after the other testing was completed), and conservation seemed easier to discover by means of the displacement problem.

Children's Explanations

When Piaget interpreted the results of his investigation he made use of children's explanations without categorizing or quantifying them as he did in early studies (Piaget 1951a). In the present study four types of explanation were distinguished. Two of these were explanations of nonconservation: (a) romancing (Piaget 1951b, introduction), it's more because "My uncle said so"; and (b) perceptual, it's more because it's "longer, thinner, thicker, wider, etc." The two types of explanation given for conservation were: (c) specific, "You didn't add any or take any away," "You can roll it back into a ball and it will be the same," and "The hot dog is longer but thinner so the same"; and (d) general, it's the same because "No matter what shape you make it into it won't change the amount."

The per cent for each type of explanation given at each age level shows that romancing and perceptual explanations decrease with age while specific explanations first increase and then level off with age. Piaget noted the same types and age trends in the explanations given by his subjects. The explanations are one type of evidence Piaget takes for his theory that as the child's thinking develops, it frees itself from its earlier domination by immediate perception. One step in this liberation is the interpretation of a perceptual effect as the result of a specific action which can be reversed (you can roll it back into a ball). A later step is to interpret a perception as but one of a great many possible instances (no matter what shape you make it into it will always be the same). These results agree with the observations upon which Piaget builds his theory of the developmental changes in the relation between thought and perception.

Discussion

The results of the present study agreed with Piaget's findings regarding the ages at which children discover the conservation of mass, weight, and volume. In both studies: the conservation of mass did not usually appear before the ages 7–8; the conservation of weight did not usually appear before the ages 9–10; and the conservation of volume did not in most cases appear before the age of 11. The discussion will briefly summarize Piaget's interpretation of these results.

Piaget's theory is that concepts of quantity develop in three stages, with the final stage earmarked by the discovery of conservation. Children at the first stage have only a general impression of quantity but are capable of judging crude weight, volume, and mass differences. In the sausage experiment they give nonconservation responses because to their general impression the sausage is different than the ball. When they are forced to break down this impression, by the explanation question, then they judge quantity by single dimensions which they are unable to coordinate one with the other.

Those children who are at the second stage have a differentiated impression of quantity and are unable to judge quantity differences two by two (long-wide, long-narrow, etc.), which Piaget calls *logical multiplication*. Children at this stage give nonconservation responses in the sausage experiment because to their differentiated impression the sausage is both more (in length) and less (in width) than the ball. They are unable to resolve the contradiction; as one child expressed it, "It's more and it's less, I'll take one of each." When these children are forced to explain their nonconservation answers they also judge quantity by single dimensions.

At the third stage children have an abstract quantity concept and judge quantity in unit terms. In the sausage experiment they immediately predict and judge conservation. Their explanations indicate either that the perceived transformation can be canceled (the sausage can be rolled back into a ball) or that the perceived differences can be equated (what the sausage gained in length it lost in width) and therefore the quantity is the same.

According to Piaget the *equation of differences* results in the formation of ratios and fixed units and underlies abstract quantity and number (Piaget 1952a) concept formation. On the perceptual plane the equation of differences enables the child to discover that an object which changes in appearance can still be the same in quantity. Piaget's theory is that once conservation is discovered it is immediately externalized and the subject has the impression that conservation is a perceptually given property of the object.

The initial appearance of the conservation of mass at ages 7–8 Piaget attributes to the development by that age of logical multiplication and equation of differences which he speaks of as *mental operations*. The time lag before the discovery of the conservation of weight at ages 9–10 and the even greater lag before the conservation of volume at ages 11–12 Piaget attributes to the quantities themselves. He argues that a quantity is difficult to conceptualize, and so to conserve, to the degree that it is associated with the subject's own action. Length, for example, was more easily dissociated from the child's action than was weight. In Piaget's theory, therefore, the discovery of conservation is limited both by the maturational level of the subject and by the properties of the object, and in this sense it is both a nature *and* a nurture theory.

CHAPTER IX

Intellectual Development

INTELLIGENCE, as a concept, has probably had more of an impact on society than any other psychological concept. Testing programs in public schools, for example, routinely include a measure of intellectual ability, particularly a measure of the "group type." In addition, many children are administered individual intelligence tests, such as the Stanford-Binet or the Wechsler Intelligence Scale for Children (WISC), by qualified psychologists. Since most children are exposed to these tests at one time or another, it is crucial that professional child workers as well as laymen understand their meaning and value.

A careful reading of Liverant's examination of the concept of intelligence reveals a persuasive argument for abandoning such traditional assumptions of IQ constancy, or the general intellectual ability factor — often referred to as Spearman's "g." In effect, Liverant argues, that scores on intelligence tests have little conceptual meaning and should be regarded solely as a basis for predicting academic behavior such as occurs in the classroom. This conclusion has important implications. Consider for a moment the criticism that intelligence tests are culturally biased in favor of middle-class children. Empirically, this is a valid criticism, and it is often used as the basis for abandoning the use of intelligence tests. Critics further argue that test scores are treated as absolutes and pigeonhole the child in a particular niche in the educational schema. The fact is, however, that intelligence tests, even the so-called "culture-free" tests, predict classroom performance at better than chance level. Thus, the public school assumes that children have certain clusters of behavioral capabilities which are found more commonly, for a variety of reasons, among middle-class children. That lower-class children do not possess these capabilities, as measured by intelligence tests, is not the fault of the tests but is rather the fault of society.

The impact of a culture lacking the stimulation found in an urban-middle-class situation is shown in the now classic study by Sherman and Key. In all likelihood the grandchildren of the youngsters included in this study now find themselves in the same impoverished condition. It may be, however, that the grandchildren will benefit from the Project Head Start program and not evidence the marked decline in test score performance shown by their grandparents.

Kagan and his associates also examined the impact of environment on test score performance. In their investigation, children whose IQ scores consistently increased over time were contrasted with children whose IQ scores declined. Apparently, children whose achievement-oriented behaviors are reinforced improve in their test performance. The results of this are, however, only suggestive, since the two groups of children were not randomly selected.

Professor Honzik's paper serves to remind us that intelligence is not entirely the result of environment. This paper further indicates that the genetic component does not emerge as a variable until later in the preschool years.

Perhaps the leading proponent of a multitrait theory of intelligence, as opposed to a general factor theory, was the late L. L. Thurstone. Through his pioneering efforts in the use of multiple factor analysis, many traits and abilities were identified and measured. Dr. Thurstone and his wife developed the Primary Mental Abilities Test consisting of at least five different more or less independent components of intellectual ability. The paper included in this chapter describes the development of each of the primary mental abilities.

Intelligence: A Concept in Need of Reexamination

Shephard Liverant

Scientific concepts sometimes lose their effectiveness as explanations because they acquire excessive meanings or because the data fail to confirm predictions derived from the concept. The late Dr. Liverant presents a careful and penetrating analysis of the scientific value of the concept of intelligence. Systematically examining the implications of the terms, he concludes that intelligence is simply a descriptive term with little, if any, explanatory or scientific value. A potentially more productive approach is an experimental and theoretical analysis of the behaviors typically included under the rubric of intelligence. He suggests that a point of departure for this analysis might be modern learning theory.

The importance of the concept of intelligence in understanding and predicting human behavior appears so obvious that the value of this term in a science of behavior has seldom been questioned by psychologists. The inadequacies inherent in present conceptions of intelligence have been made explicit by a number of authors, but the reader is left with the impression that the concept itself is essentially a useful and necessary one. By leaving open the possibility that the concept

SOURCE: Adapted and abridged from S. Liverant, "Intelligence: A Concept in Need of Re-examination." *Journal of Consulting Psychology*, 1960, 24, 101–110. (With permission of the author and the American Psychological Association.)

may be unnecessary, and even an obstacle, in explaining behavior, perhaps we can arrive at a better solution to the problems now subsumed under the rubric of intelligence.

This paper explores a number of problems over which the intelligence concept has stumbled, such as: establishing an unequivocal definition, the contribution of heredity and environment, measuring an innate capacity, situational predictions, the constancy of the IQ, intelligence as a general factor, the role of culture in defining intelligent behavior, and the function of nonintellective variables. The objective of such an exploration is to reevaluate these persistent problems by analyzing the logical and methodological adequacy of the meanings carried by intelligence.

Clinical Approach

Present uses of the term intelligence for individual prediction and the difficulties inherent in such usage are best represented in the clinical setting. Clinical case studies have produced a greatly increased awareness of the failure of an IQ (or any other behavioral appraisal) to reflect accurately a constant ability to perform at a certain level in all situations. This awareness has led to the clinical practice of considering the IQ as an index of present intellectual functioning rather than intellectual potential or capacity. However, the belief in the existence of a "true" IQ or intelligence persists, and attempts to discover it in each individual continue.

In general it appears that the host of evidence gathered over the last twenty or more years challenging the general and innate nature of intelligence has been subsumed under an interference hypothesis. Consequently, intelligence can be and still is viewed as a general and innate source of variance, but it is increasingly recognized that in order to get at it from behavioral observation one must strip away an ever increasing number of complex variables which interfere with its effects on behavior.

This point of view is illustrated by the work of the Chicago group (Eells, Davis, Havighurst, Herrick, and Tyler, 1951) who, after demonstrating the effects of culture on test performance, conclude that the answer to the problem is to develop "culture-free" intelligence tests. By contrast, Anastasi (1950) uses the same kind of evidence to question the validity of any test as a measure of an abstract conception of intelligence without regard to validation criteria. As Rotter (1963, p. 19) points out, "It is somewhat surprising that the emphasis on culture and training did not result in a discarding of the notion of over-all intelligence and the IQ in favor of a clear understanding of the value of varied tests in assessing what has been learned and what each test can predict. Rather the early trend to entitize and reify the IQ continues."

The question being raised here is what if anything will be left as a contributor to understanding behavior on a psychological level once the stripping away process is complete. If more and more of the variance which accounts for individual differences in intellectual performance can be attributed to other variables, what is intelligence?

Spiker and McCandless (1954) attempt to resolve the definitional problem by an appeal to early operationalism. In effect they conclude that intelligence is what different intelligence tests measure in different situations with different groups and the relationship of these measures to other measures. There is nothing wrong with such a definition of intelligence except that most people are not willing to accept it. Intelligence means more to most of us than a score on an intelligence test even though the "more" hasn't been made explicit (i.e., we use intelligence as a hypothetical construct whose validity depends on the verification or refutation of predictions derived from the theory which contains it).

More recent thinking on the subject suggests that the ultraempirical approach is not a satisfactory solution to the problem of definition. Several authors have argued that the construction, interpretation, and validity criteria of any test depend on the nomological network (meanings) surrounding the implicit or explicit construct(s) which the test is designed to measure. Intelligence, like any other construct, takes its meaning from the assumed antecedent conditions and subsequent responses which it mediates. The controversies over nature-nurture on the antecedent side and general versus specific factors on the response side of the relationship characterize the difficulties in arriving at an accepted definition of intelligence. Thus, the next step is to examine first the nature of the antecedent conditions and then the subsequent responses subsumed by intelligence.

Antecedent Side of the Problem

Heredity and Environment

As now evolved, the antecedents of intelligence do not refer to a set of conditions (either inherited or environmental) but rather to a conceptual model involving postulated genetic operations. Although stated in many different forms, genetic intelligence seems to embody the idea that each organism, from the moment of conception throughout the life span, has inherent within it an unmodifiable growth process determined by gene composition which if given the proper environmental stimulation at the right time will result in maximum problem-solving performance for that organism under suitable conditions of motivation, health, etc. Improper stimulation (degree and kind unspecified) may inhibit certain manifestations of this innate property, but given an adequate restoration of environmental conditions (provided structural damage has not occurred) it will proceed upon its genetically determined course. However, no amount of environmental manipulation will serve to modify the limits of intellectual performance prescribed by the genetic constituents. It is this last proposition which lends an air of crucial significance to this formulation, since knowledge of these innately fixed limits (intelligence) will permit us to predict maximum attainment under optimal conditions — predictions which are invaluable in terms of educational and vocational planning.

There are several implications of genetic intelligence which need clarification, if not complete refutation, in light of recent conceptual advances in both genetics and psychology. Paramount is the notion of intellectual limits set by heredity. As usually interpreted, this idea means that beyond a certain point (usually unspecified) any and all environmental conditions cease to make a difference as far as increments in problem solving proficiency are concerned. But the conclusions of modern day geneticists reveal a basic fallacy inherent in this line of reasoning. Geneticists postulate that the appearance of any characteristic (behavioral or otherwise) depends upon the *interaction* of a *specific* genetic structure operating within a *specific* environment. In this sense genes set the limits within any given environment, but these limits may vary as the environment varies. Without in any way arguing against the Wiesman-Morgan theory of the immutability of the germ plasm, it is no more logical to attribute a limiting role to heredity than it is to assign the same role to the environment. Perhaps the irrevocability of genetic determinants as compared to situational ones has contributed to this mode of thought, but it is one which contradicts the postulated interaction effect.

The implication of a true interaction is not that only within a limited range (set by one of the variables) does the effect of the other make a difference, but that they both operate to produce their effects over any conceivable range. Now it does appear that heredity can influence the variety of conditions which will or will not have an appreciable effect on a given characteristic. For example, it can be said that species characteristics are determined by heredity in the sense that the occurrence or nonoccurrence of an extremely wide range of external conditions does not make a difference in the morphology necessary to identify a given species. Both theoretically and empirically, however, a set of conditions could be, and in fact have been, produced which radically alter species characteristics. Feeding thyroid abstract to the young axolotl to produce a creature adapted for the land rather than the usual aquatic life is a case in point. On the other hand, intraspecies behavior is apparently affected by a much greater host of nongenetic variables. Furthermore, the importance of situational variations in determining individual differences seems to increase as one ascends the phylogenetic scale. Beach's (1956) findings regarding comparative variations in sexual behavior emphasize the ever increasing role of situational factors in determining the sexual patterns displayed by increasingly complex organisms. It is likely that the same relationship is even more predominant in the case of complex problem-solving behavior. Since the evidence points to such a great number of circumstances which can affect intellectual performance it becomes conceptually difficult to speak of heredity as the determiner of intellectual limits, particularly in the case of human beings.

From this line of reasoning it follows that although no practical way may be known to affect appreciable positive changes in an individual's performance level, it cannot be assumed that such changes are precluded by genetically determined limitations. On the contrary, the implication of genetic theorizing in this respect is that changes in any characteristic would result from sufficient environmental changes. After producing previously unknown patterns of performance in pigeons (i.e., bowling behavior), Skinner (1958, p. 96) concludes that, "It is dangerous to assert that an organism of a given species or age *cannot* solve a given problem." The implications of this reasoning in the field of mental deficiency are apparent.

A further failure to recognize the significance of the continuous interaction between genes and environment in producing behavior is indicated by the one-way effect of interaction implied by the intelligence model. The implication is that training can have an effect only after neural maturation paves the way, and that it is by controlling the maturational rate that heredity plays its vital role in the development of intelligent behavior. The "Johnny and Jimmy" type of studies (McGraw 1935) are cited as evidence in this connection. But this approach neglects the reciprocal relationship between physiological maturation and behavior. The "learning how to learn" phenomena demonstrated by Harlow (1949) strongly suggests that the rate of acquisition of problem solving ability is directly dependent on neural changes which occur as a function of previous problem solving performance. In other words, previous experience as well as genes "shapes up" the organism's maturational readiness for new training procedures.

Acceptance of the interaction thesis concerning heredity and environment invalidates the concept of innate capacity unless the term includes the operations of an environment. Consequently, the prediction of behavior based on genetic antecedents involves the problems of specifying situational conditions, a problem with which the present definition of intelligence as an inherited capacity has not dealt. There are two kinds of situational conditions which need to be specified: first, the conditions of development, growth, and learning; and second, the criterion conditions (i.e., the actual performance situations). The emphasis in this section is on the former conditions. The criterion conditions will be discussed more fully in the subsequent response section.

Environmental Specificity

Perhaps the most pronounced conceptual weakness of the present model lies in its inability to cope with environmental specificity. The position that individual differences in problem solving are a function of heredity given a relatively constant "demographic" environment (e.g., similar cultural opportunities or similar family life) grossly oversimplifies the specific and still unknown effects of the "psychological" environment on the hereditary potential.

Recent research concerned with the effects of early experience upon later behavior has brought into sharp focus the preeminent role of experiential factors in influencing problem solving processes. For example, evidence has been gathered that rats, dogs, and humans reared in impoverished perceptual and social environments show "irreversible" problem solving impairment in adulthood. Extensive clinical case material now supported by still tentative research findings indicates that much more is involved in a child's inability to profit from the most "well conducted" training procedures than lack of the proper genetic constituents. The crucial role of interpersonal relationships in the acquisition of problem solving behavior is becoming increasingly evident.

In order to avoid confusion, it is important to recognize that no amount of empirical evidence relating intelligent behavior or the lack of it to environmental events can directly invalidate the model in question. As now conceptualized, the position concerning genetic determinants is that they exist and somehow make a difference, a position which it would be absurd to deny. The most that data can accomplish is to question the usefulness of the genetic intelligence scheme and indicate lines along which a potentially more productive one may develop. The network of studies beginning to elucidate the complex set of interrelated past and present situational factors involved in determining the adequacy of intelligent behavior tends to place a heredity explanation of problem solving ability in the position of an appeal to ignorance. In the present stage of conceptualization in this area, it is the absence of knowledge concerning situational determinants which brings forth genetic ones.

The Constancy of the IQ

In the final analysis the value of any scientific approach must be judged in terms of the number of valid hypotheses which it generates. The questionable validity of one of the two major hypotheses stipulated by the genetic theory of intelligence (i.e., intelligence as a general factor) will be discussed in the subsequent response section. The inability to validate or refute the other major hypothesis concerning the constancy of the IQ represents still another instance of the essential untestability of the genetic model.

It may well be that given a theoretically constant environment, individuals would maintain the same relative position in problem solving adequacy over any given time period as a function of genetic differences. However, the indications that the *inconstancy* as well as the *constancy* of the IQ can be better explained by alternative hypotheses (other than genetic ones) seriously challenge the existing model. Disregarding individual differences in patterns of IQ change, the empirically observed "constancy" of intellectual status at the upper childhood age ranges has been accounted for on the basis of an "overlap" hypothesis. Anderson (1940) among others has proposed that the similarity in IQ from one age level to the next depends on the proportions of similar test items included in the total score at various age levels.

A more crucial test of the constancy hypothesis is provided by the longitudinal studies (Bayley 1955) explicitly considering individual differences. These conclusively demonstrate the lack of IQ constancy over any childhood period. Sontag, Baker, and Nelson (1958), in probably the most thorough and well-designed study of its kind, found that 62 per cent of their children changed more than 15 IQ points in either direction sometime during the developmental period from the age of 3 through 10 years. Most significant is the finding that the direction and degree of change in rate of "mental growth" are related to personality dimensions (primarily a need for achievement).

Reductionism

It can and has been argued that environmental explanations in and of themselves must always remain incomplete since genetic differences undoubtedly do play a role. The demand for the incorporation of genetic operations in behavioral explanatory conventions brings us to the problem of reductionism, i.e., the question of the necessity and/or feasibility of seeking explanations of the phenomena described in the language of one discipline by reference to the descriptive language of another. Reductionism, as far as psychology is concerned, usually refers to attempts to explain molar behavior in terms of physiological (i.e., neurological) events. Since genetics is still lower in the hierarchy, in the sense that its effects on behavior must be mediated through physiological processes, the criticisms cited in reference to physiological reductionism should be even more pertinent in the case of genetic reductionism. Jessor (1958) cogently argues against the logical possibility of reducing contructs designed to abstract organism-environment interactions to physiological operations, since the latter lack terms to describe the behavioral environment. This argument seems to be particularly applicable to any attempts to seek the casual antecedents of problem solving behavior (certainly a complex organism-environmental interaction) in genetic laws (certainly lacking terms to describe the behavioral environment).

Whatever the eventual relationship between genetic determinants and complex behavior proves to be, it is obvious that this relationship is a very distant one. Bridging this gap necessitates taking into account a number of intervening processes at different levels of organization. And the simpler or more molecular the process, the closer is the relationship to the genes. Thus, initial sensitivity to stimuli may be more genetically determined than differential responding to these stimuli. Since these processes preceding complex performance are continuously changing as a function of innumerable environmental variations in large part brought about by the behaving organism, the more complicated the behavior, the greater is the potential error in prediction based on genetic antecedents.

In this sense, it is not at all surprising to find a lack of correlation (Bayley 1955) between infant scales, which of necessity sample lower (more molecular) levels of behavior, and intelligence tests dependent on higher order processes. But the major conclusion to be drawn from our attempts to develop infant scales and culture-free tests is that the more we narrow our performance sample to eliminate or minimize the effects of environmental variables, the less likely we are to arrive at valid measures of intelligent behavior as we now conceptualize it.

Subsequent Response Side of the Problem

Analogous to the previous discussion of its antecedents, intelligence does not refer to a well-defined set of subsequent responses, but to an elusive set of notions concerning problem solving. Postulating intelligence as the general something (force, energy, capacity, potential) which undergirds the abilities necessary to solve problems can, of course, neither be directly validated nor invalidated. However, by examining the consequences which have followed from this formulation, one may contrast its usefulness to that of other frames of reference not including intelligence in the above sense as the basis for understanding problem solving.

Intelligence as a General Factor

Analysis of intelligence as a psychological construct raises the problem of pointing to the behavioral referents which are placed in the class, intelligence. The same analysis also requires determination of the grounds upon which certain aspects of behavior are classified. For, depending upon the basis of classification, the invented construct may fulfill its goal in expediting the understanding of behavior, or as suggested by Peak (1953, p. 248) it may prove ". . . artifactual and without systematic significance." Unfortunately it is not clear which are the behavioral referents for intelligence or which principles are involved in isolating the intelligence concept.

Intelligence as a prescientific concept (i.e., its meaning in everyday language) apparently refers to an unspecified but certainly very wide range of problem solving abilities. It is important to note that this usage does not refer directly to the behavior involved in solving problems but to the adequacy of the results of the behavior. In this sense the immediately distinguishable referents for intelligence are not *behaviors* but *problems*. The importance of all this lies in the recognition that selecting a sample of problems from an unknown universe of problems on some historical, cultural and/or common sense basis to measure intelligence (a procedure traditionally followed in intelligence test construction) may involve a number of behaviors which are not functionally related. However, the construct validity of intelligence as referring to all intellectual problems (i.e., a general factor) depends upon the functional relatedness of all or at least most of the behaviors involved in problem solving. That is, in terms of one set of operations, the describable events within the class, intelligence, must correlate as a function of a common source of variance.

Although factor analysis has repeatedly demonstrated the unrelatedness of a striking number of behaviors traditionally grouped under intelligence, there still persists the hypothesis of a general ability which now, as the result of training, interest, motivation, etc., has become differentiated into the various abilities demonstrated by correlational methods. The persistence of a general factor is based on the low but positive correlations often found between the factors which emerge from the test matrix (i.e., a second-order factor). However, even discounting similarities inherent in the content of the tests usually placed in the matrix, it cannot be assumed a priori that these correlations confirm the existence of general intelligence as usually understood. The communality which is found may, for example, be the result of the testing situation rather than any inherent property within the individual which transcends all situations. A series of studies conducted by Sarason and his coworkers (Gordon and Sarason 1955; Mandler and Sarason 1952 and 1953; Sarason and Mandler 1952) indicates that variables (test taking attitudes or test taking anxiety) operating as a function of the inter-personal competitive situation represented by the test may contribute significantly to test performance. It seems reasonable to hypothesize that these situational variables may to a large extent account for a general factor, and surely this is not what is meant by intelligence. By systematically varying the conditions under which the same tests are given to the same individuals, it may be possible to demonstrate concomitant changes in the measures as a function of these situational variables.

Regardless of the accuracy of the hypothesis concerning the role of situational factors in accounting for "g," the criticism of the existence of a general factor based on factor analytic methods stands. Guilford (1956, p. 290) in an extensive review of factor analytic studies of intellectual tests concludes that "The methods of multiple factor analysis . . . do not find a general psychological factor at the first order level and they find no second-order factor that can properly lay claim to the title of intelligence."

Cultural Definition

Whatever the most useful classification of intellectual behaviors proves to be, the very generality of intelligence makes it impossible actually to sample a unidimensional population of behaviors subsumed by intelligence, since in one way or another most, if not all, of behavior sooner or later becomes involved in problem solving. Even scratching one's epidermis may be viewed as solving the problem of itching. However, such behavior tends not to be included in the typical intelligence test. In fact, the criterion of what is or what is not intelligent behavior involves a cultural value judgment. This makes for a great deal of difficulty in arriving at a consistent sample, since by definition values are different in different cultures and tend to change with time in a given culture.

Rapaport (1953) suggests that in the case of terms having value connotations it is meaningless to ask what is x. Rather our problem becomes one of finding commonly accepted criteria for x. According to this point of view, rather than asking what is intelligence, we should be seeking established criteria for intelligent behavior which will vary from one class of situations to another. In this sense intelligence is divorced from its explanatory significance and serves a descriptive function, a state of affairs which may prove very desirable.

The Role of Nonintellective Variables

Reference to the situational context in which intellectual behaviors operate brings into focus the role of variables other than the intellectual behaviors *per se* in the problem solving process. While it is generally conceded that nonintellective factors are important in all actual measures of problem solving ability, within the intelligence model no clear conceptualization of what these variables are and how they function has yet been made. As testers, we somehow assume that by holding nonintellective variables constant (vaguely referred to as establishing rapport or providing the proper conditions) during the testing period, an index of an individual's functional capacity to solve problems can be obtained apart from these nonintellective factors. But the manifestation of any problem solving ability in or out of the testing situation must be in accord with certain laws of behavior which include the operation of these so-called nonintellective variables.

An example using the terms of Rotter's (1954) Social Learning Theory may help clarify this latter point. In social learning theory the probability of the occurrence of any behavior depends upon the individual's expectation that using this behavior in the present situation will result in a certain kind of reward and the value of that reward for him. Thus, an individual may not manifest a certain implicit or explicit skill (e.g., memory, judgment, reasoning, etc.) necessary to solve a given problem for either of two reasons: one, the level of skill required is not within his repertoire; or, two, the right combination of expectancy and reward value necessary to elicit that behavior in that situation is not operating.

Neither intelligence tests nor the intelligence model provides an objective means of making a decision regarding which of the two reasons is operating in the case of failure to solve problems. Wechsler (1958) attempts to circumvent this problem by including the operation of nonintellective variables within his practical definition of intelligence. In practice, however, it is the inability to identify and formulate the operation of these variables which results in the lower predictive validity of intelligence tests, since it is these very variables which change as the situation changes. As a consequence of these situationally modifiable variables we have the fairly common case of the child who functions so well in school but behaves so "stupidly" with his peers or, what is even more puzzling within the confines of intelligence, who does admirably on an intelligence test and abominably in school. It is only within a theory of problem solving which attempts an explicit formulation of all the variables necessary to predict behavior that these apparent contradictions become understandable.

Mental Deficiency

An adequate discussion of mental deficiency in light of the present suggestions concerning intelligence is beyond the scope of this presentation. It is mentioned at this point, however, because it is in relation to the intellectually handicapped that the discarding of intelligence as an explanatory construct may have its most far-reaching effects. Fortunately, a number of prominent students of this problem have anticipated and demonstrated the detrimental fallacy of regarding certain kinds of problem solving inadequacies as largely a matter of an inherited lack of capacity to perform any and all tasks at a certain level of difficulty. However, continued use of such terms as limited intelligence, inferior intellectual capacity, low IQ, feebleminded, mental defective, etc. (all referring to lack of intelligence as *an explanation* for inadequate performance) hinders the understanding and the development of the point of view being expressed by these authors because of the surplus meanings inherent in the term intelligence. What is necessary from our point of view is recognition of the logical basis for discarding a contradictory and outmoded terminology which persists through tradition and not through theoretical and/or empirical justification.

An Approach to Change

Inherent in the reasons for relegating intelligence to a nonexplanatory usage are suggestions for an alternative approach to understanding problem solving proficiency. Essentially what is being suggested is not that intelligence be replaced by a new term, but that it be relegated to a descriptive function applicable to certain kinds of behavior whose explanation can be attempted by the continued development of existing constructs which can better integrate data of the kind previously mentioned and direct attention to new avenues of research. As argued by some, the constructs of modern learning theories would appear to be a likely point of departure for this endeavor.

Rather than regarding intelligence tests as measures of a single dimension (general intelligence), it is more in keeping with the evidence to interpret them as assessing culturally expected standards of academic preparedness involving a number of complexly interrelated variables (e.g., implicit reaction patterns, motives, habits, expectancies, reinforcements, etc.) to account for the results. Attempting to incorporate the varieties of socially learned behaviors operating in the testing situation within the domain of developing theories of learning has the salutary effect of replacing a notion which is essentially untestable with constructs which have been selected with a view to functioning in potentially fruitful theories.

The Differential Growth of Mental Abilities

L. L. Thurstone

The late Professor Thurstone is probably best known for his pioneering work in multiple factor analysis. One outgrowth of this work was the development of the Primary Mental Abilities Test, which is widely used in the public schools today. In this report the growth of each of the primary mental abilities (Visualizing Space factor, Verbal Comprehension factor, Number factor, Reasoning factor, Perceptual Speed factor, Immediate Memory factor, and Word Fluency factor) are examined.

SOURCE: Adapted and abridged from L. L. Thurstone, *The Differential Growth of Mental Abilities*. Chapel Hill: University of North Carolina Press, 1955. (With permission of the author and the University of North Carolina Press.)

The results of the study indicate that the Space factor matures most rapidly, whereas the Verbal Comprehension and Word Fluency factors develop least rapidly. A second important contribution of this paper involves the use of a scaling technique in which the scale-intervals are derived from a defined zero point. The resulting S-shaped curves provide a better description of the growth of mental abilities than the typical negatively accelerated curve.

The purpose of this paper is to report the differential rate of growth of several mental abilities. As long as mental endowment was described in terms of a single index of intelligence it was appraised by composite tests that represented quite a number of mental abilities. It was found that the average performance increased with age until an adult average was attained at an age usually below 20. The methods of multiple factor analysis have been developed since 1930 for the purpose of isolating and identifying the components of human intelligence. The methods are still being developed and improved. Many investigators in this field have isolated a number of components of intelligence which are called primary mental abilities, and it is of interest to inquire about their differential rates of growth. The study that is reported here is a comparison of the mental growth curves of seven primary mental abilities. Data are available for large groups of children over the age span from 5 to 19.

In constructing a growth curve for a physical trait the average measure of some organ is plotted against age. A growth curve for weight shows the average weight in pounds or kilos against chronological age. The curve rises with age and becomes asymptotic toward an adult mean weight for the population studied. The unit of measurement in a physical growth curve is some unit of weight, length, or volume.

Before constructing a mental growth curve it is necessary to establish a defensible metric for mental abilities. This is known as a scaling problem. It was solved some years ago, so that we can answer questions relating to the shape of the mental growth curves. They are S-shaped for all the mental abilities that have been investigated. They have inflection points at a fairly early age, usually at about 3 to 6 or 7 years.

The adult level for the mental growth curve can be determined as the asymptote toward which the average performances approach with increasing age. The location of the zero point is a more difficult matter in dealing with the mental abilities. In working with the physical growth curve the zero point is known because it is the natural zero point of the physical measure. In the case of a psychological test of any kind a zero score does not mean the zero point of the ability in question. This is an old problem that has been solved indirectly. It has been found that the dispersion of performance increases with mean performance for successive age groups. Often this relation is roughly linear. The zero point in the study of mental abilities has been defined as that point on the scale at which the dispersion vanishes. In the nature of the case the dispersion cannot be negative. It is often possible to estimate the location of the zero point as that point on the scale at which the dispersion vanishes. This is the method that was used for most of these curves. In general the zero point is between five and six standard deviations below the mean of a particular age group. In several cases we dealt with atypicalities in the selection of the age groups, especially at the upper ages. In such cases we estimated the zero point as between five and six standard deviations below the mean test performance. In all of these cases the mental growth curves seem to be plausible when determined by these methods.

The scale which describes the increasing performance with increasing age varies from one primary mental ability to another. There is no direct translation from one to the other. For the purpose of this study we have therefore determined two limiting values, namely, the zero point and the asymptotic adult level. All of the growth curves can be reduced to this basis, so that we can say with some confidence that some of these primary mental abilities mature at an earlier age than others.

The Gompertz equation has been used to describe the mental growth curves because they are all S-shaped and they all have inflection points that are below the mean ordinates. We treat the Gompertz equation here merely as an empirical equation. It is not interpreted as a rational equation. Hence the equation is used here only for descriptive purposes.

The Gompertz equation has three parameters, namely the adult asymptote, the zero point which is defined by the distance from the asymptote to the origin, and a third parameter which describes the relative rate at which the adult asymptote is being approached with increasing age. In fitting the Gompertz equation to the growth data for each of the primary mental abilities we used the method of rectification. This method has been extended so as to handle three-parameter equations as in this case. The method of curve fitting for three parameters by rectification will be described in a separate paper.

We consider now the mental growth curves for seven primary mental abilities: Visualizing Space factor, S_1; Verbal comprehension, V; Number, N; Reasoning, R; Perceptual Speed, P; Immediate Memory, M; Word Fluency, W. Figure 9.35.1 shows the mental growth curves for each of the factors.

The first Space factor represents the ability to visualize rigid figures in three-dimensional space. The first Space factor is well represented in working with orthographic projection in ordinary mechanical drawing. Several other visualizing factors have been isolated but norms are not yet available for school populations.

The Verbal Comprehension V factor represents the ability to comprehend verbal meaning of single words or continuous text. It is undoubtedly the most important of the mental abilities for academic achievement. It can be seen that this function matures more slowly than the first Space factor.

The Number factor N is quite narrow and it represents facility in numerical manipulation. This factor does not extend to mathematical reasoning. It does not even extend to the formulation of statement problems in arithmetic. Such tasks

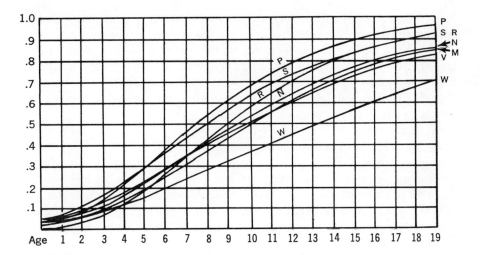

Figure 9.1 Mental growth curves for seven primary mental abilities. See text for an explanation of this graph.

involve other primary factors. The Number factor N is well represented in the work of a cashier who must handle simple numerical relations quickly and accurately.

Reasoning, R, is really a combination of two primary mental factors for induction and deduction. The inductive component here represents the ability to discover the rule or principle of the material that one is working with. An interesting characteristic of this primary factor is that it transcends the modalities. It has been shown to be the same factor whether the inductive task represents visual or verbal or quantitative tasks. The question has been raised whether the inductive factor is principally responsible for creative and inventive talent, but our present belief is that such is not the case. Individuals with good mental endowment can produce well on ordinary inductive tasks without being noticeably creative in the arts and sciences.

The Perceptual Speed factor P represents the ability to cover details in the perceptual field. This is necessarily a speed factor because practically everybody can do the perceptual tasks that are used in these tests. There are great individual differences in the speed and ease with which people can do these simple tasks. The Perceptual Speed factor has been found to be of value in selecting inspectors who must be able to spot even minor defects quickly. Although this factor is definitely in the cognitive and intellective domain it is not necessarily associated with capacity for abstract intellectual work.

Two additional factors are represented in this study, namely, the Immediate Memory factor M and the Word Fluency factor W. The Immediate Memory factor M represents the ability to memorize a set of arbitrary paired associates.

It is distinct from visual memory and incidental memory, which are different primary factors.

The Word Fluency factor W represents the ability to produce words which are required for a given context as distinguished from the ability merely to understand words that are presented. It seems likely that the Word Fluency W should be studied with some types of aphasia where the distinction between the Verbal factors V and W is much in evidence.

All of the curves in Figure 9.1 have been reduced to the same scale where unity represents the asymptotic adult performance. From this figure we can make a rough comparison of the rate of maturation of these abilities. For this purpose we note the age at which the average mental growth curve reaches four-fifths of the adult performance. With this criterion the Perceptual Speed factor P teaches 80% of the adult performance at the age of 12. The Space and Reasoning factors attain the same relative performance at the age of 14. The Number and Memory factors reach this level at about 16. The Verbal Comprehension factor develops more slowly and it reaches the same relative level at the age of 18. The Word Fluency factor W matures later than 20. It is not surprising to find the Perceptual Speed factor maturing rather early and the Verbal factors maturing quite late. In other studies it has been found that the first Spatial factor reaches adult level at about the age of 10 or 12, so that children of that age do as well on the average as educated adults.

There are interesting implications in these differences of rate of maturation of the mental abilities. It is quite likely that there are individual differences in the rate of maturation of these factors. Some children mature more rapidly in some factors than in others. It is almost certain that findings of this kind may eventually be considered seriously in preparing school curricula. It may very well happen that teaching methods will be adjusted to the imagery type of the child. Instead of trying to determine which is the best method of teaching reading, we might discover that children of different imagery types would learn to read best if the teaching method were adjusted to the child's imagery type. Some children are aided by visual devices while other children are annoyed by them.

Since it has been found that the primary mental abilities mature at different rates, it is natural to ask the parallel question about the effects of aging. If the mental abilities mature characteristically at different rates, it may also happen that there are differential rates of decline of the mental abilities because of aging. This problem can be of great national importance in adjusting retirement ages for different types of work. This problem becomes of considerable economic significance with the marked increase in longevity.

Personality and IQ Change

Jerome Kagan, Lester W. Sontag, Charles T. Baker, and Virginia L. Nelson

There is general agreement in the literature that performance on the IQ test tends to vary among individuals over time. For some individuals there is a consistent increase in performance on intellectual tasks, while for others there is a constant decrease. Many children show little or no change, or vacillate with no consistent pattern. In this paper the authors selected those children showing constant increase or decrease in IQ score from a sample of children who had been reexamined every year for 18 years, and compared them on certain personality data obtained when they were considerably younger. The results indicate that children with decreasing IQs tend to be more emotionally dependent on their parents. Children with increasing IQs tend to be more achievement-oriented and display more aggressive responses on projective tests. The results suggest that children who interact more with their environment tend to show patterns of increasing intellectual ability over time.

Research on mental development during the last twenty years has indicated that a child's IQ score does not necessarily remain constant with age. Several reports suggest that changes in environmental conditions can depress or raise IQ level, and it is sometimes implied that these changes may be explained by recourse to personality variables. The purpose of this paper is to demonstrate that changes in IQ during childhood are correlated with certain personality predispositions, as inferred from projective test data. The personality variables under study include (a) need for achievement, (b) competitive strivings, (c) curiosity about nature, and (d) passivity.

Performance on an IQ test is assumed to be a function of at least two major variables: the variety of skills and abilities that the person brings to the test situation, and his motivation to perform well on the test. Since the IQ scores of some children change markedly during the school years, it seems plausible to assume that those children who show marked increases in IQ have a very strong motivation to acquire or develop the various intellectual skills tapped by an IQ test and to perform well in a testing situation. It is suggested that need for achievement, competitive strivings, and curiosity about nature motivate the acquisition and improvement of cognitive abilities, and by so doing facilitate increases in tested IQ.

The social environment often awards praise and recognition for intellectual accomplishment, and school age children with a high need for achievement might seek to gratify this need through intellectual activity. Thus it was predicted that

SOURCE: Adapted and abridged from J. Kagan, L. W. Sontag, C. T. Baker, and Virginia Nelson, "Personality and IQ Change." *Journal of Abnormal and Social Psychology*, 1958, 56, 261–266. (With permission of the authors and the American Psychological Association.)

children showing marked increases in IQ would produce more achievement imagery on the TAT than those with minimal gains in IQ.

Secondly, the school environment emphasizes competitive intellectual activity, and children with strong competitive needs would be highly motivated to acquire the intellectual skills which result in successful competition with one's classmates. Thus it was predicted that children showing IQ gains would show more competitive strivings than children displaying minimal gains in IQ. In choosing an index of competitive strivings, besides the related measure of TAT achievement fantasy, it was decided to use aggressive content on the Rorschach. The bases for this choice rested on the assumptions that (a) incidence of aggressive imagery reflected degree of aggressive motivation, and (b) competition was a socially accepted form of aggressive behavior. For in competition, as in aggression, the child desires to defeat another individual and assert his superiority over him. The population of children in this study is predominantly middle class and apt to place strong inhibitions on direct, overt expession of aggression. Therefore, there would be a tendency for the individual with high aggressive motivation to seek socially accepted channels for aggressive expression such as competitive activity with peers. Thus it was predicted that children showing IQ gain would report more Rorschach aggressive content than those with minimal gain because of their greater competitive predisposition.

A third motive that might facilitate a child's acquisition of knowledge and skills in dealing with the environment could be curiosity about nature. Interest in birth, death, sexual anatomy, and other processes of nature is a frequent phenomenon in young children. It is suggested that the more intense this curiosity, the greater the motivation to acquire the habits which would gratify this motive. Since reading, questioning, and manipulating the environment are effective behavioral methods of gratifying one's curiosity, it might be expected that the highly curious child would be more likely to develop these skills and therefore apt to gain in IQ score. The TAT measure used to evaluate curiosity was presence of themes of interest in nature and its phenomena. For the Rorschach, it was hypothesized that concern with the body might reflect, in part, heightened interest in natural processes, and it was suggested that anatomy content might be more frequent for children who showed marked IQ gains than for those with minimal increases in IQ. It is recognized that many clinical psychologists regard anatomy content in adults as indicative of psychopathology. This study is concerned with the correlates of IQ gain rather than psychopathology, and it is not implied that children who show increases in IQ are completely free of conflict. Secondly, it was felt that the determinants of anatomy content for children might be different from those which produce this content in adults.

A final prediction dealt with the predisposition to behavioral passivity. The children who show IQ gains have been characterized as having high need achievement, competitive strivings, and curiosity about the environment. This constellation of motives implies that when these children are confronted with a problem, they would have a tendency to attack and attempt to solve the problem rather than withdraw from the situation or seek help. On this basis, it was predicted that children who showed IQ gains would be less likely than those with minimal IQ increases to characterize their TAT heroes as passive in attitude or behavior.

The Fels Research Institute is uniquely equipped to test these ideas about IQ change since it has continuous longitudinal information on the development of a sample of normal children. These data include intelligence and projective tests, observations of the children, and reports on the parent-child interaction. In a recent study, Sontag, Baker, and Nelson (1958) related personality information on a sample of children with changes in IQ and found that those children who showed marked increases in IQ were rated as more competitive, more likely to display self-initiated behavior, and less passive than those who showed decreases in IQ. The TAT and Rorschach protocols were not utilized in making these personality ratings, and the results from this study served as a major stimulus for the present investigation.

Method

A sample of 140 Fels subjects (Ss), 70 of each sex, were chosen for study because a fairly complete record of test information was available on them. From ages 2½ to 6, the Stanford-Binet intelligence test (1916 or 1937 revision) was administered to most Ss twice yearly, on their birthdays and six months after their birthdays. From ages 6 to 12, most Ss received alternately Form L or Form M of the 1937 revision annually on or near each S's birthday. All of the tests were administered by one of the authors (V. L. N.). The mean IQ of the Fels population is near 120, with standard deviation varying from 14 to 20 IQ points.

In order to obtain groups of Ss who showed the most change in IQ score from ages 6 to 10, a smoothed longitudinal plot of each S's IQ was prepared by averaging the mean of three consecutive test scores around each age. This procedure is explained in detail in other reports (Baker, Sontag and Nelson, 1955; Sontag et al. 1955 and 1958). This technique tends to eliminate erratic variations in IQ and hopefully furnishes a more valid measure of IQ changes. Then each S's smoothed IQ at age 6 was subtracted from his smoothed IQ at age 10, and this distribution of differences, positive if S gained in IQ and negative if S lost in IQ, was divided into quartiles. This report deals with the projective test information on those Ss in the two extreme groups; those who increased and those who decreased the most in IQ score. These will be called Group A, the IQ ascenders, and Group B, the IQ descenders, respectively. There was no significant difference between the mean IQ of the two extreme quartiles at age 6, the means being 119 and 116 for Groups A and D respectively. The average amount of increase in IQ for Group A was larger (plus 17 points) than the corresponding decrease for the members of Group D (minus 5 points), and while 46 per cent of Group D lost 5 or more points, every child in Group A gained 10 or more points during the years 6 through 10. The mean IQ of the entire sample of 140 tends to increase slightly from ages 6 to 10, probably as a result of practice effects with the same test. Since every S in Group D showed a decrease in IQ, it might be inferred that the members of Group D did not benefit from practice and familiarity with the test, and it is probably more accurate to view Group D Ss in this light rather than as Ss who showed marked decreases in IQ score.

The projective tests used in the analysis were the Rorschach and selected TAT pictures. Two factors governed the choice of the TAT cards which were analyzed. Because the protocols were gathered over a period of years, there was not complete comparability for all Ss for the number of cards administered. Secondly, the specific hypotheses of the study dictated the cards chosen for analysis, and Cards 1, 3 BM, 3 GF, 5, 6 BM, 12 F, 14, and 17 BM were selected for analysis. The age at which the TAT protocols were administered ranged from 8–9 to 14–6 years, with median at 11–6 and 80 per cent of the protocols obtained between the ages of 11 and 12. The age at which the Rorschachs were administered ranged from 6–5 to 13–6 years, with median at 10–5 and 63 per cent of the sample having had the test between ages 10 and 11. Since the Rorschach and TAT were administered by different examiners there was no comparability with respect to inquiry or probing. Thus, the analysis of both the Rorschach and TAT was restricted to the S's spontaneous verbalization to the stimulus before any questions or inquiry were conducted by the examiner. The protocols were scored for the following fantasy categories.

1. Need achievement on the TAT. Achievement imagery on the TAT was scored according to the definition of McClelland et al. (McClelland, Atkinson, Clark, and Lowell 1953); and themes involving a reference to competition with a standard of excellence were scored achievement imagery.

2. Rorschach aggression. The definition of aggressive content on the Rorschach included (a) people, animals, or creatures engaged in physical or verbal aggression, e.g., fighting or quarreling; (b) explosive objects or explosions, e.g., volcanoes, bombs exploding, fireworks; and (c) objects or animal parts normally regarded as instruments of aggression, e.g., spears, rifles, clubs, guns, knives, horns, and claws.

3. Intellectual curiosity about nature. For the TAT, curiosity was defined in terms of themes in which someone is interested in the processes or phenomena of nature. Curiosity on the Rorschach was restricted to anatomy or X-ray responses of internal organs or bony parts, e.g., stomach, backbone, ribs.

4. Passivity. Because of the limited amount of thematic material in the spontaneous performance, themes of passivity were limited to stories in which the central figure was described as sleepy, tired, or resting.

The fantasy categories were independently scored by the senior author and an assistant without knowledge of the S's IQ scores. Reliability was very high because of the limited amount of content scored for each response and the objectivity of the definitions. Percentage of agreement for the three TAT categories was 9 per cent, and for the two Rorschach categories 99 per cent.

Results

Although there was a total of 70 Ss in the two extreme quartiles, not all of the Ss had Rorschach or TAT data for the age range under study. Because there are approximately twice as many boys as there are girls in Group A, all comparisons were first made separately by sex and results were combined only if the direction of the result for both boys and girls in the same IQ group was in the predicted direction.

1. *Need Achievement.* All achievement themes, save one, occurred to Cards 1 and 17 BM. The typical achievement story to Card 1 concerned a boy who wanted to master the violin and/or become a famous violinist, while the typical achievement theme to 17 BM involved competitive activity with regard to rope climbing. Table 9.1 shows the percentage of Ss in each group reporting

TABLE 9.1. *Percentage of Ss Reporting Achievement Imagery to Cards 1 and 17 BM*

TAT card	Group A			Group D		
	BOYS	GIRLS	BOYS AND GIRLS	BOYS	GIRLS	BOYS AND GIRLS
Card 1	36.4	50.0	40.6	27.3	15.0	19.4
Card 17 BM	36.4	30.0	34.4	0.0	15.0	9.7
Cards 1 and 17 BM	22.7	10.0	18.8	0.0	0.0	0.0

achievement imagery plots to Cards 1, 17 BM, and to both pictures.

For both Cards 1 and 17 BM, more male and female Ss in Group A report achievement imagery than the boys or girls of Group D. For Card 1, the difference between Group A and Group D girls is reliable at the .03 level; the difference for boys is in the predicted direction but not significant. For Card 17 BM, the difference between Group A and Group D boys is significant $(p = .03)$ and in the predicted direction for girls. All p values are for one tail and were evaluated using the exact method suggested by Fisher (1934). When the sexes were pooled, comparisons between Groups A and D were significant not only for Cards 1 and 17 BM separately but also for the number of Ss telling achievement imagery to both Cards 1 and 17 BM $(p < .10, .03,$ and $.01$ respectively). Thus, the Ss who showed increases in IQ were more prone to structure Cards 1 and 17 BM in terms of achievement-oriented behavior than were the Ss in Group D.

2. *Aggressive content on Rorschach.* There was no significant difference between Groups A and D or between boys and girls with respect to the mean number of responses per protocol, and the mean for the entire sample was 27 responses. There was no difference between Group A and Group D girls with respect to percentage of each group reporting one or more aggressive responses per

protocol (30.0 per cent for Group A versus 33.0 per cent for Group D). However, the difference between Group A and D boys approached significance with 59.1 per cent of the former and 22.2 per cent of the latter reporting one or more aggressive images ($p = .07$). Thus, the prediction of a correlation between IQ increases and aggressive imagery held only for the boys. Because of the tentativeness of this result and the more speculative nature of the hypothesis relating competitive striving and aggressive content, an attempt was made to validate this finding by analyzing a later Rorschach protocol for the boys in Groups A and D. Not all of the boys had Rorschachs administered to them at a later age, and only 15 Ss in Group A and 5 in Group D were available for analysis. The median ages at the time of administration were 13–8 and 15–0 for Groups A and D respectively, and there was no significant difference in the lengths of the protocols of the two groups. The results were in the same direction for 86.7 per cent of Group A, and 20.0 per cent of Group D reported one or more aggressive images; this difference is highly significant ($p = .01$).

3. *Intellectual curiosity.* The only TAT card eliciting curiosity plots was Card 14, and the typical theme described a person gazing at or interested in the stars or the heavens. Both the boys and girls in Group A told more themes of interest in the stars or heavens than the males and females in Group D ($p = .14$, $p = .10$, respectively), and combining of the sexes yielded a highly significant difference between Groups A and D ($p < .01$).

4. *Anatomy and X-ray responses on the Rorschach.* There was no difference between Group A and Group D girls reporting one or more anatomy responses (30.0 per cent versus 38.9 per cent for Groups A and D respectively). For the boys, 31.8 per cent of Group A and 0.0 per cent of Group D reported anatomy or X-ray imagery, a difference that approached significance ($p = .06$). This finding was also validated on the same sample of 20 boys that was used to check the differences in aggressive content. The results were in the same direction with 60.0 per cent of Group A and 20.0 per cent of Group D reporting anatomy content ($p = .15$).

5. *Passivity.* Card 3 BM accounted for most of the passivity themes, and the groups were compared with respect to the incidence of stories to Card 3 BM in which the central figure was sleepy, tired, or resting. Both the boys and girls in Group D showed more passivity themes than the boys and girls in Group A. Although only the difference for the girls was significant ($p = .06$), when the sexes were pooled the difference was highly reliable ($p < .03$).

Cards 3 GF, 5, 6 BM, and 12 F did not furnish data relevant to the hypotheses under test, and these results are not summarized.

Discussion

In the main, the hypotheses about the differences between Groups A and D have been verified. Boy and girl ascenders produced more TAT achievement imagery and curiosity about nature than Group D children, and male ascenders displayed more aggressive content on the Rorschach than the boys in Group D. The higher incidence of aggressive imagery for the boys who gained in IQ was interpreted as reflecting stronger competitive motivation. Finally, the Ss in Group D were presumed to have a more passive orientation since they were more likely to perceive the ambiguous figure on Card 3 BM as sleeping or tired. The relation between Rorschach anatomy content and IQ gain was the most tentative finding.

The results are interpreted as indicating that high motivation to achieve, competitive strivings, and curiosity about nature may motivate the acquisition of intellectual skills and knowledge which, in turn, facilitates increases in tested IQ. If one accepts the generally assumed notion that boys are more competitive and achievement oriented than girls, the fact that there were twice as many boys in Group A as there were girls supports the present interpretation. A recent study using the Edwards Personal Preference Schedule found that high school boys obtained higher need achievement scores than high school girls.

These results are not interpreted as indicating that strong achievement, competitive, and curiosity motives are the only variables involved in producing gains in IQ. The Ss in this study are all average or above in IQ, and there is not adequate sampling of children with lower IQ levels. One would not expect Ss with low IQs or language handicaps to suddenly show an interest in reading, despite achievement needs or intellectual curiosity. The child who spends increased time reading because of a heightened interest in natural processes must have already learned the basic reading skills so that this behavior is not a difficult or unlikely choice for him.

Similarly, needs for achievement and successful competition should motivate attempts at improvement of intellectual abilities only in a social milieu where praise, recognition, and superior status are awarded for such accomplishment. That is, achievement-oriented children from homes in which intellectual activity was praised would probably be more likely to master intellectual skills than achievement-oriented children from homes in which such accomplishment was not rewarded. In a cultural environment where athletic ability, fighting prowess, or success with the opposite sex was highly valued, one might expect the child to choose these behavioral channels to gratify his achievement and competitive needs. The parents in the Fels population are predominantly middle class and tend to place importance on intellectual accomplishment. A large majority of the parents have attended college, and since enrollment in the Fels program is voluntary it might be inferred that only parents who valued knowledge and scientific pursuits would be predisposed to become part of the research population. Thus, the children under study tend to come from homes which value intellectual ability.

Study of the educational attainment of the parents of the Ss in Groups A and D revealed no significant difference between the groups with respect to the percentage of families in which both parents attended college (57.1 per cent for

Group A versus 42.9 per cent for Group D; $p > .30$). Although there is a slight difference favoring the educational level of Group A families, the difference was not dramatic. There may be important differences between Groups A and D with respect to the differential encouragement of intellectual achievement, but measurement of these differences would probably require variables more refined than educational level of the parents. However, even though parental emphasis on intellectual activity may increase the child's desire to improve his cognitive skills, the child's predisposition to adopt or rebel against parental values should selectively influence his motivation to strive for intellectual accomplishment. Thus, the type of relation between parent and child may be an important factor in this process.

Finally, there is the possibility that genetic and/or constitutional variables may play a role in facilitating marked IQ changes. There is considerable data indicating that genetic factors influence general IQ level, but less evidence relevant to the role of these variables in producing childhood increases in IQ score. For most of the children in our population, IQs tend to level off during the ages 6 to 10 years, and most of the marked changes in level occur during the preschool years. However, the exact relationship between genetic variables and IQ change has yet to be determined. The phenomenon of IQ increase during the school years is admittedly complex, and it is not implied that the child's motives are the major factor. However, it is suggested that personality needs may influence this process. Perhaps the most accurate generalization is that for middle-class children with average or above IQ levels, strong achievement, competitive, and curiosity needs may facilitate IQ gains by motivating the child to master intellectual skills.

The Intelligence of Isolated Mountain Children

Mandel Sherman and Cora B. Key

The concern of child psychologists for children from impoverished environments dates back to at least the late 1920's and early 1930's. It was more widely believed then that heredity was the sole factor in intellectual performance, and that little or nothing could be done in the way of intervention to help people such as those described in this study. Sherman and Key demonstrate rather clearly in their study that a human being's intellectual growth will, within limits, develop to a level commensurate with environmental demands. Thus as the children in this study grew older the discrepancy between demands of their environments and those that one might find in an urban upper-middle-class society increasingly diverged. The result was a constant decrement in performance on measures of intellectual ability.

source: Adapted and abridged from Mandel Sherman and Cora Key, "The Intelligence of Isolated Mountain Children." *Child Development*, 1932, 3, 279–290. (With permission of the authors and the Society for Research in Child Development.)

This report of the results of intelligence tests made of mountain children is part of a larger study begun in the summer of 1929 to determine the cultural influences which affect intellectual, emotional, and personality development and the influences determining the attitudes of mountain people living in relative degrees of isolation.

The communities studied were four hollows located approximately 100 miles west of Washington, D.C., in the Blue Ridge Mountains, and a small village at the base of the Blue Ridge about the same distance from Washington to the southwest. Of great significance is the ancestry of these people. The Hollows were settled in the precolonial period by English and Scotch-Irish immigrants. When German immigrants were given most of the land in the Shenandoah Valley surrounding these mountain ranges, the English and Scotch-Irish people were forced up the mountainside. The topography of this region is such that the settlers were forced further within the mountains, settling in hollows surrounded by mountain ranges. There they built their log and mud cabins many of which still remain and are inhabited. Each of the hollows selected for study, Colvin, Needles, Oakton and Rigby, are close to each other but are separated by comparatively high mountain ranges. Of these hollows, Colvin is at the lowest level in social development. This hollow is small, consisting of a small number of families living in scattered, mud-plastered log huts. There is no road, except for a trail, to the outside world. One small log and mud cabin is rented by the county school board for a school. There is no general meeting place, and the church meetings which have been held in the past have been discontinued except for a very occasional revival meeting. With three exceptions, the adults are illiterate. They are descendents of the original settlers, who married relatives and mixed very little with the people outside of the hollows. Colvin Hollow is so named because most of the inhabitants are Colvins. Many of the younger children do not know their last names. They identify themselves, for example, as Sadie's Bennie or Dicy's Willie.

Needles Hollow, adjacent to Colvin Hollow, is next in the scale of social development. It is reached by a rocky road from a small hamlet at the base of the mountains. Its patches of ground, from two to five acres on the average, surrounding the cabins, approach the status of small farms. It is a more socialized community and many of the adults are literate. The children have had good school advantages compared to Colvin Hollow.

Oakton Hollow, next higher in the social scale, is separated from Colvin Hollow by a high mountain. The road to the valley is passable for old Fords and wagons most of the year. The hollow boasts of a combined general store and post office, and many of the inhabitants receive mail and an occasional magazine. There exists a greater social consciousness than in Colvin or Needles Hollows. Oakton Hollow has had about four months of school each year for some time. The people are fairly prosperous, although they have but little surplus farm products to sell in the valley.

Rigby Hollow, culturally further developed, can be reached from the valley much more easily than any of the other three hollows. The present school was established by missionaries about nine years ago and has been conducting regular school terms. Church and Sunday School services are held regularly. The farms are larger than those of the other hollows, and there nearly always is a surplus which is sold in the valley. School terms have been about seven months each year for the past eight years, and approximately 75 per cent of the inhabitants are literate.

For purposes of comparison a small farm and sawmill town, Briarsville, was chosen. It is located at the base of the mountains to the south of the Hollows. The town has a hard-surfaced road connecting it with the principal cities of Virginia. The school building is a modern structure with four classrooms, three of which are used regularly. The school board employs three well-trained teachers. The town has a good general store, telephones, and receives newspapers.

The comparison of the intelligence test results of the mountain children with those of the children of Briarsville is especially significant in view of the origin of many of the residents of this town. Many of the inhabitants migrated from the mountains in the past to obtain work on the adjacent farms and in the sawmill. At first socially isolated from the "first" families of this town, the children now mingle freely. It was thought that a comparison of intelligence tests results of the mountain children with those of Briarsville would be much more significant than with children of an average town or city.

Intelligence tests were given to more than half of the children of the four mountain hollows and Briarsville. Not every child was tested, for some of the younger children could not be taken to the place where the tests were given, and a few of the others refused to cooperate. Nine tests were used: the Stanford-Binet; the National Intelligence Test, Scale B, Form 2; the Pintner-Cunningham Primary Mental Test. For performance tests the following were employed: Manikin, Seguin Form Board, Mare and Foal Healy Puzzle "A," the Knox Cube Test from the Pintner-Patterson scale of performance tests, and Goodenough's Draw-A-Man test.

A representative sample of the school population thus was tested. A total of 386 tests were given to the children in the mountain communities and 198 in Briarsville. The children in Briarsville were not given Stanford-Binet tests because

TABLE 9.2. *Per Cent of Children Showing Age-Grade Retardation*

AGE-GRADE RETARDATION	BRIARSVILLE	MOUNTAINS
1	22	20
2	38	17
3	16	12
4	12	16
5	4	8
6	1	8

of the difficulty in organizing the program there. One hundred and two children were examined in the mountain communities, and 81 in Briarsville. In addition to an investigation of test scores and mental age results, a qualitative analysis of the responses was made.

The per cent of children retarded in school in the mountains and in Briarsville is given in Table 9.2 taking 6 to 7 years as the age standard for first grade, 7 to 8 for second grade, and so on. Children at the grade or accelerated, and those retarded more than six grades, are not included. Only one child in the mountain communities was found to be in a grade higher than his chronological age warranted, and thirteen were "at grade."

It is difficult to estimate age-grade retardation accurately in the mountain communities because of the loose standard of requirements for grades. Grade placement depends entirely upon the judgment of the teacher, although her estimate sometimes is obtained by a formal examination. The fact that only a few children were accelerated is not a real indication of a general lack of ability but probably means that the teachers do not use the same system of promotion as in a city school. Psychological tests of intelligence and achievement have never been given in these communities and there is, therefore, no way of measuring the real abilities of the children. In many cases the older children are left to their own resources in the school room as the teacher spends most of her time with the younger children.

The distribution of the average intelligence quotients of the children in the four mountain communities and Briarsville were similar to those of children in an average community. The average intelligence quotient of the Briarsville children was higher than that of the mountain children in every test, and had a smaller standard deviation. The results give further evidence of the effect of systematic training upon intelligence test ratings, a factor often slighted in comparative studies of intelligence test scores.

The dependence of the intelligence quotients on the kind of test used is shown in a comparison of the average IQs of the mountain children on the different tests used. The highest average intelligence quotients are found in the tests presumably most independent of language and of school training, and lowest in those utilizing language ability.

When we examine the results of the tests in Briarsville, on the other hand, we find that while the highest average IQ was obtained in the performance tests, the next highest was on the National Intelligence Test — a test dependent upon language ability. This may be additional evidence that systematic and consistent training in a commuunity of a comparatively high order or social organization is a stimulus to the development of the kind of intelligence we ordinarily measure by tests.

The Stanford-Binet test at once might be considered inadequate because of its evident dependence upon language and school training. Analysis of the successes and failures on this test further showed its unadaptability for studying this type of child. Failures were most evident on items involving abstract comprehension. This sort of failure differed in degree in the various communities. The Colvin Hollow children failed most frequently in tests involving calculation, in part because the terms used were foreign to them. The difficulty of evaluating failures on simple problems is due in part to the certainty of knowing whether the children failed because of insufficient language comprehension to understand the directions. Rote memory was found to be above the average of other test results, but the most common failure in Colvin Hollow was in the reversal of numbers. Following the giving and scoring of the tests a number of children were given practice in the reversal of the number sequence 1–2–3. After it was thought that they could reverse this sequence, other numbers containing four figures were given. As an example, the sequence of 6–5–2–8 was reversed by most of the children as 6–5–4–3–2–1.

The almost universal failure of the mountain children in the ball and field test indicates their lack of ability to comprehend and solve a simple problem involving foresight and planning ability. Few of the children appeared to have a plan for finding the ball in a circular field. Usually a line was drawn in the center of the diagram and in some cases this was varied by dots indicating trees. Many children of Colvin and Needles Hollows could not understand the directions of the ball and field test. They had little comprehension of the meaning of "field" and were astonished at a ball being lost. (Most of the children never had seen a ball.) One boy of 13 made a curious effort. He drew a number of small rough circles in the enclosure which he explained as representing trees. Then he drew a line from one circle to the next connecting them. He then stated that he was hunting for the lost article under the trees. In this and other cases it was very difficult to assume, as one is forced to do in scoring the test, that the failure indicates a deficiency of innate intelligence even on that one test. Although it is not assumed that a child must have experience in the performance called for on a given test — and indeed such direct experience would mitigate the significance of the score — it can be assumed that a child must have had some approximate or similar experience. These mountain children live in an environment calling for little planning and ingenuity expected of an average child of not more than 9 years.

Evidently space and form differentiation as employed in these tests are relatively foreign to these children. Only one of the younger children in Colvin Hollow correctly copied the drawing of a diamond.

The items which the children in all the hollows passed most consistently were the mutilated pictures, counting backwards from 20, arranging weights and comprehension of pictures. In two of the hollows most of the children could not name the days of the week in correct sequence. This failure probably was due to the fact that they have no use for differentiation of days, since one day is like the next in its significance except for the days of going to school and staying at home.

An impoverished environment probably acts as a depressing factor on the development of intelligence. The problem of the effect of the environment upon the development of intelligence has attracted the attention of many psychologists in recent years. Some believe that the environment may act either as a stimulant or as a depressant to the intelligence of young children. Others believe that the capacity for the development of intelligence is influenced but little by the environment.

TABLE 9.3. *Average Intelligence Quotient on Five Tests According to Increasing Chronological Age**

| CHRONO-LOGICAL AGE | NUMBER OF CASES | | PINTNER-CUNNINGHAM | | NATIONAL INTELLIGENCE | | DRAWING OF A MAN | | PERFORMANCE SCALE | | | |
| | | | | | | | | | Year scale | | Med. M.A. scale | |
	Mountains	Briarsville	Mountains	Briarsville	Mountains	Briarsville	Mountains	Briarsville	Mountains	Briarsville	Mountains	Briarsville
6–8	12–13	8	84	94			80	93	91		89	
8–10	15–23	4–22	70	91		117	66	82	84	119	76	93
10–12	5–16	5–20	53	76	66	101	71	69	86	108	70	87
12–14	7–12	16			67	91	69	73	83		83	
14–16	8–15	14			52	87	49	70	75		73	

* The figures indicating the number of cases does not mean that every test was given to the numbers indicated. The minimum and maximum number of children given a test at the respective chronological ages is shown.

Table 9.3 gives the average intelligence quotients on various tests according to increasing chronological age. It shows a decrease in intelligence quotients with increase in chronological age for every test except the National, applied to the mountain children. The decrease in the intelligence quotients in some of the tests is as great from the sixth to the tenth year as from the tenth to the sixteenth year. In some cases the decline in intelligence for children over 10 is greater than for children between 6 and 10. An intelligence test is an indirect measure. An estimate of intelligence is based on the information the child has been able to obtain. In the mountain environment increments of information become less large with increases in age, and the 7-year-old has relatively more chance to gather information and to learn by experience than the 12-year-old in the same environment.

Another analysis shows the per cent of cases below the average intelligence of the four mountain communities studied. The analysis shows, with some slight variation, that the per cent of cases below average intelligence increases with the decrease in the cultural level of the community. In Colvin Hollow, socially lowest in the group, the percent of cases below average intelligence is considerably greater than in any of the other communities. Briarsville, the highest community culturally, had the smallest per cent of cases below average, with one exception. When each community is ranked according to the per cent of cases below average intelligence and an average rank obtained for the various tests, Rigby Hollow is second, Oakton Hollow third, and Needles Hollow fourth.

No consistent relationship between the size of the family and the average intelligence quotient was found. If these tests rate the intelligence of children fairly, it may be inferred that the size of the family has no effect on the intelligence of the children; but there are many arguments against such an interpretation. The children tested were not all of the same age. Since we have found that the intelligence rating of the mountain children depends upon the age of the child, the relationship between the size of the family and intelligence is not clear.

Parent-Child Resemblance in Intelligence

Marjorie P. Honzik

The extent to which heredity contributes to intellectual ability is often estimated by determining the degree of relationship between test score performance of children with their true parents in contrast to children and their foster parents. Another frequently used index of parental ability is their level of attained education. In this study, indices of ability were used with the mothers but only educational level was used with the fathers. The results indicate that with increasing chronological age the relationship between the child's measured ability and the ability of his parents increases. This increase in relationship occurs for children and their true parents, but not between the adopted child and the foster parents. These results are interpreted by Dr. Honzik as reflecting the importance of genetic determinants in intellectual ability. The fact that the correlations attain only modest values ($+.45$) indicates that parental ability is only one of many factors that contribute to a child's intellectual development.

A number of developmental studies have reported that the mental test scores of children under two years have little or no relationship to parental ability as measured by the number of years of schooling, ratings of intelligence, or test scores. When these same children are retested at later ages, their mental test scores are found to be significantly correlated with parental ability. A crucial question is the extent to which these age changes in relationship are due to environmental factors, or to intrinsic differences in the patterns of mental growth. One way in which this increasing resemblance can be evaluated is by comparing the age changes in the correlations which occur among children reared by their own parents in contrast to those reared apart from their parents.

SOURCE: Adapted and abridged from Marjorie P. Honzik, "Developmental Studies of Parent-Child Resemblance in Intelligence." *Child Development*, 1957, 28, 215–228. (With permission of the author and the Society for Research in Child Development.)

In this report we shall compare the age changes in relationship for two distinct groups, each of over 100 children, who were tested at various ages between 21 months and 16 years; and then contrast this trend with that reported by Skodak and Skeels for 100 adopted children who were tested four times between their second and fourteenth year.

In the Guidance Study at the University of California Institute of Child Welfare, a sample of 252 children who were representative of those born in Berkeley during an 18-month period were divided into equivalent subsamples called the "Guidance" and "Control" goups. This division of the main sample was made on the basis of certain socioeconomic variables before the mental testing program was begun. The children in the two groups were first brought to the Institute for mental tests at the age of 21 months. The tests used at this age level and at the subsequent testings during the preschool years were the California Preschool Schedules. Beginning at 6 years, the 1916 Stanford Revision of the Binet Scale was the test used, with a shift to the 1937 Revision at age 8. The parents were not given intelligence tests, but the number of years of schooling is known for both parents. In addition, the Guidance group ratings (on a seven-point scale) of the mothers' intelligence were made when the children were between 3½ and 4½ years by staff members who had had many hours of discussion with the mothers. The correlation between these ratings of the mothers' intelligence and the number of years of schooling of the mothers is $+.73$. In fact, in this study all measures which reflect the ability of the parents were inter-correlated to about the same extent (socioeconomic status correlates with both mother's and fathers' schooling $+.73$; mothers' and fathers' schooling correlate $+.74$).

The correlation between the education of the mothers and the children's mental test scores at 21 months was negligible, but between 3 and 3½ years, the relationship became significant. To check the validity of this age trend, correlations were computed separately for the two subsamples of the total Guidance Study sample. The finding that these subsamples exhibit essentially the same age changes in relationship suggests that the trend is a valid one and would be duplicated in comparable developmental studies.

In a study of 100 adopted children, Skodak and Skeels (1949) report that adopted children whose true mothers tested quite low in intelligence earned mental test scores which were substantially higher than those of their mothers. In addition, these authors report the relation of various indices of ability of the true mothers to the mental test scores of their children at four successive age levels. It is these correlations which interest us and which we wish to compare with the relationships obtained in the Guidance Study for children reared by their own mothers.

Regardless of the index used (IQ or number of years of schooling), Skodak and Skeels found that the correlation between the *true* mother's ability and her child's mental test scores at approximately two years of age is insignificant. By the time the adopted children reached four years on the average, the correlations between their IQ's and the true mothers' education and intelligence are $+.31$ and $+.28$, respectively. These correlations are significant at the 5 per cent level. In contrast these authors found *no* relationship at any age between the mental test scores of these same children, who were adopted in the first months of life, and their *foster,* or adopting, mothers' education. These highly significant results are especially interesting when compared with the findings for the groups of children who have always lived with their own parents.

In Figure 9.2 the mother-child correlations for the total Guidance Study sample (combined Guidance and Control groups) are compared with those reported by Skodak and Skeels for the adopted children. The true mother-child correlations age trends in their study and ours are alike. The similarity in the changing relationships with age for the Guidance Study group who always lived with their parents as compared with the Skodak-Skeels group who never lived with their parents is impressive. However, the final correlations between the index of maternal ability (number of years of schooling) and the children's mental test scores is only $+.35$ for the children reared by their true parents; and $+.32$ for the children not reared by their true parents, indicating that less than 15 per cent of the variance in the children's scores can be accounted for by this very rough index of the true mother's ability.

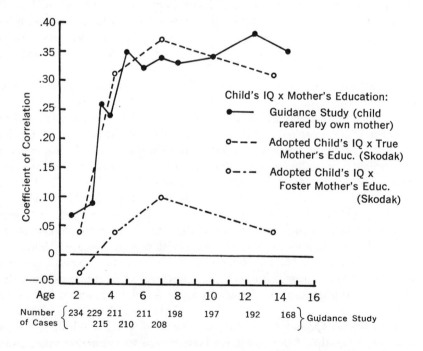

Figure 9.2 Education of mother in relation to child's IQ.

The fact that the individual differences in the adopted children's mental test scores are not related to the foster mothers' educaton at any age is also shown in Figure 9.2. This finding is surprising since the average IQ of the adopted children at 13½ years was 106, while the average IQ of their true mothers was reported as only 86. A regression upward toward the mean is to be expected, but not beyond the mean. Our interpretation of these findings is that the educational level of the true mother roughly indicates her intellectual capacity, and this capacity is at least somewhat determined by genetic factors which she, in turn, transmits to her children. The difference in the level of ability of the adopted children and their true mothers may be due in part to systematic undermeasurement of the true mothers' intelligence and in part to the generally favorable environment provided by the foster families. It is conceivable, and it seems to us probable, that in this sample certain unmeasured family variables such as the affection and emotional support given the foster children were as important as purely intellectual stimulation in nurturing the mental growth and performance of these foster children.

A better indication of the age changes in the mother-child resemblance would probably have been obtained if optimal test scores had been available for the mothers in these two studies. In the Skodak-Skeels investigation, 63 of the mothers were given individual mental tests but these mothers were tested shortly after the babies' births "usually after the mother had decided to release the baby for adoption." The authors note that "these IQs were consistent with other evidence of the mental adequacy of the mothers" and the "tests were never given when the mother was ill or obviously upset," but it is unlikely that these IQs reflect the optimum performance of which these mothers might have been capable under more favorable conditions. However, even these IQs showed age trends in relationship to the mental test scores of the children which were similar but tended to run a little higher than those obtained for the mothers' education. The mother-child correlations in the Guidance Study are higher when based on ratings of the mother's intelligence than when education is used as an index of the mother's ability. They are in the former instance, comparable with a correlation of .49 reported in a study in which testing procedures for both parents and children were carefully controlled.

In Figure 9.3 the age change in mother-child resemblance in intelligence reported by Skodak and Skeels for 63 of the adopted children is compared with the findings for the Guidance group where the measure of maternal intelligence was an averaged rating. The correlations obtained in the Guidance group are higher than those reported for the adopted children. This latter difference may be due to differential environmental stimulation by the more intelligent mothers in the Guidance group, but there is also the likelihood in the Skodak-Skeels study of an unequal effect of stress on the mothers' IQs. These findings certainly suggest that the variations in the magnitude of the correlations depend somewhat on the sensitivity of the measures of maternal intelligence, but the question of

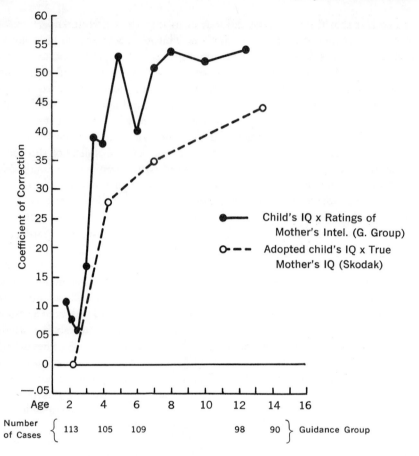

Figure 9.3   Intelligence of mother in relation to child's IQ.

whether the differences in the correlations shown in Figure 9.3 are entirely attributable to differences in the validity of the measures of mothers' intelligence cannot be answered by these studies.

The correlations between the number of years of schooling of the father and the children's mental test scores at successive ages were determined for the Guidance and Control groups separately. Although there are few coefficients which appear too high or too low in relation to the trend (e.g., the correlations of +.40 at 5 years for the Guidance group and +.43 for the Control group at 7 years), the age changes are similar to those found between the mental test scores of these children and the mothers' education. The relationship between the number of years of schooling of the father and the children's test scores is negligible at 21 months (+.07) and 3 years (+.11) but is significant at the 5 per cent level at 3½ years (+.21) and reaches a high of +.40 at 7 years, thereafter ranging from +.34 to +.39. The trend of the age changes in relationship between the children's mental test scores and the father's schooling is similar in the two groups (Guidance and Control) in spite of the above mentioned inconsistencies. The correlations for these two groups combined are compared with the findings for adopted children in relation to the education of their true fathers. The correlations between the mental test scores of the adopted children and the education of their true fathers were computed from the raw data presented by Skodak and Skeels. The impressive fact is that the trend in relationships for the adopted children resembles so closely that found for the children reared by their own parents. Since the relationships obtained in the Guidance Study are no higher than those found for the adopted children, we may infer that the more highly educated fathers do not offer differentially more stimulating environments to their children. This inference is confirmed by the correlations between foster father's education and child's IQ, which are not significantly different from zero.

The fact that the parent-child resemblance is no greater for children reared by their own parents and the further fact reported by Skodak-Skeels of no relationship between the children's mental test performance and the foster parents' ability suggest that the education of the parents *per se* is not an environmentally important factor and that the obtained parent-child correlations reflect individual differences which are largely genetically determined.

CHAPTER X

Language Development

THE ACQUISITION of language is perhaps the most important achievement of the young child. Not only does language provide the child with the symbols necessary to further his understanding of his environment, but language also provides the child with the means of communicating his own ideas. Initially, language consists of more or less random babblings in which all of the sounds necessary for a particular language are present. Subsequently, certain sounds appear more regularly while other sounds are emitted with decreasing frequency. The sounds which are maintained are those associated with the language the child hears most frequently in his environment. It is generally held by developmental psychologists that the transition from the babbling stage to actual language is continuous; that is, the formation of meaningful words derives from previously acquired speech sounds. The learning of verbal labels then becomes one of associating an object with a specific sound until the sound symbolically represents the object. Subsequent development involves the growth of vocabulary, the use of sentences, and the acquisition of grammar.

Assuming that a high output of vocalization during infancy is important to subsequent language development, it would be important to determine if environmental conditions can influence this behavior. The study by Rheingold, Gewirtz, and Ross describes the successful application of the principles of conditioning to eliciting vocalizations among a sample of infants. It is probable that the results of this study performed in a laboratory setting accurately reflect the general procedure used by parents in the home — at least among those parents who have an appreciation of the importance of language.

The paper by Dr. Berko describes the acquisition of syntax and morphology. (Syntax refers to the ordering of different parts of speech within a sentence and is especially important for effective communication. Morphology refers to the modifications in word endings that are necessary for forming the plural or past tense.) This report by Dr. Berko raises some difficult theoretical problems for psychologists because present stimulus-response theories are unable to account for many of the findings related to the acquisition of syntax and morphology.

The remaining papers, by Professor Brown and by Professors Palermo and Jenkins, generate some important questions about how children make use of words. Heretofore, it was assumed that the use of generic terms was indicative of more mature language development reflecting a higher conceptual level. Each of these papers casts serious doubt on this assumption and has implications for certain popular practices involved in intelligence testing.

The Child's Learning of English Morphology

Jean Berko

The term morphology, as used in linguistics, refers to the development of inflections and the form of word endings. Children learn the inflections and forms of word endings, at a functional level at least, during the first five or six years of life. This learning takes place without a great deal of obvious effort and is considered by some scholars to be largely a matter of imitation. Other scholars, although in fundamental agreement that the learning of inflections and word endings is largely imitative, also argue that the rules of inflection and forming word endings are internalized and are therefore capable of broad generalization. In this experiment Dr. Berko tested the ability of 5½- to 7-year-old children to form word endings. Nonsense syllables were used so that responses would not be influenced by previous experience. The results lend support to the notion that children do employ rules in the formation of word endings which are generalized to a broad variety of situations.

In this study we set out to discover what is learned by children exposed to English morphology. To test for knowledge of morphological rules, we use nonsense materials. We know that if the subject can supply the correct plural ending, for instance, to a noun we have made up, he has internalized a working system of the plural allomorphs in English, and is able to generalize to new cases and select the right form. If a child knows that the plural of *witch* is *witches,* he may simply have memorized the plural form. If, however, he tells us that the plural of *gutch* is *gutches,* we have evidence that he actually knows, albeit unconsciously, one of those rules which the descriptive linguist, too, would set forth in his grammar. And if children do have knowledge of morphological rules, how does this knowledge evolve? Is there a progression from simple, regular rules to the more irregular and qualified rules that are adequate fully to describe English? In very general terms, we undertake to discover the psychological status of a certain kind of linguistic description. It is evident that the acquisition of language is more than the storing up of rehearsed utterances, since we are all

SOURCE: Adapted and abridged from Jean Berko, "The Child's Learning of English Morphology." *Word*, 1958, 14, 150–177. (With permission of author and publisher.)

able to say what we have not practiced and what we have never before heard. In bringing descriptive linguistics to the study of language acquisition, we hope to gain knowledge of the systems and patterns used by the speaker.

In order to test for children's knowledge of this sort, it was necessary to begin with an examination of their actual vocabulary. Accordingly, the 1000 most frequent words in the first-grader's vocabulary were selected from Rinsland's listing. This listing contains the most common words in the elementary school child's vocabulary, as taken from actual conversations, compositions, letters, and similar documents. This list was then examined to see what features of English morphology seem to be most commonly represented in the vocabulary of the first-grade child. From this we could decide what kind of extensions we might expect the child to be able to make. All of the English inflexional morphemes were present.

The areas that seemed to be most promising from this examination were the plural and the two possessives of the noun, the third person singular of the verb, the progressive and the past tense, and the comparative and superlative of the adjective. The pronouns were avoided both because of the difficulty involved in making up a nonsense pronoun, and because the pronouns are so few in number and so irregular that we would hardly expect even adults to have any generalized rules for the handling of new pronouns. Moreover, we do not encounter new pronouns, whereas new verbs, adjectives, and nouns constantly appear in our vocabularies, so that the essential problem is not the same. The past participle of regular or weak verbs in English is identical with the past tense, and since the regular forms were our primary interest, no attempt was made to test for the past participle. A number of forms that might suggest irregular plurals and past tenses were included among the nouns and verbs.

The productive allomorphs of the plural, the possessive, and the third person singular of the verb are phonologically conditioned and identical with one another. These forms are /-s ∼ -z ∼ -əz/, with the following distribution:

/-əz/ after stems that end in /s z š ž č ǰ/, e.g. *glasses, watches;*
/-s/ after stems that end in /p t k f θ/, e.g. *hops, hits;*
/-z/ after all other stems, viz. those ending in /b d g v ð m n ŋ r l/, vowels, and semivowels, e.g. *bids, goes.*

The productive allomorphs of the past are /-t ∼ -d ∼ -əd/, and they are also phonologically conditioned, with the following distribution:

/-əd/ after stems that end in /t d/, e.g., *melted;*
/-t/ after stems that end in / p k č f θ š/, e.g., *stopped;*
/-d/ after stems ending in voiced sounds except /-d/, e.g., *climbed, played.*

The progressive *-ing* and the adjective *-er* and *-est* do not have variants. It might also be noted that the possessive has an addition allomorph /-ø/; this occurs after an inflexional /-s/ or /-z/, so that if the form *boy* is made plural, *boys,* the possessive of that plural form is made by adding nothing, and indicated in writing only by the addition of an apostrophe: *boys'.*

The children's vocabulary at the first-grade level also contains a number of words that are made of a free morpheme and a derivational suffix (e.g., *teacher,* or of two free morphemes, e.g., *birthday.* The difficulties encountered in this area are many. First, it might be noted that there are not many contrasts, i.e., not many cases of the same derivational suffix being added to different bases to produce form of like function. Although *beautiful* and *thankful* both appear on the list, it does not seem that these examples are numerous enough for us to expect a young child to be able to append *-ful* to a new noun in order to produce an adjective. Word derivation and compounding are furthermore often accompanied by changes in stress and pronunciation, so that the picture is additionally complicated. There seemed to be enough examples of the stress pattern ´ `, as in *bláckboàrd* as against *bláck boárd,* and of the diminutive-affectionate *-y,* the adjectival *-y,* and the agentive *-er* to warrant testing for these forms.

So far as the general picture is concerned, all speakers of the language are constrained to use the inflexional endings and apply them appropriately to new forms when they are encountered. We are not so often called upon to derive or compound new words, although by the time we are adults we can all to some extent do this. From this children's actual vocabulary we were able to make an estimate of the kind of morphological rules they might be expected to possess, and from these items a test could be constructed. It was noted, moreover, that in the child's vocabulary there are a number of compound words, like *blackboard* and *birthday.* It is entirely possible to use a compound word correctly and never notice that it is made of two separate and meaningful elements. It is also possible to use it correctly and at the same time have a completely private meaning for one or both of its constituent elements. In order to see what kind of ideas children have about the compound words in their vocabularies, it was decided to ask them directly about a selected number of these words.

Within the framework of the child's vocabulary, a test was devised to explore the child's ability to apply morphological rules to new words. He was called upon to inflect, to derive, to compound, and, lastly, to analyze compound words.

Materials and Procedures

In order to test for the child's use of morphological rules of different types and under varying phonological conditions, a number of nonsense words were made up, following the rules for possible sound combinations in English. Pictures to represent the nonsense words were then drawn on cards. There were 27 picture cards, and the pictures, which were brightly colored, depicted objects, cartoon-like animals, and men performing various actions. For reasons that will be discussed later, several actual words were also included. A text, omitting the desired form, was typed on each card. An example of the card to test for the regular plural allomorph in /-z/ can be seen in Figure 10.1.

This is a Wug.

Now there is another one.
There are two of them.
There are two ———————.

Figure 10.1   The Plural Allomorph in /-z/.

The subjects included 12 adults (7 women and 5 men), all of whom were college graduates. Many of these adults had also had some graduate training. All were native speakers of English.

The child subjects were obtained at the Harvard Preschool in Cambridge and the Michael Driscoll School in Brookline, Massachusetts. At the Preschool, each child was brought to the experimenter, introduced, and told that now he was going to look at some pictures. The experimenter would point to the picture and read the text. The child would supply the missing word, and the item he employed was noted phonemically. After all of the pictures had been shown, the child was asked why he thought the things denoted by the compound words were so named. The general form of these questions was "Why do you think a blackboard is called a blackboard?" If the child responded with "Because it's a blackboard," he was asked, "But why do you think it's called that?" The children at the Preschool ranged between 4 and 5 years in age. Twelve girls and 7 boys were asked all items of the completed test, and two groups, one of 3 boys and 3 girls and one of 5 boys and 3 girls, were each asked half of the inflexional items in preliminary testing.

At the Driscoll School, the experimenter was introduced to the class and it was explained that each child was going to have a turn at looking at some pictures. The procedure from this point on was the same as for the Preschool. All children in the first grade were interviewed. There were 26 boys and 35 girls in this group. Ages ranged from 5½ to 7 years.

The following is the order in which the cards were presented. Included is a statement of what was being tested, a description of the card, and the text that was read. Pronunciation is indicated by regular English orthography; a phonemic transcription is included for the first occurrences of nonsense words.

1. Plural. One birdlike animal, then two. "This is a wug /wʌg/. Now there is another one. There are two of them. There are two ___."

2. Plural. One bird, then two. "This is a gutch /gʌč/. Now there is another one. There are two of them. There are two ___."

3. Past tense. Man with a steaming pitcher on his head. "This is a man who knows how to spow /spow/. He is spowing. He did the same thing yesterday. What did he do yesterday? Yesterday he ___."

4. Plural. One animal, then two. "This is a kazh /kæž/. Now there is another one. There are two of them. There are two ___."

5. Past tense. Man swinging an object. "This is a man who knows how to rick /rik/. He is ricking. He did the same thing yesterday. What did he do yesterday? Yesterday he ___."

6. Diminutive and compounded or derived word. One animal, then a miniscule animal. "This is a wug. This is a very tiny wug. What would you call a very tiny wug? This wug lives in a house. What would you call a house that a wug lives in?"

7. Plural. One animal, then two. "This is a tor /tər/. Now there is another one. There are two of them. There are two ___."

8. Derived adjective. Dog covered with irregular green spots. "This is a dog with quirks /kwərks/ on him. He is all covered with quirks. What kind of dog is he? He is a ___ dog."

9. Plural. One flower, then two. "This is a lun /lʌn/. Now there is another one. There are two of them. There are two ___."

10. Plural. One animal, then two. "This is a niz /niz/. Now there is another one. There are two of them. There are two ___."

11. Past tense. Man doing calisthenics. "This is a man who knows how to mot /mat/. He is motting. He did the same thing yesterday. What did he do yesterday? Yesterday he ___."

12. Plural. One bird, then two. "This is a cra /kra/. Now there is another one. There are two of them. There are two ___."

13. Plural. One animal, then two. "This is a tass /tæs/. Now there is another one. There are two of them. There are two ___."

14. Past tense. Man dangling an object on a string. "This is a man who knows how to bod /bad/. He is bodding. He did the same thing yesterday. What did he do yesterday? Yesterday he ___."

15. Third person singular. Man shaking an object. "This is a man who knows how to naz /næz/. He is nazzing. He does it every day. Every day he ___."

16. Plural. One insect, then two. "This is a heaf /hiyf/. Now there is another one. There are two of them. There are two ___."

17. Plural. One glass, then two. "This is a glass. Now there is another one. There are two of them. They are two ___."

18. Past tense. Man exercising. "This is a man who knows how to gling /gliŋ/. He is glinging. He did the same thing yesterday. What did he do yesterday? Yesterday he ___."

19. Third person singular. Man holding an object. "This is a man who knows how to loodge /luwdž/. He is loodging. He does it every day. Every day he ___."

20. Past tense. Man standing on the ceiling. "This is a man who knows how to bing /biŋ/. He is binging. He did the same thing yesterday. What did he do yesterday? Yesterday he ___."

21. Singular and plural possessive. One animal wearing a hat, then two wearing hats. "This is a niz who owns a hat. Whose hat is it? It is the ___ hat. Now there are two nizzes. They both own hats. Whose hats are they? They are the ___ hats."

22. Past tense. A bell. "This is a bell that can ring. It is ringing. It did the same thing yesterday. What did it do yesterday? Yesterday it ___."

23. Singular and plural possessive. One animal wearing a hat, then two. "This is a wug who owns a hat. Whose hat is it? It is the ___ hat. Now there are two wugs. They both own hats. Whose hats are they? They are the ___ hats.

24. Comparative and superlative of the adjective. A dog with a few spots, one with several, and one with a great number. "This dog has quirks on him. This dog has more quirks on him. And this dog has even more quirks on him. This dog is quirky. This dog is ___. And this dog is the ___."

25. Progressive and derived agentive or compound. Man balancing a ball on his nose. "This is a man who knows how to zib /zib/. What is he doing? He is ___. What would you call a man whose job is to zib?"

26. Past tense. An ice cube, then a puddle of water. "This is an ice cube. Ice melts. It is melting. Now it is all gone. What happened to it? It ___."

27. Singular and plural possessive. One animal wearing a hat, then two. "This is a bik /bik/ who owns a hat. Whose hat is it? It is the ___ hat. Now there are two biks. They both own hats. Whose hats are they? They are the ___ hats."

28. Compound words. The child was asked why he thought the following were so named. (No pictures were used for these items.)

a. afternoon
b. airplane
c. birthday
d. breakfast
e. blackboard
f. fireplace
g. football
h. handkerchief
i. holiday
j. merry-go-round
k. newspaper
l. sunshine
m. Thanksgiving
n. Friday

It took between ten and fifteen minutes to ask a child all of these questions. No child failed to understand the nature of the task before him. It was, moveover, evident that a great number of these children thought they were being taught new English words. It was not uncommon for a child to repeat the nonsense word immediately upon hearing it and before being asked any questions. Often, for example, when the experimenter said, "This is a *gutch*," the child repeated, "*Gutch*." Answers were willingly, and often insistently, given. These responses will be discussed in the following section.

Results

In this experiment, preschool and first grade children, ranging from 4 to 7 years in age, were presented with a number of nonsense words and asked to supply English plurals, verb tenses, possessives, derivations, and compounds of those words. Our first and most general question had been: Do children possess morphological rules? A previous study of the actual vocabulary of first graders showed that they know real items representing basic English morphological processes. Asking questions about real words, however, might be tapping a process no more abstract than rote memory. We could be sure that our nonsense words were new words to the child, and that if he supplied the right morphological item he knew something more than the individual words in his vocabulary: he had rules of extension that enabled him to deal with new words. Every child interviewed understood what was being asked of him. If knowledge of English consisted of no more than the storing up of many memorized words, the child might be expected to refuse to answer our questions on the grounds that he had never before heard of a *wug*, for instance, and could not possibly give us the plural form since no one had ever told him what it was. This was decidedly not the case. The children answered the questions; in some instances they pronounced the inflexional endings they had added with exaggerated care, so that it was obvious that they understood the problem and wanted no mistake made about their solution. Sometimes they said, "That's a hard one," and pondered a while before answering, or answered with one form and then corrected themselves. The answers were not always right so far as English is concerned; but they were consistent and orderly answers, and they demonstrated that there can be no doubt that children in this age range operate with clearly delimited morphological rules.

Our second finding was that boys and girls did equally well on these items. Sometimes the girls had a higher percentage of right answers on an item, and more often the boys did somewhat better, but no pattern of differences could be distinguished and the differences were never statistically significant. These findings are at variance with the results of most other language tests. Usually, girls have been shown to have a slight advantage over boys. In our experiment, girls were no more advanced than boys in their acquisition of English morphology. Since other language tests have not investigated morphology *per se*, it is easy enough to say that this is simply one area in which there are no sex differences.

A reason for this lack of difference does, however, suggest itself: and that is the very basic nature of morphology. Throughout childhood, girls are perhaps from a maturational point of view slightly ahead of the boys who are their chronological age mates. But the language differences that have been observed may be culturally induced, and they may be fairly superficial. Some social factor may lead girls to be more facile with words, to use longer sentences, and to talk more. This can be misleading. A girl in an intellectual adult environment may, for instance, acquire a rather sophisticated vocabulary at an early age. This should not be taken to mean that she will learn the minor rules for the formation of the plural before she learns the major ones, or that she will necessarily be precocious in her acquisition of those rules. What is suggested here is that every child is in contact with a sufficiently varied sample of spoken English in order for him to be exposed at an early age to the basic morphological processes. These processes occur in simple sentences as well as in complex ones. Practice with a limited vocabulary may be as effective as practice with an extensive vocabulary, and the factors that influence other aspects of language development may have no effect on morphological acquisition. Since, moreover, this type of inner patterning is clearly a cognitive process, we might expect it to be related to intelligence more than to any other feature. Unfortunately, there were no IQs available for the subjects, so that a comparison could not be made, and this last must remain a speculation.

Our next observation was that there were some differences between the preschoolers and the first graders (see Table 10.1). These were predominantly

TABLE 10.1. *Age Differences on Inflexional Items*

ITEM (PLURAL)	PERCENTAGE OF CORRECT PRE-SCHOOL ANSWERS	PERCENTAGE OF CORRECT FIRST-GRADE ANSWERS	SIGNIFICANCE LEVEL OF DIFFERENCE
glasses	75	99	.01
wugs	76	97	.02
luns	68	92	.05
tors	73	90	—
heafs	79	80	—
cras	58	86	.05
tasses	28	39	—
gutches	28	38	—
kazhes	25	36	—
nizzes	14	33	—

on the items that the group as a whole did best and worst on: since no child in the preschool could supply the irregular past *rang*, and a few in the first grade could, this difference was significant. Otherwise, the improvement was in the direction of perfecting knowledge they already had — the simple plurals and possessives, and the progressive tense. The answers of the two groups were not qualitatively different: they both employed the same simplified morphological rules. Since this was true, the answers of both groups were combined for the purpose of further analysis.

Children were able to form the plurals requiring /-s/ or /-z/, and they did best on the items where general English phonology determined which of these allomorphs is required (see Table 10.2). Although they have in their vocabu-

TABLE 10.2. *Percentages of Children Supplying Correct Plural Forms*

ITEM	ALLOMORPH	% CORRECT
glasses	/-əz/	91
wugs	/-z/	91
luns	/-z/	86
tors	/-z/	85
heafs, -ves	/-s/ /-z/	82
cras	/-z/	79
tasses	/-əz/	36
gutches	/-əz/	36
kazhes	/-əz/	31
nizzes	/-əz/	28

laries real words that form their plural in /-əz/, in the age range that was interviewed they did not generalize to form new words in /-əz/. Their rule seems to be to add /-s/ or /-z/, unless the word ends in /s z š ž č ǰ/. To words ending in these sounds they add nothing to make the plural — and when asked to form a plural, repeat the stem as if it were already in the productive allomorphs. We may now ask about the relative status of the remaining allomorphs /-s/ and /-z/. For the items like *lun* or *cra*, where both of these sounds could produce a phonologically possible English word, but not a plural, no child employed the voiceless alternate /-s/. This is the second least common of the three allomorphs. The only places where this variant occurred were where the speaker of English could not say otherwise. So far as general English phonology is concerned a /-z/ cannot in the same cluster follow a /-k/ or other voiceless sound. Once the /-k/ has been said, even if the speaker intended to say /-z/, it would automatically devoice to /-s/. The only morphological rule the child is left with, is the addition of the /-z/ allomorph, which is the most extensive: the /-əz/ form for him is not yet productive, and the /-s/ form can be subsumed under a more general phonological rule.

What we are saying here is that the child's rule for the formation of the plural seems to be: "A final sibilant makes a word plural." The question that arises is, should we not rather say that the child's rule is: "A voiceless sibilant after a voiceless consonant and a voiced sibilant after all other sounds makes a word plural." This latter describes what the child actually does. However, our rule will cover the facts if it is coupled with a prior phonological rule about possible final sound sequences. The choice of the voiceless or voiced variant can generally be subsumed under phonological rules about final sound sequences; the exceptions are after vowels, semivowels, and /l- n- r-/. In these places where phonology leaves a choice, /-z/ is used, and so the child's conscious rule might be to add /-z/. It would be interesting to find out what the child thinks he is saying — if we could in some way ask him the general question, "How do you make the plural?"

Another point of phonology was illustrated by the children's treatment of the forms *heaf* and *kazh*. It was demonstrated here that the children have phonological rules, and the direction of their generalizations was dictated by English phonology, and not simple phonetic similarity. /-ž/ is a comparatively rare sibilant series in English, and they rarely attempted to follow it with another sibilant. The similarity between /f/ and the sibilants, did not, on the contrary, cause them to treat it as a member of this class. The final thing to be noted about *heaf* is that several children and many adults said the plural was *heaves*. This may be by analogy with *leaf: leaves*. If our speculation that the /-z/ form is the real morphological plural is right, there may be cases where instead of becoming devoiced itself, it causes regressive assimilation of the final voiceless consonant.

The allomorphs of the third person singular of the verb and the possessives of the noun are the same as for the noun plural, except that the plural possessives have an additional zero allomorph. These forms were treated in the same way by the children, with one notable exception — they were more successful in adding the /-əz/ to form possessive and verbs rather than they were in forming noun plurals. They were asked to produce three nearly identical forms: a man who *nazzes*; two *nizzes*; and a *niz's* hat. On the verb they were 48% right; on the possessive they were 49% right, and on the noun plural they were only 28% right. The difference between their performance on the noun plural and on the other two items was significant at the 1% level. And yet the phonological problem presented by these three forms was the same. For some reason the contingent rule for the formation of the third person singular of the verb and for the possessive is better learned or earlier learned than the same rule for the formation of noun plurals. The morphological rule implies meaning, and forms that are phonologically identical may be learned at different times if they serve different functions. These forms are not simply the same phonological rule, since their different functions change the percentage of right answers. Perhaps the child does better because he knows more verbs than nouns ending in /s z š ž č ǰ/, and it is possible that he has heard more possessives than noun plurals. It is also possible that for English the noun plural is the least important or most redundant of these inflexions. This is a somewhat surprising conclusion, since nouns must always appear in a singular or plural form and there are ways of avoiding the possessive inflexion: it is generally possible to use an *of* construction in place of a possessive — we can say *the leg of the chair* or *the chair's leg*, or *the chair leg*, although in cases involving actual ownership we do not say *of*. A sentence referring to *the hat of John* sounds like an awkward translation from the French. And no child said it was *the hat of the niz*. The children's facility with these forms seems to indicate that the possessive inflexion is by no means dying out in English.

Of the verb forms, the best performance was with the present progressive:

90% of all the children said that a man who knew how to *zib* was *zibbing*. Undoubtedly, children's speech is mostly in the present tense, and this is a very commonly heard form. Explanations of what is happening in the present all take this form. "The man is *running*" — or *walking* or *eating* or *doing* something.

The children's handling of the past tense parallels their treatment of the plurals, except that they did better on the whole with the plurals. Again, they could not extend the contingent rule. Although they have forms like *melted* in their vocabulary, they were unable to extend the /əd/ form to new verbs ending in /t d/. They treated these forms as if they were already in the past. They applied the allomorphs /-d/ and /-t/ appropriately where they were phonologically conditioned, and only /-d/ to a form like *spow*, where either was possible. This suggests that their real morphological rule for the formation of the past is to add /-d/, and under certain conditions it will automatically become /-t/. Many adult speakers feel that they are adding a /-d/ that devoices without their noticing it.

Whereas the children all used regular patterns in forming the past tense, we found that for adults strong pasts of the form *rang* and *clung* are productive. Since virtually all English verbs that are in the present of an *-ing* form make their pasts irregularly, this seemed a likely supposition. Adults made *gling* and *bing* into *glang* and *bang* in the past. New words of this general shape may therefore be expected to have a very good chance of being treated according to this pattern — real words like the verb *to string* for instance, have been known to vacillate between the common productive past and this strong subgroup and finally come to be treated according to the less common pattern. The children, however, could not be expected to use this pattern since we could not demonstrate that they had the real form *rang* in their repertory. They said *ringed*. At one point, the experimenter misread the card and told the child that the bell *rang*. When the child was asked what the bell did, he said, "It *ringed*." The experimenter then corrected him and said, "You mean it *rang*." The child said that was what he had said, and when asked again what that was, he repeated, "It *ringed*," as if he had not even heard the difference between these two allomorphs. Perhaps he did not.

The adults did not form irregular pasts with any other pattern, although a form was included that could have been treated according to a less common model. This was the verb *mot*, which was of the pattern *cut* or *bet*. There are some 19 verbs in English that form their past with a zero morpheme, but this group does not seem to be productive.

The cases of *gling*, which became *glang* in the past and *mot*, which became *motted*, suggest some correlates of linguistic productivity. About 19 verbs in English form their past tense with a zero allomorph. About 14 verbs form their past like *cling*, and 7 follow the pattern of *ring*. Within these last two groups there are words like *win*, which becomes *won*, and *swim*, which becomes *swam*. We can also find words similar to *win* and *swim* that are quite regular in the past: *pin* and *trim*. But virtually all of the verbs that end in *-ing* form their past in *-ang* or *-ung*. There are approximately 10 of these *-ing* verbs.

The productivity of the *-ang* and *-ung* forms proves that new forms are not necessarily assimilated to the largest productive class. Where a small group of common words exist as a category by virtue of their great phonetic similarity and their morphological consistency, a new word having the same degree of phonetic similarity may be treated according to this special rule. *Ox: oxen* is not similarly productive, but probably would be if there were just one other form like *box: boxen,* and the competing *fox: foxes* did not exist. With *mot,* the zero allomorph is not productive because although it applies to more cases than are covered by the *-ing* verbs, it is not so good a rule in the sense that it is not so consistent. The final /-t/, which is the only common phonetic element, does not invariably lead to a zero allomorph, as witness *pit: pitted, pat: patted,* and many others.

Although the adults were uniform in their application of *-er* and *-est* to form the comparative and superlative of the adjective, children did not seem to have these patterns under control unless they were given both the adjective and the comparative form. With this information, some of them could supply the superlative.

Derivation is likewise a process little used by children at this period when the derivational endings would compete with the inflexional suffixes they are in the process of acquiring. Instead, they compound words, using the primary and tertiary accent pattern commonly found in words like *blackboard.*

The last part of the experiment was designed to see if the children were aware of the separate elements in the compound words in their vocabulary. Most of these children were at the stage where they explained an object's name by stating its major function or salient feature: a blackboard is called a *blackboard* because you write on it. In the older group, a few children had noticed the separate parts of the compound words and assigned to them meanings that were not necessarily connected with the word's etymology or with the meaning the morphemes may have in later life. Not many adults feel that Friday is the day for frying things, yet a number admit to having thought so as children.

As we might expect, the greatest number of etymological responses — 23% — was given for *Thanksgiving,* which is an item that children are explicitly taught. It must be noted, however, that despite this teaching, for 67% of the children answering this item, Thanksgiving is called *Thanksgiving* because you eat lots of turkey.

The salient feature answers at first seem to have the nature of an etymological explanation, in those instances where the feature coincides with a part of the name — 72% of the answers, for instance, said that a fireplace is called a fireplace because you put fire in it. When the salient feature does not coincide with part of the name, however, the etymological aspects also drop out. For *birthday,* where to the child neither that fact that it is a day nor that it is tied to one's birth is important, the number of functional answers rises: it is called *birthday* because you get presents or eat cake. Only 2% said anything about its being a day.

These last considerations were, however, tangential to the main problem of investigating the child's grasp of English morphological rules and describing the evolution of those rules. The picture that emerged was one of consistency, regularity, and simplicity. The children did not treat new words according to idiosyncratic pattern. They did not model new words on patterns that appear infrequently. Where they provided inflexional endings, their best performance was with those forms that are the most regular and have the fewest variants. With the morphemes that have several allomorphs, they could handle forms calling for the most common that appear in a limited distribution range.

How Shall a Thing Be Called?

Roger Brown

A child's use of words is frequently taken as an indication of his level of conceptual attainment. Thus a child who labels a four-legged animal, with the specific characteristics of a dog, a "canine" is viewed as having attained a higher level of conceptual ability than another child who labels the dog "Prince." Professor Brown of Harvard University questions the validity of the inference that "canine" indicates a higher level of ability than "Prince." His analysis of the labeling practices of adults suggests that children learn labels which maximize communication in the simplest way. Thus, concrete terms may be learned before abstract; but in many instances the reverse may be true. It is not possible, therefore, to conclude that language development proceeds from the concrete to the abstract.

The most deliberate part of first-language teaching is the business of telling a child what each thing is called. We ordinarily speak of *the* names of things as if there were just one, but in fact, of course, every referent has many names. The dime in my pocket is not only a *dime*. It is also *money*, a *metal object*, a *thing*, and, moving to subordinates, it is a *1952 dime*, in fact a *particular 1952 dime* with a unique pattern of scratches, discolorations, and smooth places. When such an object is named for a very young child, how is it called? It may be named *money* or *dime*, but probably not *metal object, thing, 1952 dime*, or *particular 1952 dime*. The dog out on the lawn is not only a *dog* but is also a *boxer*, a *quadruped*, an *animate being*; it is the *landlord's dog*, named *Prince*. How will it be identified for a child? Sometimes it will be called a *dog*, sometimes *Prince*, less often a *boxer*, and almost never a *quadruped*, or *animate being*. Listening to many adults name things for many children, I find that their choices are quite uniform and that I can anticipate them from my own inclinations. How are these choices determined, and what are their consequences for the cognitive development of the child?

Adults have notions about the kind of language appropriate for use with children. Especially strong and universal is the belief that children have trouble

source: Adapted and abridged from Roger Brown, "How Shall a Thing Be Called?" *Psychological Review*, 1958, 65, 14–21. (With permission of the author and the American Psychological Association.)

pronouncing long names and so should always be given the shortest possible names. A word is preferable to a phrase and, among words, a monosyllable is better than a polysyllable. This predicts the preference for *dog* and *Prince* over *boxer, quadruped,* and *animate being.* It predicts the choice of *dime* over *metal object* and *particular 1952 dime.*

Zipf (1935) has shown that the length of a word (in phonemes or syllables) is inversely related to its frequency in the printed language. Consequently the shorter names for any thing will usually also be the most frequently used names for that thing, and so it would seem that the choice of a name is usually predictable from either frequency or brevity. The monosyllables *dog* and *Prince* have much higher frequencies according to the Thorndike-Lorge list (1944) than do the polysyllables *boxer, quadruped,* and *animate being.*

It sometime happens, however, that the frequency-brevity principle makes the wrong prediction. The thing called a *pineapple* is also *fruit. Fruit* is the shorter and more frequent term, but adults will name the thing *pineapple.* Similarly they will say *apple, banana, orange,* and even *pomegranate,* all of them longer and less frequent words than the perfectly appropriate *fruit.* Brevity seems not to be the powerful determinant we had imagined. The frequency principle can survive this kind of example, but only if it is separated from counts like the Thorndike-Lorge of overall frequency in the printed language. On the whole the word *fruit* appears more often than the word *pineapple* (and also is shorter), but we may confidently assume that, when pineapples are being named, the word *pineapple* is more frequent than the word *fruit.* This, of course, is a kind of frequency more directly relevant to our problem. Word counts of general usage are only very roughly applicable to the prediction of what will be said when something is named. What we need is referent-name counts. We don't have them, of course, but if we had them it is easy to see that they would improve our predictions. Bananas are called *banana,* apples, *apple,* and oranges *orange* more often than any of them is called *fruit.* The broad frequency-brevity principle predicts that *money* and *dime* will be preferred to *metal object, 1952 dime,* and *particular 1952 dime,* but it does not predict the neglect of the common monosyllable *thing.* For this purpose we must again appeal to imagined referent-name counts, according to which dimes would surely be called *dime* or *money* more often than *thing.*

While the conscious preference for a short name can be overcome by frequency, the preference nevertheless affects the naming act. I have heard parents designate the appropriate objects *pineapple, television, vinegar,* and *policeman;* all these to children who cannot reproduce polysyllabic words. Presumably they use these names because that is what the referents are usually called, but the adult's sense of the absurdity of giving such words to a child is often evident. He may smile as he says it, or remark, "That's too hard for you to say, isn't it?"

Some things are named in the same way by all adults for all children. This is true of the apple and the orange. Other things have several common names, each of them used by a specifiable group of adults to specifiable children. The same dog is *dog* to most of the world and *Prince* in his own home and perhaps on his own block. The same man is a *man* to most children, *policeman* to some at some times, *Mr. Jones* to the neighborhood kids, and *papa* to his own. Referent-name counts from people in general will not predict these several usages. A still more particular name count must be imagined. The name given a thing by an adult for a child is determined by the frequency with which various names have been applied to such things in the experience of the particular adult. General referent-name counts taken from many people will predict much that the individual does; but, for a close prediction, counts specific to the individual would be needed.

The frequencies to which we are now appealing have not, of course, been recorded. We are explaining imagined preferences in names by imagined frequencies of names. It is conceivable, certainly, that some of these specific word counts might be made and a future naming performance independently predicted from a past frequency. Probably, however, such frequencies will never be known, and if we choose to explain particular naming performances by past frequencies we shall usually have to infer the frequency from the performance.

Beyond the Frequency Principle

A frequency explanation is not very satisfying even when the appeal is to known frequnecies. The question will come to mind: "Why is one name more common than another?" Why is a dog called *dog* more often than *quadruped* and, by some people, called *Prince* more often than *dog*? Perhaps it just happened that way, like driving on the right side of the road in America and on the left in England. The convention is preserved but has no justification outside itself. As things have worked out, coins are usually named by species as *dime, nickel,* or *penny* while the people we know have individual names like *John, Mary,* and *Jim.* Could it just as easily be the other way around? Might we equally well give coins proper names and introduce people as types?

The referent for the word *dime* is a large class of coins. The name is equally appropriate to all members of this class. To name a coin *dime* is to establish its equivalence, for naming purposes, with all other coins of the same denomination. This equivalence for naming purposes corresponds to a more general equivalence for all purposes of economic exchange. In the grocery one dime is as good as another but quite different from any nickel or penny. For a child the name given an object anticipates the equivalences and differences that will need to be observed in most of his dealings with such an object. To make proper denotative use of the word *dime* he must be able to distinguish members of the referent category from everything else. When he learns that, he has solved more than a language problem. He has an essential bit of equipment for doing business. The most common names for coins could not move from the species level to the level of proper names without great alteration in our nonlinguistic culture. We should all be numismatists preparing our children to recognize a particular priceless 1910 dime.

Many things are reliably given the same name by the whole community. The spoon is seldom called anything but *spoon*, although it is also a piece of *silverware*, an *artifact*, and a *particular ill-washed restaurant spoon*. The community-wide preference for the word *spoon* corresponds to the community-wide practice of treating spoons as equivalent but different from knives and forks. There are no proper names for individual spoons because their individuality seldom signifies. It is the same way with pineapples, dimes, doors, and taxicabs. The most common name for each of these categorizes them as they need to be categorized for the community's nonlinguistic purposes. The most common name is at the level of usual utility.

People and pets have individual names as well as several kinds of generic names. The individual name is routinely coined by those who are disposed to treat the referent as unique, and is available afterwards to any others who will see the uniqueness. A man at home has his own name to go with the peculiar privileges and responsibilities binding him to wife and child. But the same man who is a one-of-a-kind *papa* to his own children is simply a *man* to children at large. He is, like the other members of this large category, someone with no time to play and little tolerance for noise. In some circumstances, this same man will be given the name of his occupation. He is a *policeman* equivalent to other policemen but different from *bus drivers* and *Good Humor men*. A policeman is someone to "behave in front of" and to go to when lost. To the kids in the neighborhood the man is *Mr. Jones*, unique in his way—a crank, bad tempered, likely to shout at you if you play out in front of his house. It is the same way with dogs as with people. He may be a unique *Prince* to his owners, who feed and house him, but he is just a *dog* to the rest of the world. A homeless dog reverts to namelessness, since there is none to single him out from his species. Dimes and nickels have much the same significance for an entire society, and their usual names are fixed at this level of significance. People and pets function uniquely for some and in various generic ways for others. They have a corresponding variety of designations, but each name is at the utility level for the group that uses it. Our naming practices for coins and people correspond to our nonlinguistic practices, and it is difficult to imagine changing the one without changing the other.

The names provided by parents for children anticipate the functional structure of the child's world.[1] This is not, of course, something parents are aware of doing. When we name a thing there does not seem to be any process of choice. Each thing has its name, just one, and that is what we give to a child. The one name is, of course, simply the usual name for us. Naming each thing in accordance with local frequencies, parents unwittingly transmit their own cognitive structures. It is a world in which *Prince* is unique among dogs and *papa* among men, *spoons* are all alike but different from *forks*. It may be a world of *bugs* (to be stepped on), of *flowers* (not to be picked), and *birds* (not to be stoned). It may be a world in which *Niggers*, like *spoons*, are all of a kind. A division of caste creates a vast categorical equivalence and a correspondingly generic name. *Mr.*

Jones and *Mr. Smith* do not come out of racial anonymity until their uniqueness is appreciated.

Adults do not invariably provide a child with the name that is at the level of usual utility in the adult world. An effort is sometimes made to imagine the utilities of a child's life. Some parents will, at first, call every sort of coin *money*. This does not prepare a child to buy and sell, but then he may be too young for that. All coins are equivalent for the very young child in that they are objects not to be put into the mouth and not to be dropped down the register, and *money* anticipates that equivalence. A more differentiated terminology can wait upon the age of storegoing. Sometimes an adult is aware of a child's need for a distinction that is not coded in the English lexicon. A new chair comes into the house and is not going to be equivalent to the shabby chairs already there. A child is permitted to sit on the old chairs but will not be permitted on the new one. A distinctive name is created from the combinational resources of the language. *The new chair* or *the good chair* is not to be assimilated to *chairs* in general.

Eventually, of course, children learn many more names for each thing than the one that is most frequent and useful. Sometimes a name is supplied in order to bring forward an immediately important property of the referent. A child who starts bouncing the coffee pot needs to be told that it is *glass*. Sometimes a name is supplied to satisfy the child's curiosity as to the place of a referent in a hierarchy of categories. Chairs are *furniture* and so are tables; carrots are a *vegetable* but apples are not. Probably, however, both children and adults make some distinction among these various names. *The* name of a thing, the one that tells what it "really" is, is the name that constitutes the referent as it needs to be constituted for most purposes. The other names represent possible recategorizations useful for one or another purpose. We are even likely to feel that these recategorizations are acts of imagination, whereas the major categorization is a kind of passive recognition of the true character of the referent.

The Child's Concrete Vocabulary

It is a commonplace saying that the mind of a child is relatively "concrete" and the mind of an adult "abstract." The words "concrete" and "abstract" are sometimes used in the sense of subordinate and superordinate. In this sense a relatively concrete mind would operate with subordinate categories and an abstract mind with superordinate categories. It is recorded in many studies of vocabulary acquisition that children ordinarily use the words *milk* and *water* before the word *liquid;* the words *apple* and *orange* before *fruit; table* and *chair* before *furniture; mamma* and *daddy* before *parent* or *person;* etc. Very high-level superordinate terms like *article, action, quality,* and *relation,* though they are common in adult speech (Thorndike and Lorge 1944), are very seldom heard from preschool children. Presumably this kind of vocabulary comparison is one of the sources of the notion that the child's mind is more concrete than the mind of the adult.[2] However, the vocabulary of a child is not a very direct index of his cognitive preferences. The child's vocabulary is more immediately determined by the naming practices of adults.

The occasion for a name is ordinarily some particular thing. In the naming it is categorized. The preference among possible names seems to go to the one that is most commonly applied to the referent in question. That name will ordinarily categorize the referent so as to observe the equivalences and differences that figure in its usual utilization. There are not many purposes for which all liquids are equivalent or all fruits, furniture, or parents; and so the names of these categories are less commonly used for denotation than are the names of categories subordinate to them. It is true that words like *article, action, quality,* and *relation* are rather common in adult written English, but we can be sure that these frequencies in running discourse are not equaled in naming situations. Whatever the purposes for which all articles are equivalent, or all actions or qualities, they are not among the pressing needs of children.

It is not invariably true that vocabulary builds from concrete to abstract. *Fish* is likely to be learned before *perch* and *bass; house* before *bungalow* and *mansion; car* before *Chevrolet* and *Plymouth.* The more concrete vocabulary waits for the child to reach an age where his purposes differentiate kinds of fish and makes of cars. There is much elaborately concrete vocabulary that is not introduced until one takes courses in biology, chemistry, and botany. No one has ever proved that vocabulary builds from the concrete to the abstract more often than it builds from the abstract to the concrete. The best generalization seems to be that each thing is first given its most common name. This name seems to categorize on the level of usual utility. That level sometimes falls on the most concrete categories in a hierarchy (proper names for significant people), and vocabulary then builds toward the more abstract categories (names for ethnic groups, personality types, social classes). Utility sometimes centers on a relatively abstract level of categorization (fish) and vocabulary then builds in both directions (perch and vertebrate). Probably utility never centers on the most abstract levels (thing, substance, etc.), and so probably there is no hierarchy within which vocabulary builds in an exclusively concrete direction.

In the literature describing first-language acquisition there is much to indicate that children easily form large abstract categories. There are, to begin with, the numerous cases in which the child overgeneralizes the use of a conventional word. The word *dog* may, at first, be applied to every kind of four-legged animal. It sometimes happens that every man who comes into the house is called *daddy.* When children invent their own words, these often have an enormous semantic range. Wilhelm Stern's son Gunther used *psee* for leaves, trees and flowers. He used *bebau* for all animals. Lombroso tells of a child who used *qua qua* for both duck and water, and *afta* for drinking glass, the content of a glass, and a pane of glass. Reports of this kind do not suggest that children are deficient in abstracting ability. It even looks as if they may favor large categories.

There are two extreme opinions about the direction of cognitive development.

There are those who suppose that we begin by discriminating to the limits of our sensory acuity, seizing each thing in its uniqueness, noting every hair and flea of the particular dog. Cognitive development involves neglect of detail, abstracting from particulars so as to group similars into categories. By this view abstraction is a mature rather than a primitive process. The contrary opinion is that the primitive stage in cognition is one of a comparative lack of differentiation. Probably certain distinctions are inescapable; the difference between a loud noise and near silence, between a bright contour and dark ground, etc. These inevitable discriminations divide the perceived world into a small number of very large (abstract) categories. Cognitive development is increasing differentiation. The more distinctions we make, the more categories we have and the smaller (more concrete) these are. I think the latter view is favored in psychology today. While there is good empirical and theoretical support for the view that development is differentiation, there is embarrassment for it in the fact that much vocabulary growth is from the concrete to the abstract. This embarrassment can be eliminated.

Suppose a very young child applies the word *dog* to every four-legged creature he sees. He may have abstracted a limited set of attributes and created a large category, but his abstraction will not show up in his vocabulary. Parents will not provide him with a conventional name for his category, e.g., *quadruped,* but instead will require him to narrow his use of *dog* to its proper range. Suppose a child calls all elderly ladies *aunt.* He will not be told that the usual name for his category is *elderly ladies* but, instead, will be taught to cut back *aunt* to accord with standard usage. In short, the sequence in which words are acquired is set by adults rather than children, and may ultimately be determined by the utility of the various categorizations. This will sometimes result in a movement of vocabulary toward higher abstraction and sometimes a movement toward greater concreteness. The cognitive development of the child may nevertheless always take the direction of increasing differentiation or concreteness.

The child who spontaneously hits on the category *four-legged animals* will be required to give it up in favor of dogs, cats, horses, cows, and the like. When the names of numerous subordinates have been mastered, he may be given the name *quadruped* for the superordinate. This abstraction is not the same as its primitive forerunner. The schoolboy who learns the word *quadruped* has abstracted from differentiated and named subordinates. The child he was (previously) abstracted through a failure to differentiate. Abstraction after differentiation may be the mature process, and abstraction from a failure to differentiate the primitive. Needless to say, the abstractions occurring on the two levels need not be coincident, as they are in our quadruped example.

NOTES

[1] The equivalence of dimes and their distinctiveness as a class from nickels and pennies is strongly suggested by the appearance of individual coins as well as by their names. Variations

in size, weight, and hue are far greater between classes than within a class. This, of course, is because coins are manufactured in accordance with a categorical scheme which is also represented in our names for coins. It is possible, then, that a child might structure coins in the culturally approved manner if he never heard them named at all. However, we cannot be sure that an untutored child would not put all shiny new coins into one class and all the dingy specimens into another. When the referents are not manufactured articles but are such things as dogs, people, flowers, and insects, it is clear that autochthonous factors in perception do not force any single scheme of categorization. The names applied must be the child's principal clue to the locally functioning scheme.

2 From the facts of vocabulary acquisition alone it is not possible to draw safe conclusions about cognitive development. Such conclusions rely on something like the following set of assumptions. A subject, whether animal or human, is ordinarily credited with a cognitive category when he extends some distinctive response to new instances of the category and withholds it from noninstances. Words, when used to denote new referents, are such a distinctive response. If children speak words they probably can make correct denotative use of them, and so the presence of the word in a child's vocabulary may be taken as evidence that he possesses the category to which the word makes reference. The instances of the category are presumed not to be differentiated by the child unless he uses words for such differentiations. If all of these assumptions are made it would seem to follow that the direction of vocabulary growth (from subordinate to superordinate or vice versa) reveals the direction of cognitive development. When the assumptions of such an argument are explicitly stated, it is clear that they are too many and too doubtful. Obviously words may be spoken but not understood; objects may be differentiated by nonlinguistic response even though they are not differentiated linguistically. However, it is not my purpose here to quarrel with these assumptions but rather to show that, even when they are accepted, the facts of vocabulary growth do not compel the conclusion that cognitive development is from the concrete to the abstract.

Social Conditioning of Vocalizations in the Infant

Harriet Rheingold, Jacob Gewirtz, and Helen W. Ross

A great deal of stress has been placed on the importance of parent interactions with their young children as a factor in subsequent language development. Many studies, for example, have shown that children reared in orphanages, where adult-child interactions are minimal, display a slow rate of language development. Similarly, children reared in environments that regard language as a relatively unimportant component of child development tend also to show retarded language growth. Although the vocabulary level of the parents undoubtedly plays an important role in vocabulary, it is also true that the frequency of early speech sounds is influenced by the degree to which they are reinforced by parents. In this study the investigators demonstrate the effectiveness of social reinforcement in generating greater output of vocalizations.

By 3 months of age the infant gives a well-defined social response to the appearance of adults. He looks at them intently, smiles, becomes active, and vocalizes. This behavior is repeated again and again in sequence. Adults often respond to

SOURCE: Adapted and abridged from H. Rheingold, J. Gewirtz, and H. W. Ross, "Social Conditioning of Vocalizations in Infancy." *Journal of Comparative and Physiological Psychology*, 1959, 52, 68–73. (With permission of the authors and the American Psychological Association.)

these acts of the infant; they may only look at the child, but they may also smile to him, touch or caress him, or vocalize in return. Frequently one observes "answering" social and, in particular, vocal play between mother and child. The adults' responses may therefore play an important part in maintaining and developing social responsiveness in the child. The principles of operant conditioning suggest that some of these adult responses, functioning as reinforcers, may affect the development of the child's social behavior. Thus, smiling in the infant has been shown to respond to conditioning.

The present study was an attempt to condition vocalizations in infants. Vocalizations were selected for study because they seem to provide an index of the whole social response. The reinforcing stimulus was a complex of social acts which resembled those an attentive adult might naturally make when a child vocalizes. If temporal contiguity between the infant's vocalization and the reinforcing stimulus, which follows it, brings about an increase in the vocalizations, conditioning may be said to have occurred. The possibility that the reinforcing stimulus may also have functioned as an arouser of vocalizations will be considered. In any case, the results of the study should provide further understanding about the development of social responsiveness, as well as of speech.

Method

Two parallel experiments were carried out in sequence. In the first, 11 babies (Ss) were studied, with one experimenter (E) and one observer-recorder (O), both women. In the second, 10 other Ss and one S from Experiment I were studied with the E and O of the first experiment exchanging roles. An experiment was composed of three successive units in each of which three or four Ss were studied at one time.

Subjects

The Ss were 21 infants, all residents almost from birth in the same institution. (We are grateful to Sister Thecla and the staff of St. Ann's Infant Asylum, Washington, D.C., for their generous cooperation.) Their median age was 3.0 months; three-quarters of them were no more than three days older or younger than the median. In each experiment six Ss were male, five were female. Age was the main criterion for selection. Four possible Ss were rejected: one seemed immature, two had a very high rate of vocalizing during the first baseline measure, and one was markedly fussy.

The institution offers excellent care and, as is characteristic of institutions, there are multiple caretakers. In general, the Ss were well developed, healthy, alert, and socially responsive. The Es asked for no modification in the usual caretaking routines. The caretakers knew that the Es were observing the development of social behavior, but they did not know the details of the experiment. The caretakers' usual behavior toward the Ss appeared not to be modified by the conditions of the experiment.

Experimental Conditions

Baseline. In experimental Days 1 and 2 (first and second Baseline days) E leaned over the crib with her face about 15 inches above S's and looked at him with an expressionless face, while O tallied vocalizations, out of S's sight. The E moved her head as necessary to remain in S's line of vision, a condition which obtained throughout the experiments.

Conditioning. During experimental Days 3 and 4 (first and second Conditioning days), E again leaned over the crib with an expressionless face except that when S vocalized, E made an immediate response and then resumed the expressionless face until the next vocalization. The response, or *reinforcing stimulus,* consisted of three acts executed by E simultaneously, quickly, and smoothly. They were a broad smile, three "tsk" sounds, and a light touch applied to the infant's abdomen with thumb and fingers of the hand opposed. No more than a second of time was required to administer the reinforcer.

At the beginning of the conditioning periods each vocalization was reinforced. Sometimes, as the rate of vocalizing increased, only every second, and later every third, vocalization was reinforced. In Experiment I, 72% of the reinforcers occurred after *each* vocalization; in Experiment II, 94%. Less frequent reinforcing seemed to depress the rate, at least initially, and, because of the rather severe time restrictions, was abandoned altogether by the end of the study.

Extinction. Experimental Days 5 and 6 (first and second Extinction days) were the same as Days 1 and 2; E leaned over the crib with an expressionless face and made no response to S's vocalizations.

The Vocal Response

Every discrete, voiced sound produced by S was counted as a *vocalization.* A number of other sounds characteristically made by very young infants, e.g., straining sounds and coughs, and the whistles, squeaks, and snorts of noisy breathing, were not counted as vocalizations. Sounds falling under the categories of protests, fusses, and cries (see Emotional Behavior below) were recorded separately. No attempt was made to record the phonetic characteristics of any of the sounds or their duration.

Observer agreement. Agreement between two Os on the number of vocalizations produced by Ss in 3-minute periods was high. Counts for 27 periods, using 13 different Ss, yielded a median percentage agreement of 96 (range, 67 to 100). About half of these reliability measures were obtained at the Ss' cribs, and the rest from tape recordings made during the experiment. These two techniques yielded similar percentages of observer agreement.

The unit of measurement. The unit for statistical analysis was the number of vocalizations an S gave in a 3-minute period. The counts were recorded by half-minutes and these were summed to give the score for the 3-minute period. After a rest period of 2 minutes, in which both E and O walked away from the baby's crib, another 3-minute count was made. After a second rest period a third count was made.

In each day nine such 3-minute counts were planned, distributed thus: one block of three in the first part of the morning, the second block of three in the late morning, and the third block of three after the midday meal. The minimum amount of time between blocks was 10 minutes, although usually an hour or more elapsed.

Actually, nine periods of observations were obtained during only 80% of the 132 subject-days (22 Ss $\times$ 6 experimental days). Since three or four Ss were studied at a time, it was not always possible to find nine periods in a day when each was awake, alert, and content. Further, because the experiments were carried out in the nursery which the Ss shared with 12 other infants, the presence and activities of these other babies, and of the caretakers in carrying out their routines, sometimes made it impossible to obtain the desired number of periods.

Emotional Behavior

A number of responses which seemed to be "emotional" were recorded during the observation periods. These were: "protests," discrete sounds of a whining nature; "fusses," a series of sounds separated by a catch in the voice, whimpering; "cries," continuous loud, wailing sounds; "persistent looking away from E," rolling of the head from side to side or staring to one side or the other of E; and "marked hand activity," hand play, finger sucking, or face or head rubbing. The last two activities seemed to be attempts to avoid E. Measures of observer-agreement in the recording of these responses were not made.

Each of these responses was given a credit of one for each half-minute in which it occurred. From the sum for each S a mean score was obtained for each experimental day.

Results

Similarity Between Experiments

Figure 10.2 presents the means of both experiments for the six experimental days. Each point represents the mean of 11 individual means. It was expected that the effect of the experimental conditions would be similar from experiment to experiment, but the extent to which the slopes of the curves would be congruent was not predicted.

The amount of similarity between the two experiments was estimated by an analysis of variance using Lindquist's Type VI design. The analysis reveals no evidence of a difference between Experiments. Further, no source of variation involving Experiments is significant. (The difference between the two experiments in second Extinction day means is not significant; it suggests, however, that the less frequent reinforcement in Experiment I may have made the behavior more resistant to extinction.)

Three conclusions may be drawn from such close agreement in the results of

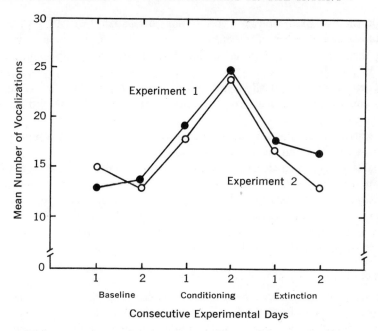

Figure 10.2   Mean number of vocalizations on consecutive experimental days.

two parallel experiments, each using different Ss and different Es: first, we are dealing with some relatively stable characteristics of three-month-old infants; second, the results may be accepted with confidence; and third, the results of the separate experiments may be pooled for all remaining analyses.

Effect of Experimental Conditions

The analysis of variance also shows that there was a difference in the effect of the three two-day experimental conditions ($p < .001$), and, also, in the effect of successive days within conditions ($p < .001$). These effects were assessed by t tests (for paired data) on the amount of change from one day to another in the mean number of vocalizations given by individual Ss. The error term was derived only from the scores for the two days being compared. The tests on the pooled sample (21 df) show that:

1. There was no statistically significant difference in the mean number of vocalizations given in a 3-minute period from the first to the second Baseline day ($t = 0.87, p > .30$).

2. The mean number of vocalizations increased from the second Baseline day to the first Conditioning day ($t = 2.69, p < .01$).

3. A further increase occurred from the first to the second Conditioning day ($t = 3.61, p < .001$).

4. On the first Extinction day, vocalizations decreased ($t = 3.19, p < .0025$).

5. The mean number of vocalizations on the second Extinction day was smaller than on the first Extinction day, but the difference was not reliable ($t = 1.35, p < .10$).

6. There was no statistically significant difference between the mean number of vocalizations given on the second Extinction day and on the second Baseline day ($t = 1.20, p > .20$).

The tests between Baseline days and between Baseline and Extinction days were two-sided tests; the others were one-sided.

If final days within conditions are compared, the differences are more marked: the mean for the second Conditioning day is higher than that of the second Baseline day at $p < .0005$ ($t = 4.80$), and the second Extinction day mean is lower than the second Conditioning day mean at $p < .0005$ ($t = 4.08$). Similar differences occur between the means of experimental conditions, obtained by averaging the first- and second-day results for each condition.

Amount of Change in Number of Vocalizations

The treatment effects have been found reliable. It seems in order, therefore, to present the means of vocalizations for each day and to calculate the amount of change produced by the experimental conditions. Under baseline conditions the three-month-old infants gave about 13 to 14 vocalizations in a 3-minute period. Individual differences were wide and ranged from 3 to 37 vocalizations. Using the social reinforcer for one day raised the rate to 18 vocalizations, an increase of 39%. A second day of conditioning elevated the rate to 25, a further increase of 34%. In all, conditioning brought about an increase of 86%. Removing the reinforcer depressed the rate to 17 during the first and to 15 during the second day, the latter approaching very closely the level of baseline performance.

Emotional Behavior

Emotional behavior, while striking when it occurred, was observed infrequently. The largest mean for any day in both experiments was 3.0, the smallest was 1.9. The order of the means by experimental days was identical in the two experiments. It was: first Extinction day, second Extinction day, second Baseline day, second Conditioning day, first Conditioning day, and first Baseline day. The greater number of emotional responses during Extinction agrees with the findings of others. Because the responses labeled emotional occurred so infrequently and because observer-agreement measures were not made, no further statistical analysis seemed warranted.

Alternative Explanation

The question raised in the introduction may now be considered. Did the reinforcing stimulus function as an arouser of vocalizations? Would infants have vocalized more often because of the stimulation it provided, even if it had *not* been made contingent upon the infant's behavior? Or, did some part of the reinforcing stimulus (say, the smile) act as a social "releaser"? The findings appear to be compatible with the conclusion that conditioning occurred: The rate of vocalizing continued to rise on the second day of Conditioning; the rate did not fall to the Baseline level on the first day of Extinction; it continued to fall on the second day of Extinction; and Ss with low Baseline rates of vocalizing gained under Conditioning, although for them there was often a relatively long time interval (30 seconds or more) between the reinforcing stimulus and the occurrence of the next vocalization. Still, the decisive answer to the question must await an experiment in which the reinforcing stimulus is administered with equal frequency, but never directly after the infant vocalizes.

Nature of the Reinforcer

The results seem to show that some everyday behavior of adults can function as a reinforcing stimulus for an infant. One would like to know from what sources its reinforcing properties arise. In the simplest case, the smiles, sounds, and caresses of adults may be reinforcing only because they provide a change in stimulation. Further information on this matter could be obtained by working with the separate parts of the reinforcing stimulus, one by one; by substituting for them lights or sounds dispensed by a machine; or by using a reinforcer of a less "affectionate" nature than the one used here appears to be. On the other hand, even for the three-month-old infant the smiles, sounds, and caresses of the adults may function as conditioned reinforcers because of their past association with caretaking acts.

It is possible that Ss of this study, living in an institution, may have had a less rich experience with adults. Institutional babies were used as Ss only because they were more readily available, because more of them could be studied at one time, and because the complicating variable of differences in maternal care could be bypassed. They did not appear, however, to be "starved" for attention or affection. Indeed, the attendants were often observed responding to babies when they vocalized. While it is possible that mothers would respond more often, in the absence of a comparative study we believe that infants in general would respond as these infants did.

Relation of Results to Theories of Speech

Since this study was limited to the vocalizing of infants in a social situation, attempts to reconcile the results with theories which account for all classes of prelinguistic utterances (babbling is the class frequently mentioned) cannot be complete. Thus, nothing in the findings of this study is incompatible with the theory that the sound which the child hears himself make has reinforcing properties; or with the theory that the adult's speech calls forth the infant's speech (a kind of imitation); or with Piaget's theory that vocalizing is perpetuated for its own sake by the processes of assimilation and accommodation. These may be labeled circular theories, for they do not postulate the necessity for any class of events prior to the moment when the infant responds to his own or another's vocalization. The theories of Miller and Dollard (1941) and of Mowrer (1960), on the other hand, are based upon the infant's associating the gratification of his needs and the accompanying vocalizations of the caretaker. Again, the results do not contradict this possibility.

The present study, however, does demonstrate the operation of still another principle: that the speech of the infant, if only in a social situation, can be modified by a response from the environment which is contingent upon his vocalizing. Hence, what happens *after* the infant vocalizes has been shown to be important.

Significance of Results

On the basis of the results of these experiments it is seen that responses of adults which do not involve caretaking can affect the vocalizing of the young in a social setting. If the results can be extended to life situations, then mothers might be able to increase or decrease the vocal output of their children by the responses they make when the children vocalize. Other kinds of social behavior in addition to vocalizing behavior should respond similarly to conditioning. It is likely that still other kinds of social behavior in babies, such as showing an interest in people, reaching out to them or turning away, perhaps even fear of the stranger, may also be affected by the responses adults make to them.

Superordinate Responses to a Word Association Test as a Function of Age

David S. Palermo and James J. Jenkins

From a developmental point of view, it is generally assumed that children's thought processes, as implied by their language usage, is fairly concrete. In a word association test, such as is used in this study, more children than adults would be expected to respond to the word "sparrow" with the word "robin," whereas more adults than children would be expected to respond with the word "bird." This expectation reflects the assumption that children's language progresses from the concrete to the more abstract. In this paper, Professors Palermo and Jenkins provide evidence that this assumption may be correct, at least with respect to responses to the word association test. Their data indicate that there is an increase from Grade 1 to Grade 6 in the use of superordinate, or abstract, responses, but after Grade 6 the frequency decreases through college age.

SOURCE: Adapted and abridged from David Palermo and J. J. Jenkins, "Frequency of Superordinate Responses to a Word Association Test as a Function of Age." *Journal of Verbal Learning and Verbal Behavior,* 1963, 1, 378–383. (With permission of the authors and the Academic Press, Inc.)

Children's language is ordinarily assumed to be concrete as opposed to being abstract in semantic content. On the basis of this assumption it might be expected that children would use subordinate rather than superordinate words more frequently in their language. The latter hypothesis has received some support. A logical extension of this analysis, made by Flavell, Draguns, Feinburg, and Budin (1958), is that superordinate responses to a word association test are more "mature" responses and, therefore, are to be expected more frequently from normal adults than from younger Ss or schizophrenics considered to be less mature for developmental or pathological reasons. In fact, there is evidence that fourth- and fifth-grade children respond less frequently with superordinates to the words on the Kent-Rosanoff association test than adults tested by Kent and Rosanoff in 1910.

The present study reports upon the frequency of superordinate responding of children from grade four through college and indicates a more complex relationship between age and frequency of superordinate responding than was evident from previous research.

Method

Procedure

All Ss were given the Kent-Rosanoff free-association test of 100 words followed by a list of 100 additional stimulus words. Only the responses to the Kent-Rosanoff list will be considered here. In Grades 4 to 6 fifty words were presented in each session. The sessions were ordinarily on consecutive school days, although for some classes a single day or a weekend intervened between sessions. All other Ss were given the Kent-Rosanoff list in one session. All tests were administered in the regular classroom by the Es.

Instructions for administration of the test placed emphasis upon: (1) giving the first response produced by the stimulus word; (2) responding with only one word; (3) E's lack of concern with spelling; and (4) speed of responding. The Ss were told that they would be timed and were requested to record the time it took them to finish the test on the back of their booklet at the end of each session. The E indicated the time on the blackboard as each minute passed during the test. Following the instructions, Ss read the stimulus words and responded by writing their associations in the spaces provided. Each page contained 25 words.

The frequency and percentage of superordinate responses for the males and females in each of the grade groups were tabulated. The behavioral definition for superordinate responses used by Jenkins and Russell (1960) was employed. In that study a written test was given to 29 undergraduate students in introductory psychology which consisted of a set of 100 sentences of the form "__ is a member of the class __." Each sentence began with one of the Kent-Rosanoff stimulus words and each S completed the sentence with a single response. A superordinate response was defined as any sentence completion that was given by 15 or more of the students taking the test.

Subjects

The word association test was administered to 250 males and 250 females in each of the grades 4–8, 10, and 12 in the Minneapolis public schools and 500 males and 500 females in introductory psychology classes at the University of Minnesota. Preliminary testing indicated that children in schools drawing from low socioeconomic levels in Grades 4 to 6 did not have sufficient facility in reading and writing skills to be used in the final sample. Therefore, the sample in these grades was limited to children attending schools which draw from middle and upper socioeconomic levels.

Following the data collection, each test was examined to determine whether it met criteria for inclusion in the final sample. Test forms were excluded from further analysis if: (1) the S had not completed the last five words on the first form given him; (2) the same response word appeared ten or more times on a page of 25 items; (3) ten or more responses appeared which were also stimulus items on a page of 25 items; (4) the S was seen to be copying response words from the blackboard or other classroom source during the test; or (5) responses to more than 10% of the total set of words were "response faults." Response faults consisted of illegible or incomplete words, omissions and sentence-like continuations from one response to the next involving four or more consecutive responses. Although these criteria appear complex and arbitrary, their development was necessitated primarily by the behavior of the youngest Ss, and they resulted in the rejection of a very small percentage of the total population tested. More than the required number of Ss was tested at each grade level. Final membership in the sample was based upon a random selection of the number specified from the total pool of tests. When a test form was rejected for one of the above reasons, a replacement was drawn at random.

Results

Figure 10.3 presents the mean percentage of superordinate responses at each grade level for the total 39 stimulus words and for the 26 stimulus words to which at least 5 per cent of the population of one of the groups responded with a superordinate response. The frequency of superordinate responses is greater in the fourth-grade children than in college students. However, examination of the entire age range makes it clear that the relationship of this type of responding to age is not a simple linear one. Considering the total 39 words represented in the lower curve, there is an increase in superordinate responses from a mean of 14.79% in Grade 4 to a mean of 15.96% in Grade 6, followed by a steady decline thereafter to the college mean level of 10.00%. In the case of the 26 stimulus words in the upper curve, there is a slight decline from the mean of 21.89% for the fourth grade to 21.79% for the fifth grade, followed by a rise to a mean of 23.40% for the sixth grade and then, again, a steady decline to a mean of 14.60% for the college students.

While the differences in absolute percentages are not extremely large, the

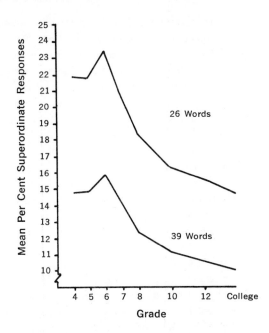

Figure 10.3 Mean per cent superordinate responses by grade for the total 39 words and the 26 words to which 5% of at least one of the groups responded with the superordinate.

consistency of these differences is impressive. Two-tailed sign tests were applied in comparisons of each adjacent grade group for the total 39 words and for those 26 words to which at least 5 per cent of the population of one of the groups responded with a superordinate response. Comparisons of Grades 5 and 6, 6 and 7, 7 and 8, and 10 and 12 all reach at least the .05 level of significance using the total 39 words. Comparisons of Grades 5 and 6, 6 and 7, 7 and 8, 8 and 10, and 12 and college all reach at least the .05 level for words which yield at least 5 per cent superordinate responses. An analysis of curves for each individual word indicates that while the peak of responding may shift to the seventh or eighth grade for some individual words, only in the case of *sickness-health* was there a complete reversal in the trend shown by the grouped data. The response of *health* to *sickness* steadily increased with age.

The males gave a larger percentage of superordinate responses than did the females at all grades except the sixth, where the mean percentage for the females is 16.04 and for the males, 15.86. Over all 312 comparisons of males and females for each word at each grade level the females exceeded the males in only 99 cases, or 32 per cent. There was only one case, *eagle-bird*, in which the females consistently responded more frequently with the superordinate response.

The data of the combined fourth and fifth grades of the present sample have been compared with the data obtained in 1916 from a comparable group of 1,000 fourth- and fifth-grade Minneapolis public school children. Since that study did not include two of the 39 words (*bitter* and *mutton*) to which superordinates could be made according to the definition used here, the data are based upon only 37 words. The mean percentage of superordinate responses for the present sample was 15.12 as compared to 11.49% in 1916. In 28 of the 37· cases the children of the present sample gave a greater number of superordinate responses: the reverse was true in eight cases, and there was one tie. A two-tailed sign test applied to these data was significant at well beyond the .05 level of confidence. The same comparisons for the 22 stimulus words to which at least 5 per cent superordinate responses were given yielded a mean percentage of 24.61% for the present sample and 18.78% for the 1916 sample. In 17 out of 22 cases the frequency of superordinate responding was greater in the present sample, which was also significant at beyond the .05 level by a two-tailed sign test.

In order to check upon this trend, a comparison was made of the frequency of superordinate responses given by the present sample and the 1916 sample on the basis of the definition used by Woodrow and Lowell. While they provide no specific definition, they did list the stimulus words and superordinate responses given with at least 5 per cent frequency by either their sample or the sample of 1,000 adults used by Kent and Rosanoff in 1910. Notice that this means that any superordinate data based upon these norms are "selected upward" for being of high frequency. Of the 35 possible superordinate responses to 29 stimulus words listed, the present sample gave the superordinate response more frequently in 23 cases, less frequently in 11 cases, and there was one tie. A sign test of this difference reaches approximately the .05 level of significance with a two-tailed test. The mean percentage of superordinate responses to each of the stimulus words was ˙13.50 in 1961 and 8.70 in 1916. The adults of the 1910 sample gave a mean percentage of 17.05 superordinate responses to the same stimulus words.

Discussion

It is clear from these data that a simple logical analysis of language which suggests that an increase in age or maturity results in an increase in the use of abstract as opposed to concrete semantic content is incorrect insofar as responses to a word association test today are concerned. Responses classified as superordinates appear to increase to a maximum at the sixth grade and decline thereafter. Perhaps the relation of age or maturity to the use of superordinates suggested by Flavell and his associates (1958) applies to young children up to the sixth grade and is succeeded by some other process which leads to a decrease in such responses. It is also possible that the sample selection necessary in the lower grades may have depressed the frequency of superordinate responses in the fourth and fifth grades. The authors are currently collecting data from children in Grades 1–4 with an individual oral test administration in order to determine the characteristics of the responses of younger children.

The fact that males give more superordinate responses than females is difficult to explain. It has frequently been reported that in most measures of language development females are generally more advanced than males. If superordinate responding is systematically related to level of language development, and if females are more advanced than males, then females should give more superordinates than males before the sixth grade and fewer superordinates than males thereafter. The data do not give appreciable support to this interpretation. At present we cannot account for the data on sex differences.

The data from the present study are in contrast to the developmental trends which may be inferred from the earlier normative studies. In the 1910 period adults gave more superordinate responses than children, while in 1961 children gave more superordinate responses than adults. Since 1910 there has been a decrease in superordinate responding for adults (independently documented by Jenkins and Russell [1960]), but during the same period there has been an increase in superordinate responding for children in Grades 4 and 5. While there may be many interpretations of these findings, the data may be accounted for in a simple fashion if it is assumed that (1) superordinate responding is curvilinearly related to linguistic development, rising to a peak during the earlier years and decreasing steadily thereafter; and (2) the rate of linguistic development is more rapid today and proceeds to a higher degree of sophistication than it did in 1910.

If these assumptions are correct, it suggests that an extensive age sampling in the 1910 period would have shown a peak of superordinate responding at an age much closer to the adult level. The fourth- and fifth-grade sample would have been relatively low in this type of responding, and the adult sample would have been relatively high. With the increasing linguistic sophistication of our culture, subsequent sampling would have indicated a movement of the peak of such responding backward toward younger ages so that in the 1961 sample the peak is found at the sixth grade, while the adult level of such responses has moved well beyond the peak and become relatively low.

The first assumption receives some support from the relation observed between frequency-of-usage of response words and the developmental curve for the use of these responses as superordinates. Superordinate responding in the case of *mutton-meat, spider-insect, butterfly-insect, heavy-weight,* and *cabbage-vegetable* does not reach a peak in frequency until the seventh or eighth grade, even in the present sample. The responses in these particular cases tend to be much lower in frequency-of-usage according to the Thorndike-Lorge Juvenile count (1944) than the other superordinates given by at least 5 per cent of the Ss. Thus, even within the limited frequency range of responses, it is the higher frequency-of-usage superordinates which peak at the earlier ages. It seems reasonable to suppose then, that higher density of linguistic exposure and increased linguistic sophistication should act to move the peak for all superordinate responding backward to the earlier years.

That today's children receive more intensive linguistic stimulation than the children of 1916 can scarcely be doubted when one considers radio, television, movies, and the rich variety of children's books and comics, but the norms furnish even more evidence. A general overview of all responses made by the fourth- and fifth-grade children today shows that they are much more similar to the responses of present-day adults than were the responses of the 1916 children to the 1910 adults. Though we cannot retrace our steps to the 1910 period and investigate our hypothesis rigorously, additional analyses of children's word associations may be made with the present hypothesis in mind.

CHAPTER XI

Emotional Development

Tʜᴇʀᴇ ᴀʀᴇ at least two approaches by which psychologists study human emotional behavior and development. The first approach involves the direct measurement of the physiological components of emotion as reflected in autonomic nervous system activity. Typically, measures of the psychogalvanic skin response, blood pressure, and cardiac reactivity are taken. Although there are several technological problems involved in measuring autonomic activity, they may nevertheless be the best indices of emotional reactivity because, being involuntary, they are more likely to accurately reflect the individual's emotional state than his overt behavior. The second approach to the study of emotional behavior is the observation of overt behavioral reactions in situations designed to be emotionally arousing. For example, a child who cringes in the corner of a room and simultaneously evidences difficulty in catching his breath when a snake is introduced is surely experiencing an emotion which an observer would label as fear. Direct observation assumes, implicitly, that the observed behavior directly reflects the emotion. Such an assumption is, at best, rather tenuous. Many more studies have been reported in the literature using the second approach, but with the advent of advances in electronic technology it is a reasonable assumption that more studies employing the first approach will be reported in the future.

The distinction between the two methods of studying emotional behavior is not merely methodological but also involves a conceptual issue. Essentially, the issue involves the distinction between emotional reactions, which are involuntary, and instrumental behaviors, which are learned. Preschool-age children, for example, often evidence behavior indicative of the emotion of anger but with little or no autonomic involvement associated with the overt behavior. Indeed, a frightened child may display behavior more characteristic of anger because, in previous situations, the child has learned that such a response leads to fear reduction. Thus, the overt behavior is instrumental and not related to a specific emotional state. Conversely, it cannot be argued that a child who does not display behavior indicative of an emotional state is not, in fact, experiencing an autonomic reaction. It is a gross oversimplification to assume that overt behavioral manifestations are directly related to emotional states. It may make better sense to view the physiological components of emotionality as stimuli which become associated with specific overt responses.

The importance of gaining more knowledge about the autonomic involvement in children's emotional behavior is demonstrated in the paper by Jost and Sontag. This experiment suggests that the strength of autonomic reactivity may be genetically determined. Observations of infants in the nursery, where presumably environmental conditions are relatively constant, reveals wide variation in emotional reactivity to stimuli. These findings have important implications for the subsequent environmental experiences of the child. For example, it seems reasonable to assume that a child who is highly reactive will encounter different reactions from his parents or teachers than the child who is less prone to intense emotional reactions. The interaction of emotional predispositions and parental child-rearing practices have not been systematically investigated. Until such data are available, we must exercise caution in ascribing variations in emotional behavior to parental practices.

The treatment of one emotional reaction, fear, is described by Jones and Jones. Essentially, the procedure involves creating a situation in which the child approaches the feared object in sufficiently small increments that an autonomic response does not occur. The procedures described by Jones and Jones are, in many respects, the basis for current innovations in conditioning therapy.

Each of the three remaining papers in this chapter are concerned with the nature of the stimulus situations that arouse emotional responses. Each study employs a different method in attacking the problem. Professor Powell derived his data from responses to a word association task while Dr. Landreth made use of direct observations in two naturalistic settings (home and school); and Dr. Meissner employed a questionnaire. These methods involve quite different assumptions, and each has its merits and its limitations.

The Genetic Factor in Autonomic Nervous System Function

H. Jost and Lester W. Sontag

A great deal of stress has been placed on the effects of child-rearing practices as they relate to emotional development of the child. These studies, by inference at least, suggest that the parents are primarily responsible for the emotional maturation of the child. Thus a child who is typically volatile and tends toward overreaction is viewed as having parents whose child-rearing practices are inferior. This approach overlooks the possibility that emotional reactivity is, to some degree, genetically determined. In this paper, the investigators demonstrate that autonomic reactivity, which is related

SOURCE: Adapted and abridged from H. Jost and L. W. Sontag, "The Genetic Factor in Autonomic Nervous System Function." *Psychosomatic Medicine,* 1944, 6, 308–310. (With permission of L. W. Sontag and Hoeber Medical Journals, Harper & Row, Publishers, Inc.)

to overt manifestations of emotionality, does indeed have an important genetic component.

This paper will present the results of an attempt to demonstrate a genetic factor in the patterns of autonomic nervous system function in children. The existence of such a genetic factor in autonomic activity or response might go far toward explaining the familial predisposition toward such psychosomatic conditions as benign essential hypertension, coronary disease, mucous colitis, Raynaud's disease, etc. — a predisposition which many workers believe they have observed.

The malfunction of an organ as the result of emotional stresses implies at once the greater than average physiological component of the individual's emotional responses to a stimulus, a lowered general threshold of stimulation, or a lowered specific organ resistance predisposing it to malfunction. By measuring the activity of certain organs which are dependent for their function on autonomic stimulus, it is possible to acquire some picture of the state of activity of the autonomic nervous system itself, and then to compare the degree of that activity and also the selective expression of it in two or more individuals. Measurement of skin resistance, systolic and diastolic blood pressure, heart rate, salivation, respiration and vasomotor persistence time form a pattern which expresses, to some degree at least, the function and state of activity of the autonomic nervous system. Inspection and statistical treatment of such measures on a large group of children make it possible to determine whether monozygotic twins closely approximate each other in autonomic pattern, whether siblings are less alike than the monozygotic twins, and finally whether random selected unrelated children, matched for age, resemble each other in autonomic pattern less closely than do the siblings and monozygotes.

Data

The data for this analysis were gathered during the years 1940–1942 at the Fels Research Institute. This is part of the longitudinal study being carried on by this group. Longitudinal scores of physical and psychological growth are taken as well as those of physiological reactivity described in this paper.

Measures of vasomotor persistence, salivary output, heart period, standing palmar conductance, reclining volar conductance, respiration period, and pulse pressure were obtained under the following standard conditions. All the measurements were made during the hours of 9–12 A.M., at least an hour after breakfast, in a quiet room in which the temperature and humidity were controlled at 74–76 degrees F. and 40% respectively. The subjects were all from the Fels study and were between 6 and 12 years of age. There were 62 subjects in the 1940 study, 74 in the 1941 study, and 81 in the 1942 study.

Vasomotor persistence was elicited by means of a firm slow stroke applied over the biceps of the left arm by a stimulator calibrated to deliver approximately 250 grams of pressure. Two strokes were made in the form of an X, the stop watch was started at the incidence of the first stroke, and the time was recorded to the nearest minute at which the location of the "crossing" was no longer a matter of certainty. The persistence time ranged from three to thirty minutes. *Salivary output* was measured for a period of five minutes. The saliva was collected in a graduated centrifuge tube by means of a simple suction pump. The subject was instructed to bring the saliva to the front of the mouth and it was taken out by the suction. *Heart period* was obtained from minute samples taken over a twenty-minute period. The heart was recorded electrocardiographically and the period consisted of the time in seconds between the QRS peaks. *Standing palmar conductance* was obtained through the use of Darrow's circuit. The electrodes were placed in the palms of each hand and the subjects were instructed to stand erect with their weight supported equally on both feet.[1] *Volar skin conductance* was made in the same manner as the measure above, except that the electrodes were placed on the forearm just above the wrist and the subjects were in a reclining position. *Respiration period:* the respiration was recorded on a polygraph moving at a speed of 3 cm per second. The period was the time between peaks on the respiratory curve. *Pulse pressure* was obtained from six measures of systolic and diastolic blood pressure taken in the twenty-minute period.

The measure of "autonomic balance" is a composite of the seven variables above. It is obtained by weighting the values of the various measures, the weights having been derived from a factor analysis. The measure expresses the degree of sympathetic or parasympathetic preponderance.

Method

Two methods of analysis were used. The first consisted of correlating the paired individuals in the three groups on the various measures. The scores of each twin were correlated with those of his partner; those of each child with those of his siblings; and a large sample of the scores of unrelated children were correlated with each other. The age factor was eliminated by the use of standard scores computed for each age level. The number of pairs for the years 1940, 1941, and 1942 were 5; 5 and 6 for the twins; 10, 19, and 25 for the siblings; and for the unrelated group, 361, 324, and 324 respectively. This unrelated group represents a random comparison of cases and is sufficiently large to be stable.

The second method of analysis consisted of difference scores. Two siblings for example, a pair of twins, might have standard scores on a particular measure of 45 and 48; in this case their difference score would be 3. Two siblings might have scores of 48 and 55; in this case the difference score with be 7. Two unrelated children might have scores of 45 and 60; here the difference score would be 15. In all instances the lowest scores indicate that the individuals are little different in the particular measurement.

Results

The correlations of the seven variables for the twins, siblings, and unrelated groups were determined. In all cases the correlations are in the direction predicted by the hypothesis that there is a genetic factor in autonomic nervous system function. The twins are more highly correlated than are the siblings, and the siblings show higher correlations than the unrelated group. The measures are also consistent over the three-year period. The correlations are not significantly different, but are suggestive in that they all point in the same direction; that is, toward a genetic factor. For the years 1940, 1941, and 1942 the twin correlations are .434, .470, and .489 respectively; the sibling correlations are .255, .406, and .288 respectively; and the unrelated group correlate .164, .017, and .080 for the three years.

Table 11.1 presents the data obtained from the differential analysis. The means, number of pairs, critical ratios, and probabilities for all the groups are given here. The more striking differences may be enumerated.

TABLE 11.1. *Means of the Differences in Physiological Measures of Monozygotic Twins Compared with Those of Siblings and Unrelated Children Plus a Similar Comparison between Siblings and Unrelated Children*

MEASURE YEAR	TWIN MEAN	N OF PAIRS	SIB'S MEAN	N OF PAIRS	UN. R MEAN	N OF PAIRS	TWIN SIB C. R.	P	TWIN UN. R C. R.	P	SIB UN. R C. R.	P
Vasomotor persistence												
'40	2.60	5	6.70	10	11.80	361	1.35	—	6.75	.01	1.80	—
'41	5.60	5	7.00	19	12.37	324	.62	—	3.98	.01	3.22	.01
'42	1.17	6	4.45	25	11.26	324	2.06	—	6.25	.01	5.25	.01
Palmar standing skin resistance												
'40	3.60	5	8.83	10	11.34	361	2.64	.05	4.07	.01	2.44	.05
'41	6.40	5	11.42	19	12.35	324	1.56	—	2.20	.05	.54	—
'42	4.67	6	8.64	25	13.40	324	2.29	.05	6.10	.01	3.88	.01
Reclining pulse pressure												
'40	3.00	5	9.00	10	11.08	361	2.61	.05	7.60	.01	.97	—
'41	6.20	5	8.68	19	8.93	324	1.00	—	1.23	—	.16	—
'42	4.50	6	8.76	25	12.98	324	2.46	.05	5.45	.01	3.36	.05
Total salivation												
'40	5.40	5	6.50	10	12.04	361	.55	—	5.22	.01	3.29	.01
'41	7.80	5	6.00	19	12.44	324	−.92	—	3.04	.05	5.20	.01
'42	8.67	6	9.24	25	9.97	324	.05	—	.41	—	.43	—
Mean respiration period												
'40	7.20	5	9.40	10	12.10	361	.56	—	1.93	—	1.56	—
'41	4.80	5	5.30	19	11.54	324	.25	—	4.24	.01	4.48	.01
'42	5.80	6	10.10	25	11.48	324	1.26	—	1.96	—	.65	—
Mean heart period												
'40	8.00	5	10.00	10	12.49	310	.62	—	1.60	—	1.51	—
'41	7.20	5	7.60	19	12.81	324	.17	—	2.72	.05	4.26	.01
'42	8.80	6	10.60	25	11.22	324	.45	—	.65	—	.34	—
Reclining volar conductance												
'40	3.60	5	11.60	10	10.54	310	2.78	.05	6.07	.01	−.40	—
'41	6.80	5	8.70	19	10.06	324	.52	—	1.00	—	.80	—
'42	5.50	6	8.70	25	7.01	324	1.28	—	.74	—	−1.09	—
Autonomic balance												
'40	4.80	5	10.50	10	11.71	144	2.27	.05	3.01	.05	.55	—
'41	11.50	5	8.28	19	13.91	129	−.21	—	.87	—	1.61	—
'42	6.17	6	11.10	25	13.78	307	1.97	—	3.25	.01	1.24	—

The measure of *vasomotor persistence* is significant at the .01 level for all the three years between the twins and unrelated groups, and at the .01 level between the sibling and unrelated group, for the last two years. The difference between the twins and siblings in this measure is not significant, but it is in the direction indicated by the hypothesis. The measure of *standing palmar skin resistance* is reliable at the .05 level between the three groups except for the 1941 measures between the twins and siblings and the siblings and unrelated groups; it is significant at the .05 level between the twin and unrelated groups for that year. *Reclining pulse pressure* is significantly different between the twins and siblings and the twins and unrelated groups for two of the three years. These are at the .05 and .01 levels for the 1940 and 1942 measures respectively. The differences between the siblings and the unrelated groups is significant at the .05 level for the 1942 measure only. All other differences are in the expected direction, but are not significant. *Total salivation* is significantly different between the twins and unrelated, and the siblings and unrelated groups in two of the three years, but there is no significant difference between the twins and siblings; in fact, there is a reversal between these groups for the 1941 measure. The measure of *mean respiration period* is significant only in the 1942 measures and then only between the twins and unrelated, and the sibling and unrelated groups. The differences for the other years, although they are not significant, are in the expected direction. *Mean heart period* is significant for the same year and groups as is the respiration period. The critical ratios for all measures are low but in the expected direction. *Reclining volar conductance* shows significant differences between the twins and siblings, and the twins and unrelated groups in the 1940 study, but no significant differences appear in the other years.

The measure *"autonomic balance,"* which is a composite score of the above variables, shows some significance between the groups. The difference between the twins and siblings in the 1940 study is at the .05 level, as is the difference between the twins and unrelated groups for the same year. All the other measures are in the expected direction except for a reversal in the 1941 study between the twins and siblings. This is due to the fact that the highly weighted measure of *total salivation* is reversed for this year.

NOTE

[1] Conductance in microohms $\times$ 1000 equals $1/R$, where R is mean resistance in thousands of ohms.

Crying Behavior in the Nursery School and the Home

Catherine Landreth

Anyone who has even casually observed the behavior of young children is aware that crying behavior occurs frequently and in a broad variety of situations. The purpose of this study by Dr. Catherine Landreth was to determine the causes of crying in children at home as opposed to the nursery school situation. Direct observations were made of 32 children in the nursery school, of whom 25 were also observed in their homes. The majority of crying behavior in the school was associated with conflicts with other children, and it was the boys who were more frequently associated with causing the crying of other children. The most frequent precipitator of crying at home occurred in the carrying out of health routines, such as brushing teeth. It was also noted that the causes of some of the crying behavior in the home derived from inconsistent and generally poor techniques in handling children.

In a previous article (Landreth 1940) a comparison was presented of different methods employed in the investigation of crying in nursery school children. Briefly, the results indicated that the four methods employed — time sampling, incident sampling, teachers' records, and teachers' ratings — were not equally valid in furnishing a measure of the incidence of this behavior; and that, in general, selection of method should be based on the characteristics of the particular behavior under investigation. Low measures of consistency further indicated that during the eight weeks of this study different factors were operating to modify the behavior investigated in individual children

The present article is concerned with analysis of these factors. The purpose of this analysis is to determine:

1. the extent to which physiological and environmental factors affected the behavior investigated;

2. the extent of variation in the home and nursery school situations in which this behavior arose.

As most studies on behavior of young children are made in a nursery school, it is of interest to determine differences in home and nursery school situations and differences in children's responses in these situations which might indicate the extent to which nursery school behavior is representative of home behavior. Data for this analysis were furnished from daily record sheets made over a period of eight weeks in the nursery school, and similar incident sampling records made over a period of five weeks in the children's homes. Home records included a daily report of variations in the child's physical condition and daily routine.

Records in the nursery school were made on 32 children, 14 girls and 18 boys,

SOURCE: Adapted and abridged from Catherine Landreth, "Factors Associated with Crying in Young Children in the Nursery School and the Home." *Child Development,* 1941, 12, 81–97. (With permission of the author and the Society for Research in Child Development.)

with an age range at the midpoint of the investigation from 2 years, 8 months to 5 years, 2 months. The children had been in attendance at the Institute of Child Welfare nursery school for periods ranging from 36 to 393 days. Mean and median IQs on the California Preschool Scale were 122 and 124 respectively. The group represented a selected socioeconomic sample in that they were drawn from middle-class homes of professional and business people. The selection arose out of the need for obtaining intelligent cooperation from the parents in the matter of record keeping. The home records were obtained on 25 of the 32 children, 8 girls and 17 boys.

Reliability of the observations expressed in terms of percentage agreement between two independent observers ranged from 100 per cent to 87 per cent, with a mean of 95 per cent.

Factors Related to Incidence of Crying

Apart from the immediate situations causing crying there are several factors which in popular opinion are considered to affect the ease and frequency with which a child becomes emotionally upset. Slight colds, digestive upsets, lack of sufficient sleep, constipation, etc., are among those most frequently cited. As a fairly complete record of each child's health routine for five weeks was obtained from the parents, it was possible to determine the relationship between each factor and the crying behavior of the children in this study.

As percentage of time spent crying was found to give the most representative measure of children's crying behavior at home and at school, all correlations were obtained between this measure and the factors listed.

Chronological Age, Length of Nursery School Attendance

For this particular group of children, chronological age and length of nursery school attendance had no significant relationship with percentage of time spent crying, either at home or at school.

Bladder Control

Irregularities of bladder control were also unrelated to the percentage of time children spent crying at home or at school.

Intelligence Quotients

There was a slight tendency for children with high IQs to cry less than those whose IQs were lower, particularly in home situations.

Slight Colds and Minor Defective Health Conditions

Slight colds and minor defective health conditions were associated with an increased amount of crying at home. That no significant relationship was obtained between this factor and crying in the nursery school is probably explained by the fact that children were not in the nursery school when their mothers considered their physical condition not normal.

Hours of Sleep

There was a tendency for children who slept more to cry more. In view of the low correlations between chronological age and percentages of time spent crying, age can hardly be considered a partial factor in this positive relationship between crying and hours of sleep. Rather, it would seem possible that a child who habitually sleeps somewhat more than the average may be suffering from a mild toxic condition which in turn may affect his emotional behavior. Further, the strain imposed on a child who has several emotional upsets during the day may make the additional time spent in sleeping a necessity for adequate recuperation.

Regular Elimination

Evidence in regard to a relationship between incidence of crying and regularity of bowel movements is inconclusive; the correlation between this factor and crying behavior in the home and school are .13 and .39 respectively.

Departures from Daily Routine

While at first sight it would seem that a certain amount of diversion and variety in the daily routine, so long as it does not interfere with the child's health program, actually favors fewer emotional upsets, this may not be the case. It is equally possible that mothers whose children are less prone to emotional upsets are more apt to take them out with them. Child 18, who has the fewest incidents and spends the least percentage of time crying at home, has the highest average number (1.7) of departures from routine per day, while Child 29, who has the highest score for incidence of crying at home, has the second lowest average number of departures from routine.

Sex Difference

The means for percentage of time spent crying at home for boys was 57 per cent as compared with 26 per cent for the girls, the critical ratio based on standard deviations being 2.04. Means for percentage of time spent crying at school for boys and girls were 34 per cent and 27 per cent respectively, with a critical ratio of .77.

The tendency for boys to cry more than girls was more apparent in the home than the school. The difference on the proportion of boys in the home and school samples was doubtless a modifying factor. It is possible that boys of this socioeconomic group are more irked than girls by complying with routines and parental restrictions of activity. Earlier findings on sex and socioeconomic differences on negativism in nursery school children during test situations would seem to support such a view.

Day of Week

The number of crying incidents per child per day present in the nursery school varied from 1.2 to 1.4 and would seem to indicate that the day of the week was not a significant factor in incidence of crying.

Hour of Day

The percentage of total incidents of crying occurring between each of the six half-hour periods of the school morning, 9 A.M. to 12 A.M., were next examined. During the first half hour 9:00 to 9:30 the children were still in process of arriving so that actually fewer children were present for this period. The last half hour, 11:30 to 12:00, was devoted to the putting away of toys and the story period. In the four periods from 9:30 to 11:30, which are comparable in terms of number of children present and type of activity engaged in, the last has the greatest percentage of incidence, indicating a rise toward the end of the morning.

Many factors undoubtedly led to differences in the amount of crying at different hours of the day in the homes. The time the children get up in the morning, the hours they were away at school, the hours they took their naps, and the time they went to bed necessarily affected the number of children on whom records were obtained for the different periods. While no analysis was undertaken of the many details involved, the data indicate a rise in the incidence of crying toward the end of the day.

Immediate Situations Causing Crying in the Nursery School

What are the immediate situations causing crying in the nursery school? Are sex and age determining factors in regard to these situations? Is there any similarity between the situations causing crying in the nursery school and those causing crying at home?

In this investigation it was found that the immediate situations causing crying in the nursery school could be classified into seven categories. Though there were marked individual differences in the distribution of crying incidents in these seven categories, the mean and median figures of 70.3 per cent and 76 per cent respectively indicated that conflicts with other children were responsible for the majority of incidents. Only five children had less than 50 per cent of their incidents attributable to this cause, and only one child, the second youngest in the school, had no instances of crying because of conflicts with other children. As he played alone during practically the entire period of observation, the lack of conflict was doubtless due to his lack of contact with other children.

Accidental injury was a much less significant cause of crying, with mean and median figures for the group 13.7 per cent and 13.1 per cent respectively. Only 3 children never cried from this cause. Mean and median figures for frustration by inanimate objects were 8.5 per cent and 1.7 per cent respectively, with 15 of the 32 children having no crying incidents associated with this situation.

Only 12 of the 32 children were recorded as crying because of conflicts with adults in the nursery school. A total of 62 incidents, less than 5 per cent, resulted from this cause; whereas in the homes, 21 per cent of the total incidents reported were directly caused by conflicts with adults, with a large percentage of the remainder doubtlessly indirectly attributable to the same cause. It is of interest that Child 29, whose record shows the highest percentage of crying due to conflicts with adults in the school, has a home record which is also the highest. As this child's intelligence quotient was only 86 and his language development somewhat retarded, it is possible that these were significant factors for his behavior in both situations.

Twenty crying incidents were attributed to fear or "insecurity" on the part of the 7 children for whom they were recorded. In the main these were associated with leaving a parent on arrival at the nursery school.

Sex Differences in Relation to Types of Nursery School Situations Which Caused Crying

In the case of crying incidents arising from conflicts with other children, the obtained means (in terms of percentage) tend to be higher for girls. However, since girls have fewer total crying incidents, the actual number of incidents due to conflicts is less in the case of girls (394) than boys (549).

A sex difference is apparently present in the category of accidental injury. Not only is the mean for girls higher, but the actual number of incidents for the girls is 75 against the boys' 44. Either the girls lack the skill and coordination to prevent as many tumbles and mishaps as the boys do, or crying because of injury receives more social disapproval and is more often inhibited in the case of boys than girls.

The boys had a higher average per cent of crying incidents arising from frustration by inanimate objects than the girls. Further, 88 of the 101 incidents of crying resulting from this cause were recorded for boys. This is possibly due to the greater activity of the boys and the type of play materials they used, a sex difference that was observed incidentally during this study and noted by Van Alstyne (1932). It would also seem from the means for situations caused by conflicts with adults that the girls as a group were somewhat less resistant to adult authority. In terms of incidents, 58 of the 62 resulting from conflict with adults were recorded for boys.

The difference between the percentage of crying incidents for boys and girls resulting from fear is doubtless attributable to the record of one boy who had 45 per cent of his crying arising from this cause. Actually, 11 of the 20 incidents of crying resulting from fear were recorded for girls.

In summary, apparent sex differences for this group were the girls' greater percentage frequency of crying because of injury and the boys' greater percentage frequency of crying because of frustration by inanimate objects and conflicts with adults.

Analysis of Children's Conflicts

As 75 per cent of the total incidents of crying in the nursery school resulted from conflicts with other children, the extent to which particular children were associated with, if not directly responsible for, crying in other children seemed a fruitful study for further investigation. The first fact which became apparent was the marked difference in the frequency with which boys and girls were associated with other children's crying. In 943 incidents of crying because of conflict with another child, the "other child" was a boy in 765 of the incidents and a girl in only 178. By reducing the total number of incidents in which a child was associated with another's crying to the average per child present, results for different children and for boys and girls were made directly comparable. The average per day per girl was .41 of an incident against 1.31 incident per boy per day, a ratio of roughly 1 to 3. This difference would seem to be due to greater aggressiveness on the part of the boys or to a sex difference in language development leading to greater use by boys of direct action in preference to speech.

Apart from the sex differences, there were considerable individual differences not only in the number of incidents of crying that children were associated with, but also in the particular children with whom they had conflicts.

Immediate Situations Causing Crying in the Home

The immediate situations causing crying in the home were found to lend themselves to classification under seventeen categories. Seven of these were concerned with the establishment of such routine habits as:

Sleeping
Taking naps
Elimination
Washing and bathing
Brushing and washing hair
Dressing and undressing
Eating

Five were associated with play activities. They were listed as:

Frustration from play materials
Frustration from pets
Conflict with siblings
Conflict with other children
Conflict with parents or adults in the home

Five which came under no general heading were:

Injury and treatment
Medical and dental examinations
Insecurity
Fussiness
Coming to the nursery school

As the classification into separate mutually exclusive categories permitted the possibility of a certain amount of subjective interpretation on the part of the investigator, a nursery school teacher also classified 105 of the 1137 home records in regard to both the situation causing crying and the type of response which the child received. Disagreement between the two classifications occurred in only 6 per cent of the situations, indicating that the classification was reasonably reliable.

As the seventeen categories listed would seem to cover practically all the situations occurring during the day, somewhat more significance attaches to the frequency with which particular situations provoked emotional upsets. A summary of both the situations and frequencies is presented in Figure 11.1.

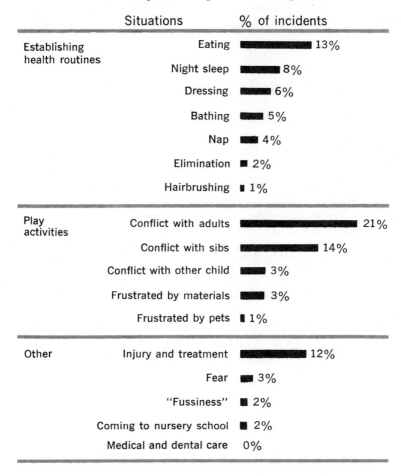

	Situations	% of incidents
Establishing health routines	Eating	13%
	Night sleep	8%
	Dressing	6%
	Bathing	5%
	Nap	4%
	Elimination	2%
	Hairbrushing	1%
Play activities	Conflict with adults	21%
	Conflict with sibs	14%
	Conflict with other child	3%
	Frustrated by materials	3%
	Frustrated by pets	1%
Other	Injury and treatment	12%
	Fear	3%
	"Fussiness"	2%
	Coming to nursery school	2%
	Medical and dental care	0%

Figure 11.1 Immediate situations causing crying in the home.

The parents' record of the situations furnished evidence that some of the difficulties arose out of inconsistencies and poor techniques in child training.

For example, some of the children who objected to going to bed had variations in their bed-hour of from one to two hours, an irregularity that would hardly make a regular bed-hour acceptable. Child 6, 42 per cent of whose crying was concerned with either going to bed or getting up, had a sleeping schedule which seemed unsuited to him. This child was usually given a three- or occasionally four-hour nap ending at 4:30 and sometimes 5:00. Seven-thirty found him unwilling to go to bed again, clamoring for toys to take to bed with him and taking an hour or more in actually getting to sleep. On being awakened at 6:00 or 6:30 after nine or nine and a half hours sleep, he was apparently unrefreshed and cried over the necessity of getting up.

The most frequent difficulty in connection with dressing and undressing occurred over the children's wishing to wear particular garments while their mothers insisted on a different choice. Typical is the case of a 4-year-old girl who cried fifteen minutes to wear a pair of red socks and then appeared at school red-eyed but in yellow socks.

Under the heading *Eating Habits* 60 per cent of the difficulties arose through conflict with the adults over eating meals or particular foods: 40 per cent represented conflicts over the manner of eating and behavior at the table.

Only one child, Number 17, cried over coming to the nursery school. Similarly, his crying in the nursery school was almost entirely due to his not wishing to stay.

Conflict with siblings occurred in every case in which the child had a sibling. The particular situations would seem to indicate that jealousy was an important factor in the cases of Numbers 19 and 25.

Only one child had no crying incidents resulting from conflict with adults in the household. Many of the difficulties encountered under this heading would also seem to reflect injudicious handling on the part of parents. Situations such as "Parent spanks child for lying over misdemeanor," "Parent spanks child for striking him," "Parent spanks child for calling him names," are not suggestive of a particularly desirable parent-child relationship on which to base mutual respect and esteem.

In fairness to the parents, it must be added that though their records frequently indicated the use of unsatisfactory methods, the very nature of this study tended to make it a record of their less successful methods of child training.

Age and Sex Differences in Certain Areas of Psychological Adjustment

Marvin Powell

Although the period of adolescence cannot be described as one of severe emotional upset, as postulated by G. Stanley Hall and others, it is reasonable to assume that a culture might create a certain amount of stress during the adolescent years. Kurt Lewin argued that the adolescent period produces stress because the individual is in an overlapping psychological situation; that is, in many respects society considers him to be a child and in other respects demands adult-like behavior. Professor Powell hypothesizes that the areas of parent-child relationships, heterosexual relationships, physical appearance, religion, social acceptability, and emotional tendencies are more likely to evidence stress during the adolescent years than during the preadolescent or early maturity years. He is suggesting, therefore, that specific areas of adjustment are more sensitive to the impact of the adolescent years than others. He also hypothesizes that, because of the more rapid rate of maturity among females than males, females will evidence stress in these adjustment areas earlier.

The purpose of this investigation was to examine experimentally a number of hypotheses related to supposed psychological changes in adolescent behavior, and to determine the chronological ages at which the greatest intensity of psychological conflict is manifested in various areas of adjustment. Since it has been demonstrated that pubescence occurs earlier for females than for males, this study also represents an attempt to determine sex differences in the age at which the greatest intensity of psychological conflicts in each area of adjustment is manifested.

Word association tests were chosen for this study as an indirect, but extremely useful, measure of psychological conflict, since previous research has demonstrated that the reaction time in such tests, as well as the type of verbal response to a "conflict" word, will differ from the reaction time and type of verbal response to a "neutral" word. A number of words, each of which was believed to be associated with one of the various areas of psychological adjustment, were selected for use in this investigation, along with a large number of "neutral" words.

These lists were then administered to a population of an equal number of males and females at yearly age levels from 10 to 17 years of age, and to groups of 21- to 25-year-old and 26- to 30-year-old married adults. In the 10- to 17-year-old groups, only those individuals with IQs of 98 or above were chosen for the experimental population. It would have been difficult to test the older groups for intelligence; therefore, only those who had graduated from high school and/or had attended college were chosen, in the expectation that they would be fairly comparable in intelligence to the younger groups.

SOURCE: Adapted and abridged from Marvin Powell, "Age and Sex Differences in Degree of Conflict Within Certain Areas of Psychological Adjustment." *Psychological Monographs,* 1955, 69, 14 pp. (With permission of author and the American Psychological Association.)

General Hypotheses Concerning Sex Differences

It was hypothesized that there are age differences in the degree of conflict which individuals experience in certain areas of psychological adjustment. Since it is generally agreed that females reach sex-social maturity at an earlier age than males, it was proposed that conflicts in certain areas of psychological adjustment will appear at an earlier age for females than for males. It was postulated on the basis of findings reported in the available research literature that these earlier conflicts for females will appear in the following adjustment areas: Parent-Child Relationships, Emotional Tendencies, Heterosexual Relations, Physical Appearance, and Social Acceptability.

Since the area of Vocational Outlook appears to be more highly related to societal demands than to sex-social maturity, it was hypothesized that the intensity of conflict in this area would be found to be greater, and appear at an earlier age, in males than in females.

Since Religious interests appear to be more closely related to general intellectual development than to sexual maturity, it was postulated that no sex differences in intensity, and age of onset, of conflict in this area would be found.

General Hypotheses Concerning Age Trends

It was hypothesized that intensity of conflict in psychological adjustment would be at a maximum during the adolescent years, as contrasted with the preadolescent or early maturity years in the following areas of psychological adjustment: Parent-Child Relationships, Emotional Tendencies, Heterosexual Relations, Physical Appearance, Religion, and Social Acceptability.

It was postulated that Vocational Outlook would become a conflict area through early maturity.

Since in our society marriage affords an opportunity for the individual to satisfy certain human needs that appear in intense forms during adolescnce, it was postulated that married individuals, in early maturity, would experience less intense conflicts in the following areas of psychological adjustment: Parent-Child Relationships, Emotional Tendencies, and Heterosexual Relations.

However, it was hypothesized that married individuals, during early maturity, would experience as great or greater intensity of conflict in the following areas of psychological adjustment: Vocational Outlook, and Social Acceptability to individuals and/or groups.

The assumptions underlying the development of the word lists are: (a) there will be a longer reaction time to words in the areas in which the individual is experiencing the more intense conflict, and (b) the type of verbal response given to a "conflict" word will differ from the type of verbal response to a "neutral" word.

Method

A total of 448 individuals (224 males and 224 females) ranging in age from

10 to 30 years participated in this study. The populations studied in the age range from 10 to 17 years were white children attending elementary school, junior high school, and high school, having IQ scores of 98 and above on either the 1937 Revision of the Stanford-Binet or the California Test of Mental Maturity. A child was placed in the age bracket which was within six months of his nearest birthday. The adult populations were composed of married white subjects who had completed high school and/or were attending college.

The area of psychological adjustment examined in this study concerned Parent-Child Relationships, Emotional Tendencies, Heterosexual Relations, Physical Appearance, Religion, Vocational Outlook, and Social Acceptability. Lists of stimulus words having emotional association with each of the above areas were selected.

In its final form for experimental use each critical list of five words was followed by a neutral list of four words. The neutral series were inserted to act as a partial control for the "generalization" effect which has been noted in previous studies (the emotional tone aroused by the critical stimulus words may extend to the subsequent reaction, thus causing the appearance of "disturbance" where no disturbance really exists).

The critical-word series and the intervening neutral-word series are presented in Table 11.2 together with the initial word series presented to each subject

TABLE 11.2. *The Various Word Series Employed in the Present Study*

Word Series for Each Area of Conflict						
Series A	*Series B*	*Series C*	*Series D*	*Series E*	*Series F*	*Series G*
PARENT-CHILD RELATION-SHIPS	EMOTIONAL TENDENCIES	HETERO-SEXUAL RELATIONS	PHYSICAL APPEARANCE	RELIGION	VOCATIONAL OUTLOOK	SOCIAL ACCEPT-ABILITY
Father	Worry	Dance	Handsome	Church	Wages	Popular
Children	Afraid	Kissing	Shabby	God	Money	Friend
Home	Unhappy	Marriage	Neat	Heaven	Employed	Lonely
Mother	Restless	Dates	Beautiful	Worship	Hire	Party
Parents	Anxious	Hugging	Ugly	Prayer	Job	Unfriendly

Word Series for the Intervening Neutral Groups						
Group 1	*Group 2*	*Group 3*	*Group 4*	*Group 5*	*Group 6*	*Group 7*
Sleep	Apple	Second	Lamp	Leaves	Daylight	Cardboard
Carpet	Window	Tree	Elevator	Fender	Photograph	Banana
Hill	Minnow	Bench	Table	Magazine	Bean	Harmonica
Flour	Piano	Sand	Balloon	Sandwich	Monday	Door

Initial Neutral Series		*Practice Series*	
Canary	Lantern	White	Man
Counter	Lighthouse	Cat	Black
Ladder	Shadow		Girl
	Tower		

to determine his average reaction time. The practice series presented in Table 11.2 was presented to each subject at the beginning of the study to familiarize him with the technique.

To control for any position effect in the experimental situation, seven different "total" lists (consisting of the seven critical and the seven intervening neutral series) were set up in such a manner that each critical series was presented in a different position and was followed by a different neutral series.

Apparatus

The subject was seated facing a large board in which there was a small door at eye level. When this door was opened by the experimenter, the stimulus word was exposed to the subject and an electric chronometer was started simultaneously. The experimenter stopped the chronometer by depressing a switch when the subject made a verbal response to the stimulus word.

Procedure

Subjects were assured that the results of the experiment would have no effect on scholastic records. The experimental room was a small, well-lighted classroom containing a table or desk and two chairs, and the experimental apparatus.

The subject was seated facing the small door, and the experimenter was seated at the left of the subject. Neither the timer nor the experimenter's control key was visible to the subject. The following instructions were given:

> I am going to give you a list of words one at a time. When I open this door (experimenter points to door) you will see a word. As soon as you see the word I want you to say the first word that comes to your mind. I will say "Ready" just before I open the door.

A short list of practice words was given before the test began and any misunderstandings in the instructions were corrected during this period.

Type of Data Obtained

1. The individual's average reaction time to the "neutral" series of words.
2. The individual's reaction time to "conflict" words in each adjustment area.
3. The verbal response of the individual to each word.

Several tests were made on the accuracy of the electric chronometer and of slight changes in the experimenter's speed in manipulating the key which stopped the electric chronometer. It was found that the experimenter's reaction speed varied within the range of 28 to 37 milliseconds, with little or no fatigue effect apparent as a two-hour session drew to a close. Since this is an extremely narrow range, this time was treated as a constant error common to all the reaction times derived in this study.

It seemed best to use each subject as his own control, and to derive a *difference score* for each critical area. This was arrived at for each individual by calculating (a) his mean reaction time to the neutral words, (b) his mean reaction time to the critical words in each area of adjustment, and (c) the *difference* between these two (a being subtracted from b); the latter is termed the subject's *difference score* in the given area, which is used in the statistical analyses in this study.

These difference scores were computed for each sex at each of the various age levels. It was hypothesized that there would be a slower reaction time to "critical" words in the various areas of psychological adjustment as the degree of conflict in these areas increased.

Results

Age and Sex Differences in Average Reaction Time to Neutral Words

Before any attempt to test for differences within and between the sexes on the various areas of psychological adjustment was made, it was decided first to determine what differences, if any, existed between the sexes in terms of average reaction time *per se,* that is, to "neutral" words. In general, it can be stated on the basis of the results that there are no statistically significant differences within or between the sexes during the adolescent and young adult age ranges, i.e., from age 12 to age 30.

Age and Sex Differences in the Psychological Adjustment Area of Parent-Child Relationships

There is a fairly steady increase in difference scores, indicative of .conflict, to the "critical" stimulus words pertaining to the psychological adjustment area of Parent-Child Relationships for both sexes, starting at age 12 and reaching a maximum between 15 and 17 years.

There is a statistically significant increase in difference scores to the "critical" stimulus words between the ages of 12 and 13 for both sexes. It is, therefore, concluded that the psychological adjustment area of Parent-Child Relationships becomes a source of conflict for both sexes between the ages of 12 and 13 years, although it would appear to be a source of greater conflict for females, since the difference for females seems to be somewhat more significant than the difference for males. It is suggested that further investigation may demonstrate that this arises as an area of conflict for females approximately one year earlier than for males.

It is further concluded that the psychological adjustment area of Parent-Child Relationships becomes a statistically significantly lesser source of conflict for both sexes in the two populations of young adults. The data also indicate a statistically significant decrease in difference scores to the "critical" words in this area between the ages of 17 and 21–25 for both sexes. There is no significant difference between the 21 to 25 and the 26- to 30-year-old groups for either sex.

Age and Sex Differences in the Psychological Adjustment Area of Emotional Tendencies

The data also indicate a steady increase in difference scores to "critical" words related to the psychological adjustment area of Emotional Tendencies. This increase reaches a peak for both sexes at 14 years of age, although there seems to be another slight increase for females at about age 17 and somewhat of a decrease for males at this same age. There are statistically significant increases in difference scores between the ages of 11 and 12, 12 and 13, and 13 and 14, for the females, while the statistically significant increase in difference scores for males occurs between the ages of 13 and 14.

These data support the hypothesis that the psychological adjustment area of Emotional Tendencies becomes a source of conflict at an earlier age for females than for males. Such conflict first begins to appear between 11 and 12 years of age for females, and between 13 and 14 years of age for males, with approximately a two-year differential between the sexes.

There is a statistically significant difference between the 17-year-old and the 21- to 25-year-old groups of both sexes, demonstrating a decrease in difference scores for the older group, but no significant difference between the two adult populations. These data tend to substantiate the postulate that the psychological area of Emotional Tendencies is no longer a source of such great conflict during the years of early maturity for either sex.

The differences between males and females at various age levels in different scores to "critical" words having reference to the psychological adjustment area of Emotional Tendencies indicate that the greatest difference between the sexes occurs at age 13, with the difference indicating a significantly greater increase in difference scores for females than for males. These data further substantiate the conclusion that there is a greater intensity of conflict for females at an earlier age than for males in this area of psychological adjustment. It appears that by age 14 both sexes show the same degree of conflict, as evidenced by the fact that there are no longer any significant differences between males and females at any of the succeeding age levels beyond age 13.

Age and Sex Differences in the Psychological Adjustment Area of Heterosexual Relations

A rather sharp increase in difference scores to "critical" words related to the psychological adjustment area of Heterosexual Relations was observed. There is a steady increase in difference scores for both sexes reaching a maximum at 15 years of age for males, with a steady decrease from 15 to 17; and reaching a maximum at 16 years of age for females with a decrease from 16 to 17, with a still greater decrease in difference scores apparent in the young adult populations. There are statistically significant differences in the increase in difference scores for females between the ages of 11 and 12, 12 and 13, and 13 and 14, and statistically significant differences for males between the ages of 12 and 13, and 13 and 14. There is also a statistically significant decrease in difference scores between the 15-year-old males and the 17-year-old males, with no difference between the 21- to 25-year-olds and the 26- to 30-year-olds of either sex.

These data support the hypothesis of earlier conflict for females than for males, demonstrating a difference in onset of conflict to this area of adjustment of about one year. For males the conflict is most apparent during the adolescent period from 12 to 17 years of age, reaching a maximum peak at 15 and declining significantly between 15 and 17. For the female population, conflict is most apparent from 11 to 17 years of age, reachng a maximum at 16 and declining from 16 to 17, although less abruptly than for the males. There seems to be relatively little conflict manifested by either of the sexes in the two adult populations.

In the comparison between the sexes at various age levels it was noted that there are statistically significant differences between males and females in difference scores to "critical" words regarding the psychological adjustment area of Heterosexual Relations at age 12 and at age 13. At both of these age levels the females show significantly greater difference scores, indicating a greater degree of disturbance than is manifested by the males at these ages. There are no other significant differences between the sexes in degree of conflict shown in response to "critical" words in this area of adjustment, although the difference between males and females at age 17 does approach statistical significance, indicating a somewhat greater decrease in difference scores for males at that age than for females.

Age and Sex Differences in the Psychological Adjustment Area of Physical Appearance

There was a fairly steady increase in difference scores to "critical" words concerned with the psychological adjustment area of Physical Appearance during the age range from 12 to 16 years of age for females and 13 to 16 years of age for males. These data seem to indicate that conflict arises approximately one year earlier for females than for males. For both sexes the peak occurs at age 16, with a slight decrease in difference scores from 16 to 17, and a statistically significant decrease in difference scores between 17 and 21–25 years of age. There are statistically significant increases in difference scores between 11 and 12, and between 12 and 13 for the females, and between 13 and 14 for the males. This would seem to support the hypothesis that conflict appears earlier for females than for males in this area of psychological adjustment. The statistically significant decrease in difference scores between the 17-year-old and 21- to 25-year-old groups suggests that the psychological adjustment area of Physical Appearance is no longer a source of so much conflict for the two populations of young adults.

The only statistically significant difference between males and females in difference scores to "critical" words regarding the psychological adjustment area of Physical Appearance occurs at the 13-year level. This, too, would demonstrate greater conflict for females at 13 years of age than for males. There seems to be some possibility that this greater degree of conflict for females than for males is present at age 12, since the tests of statistical significance closely approximate the

.05 level of confidence. By age 14, however, there is no longer a significant difference between the sexes in difference scores.

Age and Sex Differences in the Psychological Adjustment Area of Religion

The data demonstrate a relatively steady increase in difference scores for both sexes to "critical" words concerned with the psychological adjustment area of Religion. It appears that onset of the increase in difference scores occurs about one year earlier for the females than for the males; however, the males reach a maximum about one year earlier than the females. It can be seen from this there is a statistically significant increase in difference scores for females between 11 and 12, a somewhat greater increase between 12 and 13, and still another increase between 13 and 14, while for the males the increase begins between 12 and 13, and is greatest between 13 and 14.

These findings are not in accord with the postulate that there would be no differences in the age of onset of conflict in this area. Here, as in the area of psychological adjustment previously discussed, there is a one-year difference in age of onset of conflict in the direction of the female group. The statistically significant decrease in difference scores between the 17-year-old and 21- to 25-year-old groups of both sexes leads to the conclusion that little conflict is exhibited by the two young adult populations in this area of adjustment.

A further indication of the existence of a greater degree of conflict being manifested by females than by males at age 13 is shown by a statistically significant difference between males and females at age 13 in difference scores to "critical" words pertaining to the psychological adjustment area of Religion.

Age and Sex Differences in the Psychological Adjustment Area of Vocational Outlook

A steady increase in difference scores to "critical" words concerned with the psychological adjustment area of Vocational Outlook for both sexes throughout the adolescent period was found. It can be further noted that this increase in difference scores continues through the years of early maturity. There are significant increases in difference scores for females between the ages of 12 and 13, and between 13 and 14; for males, between 13 and 14, and between 14 and 15.

These results are contrary to the hypothesis that onset of conflict in this area of psychological adjustment would occur earlier for males than for females. Here there was instead approximately a one-year differential between the sexes, favoring earlier onset of conflict for females.

These results do, however, substantiate the postulate that Vocational Outlook would continue as a conflict area through early maturity, since there is no significant decrease in difference scores of either sex between the 17-year-olds and the 21- to 30-year-olds.

There were no significant differences found between the sexes at any age level in difference scores to "critical" words regarding the psychological adjustment area of Vocational Outlook. These results are also contrary to hypothesis, since it was postulated that intensity of conflict in this area would be greater for males than for females. This failure to predict may have been due to the possibility that certain of the "critical" words used in this area (e.g., money) may have had some unpleasant connotation unrelated to Vocational Outlook.

Age and Sex Differences in the Psychological Adjustment Area of Social Acceptability

There was a sharp increase in difference scores to "critical" words concerning the psychological adjustment area of Social Acceptability from age 11 to age 14 for females, and from age 12 to age 15 for males, indicating approximately a one-year difference in age of onset of conflict in this area. There are statistically significant increases for females in difference scores between the ages of 11 and 12, 12 and 13, and 13 and 14, whereas for males the statistically significant increases in difference score occur between the ages of 12 and 13, 13 and 14, and 14 and 15.

The increased difference scores for females remain at about the same level from ages 14 to 17, with a statistically significant decrease in difference scores occurring between ages 17 and 21–25. For the male population, however, the increase in difference scores appears to reach a maximum at age 15, at which time a statistically significant decrease in difference scores between ages 15 and 16 occurs. There is a further statistically significant decrease in difference scores for males between the ages of 17 and 21–25. No significant difference appears to be present between the two young adult populations of either sex.

From age 12 to age 14 females show statistically significant greater increases in difference scores to "critical" words in the Social Acceptability area than do the males. At the 15-year age level no significant differences occur between the sexes, but at ages 16 and 17 the males are demonstrating statistically significant differences from the females in the direction of decreased difference scores. There are no significant differences between the sexes at the two young adult age levels.

Sources of Anxiety in Adolescent Boys

W. W. Meissner

In this study a group of boys ranging in age between 13 and 18 years were asked a series of 217 open-ended questions related to sources of fears or worries. Responses were analyzed to determine what changes in the patterns of worries and anxieties occur during the high school years. The results indicate that the major sources of worry and anxiety for this sample of children are the school, unpopularity, sex, immoral activity, religion, vocation, and future life. It should be noted that the

SOURCE: Adapted and abridged from W. W. Meissner, "Some Indications of Sources of Anxiety in Adolescent Boys." *Journal of Genetic Psychology*, 1961, 99, 65–73. (With permission of author and the Journal Press.)

degree of concern over specific problems tends to lessen as the boys become older. Consistent with other studies, it was found that high school seniors, more than freshmen, are concerned about future vocational objectives. These results may be interpreted as meaning that during the high school years, boys are learning to assume adult male roles that will provide them with the necessary behavioral repertoire to deal with the problems of adulthood.

In understanding the adolescent's outlook on life and its problems, it is helpful to have some indication of the problem areas which are sources of worry and anxiety for him. The forces which combine to create these anxiety areas are multiple and form a dynamically shifting constellation not only in terms of the adolescent's own development and maturation, but also in terms of the social and cultural context in which that growth occurs.

Procedures and Results

The results presented in this study are drawn from a 217-item questionnaire which was administered to 1278 high school boys from nine different schools. The schools were private schools under Catholic direction and were scattered through the states of New York, New Jersey, Pennsylvania, and Maryland. The questionnaires were given in each instance with a standard set of instructions which were read to the subjects by the administrator. The test forms were sent to the respective administrators in sealed envelopes, were opened in the presence of the subjects, and immediately after completion of the test they were resealed and returned to the experimenter. The boys were selected according to classes from the school populations. As a group they represent the median range in academic achievement. The distribution according to years was as follows: 331 freshmen, 313 sophomores, 343 juniors, and 291 seniors. The age range of the total populations extended from 13 to 18 years. The average age of the freshmen was 14.3 years, the sophomores 15.2, the juniors 16.2, and the seniors 17.2. With the exception of the senior group, these age groups are roughly equivalent to the Gesell age groups. The boys were predominantly from a middle-class family background.

For the purpose of this study, eight questions were selected from the questionnaire which present some indication of the problems or areas which give high school boys occasion for worry or anxiety. The questions were all free response items. For each question the responses were ranked in the order of frequency and a rank-order coefficient was computed between the rankings for respective years. Each correlation was tested for statistical significance.

The questions selected as indicating areas of worry and anxiety were the following:

1. What are the things you worry about most?
2. What is your biggest personal problem or difficulty in life? (If you haven't any, write "None.")
3. What are the things you fear most? (If nothing, write "Nothing.")

4. What are the things you usually have doubts about?

5. When you feel sad and depressed or "down in the mouth," what generally causes this feeling?

6. When you feel lonely, what do you think are the causes?

7. Mention the difficulty or problem in your school life that puzzles you most. (If you haven't any, write "None.")

8. Please mention any problem of yours which has been omitted in these questions.

Results

The results will be discussed in reference to the individual questions and then in reference to common response categories in the whole set of questions.

Question 1. The predominant causes of worry for these boys seem to center around the school and their relation to it. The family is also a consistent source of worry. Worries about sex show a numerical increase in juniors and seniors and a significant jump in rank between junior and senior year. An indicator of changing concerns is the jump in worries about their future lives from the lower to the upper classmen and the appearance in the upper classes of worry over the subject of vocation. The correlations between the years are all significant with the exception of that between the freshmen and the seniors. This would indicate a change in the patterns of worry and concern from the beginning to the end of the high school years.

Question 2. This question indicates that the great source of personal difficulty is sex. Many boys, especially from sophomore year on, manifest difficulties not only with their relationships with girls but also in personal sex habits. Masturbation is mentioned most often in second and third years of high school. School and family become less and less a source of difficulty as the boy matures. As in the previous question, there is a rise in concern with the future and with the problem of vocation. The latter seems to be a special problem for seniors. Interestingly enough, it seems that personal difficulties with parents is a problem for a few lower classmen, but after the sophomore year it is not mentioned at all. Low correlations between freshman year and the other years and a significant correlation among the other years would indicate that the most significant changes in personal problems occur soon after the freshman year, i.e., around 14–15 years of age.

Question 3. Besides the "Nothing" response, the boys express a great fear of hell and an increasing fear of death. There is also an increase in the fear of failure and in the later years a fear of the future. The boys express a fear of God which seems to slacken among the juniors and seniors. A great many incidental responses were given to this question which are not indicated on the table: fear of punshment, responsibility, loss of parents, height, parents, pain, snakes, etc. None were mentioned with any significant frequency. Low correlations indicate a tendency for patterns of fear to shift from year to year.

Question 4. Doubts are expressed primarily about sex and religion. Doubts about sex tend to decrease as the boys mature, but at the same time doubts about religion increase. Doubts about vocation are also increasingly manifested and, in the upper years, doubts about the future. These two categories are undoubtedly related. Doubts about school and family problems, however, decrease as the boy grows older. The significant changes here also tend to occur after the freshman year as indicated by the low correlation between the ranks of this group and the other groups.

Question 5. A good many of the boys admit to feelings of sadness and depression and ascribe their depression mainly to their failures in school and to disappointment and frustration in general. A major cause of such depression is found in disappointing relations with girls, especially in the older boys. Family problems (financial, arguments with parents, etc.) are a consistent source of depression among the younger boys, but there is a significant drop in such problems among seniors. Unpopularity seems to become somewhat less of a problem as the boy grows older, although some juniors and seniors seem to become depressed about their own personality development. This seems to follow the pattern of self-centeredness described by Gesell. Arguments with friends, especially girl friends, are also listed as a source of depressed feelings. Low freshman-senior and sophomore-senior correlations suggest that patterns of depression tend to alter after sophomore year. This suggestion is reinforced by the high freshman-sophomore correlation.

Question 6. High on the list of causes of loneliness is unpopularity. There is an increased tendency in later years to look on loneliness as related to personal deficiencies (sensitivity, shyness, etc.) rather than the mere fact of being alone. Feelings of loneliness are increasingly related to sex. Boys tend to feel more and more left out of things as they grow older because they may not have a girl with whom they can engage in heterosexual social activities, i.e., dances and parties. There is a significant increase in this problem from freshman to sophomore year and another significant jump from there to the upper years. The upper years correlate highly, indicating a certain degree of stabilization as compared with the low correlations in the first two years. Freshman-junior and freshman-senior correlations are especially low, indicating significant changes.

Question 7. There is a fairly high degree of agreement in the pattern of school problems in each of the years. The greatest source of difficulty seems to be the choice of subjects studied. The boys want to know why they have to study the subjects they do and what use these subjects will be for later life. Great dissatisfaction is also had with the teachers — usually not in general, but rather it seems that every boy has his problems with one or possibly more teachers. Discipline and homework, as might be expected, are constant sources of difficulty.

Question 8. The question asked about problems which had been omitted from the questionnaire, but almost all responses repeated problems previously handled. Sex is a major problem area, but it slackens off here in the upper years. More important than sex are the problems the boys have with their studies. This seems to become more and more of a problem in the later years. A prominent place is given here to religious problems and vocational difficulties. Religious problems especially seem to become of greater importance in later years. Discipline and teacher-relations are also prominent, seeming to indicate with studies a predominance of preoccupations centering around the school and its activities. Only the correlations between second and third and again between third and fourth years are significant. This would suggest a constantly shifting pattern of interests and concerns as the boy develops from year to year. The freshman-sophomore and freshman-junior correlations are the lowest. Again the pattern of alteration between earlier and later years is manifest.

The responses reveal certain common patterns which would seem to indicate general areas of worry, concern and anxiety. The more or less frequent responses which recur in a number of questions are the following:

The school. School problems are a consistent source of worry to the high school boy. Although it remains a high source of concern, school becomes less and less a major area of concern as the boy grows older and other interests develop. His fear of failure decreases and drops significantly in senior year. He progressively manifests less doubt about the things he is required to do in school. Failure in school work is a consistent source of depression. When asked to mention a personal problem, most boys responded with difficulties about the reasons for studying certain subjects, e.g., Latin, modern language, history, etc. The biggest school problems in the order of importance were subjects, teachers, and discipline.

Sex. Sex is a consistent source of worry, difficulties, fear, and doubt. Many boys of high school age are just beginning to have heterosexual experiences and there are many things they do not know. Both in the form of heterosexual difficulties and of personal chastity, sex was listed as the major personal problem for sophomores, juniors, and seniors. Sex is not so much a source of fear as it is of doubt. Difficulty in getting along with girls is listed as a major cause of depression, as well as a source of feelings of loneliness, particularly for the older boys.

Popularity. This is a constant source of worry to the high school boy. It seems to become more frequent in the older boys when popularity takes on more social significance. As a source of fear and doubt, unpopularity is not a primary, but is a fairly consistent, problem. Feelings of depression due to unpopularity seem to decrease as the boy matures, but unpopularity is given the first rank in sophomore, junior, and senior years as a cause of loneliness. There may be some relation between the predominance of unpopularity and difficulties in relations with girls as sources of loneliness among the older boys.

Immorality and religion. From the freshman to the senior year there is an increasing amount of worry about sin, but it does not constitute a major personal problem. A fair number, especially freshmen, express their fears about sin and their doubt about it. This seems to lessen as they grow older. Immoral actions are consistently a source of depression. Religion is a cause of worry rather infrequently and is mentioned as a personal problem by only a few upperclassmen. Fear of God is mentioned by a fair number in the earlier years but takes a significant drop among seniors. However, as a source of doubt, religion becomes more and more prominent until it is listed as the primary source of doubts for juniors and seniors.

Vocation and the future. This becomes more and more a source of worry for the growing boy until for the seniors it takes a place second only to the school. Worry about vocation is expressed by a few juniors and a few seniors. There is a steady increase in the numbers who find the future and the problem of vocational choice a major personal problem. Among seniors, the choice of vocation is second only to sex as a personal problem. A few of the older boys express fears about the future but many more have doubts about the future as well as about their vocation in life. A few seniors indicate that vocation is the most puzzling problem they have.

A Study of Fear

Harold E. Jones and Mary Cover Jones

This experiment by the late Professor Harold Jones and his wife, Mary Cover Jones, both of whom were strong forces in the development of the Institute of Human Development at the University of California at Berkeley, has been rediscovered by those clinical psychologists interested in the application of conditioning therapies to a broad variety of human problems. In particular, the treatment of a child with a strong fear of white rats is described. Fundamental to the procedure is the application of the method of successive approximations; that is, the subject approaches the feared stimulus in stages that do not arouse an emotional response and where the approach response is reinforced. Over several trials, the subject is eventually able to approach the once feared object without hesitation and without any evidence of a physiological or overt emotional reaction. More recent work indicates that the procedure has considerable promise, at least with respect to certain kinds of clinical problems.

As part of a genetic study of emotions, a number of children were observed in order to determine the most effective methods of removing fear responses.

The case of Peter illustrates how a fear may be removed under laboratory conditions. His case was selected from a number of others for the following reasons:

SOURCE: Adapted and abridged from Harold Ellis Jones and Mary Cover Jones, "Fear," *Childhood Education*, 1928, 5, 136–143. (With permission of Mary Cover Jones and the Association for Childhood Education, International, 3615 Wisconsin Avenue, N.W., Washington, D. C. 20016.)

1. Progress in combating the fear reactions was so marked that many of the details of the process could be observed easily.

2. It was possible to continue the study over a period of more than three months.

3. The notes of a running diary show the characteristics of a healthy, normal, interesting child, well adjusted, except for his exaggerated fear reactions.

4. This case is a sequel to one recently contributed by Dr. J. B. Watson and furnished supplementary material of interest in a genetic study of emotions. Dr. Watson's case illustrated how a fear could be produced experimentally under laboratory conditions. A brief review follows: Albert,[1] eleven months of age, was an infant with a phlegmatic disposition, afraid of nothing "under the sun" except a loud noise made by striking a steel bar. This made him cry. By striking the bar at the same time that Albert touched a white rat, the fear was transferred to the white rat. After seven combined stimulations, rat and sound, Albert not only became greatly disturbed at the sight of a rat, but this fear had spread to include a white rabbit, cotton wool, a fur coat, and the experimenter's hair. It did not transfer to his wooden blocks and other objects very dissimilar to the rat.

In referring to this case, Dr. Watson says, "We have shown experimentally that when you condition a child to show fear of an animal, this fear transfers or spreads in such a way that without separate conditioning he becomes afraid of many animals. If you take any one of these objects producing fear and uncondition, will fear of the other objects in the series disappear at the same time? That is, will the unconditioning spread without further training to other stimuli?"

Dr. Watson intended to continue the study of Albert in an attempt to answer this question, but Albert was removed from the hospital and the series of observations was discontinued.

About three years later this case, which seemed almost to be Albert grown a bit older, was discovered in our laboratory.

Peter was 2 years and 10 months old when we began to study him. He was afraid of a white rat, and this fear extended to a rabbit, a fur coat, a feather, cotton wool, etc., but not to wooden blocks and similar toys. An abridgment of the first laboratory notes on Peter reads as follows:

> Peter was put in a crib in a play room and immediately became absorbed in his toys. A white rat was introduced into the crib from behind. (The E was behind a screen). At sight of the rat, Peter screamed and fell flat on his back in a paroxysm of fear. The stimulus was removed, and Peter was taken out of the crib and put into a chair. Barbara was brought to the crib and the white rat introduced as before. She exhibited no fear but picked the rat up in her hand. Peter sat quietly watching Barbara and the rat. A string of beads belonging to Peter had been left in the crib. Whenever the rat touched a part of the string he would say "my beads" in a complaining voice, although he made no objections when Barbara touched them. Invited to get down from the chair, he shook his head, fear not yet subsided. Twenty-five minutes elapsed before he was ready to play about freely.

The next day his reactions to the following situations and objects were noted:

Play room and crib   Selected toys, got into crib without protest
White ball rolled in   Picked it up and held it
Fur rug hung over crib   Cried until it was removed
Fur coat hung over crib   Cried until it was removed
Cotton   Whimpered, withdrew, cried
Hat with feathers   Cried
Blue woolly sweater   Looked, turned away, no fear
White toy rabbit of rough cloth   No interest, no fear
Wooden doll   No interest, no fear

This case made it possible for E to continue where Dr. Watson had left off. The first problem was that of "unconditioning" a fear response to an animal, and the second, that of determining whether unconditioning to one stimulus spreads without further training to other stimuli.

From the test situations which were used to reveal fears, it was found that Peter showed even more marked fear responses to the rabbit than to the rat. It was decided to use the rabbit for unconditioning and to proceed as follows: Each day Peter and three other children were brought to the laboratory for a play period. The other children were selected carefully because of their satisfactory adjustments in general. The rabbit was always present during a part of the play period. From time to time Peter was brought in alone so that his reactions could be observed and progress noted.

From reading over the notes for each session it was apparent that there had been improvement by more or less regular steps from almost complete terror at sight of the rabbit to a completely positive response with no signs of disturbance. New situations requiring closer contact with the rabbit had been gradually introduced and the degree to which these situations were avoided, tolerated, or welcomed at each experimental session gave the measure of improvement. Analysis of the notes on Peter's reactions indicated the following progressive steps in his degrees of toleration (See Figure 11.2):

A. Rabbit anywhere in the room in a cage causes fear reactions.
B. Rabbit 12 feet away in cage tolerated.
C. Rabbit 4 feet away in cage tolerated.
D. Rabbit 3 feet away in cage tolerated.
E. Rabbit close in cage tolerated.
F. Rabbit free in room tolerated.
G. Rabbit touched when E holds it.
H. Rabbit touched when free in room.
 I. Rabbit defied by spitting at it, throwing things at it, imitating it.
J. Rabbit allowed on tray of high chair.
K. Squats in defenseless position beside rabbit.
L. Helps E to carry rabbit to its cage.
M. Holds rabbit on lap.

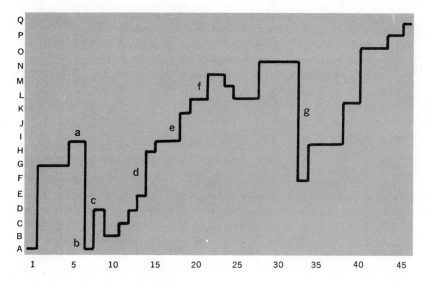

Figure 11.2 Chart indicating progressive steps in toleration. See text for definition of symbols.

N. Stays alone in room with rabbit.

O. Allows rabbit in play pen with him.

P. Fondles rabbit affectionately.

Q. Lets rabbit nibble his fingers.

These "degrees of toleration" merely represented the stages in which improvement occurred. They did not give any indications of the intervals between steps, or of the plateaus, relapses, and sudden gains which were actually evident. To show these features a curve was drawn by using the seventeen steps given above as the Y axis of a chart and the experimental sessions as the X axis. The units are not equal on either axis, as the "degrees of toleration" have merely been set down as they appeared from consideration of the laboratory notes with no attempt to evaluate the steps. Likewise the experimental sessions were not equi-distant in time. Peter was seen twice daily for a period and thence only once a day. At one point illness and quarantine interrupted the experiments for two months. There is no indication of these irregularities on the chart. For example, along the X axis, 1 represents the date December 4, when the observation began; 11 and 12 represent the dates March 10 A.M. and P.M. (from December 17 to March 7, Peter was not available for study).

The question arose as to whether or not the points on the Y axis which indicated progress to the experimenter represented real advance and not merely idiosyncratic reactions of the subject. The "tolerance series" as indicated by the experimenter was presented in random order to six graduate students and instructors in psychology to be arranged so as to indicate increase in tolerance, in their judgment. An average correlation of .70 with the experiment's arrangement was found for the six ratings. This indicates that the experimenter was justified from an a priori point of view in designating the steps to be progressive stages.

The first seven periods show how Peter progressed from a great fear of rabbit to a tranquil indifference and even a voluntary pat on the rabbit's back when others were setting the example. The notes for the seventh period (see a on chart) read:

> Laurel, Mary, Arthur, Peter playing together in the laboratory. E put rabbit down on floor. Arthur said, "Peter doesn't cry when he sees the rabbit come out." Peter: "No." He was a little concerned as to whether or not the rabbit would eat his kiddie car. Laurel and Mary stroked the rabbit and chattered away excitedly. Peter walked over, touched the rabbit on the back, exulting, "I touched him on the end."

At this period Peter was taken to the hospital with scarlet fever. He did not return for two months.

By referring to the chart at (b), it will be noted that the line shows a decided drop to the early level of fear reaction when he returned. This was easily explained by the nurse who brought Peter from the hospital. As they were entering a taxi at the door of the hospital, a large dog, running past, jumped at them. Both Peter and the nurse were very much frightened, Peter so much that he lay back in the taxi pale and quiet, and the nurse debated whether or not to return him to the hospital. This seemed reason enough for his precipitate descent back to the original fear level. Being threatened by a large dog when ill, and in a strange place and being with an adult who also showed fear, was a terrifying situation against which our training could not have fortified him.

At this point (b) we began another method of treatment, that of "direct conditioning." Peter was seated in a high chair and given food which he liked. The E brought the rabbit in a wire cage as close as she could without arousing a response which would interfere with the eating. Through the presence of the pleasant stimulus (food) whenever the rabbit was shown, the fear was eliminated gradually in favor of a positive response. Occasionally also, other children were brought in to help with the "unconditioning." These facts are of interest in following the charted progress. The first decided rise at (c) was due to the presence of another child who influenced Peter's reaction. The notes for this day read:

> Lawrence and Peter sitting near together in their high chairs eating candy. Rabbit in cage put down 12 feet away. Peter began to cry. Lawrence said, "Oh, rabbit." Clambered down, ran over and looked in the cage at him. Peter followed close and watched.

The next two decided rises at (d) and (e) occurred on the day when a student assistant, Dr. S., was present. Peter was very fond of Dr. S., whom he insisted was his "papa." Although Dr. S. did not directly influence Peter by any overt suggestions, it may be that having him there contributed to Peter's general feeling of well being and thus indirectly affected his reactions. The fourth rise on the chart at (f) was, like the first, due to the influence of another child. Notes for the 21st session read:

> Peter with candy in high chair. E brought rabbit and sat down in front of the tray with it. Peter cried out, "I don't want him," and withdrew. Rabbit was given to another child sitting near to hold. His holding the rabbit served as a powerful suggestion; Peter wanted the rabbit on his lap, and held it for an instant.

The decided drop at (g) was caused by a slight scratch when Peter was helping to carry the rabbit to his cage. The rapid ascent following shows how quickly he regained lost ground.

In one of our last sessions, Peter showed no fear although another child was present who showed marked disturbance at sight of the rabbit.

Early in the experiment an attempt was made to get some measure of the visceral changes accompanying Peter's fear reactions. On one occasion Dr. S. determined Peter's blood pressure outside the laboratory and again later, in the laboratory while he was in a state of much anxiety caused by the rabbit's being held close to him by E. The diastolic blood pressure changed from 65 to 80 on this occasion. Peter was taken to the infirmary the next day for the routine physical examination and developed there a suspicion of medical instruments which made it inadvisable to proceed with this phase of the work.

Peter has gone home to a difficult environment but E is still in touch with him. He showed in the last interview, as on the later portion of the chart, a genuine fondness for the rabbit. What has happened to the fear of the other objects? The fear of the cotton, the fur coat, feathers, was entirely absent at our last interview. He looked at them, handled them, and immediately turned to something which interested him more. The reaction to the rats and the fur rug with the stuffed head was greatly modified and improved. While he did not show the fondness for these that was apparent with the rabbit, he had made a fair adjustment. For example, Peter would pick up the tin box containing frogs or rats and carry it around the room. When requested, he picked up the fur rug and carried it to E.

What would Peter do if confronted by a strange animal? At the last interview E presented a mouse and a tangled mass of angleworms. At first sight, Peter showed slight distress reactions and moved away, but before the period was over he was carrying the worms about and watching the mouse with undisturbed interest. By "unconditioning" Peter to the rabbit, he has apparently been helped to overcome many superfluous fears, some completely, some to a less degree. His tolerance of strange animals and unfamiliar situations has apparently increased.

The study is still incomplete. Peter's fear of the animals which were shown him was probably not a directly conditioned fear. It is unlikely that he had ever had any experience with white rats, for example. Where the fear originated, and with what stimulus, is not known. Nor is it known what Peter would do if he were again confronted with the original fear situation. All of the fears which were "unconditioned" were transferred fears, and it has not yet been learned whether or not the primary fear can be eliminated by training the transfers.

NOTE

[1] "This infant was reared almost from birth in a hospital environment; his mother was a wet nurse in the Harriet Lane Home for Invalid Children. Albert's life was normal: he was healthy from birth and one of the best developed youngsters ever brought to the hospital, weighing twenty-one pounds at nine months of age. He was on the whole stolid and unemotional. His stability was one of the principal reasons for using him as a subject in this test." (Watson and Rayner, 1920, p. 1.)

CHAPTER XII

Social Interactions

THE STUDY of children's social development encompasses a broad variety of behavioral situations. There are numerous studies concerned with the bases of children's choices of friends, leadership behavior, and conformity behavior. The study of children's friendships was given impetus almost 40 years ago by the development of Moreno's technique for measuring social interactions. In general terms, the research evidence indicates that children prefer other children whose social backgrounds, intellectual abilities, social class levels, racial origins, and sex are similar to their own. These results are consistent with the hypothesis that friendships develop where the attitudes, values, and standards of social behavior are compatible. Professor Meyer, using a more recently developed instrument for measuring social relationships, demonstrates that same-sex peers are perceived more favorably than opposite-sex peers, at least in terms of two broadly defined social situations. Kuhlen and Lee show that the standards of reinforcing behaviors tend to change during the teen years and that the incorporation of these changed standards is an important component of social acceptability. Marshall and McCandless, using preschool children, show that children who are overly dependent on adults are less likely to develop social behaviors that are perceived favorably by their peers. The results of all three studies are consistent with the general hypothesis that children's friendships develop on the basis of mutually reinforcing behaviors.

The study of conformity behavior has not received wide attention primarily because of the difficulties in developing reasonably well-controlled situations. Professor Iscoe and his colleagues describe a method for use with children which is a modification of a technique that had originally been employed with adults. Although conformity is, in many situations, a desirable behavioral attribute, this study indicates that there are many children who will conform to group consensus even when they are aware that the group opinion is incorrect. It is both a scientifically and socially important matter to discover how such conforming behavior develops and to generate techniques that would foster independent thinking.

Social Needs and Heterosexual Affiliations

William J. Meyer

Studies contrasting the frequency of same-sex choices as opposed to opposite-sex choices among children ranging from Grade 1 to Grade 12 indicate significant increases in opposite-sex choices beginning with adolescence. These results may be considered, in part at least, as an artifact of the social situation upon which choices are made during the adolescent years. Thus, a typical hypothetical social situation would be, "Name four people you would like to dance with." On the basis of that type of social situation, it would be incorrect to conclude that members of the opposite sex are preferred for all situations relative to same-sex peers. Using the Syracuse Scales of Social Relations, a rating rather than a nomination procedure, Dr. Meyer demonstrates that same-sex peers are preferred over opposite-sex peers for two broadly defined social situations. These results are consistent with the hypothesis that reinforcement expectancies in social situations are greater among same-sex peers than among opposite-sex peers.

The purpose of this investigation was to examine the developmental relationships believed to exist between two social-psychological needs and the social relations structure existing between boys and girls during preadolescence and adolescence. The data to be reported concern boys' and girls' perceptions of the degree to which their same-sex and opposite-sex classmates afford satisfaction of two relatively specific social-psychological needs. Studies of developmental trends with respect to heterosexual affiliations have shown a decrease in the frequency of opposite-sex choices until Grade 6 and then an increase in such choices. These findings, derived from sociometric tests, suggest that for both sexes the relative ability of the opposite sex to satisfy social needs increases considerably after pubesence.

The present study is based on the assumption that a person is attracted to those group members who are perceived as having a high potential for satisfying one of his social-psychological needs. Rotter (1954) has postulated that a person acquires expectancies "that a particular reinforcement will occur as a function of a specific behavior on his part in a specific situation or situations." The probability that he will seek interactions with another individual in a particular social situation can be ascertained from a knowledge of his previous reinforcements with all the individuals in his group. If the behavior of the group members has been reinforcing, the probability that he will be attracted to them in similar social situations is increased.

Two relatively specific social needs were investigated for their influence on the development of heterosexual affiliations. The needs of playmirth and suc-

SOURCE: Adapted and abridged from W. J. Meyer, "Relationships Between Social Need Strivings and the Development of Heterosexual Affiliations." *Journal of Abnormal Social Psychology*, 1959, 59, 51–57. (With permission of author and the American Psychological Association.)

corance were selected because of their relative independence of each other, their relevance to children, and the existence of sex differences in appropriate social behavior for their reduction. Since the research literature indicates that sex differences exist not only in need strength but also in the behavior required for need reduction, it is anticipated that subjects of each sex will perceive others of the same sex as having a higher potential for satisfying their social need strivings. This sex differential is expected to be maintained throughout the age range included in this study. In addition to the foregoing tentative hypothesis, data relevant to boys' and girls' perceptions of the opposite sex will be examined.

Method

The Sociometric Instrument

Gardner and Thompson (1956) have published a series of rating scales that overcome some of the psychometric and psychological deficiencies of the traditional sociometric instrument. Underlying these scales is the assumption that the social desirability of a group depends upon the ability of the group members to satisfy specific social-psychological needs. The problem of comparability of social ratings within groups and between groups is resolved by requiring all Ss to construct a psychological frame of reference by identifying certain anchor points along a broad psychological continuum. The near equal-interval scaling of this continuum is established from a composite of individual ratings by a factionation procedure.

Each group member is asked to consider a specified hypothetical social situation. He is then required to think of the *one* person out of all the individuals he has ever known, including members of his group, who would be the very best individual to have as a partner for the particular activity. To aid the Ss in forming a concept of the *best* individual, a normal distribution curve is provided, with five equal-appearing intervals, set off with sufficient space to write in the appropriate names. The Ss place the name of the best individual in the box marked *most*. A similar procedure is followed for the *least* liked individual. The preferred-most and preferred-least positions define a psychological continuum common to the members within the group and also common to two or more groups. The next step requires the Ss to bisect this continuum into four equal segments by first identifying a *median* individual, and then the individuals who are half-way between the *least* and *median* positions and the *median* and *most* positions. The names, placed at equal intervals along the base line, yield an eight-point scale ranging from slightly above the *least* position to slightly below the *most* position. Ratings of individual group members are made in terms of this reference population by means of a series of forced-choice comparisons.

Separate scales were prepared for each of the two social-psychological needs. To determine the heterosexual social structure for succorance needs, the following hypothetical situation was presented to the Ss: "Sometimes you get into trouble and feel unhappy. It might be that you have been blamed for something you didn't do. Think about some time when you were very unhappy and would have liked to talk over your trouble with some kind and sympathetic person." The heterosexual social structure for the playmirth need was assessed by means of the following hypothetical situation: "Suppose you want to have a party. You especially want to invite someone who is always doing things to make people have a good time and have lots of fun." Ten graduate students, making judgments from a large number of such statements, were in unanimous agreement that these statements represent the needs for succorance and playmirth.

The individual ratings of the group members were recorded on a matrix. An average rating *made* by each individual of his classmates was computed by summing across each row of the matrix for each individual and dividing by $n-1$ to obtain the mean. The average rating *received* by each individual from his classmates was computed by summing down each column of the matrix for each individual and dividing by $n-1$.

Subjects

A total of 387 pupils, 212 girls and 175 boys, in Grades 5 through 12 in a rural community were administered the scales. The majority of these children were from lower-middle income homes. The distributions of sex, age, and intelligence are not unlike those expected in the average public school. The influence of selection due to school dropouts at the upper grade levels was minimal, since somewhat less than 15% had left school for reasons other than transfer.

Procedure

Test booklets with lists of names appropriate for each classroom were distributed. The entire sample was tested on the same day at the end of the sixth month of the school year. Average total testing time was approximately 40 minutes. Student cooperation was excellent.

Reliability indices were computed using two sixth-grade classrooms. Since the stability of sociometric scores has been shown to increase with age, it was not considered necessary to determine reliability beyond Grade 6. Both the need-playmirth and need-succorance scales were readministered two weeks after the initial testing period. Separate indices were determined for ratings given and received. The mean reliability for the ratings made on the need-succorance scales is .76; and for the ratings received, .91. For the ratings made and received on need-playmirth, the corresponding values are .69 and .84.

Results

The hypothesis that a person's perceptions of his own sex are more positive than his perceptions of the opposite sex was tested by comparing the mean ratings made by each sex of their own sex, with the mean ratings made of the opposite sex.[1] Similar analyses were made for both need situations. Since these comparisons involve the same rater making both judgments, the t test for matched pairs was used to determine statistical significance. The results of these analyses show that same-sex social ratings are generally higher regardless of the rater's sex. There are no reversals at any of the grade levels for the need-succorance situation, though there are two reversals for playmirth. These results lend support to the hypothesis that for each sex, persons of the same sex are best able to reduce social needs. They further suggest that sex differences in ability to satisfy social-need strivings are more clear-cut for succorance than for playmirth behavior.

To test for the presence of a developmental trend in the differences between same-sex and opposite-sex ratings, an analysis of variance of the difference scores was carried out. Three of the four analyses failed to show a significant effect. The generally nonsignificant between-grades effect can be interpreted as meaning that there is little change in boys' and girls' perceptions of their opposite-sex classmates' ability to satisfy their social needs. For the playmirth situation, however, the data indicate that girls perceive their male classmates as becoming increasingly more capable of satisfying their needs. The sex difference in the developmental trends for the playmirth situation suggests that beginning around Grade 7, girls shift in their perceptions of boys as social companions, though they maintain a greater preference for girls. Boys do not show a similar shift at any grade level.

An analysis of variance of opposite-sex ratings $(B \times G - G \times B)$ for each need situation revealed a significant grade level $\times$ age interaction for the playmirth situation. This interaction can be interpreted as meaning that the differences between boys' and girls' perceptions of the opposite sex decrease with increasing grade placement. Figure 12.1 shows that the decrease in the differ-

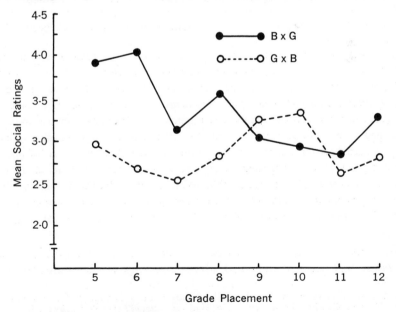

Figure 12.1 Mean opposite-sex ratings of boys and girls on the need-playmirth social situation.

ence scores can be attributed to the increasingly higher ratings of the girls after Grade 7 in contrast to the relatively constant opposite-sex rating made by the boys. The nonsignificant interaction term for the succorance situation can be interpreted as meaning that the same relative distance between the sexes is maintained over the eight grades studied.

Discussion

This study supports the hypothesis that same-sex social interactions are perceived by preadolescent and adolescent children as more reinforcing than social interactions with the opposite sex. The hypothesis that the difference between boys' and girls' perceptions of their own sex and opposite sex remains constant was upheld in the succorance-need ratings of both sexes. The hypothesis was again upheld in the boys' ratings of their own sex and opposite sex for the playmirth situation. However, the girls' ratings in the playmirth situation showed that after Grade 7, girls perceived boys as increasingly more capable of satisfying their playmirth needs although they still prefer female companions.

NOTE

[1] The *mean* made and received same-sex and opposite-sex ratings are redundant. To facilitate communication the data reported in this paper are all in terms of ratings made, i.e., a mean rating made by boys of girls.

Personality Characteristics and Social Acceptability in Adolescence

Raymond G. Kuhlen and Beatrice J. Lee

It is a reasonable assumption that the behavioral traits associated with social acceptability at one age may change considerably at a later age. The "Guess-Who" instrument used in this study by Dr. Kuhlen and Mrs. Lee is a modification of the Moreno sociometric technique. With this instrument it was possible to determine for each child a description of his social behaviors. These descriptions were then examined in terms of each child's level of social acceptability. The basic hypothesis was supported, at least with respect to some of the behavioral items. It was also found that there are consistent differences in personality characteristics among popular as opposed to unpopular children at all grade levels. In general terms, children who are active and outgoing are more likely to gain acceptance among their peers than are children who are highly talkative, bossy, and attention seeking.

It is evident that at any age an acceptable social status is an important requisite for satisfactory personal and social adjustment. Lack of such status frequently

SOURCE: From Raymond G. Kuhlen and Beatrice J. Lee, "Personality Characteristics and Social Acceptability in Adolescence." *Journal of Educational Psychology*, 1943, 34, 321–340. (With permission of authors and the American Psychological Association.)

makes for misery and unhappiness; whereas attainment of status once lacking may produce marked changes in an individual's personality and feelings of well-being. Inasmuch as emerging interest in social relationships, especially hetero-sexual relationships, seems particularly characteristic of adolescence, problems of attaining and maintaining social status may be of greater importance at that age.

The purpose of the present study was to obtain measures of social acceptability at different ages through the adolescent period, and also to get judgments from the associates of the subjects as to their personal characteristics. By examination of these data, it was hoped that some new insights into social development in adolescence might be gained, and some evidence obtained as to what particular personal characteristics are associated with, and hence might conceivably foster, social acceptability at these ages.

Procedure

In obtaining the data two instruments were used. The first, a "Guess Who" test, was used for the purpose of obtaining information regarding the personalities of the children, and contained some forty items asking for nominations of children who fit particular descriptions, such as "Here is someone who is always cheerful, jolly and good-natured, laughs and smiles a good deal." Descriptions were always in pairs representing polar traits. Thus the mate to the above sample item was: "Here is someone who always seems rather sad, worried or unhappy, who hardly ever laughs or smiles." Similar descriptive statements were presented representing the twenty pairs of characteristics listed below:

Restless — Quiet
Talkative — Silent
Active in games — Not active in games
Enjoys jokes — Does not enjoy jokes
Friendly — Not friendly
Sociable — Not sociable

Initiates games and activities — Follows in activities
Enjoys a fight — Does not enjoy a fight
Willing to take a chance — Unwilling to take a chance
Neat — Unkempt

Girl likes opposite sex — Girl avoids opposite sex
Boy likes opposite sex — Boy avoids opposite sex
Enjoys jokes on self — Does not enjoy jokes on self
Acts older than age — Acts younger than age
Seeks attention — Does not seek attention
Popular with others — Unpopular with others
Cheerful and happy — Sad and unhappy
Good-looking — Not good-looking
Enthusiastic — Listless
Always bossing others — Does not mind being bossed

The second instrument, based on Moreno's sociometric technique, was for the purpose of determining social acceptability. This blank contained directions asking each child to indicate first and second choices of companions for: (1) occupying the next seat in the classroom, (2) attending the movies, (3) going for a walk, (4) going skating, (5) making things (as model boats, dresses, etc.), (6) playing outdoor games, (7) playing indoor games, (8) studying school school work, (9) reading for fun. The only restriction was that the choices must be made from the subject's own grade, not necessarily his own classroom. Any individual could be chosen as many times as desired. An "acceptability" score for each individual was arrived at by weighting first choices 2, and second choices 1, and dividing their sum by the number of potential raters. Several mentions of a particular child by the same person received the same weight as an equal number of mentions by different children. As used in this report, "social acceptability" means social acceptability among one's own sex. Scores were determined in this manner, because it was observed that a certain individual might be exceedingly popular with his own sex but be chosen by none of the opposite sex. In other instances, individuals were popular with both sexes. It was deemed better to have the scores mean the same thing in the case of each individual, hence the restriction to popularity among one's own sex.

Subjects

Seven hundred children were studied including over 100 of each sex in each of Grades 6, 9, and 12. The sample included all of the sixth-, ninth-, and twelfth-graders in four centralized schools and the twelfth-graders in two similar schools, all in central New York. The mean ages of the three grade groups, respectively, are: boys 11.9, 14.7, and 17.4; girls 11.6, 14.3, and 17.3.

Results

Personality Characteristics and Social Acceptability

A third aspect of the study has to do with the relationship between personality characteristics and social acceptability. What personality characteristics are the most popular individuals judged to have, and what are deemed to be the characteristics of the least popular? When interpreting the data here presented it should be pointed out that judgments of characteristics were obtained first, and after these papers were collected choices were made as to desirable companions. A reversal of this procedure might have created a greater "halo effect" than probably already exists. Also, it should be remembered that here "social acceptability" means social acceptability among one's own sex.

The plan in this phase of the study was to set up for each sex and grade, groups composed of the 25 per cent most popular and the 25 per cent least popular subjects, and to contrast these extreme groups in terms of the characteristics on which judgments had been obtained. The figures in Tables 12.1 and 12.2 represent, for the two sexes, the percentage of the highly acceptable group and the percentage of the least acceptable group who received some mention by their associates as evidencing various characteristics. Thus, for the sixth

TABLE 12.1. *Changes in Desirability of Various Characteristics at Different Ages through Adolescence, as Shown by the Percentages of Those of Various Grade Groups Who Are Most Acceptable (High) and Those Who Are Least Acceptable (Low) Who Are Judged by Their Associates to Have Various Characteristics — Boys*

TRAIT	Grade VI			Grade IX			Grade XII		
	HIGH	LOW	CR	HIGH	LOW	CR	HIGH	LOW	CR
Restless	32	60	2.1	57	57	.0	46	27	1.5
Talkative	48	52	0.3	57	43	1.1	92	42	4.5
Active in Games	96	20	8.5	77	27	4.5	73	35	3.0
Enjoys Jokes	88	44	3.7	77	30	4.1	92	42	4.5
Friendly	96	4	16.7	90	20	7.7	100	19	10.5
Sociable	64	48	1.2	70	30	3.4	65	31	2.6
Initiates Games and Activities	76	8	6.7	57	7	4.9	96	15	10.1
Enjoys a Fight	60	48	0.9	80	40	3.5	62	46	1.1
Willing to Take a Chance	84	28	4.8	87	30	5.5	92	35	5.3
Neat and Clean	80	12	6.6	73	27	4.1	77	31	3.8
Likes Opposite Sex	52	12	3.4	67	17	4.6	92	27	6.4
Enjoys Joke on Self	80	4	8.5	67	17	4.6	89	27	5.8
Acts Older than Age	32	20	1.0	37	17	1.8	31	27	0.3
Seeks Attention	44	32	.6	43	47	.3	62	35	2.0
Popular with Others	92	4	13.1	93	13	10.4	96	27	7.1
Cheerful and Happy	96	0	24.6	80	27	4.9	100	31	7.6
Good-Looking	84	4	9.6	63	13	4.6	66	12	4.7
Enthusiastic	92	0	17.0	83	7	9.2	100	23	9.3
Bosses Others	24	24	.0	43	40	.3	42	23	1.5
Number of Cases	25	25	—	30	30	—	26	26	—

TABLE 12.2. *Changes in Desirability of Various Characteristics at Different Ages through Adolescence, as Shown by the Percentages of Those of Various Grade Groups Who Are Most Acceptable (High) and Those Who Are Least Acceptable (Low) Who Are Judged by Their Associates to Have Various Characteristics — Girls*

TRAIT	Grade VI			Grade IX			Grade XII		
	HIGH	LOW	CR	HIGH	LOW	CR	HIGH	LOW	CR
Restless	21	52	2.6	13	27	1.3	35	10	2.3
Talkative	38	41	.3	50	27	1.9	52	21	2.6
Active in Games	66	21	3.9	57	17	3.5	59	7	5.2
Enjoys Jokes	59	17	3.6	73	20	4.9	72	7	6.8
Friendly	97	14	11.5	93	27	7.1	93	21	8.0
Sociable	69	21	4.2	80	40	3.5	83	14	7.3
Initiates Games and Activities	76	10	6.8	80	17	6.3	59	7	5.0
Enjoys a Fight	17	28	1.0	13	13	0.0	28	7	2.2
Willing to Take a Chance	76	24	4.6	70	17	3.7	62	17	3.9
Neat and Clean	100	55	4.9	93	33	6.1	83	31	4.7
Likes Opposite Sex	69	17	4.7	67	17	4.6	83	28	5.1
Enjoys Joke on Self	72	7	6.8	60	23	3.1	72	10	6.2
Acts Older than Age	45	28	1.4	57	40	1.3	41	66	1.9
Seeks Attention	31	35	.3	27	30	.3	35	21	1.2
Popular with Others	86	14	8.0	93	13	10.4	90	17	8.0
Cheerful and Happy	83	31	4.7	90	20	7.7	83	21	6.0
Good-Looking	83	10	8.1	80	27	4.9	59	17	3.6
Enthusiastic	90	10	10.0	83	20	6.3	90	21	7.3
Bosses Others	45	45	0.0	40	23	1.4	52	21	2.6
Number of Cases	29	29	—	30	30	—	29	29	—

grade, 32 per cent of the best liked boys and 60 per cent of the least liked were rated as being restless. This difference is 2.1 times its standard error. The remainder of the Tables 12.1 and 12.2 are to be read in similar fashion.

It will be noted that in spite of the few number of cases in the extreme groups, most differences are strikingly large and highly reliable statistically. To use as examples those that show greatest differentiation for both sexes and at all grades, it is apparent that the highly accepted person is one who is judged to be popular with others, to be cheerful and happy, to be enthusiastic, to be friendly, to enjoy jokes, and to initiate games and activities. It is also interesting to note that at all ages those who are highly accepted by their own sex, were judged also to like the opposite sex.

A number of writers have emphasized the importance in adjustment through adolescence of changing values as to what traits are socially important. At one age a person may have those characteristics that make for popularity at that age and be very popular, but a year or more later may show a marked loss in popularity because new traits have assumed importance in the eyes of his age mates — traits which that person may not then possess. Thus age trends, such as are apparent in the present data, may assume considerable importance. Among items showing such trends are "Talkative," "Seeking attention," "Bossing others," and "Restless." Of these the first three do not differentiate between the highly acceptable and those not accepted at the sixth grade, but do differentiate at the twelfth grade. The agreement between the sexes add to the degree of confidence that can be placed in the statistical reliability of these trends. In the case of restlessness, it is noteworthy that a reversal has occurred. At the sixth-grade level a reliably larger proportion of the socially "unaccepted" group were judged to be restless, but by the twelfth-grade level the "popular" group were more often judged to be restless. Again, the same trends are apparent in both sex groups. It would seem from these findings that at the twelfth-grade level, more than at the sixth-grade, the highly accepted adolescent tends to be the active, socially aggressive extrovert.

Other age trends are apparent in the data, though these characteristics differentiate reliably at all ages. For both sexes, good looks seem less markedly associated with acceptability as age increases. For boys, activity in games does not differentiate between the acceptable and those not accepted as well at the twelfth-grade as at the sixth-grade level. On the other hand, liking the opposite sex seems to bear a closer relationship at adolescence than earlier. For girls, enjoying a joke and being sociable are associated with acceptability at all ages, but more clearly in adolescence. Again, the increased importance in adolescence of active social participation and greater social sensitivity, such as responding to humors, is suggested.

There is danger in evaluating findings of this sort that differences will be studied and emphasized at the expense of essential similarities. In order to provide proper perspective, it will be worth while to examine the relative rank of these traits in terms of their association with acceptability. The difference between the percentage of the most acceptable group and the percentage of the least acceptable group who evidenced a trait determined the rank of the trait. When this is done we find that the five traits most highly and least related to acceptability at the sixth- and at the twelfth-grade levels are as follows (the figures in parentheses are computed from Tables 12.1 and 12.2 and indicate differences between percentages for high and low acceptability groups):

Traits Having Highest Association with Acceptability

Boys		Girls	
SIXTH GRADE	TWELFTH GRADE	SIXTH GRADE	TWELFTH GRADE
Cheerful (96)	Friendly (81)	Friendly (83)	Popular (73)
Enthusiastic (92)	Initiates games (81)	Enthusiastic (80)	Friendly (72)
Friendly (92)	Enthusiastic (77)	Good-looking (73)	Enthusiastic (69)
Popular (88)	Cheerful (69)	Popular (72)	Sociable (69)
Good-looking (80)	Popular (69)	Initiates games (66)	Enjoys jokes (65)

Traits Having Lowest (or Negative) Association with Acceptability

Enjoys fight (12)	Seeks attention (27)	Bosses others (0)	Bosses others (31)
Acts older (12)	Restless (19)	Talkative (−3)	Talkative (31)
Seeks attention (12)	Bosses others (17)	Seeks attention (−4)	Restless (25)
Bosses others (0)	Enjoys fight (16)	Enjoys fight (−11)	Enjoys fight (21)
Talkative (−4)	Acts older (4)	Restless (−31)	Seeks attention (14)
Restless (−28)			Acts older (−25)

Similarity in relative importance of various traits at Grades 6 and 12 (also for Grade 9, though not shown) is obvious from the above list. In fact, for boys the five traits highest at the sixth grade are, with one exception, the same for the twelfth grade. "Initiates games" moved from a rank of eight at the sixth to second place at the twelfth grade; "good-looking" dropped from fifth place at the sixth grade to ninth place at the twelfth grade. Among the lowest five traits for boys, the overlap is also decided, only one characteristic, "talkative," being among the lowest five in the sixth but not in the twelfth grade. From next to the bottom at the sixth grade, it had moved up to the middle position by the twelfth. For girls, the similarity at the sixth and twelfth grade among the extremes is also clear. "Initiates games" and "good-looking" have, however, dropped from among the highest five at the sixth grade to ranks of eleventh and thirteenth place (out of nineteen) by the twelfth. "Sociable" and "enjoys jokes" have climbed from ninth and twelfth places, respectively, at sixth grade to among the first five at the twelfth grade.

It will be seen that although "bosses others," "restless," and "seeks attention" are more closely related to acceptability at the twelfth grade than at the sixth, they are, at all ages, among those traits showing least association with acceptability. But in some instances (best shown by "restlessness") the change has been from a negative relationship at the sixth grade to a fair positive relationship at the twelfth, in spite of no great change in rank. Of course, these comments simply illustrate in another fashion trends already pointed out.

Dependence on Adults and Social Acceptability

Helen R. Marshall and Boyd R. McCandless

Social acceptability among preschool children can be viewed in terms of the reinforcement a child provides in social interactions with his peers. These social behaviors are undoubtedly acquired, requiring extensive opportunities to engage in social interactions. Professors Marshall and McCandless offer the hypothesis that dependent children have fewer social interactions with their peers and more social interactions with adults than children who are more independent. Thus it is possible that the dependent child develops social behaviors that are reinforcing to adults but not reinforcing to peers. The results of this study indicate that among preschool children there is a statistically significant negative relationship between dependency on adults and social acceptability among peers. The negative relationship lends support to the notion that dependency on adults generates behaviors which are not viewed positively by peers.

The belief is widely held by those responsible for the guidance of children that extreme dependence upon adults in a nursery school situation indicates that the child has not had his needs met for satisfaction in contacts with adults, particularly his parents. It is also commonly assumed that a warm and satisfactorily dependent relationship with adults (particularly parents) must exist before a child can be secure enough to gain emotional satisfaction from social competence with and acceptance by peers. Sears' position provides some support for these points of view. He has thought of extreme preschool-aged dependency as being possibly due to weaning and feeding frustration in infancy, these having aroused anxiety associated with adults so that adults controlling and manipulating behavior is essential to the child's emotional economy. Dependency is the expression of this controlling behavior.

The opinion is seldom advanced that adult dependency in preschool situations may be due to lack of techniques for relating with peers, without other dynamic determinants. Rarely expressed also is the opinion that extremely gratifying parents may develop habits of dependency in their children (probably reinforced by the same kind of teachers), thus perhaps reducing or precluding the possibility that the children can find equivalent satisfaction with their peers.

SOURCE: Adapted and abridged from Helen R. Marshall and Boyd R. McCandless, "Relationship Between Dependence on Adults and Social Acceptance by Peers." *Child Development,* 1957, 28, 413–419. (With permission of the authors and the Society for Research in Child Development.)

To the authors' knowledge, it has not been established empirically that any relationship, positive or negative, exists between dependence on adults and competence with peers, including acceptance by them. Using the observed number of adult-child interactions as the measure of dependency, this paper asks two questions: (1) Is the degree of preschool children's dependency on adults in free play situations related to their participation with and acceptance by peers? (2) If such a relationship is found, is it affected by the progress of acquaintance in a preschool group from its inception through time?

Subjects and Procedures

Ss constituted two groups in the Laboratory Preschools of the University of Iowa's Child Welfare Research Station. Children were selected for these groups and teachers assigned by regular Station procedures, independently of the present authors. Fathers of all children were engaged in professional or business-managerial occupations. It was the first Station preschool experience for the majority of the children in each group, although three children were members of both groups. One boy of these three was absent from school too often in Group I to be used as a S, leaving 10 girls and 9 boys in Group I (I). School absence also eliminated a girl in Group II (II), leaving as Ss nine girls and 10 boys. Mean CA at the time of beginning observations for I was 4–4 years; II averaged 4–11 years at the beginning of the first of two play observation series (IIA). The two groups were combined into a single sample of 36 Ss for the correlations listed in Table 12.50.1 of this paper, and for these, Group II records and tests were used for the three children belonging to both groups. There was no teacher overlap between groups, and each group was staffed with an experienced head teacher and two graduate teaching assistants. Interactions with other adults (e.g., the present investigators, student observers, graduate assistants, parents) are included in the dependency measures.

The interactions were recorded for two-minute periods in the following categories for both peer and child-adult interactions: (a) Association: apparent mutual awareness of a common activity or interest. (b) Friendly approach or response that is neutral, pleasant, friendly, or helpful. It may be limited to one word or include many words. (c) Conversation: Ss converse in a friendly fashion for one-half minute or more of the two-minute observation time (used for II only). (d) Hostile: verbal or physical approach or response that interferes with the on-going activity of the S is a direct attack, or is judged deliberate "snubbing" withdrawal from some approach of the child or adult.

An adult dependency score was obtained for each child by adding the observed incidence of adult-child interactions, by category or combinations of categories and dividing this sum by the total number of minutes of observation for the child.

For Ss in I, a minimum of 100 minutes of observation per child was obtained over one calendar month. At least 200 minutes of observation — two 100-minute series designed as IIA (earlier) and IIB (later) — were recorded for each S of

II over six calendar weeks. In all observations, Ss were in indoor and outdoor free-play situations offering a wide variety of companions and activities. All pre-school hours and activities were included in the observations except situations where spontaneous social interactions between children were not encouraged or could not develop, such as listening to stories, testing, juice service, or dressing.

Odd-even sampling reliability of dependency scores was computed only for the friendly approach category and its combinations, since zero scores were obtained in the split halves of other categories for many Ss. Odd-even split-half dependency scores for this category and its combinations in IIA had Guttman coefficients of .69 to .72. Sampling reliability over time was computed for two different split-halves. The two 100-minute series of II had the following Guttman coefficients for dependency scores: friendly approach, .65; conversation (for the 14 Ss with scores), .84; association plus friendly approach, .74; association plus friendly approach plus conversation, .77. However, in the split of the first and second 50-minute scores of IIA, friendly approach dependency scores had a Guttman coefficient of only .16. Sampling reliability of dependency scores, then, is low to moderate, where high sampling reliability was obtained for peer interaction scores. These latter ranged from .80 to .95 in all splits of observation records.

Four measures of peer social acceptance and participation were used in this investigation: (a) Sociometric score, obtained from verbal choices of Ss, Mc-Candless and Marshall (1957). The scores in Table 12.3 were obtained from choices during the fourth of a series of four test periods for I and the third of three for II. ((b) Teacher judgment (of social status) score. The score used in Table 12.3 was obtained from judgments of teachers made at the same time that the sociometric choices were obtained. (c) Observed social acceptance score or, roughly, the sum of the number of children for whom the S was observed to be one of three peers played with most frequently in I and IIB records. (d) Peer interaction score for single and combined categories of observed inter-action. Limited to social interactions with other children, this score was obtained in the same way as the dependency score and is a measure of degree and kind of social participation with peers. For Table 12.3 analyses, scores from obser-vation records of I and IIB were used.

Results

1. Is the degree of preschool children's dependency on adults in free play situations related to measures of social acceptance by and interaction with peers?

Table 12.3 gives product-moment and biserial correlation coefficients obtained between dependency scores and measures of social acceptance and participation for the sample of 36 Ss. All but two of the 35 coefficient are negative, 15 of them being significant at the $p = .05$ or less level. When the same correlations were computed for each group separately, a similar consistency in negative direction and size of coefficients was obtained for both I and IIB. The consistency of direction and frequency of significance of these relationships indi-

TABLE 12.3. *Correlation Coefficients for Adult Dependency Scores and Peer Acceptance or Participation Scores for Sample of 36 Ss*

PEER ACCEPTANCE OR PARTICIPATION SCORES	ADULT DEPENDENCY SCORES‡				
	A		FA	A + FA	H
	r_{bis}	r†	r	r	r_{bis}§
Sociometric Scores	−.59*	−.27	−.26	−.32	−.51*
Teacher Judgment Scores	−.50*	−.21	−.39*	−.40*	−.23
Observed Social Acceptance Scores	−.13	−.25	−.49**	−.45**	−.09
Peer Interaction Scores:‡					
A	−.40	−.23	−.42*	−.45**	−.15
FA	−.54*	−.37	−.64**	−.67**	−.24
H	−.09	.16	−.11	−.07	.19
A + FA	−.50*	−.32	−.56**	−.59**	−.21

* r or r_{bis} is significant at $< .05$ level.
** r is significant at $< .01$ level.
† $N = 30$.
‡ Observation category letters are abbreviations for names of the categories, as follows:
  A = Association; FA = Friendly Approach; H = Hostile.
§ 11 Ss had zero scores in the hostile "dependency" category.

cates that dependence on adults in the preschool situation accompanies relatively low social status and group participation.

The practical importance of the significant negative correlations between dependency and the categories of association (A) and friendly approach (FA) is pointed up when it is noted the A + FA make up 86 per cent of all the observed peer social interactions of these children, A composing 36 per cent, FA 50 per cent.

The negative relation between children's sociometric scores and dependency scores differed significantly from zero for the biserial coefficients of association and hostile dependency scores, as shown in Table 12.3. All dependency scores except those for the hostile category correlated negatively and significantly with teacher judgments of social status. Observed social acceptance scores correlated significantly with dependency scores in the friendly approach category and the additive combination of categories. In general, then, negative relations were found to exist between dependency scores, and each of these three measures of social acceptance obtained after several weeks of acquaintance.

The negative relationship between dependency scores and degree of social participation with peers was most marked for the correlations of the friendly approach category peer interaction scores. This category of peer interaction scores was related negatively and significantly to all dependency scores except those of the hostile category. The product-moment rs were the largest in size of any obtained for the total sample. For the friendly approach dependency scores, the r obtained with the same category of peer interaction scores differed significantly from the rs obtained with association (.02 level) and hostile (.01 level) peer interaction scores. Hostile peer interaction scores appear to be unrelated to either friendly or hostile dependence on adults.

The conversation category of interactions with adults was recorded only in observations for II. In IIB, conversation dependency scores correlated negatively and significantly with friendly approach ($r = -.50$) and A + FA ($r = -.49$) peer interaction scores. However, the correlations with the three measures of social acceptance were not significant ($rs = -.39$ to $-.45$). Conversation peer interaction scores correlated significantly with association dependency scores ($r_{bis} = -.52$) and with the combination dependency score ($r = -.52$).

2. Is there any indication that the degree of a child's dependence on adults and its relation to other scores change as acquaintance progresses in a newly formed preschool group?

The 100 minutes of observation records of series IIA were collected for the 19 Ss in the initial three to four weeks of the group's existence. The product-moment correlation coefficients between friendly dependency scores, and other measures taken during this series, are neither significant nor consistent in direction. The only correlations approaching significance are positive relations between dependency scores and hostile peer interaction scores; these correlations hovered around zero in Observation Series IIB. These data, considered in conjunction with the data presented in the previous section, suggest that negative relations between dependence on adults and measures of social status and participation with children may come to exist only after a period of several weeks' acquaintance in a preschool group.

Additional evidence of a change in dependence on adults is furnished by test of differences in dependency scores obtained in the IIA and IIB observation series. The mean differences in scores were significant beyond the .001 level by two-tailed t tests for all categories, although the direction of the difference was not the same for all categories. Friendly approach and the additive combination dependency scores were larger in IIA than in IIB, while conservation dependency scores were higher in IIB.

Zero scores in the dependency categories of association and hostile prohibited treatment as continuous variables. Twelve Ss had no association interaction with adults in IIA, but only four Ss had zero association dependency scores in IIB. Hostile "dependency" interactions were recorded for 7 children in IIA and for 11 children in IIB.

Age, Intelligence, and Sex in the Conformity Behavior of Negro and White Children

Ira Iscoe, Martha Williams, and Jerry Harvey

Conformity behavior refers to the tendency of human beings to make responses that are compatible with those of the group but incompatible with the situation. In the laboratory, it is possible to create a situation in which the subject is exposed to information concerning the responses made by members of his group and where this information is incompatible with the reality of the situation. Such a laboratory situation was developed by Professor Iscoe and his colleagues. Comparisons of Negro and white and male and female were made at each of four age levels. The older children evidenced the least conforming behavior and the Negro female group was less conforming than the white female group. Negro males and white males were about equally conforming. It is suggested that the racial difference in conformity among females relates to different cultural expectations.

In a previous study by Iscoe, Williams, and Harvey (1963), the modification of children's judgments by a simulated group technique was investigated. The sample consisted of rural and urban white children at the ages of 7, 9, 12, and 15 years. In general, with the criterion measure used, females were found to be more conforming than males, and the relation of conformity with age was curvilinear. It was concluded that the criterion of conformity employed was a problem in this type of research and that different criteria could lead to differing interpretations of the relation between conformity and other variables. There is a need for the assessment of conformity behavior in relation to such basic variables as sex, age, and IQ using different criterion measures. Furthermore, even if a significant relation were established between conformity and a variable such as sex, this is no indication of its value for predicting such behavior. The same may be said for other commonly employed variables and certainly holds for studies in which a number of variables are employed. The present conformity study was designed to obtain an estimate of the amount of variance attributable to age, sex, race, and IQ separately and in simple interaction. A technique of multiple regression analysis was employed which permitted this determination as well as an estimate of the proportion of variance contributed by these variables to any one of several criterion measures.

SOURCE: Adapted and abridged from Ira Iscoe, Martha Williams, and Jerry Harvey, "Age, Intelligence, and Sex as Variables in the Conformity Behavior of Negro and White Children." *Child Development,* 1964, 46, 451–460. (With permission of the authors and the Society for Research in Child Development.)

Method

Subjects

Ss were obtained from segregated public schools in an urban location. Half of the Ss were Negro and half were white. Of the 128 Ss in each racial group, there were 64 males and 64 females. These were further subdivided equally into four age groupings, 7, 9, 12, and 15 years. Data on the 128 white Ss had been obtained as part of a previous study by Iscoe, Williams, and Harvey (1963). In that study rural and urban children were tested. Only the data of the 128 urban Ss were analyzed in this study in relation to data on Negro Ss who were from the same urban locale. All Ss were tested in their own school settings. Experimenter, test, and method of presentation were identical for the two racial groups. White Ss were about equally divided between lower middle class and the upper level of the lower class. It is difficult to ascertain with any precision the socioeconomic level of the Negro Ss. They are best described as coming from the lower classes. The mean family income was certainly well below that of the white Ss. The fathers performed mostly unskilled labor. Working mothers coupled with father absence was a common feature.

Procedure

The general procedure for this study has already been described by Iscoe, Williams, and Harvey (1963). Briefly, each S was first tested in an "Alone" condition in which no conformity pressures were operating. This situation provided a measure of S's initial ability to perform the task (the counting of metronome clicks delivered via earphones at the rate of 100 per minute). In the Alone and later in the "Group" condition each S responded when a light flashed in his booth. In the Group condition before the signal light flashed, each S heard what he believed to be the voices of the other three Ss, who had been brought into the room at the same time and seated in other booths. What the S actually heard was the prerecorded responses of children of the same age, sex, and race as himself. All of the Ss heard the taped voices at the same time and responded simultaneously since lights flashed in all four booths after the third taped voice had given an estimate of the number of metronome clicks delivered over the communication network. In the Alone condition (no group pressures operating) Ss listened to a series of metronome clicks. There were 12 trials in all, the number of clicks varying from 5 to 38 per trial. In the group condition there were 24 trials, 12 of which were "critical trials," that is, the simulated background gave a uniformly incorrect response varying 1, 2, or 3 clicks from the number actually presented. On the other 12 trials randomly interspersed in the group condition, the background voices responded by reporting the actual number of clicks presented. In the running of hundreds of Ss virtually no detection of the simulation has been noted.

Measures

The previous study by Iscoe, Williams, and Harvey (1963) indicated that different criterion scores might yield conflicting interpretation of the relation between conformity and other significant variables. Therefore two different criterion scores were employed and compared in the present study.

Criterion score 1. This measure was the number of times out of a possible 12 a S "conformed" by agreeing with the incorrect number of clicks reported by the three preceding (and prerecorded) voices. Level of performance in the Alone condition was not taken into account. This measure is the one that is most commonly employed in studies of conformity or yielding behavior.

Criterion score 2. This measure took into account the S's initial ability in performing the task. The measure was therefore an adjusted score wherein the number of errors made in the Alone condition was compared with the number made in the "Group, background incorrect" condition. Thus, if a S made three counting errors on the 12 Alone trials and six counting errors on the 12 trials in which there was an incorrect background, his score was 3. Errors in this sense included not only responses which agreed with the incorrect background but also other kinds of errors as well, such as "no response" errors. The rationale was that any increase in number of errors (regardless of the type of error) from the Alone to the Group condition could be attributed to the effect of the incorrect background.

Technique of Analysis

A computer-programmed iterative technique for multiple regression analysis was employed. This model permits an estimate of the contribution to total variance made by the variables employed and enables evaluation of the variables by means of the *F* statistic. It is superior to the usual analysis of variance procedure in that the obtaining of a highly significant *F* via analysis of variance does not reveal the degree to which a variable or indeed the whole set of variables may be employed as a predictor of the behavior measured.

In the present study, analysis was based on an intercorrelation matrix of 73 predictor variables and two criterion scores. The 73 predictor variables included the four "main effect" variables of sex (male, female), age (7, 9, 12, and 15 years), race (white, Negro), and IQ (80 and below, 81–100, 101–120, 121 and above, and no information). It should be noted that in the 73 predictor variable system some variables are subsets of others, and thus all 73 variables were not linearly independent. The actual number of independent predictors was 36. The 73 variable predictor system included the main effects and second order interactions.

An iterative technique for multiple regression analysis, programmed for the IBM 1604 computer, was used to treat the data in the intercorrelation matrix. Regression analysis enables the investigator to estimate the proportion of criterion variance that can be accounted for by the complete system of predictor variables or by portions of that system. One can obtain R^2 values for both complete and restricted prediction systems, and the difference between these R^2 values may be interpreted as an estimate of how much more criterion variance could be explained if the omitted variables were included in the prediction system. The estimate of the contributions of omitted variables may be evaluated by means of the F statistic. The F values obtained would be identical to those derived by the standard analysis of variance procedure.

Results

The correlation between criterion scores was .76 and suggests similarities in what the two criterion scores measure; however, it will be shown that in some instances the two criteria yield different interpretations.

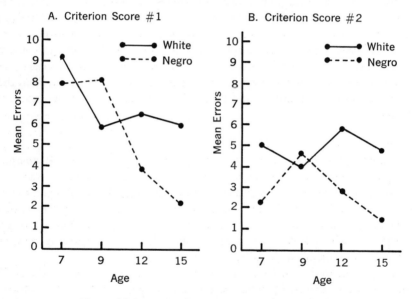

Figure 12.2   Relation of age and race to conformity.

Sex as a Factor in Conformity

Although sex was not significant, in itself, as a variable, a significant sex $\times$ race interaction was obtained. This relation is illustrated graphically in Figure 12.2. While white and Negro males were similar in conformity behavior, Negro females conformed less than white females. In a previous study by Iscoe, Williams, and Harvey (1963) of white children, girls conformed significantly more than boys. The opposite findings for females in the two racial groups in this study resulted in negating sex as a significant main effect variable.

Relation of Age to Conformity

Age is a highly significant factor. Employing Criterion 1, it would appear that conformity in our Ss is a decreasing function of age. Criterion 2 suggests that the relation is curvilinear for the ages studied. This latter finding is in keeping with previous results by Iscoe, Williams, and Harvey (1963) and illustrates the possibility of contradictory findings in studies of conformity unless various criterion scores are clearly specified and compared.

The significant age $\times$ race interaction is presented in Figure 12.2. Whereas white children increase in conformity behavior from 9 to 12 years and then decrease somewhat at age 15, the Negro children show a progressive decrease in conformity behavior after the age of 9. No other interaction including age was significant.

Comparison of Conformity Behavior of Negro and White Children

The statistical analysis for race indicates that Negroes conform less than whites. This was found regardless of the criterion used. Thus, on criterion 1 the average for whites is 6.9 and for Negroes it is 5.6; on criterion 2 the corresponding figures are 4.9 and 2.9 This difference, however, appears to be largely due to the difference between white and Negro females, for the males of both races are very similar (see Figure 12.2).

Significant interactions including race have already been discussed except for the one IQ $\times$ race interaction (Criterion Score 1). In regard to this interaction, significant at the .05 level, it should first be noted that IQ, in itself, was not a significant variable. It is difficult to interpret the race $\times$ IQ interaction. The IQ measure was the California Mental Maturity Test. The interaction appears mainly to be due to the differential behavior of Negroes and whites below 80 IQ. In this range Negro children conformed much less than did whites. However, the small number of Ss of both races within this range limits our interpretation. In the IQ ranges of 80 and above there appeared to be, as in previous studies, the suggestion of decreasing conformity behavior with increasing intelligence for both races.

Contribution of Predictor Variables

The use of regression analysis, it will be recalled, permits an examination of the effects of adding or deleting variables in terms of their contribution to prediction of a criterion. Considering all of the variables of the prediction system (age, race, sex, and IQ, and simple interactions) accounts for approximately 36 per cent of the total variance in Criterion 1, and 26 per cent in the case of Criterion 2. The main effects themselves account for roughly 19 per cent and 12 per cent, respectively, depending on the criterion score employed. Respectively deleting sex, age, race, and IQ information, it was found that the prediction system was significantly lowered as to predictive efficiency in two cases, that of age and race. It appears that age and race were two main effect variables which significantly contributed to prediction. For Criterion 1, omitting information about age from the prediction system lowered the R^2 from approximately 19 per cent to 12 per cent, which is a significant loss. The omission of race information likewise produced a significant loss. For Criterion 1 the reduction was from approximately 19 per cent to 16 per cent, and for Criterion 2, from 12 per cent to 4 per cent. The race variable became more important in the prediction system when an adjusted measure taking into account initial performance was employed (Criterion 2). Omission of sex or IQ information did not significantly reduce predictive efficiency.

The predictive efficiency gained by taking into account information supplied by simple interactions indicates that such information was quite important. The total system yielded R^2s of approximately 36 per cent (Criterion 1) and 26 per cent (Criterion 2). Deleting information contributed by simple interactions lowered predictive efficiency to approximately 19 per cent (Criterion 1) and 12 per cent (Criterion 2).

The added predictive efficiency gained by including various interactions to the "main effect" information will now be examined. The age $\times$ race information raised the R^2 value for Criterion 1 from approximately 19 per cent to 26 per cent, the greatest increase produced by inclusion of any second order interaction information. For Criterion 2 the sex $\times$ race information included in the prediction system produced the greatest increase, from approximately 12 per cent to 17 per cent, in the value of R^2.

Even when using all 73 variables as predictors, the amount of variance accounted for by this system was not great. About one third of the variance (Criterion 1) could be accounted for by knowledge of the sex, age, race, and IQ of the Ss, including simple interactions of these variables. It is important, however, to take into consideration this type of information when attempting to study conformity behavior.

Discussion

The relatively high correlation between criterion scores suggests that both criteria reflect the same behavior, namely, the tendency to yield to social pressures. These results are consistent with those reported by Blake, Helson, and Mouton (1956) with adults who report that conformity to an objective stimulus (the metronome task) is unrelated to initial ability to perform the task. Similar results have also been reported by Iscoe and Williams (1963) with children. Nonetheless, the criterion for conformity employed may be of importance when the investigators wish to determine whether the yielding behavior is a function of the group pressures rather than the inability of Ss to perform the experimental task. This is especially pertinent in developmental studies. Conformity on the part of a 7-year-old child, according to Criterion Score 1, is much greater than for the 12-year-old child. However, the underlying mechanisms may be different. The younger child may be conforming (or yielding) either because he is unable to perform the task or is unsure of the answer, whereas the 12-year-old, competent to perform the counting task, may be more sensitive to peer group pressures and yield to them. The importance of controlling for "initial competency" in research on conformity and yielding behavior has been most recently emphasized by League and Jackson (1964), who report that low self-esteem Ss (adults) under Alone conditions made significantly more counting errors than did high self-esteem Ss. In studies with children, designed to investigate the interplay of personality measures with conformity behavior, this factor should certainly be stressed. Although a relatively simple task such as the counting of metronome clicks allows for the assessment of initial ability, complications arise with such questions as the changing of attitudes or opinions via group pressure techniques.

The finding that the Negro females were less conforming than the white females can best be explained by an examination of the sex role expectancies and child-rearing practices of the two racial groups. According to Dai (1952), the father in a Negro culture is frequently absent from the home and the mother is the chief source of authority. Although there is not sufficient research to bear out this contention, behavioral scientists familiar with the Negro culture in the South generally agree that a Negro girl can get away with nonconformity more than can a white girl. The same holds true in terms of relationships between Negroes and whites. Negro females are much more independent in dealing with members of the white culture than are Negro men. White females, on the other hand, are instructed early into the virtues of conformity and "getting along." They lack, by and large, the competitiveness frequently exhibited in Negro females. Whether or not the above is sufficient explanation of the findings remains for further research.

The finding that the full model employed in this study explained approximately 36 per cent of the variance points again to the great complexity of conformity behavior and its prediction. Obviously, personality variables have to be considered in future studies of this kind. Prediction systems including information about various facets of personality, child-rearing practices of parents, classroom behavior, field independence and dependence, and the like would be extremely valuable. Personality measures, particularly, lend themselves most conveniently to the type of analysis employed in the present study.

CHAPTER XIII

The Family

GUIDING the development of a child's attitudes, values, and social behaviors is called the socialization process. This process is universal among human beings, and it is through socialization that cultures maintain continuity. Institutions such as schools and churches contribute to the socialization process as well as the child's peers, the various communication media, and his family. Because the family is almost exclusively involved in the formation of attitudes, behaviors, and values during the first five years of life, it is considered to be the most important of all influences on socialization. However, understanding of the parental role in child socialization has proven difficult for the following reasons:

1. There is no comprehensive theory of parent-child relationships which is sufficiently well defined to allow for the development of precise measurement techniques.

2. A large proportion of published reports are based on the results of parental interviews, a technique which depends upon the integrity and intelligence of the respondents.

3. Gaining access to other than upper-middle-class families has proved difficult and has, therefore, led to restricted conclusions.

4. There has been a tendency to assume that children arrive in a family *tabula rosa* and that variations in social behaviors are exclusively attributable to variations in parent-child relationships. The impact of the child's behavioral predispositions on parental child-rearing practices have been largely ignored.

Despite these difficulties, and because of the ingenuity of many investigators, some understanding of the complexities of the socialization process are beginning to emerge. Dr. Johnson, for example, proposes an especially unique hypothesis when she asserts that fathers play the most important role in defining sex-appropriate behaviors not only for their sons but for their daughters as well. The previous assumption that fathers influenced their sons while mothers influenced their daughters has not been strongly supported with respect to the mother-daughter relationship. Lesser shows, however, that mothers' attitudes do play a role at least with respect to aggression.

The investigation by Siegel and Kohn shows the effects of permissive handling of child aggression in a subsequent social situation. The results suggest that permissiveness does, in fact, lead to internalization of adult standards — a finding which should be of considerable interest to the numerous critics of permissive child-rearing methods.

The study by Brown, Morrison, and Couch examines the influence of familial affection on a number of variables that are typically grouped under the rubric of character. Although the magnitude of the resulting correlations are modest, it is possible to conclude that warm family relationships contribute positively to character development. A more detailed analysis of the affectional ties is now necessary in order to understand how familial affection influences character development.

Professor Harris and his colleagues cast serious doubt on the timeworn practice of giving children chores in order to develop in them a sense of responsibility. In all likelihood future research will create doubts about other currently accepted child-rearing practices. The fact is that the forces that interact in the development of an individual are much too complex to be explained by a single practice.

Sex Role Learning in the Nuclear Family

Miriam M. Johnson

In this theoretical analysis, the author offers a hypothesis that she believes integrates the diverse findings related to the sex role learning of children. Essentially, Dr. Johnson argues that the father is the more crucial parent in developing appropriate sex role behavior for both sons and daughters. Heretofore, it was assumed, largely on the basis of Freudian theory, that the father was crucial in the development of behaviors appropriate to the male role for his son, while the mother was crucial in the development of female behaviors in the case of the daughter. As Dr. Johnson indicates in this paper, the research evidence supports the former assumption but not the latter. Dr. Johnson contends that studies should focus on father-daughter relationships because fathers differentiate sex roles for sons and daughters to a greater degree than do mothers.

In his article, "Freudian Theories of Identification and Their Derivatives," Bronfenbrenner (1960) ends his excellent analysis and codification of identification theories with the injunction that what we need is not more theory but more empirical research. He states that elaborate theoretical explanations of assumed phenomena have been made but that in reality "very little is known about the extent of variation in the behavior of fathers and mothers towards sons and

SOURCE: Adapted and abridged from Miriam M. Johnson, "Sex Role Learning in the Nuclear Family." *Child Development*, 1963, 34, 319–333. (With permission of the author and the Society for Research in Child Development.)

daughters, and even less about the possible effects of such differential treatment." We would argue that "very little is known" about parental behavior and identification processes, not because there are no data, but because there is no adequate theoretical explanation to which existing findings can be assimilated and thereby become "known." It is the purpose of this paper to attempt to make theoretical sense out of already available findings, many of which appear anomalous from the standpoint of current orthodoxy, by proposing some simple, but we think crucial, modifications in Freudian and post-Freudian identification theory.

Theoretical Proposal

Basically, our major proposition is a simple one: we suggest that it is identification with the *father*, in the sense of internalizing a reciprocal role relationship with the father, which is crucial for producing appropriate sex role orientations in *both* males and females. In order to see how women might learn their sex role by identifying with the cross-sex parent, it is necessary to define identification, following Parsons (1958), as the internalization, not of a total personality or of personality traits, but of a reciprocal role relationship that is functional at a particular period in the child's development. As Parsons puts it:

> Only in a very qualified sense can one say that an infant learns to be like his mother. Rather, he learns to play a social role in interaction with her; his behavior — hence his motivation — is organized according to a generalized pattern of norms which define shared and internalized meanings of the acts occurring on both sides.

If one takes this view of identification, it becomes possible to postulate, as Parsons does, that the development of personality in the child involves his making a series of successive identifications with increasingly specialized and differentiated social roles. We assume, following both Parsons (1958) and Mowrer (1950), that both boys and girls identify initially with the mother but that this identification is not sex typed. The possibility we are suggesting is that it is the next identification, with the father, coming after the stage of infantile dependency on the mother, which is crucial for appropriate sex role learning in females as well as in males. Obviously, if girls are to become feminine and boys masculine, the nature of this reciprocal role relationship with the father must be different for each sex. We shall cite evidence later to show that the father does differentiate his role toward opposite-sexed children whereas the mother does not.

It is generally assumed, once the Oedipal stage is reached and beyond, that the father takes a less demanding and more "appreciative" attitude toward his daughter than toward his son, playing husband to the girl and mentor to the boy. What has not been generally accepted, however, although the empirical evidence for this too definitely exists, is that the mother does not make a distinction symmetrical to the father's. Although the mother does share common cultural values with the father about what is appropriate masculine and feminine behavior, and may assign tasks, for instance, on a sex typed basis, there is considerable evidence that she does not make a basic differentiation in her attitude toward male and female children. She neither plays wife to her son nor does she urge her daughter to "buck up and get in there and be a woman," rather she thinks of both sexes as "children" whom she treats in the light of her general nurturant and supportive role in the family.

Our theoretical reasons for expecting the father to differentiate his role along the aforementioned lines, while the mother does not, rest on certain considerations about the nature of masculinity and femininity. We think that the crux of this multifaceted differentiation is best captured by Parsons' instrumental-expressive distinction. The expressive role player is oriented toward the relationships among the actors within a system. He is primarily oriented to the attitudes and feelings of these actors toward himself and toward each other. The instrumental role player, by contrast, is oriented toward actively securing a favorable relation between the system and its environment. If we take the family as a whole as the relevant system, the mother is the expressive leader, responsible for the care of individual family members; the father is the instrumental leader, primarily responsible for providing for his family as a unit in the environment.

Motivational Requirements for Expressive and Instrumental Action

Expressiveness is characterized by an orientation toward "pleasing" in the specific sense of receiving rewarding responses from others by virtue of giving them rewarding responses.[1] For example, by being solicitous, appealing, and "understanding," a woman seeks to get a pleasurable response by giving pleasure. Theoretically, then, it seems appropriate that expressiveness, a direct sensitivity and responsiveness to the attitudes of others, should be learned through reciprocal interaction with an expressive partner in a relatively permissive context of mutual gratification.

An instrumental role player, almost by definition, cannot be *primarily* oriented to the positive and negative emotional reactions of others to him in the immediate interactional situation because his orientation involves a disciplined pursuit of goals that transcend this situation. In short, he is disposed to view the interaction as a means to an end. He must resist pressures to become affectively involved in the immediate situation itself. Certainly as Bales suggests (Parsons and Bales, 1955), one major attitudinal requisite of instrumental action would seem to be the ability "to take" the hostile reactions from others which such action is likely to generate. It seems highly unlikely that one could be masculine with the unselfconscious, self-sustaining determination required by instrumentality in order to "please" or be loved. As Arnold Green (1946) argues in his classic article, "The Middle-Class Male Child and Neurosis," the male child when made too dependent upon parental love cannot function adequately and aggressively in his peer relations even though his parents expect it of him. Bronfenbrenner's findings (1961) in an exploratory study of 400 tenth grade students have led him to the same conclusion. He suggests that: ". . . Love-oriented socialization techniques

. . . while fostering the internalization of adult standards and the development of socialized behavior, may also have the effect of undermining capacities for initiative and independence particularly in boys."

Propitiation and accommodation in order to get love and masculinity in the sense we define it would seem to be incompatible motivational systems. It would therefore seem more appropriate that an instrumental orientation be inculcated by one who bases his demands, not on love, but on objective punishment or deprivation. This view finds recent empirical confirmation in the studies of child-rearing reported by Sears, Maccoby, and Levin (1957), and by Miller and Swanson (1960). Both studies report, "love oriented" techniques seem to produce guilt while physical punishment, threats, and withdrawal of tangible privileges are likely to produce outward aggression in the child.[2]

Male socialization, we think, requires a distinctive "push" into instrumentality that female socialization does not require. A recognition of the difference in the kinds of reinforcement required for the two roles is even reflected in our everyday speech. One never says to a girl, "Screw up your courage and act like a woman," neither do the women's branches of the armed services promise that their discipline will "make a woman out of you." To males one says, "Try to be a man"; to females one simply says, "Be a woman."

Mechanisms of Internalization

It seems fairly clear that the mechanism we have deduced to be appropriate to instrumental learning is closely akin to Freud's "castration fear" or, more generally, fear of overt aggression. On the other hand, the mechanism we think appropriate to expressive learning (love reciprocity) is not quite the same thing as Freud's "anaclitic identification" or fear of loss of love. We think that there are actually three mechanisms which operate, only two of which — fear of aggression and love reciprocity — are specifically relevant to sex role learning. It would seem that "fear of loss of love" is the mechanism most appropriate to the initial, asexual (although expressive) identification made by children of both sexes with the mother. In this first identification children learn to get love rewards from the mother by pleasing her, by being "good" children. It seems likely that it is in this asexual love relationship with the mother, where the child is in a situation of maximum dependency on the rule giver, that the primary superego is formed. It has always appeared unlikely that the presence or absence of conscience should be a sex-linked characteristic. If superego formation, induced by fear of loss of mother's love,[3] *preceded* sex role identification, however, this disturbing conclusion need not arise.

The mechanisms which we think appropriate to the learning of specifically masculine and feminine orientations, then, do not directly involve "fear of loss of love." For the boy "fear of overt punishment" and positively a desire for "respect" would seem to be conducive to an instrumental orientation, and for the girl "love reciprocity" would produce mature expressiveness. In this "love reciprocity" relationship the girl is motivated by the positive desire to get love by giving love, which we think is the defining attribute of femininity.

The Father's Role

To argue that the mechanisms for learning masculine and feminine orientations must be fundamentally different does not directly support the conclusion that it is the father who manipulates these mechanisms for both sexes. This conclusion does seem justified, however, if we take into account the proposition that both sexes in order to "grow up" must become emancipated from their infantile love-dependency relationship with the mother. The father as the instrumental leader of the family as a whole represents the outside world to his children. It would seem strikingly appropriate from a psychological standpoint that the parental figure representing independence be the parent responsible for sex role learning, because it seems clear that sex role internalization should take place in a context of at least relative emancipation from infantile dependency.

This view finds support in the conclusions of Helene Deutsch (1944), a psychoanalyst. On the basis of her clinical experience with women, she says:

> As the child with gradually increasing intensity turns away from the mother and childhood dependencies in favor of active adjustment to reality, this reality is represented more and more by the father — and this is true of both boys and girls.

Contrary to our previous views, the girl's first turn toward the father has an active, not a passive character, and her passive attitude is only a secondary development.

It should be made explicit that we think the mother does play a part in her children's sex role learning. She does it, however, we suggest, in her role as mother in the family rather than by differentiating her role in the mother-daughter and mother-son subsystems of the family. If she loves her husband and defines him to the children as a worthy person, then this should enormously facilitate the success of the father in emancipating the children from the mother and in determining their sex-relevant orientations. In line with this, Helper (1955) reports that males and females are more likely to describe themselves as similar to the father if the mother approves of him as a model.

Expressive Components in Both Sexes

In their early exclusive attachment to the mother, we think that both males and females learn expressive behavior. The task of the girl, then, is to shift her expressive attachment from the mother to a more mature expressive attachment to an adult male. The task of the boy is to shift his expressive attachment to an adult female and also to learn an entirely different orientation, instrumentalness, to be capable of acting effectively upon the nonfamilial environment.

A closely related conclusion is that the masculine personality has two components while the feminine personality basically has only one. The male must be instrumental but also capable of expressiveness, while the female need only be expressive. This conclusion was arrived at on empirical grounds quite independently by Bennett and Cohen (1959) in a study of sex differences on a large adult sample using the Polydiagnostic Index. They state:

> Elements of the self-concept which are rather intense for both groups appear to be those elements which are more important to females than to males. . . . This tentatively suggests the possibility that the female self-concept is the more clearly established one and that elements of this female self-concept are those which it is possible for both men and women to feel strongly.

They also remark on the basis of their data that "masculinity is a feeling recognized more by its absence in women than by its presence in men."

In summary then we have argued theoretically for the following view of identification processes: The mother is predominantly expressive toward children of both sexes and uses, intentionally or not, "love oriented" techniques of control on both. It is in this first identification of both male and female children with the mother in a love-dependency relationship that the basic superego is laid down. Sex role differentiation then follows the initial mother identification and results from the identification of both sexes with the father in differentiated role relationships. The father adds the specifically feminine element to the female's initial expressiveness by rewarding her, by his appreciative attitude, not simply for being "good" but for being "attractive." With his son as with his daughter the father is solidary, but with his son he is also demanding, thus giving the extra push that instrumentalness requires.

NOTES

[1] When applying the expressive-instrumental distinction to a concrete situation, it is necessary to state the interactive system with which one is concerned. A mother may find it necessary to displease one family member (e.g., punish a child who refuses to share) in the interest of harmonious relations in the family as a whole. The proper classification of this act depends on which interactive system one focuses upon.

[2] It may be important to maintain a distinction between "guilt" and "resistance to temptation." Burton, Maccoby, and Allinsmith (1961) have some evidence that the two are negatively correlated and are not produced by the same conditions. Our concern here is with "guilt," and the Burton study offers further confirmation of the Sears, Maccoby, and Levin (1957) findings with respect to the positive relation between "love oriented" techniques and "guilt."

[3] Actually the technique used is probably not of primary importance in this first identification. At this undifferentiated stage, "mother" means "love" to the child, and hence almost any negative reaction on the part of the mother is likely to mean "loss of love" to the child.

Overt and Fantasy Aggression as a Function of Maternal Response to Aggression

Gerald S. Lesser

A hydraulic model of personality assumes that if an emotional reaction is not expressed overtly there will be a residual build-up of tension in the personality system. In the case of emotion, the child who is punished for overt manifestations of anger may be able to find relief only in terms of covert behavior. In this case one would expect that the correlation between a measure of overt aggression and a measure of covert aggression would be in a negative direction. In the case where the parents do not punish overt manifestations of aggression, one might expect a significant positive correlation between measures of overt and covert aggression. This study by Dr. Lesser of Harvard University confirms both hypotheses.

In recent years, a voluminous literature has developed around the problem of establishing relationships between fantasy behavior and overt behavior. Different researchers have used different drive areas, different populations, different theoretical bases, and different methods of measurement. The most conspicuous conclusion is that the empirical findings are not in agreement.

The importance of this area of investigation for both clinical practice and personality theory has been elaborated by Lindzey (1952). He concludes that one of the most important and difficult problems is the "determination of the conditions under which inferences based upon projective material directly relate to overt behavior and the conditions of the reverse." The present study concerns the differential conditions under which aggressive behavior is learned that may allow prediction of how aggressive expressions in fantasy are related to those in overt behavior.

The present study seeks to examine the comparative consequences of both encouragement and discouragement of aggression through the hypothesis that under conditions of maternal encouragement of aggression a greater degree of correspondence exists between fantasy and overt aggression of children than under conditions of maternal discouragement of aggression.

Method

Subjects

The subjects (Ss) were 44 white boys (ages 10–0 to 13–2 years) and their mothers. The boys were drawn from one fifth grade and two sixth grades in two public schools. All of the boys and their mothers in these three classes participated

SOURCE: Adapted and abridged from Gerald S. Lesser, "The Relationship Between Overt and Fantasy Aggression as a Function of Maternal Response to Aggression." *Journal of Abnormal and Social Psychology*, 1957, 55, 218–221. (With permission of the author and the American Psychological Association.)

except one mother, who refused to be interviewed. The Kuhlmann-Anderson intelligence quotients of the boys ranged from 82 to 119, with a mean of 102. The two schools are in adjacent districts and the families constitute a relatively homogeneous upper lower-class group.

Maternal Attitudes and Practices

Only one aspect of the environmental conditions of learning of aggressive behavior was measured, i.e., the maternal attitudes and practices supporting or prohibiting aggression. A structured questionnaire-interview schedule was orally administered to the mothers in their homes by a male interviewer. Questions regarding the support or prohibition of aggression constituted only one segment of the total interview. Pertinent to the present study were 8 items concerning the mother's attitudes toward aggression in children, and 13 items about the mother's practices in dealing with the aggressive behavior of her child. An illustrative item measuring maternal attitudes toward aggression is: · "A child should be taught to stand up and fight for his rights in his contacts with other children." The four response alternatives of agree, mildly agree, mildly disagree, and disagree were allowed for this item. An example of an item measuring maternal practices concerning aggression is: "If your son comes to tell you that he is being picked on by a bully at the playground who is his own age and size, there would be a number of different things you might tell him. Would you tell him to ignore him and turn the other cheek?" Response alternatives for this item were yes and no. Items that did not involve judgments on a four-point scale were transformed to have approximately the same range of scores as the items that involved four alternatives.

A single score was obtained for each mother by combining all items, and assigning plus scores to the responses indicating support of aggression, and minus scores to responses indicating discouragement of aggression. The range of scores was from $+9$ to -7, with a median score of $+2$. The corrected odd-even reliability coefficient was .80.

The distribution of scores for maternal response to aggression was dichotomized to form one group of mothers (with scores above or at the median) whose attitudes and practices were more supportive of aggressive behavior than those of the other group (with scores below the median). The hypothesis demands that the correlation between fantasy and overt aggression for the children of the mothers in the former group be significantly more positive than the corresponding correlation for the children of the mothers in the latter group.

Fantasy Aggression

Fantasy aggression in the children was measured through an adaptation of the TAT procedure. A set of ten pictures was designed. In each picture two boys are interacting. The pictures differed from one another in the degree to which the instigation to aggression was apparent.

To ensure complete and accurate transcription of the stories, tape recordings were taken. An introductory period preceding the fantasy task served both to establish rapport between the child and the male examiner, and to familiarize the child with the recording device. Instructions were:

I'm going to show you some pictures. These are pictures of two boys doing different things. What I'd like you to do is make up a story to each of these pictures. You can make up any story you wish; there are no right or wrong stories. Say what the boys are thinking and feeling and how the story will turn out.

The ten pictures, in the order of presentation, were:

1. One boy is holding a basketball and the other boy is approaching him with arms outstretched.
2. One boy is stamping upon an ambiguous object and the other boy is reaching for the object.
3. One boy is sitting behind the other boy in a classroom and is leaning toward him.
4. One boy is walking down the street and the other boy, with fists clenched, is glaring at him.
5. One boy, with fists clenched, is staring at the other boy, who is sitting, head bowed, on a box.
6. One boy is sawing a piece of wood and the other boy is leaning on a fence between them, talking to him.
7. The two boys, surrounded by a group of other boys, are approaching each other with arms upraised and fists clenched.
8. The two boys are making a fire. One boy is kneeling to arrange the wood and the other boy is approaching, laden with wood for the fire.
9. One boy, who is looking back, is running down a street and the other boy is running behind him.
10. Two boys are standing in a field. One boy, with his hand on the other boy's shoulder, is pointing off in the distance.

A fantasy aggression score was obtained for each S by counting the number of times the following acts appeared in his stories: fighting, injuring, killing, attacking, assaulting, torturing, bullying, getting angry, hating, breaking, smashing, burning, destroying, scorning, expressing contempt, expressing disdain, cursing, swearing, threatening, insulting, belittling, repudiating, ridiculing.

Fantasy aggression scores ranged from 1 to 15, with a mean of 5.3. The corrected matched-half reliability coefficient was .86; the interjudge scoring reliability coefficient was .92.

Overt Aggression

To measure overt aggression in the child, a modified sociometric device, the "Guess who" technique, was adopted. The Ss were presented with a booklet containing a series of written descriptions of children and were asked to identify each of these descriptive characterizations by naming one or more classmates. Fifteen overt aggression items were used, such as "Here is someone who is always looking for a fight." A diversity of aggressive behaviors were included; items depicted verbal, unprovoked physical, provoked physical, outburst, and indirect forms of aggressive behavior.

An overt aggression score was obtained for each S by counting the number of times he was named by his classmates. There were substantial differences among the three classes in the distributions of the overt aggression scores; in order to combine into one distribution the scores of children in different classes, overt-aggression raw scores were transformed into standard scores.

The biserial correlation coefficient between the overt aggression measure derived from the children and teacher entries for the same "Guess who" aggression items was .76 $(p < .01)$.

Results

Two Pearson product-moment correlation coefficients were obtained. For boys $(n = 23)$ whose mothers are relatively encouraging or supportive of aggression, the correlation between fantasy aggression and overt aggression is $+.43$ $(p < .05$, two-tailed test). For boys $(n = 21)$ whose mothers are relatively discouraging of aggression, the corresponding correlation is $-.41$ $(p < .10$, two-tailed test). These coefficients are statistically different $(p = .006$, two-tailed test).

When the total sample is not separated into two groups on the basis of scores for maternal response to aggression, the overall Pearson product-moment correlation coefficient is $+.07$. This coefficient is not significantly different from zero.

Discussion

Confirmation is found for the hypothesis that under conditions of relative maternal encouragement of aggression, a greater degree of correspondence exists between the fantasy and overt aggression of children than under conditions of relative maternal discouragement of aggression. Thus, the direction and extent of the relationship between fantasy and overt aggression in the child is apparently influenced by the maternal attitudes and practices surrounding the learning of aggressive behavior.

It has been predicted that those tendencies which are negatively sanctioned or prohibited will be high in fantasy expression and low in overt expression. This association is premised upon a compensatory or substitutive role of fantasy where overt expression is not allowed. A scatter plot of the fantasy and overt aggression scores for the children whose mothers discourage aggression (from which the $-.41$ coefficient is derived) reveals a considerable number of such high fantasy aggression, low overt aggression scores. However, children with low fantasy aggression and high overt aggression scores are as well represented in this scatter plot as those with high fantasy aggression, low overt aggression scores. Although mothers of children in this group were classified (relative to the others) as discouraging aggression, perhaps certain of them do so ineffectively, and thus allow the child sufficient release of aggressive feelings in overt behavior so that he may not need to express aggression in fantasy. An alternative speculation regarding the concurrence of low fantasy aggression and high overt aggression in the group exposed to maternal discouragement of aggression suggests that a child with strong aggressive needs whose mother prohibits aggression may assign this prohibitory attitude to the adult E and suppress fantasy aggression expressions in the testing situation; yet this child may find avenues for overt expression of aggression among his peers.

In the present study, only one condition related to the learning of aggressive responses and controls was assessed, maternal attitudes and practices. Other possibly critical determinants that remain to be explored include fathers' behavior and teachers' attitudes and practices. This study has sampled a limited range of maternal attitudes and practices concerning aggression. Although there is no direct manner of determining the absolute degree of punitiveness of the most prohibitive mother in this sample, it appears unlikely that extremely severe and continuous maternal punitiveness is represented. Such severe condemnation of aggression might so limit or restrict both the fantasy aggression and overt aggression expressions of the child that no correlation analysis within such a group would be possible. Both the extremes of unimpeded permissiveness and severe condemnation warrant further investigation.

The Relationship of Children's Home Duties to an Attitude of Responsibility

Dale B. Harris, Kenneth E. Clark, Arnold M. Rose, and Frances Valasek

It is almost axiomatic among parents that their children should be given "chores" in order to develop in them a sense of responsibility. Psychologically, this axiom rests on the assumption that requiring a child to perform certain household duties that are his responsibility will transfer to a broad variety of situations outside of the home. An empirical test of this axiom, as reported in this paper by Professor Harris and his colleagues, indicates that giving a child chores does not influence his sense of responsibility. Thus, children who report having a large number of home duties in contrast with those not having any home duties do not evidence any greater attitude of responsibility outside the home. In all likelihood, the variables involved in the development of an attitude of responsibility are highly complex and generally unrelated to specific parental practices such as requiring household duties.

Advisory literature to parents usually contains the assumption that giving children tasks around the house has merit in training for independence, depend-

SOURCE: Adapted and abridged from Dale B. Harris, Kenneth E. Clark, Arnold M. Rose, and Frances Valasek, "The Relationship of Children's Home Duties to an Attitude of Responsibility." *Child Development*, 1954, 24, 29–33. (With permission of the authors and the Society for Research in Child Development.)

ability, or "responsibility," as it is frequently put. These tasks are not infrequently resisted by children; common parental queries have to do with how to get children to accept their duties more willingly. Indeed, children, when asked how they think their parents would like to have them improve their behavior, mention "do my chores" as second or third in a long list of characteristics offered; this is true of boys and girls alike and at all ages from 6 to 14.

Another paper by the writers describes the measurement of responsibility in children from 9 to 18 years of age (Harris, Clark, Rose, and Valasek 1954). One measure, "Teacher's Check List," was a Thurstone-type rating scale of responsible behaviors applied individually to each child by his classroom or homeroom teacher. The other, "How I feel about Citizenship," was a series of attitude items calling for agreement or disagreement and dealing with civic responsibilities of grown-ups, children's obligations with respect to school, and a number of personality and interest characteristics, all found to be valid with respect to reputation with peers and with teachers for responsibility.

The relationship of home duties to responsibility was studied by a questionnaire entitled "What Are My Jobs," and completed by all children in our sample, somewhat more than 2000 from rural, small town, and urban settings. The "Jobs" questionnaire consisted of three major groupings of items. A number of questions related to the child's income, whether as allowance or in return for duties, and its sources and its distribution by the child. There were also some questions pertaining to the child's future educational and work plans. A second part contained 20 items relating to personal habits and skills and included such items as:

Do your parents generally have to remind you to brush your teeth?
Do your parents generally have to remind you to wash your hands and face?
Have you ever been on the school patrol?
Have you ever held an office in a school club?
Do you have your own house key?

These items generally reflect maturity and independence of self-management. The final section consisted of 100 specific duties, including 17 that would be found only in a rural environment. The child was asked to mark whether he did the job "frequently," "sometimes," or "never," and for the jobs which he frequently or sometimes did, whether he liked or disliked them.

The two attitude measures described earlier constituted our criterion of responsibility. These measures are only slightly intercorrelated; for our entire population of town and rural children ($n = 2441$), the Pearson r was $+.27$, though there was a tendency for r values to be higher for older than for younger children when correlations were computed in different age groups (Harris, et al. 1954).

The relationship to home duties may be expressed in a crude manner by simply counting the number of jobs a child says he "never" does and correlating this "score" with his scores on the criterion measures. This procedure investigates the hypothesis that more responsible children will have smaller "never" counts on the job questionnaire. Results of such an analysis for several selected age and sex groups and for the total rural and small town population certainly cannot be used to support the hypothesis that the number of home duties assumed by a child bears a substantial relation to his sense of responsibility, at least as measured in this study. Nor is there any evidence that this relationship may exist in older children, after more years of family training.

The relationship of home experience to responsibility was further investigated by an item analysis of the home duties questionnaire, on the supposition that the very crude measure used in the correlational study might obscure certain more specific relationships. Criterion groups were constituted by selecting individuals from deviate quarters of the score distributions for both criterion measures, using the correlation scattergrams between both measures. These groups were so drawn that the fourth of the children highest on both measures together and the fourth lowest on both measures together were utilized. It is obvious, of course, that the selection was based on an inspection of correlation scattergrams which did not show a great coincidence of the regression lines. These samples were selected with cognizance of the fact that a sex difference exists between boys and girls on both measures of responsibility, particularly on the teacher's rating. The samples were adjusted to equalize the sex representation on the selected deviate groups. Significance of differences between proportions of each group responding to each item were calculated.

Again the results are negative. Results were kept separate for boys and girls. For boys, five tasks differentiated between most and least responsible at the 5 per cent level of significance in terms of doing the task or not. Fourteen items differentiated on the basis of whether those reporting the items stated they liked to do it. Generally, the more responsible boys more often liked to do the work, though they were not actually more likely to do the task. For girls, eight items differentiated high and low responsibility subjects as to performance but only six items on a liking basis. These items are listed in Tables 13.1 and 13.2. Actually, the *number* of "significant" differences reported in the tables itself falls within chance expectation.

While no differences were found between most and least responsible children with regard to source or expenditure of personal income, responsible children, both boys and girls, more frequently stated they planned to get education beyond high school. To each of the questions, "Do your parents generally have to remind you to brush your teeth, wash your hands and face, change to clean clothes, or comb your hair," significantly more of the high responsibility children, both boys and girls, responded, "no." Among the rural boys more high-responsibility boys had driven a tractor in the fields. High responsibility girls responded more frequently with "yes" to the questions, "Have you ever held an office in your school class?" and "Have you ever worked on a committee?"

While these items could be viewed as expressions of special experience which has served to inculcate a sense of responsibility, they can also be viewed merely as expressions of the validity of the criterion in this instance. Children with a

TABLE 13.1. *Items Which differentiate Significantly (5% Level) Between Responsible and Less Responsible Children in Terms of Reported Participation*

ITEM	CRITICAL RESPONSE	GROUP SHOWING GREATER PERCENTAGE	SEX
Sweep floor	Sometimes	Low Responsibility	B
Keep own room neat	Regularly	High Responsibility	B, G
	Sometimes	Low Responsibility	
Empty garbage	Regularly	High Responsibility	B
Keep records or accounts for family	Never	High Responsibility	B, G
Fill root cellar	Sometimes	Low Responsibility	B
	Never	High Responsibility	
Bathe baby	Never	High Responsibility	G
Change diapers	Never	High Responsibility	G
Help select furniture or furnishings	Sometimes	High Responsibility	G
Dry dishes	Regularly	High Responsibility	G
	Sometimes	Low Responsibility	
Help with preserving food	Sometimes	High Responsibility	G
Prepare food for cooking	Regularly	High Responsibility	G

TABLE 13.2. *Items Which Differentiate Significantly (5% Level) Between Responsible and Less Responsible Children in Terms of Reported Liking or Disliking to Do Them*

ITEM	CRITICAL RESPONSE	GROUP SHOWING GREATER PERCENTAGE	SEX
Plan games for family	Don't like	Low Responsibility	B
Plan family outings or picnics	Don't like	Low Responsibility	B
Pay bills for family	Don't like	Low Responsibility	B
Keep money records for family	Don't like	Low Responsibility	B
Help select furniture or furnishings	Like	High Responsibility	B, G
Build simple furniture or furnishings	Like	High Responsibility	B
Sweep	Like	High Responsibility	B
Clean own room	Like	High Responsibility	B
Keep room neat	Like	High Responsibility	B, G
Prepare food for cooking	Like	High Responsibility	B
Make outside repairs to roof, siding, doors, etc.	Don't like	Low Responsibility	B
Help paint garage, house, or farm buildings	Don't like	Low Responsibility	B
Repair or paint toys	Like	High Responsibility	B
Plant and care for flowers, shrubs	Don't like	Low Responsibility	B
Dry dishes	Like	High Responsibility	G
Groom work animals	Like	Low Responsibility	G
Shovel snow	Like	High Responsibility	G
Rake yard	Like	High Responsibility	G
Read to younger brother and sister	Don't like	Low Responsibility	B

well-defined sense of responsibility probably do require less reminding by their parents, probably are more frequently selected for school offices, because of their more dependable behavior! Thus, this analysis affords little help in isolating the kinds of training which can be given to insure or to increase a responsible attitude in children. Certainly, there is little evidence that the routine tasks, such as washing dishes, caring for pets, house cleaning, preparation of food, repairing about the house, are associated with an attitude of responsibility.

The Effect of Adult Presence or Absence on Aggression

Alberta E. Siegel and Lynette G. Kohn

An important objective of child-rearing practices is the internalization, on the part of the child, of society's standards of acceptable behaviors. The process of internalization usually involves a program of rewards and punishments by which the parent attempts to define for the child the domains of acceptable and unacceptable behaviors. According to the authors of this experiment, children will rely on their parents to provide guidance in a particular situation rather than rely on their own internalized standards. A comparison of the frequency of aggressive behavior in the presence of an adult and without an adult present revealed lower aggression when the adult is absent. As suggested by the authors, greater parental permissiveness may have a positive effect on the internalization of socially acceptable behavior.

An adequate account of aggressive behavior must acknowledge the force of a number of influences in determining the amount and kind of aggression a child exhibits. One of these, of course, is the strength of his aggressive drive, and this is presumably a resultant of a range of experiences in his personal history and of the operation of certain characteristics of the immediate setting.

A second influence of importance is the child's own attitude toward aggression — his own evaluation of its goodness or badness. This may be presumed to be a distillation and internalization of the attitudes of significant people in his life. These two influences — the strength of the child's aggressive drive and the nature of his attitudes toward aggressiveness — together undoubtedly account for much of the variability in aggression from child to child and also for at least some of the systematic variability between the sexes.

A third influence is the expressed attitudes and values of the other people in the setting in which aggression may be displayed. In our culture, with its extremely complex code about when, where, how, and to whom aggression may appropriately be displayed, people learn to derive cues about what behavior is acceptable at any given time and place by observing the behavior and communications of others in the setting. Children learn especially to rely on adult behaviors and communications to provide hints as to what is suitable or appropriate. This third sort of influence probably accounts for many differences in children's behavior from one setting to another, and also is probably important in shaping sex differences in both incidence and modes of aggression.

A fourth influence is the expectation that aggression will elicit counter-

SOURCE: Adapted and abridged from Alberta E. Siegel and Lynette G. Kohn, "Permissiveness, Permission, and Aggression: The Effect of Adult Presence or Absence on Aggression in Children's Play." *Child Development*, 1959, 30, 131–141. (With permission of the authors and the Society for Research in Child Development.)

aggression (punishment). Presumably, such an expectation typically acts to inhibit overt expression of aggression.

It is by reference to the fourth factor that the finding of an increase in aggression from session to session has been explained. We believe that an adequate account of both session-to-session increase in an adult's absence must include reference to all of the influences which have been enumerated, and especially the second, third, and fourth.

In either the presence or the absence of an adult, we may expect wide individual differences in incidence of aggression. Because of the wide range of aggressive drives in children and because of individual differences irrespective of condition, however, we may expect systematic group differences dependent on the condition of adult presence or absence.

In the presence of a permissive adult, a child's aggression may be expected to increase because (a) he will infer from the behavior of the adult that this is a setting in which aggression is suitable or appropriate, and (b) with experience he will undergo a progressive decrease in inhibition based on fear of punishment. That is, changes in the nature of the third and fourth influences mentioned above account for an increase over time.

In the absence of any adult, however, a child's aggression may be expected to decrease from session to session. Lacking any adults to define the social situation and to express expectations of his behavior in it, the child will, after an initial "release" or testing of the limits, rely increasingly on his own learned standards of conduct (the second influence mentioned above) which, in the middle-class child, will typically be that aggression is unacceptable in social play.

Hypothesis

The study reported here was conducted to test the hypothesis, derived from the above account, concerning session-to-session differences in aggression in children's play in the absence of an adult relative to such differences in the presence of an adult. The hypothesis is that *children under the two conditions will exhibit different session-to-session changes in aggression, in that the aggression of the children under the adult-absent condition will tend to decrease in comparison to the aggression of the children under the adult-present condition, which will tend to increase.*

Method

Subjects

The Ss were boys enrolled in a university nursery school. Boys were used exclusively because the amount of aggression they display in the play setting used in the study is much greater than the amount displayed by girls, and therefore boys' aggression scores may be presumed to be more sensitive to change. The boys served in the experiment in pairs, both members of any pair being from the same play group in the school. One member of each pair was chosen from the older boys in the group (among the upper 50 per cent in age) and one from among the younger. The boys were paired by the director of the nursery school on the basis of their usual friendliness to each other and the supportiveness they could be expected to have for each other in an unfamiliar play setting. The older boy of each pair was an S in the experiment. Eighteen pairs were selected, and the older boys (Ss) in these pairs ranged in age from 4–1 (4 years, 1 month) to 5–0. The younger boys (who were not Ss — their aggression in play was not scored) ranged in age from 2–11 to 4–9, the great majority being 3-year-olds or early 4-year-olds. There were three independent play groups in the school; therefore, some minor overlap occurred between the age ranges of "older" and "younger" boys.

After the pairs had been selected, they were assigned at random (by the toss of a coin) to the two conditions: Adult-Absence and Adult-Presence. Nine pairs were assigned to each condition. The average age of Ss in both groups was 4–7.

Procedure with Subjects

Each pair participated in two play sessions. These occurred two days apart. Any pair's two sessions were held at the same time of day, insofar as this could be accomplished without destroying the informal and permissive nature of the E's interactions with the Ss. (In the Adult-Absent group, the difference between time of day for initiation of one session and time of day for initiation of the other was 22 minutes on the average, and these differences ranged from 0 to 50 minutes. In the Adult-Presence group, the average difference in time of day of initiation was 16 minutes, with a range from 0 to 40 minutes.)

All play sessions were conducted in a small playroom in the same building as the nursery school classrooms. This room is reserved for testing and research sessions, and is familiar to the children in the school.

The sessions were initiated in an identical manner for all pairs. E invited the pair to come to the playroom so that she could read a story to them and then let them play with some special toys there. As soon as the children entered the room, they were asked to be seated in two chairs, and E read a story to them.

The two stories used for the two sessions were rather similar in content, each being a simple story which was neutral with respect to aggression and which was printed in a brightly illustrated book. These stories were selected during a pilot study for their interest and appeal for young boys. A counterbalanced design determined which story was read first and which second for any pair.

After the story had been read, E invited the children to play as they wished with any of the toys in the room. The toys, selected to be similar to those used in the earlier study (Siegel 1957), were these: two rubber daggers, two small plastic toy guns, one singing spinning top, two lumps of clay, small wooden train composed of detachable cars, three small metal automobiles, five or six inflated plastic punching toys (a clown) which stood child height. The arrangement of the room, which was furnished with three chairs and a table, was the same at the beginning of each session.

For the pairs in the Adult-Presence condition, E sat quietly in a chair at one side of the playroom during both sessions. Her attitude was friendly, acceptant, interested, but nonintrusive. She did not initiate any conversations, and she replied only briefly and noncommitally to any initiations from a child.

For the pairs in the Adult-Absent condition, E followed her invitation to the children to play with another statement indicating that she had to leave the room for a while to work at her desk. (E had shown this desk to the Adult-Absent pairs while walking with them to the playroom; the desk was in a hall some distance from the room). She explained that they were to stay in the room until she returned for them. She said that she would knock at the door before entering the room upon her return, and that during her absence they would be alone and their privacy would not be disturbed. The purpose of these remarks, which were restated or amplified when necessary to assure their being understood, was to assure the children of freedom from adult intrusion, supervision, or observation during their play.

Some children under the Adult-Absent condition left the room during the play session, usually to carry some item of information to E at her desk. In such instances, E walked back to the playroom door with them, repeated her instructions, and returned them to the playroom.

Each pair remained in the room for a 14-minute play period. During this period their play was observed by an observer behind the one-way vision mirror on one wall of the room. At the conclusion of the period, E terminated the play session and walked with the children back to the nursery school. For the Adult-Absent pairs her conduct was exactly as she had told them it would be: she returned to the door of the playroom, knocked, and waited for their invitation before entering. Moreover, she ignored the state of the room, and she responded in an uninquisitive and noncommittal way to their remarks about what went on during her absence.

Scoring of Aggression

All play sessions were observed and scored by the same person, a graduate student in psychology who was kept ignorant of the purposes of the study and of the hypothesis under test. Scoring began as soon as E left the room in the Adult-Absent sessions. Paced by an electric timer and using prepared scoring sheets, O entered a rating of aggression for every 20-second interval. The rating was either a 0 (no aggression), 1 (mild or playful aggression), 2 (stronger or more forceful aggression), or 3 (intense aggression in which the child seemed highly involved). O's rating of intensity represented, by convention, the *most extreme* aggressive behavior of the child during the 20-second interval. In judging intensity, O considered both the quality of the instrumental act and the nature of the goal response; an act might be judged intensely aggressive because its aim was highly destructive or hostile or because its mode of execution was highly forceful and showed much self-involvement. Only the behavior of the older member of each pair, the S, was scored. A S's aggression score for a play session was the sum of the ratings he received for the 42 20-second intervals during that session. Thus, theoretically scores could range from 0 to 126. In fact, the observed range of scores for these Ss was from 10 to 114. In previous work (Siegel 1957) this scoring between total scores from 48 protocols of two independent observers was indicated by the Pearson correlation, $r = .97$. For the present study, pilot sessions were conducted to train O in the scoring technique and to conduct a preliminary check on interobserver reliability, which was found to be satisfactory. In the course of the experiment itself, 12 play sessions (including some of each type — first Adult-Absent session, second Adult-Absent session, first Adult-Present session, and second Adult-Present session) were observed and scored independently by a second O, and the interobserver agreement for these sessions is given by the Pearson correlation, $r = .98$.

Summary of Experimental Controls

Summarized below are the controls which were instituted in the experiment in order to enable isolation of the effects of adult-presence or adult-absence on session differences in aggression:

1. Any S's partner in play was the same child for both sessions. Thus, any differences between sessions cannot be attributed to systematic differences in interpersonal stimulation.

2. Only one member of each pair served as a S. The statistical test's requirement that the scores be independent was thus met.

3. A counterbalanced design determined which story was read first and which second for any pair, so that any possible systematic differential effect of any story would not appear as an experimental effect.

4. The pairs were assigned to the two conditions by a random procedure. Any significant differences between the Ss' behavior under the two conditions, therefore, cannot reasonably be attributed to any probable prior systematic differences between the Ss in the two groups.

5. Possible time-of-day effects on incidence of aggression were held constant; any pair participated in both sessions I and II at the same time of day.

6. Timing effects were controlled by separate sessions I and II by a constant interval of time (48 hours) for every pair.

7. Possible observer bias was controlled by keeping O ignorant of the hypothesis under test. O knew whether or not E was present at any play session, of course, but she did not know that E's presence or absence was the experimental effect under study, and she was not familiar with the research literature concerning the influence of an adult on children's play.

8. The E was the same person for all sessions, and she attempted to interact with all children similarly except with respect to those acts of hers which necessarily depended on whether she was present or absent during the play session.

Results

The hypothesis was tested by a Mann-Whitney test on the difference scores (each S's session II score for aggression subtracted from his session I score). The scores for the Ss in the Adult-Absent sessions show changes significantly different ($p = .01$) from those shown by the scores for the Ss in the Adult-Present sessions. A close inspection of the data reveals that all Ss in the Adult-Absent settings show *less* aggression in session II than in session I, whereas two-thirds of the Ss in the Adult-Present settings showed *more* aggression in session II than in session I. Thus, the hypothesis is confirmed.

This finding does not imply an overall difference in incidence of aggression under the two conditions: when each S's scores for the two sessions are considered together, the mean of these totals for the Adult-Absent Ss (124.4) is less than a point difference from the comparable mean for the Adult-Present Ss (123.7). Thus, it is not the total incidence of aggression which is shown to vary the two conditions, but rather the timing of its occurrence.

Discussion

The results of this study confirm the hypothesis drawn from the contention that adult permissiveness must be conceived in more positive terms than simply as a way of reducing S's fear of punishment.

In their discussion of ego functions, Redl and Wineman (1957) have described a phenomenon similar to that under study. They describe the "spontaneous establishment of substitute controls":

> Even in normal children, the control system of the ego does not always have to stay switched on to its full volume just to keep things from getting disorganized. Much of the time, ego control can be switched back to low, just because there are adequate outside control forces at work. In those cases, the ego gets its flow of support from the presence of authority figures, the soothing awareness of a relaxed and friendly atmosphere, the perception of existing routines or well-oiled rules and regulations. . . . Sometimes, especially when impulsivity runs high, even well-adjusted children have trouble keeping to the level on which they were performing when such "ouside controls" suddenly drop out. Thus . . . the teacher leaving the room may find noise rising in the classroom in spite of the warnings or pleas she left behind, the change over from a more highly pressured classroom to one with a wider range of permissiveness may cost ten minutes of temporary disorganization.
>
> The normal child is supposed to have some reserves to institute inside controls quickly after the outside ones have petered out. . . . In fact, we could think of no better test for the emergency vigilance of ego functions than just such of withdrawal or breakdown of outside structures or controls (Redl and Wineman, pp. 110–111).

In terms of these authors' discussion, Ss under the Adult-Absent condition in the present study were observed spontaneously to establish "substitute controls," to "switch to high," to demonstrate the "emergency vigilance of ego functions." On the other hand, Ss under the Adult-Present condition could "switch to low," and could get a flow of support from the existence of an accepting authority figure and the perception of rules and regulations consonant with their behavior. It may be suggested that a technique for assessing a child's ego strength or maturity of controls would be to compare his behavior in the two settings of this study (Adult-Absence and Adult-Presence) and especially to observe the swiftness and ease with which he "switched to high."

Also relevant is the psychoanalytic account of the relations between leader and follower. As presented by Munroe (1955), this theory sees a leader as a substitute for internalized controls. "The leader and the admonitions of the leader are substituted for the ego ideal or superego. The great man . . . takes over the individual conscience" (Munroe 1955, p. 146). In the terms of the psychoanalytic account, the present study concerns children who abdicate superego functions to an adult leader when in her presence — "Interesting enough, people usually do not feel acute remorse for actions committed under conditions of leadership conscience" (Munroe 1955, p. 146) — but who increasingly rely on their own ego ideal or superego for standards of behavior in the absence of any adult.

The importance of the presence of an adult, and the differential effects of adults in different role-relations to the Ss, have been highlighted by the findings of Levin and Turgeon (1957), who studied changes in children's aggression in two sessions of doll play. The first session was attended by only the child and the experimenter. During the second session, the child's mother was in attendance for one group of Ss and an adult woman who was a stranger to the children was in attendance for the other group. Each of the children watched by their mothers was more aggressive in the second than in the first session, whereas four-fifths of the children watched by a stranger were less aggressive. These sessions differences are in the opposite direction from what had been predicted in a hypothesis drawn from displacement theory, and it is of interest to note that Levin and Turgeon refer to the nature of superego development in the child in their attempt to account for the unexpected finding. They suggest the plausibility of a "transfer of superego" explanation, one which posits that the child returns impulse control to the mother in her presence. "Self-control is a worrisome burden for the child, so that he is ready to transfer his newly acquired control to his mother when she is available. Anecdotally, we know that mothers often complain that their children are so well behaved only when they are not around" (Levin and Turgeon 1957, p. 307).

The findings of the present study, as well as those of other related studies, also have direct methodological implications. They emphasize the significance of the behavior of any adult E in a laboratory situation with children, pointing to the *social* nature of the play situations typically used in research with young children, and demonstrating that children's play responses are extremely sensitive to variations in the social setting of the play.

Influence of Affectional Family Relationships on Character Development

Andrew W. Brown, Joan Morrison, and Gertrude B. Couch

It is a generally held belief among psychologists and other mental health specialists that family relationships characterized by warmth, mutual respect, and affection are associated with the development of good psychological adjustment. Such warm family relationships probably provide the child with strong models of behavior which, when imitated by the child, lead to positive reinforcement. The authors of this study have obtained measures of the strength of affectional relationships within a number of specific families and correlated this measure with an index of character reputation. Although the correlations between the measures are low, they are in a positive direction and statistically significant. These results suggest that family relations are important; but there is a need for a greater specification of the variables that influence character development.

The study reported here is an integral part of a larger one which is being conducted by the Committee on Human Development of the University of Chicago on factors influencing the growth of character and personality in a typical small midwestern town (to be referred to in this paper as Prairie City). The study has been going on for a number of years and is expected to continue for some time to come. Anthropologists, sociologists, educators, and psychologists are collaborating in the investigation. A particularly intensive study has been made of the children born in 1926 and those born in 1932, i.e., those who were 16 years old and 10 years old respectively when the study was initiated. These two age groups constitute the Ss of this report.

Hypothesis for This Portion of the Project

The pupose of this particular part of the research was to test one of the hypotheses set up by the Committee at the time the study was begun, namely, *that character development is determined by affectional family relationships.* As the study progressed, however, two purposes emerged:

1. To devise and validate an instrument for the measurement of these relationships within the family, and

2. To determine the extent to which affectional family relationships influence personality and character development.

The Development and Weighting of the F-R Questionnaire

An operational definition of affectional family relationships was used which

SOURCE: Adapted and abridged from A. W. Brown, J. Morrison, and G. B. Couch, "Influence of Affectional Family Relationships on Character Development." *Journal of Abnormal and Social Psychology,* 1947, 42, 422–428. (With permission of the authors and the American Psychological Association.)

had no implication of right or wrong but which merely stated the conditions believed necessary for the existence of such relationships.

Ten different areas of family interaction thought to be revealing of affectional family relationships were outlined and questions framed around each area. The areas were as follows:

1. *Common Participation in Work and Play.*

2. *Degree of Approval-Disapproval.* (On the part of the parents toward the child.)

3. *Regularity in the Home.* (By this is meant the degree to which the parents are willing to accept some restraint on their own freedom in order to maintain an optimum amount of order in the child's life.)

4. *Confidence Shared.* (The degree to which there is a mutual sharing of confidences.)

5. *Sharing in Family Decisions.* (The degree to which a *real* democratic attitude prevails in the home.)

6. *Child's Acceptance of the Standards of the Home.*

7. *Trust and Faith in Child by Parents.*

8. *Parental Attitude toward Peer Activities.* (The extent to which the parents accept and encourage the child's relations with his peers.)

9. *Interparental Relations.* (The extent to which the relations between the parents are conducive to healthy character development in the child.)

10. *Signs of Tension.* (Nervous and other physical symptoms thought to be indicative of poor family relationships.)

Items designed to determine the interfamily relationship in each of these ten areas were selected from the old questionnaire and new questions were added, with a minimum of five questions for each area. In most areas there were more than five. The questions were answered on a five-point scale, ranging from "very often" through "fairly often," "occasionally," "very seldom," to "almost never." Thus, such a question as "Do you talk to your parents about your problems and worries?" could be answered at any of five points on the scale.

The answers to the items were given weights from 5 to 1, according to their contribution to healthy character development. This contribution was determined by the independent judgments of a group of instructors and advanced students engaged in a clinical study of the 10-year-old group of Prairie City children. Each member of this conference specialized in the interpretation of one or more of the instruments dealing with character and personality development.

For example, in area 1 — *Common Participation in Work and Play* — it was agreed by those participating in the Clinical Conference that an answer of "fairly often" to a specific question indicated a more desirable relationship than "very often." Each question was weighted on the basis of these judgments. Thus, the question, "Do you do little chores around the house without complaining?" was weighted as follows:

"very often"   4
"fairly often"   5
"occasionally"   3
"very seldom"   2
"almost never"   1

The Conference considered that an answer of "fairly often" indicated a healthier relationship between parents and child than did "very often."

Development of Criteria Instruments

For the purposes of this research, character was defined as reputation, as this was the only estimate of character that could be objectively obtained. Ratings of character reputation were secured from teachers, peers, and youth group leaders in the community. These character ratings were obtained on five traits — honesty, moral courage, friendliness, loyalty, and responsibility — by the use of the following instruments:

1. *The Guess-Who.* This test consisted of 44 brief statements or word pictures, approximately 10 for each of the character traits studied, about some hypothetical individual. These statements were presented in pairs of opposites. For example, the following pair was used for honesty:

Here is someone who goes out of his way to return anything he finds.
Here is someone who will keep anything he finds.

The students were given a list of these statements and also a list of all the children in the group and were asked to match each word picture with as many names from the list as they thought fitted the description. They were told the test was anonymous and were asked not to sign their names.

2. *The Portrait Guess-Who.* This test was a variation of the Ohio Recognition Scale used by Raths and his co-workers at Ohio State University. The test consisted of two short paragraphs for each trait, one describing a person who showed a degree of the trait in question, the other describing a person who lacked it. It differs from the Guess-Who in that each portrait combined several manifestations of a trait as they might be found in a hypothetical individual. Sample portraits for the trait of responsibility are below:

a. Suppose you were going to choose boys and girls to help plan a party or to organize a campaign to sell savings stamps. You want boys and girls who have some good ideas, who will work hard and who will stick to the job till it is finished. They know how to plan and they do careful work. They try to do their very best.

b. Some boys and girls do not do their share. They are careless and they do not take very good care of things. They do not do good work on a committee. They cannot be counted on to do what they say they will. They let other people do all the hard work.

This test was given about three months after the Guess-Who. The Ss were given a list of their classmates and were asked to put the letter of each paragraph before the name of the boy or girl on the list whom they thought the paragraph described. They were asked not to rate themselves.

3. *The Check-List.* This instrument consists of a number (126) of behavioral situations in which varying degrees of the different character traits seemed to be manifested. This list was given only to teachers and other leaders in the community acquainted with the child. They were asked to check those situations which seemed most characteristic of a given individual. Examples for the trait Responsibility are as follows:

___ Keeps appointments.
___ Dawdles at his work.
___ Takes good care of school property.
___ Must be continually prodded to finish work.

4. *The Character-Sketch.* This instrument consisted of a number of short verbal sketches, each designed to represent an individual with some degree of one of the character traits studied. The sketches were submitted to adult leaders in the community who were familiar with the children. They were asked to match the sketches with the names of those in the study group. The following are examples of character sketches dealing with the trait Friendliness:

Y is a very pleasant person and people like to be with him. He will come more than half way in social relationships. Indeed, thought not out-standingly popular, he has more friends than the average person.
D is a very withdrawn person in manner and appearance. He seldom smiles and seems to try to avoid people. Since he never speaks to people or associates with them, he is almost without friends.

The items in each of these instruments were scaled on the basis of the opinions of 30 competent judges in regard to the degree to which the subjects exhibited the traits.

With the use of these four devices ratings were obtained for both age groups for each of the five character traits: honesty, moral courage, friendliness, loyalty, and responsibility. The ratings were transmuted into derived standard scores, or D-scores. Peer ratings and adult ratings were then averaged to determine the individual's rating for each trait. These constituted the criterion scores.

Administering, Weighting, and Scoring the Revised Questionnaire

The F-R Questionnaire was presented in May, 1946, to the 1932 group of children in Prairie City, who were now 13 years of age. The subjects were permitted to ask questions regarding the meaning of words in the inventory, but as the items had been worded as simply as possible, there was apparently little difficulty in understanding the items or the technique of answering.

The Questionnaire was scored by computing the average weighted score for each of the 10 sections.

The method of weighting these areas was quite arbitrary, being based upon the judgment of the 12 persons participating in the Clinical Conference on these cases. Some of the areas were given a rating of 1, some given a rating of 2, and one was given a rating of 3.

The areas concerned with (a) *Regularity in the Home,* (b) *Interparental Relation,* and (c) *Signs of Tension* were considered to have the least relation to affectional family relations and consequently were given a weight of 1 by the Conference. Thus, the highest possible average score which could be made on any of these sections was 5 and the lowest average score, 1.

Six areas were given a weight of 2 by members of the Conference. These were (a) *Common Participation,* (b) *Confidence Shared,* (c) *Trust and Faith in Child by Parents,* (d) *Sharing in Family Decisions,* (e) *Child's Acceptance of Standards of the Home,* and (f) *Parent Attitude toward Peer Activities.* In each of these areas the highest possible score was, therefore, 10 and the lowest possible was 2.

One area or section, namely, the *Degree of Approval-Disapproval of the Child by the Parents,* was given a weight of 3 — the highest possible score in this area being 15 and the lowest, 3.

Thus, with three areas yielding a high average score of 5 each, or 15, six areas yielding a high average of 10 each, or 60, and one area yielding a high average score of 15, the highest possible total score was 90 and the lowest possible score, 18. This scheme of scoring had the advantage of making possible a quantitative rating on each of the ten sections, as well as on the Questionnaire as a whole.

Results

Relation Between Affectional Family Relationships and Character Reputation Scores

The children's ratings on the revised Questionnaire was correlated with the character criteria scores previously described. These correlations are presented in Table 13.3.

TABLE 13.3. *Correlation Between Affectional Family Relations Score and Character Reputation Scores*

TRAIT	CORRELATION
Honesty	.40 ± .06
Moral Courage	.22 ± .07
Friendliness	.35 ± .06
Loyalty	.30 ± .06
Responsibility	.43 ± .05

From the correlations in the table, the following tentative conclusions may be drawn:

1. There is a substantial correlation between affectional family relationship and character reputation score as determined by these instruments.

2. The relationship seems to be higher for some traits than it is for others,

e.g., ratings on responsibility show a higher correlation with affectional family relationships than do those on moral courage.

Relation Between Various Factors in Family Relations and Character Reputation Scores

Correlations were also computed between the character criteria D-scores and the various areas of the F-R Questionnaire to determine which, if any, of the areas played the greatest part in influencing the character development of the child. These correlations are presented in Table 13.4.

TABLE 13.4. *Correlation Between Various Areas in F-R Questionnaire and Character Reputation Scores*

F-R AREA	CORRELATION
1. Common Participation	.31 ± .07
2. Degree of Approval-Disapproval	.31 ± .07
3. Regularity in the Home	.24 ± .07
4. Confidences Shared	.35 ± .06
5. Sharing in Family Decisions	.45 ± .06
6. Trust and Faith in Child by Parents	.26 ± .07
7. Child's Acceptance of Home Standards	.34 ± .06
8. Attitude toward Peer Activities	.42 ± .06
9. Interparental Relations	.42 ± .06
10. Signs of Tension	.14 ± .08
Total	.45 ± .06

The following conclusions are suggested by these correlations:

1. There is a definite positive relationship between each of the areas in the F-R Questionnaire and character development. This seems to indicate that affectional family relationships as operationally defined in this study determine to a fair degree the type of character and personality a child will possess.

2. The area of family relationships which seems to be most closely associated with character development is area five, *Sharing in Family Decisions*, i.e., the degree to which a democratic attitude prevails in the home.

3. Another area which is closely associated with the character criteria scores is the area of *Interparental Relations*. While the correlation of .42 is not high, it does indicate a substantial relationship between the attitudes of the parents toward each other and character development of the child. This confirms the experience of most clinicians.

4. A third area having a fairly high correlation with the character criteria was area eight, *Parental Attitude toward Peer Activities*. This suggests that the parents' attitude toward the child's relations with his peers may have a stronger influence on the child's character development than other areas which at first glance may appear of more importance.

CHAPTER XIV

The Socialization Process

The SOCIALIZATION process has received considerable empirical and theoretical attention in the professional journals. This is not surprising in that the child's culture helps him to define concepts of justice, right and wrong, and a sense of individual responsibility. This chapter permits an examination of some of the theoretical approaches to analyzing socialization as well as some of the various methods of investigating the problem.

There are at least two broad theoretical approaches to socialization, one of these orientations relies to a considerable degree on such terms as "conscience," "internalized moral agent," "guilt," and "identification." Thus the socialization process is seen as an incorporation of society's standards and the emergence of individualized moral and ethical codes. The internalization process occurs by means of identification with an adult representative of society and transgressions are inhibited by means of guilt; that is, a psychologically painful reaction activated by a transgression.

The alternative general model makes use of the terms just described, but in a descriptive as opposed to an explanatory sense. This general model is probably best described as a behavioristic learning model and relies very much on stimulus-response principles of learning. Anxiety, the association of a stimulus-response sequence with pain, is given a key role. Children learn, in exactly the same way as they learn everthing else, the consequences of their behavioral acts and under what stimulus conditions these acts can be displayed with immunity. Socialization is not exclusively a matter of associating behaviors with pain but also involves the substitution of negative behaviors with positive ones. Behavioral theorists are more likely to use the term "imitation" rather than "identification" in discussing the source of the ideal behaviors. Thus, children observe the behavior of others and their consequences and imitate this behavior in a similar situation. If the behavior leads to positive reinforcement, it is likely to be repeated on the next occasion. A behavioral analysis, therefore, relies as much on the principles of reinforcement (perhaps even more) as on the anxiety producing affects of punishment.

As the reader will note, much of the research is highly exploratory, which is to be expected when investigators are first involved in trying to define their terms and sharpen their operational procedures. Professor Durkin examines one aspect of Piaget's theorizing concerning the development of moral behavior. According to Piaget, children develop a general concept of justice which can be generally applied to diverse situations. Dr. Durkin offers an interesting hypothesis for the failure of her data to support the general hypothesis.

The experiment by Rebelsky and her associates are excellent examples of experimental approaches to analyzing the variables influencing moral behaviors. Systematic analyses of these variables, under controlled laboratory conditions, may provide a clearer specification of the crucial variables worth examining in a broader based research program where observations are made in a naturalistic setting.

Perhaps because aggression, dependency, and achievement are of concern to both parents and teachers, psychologists have devoted considerable effort toward understanding them. Numerous theories have emerged, gained popularity, and finally waned because they were too general or failed to account for the data. The papers by Heather, Moss et. al., and Bandura et. al. represent diverse views and methods. There seems to be agreement among these scientists, that each behavior category is largely a learned response which is acquired either through imitation or because the specific response typically achieves a specific goal. The distinction between an instrumental response (a response designed to achieve some desired goal-object that may be distinct from the apparent intent of the instrumental response; that is, a child pushes another child to be first in line but not necessarily to hurt the victim) and an emotional response (a response made for its own sake) is made by Heathers with respect to dependence and independence. A similar distinction makes sense with respect to both aggressive and achievement behaviors, as discussed in the paper by Moss et. al.; Bandura et. al.; and Lefkowitz et. al.

In considering the results of each study it would be worthwhile to recall some comments made in Chapter XI (Emotional Development) concerning apparent genetic differences in emotionality. It is conceivable that the variables examined in the present chapter, such as imitation, reward, punishment, and parental values, may operate differentially depending upon the emotional predisposition of the child. A completely adequate theoretical rationale will not be achieved until it includes the interaction of environmental variables with behavioral predispositions.

The Specificity of Children's Moral Judgments

Dolores Durkin

Jean Piaget asserts, as part of his theoretical model, that with increasing age children increasingly accept reciprocity as a principle of justice. Piaget further asserts that reciprocity as a principle of justice generalizes over a variety of specific behavior situations such as aggression and sharing property. Professor Durkin tested this hypothesis by having three age groups of children respond to four stories depicting aggression, sharing property, taking property, and defaming character. The results are not consistent with Piaget's theory but rather indicate that children have significantly different kinds of judgments about each of the different kinds of behavioral situations. After analyzing the children's reasons for nonreciprocity, Professor Durkin suggests that Piaget's definition of reciprocity may be too narrow because it fails to include more subtle forms of this principle.

In *The Moral Judgement of the Child* (1932), Piaget questioned Swiss children about two story-situations depicting acts of physical aggression, and on the basis of their responses he proposed that "children maintain with a conviction that grows with their years that it is strictly fair to give back the blows one has received" (p. 301). This increasing acceptance, with age, of reciprocity as a principle of justice assumes importance in Piaget's more general theory of moral-judgment development in children.

The present writer, in two earlier studies (Durkin 1959a, 1959b) attempted to evaluate the Piaget proposal regarding children's attitudes toward reciprocity by questioning American children of three different age groups, also about acts of physical aggression.

The findings did not substantiate Piaget's proposal concerning the child's increasing acceptance, with age, of reciprocity as a principle of justice. Also noted in the findings, however, was the fact that this group of American subjects made quite different kinds of judgments about different kinds of justice violations. As was indicated in one of the studies, "this phenomenon of specificity would tend to suggest further flaws in the Piaget theory in that the theory purports to describe the development of children's attitudes toward reciprocity on the basis of their judgments about a single kind of behavior, that of physical aggression" (Durkin 1959b, p. 295).

The purpose of the present study, therefore, is twofold: (a) to examine systematically the specificity of judgments made by this American group of subjects, and (b) to examine the reasons they give for their judgments as a way of possibly explaining the specificity.

SOURCE: Adapted and abridged from Dolores Durkin, "The Specificity of Children's Moral Judgments." *Journal of Genetic Psychology*, 1961, 98, 3–13. (Abridgement with permission of the author and the Journal Press.)

Subjects and Procedures

The 101 Ss in this study were all of the second-, fifth-, and eighth-grade chil-dren in a Midwestern community-consolidated school. Twenty-eight of the total group were in Grade II, 38 were in Grade V, and the remaining 35 were in Grade VIII. These particular grade levels were selected because in them it would be most likely to find chronological ages of 7, 10, and 13, the age-groups that correspond to what Piaget (1932) designates as "three great periods in the development of the sense of justice in the child" (p. 314). The actual mean ages of the three groups were 7.8, 10.9, and 13.9.

As was described in detail in an earlier study, Ss responses to the story situa-tions were obtained in individual, tape-recorded interviews. A total of five story-situations were used, each depicting a context in which reciprocity is possible. The five story-situations were:

(A) One day when they were out at recess, Bennett hit Van.
What should Van do?
Why?[1]

(B) One morning in school, Anton asked Cyril Hayes, the boy who sits in front of him, if he could use his eraser.
Cyril said, "No." About a week later, Cyril was the one who didn't have an eraser, so he asked Anton if he could use his.
What should Anton do?
Why?

(C) In another room a boy by the name of Keith took a ruler off Russell Holec's desk and wouldn't give it back to him.
What should Russell do?
Why?

(D)[1] One morning in school Basil copied answers from another boy's test paper, and his teacher caught him. Later when the children were out on the playground at recess time, Alf, a boy in Basil's room, ran up to Basil and called, "Hi, cheater! Hi, cheater!"
What should Basil do?
Why?
(This story was included only to provide background material for story E. Subjects' responses to it were not analyzed, or included in the study.)

(E) On another day Alf was the one who was caught cheating.
What should Basil do?
Why?

Following Piaget's definition of reciprocity as being a return of identical behavior, reciprocity responses for Story A are those which propose that if a child is hit by another, he should hit this second child in return. For Story B, a reciprocity response is one which proposes that a child should not share his property with a child who has previously refused to share his. Reciprocity responses for Story *C* are those which recommend that a child should take the property of another child who has previously taken his; and for Story *E*, reciprocity responses are those which suggest that one child has the right to defame the character of another child if he has previously defamed his.

1. Specificity of Responses

The specificity of Ss responses can be examined on the basis of their responses as a group, and as individuals. Group responses show that reciprocity responses were given by 26.7 per cent (SE = 4.2) of the subjects to Story *A*, by 40.6 per cent (SE = 4.9) of the Ss to Story *B*, by 5.0 per cent (SE = 2.2) of the subjects to Story *C*, and by 25.7 per cent (SE = 4.4) of the subjects to Story *E*. Remaining responses were of a non-reciprocity kind.

These differences in group responses to the four stories, in terms of their being reciprocity or non-reciprocity responses, were examined for significance by use of chi square tests for correlated percentages. The chi square values, corrected for continuity, show that group responses to the four stories two at a time, are, with one exception (responses to Stories *A* and *E*), significantly different.

Specificity on the basis of individual responses is shown in Table 14.1, where it can be seen that of the 27 reciprocity responses given to Story *A*, that depicting physical aggression, two or 7.4 per cent (SE = 5.0) accurately predict *S*'s response to the three subsequent stories in terms of their being either reciprocity or nonreciprocity responses (Pattern 1). It can also be seen from Table 14.1 that of the 74 nonreciprocity responses given by subjects to Story *A*, 44 or 54.5 per cent (SE = 5.8) accurately predict an individual's responses to the three subsequent stories (Pattern 2).

TABLE 14.1. *Frequency Distribution of 16 Possible Patterns of Response at 3 Different Grade Levels*

16 POSSIBLE PATTERNS OF RECIPROCITY AND NONRECIPROCITY RESPONSES TO THE 4 STORIES	GRADE II	GRADE V	GRADE VIII
1. R, R, R, R	1	1	0
2. NR, NR, NR, NR	4	14	26
3. R, NR, NR, NR	0	6	1
4. R, R, NR, NR	1	4	1
5. R, R, R, NR	0	0	1
6. NR, R, R, R	1	0	0
7. NR, NR, R, R,	0	0	0
8. NR, NR, NR, R	3	1	1
9. NR, R, NR, R	4	3	1
10. R, NR, R, NR	0	1	0
11. NR, R, R, NR	0	0	0
12. R, NR, NR, R	1	1	1
13. NR, R, NR, NR	8	5	3
14. R, NR, R, R	0	0	0
15. R, R, NR, R	5	2	0
16. NR, NR, R, NR	0	0	0

In order to examine statistically the independence of a subject's response to Story A and to each of the other three stories, chi square tests of contingency were carried out. The values of chi square, corrected for continuity, indicate that hypotheses of independence cannot be rejected at the 5 per cent level of confidence, the criterion of significance used throughout this paper.

2. Reasons Given for Responses

a. Story A (Aggressing another). A frequently noted characteristic of the reasons given by subjects for their responses to Story A was the element of negativism; that is, Ss seemed to arrive at their particular judgments more by elimination than by direct choice. Such a tendency, it was further noted, was one which significantly increased as grade level increased ($x^2 = 11.9$; $p < .01$). Specifically, negativism characterized the reasons given by four or 14.3 per cent (SE $= 6.6$) of the second graders, by 13 or 34.2 per cent (SE $= 7.7$) of the fifth graders, and by 24 or 63.2 per cent (SE $= 8.2$) of the eighth graders.

Of the 4 second-grade Ss who seemed to take this negative approach in solving the problem, 3 explained their particular responses by denouncing reciprocity ("He shouldn't hit him back."); the fourth, by denouncing the telling of a teacher about the offense. Ten of the 13 fifth graders gave as reasons for their responses a denouncement of reciprocity, while the other 3 explained, "He shouldn't tell." Of the 24 eighth-grade Ss in this group of "negativists," 21 objected to reciprocity, 2 objected to telling a teacher, and one objected to both reciprocity and telling a teacher.

Summarily, 41 or 40.6 per cent (SE $= 4.9$) of the total group of Ss explained their responses to Story A by denouncing other possible responses. Thirty-four in this group objected to reciprocity, 6 objected to telling an authority person, and one objected to both reciprocity and "telling."

A second characteristic noted in the reasons given by subjects for their particular responses to Story A was lack of articulation, a characteristic which decreased significantly as grade level increased ($x^2 = 19.09$; $p < .01$). When probed as to why a particular response was given, 16 or 57.1 per cent (SE $= 9.4$) of the second-grade subjects, and 11 or 28.9 per cent (SE $= 7.4$) of the fifth-grade subjects, could give no further or more articulated reason than, "Because he hit him."

b. Story B (Sharing property). All of the reasons given by the 41 subjects who suggested reciprocity as a solution for Story B were identical in essence: One shouldn't share property with a child who has previously refused to share his. Typical of the specific reasons given were:

> 'Cause he said no the other time.
> That other boy never let him have nothing.
> Because the other boy said no, and he might have had to use it real bad.
> Because the boy wouln't let him use his eraser, so there's no reason why he should let him use his.

While it would seem, on the surface, that nonreciprocity responses — that is, responses that proposed sharing — would be more altruistic kinds of responses, examination of the reasons given for some of them suggested, actually, a regard for one's own rather than for one's neighbor's needs. Of the 60 nonreciprocity responses given to Story B, none given by the second graders, but 10 or 43.5 per cent (SE = 10.3) of those given by the fifth graders, and 12 or 41.4 per cent (SE = 9.2) of those given by the eighth graders were explained in terms of looking out for one's own future needs. These 22 Ss suggested, for example, that one should share an eraser with a child who has previously refused to share his because:

> Maybe the other boy would feel ashamed of himself and give it to him the next time.
> The other boy would be more apt to loan his the next time.
> He can say, "The next time I don't have an eraser you can let me use yours."

More altruistic kinds of reasons were given by the other 38 Ss who also gave nonreciprocity responses to Story B. Typical of these were:

> Because it's nicer to share with other people.
> Because you should let people borrow things.
> To be nice about the deal.
> Because it would be kind if he let him borrow it.
> He should be nice instead of stingy.

c. *Story C (Taking property)*. Only 5 Ss or 5.0 per cent (SE = 2.2) of the total group of 101 Ss gave reciprocity responses to Story C. Each of the 5 explained his response by pointing out that if a child takes a ruler belonging to another child, the second child has the right to take something of his. Only one of these Ss (a second grader) specified it should be another ruler.

Eighty-nine or 92.7 per cent (SE = 2.7) of the 96 nonreciprocity responses given to Story C suggested telling an authority person about the child who has taken property belonging to another; for all but one, the authority person was the teacher.[2] Three different kinds of reasons were given by the 89 Ss for this nonreciprocity response. Twenty-nine (8 in Grade 2, 5 in Grade 5, 16 in Grade 8) identified the behavior described in Story C as stealing which, they suggested, should be reported to an authority person. Fifty-three (15 in Grade 2, 27 in Grade 5, 11 in Grade 8) saw telling an authority person as a way of getting back the property that had been taken. The remaining 7 Ss (1 in Grade 5, 6 in Grade 8) saw telling an authority person as a way of *avoiding* trouble. As one of the 7 explained, "If he tried to take it away, he might get into trouble for fighting."

d. *Story E (Defaming character)*. Of the 24 reciprocity responses given to Story E, 22 or 91.7 per cent (SE = 5.6) were explained by subjects' apparent acceptance of the principle, "Do unto others as they do unto you." Or, as they specifically put it:

You've got to take your own part. When somebody does something you got to do it back.

He did it to him, so he should do it to get even with him.

Reasons given for the other two reciprocity responses were:

To show him that your feelings can be hurt by somebody calling you a cheater.

To prove he wasn't the only one who ever copied.

The 77 nonreciprocity responses to Story E were actually "Do nothing" responses; that is, Ss proposed that a child who has been called a "cheater" by another child should do nothing when, subsequently, the second child is found to be cheating. Fifty-two or 67.5 per cent (SE = 5.3) of such responses were explained in terms of a denouncement of reciprocal behavior, and for these 52 subjects reciprocal behavior was to be avoided because:

It is wrong to tell bad things about another ($n = 17$).

It would hurt the child's feelings ($n = 9$).

It would make him lose his friends ($n = 7$).

It would lead to further trouble ($n = 7$).

Two wrongs don't make a right ($n = 5$).

It is the behavior of a tattle-tale ($n = 4$).

It would anger the child ($n = 1$).

It would lead to his seeking revenge ($n = 1$).

It would ruin his reputation ($n = 1$).

The other 25 Ss in this group of 77 explained their nonreciprocity responses directly; that is, without any reference to reciprocal behavior. Nine of them referred to and applied the Golden Rule; eight referred to the future by prophesying that if Basil said nothing now, Alf wouldn't say anything if Basil were caught cheating a second time. Seven other Ss maintained that Basil should do nothing because what Alf did was none of his business, while the final subject explained:

In the Bible it says that if you be kind to people even when they do something to you, you'll even the score. . . . Like if he hit you on the cheek and you turn your head the other way . . . that would even the score because that would hurt him. . . . He'd feel sorry and stuff like that.

Discussion

The specificity of children's moral judgments, and in particular of their attitudes toward reciprocity as a principle of justice, has been noted in a general way in a previous study. Now, when analyzed in detail, it becomes even more pronounced and emphatic. Considered as a group, the 101 Ss in this present study were found to make, with one exception, significantly different kinds of judgments about four different kinds of behavior. The exception occurred when their responses to Story A (Aggressing another) and Story E (Defaming character) were compared. Considered as individuals, their judgment about one kind of behavior (physical aggression) were shown to be consistently independent of their judgments about three other kinds of behavior. Taken together, then, these findings indicate that a child's judgments about the restoration of right order in various situations is affected by the particulars of each situation; and, therefore, that it cannot be assumed that his judgment about one is necessarily representative of what his judgments about the others would be. As was indicated earlier, this phenomenon of specificity places limitations on the general applicability of Piaget's theory regarding the development of concepts of justice in children since the theory is based on their judgments about the restoration of right order in a single kind of situation, that of physical aggression between children.

Examination of the reasons given by Ss in this present study for their particular judgments, originally proposed as a possible way of explaining the specificity, actually serves better as a way of further emphasizing it. For example, the examination of reasons given for responses to Story B (Sharing property) has demonstrated that apparently identical responses are, at a subsurface level, quite different in essence. To share one's property with another child because it would be kind to do so is, it would seem, an essentially different kind of proposal from one that suggests a child should share because it will probably mean material advantages for him in the future. Or, as in Story E (Defaming character), the proposal that one child should refrain from defaming the character of another because to do so would hurt his feelings is hardly identical to a proposal that is overtly similar in kind, but which is explained in terms of: "Don't tell on him, and he won't tell on you."

These elements of pragmatic concern for one's own future welfare have been seen as especially characteristic of reasons given by Ss for their nonreciprocity responses. As such, they tend to suggest that the apparent altruism and goodness of nonreciprocity responses, as compared with reciprocity responses, are not always substantiated in fact. This important difference between appearance and fact is further emphasized by the observation that certain nonreciprocity responses, when analyzed through the reasons given for them, could actually represent indirect forms of reciprocity. Such a possibility became especially pronounced in the response of the S who promoted the Biblical ideal of turning one's check when hit by another because, according to his interpretation, it was a way of "getting even." Perhaps, then, the Piaget definition of reciprocity as being a return of identical behavior is too narrow in that it fails to include the more subtle forms of reciprocity.

Reasons given by subjects for their judgments also point to at least two other kinds of incidental, but nonetheless noteworthy observations. That they show, for example, such frequent reference to what shouldn't be done, rather than to what should be done, tends at least to suggest that the negative side of moral codes is being emphasized to such an extent that their positive side lacks existence, or at least clarity and preciseness for some children. Frequently, in this study, subjects' responses would prompt one to say, "I know what you're against, but what are you for?" And they would also suggest, as was indicated above, that there is a real need to add positive substance to children's moral ideals.

The second incidental observation made regarding reasons given by subjects for their judgments was their lack of articulation. As was indicated earlier, some of the younger subjects were able to give, as the reason for their judgments, only a verbal repetition of the behavior depicted in the story being considered. Actually, this same kind of tendency among younger children has also been noted in Strauss' (1954) study of the development of conceptions of rules. He calls it a definitional conception of rules, and explains that "If a consequence is envisaged (by younger children), it . . . follows by definition, by a kind of direct connection between infraction and consequence that is grounded in no other rationale than its own connection" (p. 195). While data in this present study are not sufficient to verify such a proposal, nonetheless they do not contradict it. Perhaps other studies, in the light of the importance of reasons given by children for moral judgments, would do well to focus them with both persistence and depth.

NOTES

[1] Identical story-situations were presented to male and female subjects. For the female subjects, however, the story characters were always girls; for the male subjects, they were always boys.

[2] One subject suggested telling a policeman about the offense. School records showed that her father was serving time in a penitentiary for forgery.

Resistance to Temptation

Freda Gould Rebelsky, Wesley Allinsmith, and Robert E. Grinder

The scientific study of conscience development has proven to be very difficult. The concept of "conscience" itself did not originate from any psychological theory, so that the term is characterized by broad diffuse connotations. Nevertheless, most psychologists agree that children evidence behaviors indicative of some sort of internalized set of behavioral standards. In this experiment, which was conducted at Harvard University, the assumption is made that one aspect of conscience may be inferred from behavioral measures of resistance to temptation and that a second aspect of conscience may be inferred from children's use of confession. The outcome of the experiment lends support to these assumptions, but only in the case of girls; that is, there was a relationship between the use of confession and resistance to temptation among girls but not boys. As very clearly noted by the authors, the antecedents influencing resistance to temptation are very complex and not yet very well understood.

SOURCE: Adapted and abridged from Freda Gould Rebelsky, Wesley Allinsmith, and Robert E. Grinder, "Resistance to Temptation and Sex Differences in Children's Use of Fantasy Confession." *Child Development*, 1963, 34, 955–962. (With permission of the authors and the Society for Research in Child Development.)

In some recent studies of child development, evidence of confession has been used as an index of conscience. As a basis for interpreting their data, the assumption was made that the response of confession is an indication of the degree to which conscience is developed. Allied assumptions which may or may not have been in the minds of these authors are that the probability of confession is not influenced in a major way by other variables, that confession has the same meaning for all children, and that, given the same "amount" of conscience, there is the same likelihood that confession will be used.

We doubt that these assumptions are justifiable. Acts of confession may reflect complex motivations and may achieve differing results for the confessor. Among the possible motives for confession are guilt, dependency, desire for affiliation, and desire for punishment. Confession may result in absolution and foregiveness, punishment of various types, or both punishment and forgiveness. There are also important ways in which the actual behavior of confessors may differ, e.g., in the length of time elapsing between transgression and confession; in the person chosen as recipient; in the "emotionality" or contriteness of the confession.

The present study was undertaken to explore the topic of confession, using a behavioral measure of resistance to temptation and children's completions of projective stories that deal with transgression. Two topics of the study are discussed herein: (a) sex differences in the use of confession, and (b) the soundness of the use of confession as a measure of conscience.

Hypotheses

In western civilization, confession appears to be a behavior that fits more appropriately into the dependent, affiliative, verbal, manipulative framework of femininity than into the independent, motoric, less socially adept framework of masculinity. Therefore it seems probable that in our society more girls than boys would use confession. Because a well-behaved and conscientious boy might not want to use or be able to use behavior as "feminine" as confession, we predicted that girls would be more likely to confess after transgression than boys. On the grounds that development of one aspect of "conscience" may be inferred from behavioral measures of resistance to temptation, we also expected that children's use of confession in the projective stories would be positively related to their degree of resistance to temptation. At the same time we were aware of the multiple determinants of resistance to temptation.

Method

Subjects

The Ss for the study were 138 sixth grade children living in Newton and Watertown, Massachusetts. There were 69 boys and 69 girls between the ages of 11–6 and 12–6 years. Six years previously the mothers of these Ss had been interviewed extensively about their child-rearing practices.

Procedure

The children were given 10 projective story beginnings to complete. In the present report eight of the stories, those dealing with transgression by a hero (or heroine) against peers or adults, are used. Since the stories differed somewhat for the sexes, boys and girls in a given school were segregated and administered the stories simultaneously. Male *E*s administered the stories, announcing that they were from Harvard University and stating:

> We're interested in finding out what (boys/girls) your age are like. I have some stories here for you to finish. I'll read each story aloud and you can follow it in your booklet. Then you finish the story, starting where the story leaves off. This is not an English class. Don't worry about spelling. There are no right or wrong answers; you can say anything you want in your stories; we'll take them back to the University with us.

The children were then asked to turn to the first story. The *E* read it aloud, saying at the end, "Now you finish the story, telling what the people in your story are thinking and feeling, and what happens and how it turns out." The children wrote their story endings in the test booklet in the appropriate space provided for them.

From 3 to 10 days after the story session, a different male *E* administered the behavioral test of temptation to the Ss. The temptation test consisted of a shooting gallery game that was played alone by each S. Seated 7 feet away from a target box, Ss "shot" a "ray-gun" pistol at a rotating rocket, and with each shot prearranged scores from zero to five were registered by score lights, also housed in the target box. Badges were offered as prizes, motivation was high, and the game was programed so that only by cheating could a child win a prize. Ss were thus tempted to cheat.

After each S finished the temptation game, he was sent to still another *E* who gave him a second set of story beginnings to complete. The second set of stories was similar in number and in content to the first. The same instructions given previously were used, except that stories were not read aloud. Because Ss entered the experimental room at times when others who had finished the temptation test earlier were already writing, earphones were placed on the S's head when he was ready for a story beginning, and he listened to it as recorded on an audiograph machine. Several machines were on hand so that Ss did not have to wait before moving on to the next story.

The story completion items were designed to be of interest to the Ss' age group. All were written so that there was little or no possibility of the hero's being detected unless he gave himself up or gave himself way. The stories dealt with situations in which the Ss probably would not have found themselves, but in which the emotions depicted, such as the coveting of a friend's toy or a yearning to win the prize in a race, were nevertheless appropriate to the subject's age. The story stimuli given to both sexes were parallel: changes were made only in the name and sex of the major character, who was male for boys and female for girls, and in having a walking race for girls in place of a running race for boys. For each sex there were four pairs of stories which had been matched in content. One of each pair was presented before and one after the test of resistance to temptation.

Coding the Stories

The completed stories were scored by four coders in terms of several dimensions of guilt, but only the data on presence or absence of the use of confession in the story endings will be presented in this paper. Interjudge reliability of the coding of presence or absence of confession, based on a sample of the stories, was perfect. Confession in the children's completions of the story beginnings was defined as the revelation in words by the hero that he had committed the transgression. The operational definition thus excluded situations in which the hero never confessed but behaved so oddly that others were able to infer that he had transgressed. It included what others have termed "admission," i.e., acknowledgment after being suspected, interrogated, or accused. In the present data the great majority of the confessions (77 per cent) were spontaneous in the sense of occurring before there was evidence that the hero anticipated detection. That is, "admissions" were rare, and there were no differences between the sexes in the use of voluntary and nonvoluntary confessions.

The coding was done story by story, with the identity of the children masked by numbers and their behavior in the resistance to temptation situation unknown to the coders.

Data Analysis and Statistics Used

The data on confession were analyzed by sex of the child and by his behavior (cheating or not cheating) in the temptation situation. Each of these variables was examined with the other held constant. Three separate analyses were carried out: (a) the use of confession in the endings of the stories administered before the temptation game; (b) the use of confession in the endings of the stories administered after the temptation game; and (c) the use of confession in response to all eight stories. The change in the number of stories in which confession appeared from pregame to postgame was also examined. Mood's likelihood ratio, which yields a number with which one can enter a chi square table to get a probability value, was used to assess the significance of the differences in the distributions in this study. Inasmuch as we would be interested in results in either direction, all tests are two-tailed, despite prior prediction. A significance level of .05 was used.

Results

It is clear that confession was used frequently by children of this age in responding to the stories. In the eight possible stories, 131 of the 138 children depicted confession at least once, including all the girls. All but 7 of the boys portrayed confession in at least one story.

Table 14.2 summarizes the data, showing differences among various groups

TABLE 14.2. *Differences Between Various Groups in Number of Stories in Which They Portrayed Confession*

GROUPS COMPARED*	TOTAL EIGHT STORIES			FOUR PRETEST STORIES			FOUR POSTTEST STORIES		
	X^2	df	p	X^2	df	p	X^2	df	p
1. Boys / Girls†	32.27	8	.001	12.28	4	.02	10.30	4	.05
2. Cheaters / Noncheaters	19.75	8	.02	13.73	4	.01	12.17	4	.02
3. Boy cheaters / Boy noncheaters	11.72	8	.20	4.56	4	.40	6.05	4	.20
4. Girl cheaters / Girl noncheaters	10.86	8	.30	8.16	4	.10	10.17	4	.05
5. Boy cheaters / Girl cheaters	17.51	8	.05	6.48	4	.20	8.44	4	.10
6. Boy noncheaters / Girl noncheaters	17.59	8	.05	4.78	4	.50	5.91	4	.50
7. Combined X^2 (3 + 4): Cheat / Noncheat (with sex control)	22.58	16	.20	12.72	8	.20	16.22	8	.05
8. Combined X^2 (5 +6): Boys / Girls (with cheat control)	35.10	16	.01	11.26	8	.20	14.35	8	.10

NOTE: All tests are two-tailed.

* *Groups:*

Boy cheaters	$N = 52$	Total boys	$N = 69$
Boy noncheaters	$N = 17$	Total girls	$N = 69$
Girl cheaters	$N = 44$	Total cheaters	$N = 96$
Girl noncheaters	$N = 25$	Total noncheaters	$N = 42$

† The italicized groups confessed in more stories than did the nonitalicized ones.

in the number of stories in which they portrayed confession. In the three columns, (a) total number of stories, (b) the four pretemptation stories, and (c) the four posttemptation stories, girls used confession in more story endings than did boys, and noncheaters used confession more than did cheaters.

The effects of controlling sex of child and response to temptation are also given in Table 14.2. As can be seen, the sex difference holds up when response to temptation is controlled; the relation of confession to resistance to temptation turns out to be a function mainly of the girl Ss.

An analysis was made of the shift in number of confessions given by the Ss from the pretemptation test stories to the posttemptation test stories, with the same eight groups as in Table 14.2. There were no significant differences between groups, except between cheaters and noncheaters. Noncheaters tended to confess more in the pretemptation test stories, and cheaters tended to confess either the same amount or more in the posttemptation stories ($x^2 = 12.44$, 2 df, $p < .01$).

Discussion

The results indicate that the use of confession by children in completing stories about transgression differs with sex. Girls confess more. There also appears to be a relation between the use of confession and cheating behavior: those who do not cheat are more likely to depict confession in their stories than are cheaters. As anticipated, this finding is much clearer for girls than for boys. If resistance to temptation is interpreted as a major aspect of conscience and if the temptation game is judged a valid measure of the tendency to resist temptation, the data of this investigation suggest that the use of confession as a measure of conscience is more efficient — and perhaps more appropriate — in the case of girls than boys.

There are many possible reasons why confession was used in this study more by girls than by boys and why it appears to be more highly related to girls' rather than boys' resistance to temptation: (a) confession is an affiliative, dependent behavior which is more appropriate for girls than boys to use in our society; (b) girls have a greater superiority in the use of language for social influence purposes and thus use confession more readily; or (c) girls may not have been as interested in the cheating game or as involved with it or with the stories and thus were able to choose an "easy" response without really involving themselves emotionally.

If the stories had been used alone, without the benefit of the chance to cheat, the findings would have been much more limited, though it still would be clear that girls confess more than boys. We are now able to predict the girl's behavior in a temptation situation knowing their response to fantasy in pretest stories, and we can predict some aspect of fantasy knowing their behavior in the temptation test.

In a recent study of Israeli children, Luria, Goldwasser, and Goldwasser (1963), using similar stories and the same coding of confession as was used in this study, found no sex differences in the use of confession. The data in the present study were reanalyzed for Jewish and non-Jewish children. Though the sample of Jewish children is small ($n = 37$), it appears that there are no sex differences in the use of confession in Jewish children and that the sex differences reported in this paper were even more marked when the Jewish children were removed from the sample. Jewish boys in the sample were like non-Jewish boys, but the Jewish girls cheated more than did non-Jewish girls and confessed less, thus supplying additional evidence on the relation of cheating and non-confession found in girls.

In this study we had a behavioral measure of resistance to temptation and a measure of fantasy confession. We still need studies in which actual cheating (or some other measure of conscience) as related to actual behavior of confession following the cheating. We have reports of mothers about children's confession and reports of mothers and fathers about children's confession. We now have a measure of fantasy confession, but as yet have no behavioral measure of confession. It is apparent that further clarification of the use of confession and its relation to behavior and to the sex of the confessor waits upon studies in which both a behavioral measure of conscience and confession are employed. To create a plausible opportunity for Ss to confess may be a difficult task. Meantime, the clear sex differences shown in this paper, coupled with the lack of a distinct relation of confession to resistance to temptation in boys, lead to the conclusion that confession should not be used unquestioningly as a measure of conscience for both sexes in research in child development.

The data also point out the need for explorations into the use of confession among groups where the sex role differences are less clear or more clear than in our society.

Acquiring Dependence and Independence

Glen Heathers

An important distinction is made in this paper by Professor Heathers between instrumental and emotional dependence. By instrumental dependence he refers to dependency behaviors which are designed to achieve some ultimate goal. Thus a child must seek help from a parent for the purpose of satisfying a particular problem and not for the dependency relationship with the parent *per se*. In terms of emotional dependence the end-goal is the response of the adult to the child; for example, an affectionate response. A similar distinction is made with respect to the development of independence. According to Dr. Heathers's formulation, instrumental dependence develops by means of the child learning what responses on his part lead to help from others. Emotional dependence develops from acquired needs for affection, approval, and reassurance. Emotional dependence is more likely to develop in those situations that produce constant sources of conflict and anxiety in the child.

Everyone's personality develops in a social world, and every aspect of personality reflects one's relationships and experiences with others. A central aspect of the process of becoming "socialized" is developing needs, perceptions, and response patterns having to do with dependence on others, or with independence. Currently, a major research program on the development of dependence-independence in preschool children is underway at the Fels Research Institute. This paper presents the general theoretical orientation basic to the research program. Its purposes are to define certain forms of dependence-independence and to indicate how they may be learned.

Forms of Dependence and Independence

A person is dependent on others to the extent that he has needs[1] which

─────────
SOURCE: Adapted and abridged from Glen Heathers, "Acquiring Dependence and Independence: A Theoretical Orientation." *Journal of Genetic Psychology*, 1955, 87, 277–291. (With permission of the author and the Journal Press.)

require that others respond in particular ways if these needs are to be satisfied. A person is independent of others to the extent that he can satisfy his needs without requiring that others respond to him in particular ways.

One way of depending on others is *instrumental dependence,* which is present when a person seeks help in reaching goals. Thus, an infant depends on others for help in satisfying hunger and other bodily needs. When a child seeks help, as in getting food, help is the subgoal in relation to the end-goal of food.

With emotional dependence, the responses of others are the end-goals rather than means of reaching them. Thus, the need for affection is an emotional-dependence need which is satisfied by others' affectionate responses. Three forms of emotional dependence may be distinguished — needs for reassurance, for affection, and for approval. The need for *reassurance* occurs in situations when a person anticipates undesired or feared outcomes — failure, rejection, injury, etc. Seeking reassurance is a matter of placing oneself in the care of another person as a way of avoiding such outcomes. Thus, a child who fears the dark desires someone he trusts to share the darkness with him, and a child who is anxious about failing a task wants to be told that he will make out all right. A person's need for *affection* is the need for others to respond with physical signs of affection such as caresses and kisses or with words and deeds which show that they care for him. A person's need for *approval* is the need for others to make positive responses toward him either on the basis of his performance or on the basis of status-giving characteristics such as his appearance, his possessions, or his social roles.

Instrumental independence means conducting activities and coping with problems without seeking help. It is the obverse of instrumental dependence.

Emotional independence means, first, the absence of needs for reassurance, affection, or approval in particular situations. This aspect may be called "emotional self-reliance" and is the obverse of emotional dependence. In addition, emotional independence is defined to include "self-assertion" in the form of needs to master tasks, and to dominate others. It should be noted that emotional self-reliance does not assume any specific independence needs, while self-assertion does. The need to master a task is assumed to be more than the need to complete it; it is the need for self-approval on the basis of one's performance. Similarly, the need to dominate is assumed to be a need for self-approval on the basis of one's assertive behavior. These definitions of self-reliance and self-assertion assume that the behavior expressing them is not used as a means of gaining approval. When approval is the goal, as when a person dominates in order to attract attention or praise, emotional dependence rather than independence is shown.

Assumptions about the Learning Process

In offering an account of how dependence and independence are learned, it is assumed that learning takes place in relation to needs which a person tends to satisfy through making appropriate goal-directed responses. A person learns certain "meanings" of aspects of situations in relation to his needs, and he learns "predispositions" to make or not to make certain goal-directed responses when a given need is active in a situation. His overt responses depend on which of his needs are active as he enters the situation, on what *need-relevancies* he perceives in the situation, and on his *expectancies* of satisfying or not satisfying his needs by responses directed toward goals in the situation.

The need-relevancies of a situation may be divided into three categories: (a) need-arousal — a situation may evoke needs, as when a person perceives the threat of injury; (b) goals — a situation may provide opportunities for satisfying needs; and (c) goal-pathways — a situation may provide opportunities to make responses which lead to goals.

A person learns the need-relevancies of a situation through the simultaneous association of his perceptions[2] of the situation, and of his responses in the situation, with positive or negative *reinforcement*. When perceptions of the situation and of his responses to it are associated with *positive* reinforcement (achieving goals) he learns to expect a positive outcome and acquires predispositions to make the goal-directed responses which led to positive reinforcement. Conversely, when perceptions of the situation and of his responses are associated with *negative* reinforcement (failure to achieve goals, punishment, injury) he learns to expect this sort of outcome and acquires predispositions not to make the responses which led to negative reinforcement.

A point which requires special emphasis is that the reinforcement value of a goal is not determined by the goal as such but by its relation to one's expectations. Thus a child who is seeking affection from his mother may perceive her hug as rejection because she doesn't take him on her lap and caress him as she usually has done. Another child may perceive a similar hug as rewarding because it equals or exceeds what he has learned to expect.

An important aspect of learning need-relevancies is that stimuli from a situation which are associated with reinforcement acquire reinforcement value. When this has occurred, these accompaniments or "signs" of reinforcement may function as goals in the absence of the previous reinforcement. Thus, if a child's mother smiles whenever she gratifies any of his needs, her smile will come to be a goal in its own right.

When substitute goals are learned, new needs are also acquired in the sense that a person tends to seek these substitute goals in the absence of the needs which were previously active. In this article, needs for reassurance, affection, approval, mastery, and domination are considered to be acquired needs. It is assumed that the reason one comes to need affection, approval, etc., is because of a general tendency to seek positive reinforcement. So, when a person perceives the opportunity for achieving a goal (such as affection or approval) he not only has the expectancy of achieving it but also the predisposition to achieve it.

Instrumental Dependence

At birth, and during his first months, the infant is relatively helpless and is *passively* dependent on others to satisfy almost all his needs. He can breathe, and, if his supply of air is interrupted, his struggling may restore it. He can suck in and swallow liquid brought to his mouth and he can digest and eliminate. He reacts to annoying stimuli by general bodily activity which may remove the annoyance. However, beyond such reflexes and such general bodily responses, the very young infant can do nothing to satisfy his needs.

Despite his helplessness, it is wrong to say that the neonate is *actively* dependent on others, since he must first learn to associate others with the satisfaction of his needs. Neither instrumental nor emotional dependence are present until the child has learned to perceive others as related to achieving goals, and until he has learned to use certain responses as means of inducing others to attend to his needs. For example, the basis for learning to use crying as an expression of instrumental dependence is the fact that a child's mother responds to his crying by trying to discover and satisfy his needs. Learning principles predict that through this sort of experience the child comes to associate crying with his mother's responding to him, and with relieving his distress. When this learning has taken place, crying may be used as a device to express instrumental dependence.

In developing instrumental dependence on others, the child learns various devices for stimulating others to help him reach his goals. Crying is generally effective in alerting others to the fact that he wants something, and also is apt to disturb others enough to make them try to find out what he wants and "pacify" him. But crying isn't a good way of indicating *what* he wants. A child learns to indicate what he wants by looking toward it, pointing at it, naming it, etc. In this process of learning instrumental-dependence devices, each child is taught by his mother and others to use certain ways of asking for help which are acceptable to them, and to which they will respond by helping them. He is also taught not to use certain devices because these are ineffective in getting help. Thus a child may be taught to stop crying, to smile, or to say "please" as conditions for getting others to help him.

One form of instrumental dependence is imitation, in which one depends on another for his cues as to where to go or what to do in order to reach his goals. Imitation has been analyzed in detail by Miller and Dollard (1941), who showed that one child will learn to imitate another child if following the other leads to reward while not following him leads to nonreward. They showed also that imitation "generalizes" from one situation to another. That is, imitation becomes a general instrumental-dependence device which may be used in any appropriate situation as a means of reaching a goal.

It is essential that the person from whom instrumental aid is sought be motivated to give help. Very often this means that a child must "earn" the help he seeks by offering his prospective helper some inducement. Thus a mother who desires that her child show signs of "growing up" may require that he try first before she will help him. This give-and-take is obviously important in developing the socialized individual. Instead of passive, one-sided relationships it requires active, mutual relations with other peoples. Sears (1951) offers a beginning toward the systematic analysis of this interaction process in his consideration of the "dyadic group."

Emotional Dependence

Acquiring Emotional Dependence Needs

In explaining how emotional dependence develops, the first question is how others' responses become the end-goals which are sought rather than means toward end-goals as with instrumental dependence. In the analysis which follows, this will be discussed in relation to acquiring needs for reassurance, affection, and approval.

Needs for reassurance. Reassurance satisfies needs for emotional support in "anxiety" situations when a person anticipates injury, failure, or rejection. In order to anticipate unpleasant experiences in a situation, one must previously have had such experiences in situations having something in common with the present one. The need for reassurance in situations perceived as threatening develops if other people, by their presence or their responses, have given instrumental aid which prevented the threatening outcomes. In this way, other people become associated with avoiding or relieving anxiety in threatening situations. More generally, the presence and responses of others, including their verbal assurance, come to be associated with anxiety reduction in any situation. Thus a person comes to "trust" others and to count on them to prevent undesired outcomes. The need for reassurance, and responses of seeking it, thus develop as means of preventing or relieving anxiety.

Obviously a person does not learn to trust everybody, since in his experiences some people have failed to protect him from harm and some have punished him through frustrating, rejecting, or injuring him. On the basis of these differential experiences, each person learns to direct his needs for reassurances toward certain people or categories of people and not toward others.

Needs for affection. To explain how a child's needs for affection develop, it is necessary to show how affectionate responses by others become associated with the satisfaction of certain of the child's "basic" needs. The infant's earliest experiences of receiving affection have to do with being made comfortable and relaxed, and with being given pleasant sensual stimulation. One of the primary expressions of affection is when a mother holds her infant as she feeds him. Another is holding him in her arms and caressing him while rocking him to sleep. Each of these classical expressions of affection involves a comfortable posture, warmth, and mild stimulation tending to relax the child. Also each involves direct sensual stimulation to which the child responds with signs of pleasure. After a few weeks, the child experiences affection from his mother and others through being played with — being tumbled about, being surprised in games like peek-a-boo, being given toys to play with, being teased with funny faces or funny sounds, etc. On the basis of such experiences, the child comes to perceive its mother and others as sources of comfort and pleasure. Also it develops impulses toward being responded to in ways associated with such comfort and pleasure — it develops needs for affection.

While satisfying her child's need in direct physical ways the mother also smiles at her child, talks gently to him, calls him pet names, and uses other verbal expresses of her affection. Since these reponses are associated with the direct physical gratification of his needs, they come to have reward value in their own right so that needs which were satisfied originally by physical affection may now be satisfied (at least in part) by these symbolic expressions of affection.

Needs for approval. When the child first learns to depend on others for instrumental aid, for reassurance, or for affection, nothing much is required of him beyond letting others know what his needs are. In other words, if his mother understands his capacities, she won't demand that he behave in any particular way as a condition for giving him help or reassurance or affection. However, after a time, she begins to require that he act in certain ways if he is to get her to cooperate in meeting his needs. The child's choice of response in a situation thus becomes a condition of his being rewarded, ignored, or punished by others.

When the child learns that his choice of response determines whether others will satisfy his needs, he develops the need to respond in ways which others approve. When they tell him "that's fine," "you're a big boy," "you did it by yourself," etc., at the same time they reward him in other ways, their verbal expressions of approval acquire reward value. Thereafter, when the need for approval is present, these signs of approval may satisfy the need.

On the other hand, signs of disapproval (frowning, yelling at the child, saying "don't" or "that's naughty") are associated with rejection or punishment and acquire negative reinforcement value. Disapproval thus becomes a basis for learning not to do certain things even when those acts are not discouraged in any other way. Also, since disapproval is often accompanied by punishment, it will tend to arouse anxiety about being punished. This anxiety will be relieved by getting others to respond positively.[3]

Developing Response Patterns for Expressing Dependence Needs

In analyzing any need, three aspects may be distinguished: (a) a state of *tension* or expectancy which may be experienced as dissatisfaction, anxiety, or pleasant anticipation; (b) *goals* (objects, circumstances, others' responses) which are ways of satisfying the need; and (c) *response patterns* which are means of achieving these goals. The analysis to this point has dealt mainly with the tensional and goal aspects of emotional dependence. This section considers how a person develops or selects particular response patterns (devices) for stimulating others to satisfy his dependence needs.

In seeking a dependence relationship with another person, one's overtures should do three things — attract the other person's attention, indicate what is wanted, and motivate the other person to respond in the desired way. During the child's first year or so, crying is one of the most frequently used dependence devices. Crying usually induces the child's mother to approach, pick him up, and comfort him, thus satisfying needs for reassurance or for affection. One of the child's earliest learned dependence devices is turning or leaning toward his mother and reaching out his arms. This is a postural adjustment associated with being picked up; when it occurs in anticipation of being picked up it serves as a stimulus to the mother and is a dependence device. When the child is able to crawl or walk, he tends to approach his mother when seeking to satisfy dependent needs.

Language adds greatly to the child's ability to indicate what he wants and also give him further weapons for motivating others to comply with his wishes. When he learns to say "mama" and "dada" he can indicate which one he wishes to serve him. As his vocabulary grows, he can say specifically what his wishes are, or what he wants others to do: "I'm scared," "I'm tired," "come here," "carry me," "watch me," "look what I made." Each of these verbal expressions is taught the child in association with the situations or acts to which it applied, and in association with the satisfaction of the needs which were present at the same time.

Each child learns his own unique set of dependence devices according to which of his response patterns his parents and others rewarded. Thus it is not possible to present a list of dependence response patterns which applies to all children. However, there are common elements in every child's set of dependence devices which reflect the fact that each child's needs for reassurance, affection, and approval call for certain kinds of responses from others. Also, each child in a cultural group tends to be taught a set of dependence devices which reflect the values and norms of the group.

Reactions When Dependence Overtures Are Rejected

Sontag (1951) proposes that the frustration of dependent needs leads to "defenses" against further frustration of one's dependence-seeking overtures. Obviously the most radical defense against rejection is to stop trying to induce others to satisfy one's dependence needs. However, before a child adopts this sort of reaction to felt rejection, he may respond to rejection by changes in his dependence-seeking devices, or by shifting his overtures away from one person toward another. Thus, if a child's mother rejects his requests to sit on her lap but offers affection in other ways, the child will tend to modify his affection-seeking overtures correspondingly. If the child's mother almost always refuses to pick him up and play with him while his father usually does, he will tend to turn to his father rather than to his mother for this sort of expression of affection.

Sontag has indicated how overconformity may be adopted as a general device for avoiding rejection of dependence overtures. As he pointed out, through being "good" a child lessens his chances of being disapproved or punished as well as increases his chances of winning affection and approval from his parents or others. Being good, of course, means paying the price of catering to adults' standards of conduct as a way of inducing them to gratify his dependence needs.

In the cases described above, a child reacts to rejection by modifying his dependence-seeking overtures or by changing the person toward whom he directs such overtures. These types of adjustive reactions to rejection occur as the child perceives an alternative way of satisfying his dependence needs. However, if such alternative channels are not available to him, if he consistently meets rejection when he makes dependence-seeking overtures to the people around him, he may come to expect rejection generally. In such a case, expressing his emotional dependence needs becomes associated with punishing consequences (frustration) and the child tends to quit trying to induce others to satisfy these needs. Thus, constant rejection may produce a general withdrawal from seeking dependence relationships, although dependent needs may still be active. Experimental evidence in support of this point is offered by Carl (1949), who showed that the frequency of dependence responses declines when the adult toward whom these responses are directed consistently fails to respond to them.

Where consistent rejection has produced strong withdrawal tendencies, one may find the child showing evidence of a conflict between the tendency to make dependence overtures and the tendency to hold back in anticipation of being rejected. Hesitant, timorous overtures may result from these opposed impulses. The child who wants affection may start toward his mother, then stop half way and stand there. Or he may go over and stand at her side, touch her dress, then wait for an encouraging sign from her before making more definite indications of his wishes.

Instrumental Independence

When a child initiates his own activities and copes with difficulties he encounters without asking for help, he shows instrumental independence. Suppose a child starts working out a cut-out puzzle with the goal of completing it. If the puzzle is hard for him he will take quite a while and make many mistakes before he reaches his goal. The extent to which he persists in the task without asking for help may be taken as a measure of his instrumental independence.

Whether a child shows instrumental independence in a situation depends on a number of factors. The hypotheses which follow specify five of these factors and predict their effects on a child's tendencies to seek help.

(a). *The more frustration a child encounters while performing an activity, the more will he tend to seek help.* This hypothesis simply assumes that children learn to seek help as one way of overcoming obstacles in their goal-directed behavior.

(b). *The more a child expects that help is available, the more will he tend to seek it.* If a child has learned through repeated experiences that others will help him under certain conditions, he will tend to resort to help when those conditions exist. If he usually has been refused help at such times, he will tend not to expect or seek it.

(c). *The more a child expects he can reach his goal unaided, the less will he tend to seek help.* If the child has previously completed the activity or similar activities without help, he has a basis for expecting to succeed on his own and for going ahead without asking for help.

(d). *The more reassurance a child receives while performing an activity, the less is he apt to seek help.* This factor of reassurance is illustrated when someone says, "You're doing fine," or "You can finish it." The hypothesis assumes that reassurance fosters instrumental independence by lessening anxiety in instances when the child is anticipating failure.

(e). *The more a child expects approval for reaching a goal unaided, the less will he tend to seek help.* This assumes the child has the need for approval and that this need provides a positive incentive for finishing an activity without help if he expects approval upon completing it.

The development of "frustration tolerance" is an aspect of acquiring instrumental independence. The critical factor in learning to cope with frustrations is whether the child actually persists until he reaches his goal. When a parent helps a child "over the rough spots" so that he continues at the task rather than giving up, he is helping his child learn to tolerate frustration. Also, if he makes the task easy at the outset and gradually steps up its difficulty as the child's expectation of success increases along with increasing frustration, the chances are good that more and more frustration will be tolerated. Finally, if the desirability of the goal is increased, the child is more apt to persist until reaching it and so to develop the expectation of overcoming obstacles on future occasions.

In analyzing how instrumental independence develops, the role of emotional dependence deserves special consideration. If a situation is one in which the child anticipates injury or rejection, he may require reassurance (emotional dependence) in order to face the situation and so be enabled to develop instrumental independence. Also, as discussed by Stendler (1952), the child's need for approval may play a key role in motivating him to exhibit instrumental independence rather than quitting or asking for help when he encounters difficulties.

Emotional Independence

Emotional dependence and independence are relative terms. No one at any age is emotionally dependent in every situation. However, comparing children or adults of the same age, there are great differences in the types of situation, and in the proportion of all situations, where emotional dependence and independence are shown. As an individual grows older, the situations in which he shows emotional dependence and independence change. It is these differences which require explanation.

Developing Emotional Self-Reliance

A child may be called emotionally self-reliant (or self-confident) when he faces threats of injury or rejection without requiring emotional support. A lack of emotional self-reliance is shown by avoiding threat situations or by seeking emotional "props" which make one feel safer while coping with threats. These props may be means of reducing the actual threat in the situation, or "security symbols" such as the doll a child takes to bed with him, or reassurance from a trusted person.

In analyzing how emotional self-reliance is acquired, threats of injury and of rejection will be discussed separately.

Acquiring self-confidence in physical threat situations. Initially, each child is fearless in many situations where his parents know he may injure himself. When a 12-month-old crawls off the porch and tumbles to the ground he need not be showing self-confidence. He may simply not know any better. Eventually, a child will fall enough times in one situation or another to learn the painful consequences and to anticipate them whenever he is at the point of falling again. When he has learned to associate a situation with the threat of hurting himself, the issue of emotional dependence or independence in that situation is relevant. In responding to the threats he perceives in a situation where he may hurt himself, a child shows emotional independence if he copes with the situation without requiring any protective devices or without leaning on another person for reassurance.

The question of how self-confidence is learned applies in particular to situations where a child has been frightened or hurt and reacts by showing fear or avoidance, or by requiring emotional support in order to face the situation. Methods of learning self-confidence may be illustrated by ways in which children overcome the fear of deep water. Assume a child who swims a little, but is afraid to be in water over his head. Six methods of overcoming his fear are described below.

1. *Sink-or-swim method.* In this case, the child is forced to cope with the situation by being tossed into the water and left to fend for himself. If he gets to land under his own power a few times, he may perceive himself as capable of coping with the situation and lose his fear. This is a hazardous method of teaching self-confidence, since the child may panic and have to be rescued. Or the experience may intensify his fear of the water even though he makes it to land.

2. *Distraction method.* This method includes any means by which the child temporarily forgets or pushes aside his fear so that he jumps into the water and tries to swim. For example, if others say, "I dare you," or "coward," the child may be distracted from his fear long enough to plunge in. Swimming successfully under these conditions is a way for the child to replace his expectation of failure and injury with the expectation of success.

3. *Threshold method.* This is the method of starting out a stroke or two from land and going a bit farther out each time as confidence grows in one's ability

to swim back. The success of this method depends on the threat in the situation increasing slowly enough that the child's anxiety or fear does not exceed the level which he will tolerate.

4. *Overlearning method.* This method calls for practicing swimming under safe conditions to the point where one becomes so skillful and experienced that he becomes confident he can take care of himself in the deep water.

5. *Crutch method.* In this case the child uses water wings or a life belt which he relies on to keep him from sinking. With the protection this device gives him, he practices swimming until he has sufficient confidence in his ability that he will venture into water without a crutch.

6. *Reassurance method.* In this method the child depends on some person whom he trusts to protect him. The reassurance given him enables him to practice swimming and to discover that he can take care of himself.

Each of the six methods described applies to acquiring self-confidence in the great variety of physical threat situations — overcoming the fear of being alone in a room, the fear of animals, the fear of high places, the fear of fighting, etc. Acquiring self-confidence by any of these methods depends on coping with the feared situation successfully and on developing the expectation of being successful on one's own.

Acquiring "rejection-tolerance." One form of emotional self-reliance is the capacity to tolerate rejection by others. Two bases for exhibiting rejection-tolerance are proposed. First, a person may be emotionally self-reliant following instances of being rejected if he has alternative ways of satisfying his needs for affection and approval when they arise. If he has usually been successful in satisfying these dependent needs he may expect to be able to satisfy them again and so will be secure against specific instances of being rejected. Second, a person while developing channels for expressing his emotional dependence needs, learns to discriminate the people who are important sources of gratification of these needs from others who are not. When this learning has occurred, he will be able to take rejection from people who "don't matter" as long as those whom he counts on are not rejecting.

Developing Self-Assertion

Self-assertion expresses needs to master tasks or to dominate other people. In satisfying these needs the relevant goals are feelings of adequacy or superiority: "I did it," "I'm smarter than you are," "I beat him," etc. In short, it is assumed that self-assertion needs are satisfied by self-approval.

Acquiring mastery needs and behavior. A basis for explaining how mastery develops is the child's desire to win others' approval. On this basis, three aspects of the process of developing this form of self-assertion may be distinguished, as follows: (a) acquiring needs for approval, (b) learning to perform tasks with persistence, speed, or skill in order to win approval, and (c) "internalizing," i.e., adopting others' standards as to the sort of performance required to gain approval, and feeling self-approval when these standards are satisfied. The first two aspects fall under emotional dependence and have been discussed earlier in this paper. It is with the third aspect that emotional independence enters the picture since the child who has internalized his approval-seeking doesn't require approval from others to motivate his performance.

Internalization of approval may be explained as follows. After learning to do things which win others' approval, a child anticipates approval whenever he performs the acts which have been approved. It is assumed that anticipated approval is rewarding by itself, giving a feeling of security or pleasure. Since it is rewarding, it may function as a goal to reinforce the performance of the customarily approved behavior.

The degree to which a child develops mastery needs, and the activities and standards of performance he uses to express those needs, are determined by his individual learning experiences. A child will tend to express mastery needs in those activities in which he has been successful in getting approval. Getting approval, of course, depends on doing things which his parents and others value — going to the toilet, keeping clean, solving puzzles, catching a ball, reciting a rhyme, etc. Also a child learns to strive for the levels of accomplishment which others have set up as a basis for giving approval — speed, accuracy, grace, persistence, originality, etc.

Acquiring dominance needs and behavior. Learning dominance needs and behavior may be accounted for on the basis of winning others' approval in the same way that learning mastery was explained above. Once others' approval has been internalized, self-approval (from anticipated approval) serves as reinforcement for dominant behavior. The great differences in dominative behavior among children of the same age may be explained as due in part to differences in the amount of approval or disapproval others have given them for being dominant in particular ways in various situations.

A child does not have to win in order to satisfy dominance needs if approval has been given him for daring, for doing his best, or for making a good showing. However, other things being equal, the more often a child is defeated in tests for dominance, the less apt he will be to express dominative behavior. Since dominating others often has instrumental value in obtaining goals other than approval (as when two children want the same toy), being successful in competing for such goals reinforces one's tendencies toward expressing domination, while being unsuccessful sets up expectations of failure and tends to weaken those tendencies.

NOTES

[1] The term "need" is a theoretical construct which refers to perceptions and response patterns related to achieving and utilizing any goals in a particular class of goals (e.g., affection). Needs may be measured at the perceptual level by obtaining verbal reports (as in projective tests) or at the overt behavioral level by observing responses toward goals.

[2] The use of the term "perception" in this paper may cause confusion because it is conventional to restrict this term to conscious processes. The term is used in this paper to refer to all "psychological processes" which are active when a person reacts to a situation, regardless of the degree of conscious awareness or control of these processes.

[3] The present account of the development of instrumental and emotional dependence implies two basic steps in the socialization process. When the child has learned to depend on others for help, protection, reassurance, and affection, the first step — acquiring "infantile dependence" — has been made. When he learns to seek approval by conforming to others' requirements, he takes the second step, which leads him out of infantile dependence toward what may be called "social maturity." Social maturity is primarily the readiness for mutual relations with others where one tries to satisfy others' needs as a condition for their satisfying his own.

Stability of Achievement and Recognition-Seeking Behavior

Howard A. Moss and Jerome Kagan

Although developmental psychologists vary in their explanations, there is general agreement that behavior patterns are relatively stable over the life span. Some theorists, for example, explain this stability in terms of biological variables whereas others, including Drs. Moss and Kagan, employ constructs derived from learning theory. The basic data involved in this study include longitudinal observations of behavior during the first 14 years of life, during which time it was possible to establish the strength of each child's achievement recognition behaviors. These same subjects were then reassessed during the early adult years. The resulting correlations suggest that achievement recognition behaviors are fairly stable over the time period involved. It should be noted that the upper-middle-class environment from which the subjects were obtained is conducive to the maintenance of achievement-oriented behaviors and may account for the observed stability.

The supposition that selected adult response patterns are established at an early age is a primary assumption of developmental theory. Although literary documents and psychotherapy protocols have provided anecdotal support for this hypothesis, more objective validation has been difficult to obtain. The present paper is a second report that has emerged from a larger project on the stability of childhood behavior. The first paper indicated that dependent behavior in girls showed moderately high stability from the early school years through young adulthood (Kagan and Moss 1959). The present report is concerned with the developmental consistency of two related behaviors: the tendency to strive for (a) mastery of selected skills (achievement behavior), and (b) social recognition through acquisition of specific goals or behaviors (recognition behavior).

SOURCE: Adapted and abridged from Howard A. Moss and Jerome Kagan, "Stability of Achievement and Recognition-Seeking Behaviors from Early Childhood through Adulthood." *Journal of Abnormal and Social Psychology,* 1961, 62, 504–513. (With permission of the authors and the American Psychological Association.)

The achievement variable emphasizes mastery of intellectual, athletic, mechanical, and artistic skills as well as competence in specialized crafts. Social recognition is obtained through acquisition of most of the above behaviors. For intellectual competence, athletic ability, acquisition of money, and positions of power in social groups are the primary methods of obtaining social recognition in the cultural milieu of our middle-class population. Thus, the overt behaviors involved in achievement and recognition strivings overlap to some degree.

In an attempt to differentiate between these two variables, the investigators evaluated the degree to which the individual's mastery behavior was directed at satisfaction of an internal standard of excellence in order to gain self-approval (achievement motivation), in contrast to seeking approval from the social environment (recognition motivation). This is a difficult differentiation to make. The data to be presented reveal a high, positive correlation between ratings of these two behavioral variables. This interdependence suggests that it may be impossible to measure the "desire to improve at a skill" independent of the individual's "desire for social recognition" for this improvement.

Method

Subjects and General Procedure

The subjects were 36 males and 35 females from the Fels Research Institute's longitudinal population. They were enrolled in the project at birth, during the years 1929–1939. At the time of an adult assessment (1947–1959) they were between 20 and 29 years of age. The subjects came from predominantly middle-class backgrounds, over half of the group were married; 70% had college degrees or were enrolled in a college, and the majority were living within a 30-mile radius of the institute. The adult group included 55 Protestants, 15 Catholics, and 1 Jew.

The heart of this study consists of correlations between the childhood information on these subjects and their adult behavior. The childhood data included (a) longitudinal observations of the child's behavior during the first 14 years of life in a variety of settings, (b) observations of the mother-child interaction during these years, (c) TAT protocols obtained in adolescence, and (d) annual Stanford-Binet intelligence test scores during the ages 5–11. Although the data collected during adulthood (age range 20–29) sampled a variety of techniques, this report utilizes only two sources of adult information, 5 hours of interview, and a TAT protocol.

Longitudinal Observations: Birth to Age 14

As a standard procedure of the Fels longitudinal program, psychologists or psychologically trained personnel summarized their observations of the child in the home, in the Fels nursery school and day camp, and in the subject's public school. The home reports were based on a visit to the home where mother and child were observed for half-day sessions. These home visits were generally made semiannually for the first 6 years of life and annually from 6 to 12. Most of the mothers were interviewed each year for the first 14 years of the child's life. The nursery school summaries were based on semiannual, free-play sessions from ages 2.5 to 5. The sessions usually consisted of 15 consecutive half-day periods in groups of 10–12 children. Day camp typically consisted of an annual 2 week session of half-day periods during ages 6–10 in which free and structured group activities were observed. Public school visits, made semiannually, consisted of a half-day observation of the child in his routine classroom activities. Finally, the subjects of ages 6–14 were interviewed each year at the institute and a summary of the interview was prepared. All of the longitudinal reports for each subject were collated in chronological order and placed in the subject's individual file.

Scoring of longitudinal variables. A comprehensive list of rating scale variables (7-point scale) was defined for the purpose of evaluating the narrative material just outlined. The material for each subject was divided into four age periods: 0–3, 3–6, 6–10, and 10–14. The senior author, who had no knowledge of the adult psychological status of the subjects, first read all the information for each subject for age 0–3 and made those ratings for which he had adequate information. Following a period of interpolated work, he studied each subject's material for age 3–6 and again made his ratings. This procedure was repeated for ages 6–10 and 10–14. A period of approximately 6 months intervened between the evaluation of the data for any one subject for each age period. This paper deals only with the stability of achievement and recognition behaviors, and abridged definitions of these variables follow.

Childhood Variables

Achievement behavior (rated for ages 0–3, 3–6, and 6–10). This variable assessed the degree to which the subject tended to persist with challenging tasks, games, and problems, and his involvement in activities in which a standard of excellence was applicable. For 0–3, emphasis was given to persistence with perceptual-motor activities (e.g., making block towers, stringing beads, drawing, and coloring). For ages 3–6 and 6–10 the greatest weight was given to interest in and persistence with intellectual, mechanical, athletic, and fine motor activities.

For age 10–14 the general achievement variable defined above was differentiated into three variables dealing with different achievement areas (intellectual, mechanical, and athletic).

Intellectual achievement (rated for age 10–14). This variable assessed the degree to which the subject attempted to master language and numerical skills and showed involvement in the acquisition of knowledge.

Mechanical achievement (rated for age 10–14). This variable assessed the degree to which the subject attempted to master mechanical skills and manifested involvement in activities such as carpentry, construction of model vehicles, engines and motors, and craft work.

Athletic achievement (rated for age 10–14). This variable assessed the degree to which the subject attempted to master and showed involvement in athletic activities. These behaviors included swimming, hiking, baseball, football, basketball, tennis, acrobatics, and track events.

Recognition-seeking behavior (rated for ages 6–10 and 10–14). This variable assessed the subject's striving to obtain goals that led to recognition from parents, teachers, and peers. The behaviors emphasized in the rating were (a) grades in school and school honors, (b) stated desire for status-laden vocations or ostentatious material goods, (c) striving for leadership in teams or clubs, (d) attempts to get recognition from farm activities (e.g., raise the best calf, the highest corn, etc.).

Maternal Variables

Maternal acceleration of developmental skills in child (rated for ages 0–3, 3–6, and 6–10). The home visits and maternal interviews yielded information on the mother's behavior and attitudes toward her child. The maternal variable that is directly relevant to the subject's achievement behavior was called *maternal acceleration.* It was defined in terms of the degree to which the mother showed concern over the subject's cognitive and motor development, and the degree to which she exhibited desires for precocious achievement in her child. The rating reflected the degree to which the mother "pushed" the subject's development beyond his abilities and her concern with his general achievement level.

Adult Interview

The junior author, who had no knowledge of the subjects' childhood information, interviewed each subject and rated him (7-point scale) on a variety of variables. The definitions of the variables related to achievement and recognition seeking behaviors follow.

Achievement behavior. This variable evaluated the subject's behavioral attempts to master tasks for which "self-satisfaction" rather than social recognition was the *salient* goal. In achievement behavior, the subject was striving to attain a *self-imposed* standard of excellence. The rating was based on the subject's emphasis and concern with task mastery in his job and avocational pursuits.

Recognition-seeking behavior. This variable evaluated the subject's behavioral attempt to obtain symbols of status and social recognition. The rating was based on evidence of strivings for (a) vocational recognition, (b) academic awards and honors, (c) positions of leadership or recognition in community or vocational groups, (d) concern with conspicuous material display, (e) striving for upward mobility in social class position.

Concern with intellectual competence. This variable assessed the value the subject placed upon intelligence, knowledge, academic achievement, and intellectual superiority regardless of whether the goal was to satisfy inner standards or to obtain social recognition.

Reliability of Longitudinal and Adult Interview Ratings

A random sample of 32 tape-recorded adult interviews were independently studied and rated by a second judge to assess the reliability of the junior author's adult ratings. The reliabilities of the longitudinal variables were also assessed through independent ratings, by a second judge, of samples of 50–60 cases at each of the four age periods. The reliabilities of the adult and child ratings were determined by product-moment correlation coefficients.[1] For the adult ratings of achievement behavior, recognition behavior, and intellectual concern the reliability coefficients were .84, .99, and .98, respectively. With the exception of one child behavior variable, the reliabilities of the longitudinal ratings ranged from .74 to .90 with a median coefficient of .81. The one low longitudinal reliability was for child's achievement for age 0–3 ($r = +.35$; $p < .01$; two-tailed).

TAT Achievement Fantasy: Adolescent and Adult Protocols

Early adolescent (median age of 14–6 years) protocols were available for 67 of the 71 subjects, and all 71 subjects were administered TAT stimuli following the adult interview. The adolescent protocol was based on seven cards from the Murray (1943) series (Cards 1, 5, 14, 17BM, 3BM, 6BM, and 3GF). The male adult protocol was based on 13 cards (4, 8BM, 7BM, 6BM, 12M, 17BM, 13MF, 14, 3BM, 5, 1, 3GF, and 18GF). The adult females were also administered 13 cards (4, 6GF, 12F, 2, 8GF, 17BM, 13MF, 14, 3BM, 5, 1, 3GF, and 18GF). For both the adolescent and adult protocols achievement themes were scored according to the scheme described by McClelland, Atkinson, Clark, and Lowell (1953). Since incidence of the subcategories of the McClelland scoring system were infrequent, only stories in which achievement behavior was the major aspect of the plot were considered. These are scored Ach Th in the McClelland scheme. For the adolescent protocol, there was a lack of comparability among the examiners with respect to the inquiry questions and only the spontaneous verbalization of the subject was scored. Agreement between two independent coders was 95%. The longitudinal and interview ratings of achievement and recognition behavior were made *without knowledge* of the subject's adolescent or adult TAT stories. Thus, the behavior and interview ratings were independent of each other and of the TAT thematic scores.

IQ Change

Each child was given the Stanford-Binet, Forms L and M alternately, annually from ages 5 through 11 by the same psychologist. The mean IQ for the entire Fels population is about 120 (SD of 15). For each subject, a smoothed plot of his IQ scores was obtained by averaging his three IQ scores around each age. For example, a child's smoothed or average IQ at age 6 was the result of averaging his IQ scores at ages 5, 6, and 7; his smoothed IQ at age 10 was the average of his IQs at ages 9, 10, and 11. This procedure tends to remove the chance variation associated with any one IQ score. Each S's smoothed IQ at age 6 was then subtracted from his smoothed IQ at age 10 and the resulting difference was used as a measure of IQ change. As with achievement themes, the child and adult achievements ratings were made without knowledge of the S's IQ or his IQ change score.

In summary, four independent scources of data were analyzed: child and maternal behaviors for the first 14 years of life, adult behavior, adolescent and adult achievement themes, and childhood IQ change scores.

Statistical Analysis

Relationships among the following variables were evaluated: (a) childhood achievement and maternal acceleration ratings with the adult interview ratings, (b) adolescent achievement themes with adult achievement themes, (c) adolescent and adult achievement themes with the longitudinal and adult ratings, and (d) IQ change scores with the childhood and adult ratings. Product-moment correlations were used except when the TAT achievement score was involved. Since achievement themes were not normally distributed, contingency coefficients[2] were used for all tests of association using this variable. Mechanical achievement for age 10–14 was the only variable for which there was a significant sex difference; the boys having a higher mean rating than the girls ($p < .05$; two-tailed).

Results

Stability of Achievement and Recognition Behaviors

Table 14.3 presents the relationships between the child and adult ratings of

TABLE 14.3. *Relation Between Longitudinal Ratings of Childhood Achievement and Early Maternal Acceleration with Adult Achievement Behavior (Product-Moment Correlations)*

Childhood Variables		Adult Variables					
	Age	Achievement		Recognition		Intellectual Concerns	
		MALES	FEMALES	MALES	FEMALES	MALES	FEMALES
Recognition	6–10	.47[3]	.40[2]	.42[2]	.48[3]	.37[2]	.55[4]
	10–14	.25	.20	.36[1]	.39[2]	.24	.40[2]
Achievement	0–3	−.12	−.02	.01	−.22	−.08	−.02
	3–6	−.03	.45[2]	−.11	.49[3]	.13	.44[2]
	6–10	.46[3]	.38[2]	.57[4]	.51[3]	.69[4]	.49[3]
Achievement							
Intellectual	10–14	.40[2]	.42[2]	.60[4]	.56[3]	.66[4]	.49[3]
Mechanical	10–14	.20	.20	.46[2]	.02	.47[2]	.27
Athletic	10–14	−.18	.01	−.17	−.09	−.47[2]	.02
Maternal Acceleration	0–3	.22	.36[1]	.44[1]	.41[1]	.09	.36[1]
	3–6	.31	.09	.24	.12	.42[2]	.12
	6–10	.14	.33[1]	.16	.23	.32[1]	.43[2]

[1] $p < .05$; one-tailed   [2] $p < .02$; one-tailed   [3] $p < .01$; one-tailed   [4] $p < .001$; one-tailed

achievement and recognition behavior, as well as the relation between maternal acceleration and adult achievement variables. There are several important results in this table. The rating of achievement behavior for age 6–10 showed a significant, positive association with all three adult variables for both sexes. The rating of achievement for age 3–6 was predictive of adult behavior for the females but not for the males, a finding that suggests the earlier emergence of stable achievement strivings in girls' development than in boys.' Of the three achievement behaviors rated for age 10–14, only intellectual mastery was predictive of adult achievement for both sexes. Involvement in mechanical activities was predictive of adult achievement for boys but not for girls. Athletic achievement showed no relationship to the rating of general adult achievement, and was negatively associated with intellectual concern for adult males ($p < .02$).

Recognition-seeking behavior for age 6–10 was also predictive of adult achievement behavior. A few of the child variables were moderately intercorrelated and the three adult variables were highly intercorrelated. This lack of independence makes some of the stability correlations between childhood and adulthood somewhat redundant.

Maternal Acceleration and Adult Behavior

Maternal concern with the child's developmental progress during the first 10 years of life showed low to moderate correlations with adult achievement behavior. The maternal rating for age 6–10 was not a better predictor of adult behavior than the maternal rating for the first 3 years of life. Moreover, the age 0–3 rating was associated with all three adult, achievement variables for girls, while it predicted only recognition behavior for adult males.

Stability of TAT Achievement Fantasy

Although different sets of TAT pictures were used in obtaining the adolescent and adult protocols, the three pictures that usually elicited achievement stories were presented at both administrations. Cards 1, 14, and 17BM, which elicited 77% of all the achievement themes, were common to both protocols.

The stability of the TAT achievement score between the adolescent and adult protocols was determined through the use of contingency coefficients. The stability coefficients were .34, .36, and .31 for boys, girls, and total group ($p < .10$, $< .05$, $< .02$; one-tailed). Thus, achievement themes also showed some degree of stability over this 10-year period. These data extend the findings of an earlier investigation (Kagan and Moss 1959), in which the authors reported a 3 year stability coefficient of .32 ($p < .01$) for achievement themes obtained at median ages of 8–9 years and 11–6 years. The stability coefficients between the adolescent and adult protocols are of the same magnitude as those found for the earlier age period.

Validity of Achievement Themes: Relations with Child and Adult Behavior

Contingency coefficients were computed relating the occurrence of adolescent and adult achievement themes with the longitudinal and adult achievement ratings. The highest and most consistent relations were between the adult achievement themes and adult interview ratings. The only significant relation between adult themes and the childhood ratings held for mechanical achievement ($C = +.63$; $p < .001$ for boys, and $-.50$; $p < .02$ for girls).

The adolescent TAT was also more predictive of adult behavior than it was of the childhood ratings. Adolescent achievement themes predicted adult achievement behavior for women ($C = +.44$; $p < .01$) and intellectual concerns for men ($C = +.44$; $p < .01$). Adolescent achievement themes showed minimal association with the child's achievement behavior. The only significant positive association was with age 3–6 achievement for boys. Once again the rating of mechanical achievement for girls was negatively associated with achievement themes. This negative correlation may be due to the fact that this is the only variable for which markedly different behavioral referents were used in rating the two sexes. For boys, involvement in carpentry, engines, motors, and model airplanes was emphasized in the rating. These activities are sex typed and girls showed no interest in them. Participation in craft work (making jewelry, leather articles) and sewing was also used as evidence of involvement in mechanical activities and girls tended to choose these behaviors.

Maternal acceleration during the first 10 years of life showed suggestive relationships with the adolescent achievement themes. For example, maternal acceleration for age 0–3 predicted achievement themes at adolescence for girls ($C = +.51$; $p < .02$), but not for boys. Maternal acceleration for age 6–10 predicted adolescent achievement themes for boys ($C = +.51$; $p < .01$) and adult achievement themes for girls ($C = +.41$; $p < .05$).

In summary, the adult and adolescent TAT stories showed moderate correlations with adult achievement but minimal association with the childhood achievement ratings. Maternal acceleration was associated, to some degree, with adolescent achievement themes.

IQ Increase and Achievement Behavior

Table 14.4 presents the correlations between changes in IQ during age 6–10 and the longitudinal and adult behaviors. The amount of IQ increase was a fairly sensitive predictor of both intellectual achievement for age 10–14 ($r = .37$ and $.41$ for boys and girls; $p < .01$); and concern with intellectual competence in adulthood ($r = .49$ and $.42$; $p < .01$). These results support and extend the earlier studies and indicate that amount of IQ increase during the first four years of school is a moderately accurate index of the subject's motivation to master intellectual tasks during adolescence and early adulthood. It is important to note that IQ change showed no relation to mechanical or athletic strivings for boys, and was negatively associated with athletic achievement for girls ($r = -.46$; $p < .02$). Thus, IQ increase is not a general measure of achievement strivings for all areas of task mastery. The IQ change measure predicts all three adult achievement ratings because the three adult variables are heavily

TABLE 14.4. *Relation Between IQ Change and Childhood and Adult Achievement Variables (Product-Moment Correlations)*

LONGITUDINAL VARIABLES	AGE	MALES	FEMALES
Recognition	6–10	.24	.21
Recognition	10–14	.41[2]	.09
Achievement	0–3	.13	.04
Achievement	3–6	−.02	.24
Achievement	6–10	.39[4]	.47[3]
Achievement-intellectual	10–14	.37[1]	.41[2]
Achievement-mechanical	10–14	.15	.14
Achievement-athletic	10–14	−.16	−.46[2]
Maternal acceleration	0–3	−.06	.20
Maternal acceleration	3–6	−.03	−.12
Maternal acceleration	6–10	.10	.54[3]
ADULT INTERVIEW VARIABLES			
Recognition		.48[3]	.25
Achievement		.38[3]	.38[2]
Intellectual concern		.49[3]	.42[3]

[1] $p < .05$; one-tailed   [2] $p < .02$; one-tailed   [3] $p < .01$; one-tailed

weighted with concern over intellectual competence. Finally, the maternal acceleration rating for age 6–10 showed a positive relation with IQ change for girls ($r = +.54$; $p < .01$) but not for boys.

Intercorrelations among the Measures

For all three age periods there were high, positive correlations among the achievement and recognition variables. For age 10–14, recognition behavior was highly correlated with achievement strivings in the intellectual area, but only minimally related to mechanical or athletic achievement. This finding suggests that, for this middle-class sample, mastery of intellectual skills is the primary method chosen to obtain social recognition. Perhaps for lower-class samples this generalization might be less valid. The high correlations between recognition behavior and intellectual concern in adulthood, together with the fact that maternal acceleration predicted both variables, suggests that it is difficult to separate "recognition-seeking behavior" from "attempts to improve intellectual competence."

Discussion

Stability of Achievement Strivings

The results indicate that strivings for intellectual mastery are moderately stable from the school years through early adulthood. This behavioral disposition emerges as a stable phenomenon at ages 3–6 for girls and 6–10 for boys. The stability of the behavior ratings is paralleled by the moderate stability of TAT achievement stories over a shorter age span. Moreover, achievement stories in adolescence and adulthood also predicted the adult behavior ratings. This consistent cluster of correlations adds construct validity to the TAT achievement variable and support to the conclusion that this class of behaviors is stable over time.

Involvement in athletics for age 10–14 showed no strong, positive relation to either IQ increase or adult achievement behavior and, in a few instances, negative relationships occurred. This was not because the interviewer failed to assess adult involvement in this particular activity. Rather, many of the adults who had been involved in athletics as early adolescents were not overly concerned with task mastery as adults and they tended to avoid intellectual activities.

The majority of the sample regarded positions of responsibility, intellectual challenge, and knowledge of the environment as highly desirable goals. If a subject had strong achievement motives he tended to gratify them through intellectually oriented endeavors. It is suggested that the mass media and social environment differentially emphasized the importance of different skills in accordance with the sex and age role characteristics of the individual. For adults, there tends to be an emphasis on intellectual competence and a de-emphasis on active mastery of athletic skills. Moreover, intellectual mastery is less involved in potential sex role conflict than mechanical or athletic behaviors. To excel at sports is one of the defining characteristics of masculinity. Some boys become involved in athletics in order to maintain their sex role identity and avoid peer rejection. An athletic girl will be subject to peer rejection for excessive participation in athletics. Thus, athletic mastery is under the control of motives and conflicts related to sex role identification in addition to needs for task mastery.

This latter point raises the question of the appropriate definition of achievement behavior and motivation. It is suggested that the concept of a general achievement motive is too broad a term, and it may be useful to replace this construct with a series of variables that relate to more specific behaviors. It seems more reasonable to talk about "desire to improve intellectual skills," or "desire to improve athletic skills" than to use the more global concept of need achievement. Individuals strive to perfect skills in different areas, and the motivations for these strivings are multiple. Prediction and comprehension of these phenomena might be facilitated if there was some differentiation among the behaviors and motives that are involved in task mastery.

The lack of predictive power of age 0–3 mastery behavior might have been due to the greater difficulty in rating this variable (the interrater reliability was .35). On the other hand, the behavioral referents for this rating differed from those used to assess mastery for the older age periods. Since 2-year-olds do not initiate intellectual or athletic mastery behavior, persistence with simple, perceptual-motor tasks (stringing beads, building towers) was the basis for this early rating. A high rating for 0–3 reflected a high threshold for satiation with simple, sensorimotor activities. At the older ages, the achievement rating was based on involvement with problem-solving behaviors that were more similar in form to adult achievement behavior. The age 0–3 rating is dynamically different from the symbolic behaviors that characterize achievement during the preschool and school years. This statement is supported by the fact that achievement for age 0–3 was negatively correlated with achievement for age 3–6 ($r = -.20$) and age 6–10 ($r = -.30$), and showed no relationship to achievement themes or IQ change. Persistence with simple sensorimotor tasks during the first 2 or 3 years of life is not an index of future intellectual, achievement strivings. The 2-year-old who will sit for 20 minutes trying to put a peg in a hole is not necessarily the ambitious scholar of the fifth grade.

Maternal Acceleration and Achievement

The ratings of maternal concern with the child's developmental skills were heavily weighted with encouragement of intellectual progress. The most consistent correlates of maternal acceleration were found with the ratings of adult concern with intellectual competence. Maternal acceleration for age 0–3 was slightly more predictive of adult behavior for girls than for boys. Similarly, maternal acceleration for age 6–10 was more predictive of IQ increase for daughters than for sons. The sex difference between these latter two correlations was significant at the .05 level. It is suggested that since the girl was more likely than the boy to identify with the mother, maternal encouragement of intellectual mastery should have had a greater effect on the development of the girl than on the boy.

TAT Achievement Stories

Achievement themes on the TAT were moderately stable and were correlated with adult achievement behavior. The fact that the correlations were as high for females as for males, although the three critical cards illustrated male heroes, raises some question concerning the validity of the hero hypothesis. Since Cards 1, 14, and 17BM all picture a male in a potential achievement situation, one might expect that achievement themes for women would not be highly correlated with their achievement behavior. The present results indicate that the production of achievement themes may be more influenced by the subject's conception of what behaviors are appropriate for the hero, than by the degree of identification of storyteller with hero. Perhaps high achievement girls conceptualize the male role as being more associated with task mastery than do low achievement girls.

The achievement variables used in this study (ratings of overt behavior, IQ increase scores) measured "real life" behaviors that would be expected to engage the subject's motivation. The positive correlations obtained indicate that achievement themes are valid indices of intellective mastery when the conditions under which the behavioral samples are obtained are motive arousing.

Limitations on Generalizability

Although the stability correlations for achievement behavior are fairly high, the nature of this particular sample favored stability. The social milieu of these subjects remained constant throughout the first 17 years of their lives, and the parents and peers of these subjects retained their same values. The degree of stability obtained with this sample might not hold for populations that are more mobile, for different ethnic or social class groups, or for children subjected to major developmental traumata.

Social Reinforcement and Stability

The stability of achievement behavior is congruent with general reinforcement theory. Each time achievement strivings are rewarded through social approval or internal feelings of satisfaction, the strength of this behavioral tendency should be increased. If achievement strivings lead to failure, these behaviors should extinguish. The child who attains scholastic honors through effort is rewarded by the social environment, and this experience frequently leads to an expectancy of future success for similar behavior. This rewarding experience, coupled with the strong cultural approval for intellectual competence, increases the probability that the child will continue to engage in intellectual tasks. On the other hand, persistent failures in intellectually challenging situations are likely to lead to an expectancy of failure, and these expectancies can result in avoidance and/or withdrawal from involvement in intellectual behavior.

NOTES

[1] All correlations were corrected for restricted range of scores.

[2] The contingency coefficients were based on chi squares computed from Mood's likelihood ratio test for a 3×2 distribution.

Imitation of Film-Mediated Aggressive Models

Albert Bandura, Dorothea Ross, and Sheila A. Ross

Considerable controversy has developed over the appropriateness of many children's television programs depicting aggressive behavior. According to the critics, children who view these programs are stimulated in the direction of performing overtly hostile acts. Professor Bandura and his colleagues provide experimental evidence indicating that children in fact will imitate the overt acts of aggression performed by adults. They do not take the position that viewing adult aggressive behavior increases the frequency of aggression; but they do argue that under appropriate conditions, children will express their anger employing behaviors consistent with an adult model. This is probably one reason why children whose parents use physical punishment are typi-

SOURCE: Adapted and abridged from Albert Bandura, Dorothea Ross, and Sheila A. Ross, "Imitation of Film-Mediated Aggressive Models." *Journal of Abnormal and Social Psychology,* 1963, 66, 3–11. (With permission of the authors and the American Psychological Association.)

cally rated as being more aggressive than children whose parents use other modes of punishment.

Most of the research on the possible effects of film-mediated stimulation upon subsequent aggressive behavior has focused primarily on the drive-reducing function of fantasy. While the experimental evidence for the catharsis or drive reduction theory is equivocal, the modeling influence of pictorial stimuli has received little research attention.

An incident in which a boy was seriously knifed during a re-enactment of a switchblade knife fight the boys had seen the previous evening on a televised rerun of the James Dean movie, *Rebel Without a Cause*, is a dramatic illustration of the possible imitative influence of film stimulation. Indeed, anecdotal data suggest that portrayal of aggression through pictorial media may be more influential in shaping the form which aggression will take when a person is instigated on later occasions, than in altering the level of instigation to aggression.

Aggressive models can be ordered on a reality-fictional stimulus dimension with real-life models located at the reality end of the continuum, nonhuman cartoon characters at the fictional end, and films portraying human models occupying an intermediate position. It was predicted, on the basis of saliency and similarity of cues, that the more remote the model was from reality, the weaker would be the tendency for Ss to imitate the behavior of the model.

Of the various interpretations of imitative learning, the sensory feedback theory of imitation recently proposed by Mowrer (1960) is elaborated in greatest detail. According to this theory, if certain responses have been repeatedly positively reinforced, proprioceptive stimuli associated with these responses acquire secondary reinforcing properties and thus the individual is predisposed to perform the behavior for the positive feedback. Similarly, if responses have been negatively reinforced, response-correlated stimuli acquire the capacity to arouse anxiety, which in turn inhibits the occurrence of the negatively valenced behavior. On the basis of these considerations, it was predicted that Ss who manifest high aggression anxiety would perform significantly less imitative and nonimitative aggression than Ss who display little anxiety over aggression. Since aggression is generally considered female inappropriate behavior, and therefore likely to be negatively reinforced in girls, it was also predicted that male Ss would be more imitative of aggression than females.

To the extent that observation of adults displaying aggression conveys a certain degree of permissiveness for aggressive behavior, it may be assumed that such exposure not only facilitates the learning of new aggressive responses but also weakens competing inhibitory responses in Ss and thereby increases the probability of occurrence of previously learned patterns of aggression. It was predicted, therefore, that Ss who observed aggressive models would display significantly more aggression when subsequently frustrated than Ss who were equally frustrated but who had no prior exposure to models exhibiting aggression.

Method

Subjects

The Ss were 48 boys and 48 girls enrolled in the Stanford University Nursery School. They ranged in age from 35 to 69 months, with a mean age of 52 months.

Two adults, a male and a female, served in the role of models both in the real-life and in the human film-aggression condition. One female E conducted the study for all 96 children.

General Procedure

Ss were divided into three experimental groups and one control group of 24 subjects each. One group of experimental Ss observed real-life aggressive models, a second group observed these same models portraying aggression on film, while a third group viewed a film depicting an aggressive cartoon character. The experimental groups were further subdivided into male and female Ss so that half the Ss in the two conditions involving human models were exposed to same-sex models, while the remaining Ss viewed models of the opposite sex.

Following the exposure experience, Ss were tested for the amount of imitative and nonimitative aggression in a different experimental setting in the absence of the models.

The control group Ss had no exposure to the aggressive models and were tested only in the generalization situation.

Ss in the experimental and control groups were matched individually on the basis of ratings of their aggressive behavior in social interactions in the nursery school. The E and a nursery school teacher rated the Ss on four 5-point rating scales which measured the extent to which Ss displayed physical aggression, verbal aggression, aggression toward inanimate objects, and aggression inhibition. The latter scale, which dealt with the Ss' tendency to inhibit aggressive reactions in the face of high instigation, provided the measure of aggression anxiety. Seventy-one per cent of the Ss were rated independently by both judges so as to permit an assessment of interrater agreement. The reliability of the composite aggression score, estimated by means of the Pearson product-moment correlation, was .80.

Data for Ss in the real-life aggression condition and in the control group were collected as part of a previous experiment (Bandura, Ross, and Ross 1961). Since the procedure is described in detail in the earlier report, only a brief description of it will be presented here.

Experimental Conditions

Subjects in the Real-Life Aggressive condition were brought individually by the E to the experimental room and the model, who was in the hallway outside the room, was invited by the E to come and join in the game. The S was then escorted to one corner of the room and seated at a small table which contained potato prints, multicolor picture stickers, and colored paper. After demonstrating how the S could design pictures with the materials provided, the E escorted the model to the opposite corner of the room which contained a small table and chair, a tinker toy set, a mallet, and a 5-foot inflated Bobo doll. The E explained that this was the model's play area and after the model was seated, the E left the experimental room.

The model began the session by assembling the tinker toys but after approximately a minute had elapsed, the model turned to the Bobo doll and spent the remainder of the period aggressing toward it with highly novel responses which are unlikely to be performed by children independently of the observation of the model's behavior. Thus, in addition to punching the Bobo doll, the model exhibited the following distinctive aggressive acts which were to be scored as imitative responses:

The model sat on the Bobo doll and punched it repeatedly in the nose.

The model than raised the Bobo doll and pommeled it on the head with a mallet.

Following the mallet aggression, the model tossed the doll up in the air aggressively and kicked it about the room. This sequence of physically aggressive acts was repeated approximately three times, interspersed with verbally aggressive responses such as "Sock him in the nose . . . ," "Throw him in the air . . . ," "Hit him down . . . ," "Kick him . . . ," and "Pow."

Ss in the Human Film-Aggression condition were brought by the E to the semidarkened experimental room, introduced to the picture materials, and informed that while the Ss worked on potato prints, a movie would be shown on a screen, positioned approximately 6 feet from the Ss table. The movie projector was located in a distant corner of the room and was screened from the Ss' view by large wooden panels.

The color movie and a tape recording of the sound was begun by a male projectionist as soon as the E left the experimental room and was shown for a duration of 10 minutes. The models in the film presentations were the same adult males and females who participated in the Real-Life condition of the experiment. Similarly, the aggressive behavior they portrayed in the film was identical with their real-life performances.

For subjects in the Cartoon Film-Aggression condition, after seating the S at the table with the picture construction material, the E walked over to a television console approximately 3 feet in front of the S's table, remarked, "I guess I'll turn on the color TV," and ostensibly tuned in a cartoon program. The E then left the experimental room. The cartoon was shown on a glass lens screen in the television set by means of a rear projection arrangement screened from the S's view by large panels.

The sequence of aggressive acts in the cartoon was performed by the female model costumed as a black cat similar to the many cartoon cats. In order to heighten the level of irreality of the cartoon, the floor area was covered with artificial grass and the walls forming the backdrop were adorned with brightly colored trees, birds, and butterflies creating a fantasyland setting. The cartoon began with a close-up of a stage on which the curtains were slowly drawn revealing a picture of a cartoon cat along with the title, *Herman the Cat*. The remainder of the film showed the cat pommeling the Bobo doll on the head with a mallet, sitting on the doll and punching it in the nose, tossing the doll in the air, and kicking it about the room in a manner identical with the performance in the other experimental conditions except that the cat's movements were characteristically feline. To induce further a cartoon set, the program was introduced and concluded with appropriate cartoon music, and the cat's verbal aggression was repeated in a high-pitched, animated voice.

In both film conditions, at the conclusion of the movie the E entered the room and then escorted the S to the test room.

Aggression Instigation

In order to differentiate clearly the exposure and test situations Ss were tested for the amount of imitative learning in a different experimental room which was set off from the main nursery school building.

The degree to which a child has learned aggressive patterns of behavior through imitation becomes most evident when the child is instigated to aggression on later occasions. Thus, for example, the effects of viewing the movie, *Rebel Without a Cause*, were not evident until the boys were instigated to aggression the following day, at which time they reenacted the televised switchblade knife fight in considerable detail. For this reason, the children in the experiment, both those in the control group, and those who were exposed to the aggressive models, were mildly frustrated before they were brought to the test room.

Following the exposure experience, the E brought the S to an anteroom which contained a varied array of highly attractive toys. The E remarked that these were her very best toys, that she did not let just anyone play with them, and that she had decided to reserve these toys for some other children. However, the S could play with any of the toys in the next room. The E and the S then entered the adjoining experimental room.

It was necessary for the E to remain in the room during the experimental session; otherwise, a number of the children would either refuse to remain alone or would leave before the termination of the session. In order to minimize any influence her presence might have on the S's behavior, the E remained as inconspicuous as possible by busying herself with paper work at a desk in the far corner of the room and avoiding any interaction with the child.

Test for Delayed Imitation

The experimental room contained a variety of toys, some of which could be used in imitative or nonimitative aggression, and others which tended to elicit predominantly nonaggressive forms of behavior. The aggressive toys included a 3-foot Bobo doll, a mallet and peg board, two dart guns, and a tether ball with a face painted on it which hung from the ceiling. The nonaggressive toys, on the other hand, included a tea set, crayons and coloring paper, a ball, two dolls, three bears, cars and trucks, and plastic farm animals.

In order to eliminate any variation in behavior due to mere placement of the toys in the room, the play material was arranged in a fixed order for each of the sessions.

The S spent 20 minutes in the experimental room, during which time his behavior was rated in terms of predetermined response categories by judges who observed the session through a one-way mirror in an adjoining observation room. The 20-minute session was divided in 5-second intervals by means of an electric interval timer, thus yielding a total number of 240 response units for each S.

The male model scored the experimental sessions for all Ss. In order to provide an estimate of interjudge agreement, the performances of 40% of the Ss were scored independently by a second observer. The responses scored involved highly specific concrete classes of behavior, and yielded high interscorer reliabilities, the product-moment coefficients being in the .90s.

Response Measures

The following response measures were obtained:

Imitative aggression. This category included acts of striking the Bobo doll with the mallet, sitting on the doll and punching it in the nose, kicking the doll, tossing it in the air, and the verbally aggressive responses, "Sock him," "Hit him down," "Kick him," "Throw him in the air," and "Pow."

Partially imitative responses. A number of Ss imitated the essential components of the model's behavior but did not perform the complete act, or they directed the imitative aggressive response to some object other than the Bobo doll. Two responses of this type were scored and were interpreted as partially imitative behavior:

Mallet aggression. The S strikes objects other than the Bobo doll aggressively with the mallet.

Sits on the Bobo doll. The S lays the Bobo doll on its side and sits on it, but does not aggress toward it.

Nonimitative aggression. This category included acts of punching, slapping, or pushing the doll, physically aggressive acts directed toward objects other than the Bobo doll, and any hostile remarks except for those in the verbal imitation category; for example, "Shoot the Bobo," "Cut him," "Stupid ball," "Knock over people," "Horses fighting, biting."

Aggressive gun play. The S shoots darts or aims the guns and fires imaginary shots at objects in the room.

Ratings were also made of the number of behavior units in which Ss played nonaggressively or sat quietly and did not play with any of the material at all.

Results

Since the distributions of scores departed from normality and the assumption of homogeneity of variance could not be made for most of the measures, the Freidman two-way analysis of variance by ranks was employed for testing the significance of the obtained differences.

Total Aggression

The mean total aggression scores for Ss in real-life, human film, cartoon film, and the control groups are 83, 92, 99, and 54, respectively. The results of the analysis of the variance performed on these scores reveal that the main effect of treatment conditions is significant ($x_r^2 = 9.06, p < .05$), confirming the prediction that exposure of Ss to aggressive models increases the probability that Ss will respond aggressively when instigated on later occasions. Further analyses of pairs of scores by means of the Wilcoxon matched-pairs signed-ranks test show that Ss who viewed the real-life models and the film-mediated models do not differ from each other in total aggressiveness, but all three experimental groups expressed significantly more aggressive behavior than the control Ss.

Imitative Aggressive Responses

The Freidman analysis reveals that exposure of Ss to aggressive models is also a highly effective method for shaping Ss' aggressive responses $x_r^2 = 23.88$, $p < .001$). Comparisons of treatment conditions by the Wolcoxon test reveal that Ss who observed the real-life models and the film-mediated models, relative to Ss in the control group, performed considerably more imitative physical and verbal aggression.

Illustrations of the extent to which some of the Ss became virtually "carbon copies" of their models in aggressive behavior are present in Figure 14.1. The top frame shows the female model performing the four novel aggressive responses; the lower frames depict a male and a female subject reproducing the behavior of the female model they had observed earlier on film.

The prediction that imitation is positively related to the reality cues of the model was only partially supported. While Ss who observed the real-life aggressive models exhibited significantly more imitative aggression than Ss who viewed the cartoon model, no significant differences were found between the live and film, and the film cartoon conditions, nor did the three experimental groups differ significantly in total aggression or in the performances of partially imitative behavior. Indeed, the available data suggest that, of the three experimental conditions, exposure to humans on film portraying aggression was the most influential in eliciting and shaping aggressive behavior. Ss in this condition, in relation to the control subjects, exhibited more total aggression, more imitative aggression, more partially imitative behavior, such as sitting on the Bobo doll and mallet aggression, and they engaged in significantly more aggressive gun play. In addi-

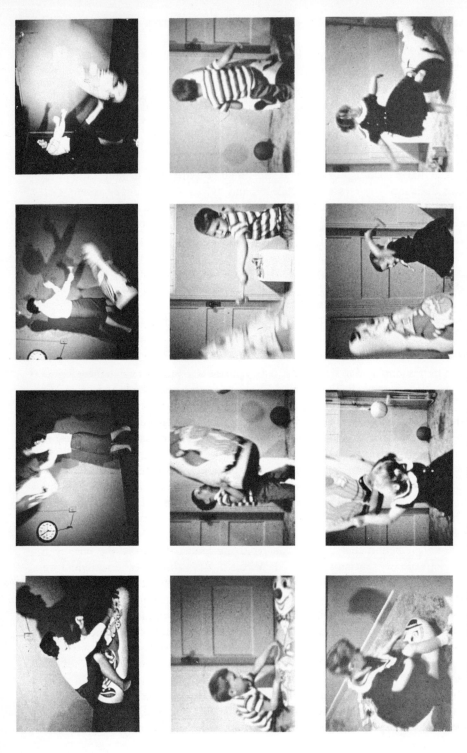

Figure 14.1   Photographs from the film, Social Learning of Aggression through Imitation of Aggressive Models.

tion, they performed significantly more aggressive gun play than did Ss who were exposed to the real-life aggressive models.

Influence of Sex of Model and Sex of Child

In order to determine the influence of sex of model and sex of child on the expression of imitative and nonimitative aggression, the data from the experimental groups were combined and the significance of the differences between groups was assessed by t tests for uncorrelated means. In statistical comparisons involving relatively skewed distributions of scores the Mann-Whitney U test was employed.

Sex of Ss had a highly significant effect on both the learning and the performance of aggression. Boys, in relation to girls, exhibited significantly more total aggression ($t = 2.69$, $p < .01$), more imitative aggression ($t = 2.82$, $p < .005$), more aggressive gun play ($z = 3.38$, $p < .001$), and more nonimitative aggressive behavior ($t = 2.98$, $p. < .005$). Girls, on the other hand, were more inclined than boys to sit on the Bobo doll but refrained from punching it ($z = 3.47$, $p < .001$).

The analysis also disclosed some influences of the sex of the model. Ss exposed to the male model, as compared to the female model, expressed significantly more aggressive gun play ($z = 2.83$, $p < .005$). The most marked differences in aggressive gun play ($U = 9.5$, $p < .001$), however, were found between girls exposed to the female model ($M = 2.9$) and males who observed the male model ($M = 19.8$). Although the overall model difference in partially imitative behavior, Sits on Bobo, was not significant, Sex $\times$ Model subgroup comparisons yielded some interesting results. Boys who observed the aggressive female model, for example, were more likely to sit on the Bobo doll without punching it than boys who viewed the male model ($U = 33$, p $< .05$). Girls reproduced the non-aggressive component of the male model's aggressive pattern of behavior (i.e., sat on the doll without punching it) with considerably higher frequency than did boys who observed the same model ($U = 21.5$, $p < .02$). The highest incidence of partially imitative responses was yielded by the group of girls who viewed the aggressive female model ($M = 10.4$), and the lowest values by the boys who were exposed to the male model ($M = 0.3$). This difference was significant beyond the .05 significance level. These findings, along with the sex of child and sex of model differences reported in the preceding sections, provide further support for the view that the influence of models in promoting social learning is determined, in part, by the sex appropriateness of the model's behavior (Bandura et al. 1961).

Aggressive Predisposition and Imitation

Since the correlations between ratings of aggression and the measures of imitative and total aggressive behavior, calculated separately for boys and girls in each of the experimental conditions, did not differ significantly, the data were combined. The correlational analyses performed on these pooled data failed to yield any significant relationships between ratings of aggression anxiety, frequency of aggressive behavior, and the experimental aggression measures. In fact, the array means suggested nonlinear regression although the departures from linearity were not of sufficient magnitude to be statistically significant.

Discussion

The results of the present study provide strong evidence that exposure to filmed aggression heightens aggressive reactions in children. Ss who viewed the aggressive human and cartoon models on film exhibited nearly twice as much aggression than did subjects in the control group who were not exposed to the aggressive film content.

In the experimental design typically employed for testing the possible cathartic function of vicarious aggression, Ss are first frustrated, then provided with an opportunity to view an aggressive film following which their overt or fantasy aggression is measured. While this procedure yields some information on the immediate influence of film-mediated aggression, the full effects of such exposure may not be revealed until Ss are instigated to aggression on a later occasion. Thus, the present study, utilizing a design in which Ss first observed filmed aggression and then were frustrated, clearly reveals that observation of models portraying aggression on film substantially increases rather than decreases the probability of aggressive reactions to subsequent frustrations.

(Filmed aggression not only facilitated the expression of aggression, but also effectively shaped the form of the Ss' aggressive behavior.) The finding that children modeled their behavior to some extent after the film characters suggests that pictorial mass media, particularly television, may serve as an important source of social behavior. In fact, a possible generalization of responses originally learned in the television situation to the experimental film may account for the significantly greater amount of aggressive gun play displayed by Ss in the Film condition as compared to Ss in the Real-Life and control groups.) It is unfortunate that qualitative features of the gun behavior were not scored since Ss in the Film condition, unlike those in the other two groups, developed interesting elaborations in gun play (for example, stalking the imaginary opponent, quick drawing, and rapid firing), characteristic of the Western gun fighter.

The view that the social learning of aggression through exposure to aggressive film content is confined to deviant children finds little support in our data. The children who participated in the experiment are by no means a deviant sample; nevertheless, 88% of the Ss in the Real-Life and in the Human Film condition, and 79% of the Ss in the Cartoon Film condition, exhibited varying degrees of imitative aggression. In assessing the possible influence of televised stimulation on viewers' behavior, however, it is important to distinguish between learning and overt performance. Although the results of the present experiment demonstrate that the vast majority of children *learn* patterns of social behavior through pictorial stimulation, nevertheless, informal observation suggests that children do not, as a rule, *perform* indiscriminately the behavior of televised characters, even those they regard as highly attractive models. The replies of parents whose children participated in the present study to an open-end questionnaire item concerning their handling of imitative behavior suggest that this may be in part a function of negative reinforcement, as most parents were quick to discourage their children's overt imitation of television characters by prohibiting certain programs or by labeling the imitative behavior in a disapproving manner. From our knowledge of the effects of punishment on behavior, the responses in question would be expected to retain their original strength and could reappear on later occasions in the presence of appropriate eliciting stimuli, particularly if instigation is high, the instruments for aggression are available, and the threat of noxious consequences is reduced.

A question may be raised as to whether the aggressive acts studied in the present experiment constitute "genuine" aggressive responses. Aggression is typically defined as behavior, the goal or intent of which is injury to a person, or destruction of an object. Since intentionality is not a property of behavior but primarily an inference concerning antecedent events, the categorization of an act as "aggressive" involves a consideration of both stimulus and mediating or terminal response events.

According to a social learning theory of aggression proposed by Bandura and Walters (1963), most of the responses utilized to hurt or to injure others (for example, striking, kicking, and other responses of high magnitude), are probably learned for prosocial purposes under nonfrustration conditions. Since frustration generally elicits responses of high magnitude, the latter classes of responses, once acquired, may be called out in social interactions for the purpose of injuring others. On the basis of this theory it would be predicted that the aggressive responses acquired imitatively, while not necessarily mediating aggressive goals in the experimental situation, would be utilized to serve such purposes in other social settings with higher frequency by children in the experimental conditions than by children in the control group.

Punishment, Identification, and Aggression

Monroe M. Lefkowitz, Leopold O. Walder, and Leonard Eron

An understanding of the antecedent conditions influencing the socialization of aggression is important for both theoretical and pragmatic reasons. Recent studies, such as this one indicate that the process is more complex than some original formulations suggested. In pragmatic terms the socialization of aggression is perceived by parents, educators, and mental health workers as one of the most important processes for the long-term adjustment of children. The results of this study indicate that the amount of aggression among children increases as the dependence of the parents on physical punishment for controlling aggression increases. Identification, which in this study is an indication of degree of socialization, decreases as a function of increased use of physical punishment.

The aim of the current research is to examine some of the relationships obtained among punishment, identification, and aggression when the measure of aggression is derived independently of the punishment and identification measures and when punishment is examined by two analyses. One analysis of punishment would be as a dichotomy between its physical and nonphysical aspects and would necessitate the combining of fathers and mothers into groups which say they use no physical punishment, as compared to those in which either parent admits to any use of physical punishment. The other analysis would deal with punishment as a scaled quantity ranging from zero to four physical punishments. Treating punishment as a continuous variable and then observing changes in aggression and identification at different points on the punishment continuum, should yield further information concerning the inhibiting or instigating effects of punishment on aggression. In addition, data pertaining to the effect of increasing punishment on confessing behavior (the measure of identification) may be obtained and the covariation between confessing and aggression may be observed. Dichotomization of punishment into physical and nonphysical categories would render data on the efficiency of these two kinds of disciplinary techniques as "conscience-building" phenomena.

Method

Subjects

The subject population was comprised of all the third grade boys and girls in a semi-rural area of Columbia County, in the State of New York, as of 1959–1960. These children were approximately 8 years of age. Data were also gathered from

SOURCE: Adapted and abridged from Monroe M. Lefkowitz, Leopold O. Walder, and Leonard Eron, "Punishment, Identification, and Aggression." *Merrill-Palmer Quarterly,* 1963, 9, 159–174. (With permission of the authors and *Merrill-Palmer Quarterly.*)

as many of the parents of these children as would consent to be interviewed. The pool of Ss involved consisted of 875 children, 555 fathers and 699 mothers.

Measuring Devices and Procedure

Punishment. All parents interviewed were asked to respond to 24 precoded questions dealing with punishment for specific acts. Of the 24, four were concerned solely with physical punishment:

1. If you heard (*name*) say mean things to another child, would you wash out his mouth with soap? (no, yes, cannot respond).

2. If (*name*) were rude to you, would you wash out his mouth with soap? (no, yes, cannot respond).

3. Would you spank (*name*) until he cries — if he were rude to you? (no, yes, cannot respond).

4. If (*name*) got very mad at you, would you slap him in the face? (no, yes, cannot respond).

The remaining 20 items were categorized under love withdrawal, restraint, isolation, shame, threat, and reasoning. Parental punitiveness was assumed to vary directly with the number of "yes" responses to the four physical punishment items. Due to the importance of the father in socialization of the child (Eron, Banta, Walder, and Laulicht 1961), classification by number of physical punishment items chosen (where the number could range from zero to four) was performed separately for mothers and fathers.

Identification. As part of the interviewing procedure, all parents were asked questions designed to elicit information concerning their child's internalization of the socialized agents' interdictions. Confessing behavior, it was assumed, would tap this function. Consequently the following two items — modification of two questions in the Sears, Maccoby, and Levin study (1957) — were used:

1. When you ask (*name*) about something naughty he has done, how often does he deny it? Does he deny it: 1. all of the time? 2. most of the time? 3. some of the time? 4. almost never? 5. never?

2. When (*name*) has done something naughty and you haven't seen him do it, how often does he come and tell you about it without you having to ask him? 1. never? 2. almost never? 3. some of the time? 4. most of the time? 5. all of the time?

Aggression. This measure, a peer-rating sociometric technique, patterned after the "Guess Who" format, enabled aggression ratings to be obtained independently of the parents. Essentially, every child in a class rates every other child in that class on ten items dealing with aggression. This aggression index has been described in detail elsewhere (Walder *et al.* 1961).

Social Status. A measure of social status — occupation — was employed in order to determine what relationship, if any, obtained between severity of punishment and social status. There is evidence that both middle- and working-class parents make use of physical punishment with about the same frequency. However,

Bronfenbrenner reports (1958) that ". . . working-class parents are consistently more likely to employ physical punishment, while middle-class families rely more on reasoning, isolation, appeals to guilt, and other methods involving the loss of love" (p. 424).

The measure in the present study was obtained from the parental interviews by determining the father's occupation and classifying the response according to the listing in the 1950 Census of Population, Classified Index of Occupations and Industries. In this classification, the ratings vary from zero, comprising professional, technical, and kindred workers, to nine, the category for laborers. Lower ratings correspond to higher social status job categories.

Results

Table 14.5 lists the range of physical punishment alternatives, shows the

TABLE 14.5. *Mean Aggression and Confessing Scores Classified According to Number of Physical Punishment Items Admitted by Parents*

PHYSICAL PUNISHMENT	N	AGGRESSION	CONFESSING	BOYS	GIRLS
			Mothers		
0	428	11.03	6.30	219	209
1	180	13.71	5.82	94	86
2	63	16.19	5.52	35	28
3, 4	28	18.39	5.46	18	10
			Fathers		
0	353	9.79	5.96	167	186
1	138	14.96	5.19	80	58
2	45	15.16	5.78	28	17
3, 4	19	14.89	5.16	11	8

number of mothers or fathers choosing any one classification, and shows the number of boys and girls within each punishment alternative. Regarding sex differences, it was found that boys make significantly higher scores than girls on the peer-rating measure of aggression. In an analysis of directional tendencies, however, the findings for boys and for girls on punishment and aggression are consistent with the overall pattern with the exception of those groups in the highest physical punishment category. Since the Ns in this category are small (Table 14.5), the reliability of this finding is questionable. Consequently, no separate analysis for boys and girls was undertaken in this study.

Illustrated in Table 14.5 is the consistent increase in children's mean aggression scores as the number of physical punishment items chosen by mothers varies from zero out of four possibilities to three and four out of four possibilities. (Categories three and four were combined because of the small ns when considered separately.) In order to determine whether or not these mean aggression scores were significantly different from each other, an analysis of variance for randomized groups was performed. The obtained F ratios of 5.30 for mothers, and 7.26 for fathers are significant beyond the .01 level of confidence, indicating that in both cases the four aggression means are not all estimates of a common population mean.

To answer the question of how these means differ, t tests comparing each mean with every other mean were performed. These data show that the children's mean aggression scores differ significantly when mothers report using no physical punishment as against their choices of one, two, three, and four physical punishment items. When mothers report using any degree of physical punishment, however, children's mean scores in these categories do not differ significantly from each other.

In the case of fathers, the increase in aggression is not as consistent as for mothers in that the largest aggression mean coincides with the next to the largest number of physical punishment items. Although the F ratio is significant, indicating that the four means represent different populations, the t test analysis indicates that significant differences exist between mean aggression scores only when fathers admit to using no physical punishment as compared to their choice of one and two of the four physical punishment items. There is no significant difference in aggression scores, however, between the use of physical punishment and the choice of three or four physical punishments.

In observing the mean scores of the items designed to measure children's confessing behavior as reported by mothers, Table 14.5 depicts a consistent decrease in these scores alongside the increase in both physical punishment items and aggression scores. An analysis of variance yields an F ratio equal to 7.61, significant beyond the .01 level of confidence, implying that these means are not estimates of a common population mean.

Insofar as children's confessing behavior as reported by fathers is concerned, a glance at Table 14.5 shows an inconsistent decrease in these scores paralleling the increase in aggression scores. However, analysis of variance yielded an F ratio of 8.33 which is significant beyond the .01 level of confidence, indicating that the mean confessing scores did not arise from the same population. When the relationship between confessing behavior and aggression is considered, inspection of the Pearson Product Moment correlations in Table 14.6 shows that these measures are negatively related for all classifications of punishment. In the case of mothers, confessing behavior and aggression are inversely related and statistically significant at the .01 level in the zero physical punishment class and in the maximum physical punishment class; significance is at the .05 level of confidence in the second punishment category. For fathers, Table 14.6 shows that the negative relationship between confessing and aggression is significant at the .05 level of confidence only in the category of maximum punishment. Finally, it may be observed that with one exception, for the case of fathers, all the correlations increase in absolute value as the degree of punishment increases.

In analyzing children's aggression and confessing scores as they relate to

TABLE 14.6. *Correlations Between Peer-Rating Measure of Aggression and Children's Confessing Scores Reported by Parents*

PHYSICAL PUNISHMENT	N	r	t	p
			Mothers	
0	428	—.13	2.60	.01
1	180	—.15	2.05	.05
2	63	—.23	1.82	n.s.
3, 4	28	—.50	2.93	.01
			Fathers	
0	353	—.07	1.26	n.s.
1	138	—.16	1.88	n.s.
2	45	—.14	.93	n.s.
3, 4	19	—.52	2.49	.05

physical punishment, the question arose as to how nonphysical relates to physical punishment. For each category of punishment, therefore, and for both parents, the mean number of punishment items other than physical was computed. These data show that the mean number of nonphysical punishment items used by parents increases directly with their choice of physical punishment items. The analysis of variance of these means presents F ratios of 23.25 and 25.47 for mothers and fathers respectively. Significant beyond the .01 level of confidence, the analysis indicates that these mean scores did not arise from the same population.

To answer the question of whether degree of physical punishment is confounded with social status, the means of fathers' occupational ratings on the 1950 census listing of occupations were computed for each class of punishment. The analyses of variance resulted in F ratios of 1.16 for mothers and 1.64 for fathers. Since neither of these ratios is statistically significant, the null hypothesis that these means arose from a common population cannot be rejected. Therefore, it may be concluded that social status as measured by fathers' occupation is not a factor entering into the number of physical punishment items chosen by parents.

Heretofore, analyses have been performed separately for mothers and fathers. But since mothers and fathers of the same family do not necessarily agree in their statements about punishment, analyses of the same variables were performed for families. Such analyses meet the condition, discussed earlier in this report, of dichotomizing physical and nonphysical punishment. In 233, or 43 per cent of the families, *both* mother and father chose zero out of four physical punishments. Furthermore, there were 312 families, or 57 per cent, in which either father or mother chose one or more physical punishments. Mean aggression scores as well as mean confessing scores differ significantly for both groups. Aggression and confessing scores are not significantly correlated in the case of zero physical punishment but are significantly correlated negatively when either father or mother admit to the use of one of more physical punishments. The t of 4.03, significant beyond the .01 level of confidence, indicates that the null hypothesis of zero correlation in the population may be rejected.

Because of the positive relationship between the number of physical and nonphysical punishment items chosen by parents, the bearing of solely physical punishment on aggression and confessing is unclear. Consequently, Pearson Product Moment correlation coefficients were computed between other-than-physical punishment scores, and scores on aggression, and scores on confessing. This analysis was done for 232 of the 233 families, and the other-than-physical punishment score was the sum of nonphysical punishment items chosen by mother and father. Other-than-physical punishment correlates .03 with children's aggression and .01 with children's confessing. Neither of these coefficients is statistically significant.

Finally, those families choosing zero physical punishment also use significantly ($t = 5.60$) less other punishments than those families choosing one or more physical punishments. Again, mean scores on social status do not differ significantly between these groups.

Discussion

The almost consistent increase in children's mean aggression scores, paralleling the increase in physical punishment, suggests that punishment enhances rather than inhibits the expression of aggression. It appears that even when parents responded that they used all of the physical punishment choices available, aggression anxiety was not produced in their children. Generally, these findings support the results of other studies showing the more punishment, the more aggression.

The increase in aggression with the increase in physical punishment seems to support the concept of imitation or role-modeling as illustrated by the studies of Bandura and Huston (1961) and Bandura, Ross, and Ross (1961). On the other hand, increases in the choice of physical punishment items by parents is associated with a decrease in the amount of confessing behavior of their children. In short, physical punishment seems *not* to foster the kind of identification which is measured by items dealing with the internalization of guilt. Rather, the children of those families choosing no physical punishments have significantly lower aggression scores than those whose families choose one or more of the physical punishments. Thus, punishment other than physical seems more effective in the devolpment of conscience — or in socialization. These results are consistent with earlier findings. Moreover, the data of the present study take into account the responses of both parents.

The negative correlations between aggression and confessing scores indicate that those children who have internalized the interdictions of the socialized agent are less aggressive than those who have not. Moreover, since the absolute value of these correlations increases with the increasing use of physical punishment, the role of the latter as a socialized technique becomes manifest. Specifically, the more the use of physical punishment by the parents, the less likely is the aggressive child to have incorporated those qualities which are assumed to comprise the construct termed "conscience." The results are not completely unequivocal: for mothers, the small but significant negative correlation within the category of zero physical punishment (Table 14.6) suggests that physical punishment may not always be a necessary aspect of the high-aggression, low-identification pattern.

Categorizing family units into physical and nonphysical punishment groups (since parents do not always use the same form of punishment) leads to a more conclusive analysis of the aggression-identification relationship. When both father and mother choose none of the physical punishment alternatives, the correlation between aggression and confessing is not significant. On the other hand, when either father or mother admits to the use of one or more physical punishment, the correlation is low, but significant. Thus, it appears probable that physical punishment has an important effect on the relationship between aggression and confessing. To eliminate equivocation concerning the relationship of physical punishment to aggression and confessing, it was attempted to show that punishment other than physical is unrelated to these child variables. Such lack of relationship was found to be the case. Therefore, within the context of this study, it seems reasonable to conclude that it is not punishment generally, but physical punishment specifically, which is related positively to aggression and negatively to identification.

It should be emphasized that in the separate analyses for mothers and fathers, several of the correlations under discussion are not statistically significant. Yet it is instructive to note that both significance and the greatest magnitude of correlations occur in the maximum categories of physical punishment (Table 14.6). This observation seems to underscore, again, the importance of physical punishment in the foregoing correlations.

Considering that mothers and fathers were interviewed separately, the close agreement in the choice of punishment items may be construed as a kind of reliability of this questionnaire technique, in obtaining information about child-rearing practices such as punishment. Also, these data dispute the notion that fathers employ harsher disciplinary techniques than mothers. That such a relatively high percentage of parents choose none of the physical punishment items is open to several interpretations: the use of physical punishment may be believed by the parent to be socially unacceptable to the interviewer; the range of physical punishments offered was too narrow; or, parents are considerably sophisticated and are aware of the implications of physical versus non-physical punishment as it relates to child behavior and personality. Which is the correct interpretation cannot be determined from the current analysis.

Finally, the finding that there was no difference in fathers' mean occupation scores among the different categories of physical punishment is consistent with Kohn's results, (1959), but inconsistent with those of Bronfenbrenner (1958).

Actually, Bronfenbrenner's finding that lower social status families are more inclined to use physical punishment than those families in the middle and upper social status categories seems to parallel a generally held notion about child-rearing practices within these classes. The current results in conjunction with Kohn's data — which show that working and middle-class parents use physical punishment approximately to the same extent — suggest that physical punishment may not be a class-bound phenomenon. From the present data, it seems reasonable to conclude that social status as measured by father's occupation is not a determinant in the amount of physical punishment chosen by parents. Actually, Bronfenbrenner (1958) suggests that a change may be occurring in the disciplinary techniques employed by the working-class and he hints at a reduction in "cultural lag." Evidence from the present study is consistent with his hypothesis that the working-class parent, as a result of greater income and education, is emulating the disciplinary techniques of the middle-class.

References

ANASTASI, ANNE. "Some Implications of Cultural Factors for Test Construction." *Proceedings of the 1949 Conference on Testing Problem, Educational Testing Service,* 1950, 13–17.

ANASTASI, ANNE. *Differential Psychology.* New York: Macmillan, 1958.

ANASTASI, ANNE, and FOLEY, J. P., JR. "A Proposed Reorientation in the Heredity-Environment Controversy." *Psychological Review,* 1948, 55, 239–249.

ANDERSON, J. E. "The Prediction of Terminal Intelligence from Infant and Preschool Tests." *39th Yearbook of the National Society for the Study of Education,* 1940, Part I. 385–403.

ANDERSON, J. E. "Dynamics of Development: Systems in Progress." In D. B. Harris (ed.), *The Concept of Development.* Minneapolis: University of Minnesota Press, 1957.

BAKER, C. T., SONTAG, L. W., and NELSON, VIRGINIA L. "Specific Ability in IQ Change." *Journal of Consulting Psychology,* 1955, 19, 307–310.

BALDWIN, A. L. *Behavior and Development in Childhood.* New York: Dryden, 1955.

BANDURA, A., and HUSTON, ALETHA C. "Identification as a Process of Incidental Learning." *Journal of Abnormal and Social Psychology,* 1961, 63, 311–318.

BANDURA, A., ROSS, D., and ROSS, S. A. "Transmission of Aggression Through Imitation of Aggressive Models." *Journal of Abnormal and Social Psychology,* 1961, 63, 575–583.

BANDURA, A., and WALTERS, R. H. *Adolescent Aggression.* New York: Ronald, 1959.

BANDURA, A., and WALTERS, R. *Social Learning and Personality Development.* New York: Holt, Rinehart and Winston, 1963.

BARKER, R. G., and WRIGHT, H. F. *Midwest and Its Children: The Psychological Ecology of an American Town.* New York: Harper and Row, 1955.

BARKER, R. G., WRIGHT, BEATRICE A., MYERSON, L., and GONICK, MOLLIE R. "Adjustment to Physical Handicap and Illness: A Survey of the Social Psychology of Physique and Disability." *Social Science Research Council Bulletin,* 1953, No. 55 (Rev.).

BAYLEY, NANCY. "On the Growth of Intelligence." *American Psychologist,* 1955, 10, 805–818.

BEACH, F. A. "Characteristics of Masculine Sex Drive." In M. R. Jones (ed.), *Nebraska Symposium on Motivation.* Lincoln: University of Nebraska Press, 1956, 1–32.

BENNETT, E. M., and COHEN, L. P. "Men and Women: Personality Patterns and Contrasts." *Genetic Psychology Monographs,* 1959, 59, 101–155

BENZER, S. "On the Topology of the Genetic Five Structure." *Proceedings of the National Academy of Science,* 1961, 47, 403–415.

BENZER, S., and CHAMPE, S. P. "Ambivalent rII mutants of phage T4." *Proceedings of the National Academy of Science,* 1961, 47, 1025–1038.

BLAKE, R. R., HELSON, H., and MOUTON, J. "The Generality of Conformity Behavior as a Function of Factual Anchorage, Difficulty of Task, and Amount of Social Pressure." *Journal of Personality,* 1956, 25, 294–305.

BLODGETT, H. C. "The Effect of the Introduction of Reward upon the Maze Performance of Rats." *University of California Publications in Psychology,* 1929, 4, 113–134.

BRADWAY, KATHERINE. "IQ Constancy on the Revised Stanford-Binet from the Preschool to the Junior High School Level." *Journal of Genetic Psychology,* 1944, 65, 197–217.

BRELAND, K., and BRELAND, M. "The Misbehavior of Organisms." *American Psychologist,* 1961, 16, 681–684.

BRIM, O. G., JR. "The Parent-Child Relation as a Social System: I. Parent and Child Roles." *Child Development,* 1957, 28, 343–364.

BRONFENBRENNER, U. "Socialization and Social Class Through Time and Space." In E. E. Maccoby, T. M. Newcomb, and E. L. Hartley (eds.), *Readings in Social Psychology.* New York: Holt, 1958, 400–425.

BRONFENBRENNER, U. "Freudian Theories of Identification and Their Derivations." *Child Development,* 1960, 31, 15–40.

BRONFENBRENNER, U. "The Changing American Child — A Speculative Analysis." *Merrill-Palmer Quarterly,* 1961, 7, 73–83.

BROWN, J. S. "Problems Presented by the Concept of Acquired Drives:" In *Current Theory and Research in Motivation: A Symposium.* Lincoln: University of Nebraska Press, 1953.

BROWN, J., and FARBER, I. "Emotions Conceptualized as Intervening Variables — with Suggestions Toward a Theory of Frustration." *Psychological Bulletin,* 1951, 48, 465–495.

BRUNSWICK, E. "Organismic Achievement and Environment Probability." *Psychology Review,* 1943, 50, 255–272.

BUCHWALD, A. M. "Supplementary Report: Alteration in the Reinforcement Value of a Positive Reinforcer." *Journal of Experimental Psychology,* 1960, 60, 416–418.

BURTON, R., MACCOBY, E. E., and ALLINSMITH, W. "Antecedents of Resistance to Temptation in Four-Year-Old Children." *Child Development,* 1961, 32, 689–710.

BUXTON, C. E. "Latent Learning and the Goal Gradient Hypothesis." *Contributions to Psychological Theory,* 1940, 2, No. 2, 3–75.

CARL, L. J. "An Experimental Study of the Effect of Nurturance on the Preschool Child." Unpublished doctoral dissertation, State University of Iowa, 1949.

CASTANEDA, A., MCCANDLESS, B. R., and PALERMO, D. S. "The Children's Form of the Manifest Anxiety Scale." *Child Development,* 1956, 27, 317–326.

DAI, B. "A Socio-Psychiatric Approach to Personality Organization." *American Sociological Review,* 1952, 17, 44–49.

DAVIDSON, HELEN. "A Study of the Confusing Letters B, D, P, and Q." *Journal of Genetic Psychology,* 1935, 47, 458–468.

DAVIS, A. "American Status Systems and the Socialization of the Child." *American Sociological Review,* 1941, 6, 345–354.

DAVIS, A. "Child Training and Social Class." In R. G. Barker, J. S. Kounin, and H. F. Wright (eds.), *Child Behavior and Development.* New York: McGraw-Hill, 1943.

DAVIS, A., and HAVIGHURST, R. J. "Social Class and Color Differences in Child Rearing." *American Sociological Review*, 1946, 11, 698–710.

DEUTSCH, H. *The Psychology of Women.* Vol. I., New York: Grune & Stratton, 1944.

DOBZHANSKY, T. "The Genetic Nature of Differences Among Men." In S. Persons (ed.), *Evolutionary Thought in America.* New Haven: Yale University Press, 1950, 86–155.

DOBZHANSKY, T. "Genetics and Equality." *Science,* 1962, 137, 112–115.

DOLLARD, J., DOOB, L. W., MILLER, N. E., MOWRER, O. H., and SEARS, R. R. *Frustration and Aggression.* New Haven: Yale University Press, 1939.

DOLLARD, J., DOOB, L. W., MILLER, N. E., MOWRER, O. H., and SEARS, R. R. "The Frustration-Aggression Hypotheses." *Psychological Review,* 1941, 48, 337–342.

DURKIN, D. "Children's Concepts of Justice: A Comparison with the Piaget Data." *Child Development,* 1959a, 30, 59–67.

DURKIN, DELORES. "Children's Acceptance of Reciprocity as a Justice-Principle." *Child Development,* 1959b, 30, 289–296.

EELLS, K., DAVIS A., HAVIGHURST, R. J., HERRICK, V. E., and TYLER, R. W. *Intelligence and Cultural Differences: A Study of Cultural Learning and Problem Solving.* Chicago: University of Chicago Press, 1951.

ELKIND, D. "The Development of Quantitative Thinking: A Systematic Replication of Piaget's Studies." *Journal of Genetic Psychology,* 1961, 98, 37–46.

EMMERICH, W. "Young Children's Discriminations of Parent and Child Roles." *Child Development,* 1959a, 30, 403–419.

EMMERICH, W. "Parental Identification in Young Children." *Genetic Psychology Monograph,* 1959b, 60, 257–308.

ERON, L. D., BANTA, T. J., WALDER, L. O., and LAULICHT, J. H. "Comparison of Data Obtained from Mothers and Fathers on Child-Rearing Practices and Their Relation to Child Aggression." *Child Development,* 1961, 32, 457–472.

FISHER, R. A. *Statistical Methods for Research Workers.* 5th ed. Edinburgh: Oliver and Boyd, 1934.

FLAVELL, J. H., DRAGENS, J., FEINBERG, L. K., and BUDIN, W. A. "A Microgenic Approach to Word Association." *Journal of Abnormal and Social Psychology,* 1958, 57, 1–7.

FORGAYS, D. G., and FORGAYS, J. W. "The Nature of the Effect of Free Environmental Experience on the Rat." *Journal of Comparative and Physiological Psychology,* 1952, 45, 322–328.

FULLER, J. L., and THOMPSON, N. R. *Behavior Genetics.* New York: Wiley, 1960.

GARDNER, E. F., and THOMPSON, G. G. *Social Relations and Morale in Small Groups.* New York: Appleton-Century-Crofts, 1956.

GARRETT, H. E. "Racial Differences and Witch Hunting." *Science,* 1962, 135, 982–

GEWIRTZ, J. L. "A Program of Research on the Dimensions and Antecedents of Emotional Dependence." *Child Development,* 1956, 27, 208–221.

GEWIRTZ, J. L. "Social Deprivation and Dependency: A Learning Analysis." Paper presented at the Annual Meeting of the American Psychological Association, New York, 1957.

GEWIRTZ, J. and BAER, D. The effect of brief social deprivation on behaviors for a social reinforcer. *Journal of Abnormal and Social Psychology,* 1958a, 56, 40–56.

GEWIRTZ, J., and BAER, D. Deprivation and satiation of social reinforcers as drive conditions. *Journal of Abnormal and Social Psychology*, 1958b, 57, 165–172.

GIBSON, ELEANOR J., and WALK, R. "Visual Cliff." *Scientific American*, April 1960.

GORDON, E. M., and SARASON, S. B. "The Relationship Between 'Test Anxiety' and 'Other Anxieties.'" *Journal of Personality*, 1955, 23, 317–323.

GREEN, A. W. "The Middle-Class Male Child and Neurosis." *American Sociological Review*, 1946, 11, 31–34.

GUILFORD, J. P. "The Structure of Intellect." *Psychological Bulletin*, 1956, 53, 267–293.

HANEY, G. W. "The Effect of Familiarity on the Maze Performance of Albino Rats." *University of California Publications in Psychology*, 1931, 4, 319–333.

HARLOW, H. F. "The Formation of Learning Sets." *Psychological Review*, 1949, 56, 51–65.

HARRELL, RUTH F., WOODYARD, ELLA, and GATES, A. I. *The Effects of Mothers' Diets on the Intelligence of the Offspring.* New York: Bureau of Publications Teachers College, Columbia University, 1955.

HARRIS, D. B., CLARK, K. E., ROSE, A. M., and VALASEK, FRANCES. "The Measurement of Responsibility in Children." *Child Development*, 1954, 25, 21–28.

HARRIS, D. B., and TSENG, S. C. "Children's Attitudes Toward Peers and Parents as Revealed by Sentence Completions." *Child Development*, 1957, 28, 401–411.

HEBB, D. O. *The Organization of Behavior.* New York: Wiley, 1949.

HEIDER, F. *The Psychology of Interpersonal Relations.* New York: Wiley, 1958.

HELPER, M. M. "Learning Theory and the Self-Concept." *Journal of Abnormal and Social Psychology*, 1955, 51, 184–194.

HIRSCH, J. "Individual Differences in Behavior and Their Genetic Basis." In E. Bliss (ed.), *Roots of Behavior.* New York: Hoeber, 1962.

HIRSCH, J., and TRYON, R. C. "Mass Screening and Reliable Individual Measurement in the Experimental Behavior Genetics of Lower Organisms." *Psychological Bulletin*, 1956, 53, 402–410.

HORWITT, M. K. "Facts and Artifacts in the Biology of Schizophrenia." *Science*, 1956, 124, 429–430.

HULL, C. L. *Principles of Behavior.* New York: Appleton-Century, 1943.

HULL, C. L. *A Behavior System.* New Haven: Yale University Press, 1952.

INHELDER, B. "Some Aspects of Piaget's Genetic Approach to Cognition." *Monographs of the Society for Research in Child Development*, 1962, 27, No. 2, Serial No. 83, 19–34.

INHELDER, B., and PIAGET, J. *The Growth of Logical Thinking from Childhood to Adolescence.* New York: Basic Books, 1958.

ISCOE, I., and WILLIAMS, M. "Experimental Variables Affecting the Conformity Behavior of Children." *Journal of Personality*, 1963, 31, 234–246.

ISCOE, I., WILLIAMS, M., and HARVEY, J. "The Modification of Children's Judgments by a Simulated Group Technique, a Normative Developmental Study." *Child Development*, 1963, 34, 963–978.

JEFFREY, W. E. The effects of verbal and non-verbal responses in mediating an instrumental act. *Journal of Experimental Psychology*, 1953, 45, 327–333.

JENKINS, J. J., and RUSSELL, W. A. "Systematic Changes in Word Association

Norms: 1910–1952." *Journal of Abnormal and Social Psychology,* 1960, 60, 293–304.

JESSOR, R. "The Problem of Reductionism in Psychology." *Psychological Review,* 1958, 65, 170–178.

KAGAN, J., and Moss, H. A. "The Stability and Validity of Achievement Fantasy." *Journal of Abnormal and Social Psychology,* 1959, 58, 357–364.

KAGAN, J., SONTAG, L. W., BAKER, C. T., and NELSON, VIRGINIA L. "Personality and IQ Change." *Journal of Abnormal and Social Psychology.* 1958, 26, 261–266.

KALLMANN, F. J. *Heredity in Health and Mental Disorder: Principles of Psychiatric Genetics in the Light of Comparative Twin Studies.* New York: Norton, 1953.

KALLMANN, F. J. (ed.). *Expanding Goals of Genetics in Psychiatry.* New York: Grune and Stratton, 1962.

KENT, GRACE H., and ROSANOFF, A. J. "A Study of Association in Insanity." *American Journal of Insanity,* 1910, 67, 37–96, 317–390.

KESSEN, W. "Research Design in the Study of Developmental Problems." In P. H. Mussen (ed.), *Handbook of Research Methods in Child Development.* New York: Wiley, 1960, 36–71.

KOHN, M. L. "Social Class and the Exercise of Parental Authority." *American Sociological Review,* 1959, 24, 352–366.

KOLZOVA, M. M. *On the Formation of Higher Nervous Activity in Children.* Leningrad: State Medical Literature Press (MEDGIZ), 1958.

LANDRETH, CATHERINE. "Consistency of Four Methods of Measuring One Type of Sporadic Emotional Behavior (Crying) in Nursery School Children." *Journal of Genetic Psychology,* 1940, 57, 101–118.

LEAGUE, B. J., and JACKSON, D. N. "Conformity, Veridicality and Self Esteem." *Journal of Abnormal and Social Psychology,* 1964, 68, 113–115.

LEVIN, H., and TURGEON, VALERIE F. "The Influence of the Mother's Presence on Children's Doll Play Aggression." *Journal of Abnormal and Social Psychology,* 1957, 55, 304–308.

LEWIN, K., LIPPITT, R., and WHITE, R. K. "Patterns of Aggressive Behavior in Experimentally Created 'social climates.'" *Journal of Social Psychology,* 1939, 10, 271–299.

LINDQUIST, E. F. *Design and Analysis of Experiments in Psychology and Education.* Boston: Houghton-Mifflin, 1953.

LINDZEY, G. "Thematic Apperception Test: Interpretive Assumptions and Related Empirical Evidence." *Psychological Bulletin,* 1952, 49, 1–25.

LIPSITT, L. P., and DeLUCIA, C. A. "An Apparatus for the Measurement of Specific Response and General Activity of the Human Neonate." *American Journal of Psychology,* 1960, 73, 630–632.

LURIA, Z., GOLDWASSER, M., and GOLDWASSER, A. "Response to Transgression in Stories by Israeli Children." *Child Development,* 1963, 34, 371–380.

MAIER, N. *Frustration: The Study of Behavior Without a Goal.* New York: Mc-Graw-Hill, 1949.

MANDLER, G., and SARASON, S. B. "A Study of Anxiety and Learning." *Journal of Abnormal and Social Psychology,* 1952, 47, 166–173.

MANDLER, G., and SARASON, S. B. "The Effect of Prior Experience and Subjective Failure on the Evocation of Text Anxiety." *Journal of Personality*, 1953, 21, 336–341.

MARGOLIUS, G. "Stimulus Generalization of an Instrumental Response as a Function of the Number of Reinforced Trials." *Journal of Experimental Psychology*, 1955, 49, 105–111.

MAYR, E. *Animal Species and Evolution*. Harvard University Press, Cambridge, 1963, p. 5.

McCANDLESS, B. R., and MARSHALL, HELEN R. "A Picture-Sociometric Technique for Preschool Children and Its Relation to Teacher Judgments of Friendship." *Child Development*, 1957, 28, 139–147.

McCANDLESS, B. R., and SPIKER, C. C. "Experimental Research in Child Psychology." *Child Development*, 1956, 27, 75–80.

McCLELLAND, D. C., ATKINSON, J. W., CLARK, R. A., and LOWELL, E. L. *The Achievement Motive*. New York: Appleton-Century-Crofts, 1953.

McGRAW, MYRTLE. *Growth: A Study of Johnny and Jimmy*. New York: Appleton-Century, 1935.

MEYER, W. J., and OFFENBACH, S. I. "Effectiveness of Paired Verbal Reinforcers as a Function of Task Complexity." *Journal of Comparative and Physiological Psychology*, 1962, 55, 532–543.

MEYER, W. J., and SEIDMAN, S. "Age Differences in the Effectiveness of Different Reinforcement Combinations on the Acquisition and Extinction of a Simple Concept Learning Problem." *Child Development*, 1960, 31, 419–429.

MILLER, D. R., and SWANSON, G. E. *Inner Conflict and Defense*. New York: Holt, Rinehart and Winston, 1960.

MILLER, N. E., and DOLLARD, J. *Social Learning and Imitation*. New Haven: Yale University Press, 1941.

MILLER, N. S. Theory and experiment relating psychoanalytic displacement to stimulus-response generalization. *Journal of Abnormal and Social Psychology*, 1948, 43, 155–178.

MILNER, ESTER A. "A Study of the Relationships Between Reading Readiness in Grade One School Children and Patterns of Parent-Child Interaction." *Child Development*, 1951, 22, 95–112.

MOTE, F. A., and FINGER, F. W. "Exploratory Drive and Secondary Reinforcement in the Acquisition and Extinction of a Simple Learning Response." *Journal of Experimental Psychology*, 1942, 31, 57–68.

MOWRER, O. H. *Learning Theory and the Symbolic Processes*. New York: Wiley, 1960.

MOWRER, O. H. *Learning Theory and Personality Dynamics*. New York: Ronald Press, 1950.

MUNROE, RUTH L. *Schools of Psychoanalytic Thought*. New York: Dryden, 1955.

MURRAY, H. A. *Thematic Apperception Test Manual*. Cambridge: Harvard University Press, 1943.

MUSSEN, P. (ed.). *Handbook of Research Methods in Child Psychology*. New York: Wiley, 1960.

NISSEN, H. W. "A Study of Exploratory Behavior in the White Rat by Means of the Obstruction Method." *Journal of Genetic Psychology*, 1930, 37, 361–376.

Parsons, T. "Age and Sex in the Social Structure of the United States." *American Sociological Review*, 1942, 7, 604–616.

Parsons, T. "A Revised Analytical Approach to the Theory of Social Stratification." In R. Bendix and S. M. Lipset (eds.), *A Reader in Social Stratification*. Glencoe, Ill.: Free Press, 1953, 92–128.

Parsons, T. "Social Structure and the Development of Personality: Freud's Contribution to the Integration of Psychology and Sociology." *Psychiatry*, 1958, 21, 321–340.

Parsons, T., and Bales, R. F. *Family, Socialization and Interaction Process*. New York: Free Press, 1955.

Pasamanic, B., Knobloch, Hilda, and Lilienfeld, A. M. "Socioeconomic Status and Some Precursors of Neuropsychiatric Disorders." *American Journal of Orthopsychiatry*, 1956, 26, 594–601.

Peak, Helen. "Problems of Objective Observation." In L. Festinger and D. Katz (eds.), *Research Methods in the Behavioral Sciences*. New York: Dryden, 1953, 243–299.

Piaget, J. *The Moral Judgement of the Child*. London: Harcourt, Brace, 1932.

Piaget, J. *The Psychology of Intelligence*. London: Broadway, 1950.

Piaget, J. *Judgement and Reasoning in the Child*. London: Routledge, 1951a.

Piaget. J. *The Child's Conception of the World*. London: Routledge, 1951b.

Piaget, J. *The Child's Conception of Number*. London: Routledge, 1952a.

Piaget, J. *The Origins of Intelligence in Children*. New York: International University Press, 1952b.

Piaget, J. *The Construction of Reality in the Child*. New York: Basic Books, 1954.

Piaget, J. "Les Stades du developpement intellectuel de l'enfant et de l'adolescent." In P. Osterrieth *et al.*, *Le Probleme des stades en psychologie de l'enfant*. Paris: Presses Universitaires de France, 1956, 33–49.

Piaget, J. *Logic and Psychology*. New York: Basic Books, 1959.

Piaget, J., and Inhelder, B. *Le Developpement des quantites chez l'enfant*. Paris: Delachaux and Niestle, 1940.

Prader, A., Tanner, J. M., and von Harnack, G. A. "Catch-up Growth Following Illness or Starvation: An Example of Development Canalization in Man." *Journal of Pediatrics*, 1963, 63, 646–659.

Rapaport, A. *Operational Philosophy*. New York: Harper, 1953.

Ray, W. S. "A Preliminary Report on a Study of Fetal Conditioning." *Child Development*, 1932, 3, 175–177.

Redl, F., and Wineman, P. *The Aggressive Child. I. Children Who Hate*. Glencoe, Ill.: Free Press, 1957.

Reynolds, B. A. "A Repetition of the Blodgett Experiment on 'Latent Learning.'" *Journal of Experimental Psychology*, 1945, 35, 504–516.

Rotter, J. B. *Social Learning and Clinical Psychology*. New York: Prentice-Hall, 1954.

Rotter, J. B. "A Historical and Theoretical Analysis of Some Broad Trends in Clinical Psychology." In S. Koch (ed.), *Psychology: A Study of the Science. Study II: Empirical Substructure and Relations with Other Sciences*. Vol. V. New York: McGraw-Hill, 1963.

SARASON, S. B., and MANDLER, G. "Some Correlates of Test Anxiety." *Journal of Abnormal and Social Psychology*, 1952, 47, 810–817.

SCOTT, J. P., and CHARLES, MARGARET. "Some Problems of Heredity and Social Behavior. *Journal of Genetic Psychology*, 1953, 48, 209–230.

SCOTT, J. P., and FULLER, J. L. "Research on Genetics and Social Behavior at the Roscoe B. Jackson Memorial Laboratory. 1946–1951. A Progress Report." *Journal of Heredity*, 1951, 42, 191–197.

SEARLES, L. V. "The Organization of Hereditary Maze-Brightness and Maze-Dullness." *Genetic Psychology Monographs*, 1949, 39, 279–328.

SEARS, R. R. "A Theoretical Framework for Personality and Social Behavior." *American Psychologist*, 1951, 6, 476–483.

SEARS, R. R. "Identification as a Form of Behavioral Development." In D. B. Harris (ed.), *The Concept of Development*. Minneapolis: University of Minnesota Press, 1957.

SEARS, R. R., MACCOBY, E. E., and LEVIN, H. *Patterns of Child Rearing*. New York: Row, Peterson, 1957.

SIEGEL, ALBERTA E. "Aggressive Behavior of Young Children in the Absence of an Adult." *Child Development*, 1957, 28, 371–378.

SIMMONS, K., and TODD, T. W. "Growth of Well Children: Analysis of Stature and Weight 3 Months to 13 Years." *Growth*, 1938, 2, 93–134.

SIMON, B. *Psychology in the Soviet Union*. Stanford, Calif.: Stanford University Press, 1957.

SIMON, H. A., and NEWELL, A. "Computer Simulation of Human Thinking and Problem Solving." *Monographs of the Society for Research in Child Development*, 1962, 27, No. 2, Serial No. 83, 117–150.

SKINNER, B. F. *Science and Human Behavior*. New York: Macmillan, 1953.

SKINNER, B. F. "Reinforcement Today." *American Psychologist*, 1958, 13, 94–99.

SKODAK, MARIE, and SKEELS, H. M. "A Final Follow-Up of One Hundred Adopted Children." *Journal of Genetic Psychology*, 1949, 75, 85–125.

SONTAG, L. W. "Dynamics of Personality Formation." *Journal of Personality*, 1951, 6, 119–130.

SONTAG, L. W., BAKER, C. T., and NELSON, VIRGINIA L. "Personality as a Determinant of Performance." *American Journal of Orthopsychiatry*, 1955, 25, 555–562.

SONTAG, L. W., BAKER, C. T., and NELSON, VIRGINIA L. "Mental Growth and Personality Development: A Longitudinal Study." *Monographs of the Society for Research in Child Development*, 1958, 23, (No. 68).

SPENCE, K. W. *Symposium on Relationships Among Learning Theory, Personality Theory and Clinical Research*. New York: Wiley, 1953.

SPIKER, C. C. "The Effects of Number of Reinforcements on the Strength of a Generalized Instrument Response." *Child Development*, 1956, 27, 37–44.

SPIKER, C. C. "The Stimulus Generalization Gradient as a Function of the Intensity of Stimulus Lights." *Child Development*, 1957, 27, 85–98.

SPIKER, C. C., and McCANDLESS, B. R. "The Concept of Intelligence and the Philosophy of Science." *Psychological Review*, 1954, 61, 255–266.

STENDLER, CELIA B. "Critical Periods in Socialization and Over-Dependency." *Child Development*, 1952, 23, 3–12.

STEVENSON, H. W. "Social Reinforcement with Children as a Function of CA, Sex of Experimenter, and Sex of Subject." *Journal of Abnormal and Social Psychology,* 1961, 63, 147–154.

STEVENSON, H. W., and FAHEL, LEILA S. "The Effect of Social Reinforcement on the Performance of Institutionalized and Non-Institutionalized Normal and Feeble-Minded Children." *Journal of Personality,* 1961, 29, 136–147.

TANNER, J. M., and INHELDER, B. (eds.), *Discussions on Child Development.* Vol. 1. London: Tavistock, 1956.

TANNER, J. M., and INHELDER, B. (eds.), *Discussions on Child Development.* Vol. 4. London: Tavistock, 1960.

TERRELL, G., JR. "The Role of Incentive in Discrimination Learning in Children." *Child Development,* 1958, 29, 231–236.

TERRELL, G., JR., and KENNEDY, W. A. "Discrimination Learning and Transposition in Children as a Function of the Nature of the Reward." *Journal of Experimental Psychology,* 1957, 53, 257–260.

THORNDIKE, E. L., and LORGE, I. *The Teacher's Word Book of 30,000 Words.* New York: Columbia University Press, 1944.

TOLMAN, E. C. "Motivation, Learning and Adjustment," *Proceedings of the American Philosophical Society,* 1941, 84, 543–563.

TOLMAN, E. C., and HONZIK, C. H. "Introduction and Removal of Reward and Maze Performance in Rats." *University of California Publications in Psychology,* 1930, 4, 257–275.

TRYON, R. C. "Genetic Differences in Maze-Learning Ability in Rats." *Year-book of the National Society for Studies in Education,* 1940, 39, Part I, 111–119.

TRYON, R. C. "Psychology in Flux: The Academic Professional Bipolarity." *American Psychologist,* 1963, 18, 134–143.

VAN ALSTYNE, DOROTHY. *Play Behavior and Choice of Play Materials of Pre-School Children.* Chicago: University of Chicago Press, 1932.

WALDER, L. O., ABELSON, R. P., ERON, L. D., BANDA, T. J., and LAULICHT, J. N. "The Development of a Peer Rating Measure of Aggression." *Psychological Reports.* Monograph Supplement 4, (9), 1961.

WATSON, J. B. *Behaviorism.* Chicago: University of Chicago Press, 1959.

WATSON, J. B., and RAYNER, R. Conditioned Emotional Reactions, *Journal of Experimental Psychology,* 1920, 3, p. 1.

WECHSLER, D. *The Measurement and Appraisal of Adult Intelligence.* Baltimore: Williams & Wilkins, 1958.

WEISS, P., and KAVANAU, J. L. "A Model of Growth and Growth Control in Mathematical Terms." *Journal of Genetic Physiology,* 1957, 41, 1–47.

WERNER, H. "The Organismic Concept of Development." In D. H. Harris (ed.), *The Concept of Development.* Minneapolis: University of Minnesota Press, 1948.

WERNER, H. *Comparative Psychology of Mental Development.* (Rev.) Chicago: Follett, 1948.

WILLIAMS, JUDITH R., and SCOTT, R. B. "Growth and Development of Negro Infants: IV. Motor Development and Its Relationship to Child Rearing Practices in Two Groups of Negro Infants." *Child Development,* 1953, 24, 103–121.

WILLIAMS, R. J. *Biochemical Individuality.* New York: Wiley, 1956.

ZIGLER, E. "Rigidity in the Feebleminded." In E. P. Trapp and P. Himelstein (eds.), *Research Findings on the Exceptional Child.* Appleton-Century-Crofts, 1962.

ZIPF, G. K. *The psycho-biology of language.* Boston: Houghton Mifflin, 1935.

Index